THE GREENWOOD ENCYCLOPEDIA OF
ROCK HISTORY

The Greenwood Encyclopedia of Rock History

Volume 1
The Early Years, 1951–1959
Lisa Scrivani-Tidd

Volume 2
Folk, Pop, Mods, and Rockers, 1960–1966
Rhonda Markowitz

Volume 3
The Rise of Album Rock, 1967–1973
Chris Smith

Volume 4
From Arenas to the Underground, 1974–1980
Chris Smith with John Borgmeyer, Richard Skanse, and Rob Patterson

Volume 5
The Video Generation, 1981–1990
MaryAnn Janosik

Volume 6
The Grunge and Post-Grunge Years, 1991–2005
Bob Gulla

THE GREENWOOD ENCYCLOPEDIA OF
ROCK HISTORY

The Early Years, 1951–1959

LISA SCRIVANI-TIDD

GREENWOOD PRESS
Westport, Connecticut • London

Library of Congress Cataloging-in-Publication Data

The Greenwood encyclopedia of rock history.
   p. cm.
   Includes bibliographical references and index.
   ISBN 0–313–32937–0 ((set) : alk. paper)—ISBN 0–313–32938–9 ((vol. 1) : alk. paper)—ISBN
0–313–32960–5 ((vol. 2) : alk. paper)—ISBN 0–313–32966–4 ((vol. 3) : alk. paper)—ISBN
0–313–33611–3 ((vol. 4) : alk. paper)—ISBN 0–313–32943–5 ((vol. 5) : alk. paper)—ISBN
0–313–32981–8 ((vol. 6) : alk. paper)   1. Rock music—History and criticism.
  ML3534.G754 2006
  781.66'09—dc22   2005023475

British Library Cataloguing in Publication Data is available.

This book is included in the *African American Experience* database from Greenwood Electronic
Media. For more information, visit www.africanamericanexperience.com.

Library of Congress Catalog Card Number: 2005023475

ISBN: 0–313–32937–0 (set)
      0–313–32938–9 (vol. 1)
      0–313–32960–5 (vol. 2)
      0–313–32966–4 (vol. 3)
      0–313–33611–3 (vol. 4)
      0–313–32943–5 (vol. 5)
      0–313–32981–8 (vol. 6)

First published in 2006

Greenwood Press, 88 Post Road West, Westport, CT 06881
An imprint of Greenwood Publishing Group, Inc.
www.greenwood.com

Printed in the United States of America

The paper used in this book complies with the
Permanent Paper Standard issued by the National
Information Standards Organization (Z39.48–1984).

10 9 8 7 6 5 4 3 2 1

CONTENTS

 # SET FOREWORD

Rock 'n' roll, man, it changed my life. It was like the Voice of America, the real America, coming to your home.

—Bruce Springsteen[1]

The term *rock 'n' roll* has a mysterious origin. Many have credited legendary disc jockey Alan Freed for coining the term. Some claim that it was actually a blues euphemism for sexual intercourse, while others even see the term rock as having gospel origin, with worshippers "rocking" with the Lord. In 1947, DeLuxe Records released "Good Rocking Tonight," a blues-inspired romp by Roy Brown, which touched off a number of R&B artists in the late-1940s providing their own take on "rocking." But many music historians point to the 1951 Chess single "Rocket 88" as the first rock record. Produced by Sam Phillips and performed by Jackie Brenston and Ike Turner's Kings of Rhythm (though released under the name Jackie Brenston & His Delta Cats), the record established the archetype of early rock and roll: "practically indecipherable lyrics about cars, booze, and women; [a] booting tenor sax, and a churning, beat-heavy rhythmic bottom."[2]

Although its true origins are debatable, what is certain is that rock 'n' roll grew into a musical form that, in many ways, defined American culture in the second half of the twentieth century. Today, however, "rock 'n' roll" is used with less and less frequency in reference to the musical genre. The phrase seems to linger as a quaint cliché co-opted by mass media—something that a *Top Gun* pilot once said in voicing high-speed, mid-air glee. Watching MTV these days, one would be hard-pressed to find a reference to "rock 'n' roll," but the term *rock* survives, though often modified by prefixes used to denote the growing hybridization of the genre: There is alternative rock, blues rock, chick rock, classic rock, folk rock, funk rock, garage rock, glam rock, grunge rock, hard rock, psychedelic rock, punk rock, roots rock, and countless other sub-genres of rock music. It seems that musicians found more and more ways to rock but, for some reason, stopped rolling—or to paraphrase Led Zeppelin's "Stairway to Heaven," the music world opted to rock, but not to roll.

Call it what you will, rock music has never existed within a vacuum; it has always reflected aspects of our society, whether it be the statement of youth culture or rebellion against adult society; an expression of love found, lost, or never had; the portrayal of gritty street life or the affirmation of traditional American values; the heady pondering of space-age metaphysics or the giddy nonsense of a one-hit wonder, rock music has been an enduring voice of the people for over five decades. *The Greenwood Encyclopedia of Rock History* records not only the countless manifestations of rock music in our society, but also the many ways in which rock music has shaped, and been shaped by, American culture.

Testifying to the enduring popularity of rock music are the many publications devoted to covering rock music. These range from countless single-volume record guides providing critics' subjective ratings to the multi-volume sets that lump all forms of popular music together, discussing the jazz-rock duo Steely Dan in the same breath as Stravinsky, or indie-rock group Pavement with Pavarotti. To be sure, such references have their value, but we felt that there was no authoritative work that gives rock music history the thorough, detailed examination that it merits. For this reason, our six-volume encyclopedia focuses closely on the rock music genre. While many different forms of rock music are examined, including the *influences* of related genres such as folk, jazz, soul, or hip-hop, we do not try to squeeze in discussions of other genres of music. For example, a volume includes the influences of country music on rock—such as folk rock or "alt.country"—but it does not examine country music itself. Thus, *rock music* is not treated here as synonymous with *popular music*, as our parents (or our parents' parents) might have done, equating whatever forms of music were on the charts, whatever the "young kids" were listening to, as basically all the same, with only a few differences, an outsiders' view of rock, one that viewed the genre fearfully and from a distance. Instead, we present a six-volume set—one that is both "meaty" and methodical—from the perspective of the rock music historians who provide narrative chapters on the many different stories during more than five decades of rock music history.

The Greenwood Encyclopedia of Rock History comprises six information-packed volumes covering the dizzying evolution of this exciting form of music. The volumes are divided by historical era: *Volume 1: The Early Years, 1951–1959,* spans from the year "Rocket 88" (arguably the first rock single) was released to the year of the infamous "Day the Music Died," the fatal airplane crash that took the lives of Buddy Holly, Ritchie Valens, and J. P. Richardson (a.k.a. The Big Bopper). *Volume 2: Folk, Pop, Mods, and Rockers, 1960–1966,* covers the period when the British Invasion irrevocably changed the world, while such American rock scenes as Motown and surf rock held their own. In *Volume 3: The Rise of Album Rock, 1967–1973*, Chris Smith chronicles the growing experimentation during the psychedelic era of rock, from *Sgt. Pepper* to *Dark Side of the Moon* and everything in between. In *Volume 4: From Arenas to the Underground, 1974–1980*, Smith et al., record how rock became big business while also spawning hybrid forms and underground movements. *Volume 5: The Video Generation, 1981–1990* starts with the year of MTV's debut and captures the era when video threatened to kill the radio star. Finally, in *Volume 6: The Grunge and Post-Grunge Years, 1991–2005*, Bob Gulla captures the many innovations of millennial rock music and culture. Within each volume, the narrative chapters are supplemented by a timeline, discography, bibliography, and a glossary of encyclopedia entries for quick reference.

We hope that librarians, researchers, and fans alike will find endless nuggets of information within this reference. And because we are talking about rock, we hope you will find that reading *The Greenwood Encyclopedia of Rock History* will be a whole lot of fun, too.

Rock on.

Rob Kirkpatrick
Greenwood Publishing Group

NOTES

1. Rock and Roll Hall of Fame and Museum home page, http://www.rockhall.com.
2. All Music Guide entry for Jackie Brenston, http://www.allmusic.com.

PREFACE

This book covers the genesis and evolution of the most popular music in the United States—rock and roll. This historical overview is intended for students, teachers, enthusiasts, and listeners. Included are '50s artists and groups and their predecessors as diverse as Little Richard and Pat Boone, the Platters and the Chipmunks, and Robert Johnson and Jimmie Rodgers, all of whom helped shape the new music in the '50s, leaving behind a marvelous repertoire. I am continuously reminded by my students how important this music still is to us. Not only did it shape the teens of the '50s, but now, some fifty years later, the genre continues, as strong as ever, and it is unimaginable to think about how life would be without it. The rock and roll of the '50s set the foundation for this music. Without Chuck Berry, perhaps there would have been no Beatles, Rolling Stones, Jimi Hendrix, or Bruce Springsteen.

Just as in the '50s, today's youth enjoy a good song. As more and more people realize the substance of rock and roll, they are turning to these classics for enjoyment. As a firm believer in and practitioner of enthusiastic teaching to motivate students, I feel strongly about sharing the vast repertoire of music history with others: teachers, students, and fans alike. As a pedagogue who regularly encourages educators of all disciplines to teach with music to inspire students, I am happy to present this book. To marry excitement and learning by using Chuck Berry's "School Day" in English classes, Billy Lee Riley's "Flying Saucers Rock and Roll" in science courses, or Bo Diddley's "Bo Diddley" in music classrooms can be an innovative approach to teaching.

Almost 200 sources were researched and validated for this book, ranging from books and articles to films and recordings, Web sites and museum archives. For all sources, but especially when discrepancies were discovered even in highly reputable ones, multiple publications were consulted to verify accuracy of information. I am indebted to many scholars and writers for their valuable resources; without these, a book of this scope would be impossible.

All information concerning record positions on the charts came from Joel Whitburn's Record Research publications, which compile *Billboard* charts' information of the rock and roll era. These books are widely acknowledged authoritative sources on the topic, and I am greatly indebted to Whitburn and his staff, who engage in painstaking efforts to collect the data:

> Whitburn, Joel. *The Billboard Book of Top 40 Albums.* 3rd ed., rev. and enl. New York: Billboard Books, 1995.
>
> Whitburn, Joel. *The Billboard Book of Top 40 Hits.* New York: Billboard Books, 2000.
>
> Whitburn, Joel. *Joel Whitburn Presents a Century of Pop Music.* Menomonee Falls, WI: Record Research, 1999.
>
> Whitburn, Joel. *Joel Whitburn Presents Billboard #1s, 1950–1991.* Menomonee Falls, WI: Record Research, 1991.
>
> Whitburn, Joel. *Joel Whitburn Presents Top R&B/Hip-Hop Singles, 1942–2004.* Menomonee Falls, WI: Record Research, 2004.
>
> Whitburn, Joel. *Joel Whitburn's Top Pop Singles, 1955–2002.* Menomonee Falls, WI: Record Research, 2003.

Chronicling the history of '50s rock and roll in American culture, this study focuses on the literature and artists of the United States. The book briefly traces the origins of rock and roll in various roots from classical music and the blues, jazz and rhythm and blues, gospel and country music, and folk and pop music—all coming together in the '50s to give birth to rock and roll. A fascinating tour through rock and roll's early days, this book includes a discussion of the first rock and roll records, a detailed account of the music industry, rock and roll's triumphant rise to being a major force, and its unpredicted downfall toward the end of the decade. Material is presented by subgenres, such as rhythm and blues-based rock and roll, rockabilly, and doo-wop, with emphasis on artists and their music. Included are sidebars—diagrams, musician biographies, and lists of songs and artists—to highlight key information and provide in-depth explanations. The timeline features significant events from rock's first decade. The A-to-Z glossary is intended for quick reference to significant artists, producers, records, and events from the era. The lists of top-selling and most significant '50s records provide a guide to the songs, artists, and groups that helped shape the decade, and the Reference Guide suggests materials for further reference, including print resources, Web sites, museum archives, events, films, and recordings.

ACKNOWLEDGMENTS

I would like to acknowledge the following people who were important to me as I completed this project. First and foremost, I am indebted to the founding fathers of rock and roll, who gave me the impetus to write this book. I want to extend a gracious "thank you" to Bob Santelli, former Vice President of Education and Public Programs at the Rock and Roll Hall of Fame and Museum in Cleveland and current Director of Public Programs at the Experience Music Project in Seattle, for sharing his enthusiasm and inspiring me with his knowledge. Many thanks to the President of SUNY (State University of New York) at Jefferson, Joe Olson, for granting me a sabbatical from my teaching post, allowing me not only to write this book but also to be home with my new babies. Thank you to my colleagues at SUNY Jefferson's Melvil Dewey Library, who provided me with innumerable sources for my research. I am grateful to Rob Kirkpatrick, formerly at Greenwood, for his commitment to and unwavering support of this monumental series; he is to be commended for initiating this milestone that promises to enlighten students for years to come. Many thanks to Anne Thompson, development editor, for her guidance and remarkable patience. Sincere appreciation goes to my dear friend and colleague, Joanna Chrzanowski, for her valuable suggestions, comments, and reading of the manuscript. I am honored and grateful that such a respected master of the written word gave freely of her time to assist me with this project. I would like to thank my family: sister Janice, brother David, and parents, Angela and Severino, for their continued enthusiasm and encouragement, and constant love and support, over the years. They have always believed in me and encouraged my talents. Thanks are in order for Chloe's company; she stayed by my side all day and all night, week after week, month after month, while I was writing this manuscript, her four furry little feet curled up next to mine.

With heartfelt appreciation, I dedicate this book to my immediate family: my precious sons, Cristofer and Dominic, and my beloved husband, Roderick. I express enormous gratitude for their love and support, which allowed me to write this book. They are absolute treasures. My tender thanks go to my three boys for understanding and making me smile.

TIMELINE: 1951–1959

1951

Bluesman Muddy Waters has numerous hit records, among them "Louisiana Blues," "Long Distance Call," and "Honey Bee." Memphis radio station WDIA disc jockey and bluesman B. B. King records "Three O'Clock Blues," which becomes his first No. 1 R&B hit early in 1952.

March 5: Widely considered the first rock and roll record, "Rocket 88" is recorded at the Memphis Recording Service by Jackie Brenston and Ike Turner's band, the Kings of Rhythm. Sam Phillips leases the recording to Chess Records, and "Rocket 88" becomes the label's first No. 1 hit, one of the most successful R&B records of the year, and a model for future rock and roll records.

May 26: The Dominoes' "Sixty Minute Man" enters the R&B charts, where it holds the No. 1 spot for fourteen weeks.

July 11: Calling himself Moondog, disc jockey Alan Freed makes his debut on Cleveland radio station WJW, hosting *The Moondog Rock 'n' Roll Party*, a rhythm and blues show.

1952

Los Angeles rhythm and blues record specialty shop Dolphin Record Store reveals a new trend; sales show that whites are now purchasing R&B recordings.

March 1:   At his Memphis Recording Studio, Sam Phillips launches Sun Records, with the release of Johnny London's "Drivin' Slow." Sun Records will become the nucleus of the early development of rockabilly—a place where legendary rockabilly artists will make some of the greatest records in the history of rock and roll.

March 21:   In Cleveland, Alan Freed organizes and hosts the Moondog Coronation Ball, which takes place at the Cleveland Arena on Euclid Avenue. Widely regarded as the first rock and roll concert, the show is promoted by Freed and Lew Platt, and is sponsored by the Record Rendezvous record store. The first of Freed's many sponsored rock music shows, it is closed down by the police and fire departments after the crowd becomes rowdy.

May: After Les Paul launches the Les Paul guitar, Gibson begins to build and market it. Also this year, Paul invents the eight-track tape recorder, which helps pioneer multitrack recording and overdubbing.

May 13:   Promising young music entrepreneur and television and radio personality Dick Clark is hired by radio station WFIL in Philadelphia.

July 12:   Lloyd Price's "Lawdy Miss Clawdy" hits No. 1 on the R&B charts, where it remains for seven weeks. The recording will be the source of numerous cover versions.

October 7:   First broadcast as a local radio show on station WFIL in Philadelphia, *Bob Horn's Bandstand* makes its television debut on the local WFIL-TV, hosted by Bob Horn and Lee Stewart.

1953

The Top 40 radio format is introduced by Gordon McLendon and Todd Storz, owners of various radio stations.

February 14:   Recorded with a band led by Ray Charles, Ruth Brown's "(Mama) He Treats Your Daughter Mean" enters the R&B charts, where it stays at No. 1 for five weeks. Brown's series of hits enables Atlantic Records to secure its place in the record industry. It is referred to as "The House That Ruth Built."

April 18:   Written for her by Jerry Leiber and Mike Stoller, Big Mama Thornton's "Hound Dog," one of the seminal records in rock and roll history, spends its first of seven weeks atop the R&B charts. Sun Records scores its first national hit with Rufus Thomas's reaction song to it, "Bear Cat." Thomas's recording enters the R&B charts this week; it eventually peaks at the No. 3 position.

May 13:   Jerry Wexler, former *Billboard* magazine journalist credited with replacing the term "race music" with "rhythm and blues," joins Atlantic Records as a producer. Wexler later becomes vice president of the company and produces R&B music.

May 23:   Bill Haley and the Comets' "Crazy Man, Crazy" is the first rock and roll record to appear on the pop charts.

July 18:   At Sam Phillips's Memphis Recording Service, a shy, young Elvis Presley records "My Happiness" and "That's When Your Heartaches Begin" as a birthday present for his mother.

August 9: Clyde McPhatter and the Drifters record "Money Honey," the first of their four R&B No. 1 hits during the '50s, and the best-selling R&B record of the year. The Drifters are the first group produced by newly appointed Atlantic Records vice president Jerry Wexler.

August 22: The Orioles achieve their greatest success, a No. 1 hit on the R&B charts, with their landmark record "Crying in the Chapel." The recording is one of the first crossover hits, signaling the coming explosion of R&B music gracing the pop charts.

1954

Leo Fender unveils the Stratocaster electric guitar with a contoured body that becomes a favorite of many virtuoso rock guitarists. Sam Phillips signs Elvis Presley to his Sun label and releases Presley's first single.

February 1: Having signed a contract with Atlantic Records in 1951, R&B singer Big Joe Turner records "Shake, Rattle and Roll." On June 12, the single sits atop the R&B charts as Turner's second chart-topper; his "Honey Hush" was No. 1 in 1953.

April 10: The Crows' landmark record "Gee," recorded in 1953, enters the R&B charts, where it reaches No. 2. This significant recording becomes one of the first crossover records by a black group when it becomes a No. 14 pop hit.

April 12: In New York City, Bill Haley and the Comets record "(We're Gonna) Rock Around the Clock," a recording that marks the birth of rock and roll. Decca Records releases this record in May, and it becomes a minor hit. After it is included on the sound track of the 1955 movie *The Blackboard Jungle* and is re-released in 1955, it becomes an international sensation.

April 24: The first recording of Hank Ballard and the Midnighters' Annie Trilogy, "Work with Me Annie" enters the R&B charts,

	where it becomes a No. 1 hit. Later in 1954, the Midnighters follow with another chart-topper, "Annie Had a Baby," and a No. 10 hit, "Annie's Aunt Fannie."
July 3:	The Chords' "Sh-Boom," released on Atlantic's Cat subsidiary label, enters the R&B charts, where it peaks at No. 2. Its crossover appeal places it on the pop charts this summer at No. 5; however, it is the only commercially successful record by the vocal group. The Crew-Cuts' version of this song rests at No. 1 on the pop charts for nine weeks this summer, an early example of the cover practice.
July 5:	With Scotty Moore and Bill Black, Elvis Presley records "That's All Right," widely considered the first rock and roll record, at Sun Records. Coupled with "Blue Moon of Kentucky," Presley's debut Sun single is released on July 19, the first of five groundbreaking singles to be recorded at Sun.
September 8:	Radio personality Alan Freed, known as Moondog, makes his debut on New York's WINS. In November, blind street musician Louis Hardin, known as "Moondog" since 1947, successfully sues Freed, prohibiting the deejay from using the name "Moondog" on his radio show.
September 22:	Presley's second Sun single, "Good Rockin' Tonight" with "I Don't Care if the Sun Don't Shine," is released.

1955

Columbia Records establishes the Columbia Record and Tape Club, an attempt by major record companies to regain the record market from independents.

January 8:	Presley's third Sun single, "You're a Heartbreaker" with "Milkcow Blues Boogie," is released on his twentieth birthday. It is followed on April 25 by his fourth record, "I'm Left, You're Right, She's Gone" backed with "Baby Let's Play House." His last Sun single, "Mystery Train" with "I Forgot to Remember to Forget," his first No. 1 country hit, is released on August 1.
January 15:	The Penguins' "Earth Angel," recorded in 1954, tops the R&B charts. This doo-wop song crosses over to the pop charts, and remains one of the most popular oldies. In February, the Crew-Cuts cover the song and achieve their second million-selling single and a No. 3 pop hit.
January 22:	The Moonglows' first Chess release, their trademark song "Sincerely," becomes a No. 1 R&B hit. Recorded in 1954, it is their biggest success, showcasing the group's exquisite vocal blend.

March 2: Bo Diddley's first recording session with Chess Records yields "Bo Diddley" backed with "I'm a Man." The first of a string of classic hits presenting his distinctive rhythmic sound called the Bo Diddley beat, "Bo Diddley" tops the R&B charts in June.

March 15: Fats Domino records "Ain't That a Shame," his first crossover hit and the first of a string of classic hits for Imperial Records. On June 11, the single begins its eleven-week stay atop the R&B charts. Domino follows in 1956 with "Blueberry Hill" and "Blue Monday," and then with "I'm Walkin'" and "Valley of Tears" (1957), "Whole Lotta Loving" (1958), "I Want to Walk You Home" (1959), and "Walking to New Orleans" (1960).

April 12: Deejay Alan Freed presents his first concert at the Paramount Theater in downtown Brooklyn. Both black and white artists are on the roster, and tickets cost 90 cents. This week, Freed's Rock and Roll Easter Jubilee features LaVern Baker, the Moonglows, and the Penguins, among others. Over the next few years Freed will showcase the biggest stars of the era with several daily concerts at the Paramount.

May 21: Chuck Berry's "Maybellene," recorded by Chess Records, helps lay the groundwork for the new rock and roll sound by combining blues and country music characteristics. In August, "Maybelline" shoots to No. 1 on the R&B charts, where it will rest for eleven weeks. The recording also marks Berry's debut on the pop charts, at No. 5. Over the next few years, Berry follows with several other classics, including "Roll Over Beethoven" (1956), "School Day" (1957), "Rock and Roll Music" (1957), "Sweet Little Sixteen" (1958), and "Johnny B. Goode" (1958).

May 22: In Bridgeport, Connecticut, the police cancel a rock and roll show headlined by Fats Domino. In March, after a teenage rock and roll dance in New Haven resulted in a brawl with several teens arrested, the cities of Bridgeport and New Haven applied the first bans on live rock music concerts.

July 9: Bill Haley and the Comets' "(We're Gonna) Rock Around the Clock" is re-released after it is included in the MGM movie *The Blackboard Jungle*. The single becomes the first No. 1 rock and roll hit on the *Billboard* charts, where it remains for eight weeks, and the best-selling record of the year. Marking the beginning of the rock era, it is the first internationally known rock and roll recording and has a huge impact on American culture.

September 14: With the Crescent City rhythm section, Little Richard records "Tutti Frutti" at Cosimo Matassa's J&M Studio in New Orleans. Early in 1956 this No. 2 R&B hit, complete with wild vocals and pounding piano, marks Little Richard's debut on the pop charts. The recording is followed by a string of classics over the next three years: "Long Tall Sally" and "Rip It Up" (both No. 1's in 1956); "Lucille," "Jenny, Jenny," and "Keep a Knockin'" (1957); and "Good Golly, Miss Molly" (1958).

September 17: Pat Boone's highly successful cover of Fats Domino's "Ain't That a Shame" tops the pop charts and crosses over to the R&B charts, resting at No. 14. Boone will settle into his niche and regularly cover R&B hits, turning them into cleaned-up pop arrangements. He will have four more No. 1 pop hits over the next two years.

November 12: The first 100-position pop chart is published by *Billboard*; the Top 100 combines sales, airplay, and jukebox play. Also in 1955, *Billboard* debuts the Most Played by R&B Disk Jockeys chart, previously the Harlem Hit Parade (debuted in 1942), which evolved into the Most-Played Juke Box Race Records chart (1945); the Best Selling Retail Race Records chart was introduced in 1948.

November 21: Sam Phillips sells Elvis Presley's Sun Records contract for $35,000 to RCA-Victor, Hill & Range Music Publishing, and Colonel Tom Parker, who arranged the deal. Other terms of the agreement call for Presley to receive $5,000 in back royalties and for Parker to replace Bob Neal as Presley's manager.

1956

In this "Year of Elvis," *Variety* bestows the title "King of Rock and Roll" upon Elvis Presley, who explodes onto the music scene. His music, appearance, and unique stage manner bring unprecedented fame. Presley records numerous hits this year, among them "Heartbreak Hotel," "Blue Suede Shoes," "I Want You, I Need You, I Love You," "My Baby Left Me," "Don't Be Cruel," "Hound Dog," "Love Me Tender," and "Anyway You Want Me (That's How I Will Be)." Also this year, the pioneering songwriter-producer team of Jerry Leiber and Mike Stoller signs a contract with Atlantic Records as independent producers, the first production deal of this sort in rock history.

January 10: At his first RCA session in Nashville, Elvis Presley records "Heartbreak Hotel," his first No. 1 smash.

January 23: James Brown and the Famous Flames sign a recording contract with Ralph Bass of Federal Records. Brown becomes a prolific recording artist, helping establish the '60s soul subgenre. He has three major hits before the end of the decade: "Please, Please, Please," "Try Me," and "I Want You So Bad."

February 18: Frankie Lymon and the Teenagers enter the charts with "Why Do Fools Fall in Love," recorded in late 1955. This vocal group classic becomes a No. 1 R&B hit and makes Lymon the first black teenage pop star. The record is a standard by which the doo-wop style is defined.

February 18: The Platters' "The Great Pretender" is the first No. 1 doo-wop song to appear on the pop charts; in January it peaked on the R&B charts at No. 1, beginning an eleven-week stay there and establishing the groundwork for this R&B vocal group's series of hits.

March 3: Rockabilly Carl Perkins's "Blue Suede Shoes" enters the pop charts, where it peaks at No. 2 and becomes the biggest hit of Perkins's career. Sun Records' first million-seller record, the smash launches Perkins's career and becomes the rockabilly signature song. "Blue Suede Shoes" makes history by being the first across-the-board chart hit, simultaneously reaching the Top 5 on the pop, country, and R&B charts. With this single, Perkins is the first country artist to reach the national R&B charts; Presley follows with "Heartbreak Hotel" in three weeks.

April 9: Gene Vincent and the Blue Caps record "Be-Bop-a-Lula" at radio station WCMS in Norfolk, Virginia. They soon sign a deal with Capitol Records and follow with other hits: "Blue Jean Bop," "Lotta Lovin'," and "Dance to the Bop."

June 5: Elvis Presley performs "Hound Dog" on the *Milton Berle Show* and causes a national furor with his performance actions, horrifying adults while delighting teenagers.

July 1: A humiliated Elvis Presley performs "Hound Dog" on the *Steve Allen Show*. Clad in a tuxedo, Presley sings to a basset hound dressed in the likes of a tuxedo—an attempt by the show's producers for a tamer Presley performance.

July 2: Elvis Presley records "Hound Dog" backed with "Don't Be Cruel." Both songs reach the top position on all three charts—pop, country, and R&B—and become the biggest hits in music history to date. In 1957, Presley follows with three more recordings that will do the same: "All Shook Up," "(Let Me Be Your) Teddy Bear," and "Jailhouse Rock."

July 9: Dick Clark is the new host of Philadelphia's WFIL-TV *Bandstand* show.

September 9:   Elvis Presley makes the first of his three appearances on the *Ed Sullivan Show*. The others are on October 28 and January 6, 1957. The three shows launch Presley into national consciousness.

November 10:   The Dells mark the beginning of their successful, lengthy career when "Oh What a Nite" enters the R&B charts and reaches the No. 4 position. In 1969, the R&B vocal group will record a new version of the song as "Oh, What a Night," which will peak at No. 1.

November 14:   At Sun Records, Jerry Lee Lewis records his first single, "Crazy Arms," paired with "End of the Road" (credited to Jerry Lee Lewis and His Pumping Piano), which establishes him as the only artist who could threaten Presley. Lewis follows with a string of explosive hits, including "Whole Lot of Shakin' Going On" (1957), "Great Balls of Fire" (1957), "Breathless" (1958), and "High School Confidential" (1958).

November 15:   Elvis Presley stars in the first of his thirty-one movies, *Love Me Tender*, which premiers at the Paramount Theater in New York City. He stars in three more before the end of the decade: *Loving You* (1957), *Jailhouse Rock* (1957), and *King Creole* (1958).

1957

The teen idol phenomenon flourishes and lasts into the early 1960s. This subgenre has numerous popular performers in the late 1950s, including Frankie Avalon, Bobby Rydell, Fabian, Paul Anka, Bobby Darin, Bobby Vee, Annette Funicello, Connie Francis, Neil Sedaka, and Ricky Nelson. Also this year, stereophonic sound is introduced by the recording industry; most companies will use it by 1958, and it will replace monophonic records in the '60s. Presley mania sweeps the world. Once again, Elvis Presley has an impressive list of hits that includes "All Shook Up," "(Let Me Be Your) Teddy Bear," "Loving You," and "Jailhouse Rock."

February 25:   At Norman Petty's studio in Clovis, New Mexico, Buddy Holly and the Crickets record "That'll Be the Day," which shoots to the top of the pop charts. They will follow their success with a series of Top 40 rockabilly tunes, including the classics "Peggy Sue," "Rave On," "Not Fade Away," "Maybe Baby," and "Oh, Boy!"

March 1:   The Everly Brothers record "Bye Bye Love" at the RCA-Victor studio in Nashville. The song establishes their trademark sound with close vocal harmonies, acoustic guitars, and the rock and roll backbeat. This is the first of their steady stream of hit records that cross over from country to pop and to the R&B charts. The Everlys have three chart-toppers before the end of the decade: "Wake Up Little Susie," "All I Have to Do Is Dream," and "Bird Dog."

April 10: Rockabilly Ricky Nelson performs Fats Domino's "I'm Walkin'" on ABC's *The Adventures of Ozzie and Harriet* television show, resulting in a wild teenage response. His performance turns him into a popular teen idol.

May 21: Canadian Paul Anka makes his first ABC-Paramount recording, "Diana," which becomes a No. 1 R&B and pop hit. In 1959, Anka follows with his next chart-topper, "Lonely Boy."

June 1: Sam Cooke records his first solo song, "You Send Me," which tops the R&B and pop charts. He will follow with many other huge hits, including 1957's "I'll Come Running Back to You," a No. 1 recording.

June 24: Jerry Lee Lewis's second single and first hit, "Whole Lot of Shakin' Going On," enters the pop charts, eventually settling at the No. 3 position while topping the R&B and country charts. In November, "Great Balls of Fire" enters the charts and becomes a No. 2 pop and No. 1 country hit in 1958; it is the best-selling record in Sun Records' history. These recordings help establish Lewis as an international celebrity.

August 5: With Dick Clark as host, the hugely successful *American Bandstand* makes its national network debut, with millions of viewers, on ABC-TV.

September 1: The Biggest Show of Stars tour begins; the first five nights are at the Paramount Theater in Brooklyn. The tour features numerous artists, including Chuck Berry, Buddy Holly and the Crickets, Paul Anka, Frankie Lymon and the Teenagers, the Drifters, the Everly Brothers, and Clyde McPhatter. It closes on November 24 in Richmond, Virginia.

September 16: The Tuneweavers' "Happy, Happy Birthday Baby" enters the pop charts. It reaches No. 5 and today is one of the most popular oldies dedication songs.

September 30: The Bobbettes achieve a No. 1 R&B hit with their debut single, "Mr. Lee." In 1959, they record their Mr. Lee sequel, "I Shot Mr. Lee."

December 19: Elvis Presley receives a draft notice for the army; he will report for duty in March 1958.

1958

This year, when the music industry organizes against rock and roll, Frank Sinatra refers to rock music as an ugly and vicious form of expression while testifying before Congress. The novelty song craze peaks with David Seville's "Witch Doctor" and "The Chipmunk Song," Sheb Wooley's "The Purple People Eater," and the Royal Teens' "Short Shorts." Rock instrumentals come of age with the Champs' "Tequila," the first No. 1 rock instrumental, that is 1958's biggest instrumental hit and the No. 8 song. Popularized on *American Bandstand*, the Stroll becomes the first rock and roll group dance, complete with its own song by the Diamonds, "The Stroll."

January 6:	On the final day of the Alan Freed Christmas Jubilee in New York, Danny & the Juniors perform "At the Hop." The single becomes the first No. 1 record of the year. Their "Rock and Roll Is Here to Stay" is written in response to attacks against rock and roll and becomes an anthem for teenagers.
January 12:	St. Louis radio station KWK announces the start of its Record Breaking Week. The station plays each rock and roll record once, followed by the deejay's breaking it on the air, so listeners can hear it.
January 20:	The Silhouettes' "Get a Job" enters the charts and becomes an instant hit. Recorded late in 1957, the song is immensely popular, and simultaneously tops the R&B and pop charts in February.
January 27:	The Chantels' "Maybe" enters the R&B charts. The recording is this female vocal group's biggest hit and earns them an appearance on *American Bandstand* and inclusion on one of Alan Freed's package tours. The Chantels become one of the first all-girl groups to sustain success beyond one hit, and they greatly influence the girl groups in the early 1960s.
February 15:	*The Dick Clark Show*, a Saturday-night television show broadcast from ABC's Little Theatre in New York City, debuts to millions of viewers.
March 17:	The Coasters record "Yakety Yak," a No. 1 hit about youthful rebelliousness that helps define rock and roll by appealing to and reflecting America's teens. The Coasters will release classic singles in 1959: "Charlie Brown," "Along Came Jones," "Poison Ivy," and "That Is Rock & Roll."
March 17:	With his backup band, the Rebels, Duane Eddy brings his trademark twangy guitar sound to the world and begins an impressive string of hits with "Moovin' 'n' Groovin'," the single that introduces him to the pop charts. He follows this year and

in 1959 with the hits "Rebel-'Rouser," "Ramrod," "The Lonely One," and "Forty Miles of Bad Road."

March 29: Teen idol Connie Francis has her first hit, "Who's Sorry Now," which reaches the No. 4 position on the pop charts. Labeled as pop music's No. 1 female vocalist from the late 1950s to the mid-1960s, she follows with the popular hit "Where the Boys Are" in 1961.

April 10: Teen idol Bobby Darin records the novelty song "Splish Splash," which becomes a smash, and "Queen of the Hop." His big hits of 1959 will be "Dream Lover" and "Mack the Knife," his signature song.

May 3: When violence erupts outside the Boston Arena after an Alan Freed show, local authorities indict the disc jockey for inciting a riot. The next week, Freed resigns from WINS because of the station's lack of support following his indictment.

May 5: Entering the charts this week, Chuck Berry's highly influential "Johnny B. Goode" becomes one of the first anthems of rock and roll. The song's famous guitar-solo introduction is one of the most copied rock and roll riffs.

May 19: After Dion DiMucci forms Dion and the Belmonts in the Bronx, New York, their "I Wonder Why" enters the charts. The recording earns them a reputation as the best street corner singers in the area. In 1959 they follow with "A Teenager in Love."

June 2: The Everly Brothers' "All I Have to Do Is Dream" simultaneously tops the pop, R&B, and country charts. The single is the only record by someone other than Elvis Presley to do so.

July 5: Ray Charles performs at the annual Newport Jazz Festival in Rhode Island. The festival is inaugurating its first blues night, and Chuck Berry, Big Joe Turner, and Big Maybelle also perform.

July 12: Alan Freed's *The Big Beat* television show premieres on ABC.

August 4: *Billboard* introduces the Hot 100 chart, the first chart to fully integrate the hottest-selling and most-played pop singles—the definitive industry chart. Ricky Nelson's "Poor Little Fool" is the first No. 1 song to appear on the Hot 100. The new chart replaces the Top 100.

August 4: Eddie Cochran's rockabilly anthem of teen disenchantment, "Summertime Blues," enters the pop charts; it will be his most successful record. He follows this with "C'mon Everybody," and in 1959 with "Somethin' Else."

October 20:   *Billboard*'s Best Seller and Disk Jockey charts are replaced by one all-inclusive Top 30 R&B singles chart titled Hot R&B Sides; it later becomes the Hot R&B/Hip-Hop Singles & Tracks chart.

November 24:   Latino rocker Ritchie Valens's "Donna" enters the charts; it is a No. 2 pop hit by early 1959 and brings him stardom. The record's flip side, "La Bamba," is the song with which he becomes identified. This double-sided record is often called one of the greatest '50s rock and roll singles.

December 1:   The Teddy Bears score their only No. 1 hit, "To Know Him, Is to Love Him," written, arranged, and produced by one of the trio's members, Phil Spector. Although it is considered a one-hit wonder, the group introduces Spector to the music world. He becomes one of the greatest producers of rock and roll.

December 15:   Jackie Wilson's "Lonely Teardrops" reaches the No. 1 position on the R&B charts, where it remains for seven weeks; it also reaches No. 7 on the pop charts. Wilson follows with hit after hit into the mid-1970s and becomes one of the premier voices of this time.

1959

The teen idol craze continues, with Dick Clark and *American Bandstand* taking an active role in the new sound in Philadelphia with clean-cut idols Frankie Avalon, Bobby Rydell, and Fabian. Despite being stationed in Germany with the U.S. Army, Elvis Presley generates four more hits this year. The payola scandal erupts, attacking BMI and the rock music it licenses; many rock and roll disc jockeys lose their jobs. Several of the major rockers disappear from the music scene, and soul music continues to evolve. New subgenres begin to emerge, including the surf sound, aided by the instrumental group the Ventures with their "Walk—Don't Run," and the girl group sound, promoted by the all-female Shirelles with their "Dedicated to the One I Love." Also this year, both the Grammy Awards and the Newport Folk Festival are inaugurated.

February 3:   Buddy Holly, Ritchie Valens, and the Big Bopper perish in a plane crash while traveling between engagements on the 1959 Winter Dance Party tour of the Midwest. Singer-songwriter Don McLean will immortalize the musicians and label that day as "the day the music died" in his 1971 No. 1 hit, "American Pie."

February 10:   Link Wray & His Ray Men, known for their first instrumental hit, "Rumble," appear on *American Bandstand*, performing "Raw-Hide."

March 3:	In New York, Ben E. King and the Drifters record "There Goes My Baby," which reflects their new music style, complete with orchestral string accompaniment. They will follow with numerous hits, such as this fall's "Dance with Me," 1960's "This Magic Moment" and "Save the Last Dance for Me," "Up on the Roof" (1962), "On Broadway" (1963), and "Under the Boardwalk" (1964).
March 9:	Teen idol Frankie Avalon achieves his first No. 1 hit on the pop charts with "Venus." He follows in December with his second chart-topper, "Why."
March 12:	Fabian makes his television debut on *American Bandstand*, performing "Turn Me Loose," his fast-climbing hit that will reach the No. 9 position on the pop charts. He achieves his second Top 10 hit this summer, "Tiger," which peaks at No. 3.
April 24:	*Your Hit Parade* broadcasts for the last time. Consisting of a countdown of each week's most popular songs, the radio show had premiered on April 12, 1935. It spawned a television series in 1950.
May 4:	In Los Angeles, the National Academy of Recording Arts and Sciences holds the first Grammy Award ceremony, at which the Champs' "Tequila" is named Best Rhythm & Blues Performance, and the Kingston Trio's "Tom Dooley" is named Best Country & Western Performance. Notably absent from the award and guest lists are the era's leading rock and roll stars.
August 3:	Ray Charles's "What'd I Say (Part I)" tops the R&B charts. The song represents the culmination of this R&B genius's creation of soul music. Charles paves the way for the funky '60s sound that will emerge with Sam Cooke, Jackie Wilson, James Brown, Wilson Pickett, the Isley Brothers, and more.
September:	Radio station WLEV in Erie, Pennsylvania, rents a hearse, packs it with 7,000 rock records, and stages a mock funeral procession to Lake Erie, where station personnel dump all the discs into the water.
October 12:	Composer teen idol Neil Sedaka's "Oh! Carol," which he wrote for Carole King, enters the pop charts, where it will settle at No. 9. Sedaka will follow with several hits recorded by him into the mid-1970s, including the early '60s' "Calendar Girl," "Happy Birthday, Sweet Sixteen," and No. 1 "Breaking Up Is Hard to Do."
November 20:	The payola investigation affects deejay Alan Freed, who is fired from New York radio station WABC after he refuses to sign a statement that he never received money or gifts for plugging

records. He continues to claim his innocence with regard to payola, and three days later Freed is fired from his daily *The Big Beat* television show on WNEW-TV.

November 29: The second Grammy Awards ceremony is held. Teen idol Bobby Darin receives the Record of the Year award for "Mack the Knife," and he is also named Best New Artist of 1959.

FIFTIES PRELUDE: "JUST GIVE ME SOME OF THAT ROCK AND ROLL MUSIC"

FIFTIES CULTURE AND POST–WORLD WAR II SOCIETY

Sometimes known as the fabulous '50s, the years between 1950 and 1959 were a thriving era of well-being in the United States compared with the decades that preceded and followed. After the Great Depression of the late '20s to late '30s, and World War II in the early '40s, the '50s witnessed the country bursting with exhilarating progress, not only in science, technology, and business, but also in music. During the presidencies of Harry Truman (1945–1953) and Dwight Eisenhower (1953–1961), America became the most powerful nation in the world. Reflecting the culture from which it came, rock and roll music emerged during this period and began its development into one of the most popular and significant exports of the United States. In the '60s, the country faced one of the most turbulent times in its history: social and political unrest and the Vietnam War. Compared with the '40s and '60s, the 1950s proved to be a pivotal decade of excitement and interest, one of social, political, and economic change in America, along with cultural explosions resulting in rock and roll music.

Tensions between the American-led West and the Communist Soviet Union and its allies triggered a number of events during the decade, such as the Cold War, the Korean War, McCarthyism, the arms race, and space exploration. America could not have known that when peace talks ended the Korean War in July 1953, its popular music would change forever because that same summer a young Elvis Presley would walk into the Memphis Recording Service and make a record for his mother. In 1950, when President Truman ordered the development of the hydrogen bomb, society hadn't yet realized the impact of one of the most important early rock and roll songs, recorded by Antoine Domino (Fats Domino) late in 1949. As the United States entered the jet age, developed early computers, saw a multitude of technological advancements and scientific discoveries, and experienced medical progress, the popular music industry witnessed enormous growth as more and more people gravitated to the new rock and roll music. Society's affluence helped revolutionize attitudes about sex, as evidenced in movies with the sex goddess Marilyn Monroe, in print with Hugh Hefner's *Playboy* magazine, and with Alfred Kinsey's publication of the *Kinsey Report*, a study of American sexual habits. This beginning of greater sexual freedom coincided with and assisted in America's embracing the exciting musical sounds of Richard Penniman's (Little Richard) risqué rhythm and blues-based recordings, allowing for an even freer American sexual attitude and more musical changes in the 1960s.

While America's innovative musicians were brewing these fresh musical sounds in the '50s, another significant societal phenomenon developed, the movement against racial segregation, which was commented on by '60s soul musicians. With boycotts, marches, sit-ins, and demonstrations as blacks sought to overturn laws protecting segregation, landmark events and decisions occurred, marking the genesis of the Civil Rights Movement in America. With the 1954 *Brown v. Board of Education of Topeka, Kansas* Supreme Court ruling that segregation meant inequality and that separate schools for blacks and whites were unconstitutional, integration of the nation's public schools occurred the same year that some of what are considered the first rock and roll records were created by Bill Haley and the Comets, Elvis Presley, Big Joe Turner, and the Chords. The orders by President Eisenhower and a federal judge that Governor Orval Faubus integrate schools in the city of Little Rock, Arkansas, in 1957 (when Elizabeth Eckford was barred from entering Central High School) took place the same year the Everly Brothers recorded their first influential rockabilly songs. The elimination of segregated public transportation with the 1955 Supreme Court ruling (as in the Topeka school case) that "separate but equal" was not legal, and the city of Montgomery, Alabama, bus segregation law being declared unconstitutional (when a bus boycott was organized after Rosa Parks was arrested for not moving to the back of a bus) occurred the same year as Charles Edward Anderson Berry's (Chuck Berry) first rock and roll hit.

As the Little Rock situation unfolded and the national media focused on civil rights issues, leaders of the movement learned how to battle segregation in front of television cameras. As Martin Luther King Jr., and others exposed racial prejudices in front of the country and the Jim Crow ways of the South were doomed, the new music was integrating American society with the blending of black and white roots music styles, in addition to the mixing of races at Alan Freed's rock and roll dances. During the mid-'50s, television networks were just coming of age, and television galvanized the political and social change in America. These and other racial events were the beginning of a period of astonishing change in America, not only in civil rights, but also in social behavior—for instance, with rock and roll artists entering America's homes via popular television programs. These changes coincided with the beginning of a new era—one that fostered a climate that allowed for novel cultural expressions, such as rock and roll music.

Because of racial segregation, poverty, and the boll weevil's devastation of cotton crops, more than 1.5 million blacks, many of them musicians, were driven from their rural homes in the early twentieth century. Between 1915 and 1965, black migrants left the South in two great waves, in pursuit of the American Dream. In the '40s, when the second wave began, many poor black sharecroppers were put out of work by new and more efficient mechanized cotton pickers as the South embraced the Machine Age. Hungry, poor, and mostly uneducated, they dreamed of going north, and those lucky enough to do so left the Southern cotton fields for the North and West after World War II, hopping on buses or trains in search of a better life—jobs with much better pay. Finding work with wages as much as six times what they earned in the South, these laborers and their families filled Northern industrial cities such as Chicago, Detroit, Pittsburgh, Cleveland, and Buffalo. Blacks from Georgia and the Carolinas generally migrated to Washington, D.C., Baltimore, Philadelphia, or New York, while those from Alabama mostly went to Detroit. Migrants from Texas and Louisiana traveled to California; those from Mississippi preferred Chicago.[1]

Many bluesmen moved to Chicago from rural Mississippi, including McKinley Morganfield (Muddy Waters) and Chester Arthur Burnett (Howlin' Wolf). With steel mills, heavy metal shops, stockyards, and meatpacking houses, many jobs were available there; Chicago was the best place to find employment, and the city was referred to as "heaven" by black laborers moving there by the thousands. A great manufacturing center and a railroad hub, during World War II's desperate need for labor Chicago relied on employment agents who traveled south to entice blacks to move north and fill the abundant vacancies. Thus numerous bluesmen traveled north through Memphis, Tennessee, to St. Louis, Missouri, until they reached their dream city—Chicago. They settled in Bronzeville (referred to as the Harlem of the Heartland), Chicago's South Side, which became home to many clubs where the bluesmen performed the music of their native South. It was one of the many new black communities created by the migrants, paralleling developments in East St. Louis, North Philadelphia, Detroit's Paradise Valley, and New York's Harlem. People arrived by carloads every day, searching for places to live. After World War II, the number of people living on the South Side of Chicago doubled. With Lake Michigan forming a natural boundary to the east and a white neighborhood creating a human boundary to the west, migrating blacks had little choice but to settle in the city, so they moved farther south in that urban region. The result was a segregated Chicago mimicking Southern segregation, although for many the American Dream had been realized; they became the cornerstone of a new black middle class, complete with the sounds of their blues voices and guitars.

With World War II having changed the social structure and cultural geography of America, the pace of life accelerated and cultural groups intermingled in the '50s. The American economy stabilized with little inflation, and a feeling of well-being permeated the nation. People were able to settle down and continue with life after years of depression and war. More and more Americans achieved prosperity, and many of the comforts and conveniences taken for granted today became a part of everyday life. Americans found themselves with plenty of time and money for leisure, which resulted in the middle class becoming avid consumers of products such as cars and entertainment. A demand for automobiles skyrocketed after the war, with General Motors leading a revolution of consumer affluence. With newfound wealth, families could afford to own multiple cars, making teenagers more mobile and able to put distance between themselves and their parents—a situation that benefited the new music. General Motors was a symbol of America's industrial strength in the '50s. It was the largest, richest corporation in the world—the first corporation in history to gross a billion dollars. After Congress passed the Interstate Highway Act in 1956, which made automobile travel easier and safer with the creation of the interstate highway system, carhops and drive-ins emerged from the '50s "car culture." Cars were equipped with a built-in entertainment system—the AM radio—that brought the sounds of America's new music to teens, who were avid consumers of records, boosting the music industry to heights it had never before seen.

Americans envisioned a better life after the war. Families looked forward to a stable and relatively predictable future. The overall goal was to succeed in school, attend college, marry, and raise a family. Men immersed themselves in their careers and provided for their families while women kept a clean, stable environment at home. Personal happiness and professional success were expected rewards of such a lifestyle, and owning a house was at the core of Americans' dreams. Following the arrival of black Southerners in some areas, middle- and upper-class families inhabiting the cities fled to the country, creating suburbs. As a result, American society became fragmented; city life declined and divisions of class, race, and geography appeared—an important factor that helped set the stage for the beginning of the era's evolving musical sounds. With the new network of roads and highways having opened up vast areas of farmland surrounding cities, the ultimate American Dream quickly became reality with suburban developments constructed by William Levitt and his mass-production construction teams providing inexpensive, attractive houses for middle-class America. Before long, complete neighborhoods were developed in the suburbs. The trend of relocation to the suburbs began in the '50s as more and more people moved from cities to the country, a trend that continued for approximately thirty years.[2]

With the new highway system crossing the country, Americans found themselves traveling more as affluent '50s society witnessed the birth of the credit card, the first hotel chains (Holiday Inns), and fast food restaurants (McDonalds), as well as the sweet harmonic sounds of such vocal groups as the Drifters and the Platters. Artists and groups could travel the nation's highways night after night, performing on popular tours and bringing their musical talents to much larger audiences. By the mid-'50s, families were vacationing at Disneyland in Anaheim, California, and enjoying the energetic, rhythmic sounds of Otha Ellas Bates McDaniel (Bo Diddley) and Charles Hardin Holley (Buddy Holly).

Emergence of Television

The postwar economic boom saw Americans purchasing newly invented products, home appliances, and furniture in abundance with the extension of credit—the new phenomenon of buying on time. Consumerism was thriving on all levels. Middle-class families were able to own their own homes, buy new cars, take vacations, and purchase the newest and hottest entertainment items—television sets, a technological breakthrough that transformed the communications industry. During the 1950s, the television ceased to be a luxury and became an essential household item; by 1952 there were millions of television sets in America's homes.

Society in the '50s was fascinated with television, whose programming was conservative and consisted of good, clean family entertainment: children's shows and variety shows, family comedies, mysteries, westerns, dramas, news, cartoons, and sports. They could see comedians (Milton Berle and Jack Benny) and situation comedies (*I Love Lucy*). Family sitcoms, such as *The Adventures of Ozzie and Harriet*, *Leave It to Beaver*, and *Father Knows Best*, portrayed the perfect '50s American lifestyle. These shows reflected contemporary society's values: families whose members respected and loved each other, mothers who stayed home and took care of their children, fathers who did white-collar work to support their families—in a happy and beautiful suburban neighborhood. Television programs displayed the conventional middle-class lifestyle in a very conservative and comfortable manner—a way that made them very popular, especially with parents, because they reflected the sweet and idealized '50s family life.

Eric Hilliard Nelson (Ricky Nelson; later known as "Rick" Nelson), one of the two sons on *The Adventures of Ozzie and Harriet*, helped smooth over the controversy created by the new sounds of rock and roll music. Disagreement between youngsters and their parents about what kind of music teenagers could listen to had begun in the late '40s, when adolescents discovered exciting rhythm and blues (R&B) music. Arguments arose when parents preferred that their children listen to the calm, soothing, popular music of the era, such as Frank Sinatra and Bing Crosby, and avoid the risqué "race music"—music performed by such African Americans as Big Joe Turner and Little Richard and marketed to African Americans. Keeping this in mind, Ozzie Nelson, Ricky's father, who had been a bandleader and who also wrote, produced, and directed *The Adventures of Ozzie and Harriet*, decided to incorporate Ricky's love for rock music into the show. Ricky began to perform rock and roll songs on the program, singing and playing his guitar in a calm, soothing manner that Ozzie knew parents would approve of Ozzie's ingeniousness resulted in instant success. He had created a sensation as he brought together two of the most powerful forces affecting teenagers of the time—television and rock music. This helped create a more positive reception of the new and daring rock and roll music that was evolving from black R&B roots. If rock and roll was okay for Ozzie Nelson's family on television, it was okay for many other families.

Another merger of '50s television and music was evident in the national television phenomenon known as *American Bandstand*, based in Philadelphia, Pennsylvania. Originally a local radio show first broadcast in 1952, Bob Horn's *Bandstand* was a popular radio program on station WFIL. Upon its change to a television show, *Bandstand* played filmed musical performances by conservative popular artists of the day, such as Norma Jean Egstrom (Peggy Lee) and Nathaniel Adams Coles (Nat "King" Cole). As rock and roll swept the nation, the format of the television show changed to incorporating teens dancing to the new hit records live. *American Bandstand* was broadcast live after school and featured teenagers doing current dances—the stroll, twist, cha-lypso, and jitterbug—to the hottest records of the day. In 1956, a radio deejay, Richard Wagstaff Clark (Dick Clark), became host of this extremely popular television show that appealed to a teenage audience at home who danced along. In 1957, the program went national. It was one of the few programs specifically designed for teenagers and one of the few outlets for rock and roll music on television. *American Bandstand* was television's longest running and most popular dance program. Airing from 1952 to 1989, it became extremely influential with youth culture and the history of rock and roll.[3] (See chapter 8 for further information.)

A new method of mass communication and entertainment that reached most homes, television had a profound effect on American society. It became *the* advertising medium. Products and performers appearing on television had an instant impact on the entire nation (which continues today). This significant shift to television as the favored entertainment medium in the '50s paved the way for changes in radio. Rhythm and blues music, craved by America's youth, was emphasized on the radio. Teenagers listened to the radio throughout the decade, and by 1959 radios numbered three times the television sets in America's homes.[4]

Importance of Radio

A loosening of Federal Communications Commission regulations in the '50s reduced the dominance of national radio networks and opened the door to dozens of new radio stations targeted to African American listeners. By mid-decade, approximately 600 local stations were broadcasting the complete range of black popular music. WDIA, located in Memphis, Tennessee, was the first of

An orchestra broadcasting on the radio, 1951. Courtesy of the Library of Congress.

these stations. It went on the air in 1949, bringing black music to the region's African American residents. Increasing numbers of white teens tuned their radios to AM stations favoring the black music sound. They discovered a style of music that seemed to speak directly to them. Their parents and teachers were appalled by this race music and felt that it corrupted youth.

Radio was a portable, all-purpose form of entertainment at the beginning of the decade. Many radio series, such as soap operas and comedies, moved to television, leaving airtime for the new trend in radio programming—playing music. Diverse music appeared on the radio, from classical to country and R&B to pop. And that music became very portable with car radios, which became standard equipment beginning in the '50s, in addition to the battery-operated transistor radio, which allowed music fans to take their radios anywhere. The smaller transistor radio, which helped to replace the large console radio, permitted teens to listen to music just about anywhere they wanted—in school, on the beach, or in their bedroom. They could listen to their music of choice, black R&B, in privacy, without their parents' knowledge or interruption. Portable radios and record players gave American teens independence, allowing them to escape from the large console radio or television set in the living room, where their parents controlled the programming. The transistor radio's invention in 1954 assisted in the birth of rock music by bringing exciting black R&B

musical sounds over the airwaves. Radio's popularity established the careers of disc jockeys during the decade. These advocates of rock and roll music continued to play the new, provocative songs on their stations.

Technological accomplishments of the time made professional-quality recording equipment available and more affordable. In addition to the invention of stereo sound, the heavy, awkward 78-revolutions-per-minute (RPM) records became extinct during the '50s as the smaller, lighter, and more affordable 45-RPM records took precedence. As a result, many small, independent record labels (indies) emerged in cities such as Memphis, Chicago, Cincinnati, New York, and Los Angeles, creating and recording hit after hit in the 45-RPM format. Local radio stations became the most effective and accessible way for indies to promote new rock talent. These small companies, such as Chess, King, Atlantic, and Specialty, recorded many R&B singles on 45s that eventually appeared on the radio and in jukeboxes, which were prominent fixtures in bars and restaurants in black communities. These companies had tight budgets and distribution systems, and counted on radio deejays to spin their discs on the air. The Top 40 radio concept evolved with radio's new role in the '50s. Disc jockeys constantly rotated only the forty top-rated recordings (as determined by *Billboard* magazine). This allowed listeners to hear music they liked whenever they tuned in to their favorite radio stations.

Dolores Williams (LaVern Baker), 1952. Courtesy of the Library of Congress.

Many pioneer disc jockeys with a passion for the new music emerged and placed the music into national consciousness. They played exciting R&B and the new sound of rock and roll by such artists as Chuck Berry, Buddy Holly, Little Richard, Fats Domino, Dolores Williams (LaVern Baker), Jerry Lee Lewis, Bo Diddley, Sam Cooke, Elvis Presley, and the Moonglows. These early jockeys included Alan Freed at WJW in Cleveland and WINS in New York; "Symphony Sid" Torin at WHOM and WOV in New York; "John R." Richbourg and Gene Nobles at WLAC in Nashville; Hunter Hancock at KFVD and KGFJ in Los Angeles; and George "Hound Dog" Lorenz at WKBW in Buffalo. Other early and daring deejays were "Jumpin'" George Oxford at KSAN, KDIA, and KWBR in San Francisco and Oakland; Porky Chedwick at WAMO in Pittsburgh; Pete "Mad Daddy" Myers at WHK in Cleveland and WINS in New York; Dewey Phillips at WHBQ and

WDIA in Memphis; Georgie Woods at WHAT and WDAS in Philadelphia; and Zenas "Daddy" Sears at WGST and WAOK in Atlanta. This first wave of radio deejays is responsible for having played black R&B music on the air and for having discovered that America wanted to hear this music, even before the Top 40 radio format became popular in the mid-'50s.[5] (See chapter 8 for further information.)

NEW CULTURAL EXPRESSIONS

A Changing Culture and America's Youth

Increased prosperity and ample leisure time generated a new consumer market in the '50s that had not been anticipated—America's youth. The powerful post–World War II youth market had a far-reaching effect on the music industry. Prosperity trickled down to teenagers who were not burdened by the work-to-survive demands of the Great Depression and had more

Promotional photo of Hunter Hancock, c. 1955. Courtesy of the Library of Congress.

leisure time than their predecessors. They were financially better off, many of them receiving allowances and holding after-school jobs. This phenomenon led to the emergence of a new teen subculture, complete with its own role models—the regulars appearing on *American Bandstand*—and print sources, such as *Teen Magazine* and *16 Magazine*. America's adolescents developed definite social, economic, and musical tastes that they made clear to adults. They began to purchase records by Chuck Berry and Little Richard and other black musicians. A wide generation gap between teenagers and their parents appeared in the '50s, as American youths spent their money on their favorite new style of music—rock and roll.

As these youths became an economic and cultural force, they rejected their parents' values. Teenagers rebelled in many ways—by being anti-high school; by idolizing actors such as Marlon Brando and James Dean, who assumed anti-establishment roles; and, to a certain point, by rejecting the conventions of society. Movies that concentrated on the generational conflicts of the time appeared, such as *Rebel Without a Cause* (1955), featuring James Dean. These films provided characters and stories with which adolescents could identify. In *Rebel*, Dean played a misunderstood son, the victim of insensitive and careless parents. He symbolized a common adolescent belief that, because they were

A scene from *The Blackboard Jungle*, showing teens out of control, 1955. © MGM/The Kobol Collection.

young, teens were misunderstood. What Dean had learned from Brando, Elvis Presley would borrow and apply to music as he became known as the rebel of rock and roll. The 1955 release of the movie *The Blackboard Jungle* gave teenage rebellion its first theme song, "Rock Around the Clock," by Bill Haley and the Comets. The film helped launch this monumental song as the first No. 1 rock and roll hit on the *Billboard* charts.

Though teenagers were preoccupied with their cars, spent a lot of money on them, and used them to help establish their newfound freedom from their parents, they used music as the biggest symbol of their revolt against the status quo. Rhythm and blues and rock and roll music epitomized this new rebellious attitude. By 1950s standards, the music of teenagers was too coarse, and many adults were not happy that it was black or black-inspired music. Thus, parents attributed the rebellion of kids to rock and roll music. They believed that the music was too loud and that it influenced their children to be destructive, since riots erupted at rock and roll parties. In addition, some songs treated sex and other taboo topics. Parents also did not approve of the dress and actions of popular '50s rockers such as Elvis Presley, Jerry Lee Lewis, and Chuck Berry. Performing on stage using Presley's hip gyrations or engaging in Berry's duckwalk was not permissible. Likewise, Little Richard's high-pitched screams were considered inappropriate. The music, lyrics, and looks of early rock and roll music and its musicians appalled the rigid parents of '50s teenagers. These factors deepened the generation gap, which still exists today, between America's youths and their parents.

Races Mix

Racial barriers began to disintegrate in the '50s, partly due to teenagers' boredom with adult pop music and their yearning for exciting music that stirred their emotions. They wanted music that spoke to them, that they could dance to and have fun listening to. Black music filled the bill—it was exciting, it was rhythm and blues. As America's white youths purchased records by artists such as Chuck Berry and Little Richard, they started to dance to the music. Advocates of the music promoted it to teenagers, who started to attend racially integrated rock and roll concerts. Thus the music helped integrate America. Because of their love for black music, teenagers began to accept African American culture and broke down barriers—those same barriers the U.S. Supreme Court was working on.

With the demise of the big bands that had flourished in the '30s and '40s, the R&B music of black musicians took the forefront after World War II. Performed by artists such as Big Joe Turner, Izear Luster Turner (Ike Turner), and Louis Jordan, this style differed from music of the swing era, mostly because of its roots. Black R&B made people want to dance in a different way from the older styles of music. Unlike the slower, more graceful swinging of dancers to the large jazz bands, R&B music allowed people to move to a quicker beat—one that stressed every other beat, the backbeat. The music had exhilarating, growling saxophone solos that stirred the interest of listeners and dancers both; R&B attracted white teenagers who demanded it over the music of their parents.

Popular Music Becomes Rock and Roll

The popular music of the early '50s that most of the nation was listening to was referred to as "pop." It was a continuation of popular styles of earlier decades, stemming from the Tin Pan Alley repertoire. It was relaxing music with no threatening musical content and lyrics that were mostly about innocent, young love. Pop music, in general, was comfortable and pleasant, like '50s society. The music expressed a society's desire to enjoy the good life, unthreatened by the turmoil and controversy of previous decades. Songs of this genre included such megahits as Frank Sinatra's "I Only Have Eyes for You" and Bing Crosby's "Out of Nowhere." Other crooners creating pop hits of the day included Perry Como, Nat "King" Cole, Andy Williams, Sammy Davis Jr., and Doris Day. This was the music that America's teens rejected, in pursuit of exciting, black R&B—the music that they tuned in to race radio stations to hear.

Pop music was still topping the charts in the '50s, though it waned in popularity as rhythm and blues emerged as the new preference. Threatened by R&B with its faster tempos, strong backbeats, and fast-selling records, pop artists grew to dislike the new sound. The music industry's large record companies that recorded pop artists started to retaliate by having such white artists as Charles Eugene Boone (Pat Boone) record cover versions (recordings made subsequent to an original version) of the popular R&B songs. Frank Sinatra referred to rock music as an ugly and vicious form of expression when he testified before Congress in 1958. The disc jockeys of pop and classical radio programs who lost their listening audiences to rock and roll stations also spoke out against the competition, as did songwriters in the American Society of Composers, Authors, and Publishers (ASCAP) who lost work, since R&B performers usually wrote their own songs. Though it put up a good battle, the music industry did not succeed; rock and roll became ever more popular as time passed.

Memphis Rhythm and Blues and Rockabilly

A wealth of rhythm and blues music flowed from Memphis, Tennessee, one of the first cities where rural bluesmen stopped on their migration north to urban centers. In the southwest corner of Tennessee, situated on the east bank of the Mississippi River, Memphis is the largest river city between New Orleans and St. Louis and the major city of the large rural region that surrounds it. Memphis was a major stop of the Illinois Central Railroad, which ran between New Orleans and Chicago. It was a natural crossroad in the South; the Mississippi Delta region, where the country blues musicians came from, lay below it. Those who came by car traveled what became known as "Blues Highway 61," which led into downtown Memphis; others came by boat. Some of them settled in Memphis; others continued to St. Louis and Chicago, among other urban centers. Today, the city of Memphis has a distinguished blues tradition that goes back to the 1920s.

Many of the country blues musicians settled in this innovative city, where their acoustic Delta blues music changed. The jug band was one of the most popular forms of the blues in Memphis in the early 1900s, using primitive instruments such as jugs, kazoos, and washboards. These bands also used the harmonica, which with time became a staple in urban blues bands. Blues musicians learned to amplify their music, creating a different sound—the urban blues. What originally was a solo blues act in the Delta region turned into a blues band in Memphis. Guitarists began to play together, one playing lead and the other providing bass and chords. In addition, the music's rhythms became heavier, quicker, and more insistent, as implied in the name "rhythm and blues." The rhythms of Memphis blues songs were harder and steadier than those of blues songs from the Delta and other surrounding areas.[6]

Memphis emerged from the Great Depression as an important blues recording center. While nationwide the record industry was damaged by the Depression, during the '40s, the city revived as a blues recording center, partly due to the pioneering black radio station WDIA. In the late '40s this station abandoned playing country, classical, and pop music. Instead, WDIA played R&B, broadcasting the exciting black music sound as far away as Canada. The station modeled itself somewhat after KFFA in Helena, Arkansas, which in 1941 started a blues show, *King Biscuit Time*, and featured a staff blues band that played at midday during the week. By 1949, WDIA was the first radio station in the country to have only black disc jockeys, including blues musicians Rufus Thomas and Riley "Blues Boy" King (B. B. King), who played race records and performed on the air.

Memphis station WHBQ employed Dewey Phillips as a deejay. The wild and crazy Phillips hosted a show, *Red, Hot & Blue*, every evening from nine to midnight. As Dewey stated, it was "the hottest thing in the country." He played race music that he loved on the air, and sometimes he repeated songs several times in one evening. He was the first disc jockey to play Elvis Presley's first single, "That's All Right," on the air after it was recorded by Sun Records. Daddy-O, as B. B. King called Dewey, served as the test market for many new record releases in the Memphis area. When he played songs on the air, teenagers listened. They not only paid attention to the music, but also listened quite carefully to him ramble between songs. Dewey's comments and phrases immediately became the new street lingo.[7]

One could hear blues music in the many clubs on Beale Street in downtown Memphis. On any given night such artists as Rufus Thomas, B. B. King, Robert Calvin Bland (Bobby "Blue" Bland), John Alexander (Johnny Ace), and Howlin' Wolf gave compelling performances. The thriving music scene was a result of the many blues performances on Beale Street—not only in clubs, but also on street corners, in theaters, at parties, and in railroad stations. Memphis blues musicians attracted and nurtured regional talent and were responsible for the two important record companies in town: Sun Records in the '50s and Stax Records, which became a mecca for soul music, in the '60s.

In 1950 Sam Phillips, a white disc jockey and engineer from Florence, Alabama, opened the Memphis Recording Service, where he recorded black urban blues singers. The success of these recordings led him to form Sun Records in 1952. Though he had previously recorded jazz swing bands, he decided instead to record music that excited him. Phillips initially recorded blues styles of artists such as Howlin' Wolf, B. B. King, Herman Parker Jr. (Little Junior Parker), and Ike Turner because he felt they had not been given the opportunity to reach an audience. He also recorded R&B, country, and gospel music.

Sun Records became very important in the early development of rockabilly, one of the early styles of rock and roll. Rockabilly artists, such as Jerry Lee Lewis, Carl Perkins, Roy Orbison, and Elvis Presley, were recorded there, in addition to the legendary country musician Johnny Cash. Phillips is credited with having discovered Elvis Presley; he had been looking for a white fellow who could sing with the black sound. In Elvis, he found that person. Presley had lived in Memphis since the age of thirteen, and the young singer saw and heard black bluesmen as they performed on Beale Street. Elvis hung out in the neighborhood, learning the blues sound from blues greats. He blended that knowledge with his gospel, country, and pop music background for an exciting vocal sound—one that Sam Phillips brought to America's attention—that would make Sun Records one of the most significant forces in rock history. (See chapter 5 for further information.)

Chicago: A Home for the Blues

Chicago was the end of the Illinois Central Railroad and the final destination of many Southern African Americans who brought the blues to cities in the North. Thousands settled in the Windy City. As they found jobs in the steel mills, stockyards, and food-processing plants, many made the city's South Side their home—just as in the 1920s, jazz musicians such as Joe "King" Oliver and Louis Armstrong had done. Early migrants and fathers of Chicago blues included guitar greats Hudson Whittaker (Tampa Red), Big Bill Broonzy, Sleepy John Estes, and popular blues harmonica player John Lee "Sonny Boy" Williamson (Sonny Boy Williamson #1). These musicians greatly influenced the next generation of bluesmen in the city and helped bridge the gap between country and urban blues before World War II.

The next generation included blues musicians Muddy Waters, Howlin' Wolf, Marion Walter Jacobs (Little Walter), and Rice Miller (Sonny Boy Williamson #2). Originally from Mississippi with such Delta blues mentors as Robert Johnson and Son House, Muddy Waters was the father of post–World War II Chicago blues. He led one of the most compelling blues bands during the '50s. Waters perfected the transformation of the Mississippi Delta blues to the urban, electric Chicago blues. The Muddy Waters Band used heavy amplification and included piano, harmonica, guitar, and drums to provide a prominent dance beat. The band influenced other Chicago blues groups. By combining the qualities of both the country and the city in Chicago, Muddy Waters created the R&B sound.

Chess and Vee Jay Records were two important Chicago recording companies in the '50s. Founded by Leonard and Phil Chess, Chess Records began as Aristocrat Records in 1947. A couple of years later, it changed its name to Chess, which, with its subsidiary label Checker, recorded Chicago blues, R&B, and rock and roll. Artists on their roster included Muddy Waters (the label's biggest and most influential artist), Howlin' Wolf, Willie Dixon, Little Walter, Elmore Brooks (Elmore James), and Sonny Boy Williamson #2, all influential musicians in the development of rock and roll. Other important Chicago artists—Chuck Berry, one of rock and roll's first great stylistic innovators, and Bo Diddley, famous for his signature rhythmic sound known as the "Bo Diddley beat"—recorded with Chess. They combined rockabilly guitar influences with strong backbeat rhythms to create some of the first rock and roll music—some of which rose to the top of the pop charts as well as the R&B charts. With Chess Records being the rhythm and blues recording pioneer, it is only right that the company acquired Jackie Brenston's 1951 recording of "Rocket 88" with Ike Turner's band from Sam Phillips (who produced it at his Memphis Recording Service and distributed it through Sun Records) while Leonard Chess was talent hunting for bluesmen in the South. "Rocket 88" is considered by many to be the first rock and roll record.

Chess Records also purchased some Howlin' Wolf songs from Sam Phillips, who recorded them at Sun Records in Memphis in the early '50s. Originally from the Mississippi Delta, in 1948 the Wolf founded a band in West Memphis, Arkansas, just across the river from Memphis, Tennessee, with bluesmen James Cotton, the harmonica wizard who later played in the Muddy Waters Band in Chicago, and Little Junior Parker, who composed "Mystery Train," the song that Elvis Presley covered in 1955 at Sun Records. Wolfs band secured a spot playing blues on local radio station KWEM, and began attracting attention before joining the exodus to Chicago in the early '50s. The Wolf called Chicago home for the rest of his life. Howlin' Wolfs blues style was rooted in the traditions of the country bluesmen he had traveled and performed with in the Delta region. His performances set the stage for later rock and roll antics. Wolf would act out his blues songs, jumping all over the stage with moaning, groaning, vocal yodels, and screams to the audience, similar to the vocal sounds of blues-influenced country singer James Charles Rodgers (Jimmie Rodgers) and the early Delta bluesman Tommy Johnson. While in Chicago, the Wolf established himself among the R&B crowd while competing with Muddy Waters. He had a series of hits that later influenced the course of rock and roll. His famous recording of "Moanin' at Midnight" was later covered by Jimi Hendrix; "How Many More Years" became Led Zeppelin's "How Many More Times"; "I Ain't Superstitious" was covered by Jeff Beck; and "Smokestack Lightning" was later popularized by the Yardbirds.

Many other independent record labels, all of which recorded R&B in the 1950s, appeared to compete with Chess Records. One of them, also in the Windy City, was Vee Jay Records, formed in 1953 by Vivian Carter and James Bracken. Originally a gospel recording label, Vee Jay recorded bluesmen John Lee Hooker and Mathias James Reed (Jimmy Reed). Originally from Mississippi, Reed was one of the biggest-selling bluesmen in the '50s. By the mid-'50s, other indies sprouted in major urban areas throughout the country, such as King, Savoy, Specialty, Atlantic, Imperial, Aladdin, and Modern and its subsidiaries RPM, Meteor, and Flair. These independent companies produced more than 80 percent of R&B recorded music in 1953, and by 1955 they were responsible for 92 percent of the rhythm and blues market.[8]

Cleveland, Ohio, and Alan Freed

One of the most famous rhythm and blues disc jockeys in the 1950s was Alan Freed, a classically trained trombone player who grew up in Salem, Ohio. Referred to as the "Father of Rock 'n' Roll," Freed played a major role in popularizing R&B among white teenagers. After appearing on local stations, on July

Alan Freed, 1958. Courtesy of the Library of Congress.

11, 1951, he made his debut on Cleveland radio station WJW, hosting an R&B program with his "Moondog" persona. Acting on the advice of Leo Mintz, owner of the Record Rendezvous shop in Cleveland and sponsor of a radio program on station WJW, Freed created *The Moondog Rock 'n' Roll Party*. The wild and crazy Moondog devoted the entire show to R&B music. With his unique style of howling like a dog, talking over the music, pounding on phone books, and clanging a cowbell, he became very popular. Freed would greet his listeners with phrases such as "Hello everybody. . . . How y'all tonight? This is Alan Freed, the ol' King of the Moondoggers, and it's time for some blues and rhythm records for all the gang in the Moondog Kingdom."[9]

Freed's show received much attention in 1951 and caused other stations in Cleveland to add R&B to their playlists. On March 21, 1952, Freed, Mintz, and Lew Platt, a booking agent and promoter, organized the Moondog Coronation Ball at Cleveland Arena. This was a landmark event in the birth of rock and roll. It was intended as an R&B concert starring the Dominoes, Paul Williams, and Vanetta Dillard. Though it was advertised only on Freed's radio show, nearly 20,000 people attended—mostly black, and twice the capacity of the Arena. By 11:30 p.m., the crowd had become rowdy, and the police and fire departments closed down the show. The riot soon became national news, and Freed's popularity escalated. Many cite the Coronation Ball as the first rock and roll concert. As another Cleveland disc jockey, Bill Randle, pointed out, "It was the beginning of the acceptance of black popular music as a force in radio. It was the first big show of its kind where the industry saw it as big business."[10]

Alan Freed is credited with coining the phrase "rock and roll." Though he claims he invented the phrase to describe the beat of the music he played, it is more likely that Freed appropriated the term from the R&B records that he played on the radio. The phrase had been in use for years as a code phrase for sexual intercourse on race records of the late '40s and early '50s. In 1955, when Freed held his first live New York City concert, he called it "The Rock 'n' Roll Jubilee Ball." Concert advertisements referred to the musicians on the program as rock and roll artists, and there was no mention of "rhythm and blues." The music establishment noticed and used Freed's coined phrase. In

1955, *Billboard* and *Variety* referred to Freed as a rock and roll disc jockey. Also, record companies began to describe R&B music in trade publications as "rock and roll." In a matter of months, Freed's phrase became an established and somewhat generic term to describe American teenagers' popular music. It is still widely used today.

In late 1954, Freed was hired as a deejay by radio station WINS and took his show to New York City. While there, he continued to spread the gospel of rock and roll. He introduced thousands of white teens on the East Coast to his favorite African American music recorded by indies. He organized and promoted many increasingly integrated rock and roll concerts at Brooklyn's Paramount Theater from 1955 to 1959. The shows included the most popular artists of the day, including the Penguins, the Moonglows, the Clovers, B. B. King, LaVern Baker, Count Basie's Orchestra, Jerry Lee Lewis, Chuck Berry, Buddy Holly, Fats Domino, Ruth Weston (Ruth Brown), Bo Diddley, Frankie Lymon, the Platters, and the Everly Brothers. Freed embarked on his film career in New York, appearing in such rock and roll movies as *Rock Around the Clock, Don't Knock the Rock, Rock, Rock, Rock!, Mister Rock and Roll,* and *Go, Johnny, Go!* Complete with multiple performances by the top artists and groups of the day, these films played a great role in promoting rock and roll to a wide audience in the '50s.

After violence erupted at one of Freed's live stage shows in Boston, WINS ended his employment in 1958. The disc jockey went to WABC radio but was fired in 1959 because of the developing payola scandal. He was not alone in the "play for pay" system of the 1950s, whereby disc jockeys were given cash or gifts in exchange for playing specific records. The indies relied on payola to have their songs played on the radio. Payola was a way of leveling the playing field, allowing small labels to compete with the industry giants, such as Columbia and RCA-Victor. In 1962, the Father of Rock and Roll pleaded guilty to two counts of bribery and was fined $300. Three years later he died, a broken man.[11]

Today, Alan Freed is honored as a rock and roll legend at the Rock and Roll Hall of Fame and Museum in Cleveland, Ohio. In 1983, leaders in the music industry joined together to establish the Rock and Roll Hall of Fame Foundation. One of the Foundation's many functions is to recognize the contributions of those who have had a significant impact on the evolution, development, and perpetuation of rock and roll by inducting them into the Hall of Fame. Freed was inducted into the Rock and Roll Hall of Fame in 1986 as a member of the first class of inductees. The world's first museum dedicated to the living heritage of rock and roll, the Rock and Roll Hall of Fame and Museum opened in 1995 and seeks to educate the public on the history and importance of the music in American culture. A memorial to Alan Freed has been added as a permanent exhibit in the museum, where the ashes of the Father of Rock 'n' Roll are housed. The deejay did more to spread the gospel of rock and roll during its infancy than any other person. (See chapter 8 for further information.)

NOTES

1. *Goin' to Chicago*, dir. George King, narr. Vertamae Grosvenor, 71 min., University of Mississippi, 1994, videocassette.

2. David Halberstam, *The Fifties* (New York: Villard Books, 1993), 132–142.

3. Dick Clark and Fred Bronson, *Dick Clark's American Bandstand* (New York: Collins, 1997), 13–22.

4. Glenn C. Altschuler, *All Shook Up: How Rock 'n' Roll Changed America* (New York: Oxford University Press, 2003), 15.

5. Ben Fong-Torres, *The Hits Just Keep on Coming: The History of Top 40 Radio* (San Francisco: Backbeat Books, 2001), 21–27.

6. Robert Palmer, "Rock Begins," in *The Rolling Stone Illustrated History of Rock & Roll*, 3rd ed., ed. Anthony DeCurtis, James Henke, and Holly George-Warren (New York: Random House, 1992), 7–8.

7. Robert Gordon, *It Came from Memphis* (New York: Pocket Books, 1995), 15–17.

8. David P. Szatmary, *Rockin' in Time: A Social History of Rock-and-Roll*, 5th ed. (Upper Saddle River, NJ: Prentice Hall, 2004), 10–15.

9. "The Big Beat: Alan Freed," permanent exhibit (Cleveland: Rock and Roll Hall of Fame and Museum, May 26, 2003).

10. Ibid.

11. "Alan Freed: King of the Moondoggers," temporary exhibit (Cleveland: Rock and Roll Hall of Fame and Museum, May 10, 2003).

2

ORIGINS OF ROCK AND ROLL: "THE BLUES HAD A BABY"

BACKGROUND OF ROCK AND ROLL

Influential Early Music Forms

When America's most popular music genre, rock and roll, came of age in the '50s, it had evolved slowly and from many different American music forms. It melded popular music styles, many of which dominated America's Southland. Though the Tin Pan Alley repertoire of pop music was centered in New York, most other precursors of rock and roll came from the South. Chief among the Southern pre-rock and roll styles were the blues from the Mississippi Delta region, jazz from New Orleans, gospel music from white and black Southern churches, rhythm and blues from the Memphis area, and folk and country music from Oklahoma, Tennessee, Texas, and many other parts of the South. These substantial American popular music genres formed from other preexisting types of music, ranging from European classical music and musical theater to work songs and spirituals, each with its unique contributions to rock and roll.

European classical music dominated American culture when British and other European settlers inhabited the colonies. They brought classical music (art music) of master composers from Europe to America, and it became the popular music of colonial America. French settlers in New Orleans favored French grand opera and produced large, spectacular opera performances. Many of the first songs published in America were derived from theater, such as English ballad opera, which mixed music with spoken dialogue in performance. Along with opera recitatives and arias, these paved the way for the birth of the

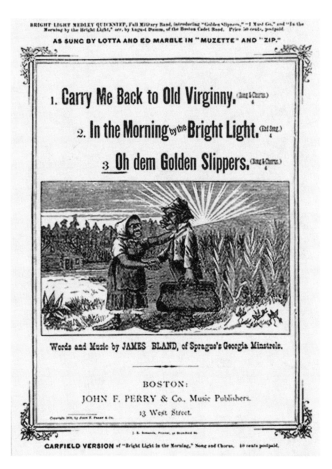

The cover of an 1879 songbook featuring the music of James Bland, an African American composer of minstrel pieces. Jerry Lee Lewis would later release "Carry Me Back to Old Virginny" as his final Sun Records single. Courtesy of the Library of Congress.

American musical, a rich source of American popular song. Much of the earliest American music was composed for church services, such as hymns and psalms. William Billings, an important early American composer, wrote hundreds of psalm settings, hymn tunes, and other vocal music for choirs. A school of religious song known as shape note hymnody thrived in colonial America. This body of sacred music ultimately influenced country music, one of the major roots of rock and roll.

Settlers from the British Isles and Ireland brought music to the United States from those regions. Although Americans modernized and localized stories told in their ancestors' songs, most often they continued singing them to the original melodies. A repertoire of indigenous folk music began to appear in America, and musicians of later genres followed this common practice. Stephen Foster of the Civil War era, Woodrow Wilson Guthrie (Woody Guthrie) of the Depression era, Robert Zimmerman (Bob Dylan) and the Kingston Trio of the 1960s folk revival, and Bruce Springsteen and Tracy Chapman of 1980s rock fame reused folk songs, replacing their texts with important social and political issues of the day.

Minstrelsy, the forerunner of the musical comedy, made its appearance in America shortly after the War of 1812. Having thrived from the 1840s to the 1870s, the minstrel show was America's most popular form of entertainment. Beginning in the 1820s, it featured white entertainers who darkened their skin with burnt-cork makeup and entertained audiences with caricatures of African American music, movement, and manners. The shows consisted of songs, dances, skits, and jokes that ridiculed African Americans with exaggerated stereotypical images. A new declamatory singing style that brought the spoken and sung word together arose from minstrel shows—one that stressed the communication of words (instead of the European refined classical music singing style)—and entered American popular music.

Though minstrelsy's demeaning and harmful stereotypes of black culture were difficult to shatter, with time the popularity of the shows allowed for more acceptance of African American performers by white audiences. Thus, minstrel shows helped establish black entertainers, as well as blues and jazz, in America. In the early 1900s, black musicians and entertainers, such as Gertrude Pridgett (Ma Rainey), Bessie Smith, William Christopher Handy (W. C. Handy), and Ferdinand Joseph Lamothe (Jelly Roll Morton) were among the first to expose audiences to a positive image of African American culture as they traveled, performed, and gained exposure to diverse influences and audiences. Minstrelsy, having blended black and white cultures in a simple way, originally began as a fascination with black culture, but later represented an integration of culture and music in a base form—something that rock and roll would also accomplish later. The minstrel show was one of the most significant genres in the early development of popular American entertainment; it influenced many theater and film musicals, in addition to television variety shows.

American popular music progressed from minstrelsy to vaudeville, which flourished from the mid-nineteenth century into the twentieth century and was a more appropriate form of family entertainment than minstrelsy. It was the most popular type of live entertainment in the country until it was overshadowed by radio and television during the twentieth century. Vaudeville shows usually included performances of sentimental ballads, thus creating a demand for songs and, ultimately, the pop song industry (Tin Pan Alley), another predecessor of rock and roll.

America started to create its own form of musical theater in the nineteenth century as an important outgrowth of vaudeville and the influential British operettas, such as those by Gilbert and Sullivan. Victor Herbert and Franz Lehar followed with American operettas; Edward Harrigan and Tony Hart pioneered American musical comedies. George M. Cohan's musicals paved the way for American musical theater, another source of American popular song. American musicals began to follow unified plots, and their songs and dances were related to that story line. Twentieth-century American musical theater composers included Jerome Kern, George and Ira Gershwin, Richard Rodgers and Oscar Hammerstein II, and others. Their unique American musical theater created a large repertoire of American popular music.

West African Seeds: Early African American Music Forms

The history of rock and roll can be traced to 1619, the year when the first slaves arrived at the English colony of Jamestown, Virginia. These slaves from West Africa planted the first seed of rock and roll by bringing their culture to America, complete with musical traditions. They came from areas now called Cameroon, the Democratic Republic of Congo, Gambia, Ghana, Guinea, Ivory Coast, Nigeria, and Sierra Leone. Although forcibly removed from their homeland with only the clothes on their backs, slaves retained their music traditions, which helped them survive mentally and emotionally in America. Having been denied their rituals of worship, the slaves adapted the imposed Christian teachings of their captors, resulting in a blending of the West African and British cultures in America—European psalms and hymns merged with songs, rituals, and deities of Africa—that maintained the format and chord structures of African music. Two chief traditions of this music were work songs and spirituals.[1]

Many characteristics of West African music have appeared throughout America's rich history of popular music, the most important being rhythm. Complex rhythms, syncopations, and polyrhythms (the simultaneous use of two or more rhythms), in addition to motor rhythms for dancing, have pervaded American music. Other common elements passed on to rock and roll from African roots include improvisation (the spontaneous creation of music); blue notes (altering the third and seventh notes of the major scale by flattening them), a melodic technique that was at the core of field hollers, work songs, spirituals, and later the blues, especially the Delta blues; swing, a relaxed rhythmic feeling; and whooping (a type of yodel that survived in the rural South well into the twentieth century in field hollers and blues).

Call-and-response, a very basic technique used in West African music, can be found in the blues and throughout the rock and roll repertoire. In days past, a leader sang music and a group responded, whereas in rock and roll a lead singer sings a phrase, followed by a response on his or her instrument. With guitars in their hands, singers established a rhythmic interplay between their voices and musical instruments, thus making the work song, which exploited call-and-response, an essential ingredient of the blues. Though it is a technique that can be found worldwide, call-and-response is commonly found in the blues, as well as throughout many rock and roll genres that appeared years later.

Two important predecessors of the blues that incorporated call-and-response were the slaves' work songs and field hollers. Work songs were secular songs performed very rhythmically, with hypnotic repetition, while doing a particular task, such as cutting trees or driving railroad spikes. A leader called out phrases and other workers responded. In contrast, field hollers were freely chanted and nonrhythmical, usually with narrative lyrics that told stories, and mostly sung by single workers while plowing or harvesting. Many field hollers were melancholy songs describing hard work and unfortunate aspects of the worker's condition; some of them also were performed in call-and-response. Both song types were repetitive, in verse-chorus format. The folklorist John Lomax and his son, Alan Lomax, went south to record these early songs in prisons, since prisoners knew and performed all the songs of the day. A 1934 expedition by the Lomaxes to the state penitentiary in Huntsville, Texas, resulted in historic recordings of this genre of black folk music.

Though they were popular before the Civil War, Negro spirituals became even more prevalent in the postwar period. These sacred folk songs of redemption and salvation composed by African Americans, which expressed religious feelings on the surface, contained coded messages about escaping slavery that whites could not understand—as in "Nobody Knows the Trouble I've Seen" and "Wade in the Water." When blacks were cast out of churches in the South, they were forced to form their own churches and to create music, based upon white hymns, for their churches. Black spirituals were similar to work songs and field hollers in performance style—repetitive and using improvisation, pitch bends, and other musical practices reminiscent of African origins. Some spirituals gradually took on a more secular form, abandoning their religious character, because slaves seldom regarded the separation of sacred and secular music. Later, secularization carried over to the bluesmen; it was not uncommon to hear them on a street corner in Memphis, singing spirituals, for their repertoire constantly mixed sacred and secular songs.

Ragtime

Ragtime (a forerunner of jazz and a building block of the blues), an African American style of popular music that flourished from approximately 1896 to 1918, was a blend of black and white music and culture. Having grown out of "coon" songs (with whooping and hollering from minstrelsy) and the instrumental marches and dances of the late 1800s known as the cakewalk (a popular precursor of the piano rag, which originated as a dance in plantation life and then appeared in minstrel shows and in piano sheet-music form), the sophisticated and technically demanding ragtime music had ragged or syncopated rhythms as a main identifying trait. The pianist's left hand accompanied the syncopated right-hand melody with the alternation of low bass notes or octaves on the beat and midrange chords between, resulting in a very steady beat.

Ragtime was an important influence on blues and jazz. The twelve-bar formal structure that became common in blues compositions originated in ragtime music. Jelly Roll Morton, a 1998 Rock and Roll Hall of Fame inductee, broadened the appeal of ragtime with a more free-flowing style, known as stomp piano. The ragtime of James P. Johnson, the creator of stride piano (an accompanimental style that modified the steady left-hand beat with swing rhythms), resembled jazz and blues even more, and Charles Davenport (Cow Cow Davenport) pioneered the boogie-woogie piano style from his exposure to ragtime. Scott Joplin, whose "Maple Leaf Rag" (1899) set off a national ragtime craze, was known as the King of Ragtime. By the 1920s, ragtime evolved into jazz, one of the major roots of rock and roll.

ROOTS OF ROCK AND ROLL

Rock and roll had a number of roots: blues, jazz, gospel, rhythm and blues, folk, country, and pop music. There were also other influences, such as the influential early music forms previously mentioned, and the popular patriotic music of John Phillip Sousa, but these seven major genres constitute the most important roots of rock and roll music. Each of these styles of American popular music influenced rock in a unique way. The stylistic merging of these black and white music genres with black and white cultures in the early '50s was extremely important in the development of rock and roll. Rock is considered by many to be the first popular music to attack segregation in America, a result achieved by such important pioneers as Alan Freed, who mixed musics and cultures at his rock and roll concerts.

Blues

As B. B. King stated in the early 1990s, the blues is the mother of American music—the source. Indeed, most other genres of American popular music evolved from the blues, so it is an extremely important and influential root of rock and roll music. Without the blues, there would not have been many of the great artists and groups of American jazz or rock and roll, including Louis Armstrong, Miles Davis, the Beatles, Jimi Hendrix, Led Zeppelin, James Brown, Stevie Wonder, Pink Floyd, Frank Zappa, and Nirvana.

No one knows exactly when or where the blues were born. They seem to have evolved from various black music forms in the Mississippi Delta in the latter part of the nineteenth century. Many scholars believe that by 1870 the blues were well established across the South, though some historians argue that they began in the 1890s, and were brought to the cities by migrants from the plantations and farms. It seems unlikely that in the nineteenth century the genre traveled to the cities so quickly, since there is plenty of evidence of blues music prior to 1900. Therefore, the birth of the blues about 1870 seems much more likely. In *Deep Blues*, Robert Palmer points out: "Since blues was so firmly rooted in earlier black folk music . . . it's difficult to say with any certainty at what point it became blues."[2] And, as Bill Wyman affirms: in his *Blues Odyssey*: "We can . . . never know who wrote the first blues song. . . . it is absolutely certain that no one actually 'wrote' the earliest songs, as the blues emerged from the complex oral tradition of African-based music, developing rapidly during the last 40 years of the 19th century."[3]

In 1903, W. C. Handy, a trained musician, performer, and publisher who later published the first blues song, met a poor bluesman while waiting for a train in Tutwiler, Mississippi, a small town between Greenwood and Clarksdale in the Mississippi Delta. While the man was singing and playing the guitar, Handy realized that he had never heard the guitar played in such a manner. This Delta bluesman did not finger the strings in the customary fashion; instead, he slid a pocketknife against the strings to create a timbre similar to that created by Hawaiian guitarists pressing a steel bar to the strings. The man sang repeated lyrics in a very emotional and compelling manner, with a wailing, moanlike voice: "Goin' where the Southern cross the Dog." He was singing about Moorhead, where "the Southern" (local slang for the railroad) and "the Dog" (the Yazoo Delta line) intersected. Handy wrote about this important event in his autobiography, *Father of the Blues*, almost forty years later. He realized that evening that he had witnessed the blues. What he thought constituted music was changed by what he heard informally performed on that railroad platform and by Mississippi string bands. Handy later wrote a political campaign song, "Mr. Crump," for the mayor of Memphis in 1909 (changed to "The Memphis Blues" when published in 1912). Commercialism of the blues had begun. Later, Handy wrote many blues songs, such as "The St. Louis Blues," "Joe Turner Blues," "The Hesitating Blues," "Yellow Dog Blues," and "Beale Street." The commercial success of this type of music proved that the blues could exist in mainstream culture. As historian Robert Santelli has acknowledged, "The blues had arrived, thanks to W. C. Handy. American music would never be the same."[4]

By 1900, the blues had developed into a somewhat predictable format resulting from a blending of African techniques and characteristics found in spirituals, work songs, field hollers, and minstrel songs with European song forms and hymns. Most blues songs incorporated a set format, today commonly referred to as the twelve-bar blues pattern, that was repeated throughout songs. It consisted of three four-bar phrases with a set chord pattern that was often varied. A fairly consistent formal structure of repeated and contrasting phrases of text and repeated harmonies evolved. The simple form used most often is referred to by musicologists as AAB: the first A is the first phrase of melody, usually four measures long with a first line of text accompanied by harmony consisting of the tonic (I) chord (built upon the first tone of a major scale); the second A is a repetition of the same melody and text, usually four measures long, accompanied by the subdominant (IV) chord (built upon the fourth tone of a major scale) and tonic chords; and the B is a different melody and a contrasting phrase of text that often rhymes with the A line and usually is four measures long, accompanied by the dominant (V) chord and sometimes the dominant seventh (V^7) chord (both built upon

Son House, one of the creators of the Delta blues sound and a great influence on many musicians who followed, including blues greats Robert Johnson and Muddy Waters. Courtesy of the Library of Congress.

the fifth tone of a major scale), subdominant, and tonic chords, and functions as a response to the words and melody of the A sections. The three important chords that created the blues harmonic progression (tonic, subdominant, and dominant) came from hymns. These simple European harmonies merged with the African music characteristics and performance practice of black folk music forms, such as complex and swing rhythms (uneven subdivisions of the beat—though written as even eighth notes, they sounded more like triplets, producing a more relaxed sound), blue notes, improvisation, and call-and-response to create the blues in America. (See sidebar, "Twelve-Bar Blues Structure," for an example and pictorial explanation of customary blues format.)

The lyrics of blues songs were very repetitive and usually had two phrases of text, the first of which was repeated, followed by a contrasting phrase, resulting in the three-line stanza that was very popular among blues artists. For example, the text of W. C. Handy's "St. Louis Blues" begins with the AAB pattern: "I hate to see the evening sun go down; I hate to see the evening sun go down; It makes me think I'm on my last go 'round." And the second verse continues: "Feelin' tomorrow like I feel today; Feelin' tomorrow like I feel today; I'll pack my grip and make my getaway." The blues vocal style was derived from work songs and incorporated call-and-response; early blues guitar players developed the style further by singing a phrase and then answering it with their guitar before progressing to the next phrase. Musicians often sang when they were feeling sad or depressed, and by 1910, "blues" was commonly used in the South to describe the blues musical tradition.

The blues progression infiltrated rock and roll music and could be heard throughout the repertoire. In the '50s, Bill Haley's "Rock Around the Clock,"

TWELVE-BAR BLUES STRUCTURE

A Harmony:	Sung Text (Call)		Instrumental Fill (Response)	
	[1] Tonic Chord (I)	[2] Tonic Chord (I)	[3] Tonic Chord (I)	[4] Tonic Chord (I)
A Harmony:	Sung Text (Call)		Instrumental Fill (Response)	
	[5] Subdominant Chord (IV)	[6] Subdominant Chord (IV)	[7] Tonic Chord (I)	[8] Tonic Chord (I)
B Harmony:	Sung Text (Call)		Instrumental Fill (Response)	
	[9] Dominant Chord (V)	[10] Subdominant Chord (IV)	[11] Tonic Chord (I)	[12] Tonic Chord (I)

Jerry Lee Lewis's "Whole Lot of Shakin' Going On," and Chuck Berry's "Johnny B. Goode" incorporated it. Other '50s songs included the pattern in common variants, such as Gene Vincent's "Be-Bop-a-Lula," Little Richard's "Tutti Frutti," and Fats Domino's "Ain't That a Shame." Songs by Buddy Holly, the Everly Brothers, the Beach Boys, the Beatles, the Rolling Stones, and many more artists and groups used the blues progression, although, with time, the conventionalized AAB pattern of the lyrics was dropped.

Country Blues

The Mississippi Delta is the area from just south of Memphis, Tennessee, south to Vicksburg, Mississippi, west to the Mississippi River and about eighty-five miles to the east of the river, to the state's central hills, at its widest point. Though the area is not a true river delta, it is a very fertile area that housed many plantations. With the commercial success of cotton after the Civil War, acres upon acres of cotton were planted and picked by black workers. The cotton crops guaranteed work for thousands of black laborers, increasing the ratio of blacks to whites in the Delta to nearly ten to one. Though black workers had their freedom, they were still bound to plantations and working for low wages. With prejudice, lynching, Jim Crow laws, and the rise of such racist organizations as the Ku Klux Klan, they could not enjoy their freedom. The blues music they created represented their cruel existence, and it documented African American anguish better than any other form of cultural expression.

Some of the earliest places to hear the blues in the Delta were at picnics, socials, parties, and fish fries, as well as juke joints, which were shacks on the outskirts of plantations where blacks met on Saturday nights to drink and dance. It is thought that the earliest bluesmen were probably local plantation workers who owned music instruments, such as a guitar or banjo, and enjoyed singing and entertaining. And as the blues matured and became more popular, bluesmen began traveling and entertaining at different juke joints, living a life of whiskey, song, women, and wandering. By the turn of the twentieth century, the blues not only thrived in the Delta, but had spread throughout the South: to the west (Arkansas, Louisiana, and Texas) and to the east (Georgia and the Carolinas). Blues musicians had no way of knowing how important their music would become, that it would have implications far beyond their local juke joints, and that it would become the foundation for almost every American popular music style, from jazz and rhythm and blues to rock and roll.

The 1930s was a crucial period in the development of the blues, when early Mississippi Delta blues performers traveled throughout the South. These included Charley Patton, the first great Delta bluesman; Eddie James Jr. (Son House), one of the originators of the Mississippi Delta blues style; and Robert Johnson, perhaps the most famous blues artist in history. They spread the sound of the Delta blues while performing songs about their despair, freedom, love, and sex. Meanwhile, on the East Coast, musicians were developing the East Coast or Piedmont blues style (a more folklike and finger-picking style).

Among them were Fulton Allen (Blind Boy Fuller), one of the Southeast's most popular blues guitarists and singers; Saunders Terrell (Sonny Terry), one of the best harmonica players in the Southeast; and Rev. Blind Gary Davis, a gospel and blues singer and guitarist.

Charley Patton, recognized as the first star of Delta blues, was an entertainer who played plantation dances and juke joints throughout the Mississippi Delta during the early 1920s. He was, in essence, the ideal rock star—his showmanship combined a high-energy performance style with his music; he often played the guitar in a loud and rough manner, held between his knees or behind his back, while jumping around. Patton's performances reflected the characteristics of Delta blues—from his coarse, rough voice that reflected hard times and hard living to his similarly rough and percussive guitar style. His slide guitar playing helped make the technique a major characteristic of Delta blues. Patton also represented a chief characteristic of the genre—one musician singing and accompanying himself on an acoustic guitar. He moved frequently and lived the life of a bluesman: plenty of drinking and smoking, multiple marriages, and some jail time. He wrote songs with lyrics that dealt with much more than disastrous love experiences. He interspersed personal viewpoints throughout his music and explored issues such as nature, imprisonment, mortality, and social mobility—as evident, respectively, in his remarkable songs "High Water Everywhere," "High Sheriff Blues," "Oh Death," and "Pony Blues." Patton's influence on other blues musicians has been enormous and his stature in blues history is immense. As far as the country blues go, Charley Patton and Deacon L. J. Bates (Blind Lemon Jefferson) were most influential on the future of the blues.

During the 1920s, though the country blues were flourishing in the Mississippi Delta, a very influential street musician from Texas, Blind Lemon Jefferson, helped the country blues reach commercial success and was, along with Arthur Phelps (Blind Blake) from Florida, one of the most popular male blues artists of the time. Jefferson, whose musical personality is reflected in most blues music that appeared after him, was one of the genre's first commercially successful recording artists, having recorded approximately 100 titles between 1926 and 1929. Jefferson performed all types of music, from hymns and spirituals to work songs and folk songs, on the street corners of Dallas for change. His characteristic guitar playing and jazzlike improvisations gave his music color. Fellow musicians admired his guitar playing, but it was Lemon's extraordinary whining vocal style that made him popular everywhere he went. Jefferson traveled extensively throughout the North and South, including the Delta, meeting a great many bluesmen, recording for Paramount, and establishing his fame with such blues songs as "Corrina Blues," "Boll Weevil Blues," "Match Box Blues," and "That Black Snake Moan." His legendary "See That My Grave Is Kept Clean," an early blues spiritual tune that has been interpreted by countless blues musicians, became a permanent fixture in the country blues repertoire. Many blues artists were influenced by Lemon's striking music style, and a handful of them—Aaron Thibeaux Walker (T-Bone Walker), Sam Hopkins (Lightnin' Hopkins), B. B. King, Rev. Blind Gary Davis, and Blind Willie McTell—later carried his country blues elements to other forms of the genre. Many of Jefferson's songs became standards, recorded hundreds of times—and the source of rock and roll hits by such artists as Bob Dylan and the Beatles.

Jefferson, who wrote his own songs, permanently changed the relationship that blues singers of the time had with professional songwriters, since prior to Jefferson, female classic blues singers in particular relied on songs written by others. He wrote and sang vivid lyrical accounts of early 1900s black culture in the South. It was Lemon's recording success that led Paramount Records to search for other male bluesmen, and to discover Blind Blake in late 1926. Blake and Jefferson provided Paramount with the two biggest-selling country blues-men of the decade, and their success enabled other male blues artists to secure recording contracts at a time when the genre was dominated by female classic blues singers, such as Ma Rainey, Bessie Smith, and Ida Prather (Ida Cox).

Son House, another major innovator of the Delta blues style, brought an extraordinary degree of emotional power to his music, as evident in his singing and slide guitar playing in the 1920s and 1930s, recordings of "My Black Mama," "Walkin' Blues," and his powerfully autobiographical "Preachin' the Blues." In 1930 House, a main source of inspiration for blues greats Robert Johnson and Muddy Waters, traveled with Charley Patton and Willie Brown to Grafton, Wisconsin, where they recorded for the Paramount label. Born on a Delta plantation outside Clarksdale, Mississippi, House, once a Baptist minister, performed both sacred and secular music at Delta juke joints and house parties until 1928, when he was found guilty of having shot and killed a man. After Son spent time that year at Parchman Farm, a renowned Mississippi penitentiary, a judge overturned the conviction, and he was released from prison and resumed performances both as a solo artist and with Patton and Brown. In 1941, and again in 1942, Alan Lomax recorded House on location in Mississippi for the Library of Congress. After moving to Rochester, New York, in 1943 and disappearing from the blues scene for many years, House was rediscovered during the 1960s blues and folk revival, when he appeared at the 1964 Newport Folk Festival and became an attraction on the folk blues coffeehouse network. In 1965, he performed at Carnegie Hall in New York City and signed a recording contract with CBS Records. His 1965 recording of "Death Letter" is one of the most sorrowful and emotional songs of the Delta blues repertoire and has been covered by artists ranging from David Johansen and Cassandra Wilson to Derek Trucks and the White Stripes.

Son House had a direct influence on the legendary bluesman Robert Johnson, perhaps the most celebrated and mythic figure in Delta blues and considered by most blues scholars and critics to be a musical genius. Johnson, a virtuoso guitarist whose stunning technique was due in part to his extremely large hands, developed a unique finger-style approach to guitar playing. Legend has it that one night Johnson made a pact with the Devil at the crossroads in order to become a better guitar player. Whether or not that is folklore, Johnson's incredible skills as both a guitarist and a blues singer and songwriter, achieved in a remarkably brief time, became obvious to all as he traveled and performed not only within the Delta but also in cities such as Memphis, St. Louis, Chicago, Detroit, and New York, stunning other bluesmen with his talent. His reputation as a guitarist spread as he wandered the Delta as an itinerant solo bluesman, though occasionally he traveled with bluesman Johnny Shines and met others on the road, such as David "Honeyboy" Edwards and Robert Jr. Lockwood (Johnson's stepson, who was taught by the master himself).

Johnson learned his exceptional guitar playing from many. Delta musicians Charley Patton, Willie Brown, and Son House influenced his slide guitar technique; boogie-woogie piano players are thought to have inspired his use of walking bass lines (the bass sounds a note on every beat); Alonzo Johnson (Lonnie Johnson) influenced his guitar tone and texture; and other bluesmen impacted his melodies and rhythms—all of these mixing to give him his unique guitar mastery. Johnson's songs, like those of others from the Delta, originated in work songs, field hollers, and spirituals, as their structure reveals. His performances were complete with call-and-response phrases with a rough and nasal vocal quality melting into acoustic guitar sliding-note fills.

Johnson recorded a total of only twenty-nine tracks, in two recording sessions in 1936 and 1937. The first session, with the American Record Company in a San Antonio, Texas, hotel room in November 1936, yielded such classic songs as "Cross Road Blues," "I Believe I'll Dust My Broom," "Sweet Home Chicago," "Terraplane Blues," "Come on in My Kitchen," and "Walkin' Blues." The second session, in a Dallas warehouse in June 1937, generated classics such as "Hell Hound on My Trail," "Me and the Devil Blues," "Traveling Riverside Blues," and "Love in Vain Blues."

Although Johnson died at the age of twenty-seven on August 16, 1938, he cleared the path for all other blues musicians to follow, and his style entered modern blues and rock. His music and performance style had a profound effect on many blues and rock musicians, including Jimmy Reed, Muddy Waters, Elmore James, Theodore Roosevelt Taylor (Hound Dog Taylor), B. B. King, Eric Clapton, Keith Richards, Jimi Hendrix, Stevie Ray Vaughan, and hundreds of others. His blues standards have been covered by the Rolling Stones, Led Zeppelin, Cream, Eric Clapton, Steve Miller, and Cassandra Wilson. As historian Robert Santelli declares, "Johnson remains a vital source of inspiration, not to mention frustration, for those who seek to take blues guitar to a new, more spectacular level. Few other blues guitarists are held in higher esteem. It is also safe to say that no one who has surfaced since his passing has been able to match his unconventional guitar accomplishments, save, perhaps, Jimi Hendrix."[5]

Today, Robert Johnson is honored for his influence on the evolution of the blues. In 1980, the Blues Foundation established the Blues Hall of Fame, into which new members are inducted annually for their historical contributions, impact, and overall influence on the blues. According to the foundation's Web site, members are inducted in five categories: Performers, Non-Performers, Classics of Blues Literature, Classics of Blues Recordings (Songs), and Classics of Blues Recordings (Albums).[6] Robert Johnson was inducted into the Blues Hall of Fame in 1980. To honor his influence on rock and roll, he was inducted into the Rock and Roll Hall of Fame in 1986 as a member of the first class of inductees.

Other major early country blues musicians included Nehemiah James (Skip James), Booker T. Washington White (Bukka White), Mississippi John Hurt, Mississippi Fred McDowell, Robert Jr. Lockwood, and Johnny Shines. Skip James, from Mississippi, sang in a high falsetto accompanied by his complicated fingerpicking guitar technique. He influenced many Mississippi bluesmen, including Robert Johnson, and was rediscovered after his performance at the 1964 Newport Folk Festival in Rhode Island. Bukka White, a Delta musician whose coarse vocals and slide guitar playing are reminiscent of blues primitivism, was recorded by Alan Lomax for the Library of Congress while at Parchman Farm, serving time for having shot a man. Bob Dylan arranged one of White's songs, "Fixin' to Die Blues." The classic country bluesman was rediscovered during the '60s blues and folk revival, and performed at the 1966 Newport Folk Festival. Mississippi John Hurt, a performer of blues songs, folk songs, and ballads, lived most of his life in obscurity until being rediscovered in the '60s. He influenced many folk artists from that era and appeared at the Newport Folk Festival in 1963, 1964, and 1965. Mississippi Fred McDowell, from Tennessee, had

 ROBERT JOHNSON (1911–1938)

Robert Johnson, one of the most celebrated figures in blues history, was born on May 8, 1911, in Hazelhurst, Mississippi, the child of Julia Dodds and Noah Johnson. Sent to live in Memphis, Tennessee, with his mother's husband, Charles Dodds (who had changed his name to Charles Spencer), Robert was known in his youth as Robert Spencer. Upon learning the identity of his birth father, he assumed the name Johnson. Robert learned the rudiments of guitar playing from his older brother, Charles, and he taught himself to play the harmonica.

By 1930, Johnson had married, and soon after, his wife died in childbirth. He then met Son House and decided to become a bluesman. He learned from watching Son House, Charley Patton, and Willie Brown perform at picnics and parties in the Delta. After marrying Caletta Craft in 1931, Johnson spent most of his time performing and roaming the Delta, eventually deserting her. He later based himself in Helena, Arkansas, where he lived the life of an itinerant bluesman, meeting other great blues musicians and creating his legend. His love of women and alcohol was almost as well known as his music. Shortly after his second recording session, he died in Greenwood, Mississippi, on August 16, 1938, three days after he was supposedly poisoned because of an affair with the wife of a local juke joint owner.

To celebrate Johnson's significant impact on blues music and culture, Columbia Records launched its Roots 'n' Blues Series with *The Complete Recordings of Robert Johnson* (1990), a two-disc boxed set complete with extensive liner notes and rare photos, offering a new study of his music. The extremely popular release won a Grammy, not only placing Robert Johnson and his musical contributions at the forefront of music history, but also stirring the reissuing of classic blues albums on compact discs by many other record companies. Johnson's legacy so greatly impacted society that the feature film *Crossroads* (1986), was based loosely on his life.

a very coarse voice and played the guitar with a rough bottleneck style (originally blues musicians slid the neck of a beer bottle and later other objects over their finger to produce a sliding or whining sound on the strings), reminiscent of the Delta style of Charley Patton and Son House. McDowell influenced blues-based rock artists and groups, such as Bonnie Raitt and the Rolling Stones. Arkansan Robert Jr. Lockwood has carried on the guitar legacy of his stepfather, Robert Johnson, who taught him to play the guitar. Lockwood traveled the Mississippi Delta, playing juke joints and house parties with Sonny Boy Williamson #2, then moved back and forth between Chicago and Helena, Arkansas; returned to Chicago, where he was a sideman for Chess Records; and finally settled in Cleveland, Ohio, where he still performs. Along with Lockwood, Johnny Shines, in addition to traveling and performing with Robert Johnson in the 1930s, has carried on the Johnson legacy. Raised in Arkansas, Shines performed in juke joints and at Saturday night fish fries. He eventually moved to Chicago and later to Holt, Alabama, touring and giving audiences the authentic sounds of the Delta blues.

Though men dominated the country blues, Lizzie Douglas (Memphis Minnie; also known as Minnie McCoy) sang in the style and was the first female blues performer to become popular after the classic blues singers (Ma Rainey, Bessie Smith, Victoria Spivey). Memphis Minnie ranks with these blueswomen and Willie Mae Thornton (Big Mama Thornton) as one of the blues' most influential and historically significant female artists. During the 1920s, Minnie was active in Memphis's Beale Street blues scene, where a talent scout for Columbia Records discovered her. She created her own fusion of country and urban blues and became a major figure in the blues, as well as one of the most recorded and most popular personalities of the 1930s and 1940s. After she moved to Chicago in 1930 with her second husband, Joe McCoy (Kansas Joe), she helped the country blues develop into the urban blues along with Big Bill Broonzy, Tampa Red, and Leroy Carr.

A renewed interest in Delta or country blues in recent years has been generated by the work of guitarists and singer-songwriters, such as Kevin Moore (Keb' Mo'), Corey Harris, Guy Davis, Eric Bibb, and Alvin Youngblood Hart. These musicians have blended the acoustic blues style of the Delta with a more contemporary and pop-oriented music. Others, such as Mississippi-based musicians Big Jack Johnson, R. L. Burnside, and Roosevelt Barnes (Booba Barnes), have created a rougher, electrified version of the Delta blues sound.

Robert Palmer sums up the country genre in his *Deep Blues*:

> The significance of Delta blues is often thought to be synonymous with its worldwide impact. According to this line of reasoning, the music is important because some of the world's most popular musicians—the Rolling Stones, Bob Dylan, Eric Clapton—learned to sing and play by imitating it and still revere the recorded works of the Delta masters. It's important

because rock guitarists everywhere play with a metal or glass slider on their fingers, a homage, acknowledged or not, to Delta musicians like Muddy Waters and Elmore James. It's important because Delta guitarists were the first on records to deliberately explore the uses of feedback and distortion. It's important because almost everyone who picks up a harmonica, in America or England or France or Scandinavia, will at some stage in his development emulate either Little Walter or a Little Walter imitator. It's important because bass patterns, guitar riffs, and piano boogies invented in the Delta course through a broad spectrum of Western popular music, from hard rock to singer-songwriter pop to disco to jazz to movie soundtracks. It's important because Delta bluesmen like Muddy Waters and Robert Johnson have become icons, larger-than-life figures who seem to have articulated some of contemporary America's highest aspirations and darkest secrets with incomparable immediacy in music they made thirty or forty years ago.[7]

Classic Blues

In the early twentieth century, blues music spread throughout the South, thanks to itinerant blues musicians carrying their music from one place to another and to the many traveling medicine and minstrel shows using musicians who played the blues. The blues gained more exposure around the turn of the twentieth century when entrepreneurs began to market prerecorded music and record companies (e.g., Columbia Records and the Victor Company) began selling discs targeted to white consumers. This breakthrough in recorded music allowed the race record industry to emerge in 1920, when the black pianist and composer Perry Bradford convinced OKeh Records to record his "Crazy Blues." On August 10, 1920, Mamie Smith, an African American vaudeville and cabaret singer, accompanied by the Jazz Hounds, recorded the song, which became a huge hit. The success of this first blues record helped the genre soar in popularity and caused other record companies, such as Black Swan, to sign black female singers to make blues

Known as the Empress of the Blues, Bessie Smith was the greatest and most influential singer to emerge from the classic blues era. Courtesy of the Library of Congress.

records. Mamie Smith paved the path for other female blues vocalists, most of them from the South and familiar with the country blues. These so-called classic blues singers included Ma Rainey, Bessie Smith (no relation to Mamie), Alberta Hunter, Ida Cox, Clara Smith (no relation to either Mamie or Bessie), Victoria Spivey, Sara Martin, and Ethel Waters—all of them thriving during the 1920s, the classic blues period.

While early blues musicians generally accompanied themselves on guitar and occasionally a banjo or mandolin, sometimes they used a harmonica or sang a cappella, depending on how poor they were. Though duos were not uncommon, the blues musician was initially a solo artist. As blues music grew in popularity, string bands and small orchestras, such as those led by W. C. Handy, began to play the blues. Handy successfully published blues songs in sheet music format and extended the blues beyond the poor black community. Black piano players began adding the blues to their repertoires as they performed in saloons and bordellos in Southern cities, whereas in New Orleans, musicians played wind instruments and piano more than guitars and harmonicas, so they jazzed up the blues with these instruments. Small jazz bands became the customary accompaniment for classic blueswomen singing on recordings throughout the 1920s. Such jazz greats as Louis Armstrong, Coleman Hawkins, James P. Johnson, and Fletcher Henderson accompanied and absorbed blues characteristics into their jazz from the classic blues as they performed accompaniments to blueswomen on many recordings.

Along with Bessie Smith, Ma Rainey is regarded as the best of the classic blues singers of the '20s. A 1990 Rock and Roll Hall of Fame inductee, Rainey is known as the Mother of the Blues because she inspired many female blues singers who followed. She is thought to have been the first woman to incorporate blues into minstrel and vaudeville stage shows as early as 1902. Her classic blues recordings included "C. C. Rider," "Ma Rainey's Black Bottom," and "Jelly Bean Blues." The greatest and most influential singer to emerge from the classic blues era, Bessie Smith has influenced every female blues and blues-related artist since, including gospel great Mahalia Jackson and blues rocker Janis Joplin. In 1923, while living in the fast lane—drinking, having sex, traveling, and performing—Smith successfully debuted with Columbia Records with a cover of Alberta Hunter's "Down Hearted Blues." Empress of the Blues, Smith was one of the most prolific artists of the classic blues period, recording more than 150 songs, including the classics "'Taint Nobody's Bizness if I Do," "Back Water Blues," "Mama's Got the Blues," "Poor Man's Blues," and "Nobody Knows You When You're Down and Out," all songs that illustrate her blues vocal mastery and her ability to evoke feelings while explaining 1920s black culture. Smith was inducted into the Rock and Roll Hall of Fame in 1989.

Among the many other contemporaries of Rainey and Smith were Alberta Hunter, who in the 1920s helped bridge the gap between the classic blues and cabaret pop music while introducing white audiences to the expressive power of the blues; Ida Cox, billed as the Uncrowned Queen of the Blues, who was known for the gloomy songs she composed; Clara Smith, called the Queen of the Moaners, who was a vaudeville blues singer and a popular performer on the Theater Owners Booking Agency (TOBA) circuit known for her melancholic songs about lost love and betrayal; Victoria Spivey, whose moanlike vocal qualities reflected her Texas roots in country blues, and who wrote "Dope Head Blues," perhaps the first recorded blues song about cocaine; Sara Martin, known for her extravagant costumes and jewelry; and Ethel Waters, known as Sweet Mama Stringbean, who later became a stage and film actress. All these women made unique contributions to the classic blues.

Blues Piano

Boogie-woogie was a blues piano style pioneered before World War I by such rent-party pianists as Romeo Nelson, Arthur Montana Taylor, and Charles Avery. The style emerged in cities as entertainment at rent parties. Blacks gave parties at which guests were invited to contribute toward the rent to offset excessive rents charged for their apartments. These early pianists were forgotten in the Depression years until record producer and critic John Hammond discovered the Chicago musicians Albert Ammons and Meade Lewis (Meade Lux Lewis) and the Kansas City musician Pete Johnson. Known as the Boogie Woogie Trio, they, along with Johnson's singer, Big Joe Turner, became very popular. This blues piano style received its name from the 1928 song credited as the first boogie-woogie record, "Pine Top's Boogie Woogie," by Clarence Smith (Pine Top Smith).

The boogie-woogie craze swept the country in the late 1930s and 1940s. This blues piano style consisted of the blues chord progression, a repetitive left-hand bass figure, and a strong percussive rhythmic sense. The Boogie Woogie Trio brought this popular style out of the clubs and onto the stages, laying the groundwork for rhythm and blues and rock and roll. Boogie-woogie has been one of the most enduring elements of blues performance practice, having entered the urban blues, R&B, and rock and roll. It became popular with musicians from Muddy Waters and Howlin' Wolf to Little Richard and Jerry Lee Lewis. In 1986, the Rock and Roll Hall of Fame Foundation acknowledged the importance of blues piano in the birth of rock and roll in the '50s, inducting Jimmy Yancey, a pioneering Chicago boogie-woogie pianist whose distinctive keyboard style influenced the music of the '50s, into the Rock and Roll Hall of Fame.

Urban Blues

As the northward migration continued and peaked in the '50s, and bluesmen moved north, some went only as far as Memphis or St. Louis and Kansas City, while others continued to Chicago, Detroit, Cleveland, Pittsburgh, Philadelphia, Newark, New Jersey, and New York City. Some went west to Los Angeles, Oakland, San Francisco, or Seattle, but no matter what their final destination was, these musicians brought their rural customs with them to their new urban settings. As a result, blues music developed into the urban or electric blues; it became extremely popular and launched the careers of some of the greatest bluesmen. Chicago became the nucleus of the new electric blues as many early Delta country blues musicians (Big Bill Broonzy, Tampa Red, Memphis Minnie, and others) came there in search of recording opportunities. After World War II and the urban blues explosion, Chicago became a mecca for the blues; the music remains there and thrives to this day. As Peter Guralnick declares in *Feel like Going Home: Portraits in Blues and Rock 'n' Roll*: "the blues came out of Mississippi, sniffed around in Memphis and then settled in Chicago where it is most likely it will peacefully live out the rest of its days."[8]

Urban blues was simple music, compared with rhythm and blues, with saxophone-led jump style combos and blues singers that had been popularized after World War II by Louis Jordan, Wynonie Harris, Amos Milburn, and Big Joe Turner. The jump blues R&B style influenced urban blues by introducing backbeats and bass riffs; however, in urban blues the amplified harmonica substituted for the jump blues saxophone, which was a prominent instrument in the R&B combos. The urban blues sound was not as polished as the jump blues, which included jazz and pop elements. Instead, the new urban blues sound was still the country blues, but electrified. In Northern cities, blues bands replaced the acoustic sounds of solo bluesmen of the South. A remarkable transformation of the blues occurred in the 1940s and 1950s when the older country styles of Charley Patton, Son House, and Robert Johnson were changed into the dynamic city styles of younger bluesmen, such as Muddy Waters, Willie Dixon, Howlin' Wolf, Little Walter, Jimmy Reed, Elmore James, Sonny Boy Williamson #2, B. B. King, John Lee Hooker, T-Bone Walker, and Lightnin' Hopkins; the electric blues was in full swing, being played to packed houses in major cities.

Brilliant blues artist Muddy Waters is considered the founder of post–World War II Chicago blues. Waters left the Mississippi Delta for Chicago in 1943 with hopes of becoming a commercial recording artist. The master guitarist, singer, songwriter, bandleader, and recording artist played a critical role in linking the Mississippi Delta blues and urban electric blues. He transformed the blues guitar sound as he blended the old and new blues with his innovative use of the electric guitar. He played the instrument with the same urgency and excitement as his Delta mentors, Robert Johnson and Son House. Waters began playing the electric guitar in 1944 out of necessity. An acoustic guitar was adequate for apartment parties, but to be heard in a crowded city club, amplification was necessary. It gave Waters's sound weight and density and brought out subtleties in his slide guitar playing (still Delta blues, but reincarnated), resulting in a louder, harder-edged, and bigger sound.

Waters changed music history when he began playing with a band because the blues had almost always been a solo act. He and his band changed the blues from the lonely, rural sound to the lively, urban blues, filling dance floors in

South Side clubs. For Leonard and Phil Chess at Aristocrat and then Chess Records, in 1951 he recorded such songs as "Louisiana Blues," "Long Distance Call," and "Honey Bee," which defined the sound of the new Chicago blues. In 1954, Waters made the biggest hits of his career, "I'm Your Hoochie Coochie Man," "Just Make Love to Me," and "I'm Ready," written for him by fellow Mississippi bluesman and superb songwriter Willie Dixon. These songs featured stop-time riffs (melodic ideas with silence built in to interrupt accompaniment rhythms and to feature the voice), with the whole band phrasing them in unison—similar to jazz riffs and those that Ray Charles Robinson (Ray Charles), who was creating hits in 1954 in his new, heavily gospel-based R&B style, was so fond of. The riffs from Waters's songs were picked up by the songwriters-producers Jerry Leiber and Mike Stoller, who were writing R&B songs and producing records by black vocal groups for their Spark record label. Leiber and Stoller recorded "Riot in Cell Block Number Nine" with the Robins, using a Muddy Waters stop-time riff; it was the first R&B hit to feature extensive use of sound effects and precisely timed comedy. The following year, Leiber and Stoller formed the Coasters, which became one of the most popular black groups of the rock and roll era and very effectively used the stop-time riff. With time, Waters's rhythmic innovation was absorbed into blues, jazz, R&B, and rock and roll, as was his other rhythmic innovation—the backbeat (emphasis on the second and fourth of every four beats). Others followed using a strong backbeat, and the sound eventually permeated rock and roll. Through all of Waters's changes to the blues (rhythmic excitement, flashy lyrics, and more flamboyant performance style), he never lost sight of his Delta roots and his slide guitar tradition.

Muddy Waters redefined the blues, making it contemporary music. He helped in the birth of rock and roll in the early 1950s and inspired countless young guitarists to play the blues in the early 1960s. The exceptional bluesman kept the blues alive in the '70s and forever changed the face of American music because the blues influenced most popular music forms. In 1980, Muddy Waters was inducted into the Blues Foundation's Hall of Fame, and in 1987 he was inducted into the Rock and Roll Hall of Fame.

Willie Dixon, who often played bass with Waters, helped define the Chess sound

Muddy Waters performing at the Conway Hall in London, 1958. © Terry Cryer/Corbis.

MUDDY WATERS (1915–1983)

Born McKinley Morganfield on April 14, 1915, in Rolling Fork, Mississippi, Muddy Waters (nicknamed for his playing near a muddy creek) was raised by his grandmother on Stovall's Plantation, just outside Clarksdale. He learned how to sing in the cotton fields, where he worked for 50 cents a day. He learned how to play the harmonica at seven and to play the guitar at seventeen, and soon afterward he was performing at house parties and fish fries, developing his guitar style from hearing Son House and Robert Johnson play country blues.

In 1943, Waters moved to Chicago with one suitcase and one guitar (purchased from Sears Roebuck, where many bluesmen bought them). After settling in an apartment near Maxwell Street, Waters played occasionally in the neighborhood, where blues musicians sang and played guitars, harmonicas, and drum sets (even amplified) on curbs, on corners, in the alleys, and in vacant lots for tips. Blues musicians just in from the South performed there, as well as for informal house parties, which were their principal sources of musical employment.

Waters became one of the most popular and best-selling artists of Aristocrat and Chess Records. He and his band made blues a raw, ferocious, and physical music, rather than merely making it louder. They spearheaded the transformation of Delta blues from music with a large black following to music with a white following, and finally to music with a worldwide following. Before Waters established himself in Chicago, Delta blues was music by and for Delta blacks. One of Waters's famous songs, "Rollin' Stone," inspired the name of an English rock group (the Rolling Stones), the name of a leading rock magazine (*Rolling Stone*), and songs by other rockers, such as Bob Dylan's "Like a Rolling Stone." A multiple Grammy winner, Muddy Waters died in Chicago on April 30, 1983, after a lifetime filled with deserved recognition and honors.

after the Chess brothers hired him in 1948. He backed quite a few blues performers, especially when they were playing his songs. Besides composing songs, he arranged them, secured musicians for recording sessions, and led the house band at Chess. A 1994 inductee of the Rock and Roll Hall of Fame, Dixon was an extremely important behind-the-scenes Chicago bluesman. He also served as talent scout and helped fellow Mississippian Howlin' Wolf by writing songs for him.

The most electrifying performer in modern blues history, Howlin' Wolf, served in the U.S. Army during World War II. After completing his military duties, Wolf returned to Mississippi for a short while, then moved to West Memphis, Arkansas, in 1948 to pursue record deals. Ike Turner discovered him there, and Sam Phillips recorded his "Moanin' at Midnight" and "How Many More Years." Phillips leased these recordings to Chess Records, which released them on the Chess label. In 1953, Wolf moved to Chicago, where he was in healthy competition with Muddy Waters. Dixon gave Wolf his songs "Spoonful," "Little Red Rooster," "Back Door Man," and "Superstitious." Though he was not known for his composition skills, the Wolf wrote some of his own songs, such as "Smokestack Lightning" and "Killing Floor." Inducted into the Rock and Roll Hall of Fame in 1991, Howlin' Wolf left his mark on the music world by having injected power and frustration into the blues with his wild performances, complete with vocal timbres ranging from whooping and howling to moaning and groaning, and his wild theatrics on stage.

Considered to be the greatest and most influential of the post–World War II harmonica players, Little Walter, in addition to being a talented songwriter, arranger, bandleader, and singer, had a much calmer personality than Howlin' Wolf. He made the blues harp an essential part of the urban blues sound, having demonstrated its effectiveness when amplified in a band setting and as a solo instrument. Arriving in Chicago from rural Louisiana in the mid-1940s, he worked with Big Bill Broonzy and Tampa Red in addition to playing in the Muddy Waters Band. The release of his very successful song "Juke" resulted in Little Walter taking over the Aces, one of the earliest and most influential of the Chicago blues bands. Another harp player who had led the Aces was Junior Wells, who took Little Walter's spot in the Muddy Waters Band. Little Walter called his new group Little Walter and His Night Cats until 1953, when he changed the name to Little Walter and His Jukes. It was with the Jukes that he rose to the top of Chicago blues.

A 1991 Rock and Roll Hall of Fame inductee, Jimmy Reed had an even calmer personality and performance style than Little Walter. His laid-back singing style appealed to a broad spectrum of people—white country and rock and roll fans as well as blacks who usually preferred blues with a more vigorous sound. Along with B. B. King, Reed sold the most blues records in the 1950s and 1960s; his records received airplay on stations with white disc jockeys and rock and pop formats. He had a profound impact on rock and roll artists and groups with his relaxed blues that regularly crossed over to the pop charts. His childhood friend and guitarist, Eddie Taylor, supplied the driving rhythms for most of Reed's recordings in the '50s, which they did for the Vee Jay label, and Reed's wife, Mary Lee (Mama Reed), wrote many of his songs. His impressive string of hits included "You Don't Have to Go," "Ain't That Lovin' You Baby," "You've Got Me Dizzy," "Baby What You Want Me to Do," and "Big Boss Man."

A 1992 Rock and Roll Hall of Fame inductee considered to be the most important slide guitar stylist of the postwar era, Elmore James was a disciple of Robert Johnson who bridged the gap between urban Chicago and rural Delta blues. His most important recording was "Dust My Broom" (1952). He and his band, the Broomdusters, recorded for Meteor Records, a subsidiary of the Modern label. James performed with Sonny Boy Williamson #2, one of the most influential blues harmonica players.

Aleck "Rice" Miller, called Sonny Boy Williamson #2 (after John Lee "Sonny Boy" Williamson), was an important harmonica player of the 1930s and 1940s. He influenced numerous blues musicians via his daily performances on the radio show, *King Biscuit Time*, on KFFA, in Helena, Arkansas, and with Little Walter shaped the course of post–World War II modern harp playing.

There were many bluesmen of note on the Memphis blues scene, both solo performers and the informal group that recorded and broadcast together, known as the Beale Streeters: Bobby "Blue" Bland, Little Junior Parker, Roscoe Gordon (Rosco Gordon), Earl Forest, Johnny Ace, and B. B. King. Of this group, King became the blues' bright future; he was the genre's most successful concert artist and ambassador. Over the years, King brought the blues to America's eyes and ears through his passion for the music. No other blues artist has done as much for the genre. Thanks to his active performance career—hundreds of blues performances every year since the 1950s—blues music and culture have won great respect, gained a wide audience, and been performed around the world.

King has received more awards and honorary degrees than any other bluesman in history, including multiple Grammy Awards and the Presidential Medal of the Arts. In 1980, he was inducted into the Blues Foundation's Hall of Fame, and, in 1987, he was inducted into the Rock and Roll Hall of Fame. On his beloved guitar, known as Lucille, King pioneered vibrato and note-bending techniques that are used today by all blues lead-guitar players. He has also had a profound effect on rock guitarists—having influenced such rockers as Eric Clapton, Jeff Beck, Jimmy Page, Johnny Winter, and Stevie Ray Vaughan. King's guitar style, a blend of Mississippi blues and jazz mixed with gospel, rock, and pop, is heard in his many hits, including the No. 1s from the '50s: "Three O'Clock Blues" (1951), "You Know I Love You" (1952), "Please Love Me" (1953), and "You Upset Me Baby" (1954). King elevated the blues guitar solo to an art form with his exquisite use of vibrato and pitch bending, mixed with his eloquent treatment of solo passages. He brought the blues out of juke joints, clubs, and roadhouses by performing in concert halls.

B. B. King, c. 1951. Courtesy of Photofest.

In the '60s, when rock groups acknowledged King's musical influence, his audience became even larger, encompassing rock fans, and he recorded with, and performed in rock venues alongside many rock and roll artists and groups, including the Rolling Stones, Stevie Wonder, the Marshall Tucker Band, and U2, all the while spreading rock and roll's most important root, the blues, throughout America and overseas.

John Lee Hooker is one of the notables of post–World War II blues, along with Muddy Waters, B. B. King, Willie Dixon, Howlin' Wolf, and Lightnin' Hopkins. With King, Hooker is one of the most famous and successful bluesmen in history. The Father of the Boogie, as he is called for his trademark sound (the constant use of intense, one-chord guitar rhythm patterns and the rhythmic stomping of his feet), was born in Clarksdale, Mississippi, and in 1943 migrated to Detroit. The Motor City's most popular blues star was an enormous influence on many British and American blues and rock musicians, among them the Animals, the Rolling Stones, Canned Heat, Jimi Hendrix, John Mayall and the Bluesbreakers, Fleetwood Mac, Johnny Winter, George Thorogood, Bonnie Raitt, and Bruce Springsteen.

Hooker, a 1991 Rock and Roll Hall of Fame inductee, began his recording career in 1948 with "Boogie Chillen," released on the Modern label, a hit that soared to No. 1 on the R&B charts in 1949 and is today considered one of the classic songs in the blues repertoire. He recorded extensively between 1949 and 1952, quite often under a number of pseudonyms (Birmingham Sam, Delta John, Texas Slim, Boogie Man, and John Lee Booker), to escape contractual obligations, but his distinctive sound never changed. In 1949, Modern released Hooker's classic, "Crawlin' Kingsnake," followed in 1951 by his biggest hit, "I'm in the Mood." Before switching to Vee Jay Records in the late '50s, he recorded for Chess Records early in the decade, when he was touring with Muddy Waters. A Grammy winner and blues legend, Hooker remained active as a recording artist and live performer through the late 1980s, exerting a tremendous influence on many phases of popular music.

Inducted into the Rock and Roll Hall of Fame in 1987, T-Bone Walker was recognized for his outstanding blues accomplishments and influence on nearly every major post–World War II guitarist, including B. B. King, Jimi Hendrix, Freddie Christian (Freddie King), Albert Nelson (Albert King), George Guy (Buddy Guy), Otis Rush, Eric Clapton, and Stevie Ray Vaughan. He had

 B. B. KING (B. 1925)

Born in the land of the country blues near Indianola, Mississippi, on September 16, 1925, King was a farmhand in the Delta. Having been born into a life of picking cotton and driving tractors, he learned hard work while a youngster—something that would carry over into his stunningly active performance career. His mother died when he was a young boy, and his father kept his distance after he started a second family. King's early interest in music came from the church, where he learned to sing gospel music and performed with gospel groups. His minister was the first to teach him a few chords on the guitar, the three basic blues chords—tonic, subdominant, and dominant. Interested in jazz, King was taken and greatly influenced by the music of jazz guitarist Charlie Christian. The unique sound of King's band came from his interest in big band music; he has almost always performed with a band of ten to fourteen members, complete with horns.

At twelve years old, when he had made enough money working in the fields to afford a guitar of his own, King began to teach himself how to play the instrument by listening to his aunt's record collection of bluesmen Blind Lemon Jefferson and Lonnie Johnson. In 1949, he became a full-time disc jockey on Memphis radio station WDIA (where he received the nickname "Beale Street Blues Boy," later shortened to B. B.), a job that brought him a following and performances in Beale Street blues clubs. In December 1949, while performing at a nightclub in Twist, Arkansas, he gave his guitar the nickname Lucille after the building caught on fire and he ran back in to save his guitar. Two men had had a fight over a woman named Lucille that evening and caused the fire that King and his guitar barely escaped. King has gone through a number of Lucilles as he has shared his passion for the blues with the world.

an immense impact on the course of blues guitar history and is credited as a creator of modern blues and a pioneer in the development of the electric guitar sound that shaped practically all popular music in the postwar period. He experimented with the prototype electric guitar in the mid-1930s and was one of the first guitarists to play the instrument in public. Walker created the electric blues guitar style. Like Charley Patton, he often incorporated guitar-playing antics into his performances by playing the guitar behind his back and neck and between his legs, while doing splits and twists. Walker's showmanship highly influenced rock and roll artists Chuck Berry and Jimi Hendrix, who learned how to engage in performances full of excitement from him.

Walker was also well known for his first-rate singing voice and was a noted composer of blues tunes; his single most famous title and massive hit was "Call It Stormy Monday (But Tuesday Is Just as Bad)," which is generally considered to be one of the greatest blues songs of all time. Other seminal hits from the late 1940s included "T-Bone Shuffle," which became an essential song in every blues guitarist's repertoire, and "I'm Still in Love with You." Walker recorded with labels including Capitol, Black & White, Imperial, and Atlantic Records. He remained a favorite artist in both America and Europe, performing in major venues and at blues festivals throughout the 1960s.

Lightnin' Hopkins, a native of East Texas, was one of the blues' greatest talents and perhaps the blues artist with the most recordings. He recorded for more than twenty labels. As one of the most influential country blues artists of the post–World War II era, along with Blind Lemon Jefferson and T-Bone Walker, he had a major impact on Texas's blues legacy. Hopkins performed a simple and traditional interpretation of the blues that influenced many white folk blues artists and became even more popular during the folk blues revival of the early 1960s. He performed at Carnegie Hall with Pete Seeger and Joan Baez, and headlined concerts with rock and roll groups such as Jefferson Airplane and the Grateful Dead.

The importance of the blues in the history of rock and roll cannot be overemphasized. The genre had an incredible influence on the birth of rock and roll in the '50s, summed up by Muddy Waters as he sang, "The blues had a baby, and they called it rock and roll." The music provided the formal basis for rock and roll; it inspired and informed the music of key artists ranging from Cream and the Rolling Stones to Bonnie Raitt and Stevie Ray Vaughan. Blues artists left behind a wealth of music that is still imitated, adapted, and synthesized into new sounds. The emotional power of the blues continues to speak to all ages, races, and cultures. It still influences almost all new forms of popular music, and outlasts most of them, while keeping its identity and dignity. Both rural and urban blues are still celebrated around America in blues festivals and concerts, as evidenced by the latest generation of artists: Keb' Mo', Alvin Youngblood Hart, Corey Harris, Kenny Wayne Shepherd, Jonny Lang, Susan Tedeschi, and the North Mississippi All-Stars. These newer artists often perform concerts with established blues artists, such as Buddy Guy, Taj Mahal,

R. L. Burnside, Bonnie Raitt, John Lee Hooker, and B. B. King. These, and many other artists and groups, continue to draw fans to the blues, and independent record labels release hundreds of blues recordings each year, which has allowed the music to cross into the twenty-first century, secure in its importance in American music history.

Jazz

Jazz is another root of rock and roll that evolved out of performance practice introduced and developed early in the twentieth century by African Americans. The family of jazz genres derived from and coexisted with the blues, which were about ten to fifteen years its elder. Sophisticated blues musicians made livelier music, using exciting rhythmic devices and different combinations of instruments. Early jazz great Sidney Bechet described black American jazz as an expression of pride and happiness that followed emancipation; it was no longer suffering music, but joyous music. The new energetic, blues-tinged style derived from Southern black performance traditions, some of them the same as those that shaped the blues. Though there have been some very successful white musicians in jazz's past, black Americans have been the leading innovators and the most authoritative practitioners of jazz, and for the most part it is considered a black root of rock and roll. The two most important jazz genres to influence rock and roll were New Orleans jazz, often referred to as Dixieland jazz, and swing jazz.

New Orleans Jazz

Jelly Roll Morton claimed that in 1902 he invented jazz in the Storyville area of New Orleans. Though Morton played a great role in the evolution of the style, many other musicians also contributed.[9] The music's foundations were established in the cultural melting pot of New Orleans, one of the richest and most cosmopolitan cities in America during the early 1800s, where every kind of music could be heard, from European opera and orchestral music to minstrel tunes and plantation melodies. Music from the West Indies mingled with African polyrhythms carried to America by

Ferdinand "Jelly Roll" Morton, self-proclaimed "originator of jazz," is shown in Washington, D.C., recording the priceless Library of Congress documentaries for the Library's archivist Alan Lomax, 1938. © AP/Wide World Photos.

slaves and European classical music played by immigrants from Italy, Germany, Ireland, France, Mexico, and Cuba, as well as by New Orleans Creoles (the light-skinned descendants of European colonists and their African wives and mistresses). Many Creole musicians were classically trained; they identified with their European, not their African, ancestors. Music types that mixed in New Orleans included minstrel songs, plantation songs, work songs, spirituals, and ragtime as well as the sound of brass bands, which were popular in Crescent City parades. Brass bands often performed at weddings, funerals, and picnics, and also during the Carnival season leading up to Lent. Rhythmic and melodic elements from Cuba and the West Indies also mixed with the musics of this city. New Orleans had a reputation for maintaining a party atmosphere from the pageantry of Mardi Gras and the activity of its Storyville prostitution district, culminating in its unofficial motto: "Let the good times roll." The 1896 landmark *Plessy v. Ferguson* decision by the U.S. Supreme Court helped change the music of New Orleans forever because the "separate but equal" ruling forced classically trained Creole musicians into black communities, where they merged their technical instrumental abilities with the blues-influenced music of black bands. Together, New Orleanians integrated cultures and music styles, creating a new music initially called "hot music" because of its fiery nature, then referred to as "jass," and eventually "jazz."

As musicians in the city developed new ways of interpreting different kinds of music, from marches and dance music to popular songs, traditional hymns, and spirituals, a loosening of performance structures evolved. In nineteenth-century marches, ragtime, and cakewalks, rhythms were interpreted more freely than in the past, and musical phrases were played in a more relaxed manner and with swing rhythms. Drummers introduced syncopated patterns and players began embellishing and ornamenting melodies, using countermelodies and blue notes. The call-and-response tradition of West African music was retained, as were polyrhythms and improvisation within a group, derived from African drumming ensembles. These groups regularly performed in New Orleans at Congo Square, where slaves gathered to re-create their drumming and dancing traditions.

From this rich cultural blend came the pioneering jazz musicians of the twentieth century, including clarinetist Sidney Bechet, pianist Jelly Roll Morton, and cornetists Charles "Buddy" Bolden, Freddie Keppard, Joe "King" Oliver, and Louis Armstrong. Their music had two functions, both of which carried over into rock and roll: it accompanied dancing and it provided entertainment (with visually stimulating antics and physical activity in performances). By 1925, Armstrong, Bechet, and a few other musicians had altered the music's format with improvised solos and established the standards of virtuosity, two characteristics that rock music would later borrow.

Louis Armstrong heightened the artistic merit of jazz in the 1920s with his trumpet playing; his extraordinary range and superb phrasing, combined with his expansion of improvisation, left their mark on the music world. This first improvisatory genius of jazz performed with Fletcher Henderson's orchestra and then made recordings of the classic jazz repertoire with his Hot Five and Hot Seven bands (such songs as "West End Blues," "Hotter Than That," and "Potato Head Blues," with timbres of the typical New Orleans jazz band sound: trumpet, trombone, clarinet, banjo, piano, guitar, drums, tuba, sometimes a string bass, and scat singing— a vocal imitation of instruments). In the absence of drums in hot jazz, the banjo often supplied rhythm, while the music usually consisted of an upbeat tempo with exciting, syncopated rhythms and multiple instrumental solos and improvisations, a trademark that would carry on in rock and roll music. Another contribution to rock music by Armstrong, a 1990 Rock and Roll Hall of Fame inductee, was his singing with blues- and jazz-inflected interpretations, which broadened the expressive range of popular singing. His singing style influenced not only singers of the next genera-

Louis Armstrong. Courtesy of Photofest.

tion (including Frank Sinatra, Nat "King" Cole, and Peggy Lee) but also musicians of the early era of rock, such as Ray Charles and many members of doo-wop groups. By 1935, the New Orleans-style jazz band had become outdated, and big bands became popular with their sections of brass and saxophones that played written arrangements and with a typical rhythm section of piano, string bass, and drums.

Swing Jazz

In the '30s, the change from Dixieland jazz to big-band jazz (with groups of approximately six to approximately twelve players) resulted in more sophisticated and more conservative music. Typical big bands consisted of three trumpets, two trombones, three reed instruments (saxophones doubling on clarinets), and four rhythm instruments. By the 1930s, the tuba and banjo of New Orleans jazz were replaced by the string bass and the guitar, respectively. The black pioneers of swing jazz were James Fletcher Henderson (Smack Henderson), William Basie (Count Basie), and Edward Kennedy Ellington (Duke Ellington). As black big bands gained attention with their rhythmical hot jazz, these pioneers and others (including Bennie Moten and McKinney's Cotton Pickers) created big-band arrangements. Arrangers of swing jazz became important. They began to notate scores and incorporate such

Count Basie. Courtesy of Photofest.

techniques of older black American musical forms as call-and-response into their music as they created short, repeated phrases, called riffs, to accompany solos. They lightened the textures of the music with fewer doubled parts and streamlined harmonies (compositional techniques that resulted in speed and grace, making the rhythm light and catchy), and called it swing. It was an appropriate nickname for the music because it spurred a swing dance craze as the public enjoyed listening and, most important, dancing to it (swinging around the dance floors). The swing era lasted from approximately 1935 to 1945.

Count Basie, one of the finest swing musicians, gained his music experience in vaudeville and clubs around New Jersey and New York, where he listened to many of the Harlem stride pianists (jazz pianists of the 1920s who modified the steady beat of ragtime with swing rhythms, such as James P. Johnson and Fats Waller) before settling in Kansas City, Missouri, in 1927. In 1935, he formed his Kansas City-based orchestra, which became one of the most dynamic and creative blues- and riff-based swing bands of the time. Known as "the band that plays the blues," Basie's group concentrated almost exclusively on the twelve-bar blues form, and often played "head" arrangements, blues riffs developed spontaneously by band members. Basie and other Southwestern bands played music with a danceable, four-beat meter, which replaced the two-beat meter of Dixieland jazz.[10] Two excellent examples of the style are his 1938 songs "Doggin' Around" and "Jumpin' at the Woodside." Basie's style incorporated sounds of the dance halls, roadhouses, and juke joints of Texas, Oklahoma, Kansas, and Missouri. And though large ensembles were thriving, small-group swing was played by sidemen eager for more solos than they were given in the big bands. Two extraordinary musicians from Basie's band (saxophonist Lester Young and singer Billie Holiday) created some of the best swing of the small ensembles. Swing played by small combos developed from the small size of many clubs in New York City, particularly in Manhattan, where the size of clubs on Fifty-second Street demanded smaller groups. That street between Fifth and Sixth Avenues became known as Swing Street—a neighborhood where jazz by many of the best artists in small-band ensembles (trios, quartets, and quintets) could be heard.

Another swing great, Duke Ellington, emerged as the leading composer of jazz during the late 1920s and early 1930s, creating such classics as "Mood Indigo," "It Don't Mean a Thing (if It Ain't Got That Swing)," and "Satin Doll." The influence of blues on the Duke is evident in his large output of original works (more than 2,000 compositions), and his orchestra was known for its signature muted brass timbres, thick polyphonic textures, and a high level of dissonance, exemplified by 1926's "East St. Louis Toodle-oo" and 1940's "Ko-Ko." Ellington led the most stable big band in jazz history; it remained intact for fifty years. As an arranger, his greatest skill was writing parts suited to the particular sounds and capabilities of the players in his band. Along with other band directors, Ellington and Artie Shaw were influenced by classical music, particularly the instrumental concerto, when they wrote for soloists in their ensembles. They also wrote extended jazz works. By the late 1930s, as these jazz geniuses gained international reputations, jazz gained respect as an American musical tradition.

Bandleader Benny Goodman did for swing music what Elvis Presley later did for rock and roll. A white musician, Goodman successfully introduced this black American music genre, which previously had only a black audience, to a large white audience. Jazz historians place the beginning of the swing era with one of Goodman's appearances on the national radio show *Let's Dance* in August 1935. Goodman, a clarinet virtuoso, practiced integration: his band performed music written by black Americans, and he hired and performed with black musicians on stage and in the recording studio. Black guitar virtuoso Charlie Christian (a 1990 Rock and Roll Hall of Fame inductee who influenced every guitarist into the '60s, including B. B. King) became a member of Benny Goodman's band and gave solo guitar the stature of a jazz horn. Many white big bands also formed (among them, those of the Dorsey brothers, Tommy and Jimmy; Glenn Miller; Artie Shaw; Woody Herman; Stan Kenton; and Harry James). In the 1930s, as swing became the music of choice, it helped domesticate jazz as many of the well-dressed big bands (often referred to as orchestras) with their clean-cut leaders entered America's middle-class households on the radio and Victrola and appeared across the country in performance on theater, night club, dance hall, and military base tours. Jazz no longer was associated only with bars and clubs, or smoking, sex, alcohol, and drugs. It finally enjoyed a clean reputation as swing music spread across the country.

Big bands trained not only instrumentalists but vocalists as well. In the 1930s and 1940s, it became standard practice for ensembles to incorporate a solo singer or small vocal group to expand the timbres of the band, adding musical variety and glamorous presence to the orchestra. Singers performed melody lines and supplied background harmonies; many of them became famous and launched solo careers after their discovery with the big bands. Orchestra singers toured with the bands: Billie Holiday with Count Basie, Benny Goodman, and Artie Shaw; Peggy Lee with Benny Goodman; Frank Sinatra with Harry James and Tommy Dorsey; Ivie Anderson with Duke

Ellington; Ella Fitzgerald with Chick Webb; Sarah Vaughan and Billy Eckstine with Earl Hines; and Mildred Bailey and the Rhythm Boys (Bing Crosby, Harry Barris, and Al Rinker) with Paul Whiteman. Singers who had launched careers with swing bands were successful as soloists performing and recording with orchestral accompaniment outside of jazz in the late 1940s and 1950s. These singers influenced the teen idols, the pop rock singers of the late '50s and early '60s.

Throughout World War II, swing remained the music of choice in America, along with a craze for the blues-based boogie-woogie. However, the big-band style began to fade in the '40s, partly because of the war, which made it difficult to keep the large bands together. The shift in taste toward R&B with an emphasis on singers, and solo pop singers, in conjunction with the beginning of rock and roll, also contributed to the decline, as did the postwar generation's preference for different music for dancing and listening. Jazz experienced dramatic changes as some of the musicians who had brought virtuosity to the genre (such as John Birks Gillespie (Dizzy Gillespie), Thelonious Monk, Charlie Christian, Charlie Parker (Yardbird Parker), and Max Roach) created the new musically advanced, quick tempo, improvisatory style known as bebop in response to the white takeover of swing. This change coincided with a return to smaller bands and the appearance of the R&B combo with its more rhythmic and black sound.

Swing helped popular music move closer to rock and roll in many ways: the use of complex, syncopated rhythms and riffs over a steady beat anticipated the thick textures in rock; the use of call-and-response that often occurred between horn sections anticipated the interplay between lead and backup singers or melody instruments in rock; the use of melodies created from a repeated riff anticipated the same by Chuck Berry in rock; and the use of simple harmony in the jazz genre anticipated the harmonic content of rock songs. Of these characteristics, the use of swing's horns playing riffs in a bluesy style, with vigorous saxophone solos and a driving rhythm, was one of the most important, and led to rock and roll.

Gospel Music

Gospel music refers to sacred song with lyrics reflecting personal religious experiences of Protestant evangelical groups. It has existed in America since the mid-nineteenth century. First appearing in religious revivals during the 1850s, gospel songs came to be included in most American Protestant hymnals and were spread throughout the world by missionaries. By the mid-twentieth century, "gospel music" also referred to a distinct type of popular song without religious association, performed by gospel musicians in concert; it had its own publishing and recording companies. There are generally two forms of this root of rock and roll: white gospel and black gospel, each of which has left its mark on rock and roll music.

White Gospel

With its lengthy history in America, white gospel music includes a large repertoire of music passed down through hymn collections for use in Sunday schools to teach the Gospel to children until the mid-1870s. Between 1875 and 1910, the preacher Dwight L. Moody and the musician Ira D. Sankey led revivals, bringing gospel hymns to the forefront of religious music in America and abroad. After Moody, many American evangelists were active in revivalism in the early twentieth century. After World War I, professional revivalism declined until Billy Graham acquired a wide following in the 1950s.

Gospel music at pre–Civil War revivals was intended to touch people with the messages of the Gospel; its performances included regular emotional outbursts; in contrast, the songs during Moody and Sankey's time were

A. P. Carter (1891–1960) sings with his wife Sara (1898–1979), who plays an autoharp and his sister-in-law Maybelle (1909–1978), who plays guitar, Poor Valley, Virginia, 1941. © Eric Schaal/Time Life Pictures/Getty Images.

calmer, with less passionate singing and less emotion. The rural gospel music of mountain singers was emotionless, in the nasal, plain, and nonvibrato Southern white vocal style. White gospel groups (such as Ernest Phipps's Holiness Quartet) performed in this style, accompanied by fiddle and guitar. Other groups (such as the Carter Family, consisting of Alvin Pleasant; his wife, Sara; and his sister-in-law, Maybelle) blended the sacred and the secular during the 1930s by incorporating elements of ballads and sentimental, cowboy, and mountain songs into their hymns, creating gospel music distinct to the Blue Ridge Mountains. Carter Family gospel music was performed by two or three voices with guitar, fiddle, mandolin, or banjo accompaniment. Hillbilly and later country singers often performed both sacred and secular music, resulting in a blending of the two styles (as did black blues musicians). Some groups went as far as recording the two types of music under different names so as not to disappoint their audiences. The performance of gospel music during the 1940s resulted in the popularity of rural gospel quartets in the South; singing families and gospel concerts merged after the model of the *Grand Ole Opry* traveling show. In the 1950s, singers (such as Elvis Presley and Jerry Lee Lewis) began performing with gospel quartet backup groups, drawing national attention to gospel music. The Oak Ridge Boys, the Statler Brothers, and the Gatlin

Brothers began to represent the secularization of rural gospel music. Commercial white gospel recordings have been stylistically indistinguishable from pop, country and western, and rock music, except for their sacred texts and occasional imitations of black gospel singing.

White gospel music contained many of the elements of American popular song, and characteristics from both genres influenced rock and roll. The hymns were simple songs set in strophic form (verse after verse telling a story, all sung to the same melody) with recurrent refrains; often they were in major keys with simple harmonies in four-part settings of homophonic texture (a simple melody with harmonic accompaniment), the same formula adopted by rock and roll. The rhythm of gospel songs often consisted of repeated patterns with dotted notes, the rhythmic techniques of secular songs of the later nineteenth century. While known for its use of country guitar playing, hillbilly vocal inflections, and close harmonies (as found in barbershop quartet singing), white gospel music sometimes borrowed elements of its black counterpart. As black gospel singing developed and black gospel quartets became popular, white groups imitated them, incorporating exciting rhythmic drive into performances and making the music even more popular.

Black Gospel

With the rise of the Pentecostal churches at the end of the nineteenth century, black American gospel music appeared at approximately the same time as ragtime, blues, and jazz, and blended native music of Africa with Christian hymns. Black sources of the music included camp meeting spirituals composed by slaves, sorrow songs of the mid-1800s, and postemancipation jubilee spirituals. White sources included hymn texts of Isaac Watts and Fanny Jane Crosby, and anonymous texts from shape-note hymnals. The melodies were borrowed from many white sources and transformed by black American performance practice through the addition of syncopation to rhythms, blue notes to pitches, quartal and quintal sonorities to harmony, and call-and-response technique to performance. As Claudia Perry affirms in the essay "Hallelujah: The Sacred Music of Black America," African American slaves found solace in Christianity: "Brutally cut off from their cultures, families, and homes,

Gospel singer Mahalia Jackson was the featured artist at the May 17 Prayer Pilgrimage for Freedom in Washington, D.C., 1957. Courtesy of the Library of Congress.

the earliest African slaves found in the figure of the martyred Christ and the religion's promises of deliverance and redemption an iconography and a world-view that spoke to their own plight."[11]

A new kind of black sacred music, the gospel hymn arose in the late nineteenth century. These songs consisted of sophisticated texts, similar to those of spirituals, set to music in the white hymn tradition of Lowell Mason and others, with the addition of syncopated, African American rhythms. Fundamentalist Pentecostal churches were established in the late nineteenth and early twentieth centuries, and their gospel hymns were aimed at poor and often uneducated black Christians. These songs typically consisted of a verse-refrain format and were based upon the pentatonic scale with simple harmony. Gospel music flourished in the 1920s and especially during the Depression years of the 1930s, when African Americans longed to escape poverty, yearned to find comfort in Jesus and the Lord, and hoped for a brighter future. In the 1930s and 1940s, gospel songs and spirituals became an important part of congregational participation in black churches, a trend that continued through the postwar era, when a new style of gospel music (such as Edwin Hawkins's "Oh Happy Day") started to be sung in church. By the 1950s, the performance of black gospel music was no longer restricted to churches and schools. It also occurred in concert halls and stadiums, and on television, and became established in Chicago, Detroit, Philadelphia, New York City, and Birmingham, Alabama. Often called anniversaries, Gospel extravaganzas featured fifteen to twenty artists and groups, and lasted four to six hours.

The blues pianist who accompanied Ma Rainey, played with the great Bessie Smith, and performed as Georgia Tom with Tampa Red, Thomas A. Dorsey turned to religious music and followed in the footsteps of Rev. C. Albert Tindley, the Methodist minister and songwriter who is credited with being an originator of gospel music. The Father of Gospel Music, Dorsey is responsible for creating the music and the environment for black gospel music to flourish; he wrote many gospel songs, established the Thomas A. Dorsey Gospel Songs Music Publishing Company, and founded the National Convention of Gospel Choirs and Choruses. The composer of the famous song "Precious Lord," he coined the term "gospel songs" for the songs that had previously been called evangelistic songs.

The fiery and stirring performance style of twentieth-century black gospel music originated in Memphis, Tennessee, around 1907, when the founders of the Sanctified Pentecostal Church of God in Christ began holding services after being inspired by a revival in Los Angeles. Often the music was improvised and sung in a highly emotional manner (much more so than white gospel music) by vocalists who were preachers, congregation members, soloists, singer-guitarists, quartets and quintets, or choirs. Black gospel singers embellished simple melodies while dramatically emoting as the music moved them by shouting, growling, moaning, whispering, screaming, and crying. By adding florid melismas to songs and altering music pitches with blue notes and glissandos, performers extended or repeated fragments of text by adding improvised comments that sometimes alternated with phrases of text. The music evoked emotional responses and embraced both singers and listeners in a rapturous manner; while rejoicing, the vocalists sang and cried "Amen!," "Hallelujah!," "Yes, Lord!," or "Praise His Name!" Spontaneous and choreographed dancing, hand clapping, and foot stomping often accompanied the music, and, when instrumental accompaniment was available, it was provided by piano, electronic organ (quite often a Hammond organ), or guitar (which replaced the banjo in the 1920s), alone or with bass, and percussion consisting of bass and snare drums, triangle, and tambourine. The trombone, trumpet, and saxophone appeared occasionally.

Gospel performances spotlighted female vocalists, and popular soloists in the black gospel style, such as Mahalia Jackson, Clara Ward, and Marion Williams, sang music consisting of harmonic language derived from nineteenth-century European hymns. They performed in a blues-tinged vocal style with blues harmonies, sometimes accompanied by two keyboards—the Hammond organ and piano. Mahalia Jackson, the Queen of Gospel Music, was a native of New Orleans who moved to Chicago. She is considered by many to be the greatest gospel singer of all time. Jackson absorbed the sounds of blues singers Ma Rainey and Bessie Smith, as is evident in her numerous hits, such as "How I Got Over," which used a call-and-response interaction of organ accompaniment with background choir, and "Move On Up a Little Higher," which displayed a blueslike vocal quality and expressive melismas. These vocal techniques were important foundations that rock and roll borrowed from gospel music. Jackson was inducted into the Rock and Roll Hall of Fame in 1997. Major singer-guitarists of black gospel included Sister Rosetta Tharpe (whose 1938 hit "Rock Me" was the first gospel song to become a best-selling record), Blind Willie Johnson, and Rev. Blind Gary Davis (also known for their secular music), whose emotive singing and powerful guitar playing successfully brought together sacred and secular music as few others were able to do.

Vocal ensembles have been an important part of gospel music. Beginning in the 1910s, black churches fostered male quartets or larger ensembles of soloists that performed a wide repertoire of black sacred music. Among the popular black gospel male quartets and ensembles were the Golden Gate Quartet, the Dixie Hummingbirds, the Soul Stirrers, and the Five Blind Boys of Alabama. One of gospel music's greatest innovators was the Golden Gate Quartet, formed in 1934, which performed powerful spirituals with intricate vocal harmonies and swing rhythms. The group used the voice as a rhythm instrument, with singers repetitively performing background rhythmic riffs to a lead singer's solo, as in 1937's "Golden Gate Gospel Train." Featuring Sam Cooke as lead singer, the Soul Stirrers engaged in the same type of singing, but with a more contemporary sound, in such songs as "Jesus, I'll Never Forget," which contained exceptional rhythmic freedom in the solo vocal part above the rhythmic background voices. The Soul Stirrers introduced falsetto singing into the quartet style. These black gospel music techniques carried over into doo-wop rock and roll.

Black gospel music helped create the vocal portion of rock and roll music. Many black gospel artists who learned how to sing in church (by bringing out their heart and soul in their voice) transferred their talents to secular music. They crossed over into pop music from the church and brought the exciting gospel vocal style with them. Aretha Franklin, James Brown, Sam Cooke, and Ray Charles are but a few examples of black gospel singers who have done so effectively. Brown incorporated the drama of gospel music into his performances with such antics as his staged heart attacks. Many distinguished rock and roll artists, from Mick Jagger to Bruce Springsteen, have studied gospel music, which has influenced them to sing in an emotional and exciting manner. The early '50s rock and roll musicians Little Richard, Elvis Presley, and Ray Charles were greatly influenced by the gospel music tradition. Charles mixed sacred with secular music when he transformed the gospel song "My Jesus Is All the World to Me" into the secular song "I've Got a Woman," and "This Little Light of Mine" into "This Little Girl of Mine." Charles and other black gospel musicians reached the new music audience with excitement and emotions in their secular songs. Their music illustrates that the gospel repertoire was the basis for R&B as well as later genres of rock and roll, including soul music.

Rhythm and Blues

In 1949, *Billboard* reporter Jerry Wexler introduced the term "rhythm and blues" to replace "race music," which had been used for music intended for distribution in the African American community since the beginning of sound recording. The old term became unacceptable, and had already been replaced with others, such as "ebony" and "sepia," by some record companies. The independent record labels devoted to rhythm and blues and the R&B series of major record companies included the gamut of African American music: blues, jazz, gospel music, and popular vocal groups. "Rhythm and blues" became a catchall term for African American music in general, especially the styles emerging during the mid-to-late '40s and '50s.

Lionel Hampton, 1952. Courtesy of the Library of Congress.

Louis Jordan, 1946. Courtesy of the Library of Congress.

Blues-based big bands evolving from the swing jazz movement (such as those of Jay McShann, Lucky Millinder, Erskine Hawkins, and Buddy Johnson) and the jump bands that flourished in the late swing period (such as those of Louis Jordan, Roy Milton, John Veliotes [Johnny Otis], and Joe Liggins) were predecessors of the R&B genre. These innovative musicians created music with an emphasis on an insistent beat that used the formal and harmonic plan of the blues. They highlighted blues vocals and instrumental solo work, incorporating an abundance of emotions and rhythmic excitement into their music and placing more emphasis on singers than on instrumentalists. Their music was a reaction to the new bebop jazz that did not catch on with the general public but was appreciated by musicians. As the country and city blues began to mix with big-band jazz and R&B music was born, these artists insisted on making music for the public. The new style developed a large following, especially on the dance floor. Rhythm and blues was dance music with a rhythmic presence emphasizing the beat, especially the backbeat. It was highly danceable and hugely popular during the '40s, when people were infatuated with rhythm—which had helped create the setting for the birth of R&B.

As the rhythm and blues style developed, two tendencies appeared in the music: the emphasis on the saxophone featured in exciting solos (referred to as honking) and the emphasis on the voice throughout songs (referred to as shouting, as in the jump blues). Musicians still used the traditional call-and-response blues technique, but it was varied, with singers and saxophonists exchanging phrases and passages of music. Battiste Illinois Jacquet (Illinois Jacquet), Cecil James McNeely (Big Jay McNeely), Earl Bostic, Talmadge Smith (Tab Smith), Eddie Chamblee, Willis Jackson, Al Sears, and Maxwell Davis were some of the superb saxophonists of the era. Big Joe Turner, Jimmy Witherspoon, Wynonie Harris, Roy Hawkins, and Eddie "Cleanhead" Vinson were prominent blues shouters featured by bands of the late swing era.

Many of the styles embraced by the term "rhythm and blues" played a part in the development of rock and roll when the music was marketed to teenagers in the mid-1950s. African Americans were listening to this black music on "race" radio stations. And this was the music that Alan Freed referred to as rock and roll when he marketed it to the radio public. With time, many black artists began to simplify their music and eliminate adult themes from the lyrics, making it more accessible and acceptable to a wider audience that included white listeners. Many music historians agree that when this blending of black and white music and culture occurred, rock and roll was born. Bo Diddley, Chuck Berry, Fats Domino, and Little Richard were some who blurred the fine line between R&B and rock and roll as genres were mixed together in the '50s. Once the blending of rhythm and blues and country music occurred, there was more of a distinction between R&B and rock and roll.

In the late '40s, musicians made the transition from the big bands of swing jazz to the smaller combos of rhythm and blues. Swing bands grew smaller when big-band music waned after World War II, and R&B combos became very popular. The new combos' sound was leaner than the big band's, was devoid of the large, brassy timbres, and featured vocals. The typical combo had six to eight pieces: one or two horns (including saxophone and trumpet), electric guitar, bass, drums, and vocals. Wind instruments were borrowed from big bands, and saxophone solos became very prominent. Lionel Hampton and Louis Jordan helped create the new R&B genre, particularly the jump blues style. A riff-based song with a heavy beat, Hampton's 1942 hit, "Flying Home," featured a rough, screaming saxophone solo. Jordan combined the popular boogie-woogie rhythm with a rougher version of swing saxophone style, and humorous lyrics were frequently garnished with jive talk. The composite sound that Hampton and Jordan created in the '40s brought together elements of blues and jazz to create the song-based qualities of R&B, anticipating rock and roll by a decade. Gospel music influenced R&B, as is evident in the importance of the lead singer's voice in songs of this style, and the lyrics in the new genre were fun and about light topics—quite often including sexual references. Rhythm and blues combos capitalized on the electric guitar and the new amplification technology of the time.

Along with Louis Jordan, Big Joe Turner, and other major R&B figures, Johnny Otis, Roy Milton, and Joe and Jimmy Liggins, with Roy Brown, Amos Milburn, Rufus Thomas, and Charles Brown, left their mark on rhythm and blues in the '40s and '50s. Ruth Lee Jones (Dinah Washington), Esther Mae Jones (Esther Phillips), and LaVern Baker were among the successful rhythm and blueswomen of the era. These artists were influential in setting the stage for rock and roll.

Johnny Otis, a 1994 Rock and Roll Hall of Fame inductee, achieved success when he downsized his big band, the Johnny Otis Orchestra, to nine instruments, which became the model for future R&B combos with small horn sections. He discovered two talented female rhythm and blues vocalists: Jamesetta Hawkins (Etta James) and Esther Phillips; produced records of Johnny Ace and Big Mama Thornton; and wrote R&B classics, such as "Every Beat of My Heart" and "Willie and the Hand Jive." With Etta James, Otis wrote the 1955 No. 1 R&B hit, "Roll with Me, Henry," changed later to "The Wallflower." His

Rhythm & Blues Caravan revue showcased R&B and early rock and roll artists. Roy Milton, another shaper of R&B music, also grew out of big-band swing. His group, the Solid Senders, consisted of a small horn section and a boogie-woogie rhythm section that supplied explosive rhythms and driving backbeats that helped create rock and roll with such hits as "R.M. Blues," "Milton's Boogie," and "Hop, Skip, and Jump." Two other R&B pioneers influenced by big-band swing, the Liggins brothers, with their bands, created classics: Joe Liggins and His Honeydrippers found success with No. 1 hits "The Honeydripper" (1945), the first R&B million-selling instrumental, and "Pink Champagne"; Jimmy Liggins and His Drops of Joy excelled with such classics as "Cadillac Boogie" (the song that inspired Jackie Brenston's "Rocket 88"), and "I Ain't Drunk." These and many other R&B bands created the jump blues sound and filled the gap between swing and early rock and roll.

Singer and pianist Roy Brown, known as a crier of the blues rather than a shouter, was one of the originators of the New Orleans sound (a regional branch of early rock and roll). His 1947 song, "Good Rocking Tonight," was a No. 11 R&B hit; however, it was fellow rhythm and bluesman, Wynonie Harris, who made it ("Good Rockin' Tonight") a No. 1 R&B record in 1948. Elvis Presley and Pat Boone also recorded hit covers of it in the '50s. Brown was a very successful recording artist in the late '40s and early '50s when he had several Top 10 R&B hits, including the No. 1 records "Long About Midnight" (1948) and "Hard Luck Blues" (1950). Amos Milburn, who often performed with Johnny Otis and Charles Brown throughout the '50s, recorded jump blues songs with boogie-woogie piano and saxophone that led directly to the birth of rock and roll. Many of Milburn's late '40s and early '50s recordings focused on alcohol topics. His No. 1 hits included "Chicken-Shack Boogie" (1948), "Bewildered" (1948), "Roomin' House Boogie" (1949), and "Bad, Bad Whiskey" (1950). Rufus Thomas, a Memphis radio station WDIA disc jockey known for his outrageous performance costumes, recorded for Sun Records. His 1953 recording of "Bear Cat" (a reaction song to Big Mama Thornton's "Hound Dog") became Sun's first national hit. Charles Brown, one of the most popular R&B artists of the late '40s and early '50s, made the blues ballad style (nightclub strain of blues) popular and was a great influence on singer and pianist Ray Charles. A 1999 Rock and Roll Hall of Fame inductee, Brown created smooth, urban arrangements of songs with his calm voice and small combos. Unlike Big Joe Turner and other blues shouters, Brown was a vocal crooner, and his piano-playing style was very mellow compared with the harsh piano playing found in other blues styles. In 1944, he joined Johnny Moore's Three Blazers and recorded such popular hits as "Driftin' Blues" and "Merry Christmas, Baby"; in 1949 he formed the Charles Brown Trio and recorded such hits as the R&B No. 1s "Trouble Blues" (1949) and "Black Night" (1951).

Dinah Washington was one of the most successful '50s R&B recording artists; her vocal talents placed her in the same esteemed category as Bessie Smith, Billie Holiday, and other great blues-based black female vocalists. Washington had forty-two hits on the R&B charts during the '40s and '50s, two of them No. 1s: "Am I Asking Too Much" (1948) and "Baby Get Lost" (1949). Hailing from a gospel background, this 1993 Rock and Roll Hall of Fame inductee's bluesy and emotional voice influenced many other female artists, including Esther Phillips and LaVern Baker. Phillips, who first sang and recorded with Johnny Otis's band and was known as "Little Esther," was the youngest female vocalist (at fifteen) to have a No. 1 record on the R&B charts—"Double Crossing Blues" (1950). She followed with a string of successes, including the No. 1s "Mistrustin' Blues" (1950) and "Cupid Boogie" (1950). Baker, another gospel-influenced female R&B singer, enjoyed success with Atlantic Records, having recorded the song "Tweedlee Dee," which was one of the first R&B records to cross over onto the pop charts in 1955. She followed with many other crossovers, including "Jim Dandy" (No. 1 in 1956) and "I Cried a Tear" (No. 2 in 1958). Baker was a key artist on Alan Freed's Rock 'n' Roll Jubilee shows and appeared in two of his movies, *Mister Rock and Roll* and *Rock, Rock, Rock!* One of the most popular of the rhythm and blueswomen of early rock and roll, Baker was inducted into the Rock and Roll Hall of Fame in 1991.

Big Joe Turner, one of the first major figures in rhythm and blues and a founding father of rock and roll, reflected once on the fleeting nature of popular music trends. He declared that rock and roll was not different from the blues and that they (musicians) just pepped it up a lot.[12] Post–World War II rhythm and blues played the biggest role in forming rock and roll, leading right into the new style. This dance music expressed the enjoyment of life and displayed it in energetic stage shows, quite often complete with saxophone players engaging in fun-to-watch antics (swiveling their hips, lowering themselves to the floor and into the audience, and rolling around on their backs while playing) predating those of rock and roll bands. Rhythm and blues singers shouted out their frequently sexually suggestive lyrics with a high level of physical activity accompanied by the accented backbeats of the rhythm, and the excitement and energy of R&B formed the basis for '50s rock and roll. This enticing music filling the airwaves of black radio stations in the late 1940s was very different from the sounds of prewar America. As rock and roll supplanted R&B in the mid-1950s, such early rock and roll artists as Bo Diddley, Chuck Berry, Fats Domino, and Little Richard continued the R&B tradition, reaching mainstream America with their exciting musical sounds. (See chapter 4 for more discussion on this musical style.)

Folk Music

The definition of folk music has been a very controversial issue among scholars over the years; however, one simple explanation is sufficient to understand the genre's influence on rock and roll. "Folk music" is a general term referring to the music traditions of a country or region in regard to songs learned informally through sharing within families and communities. It is simple

Undated portrait of Stephen Collins Foster. Courtesy of the Library of Congress.

music, mostly of rural origin, used and understood by the general public and usually transmitted in an oral tradition. As folk songs were passed from generation to generation, they underwent multiple changes, a natural process for music not written down, resulting in different versions of songs in terms of their length, melodies, rhythms, and form. Folk music has often been used to accompany activities in society. A strophic song containing stanzas of two to eight lines (with four being the most common) and dealing with a single story or event, the ballad is the type of folk music most often referred to today as folk music, though folk music also embraces children's songs, work songs, religious songs (performed outside of church), and instrumental dance music.

America has a rich tradition of Anglo-Scottish-Irish folk songs that were the pop songs of the colonial period. This large repertoire of secular music was very popular (many of the songs are still sung today) and consisted of approximately 300 British ballads, known today as the Child Ballads, named after the ballad collector Francis James Child. By the mid-eighteenth century, Americans began creating their own popular ballads, such as "Springfield Mountain," which told the story of the death of a Massachusetts man from snakebite. In the nineteenth century, many American songwriters continued the tradition of telling a story in song. Among them was Stephen Collins Foster from Lawrenceville, Pennsylvania. Many scholars claim that Foster was America's first great songwriter. He composed more than 180 household and minstrel show songs about pre–Civil War life in America, including some of the popular folk songs still enjoyed today: "Camptown Races," "Oh! Susanna," and "Old Folks at Home." Some say that Foster was the first rock and roll songwriter because he was fascinated by and loved black American culture, especially the music, and brought black music into white culture. Unfortunately, in nineteenth-century America, folk music was not appreciated. The twentieth-century folk music revival finally brought the large body of folk music to the nation's attention.

Folk Music Revival

The U.S. folk music revival dates back to the 1930s. It consisted of the documentation of musicians in the field—the collecting and recording of songs by

Portrait of Bunk Johnson, Lead Belly, George Lewis, and Alcide Pavageau playing at the Stuyvesant Casino in New York, c. 1946. Courtesy of the Library of Congress.

Carl Sandburg, John and Alan Lomax, and others. The revival presented folk music to the people, bringing the extensive music repertoire of such singers as Huddie Ledbetter (Lead Belly or Leadbelly) and Woody Guthrie to the attention of the general public, and led to the rediscovery of bluesmen and recording artists such as Mississippi Fred McDowell, Son House, and Mississippi John Hurt. The revival caused the imitation of the folk repertoire and its styles—for instance, the formation of new folk groups that were based on the Weavers' success, such as the Kingston Trio, the Limeliters, and the Chad Mitchell Trio. It also caused the rise of solo singers who sang ballads and their own compositions, such as Joan Baez, Caroline Hester, and Judy Collins, as well as others who accompanied themselves on guitar, such as Joni Mitchell, Tom Paxton, Phil Ochs, Paul Simon, and Bob Dylan.

With the invention of recording, folk communities standardized folk tunes and performances. And as recording technology improved, the music was widely accessed; cultural documentation transmitted music performances to distant places and people. Only after ethnologists recorded the Passamaquoddy Indian songs and stories on Edison's newly invented wax cylinder phonograph in the late nineteenth century did America realize the potential for field recordings to preserve its cultural communities. In 1939, Moses Asch founded Asch Records, which was renamed Folkways Records, the label on which Lead Belly

John Lomax (top) and Alan Lomax. Courtesy of the Library of Congress.

and Woody Guthrie were documented through recordings. Notated folk music, performances, and recordings of the literature appeared. In the twentieth century, folk and popular music styles began to merge when the oral tradition was replaced and supplemented by written and recorded traditions. Professional singers began to sing versions of folk songs and to compose new songs with folk elements in them.

One of the earliest collectors who used sound recordings to document music in America was the folklorist John Lomax. He recorded traditional cowboy songs and shared the repertoire with a wider audience through his collections *Cowboy Songs and Other Frontier Ballads* and *Songs of the Cattle Trail and Cow Camp*, in which he preserved such classics as "Home on the Range" and "The Old Chisholm Trail." In 1933, Lomax became curator of the Archive of American Folk Song for the Library of Congress and immediately began field expeditions in Texas and other areas of the South. On his excursions Lomax recorded various types of music, including black field and folk songs, cowboy songs, prison work chants, spirituals, and the blues, making approximately 10,000 recordings for the Library of Congress.

During the early years of the Depression, with the help of his son Alan, Lomax traveled the South with primitive equipment, recording itinerant bluesmen, prison inmates, and laborers. This led to his 1934 book, *American Ballads and Folksongs*. On these trips, the Lomaxes discovered remarkable musicians preserving America's rich musical heritage, including Lead Belly, Muddy Waters, and Jelly Roll Morton. In 1936, John wrote *Negro Folk Songs as Sung by Lead Belly*, followed in the early 1940s by *Our Singing Country*; these books helped spark interest in American folk music and blues, and established the foundation upon which future musicologists would build.

In addition to becoming assistant archivist at the Library of Congress, Alan continued his father's work by conducting fieldwork in the United States, the Caribbean, and elsewhere, creating multiple volumes of recordings throughout the '50s and '60s. He recorded songs and autobiographies of musicians such as Aunt Molly Jackson from eastern Kentucky, Jelly Roll Morton from New Orleans, and Woody Guthrie from Oklahoma. Alan produced concerts of folk music and wrote *The Penguin Book of American Folksongs* and *Folk Song Style and Culture*. He also produced the documentary series *American Patchwork*, which included the film *The Land Where the Blues Began*, which was about field hollers and work songs and the beginnings of the blues in the Mississippi Delta; he adapted the film as a book in 1993. Together, the Lomaxes accomplished their mission to preserve the dying elements of American folk music. They made folk music available to the people who had forgotten it, thus playing a key role in the early part of the folk song revival.

In 1933, when the Lomaxes were recording in the field, they discovered Lead Belly at the Angola Prison Farm in Louisiana; he amazed the two folklorists with his powerful voice, his extensive repertoire of black folk songs, and his rhythmic guitar playing. A black folk singer from Louisiana called the King of the Twelve-String Guitar, Lead Belly played folk ballads, dance tunes, spirituals, pop songs, prison songs, and the blues. He wrote original blues and folk songs, and preserved and brought to the attention of the public music that otherwise might have been lost forever. Lead Belly lived the life of a bluesman: traveling the South, performing alone and with others (most notably Blind Lemon Jefferson), and getting in trouble with the law multiple times.

Lead Belly's greatest contribution to American music was in folk music: "Goodnight Irene," "Rock Island Line," "The Midnight Special," and "Cotton Fields." After the Lomaxes helped free Lead Belly from prison in 1934, he settled in New York City. There he became friends and music partner with Woody Guthrie and Pete Seeger and bluesmen Sonny Terry and Walter McGhee (Brownie McGhee); they played clubs and coffeehouses appealing to white liberal audiences. Lead Belly became involved in politics and wrote songs with political messages, such as "Bourgeois Blues" and "Scottsboro Boys."

Lead Belly has been a great influence on generations of musicians—from other folk musicians, such as Woody Guthrie, to rock and roll musicians such as Led Zeppelin and Kurt Cobain. In 1950, the Weavers, a folk group led by Pete Seeger, recorded Lead Belly's signature song, "Goodnight Irene," which became a No. 1 hit on *Billboard*'s pop charts. Led Zeppelin paid homage to Lead Belly by regularly performing his version of an old British ballad, "The Gallows Pole," in their live shows. Nirvana's frontman, Cobain, who declared Lead Belly his greatest influence, ended the band's *MTV Unplugged* appearance (broadcast shortly before he committed suicide) with a cover of Lead Belly's "Where Did You Sleep Last Night?" In cooperation with Columbia Records, the Smithsonian Institution honored Lead Belly and Woody Guthrie by issuing a commemorative album of their songs, *Folkways: A Vision Shared*, in 1988. Singers and groups that had been touched by Lead Belly and Guthrie performed on the album, including Bob Dylan, Bruce Springsteen, Willie Nelson, Brian Wilson, U2, John Mellencamp, Emmylou Harris, Sweet Honey in the Rock, Taj Mahal, Little Richard, Doc Watson, Pete Seeger, and Arlo Guthrie (Woody's son). That same year Lead Belly and Woody Guthrie were inducted into the Rock and Roll Hall of Fame as two of rock music's early influences.

Guthrie, born in Okemah, Oklahoma, was a prolific songwriter and performer in the '30s and '40s. He lived a life of travel, commenting in his songs on economic, political, and social topics as he sang for everyday folks in America. His early ballads touched on the human misery of the Dust Bowl—the devastating drought that struck the South and West during the '20s and caused thousands of bankrupt farmers to migrate west in hope of better economic opportunity. Guthrie's most famous song, "This Land Is Your Land," considered to be the folk national anthem, was a reaction to Irving Berlin's sentimental patriotic song, "God Bless America." Guthrie's songs were linked with politics, as so many folk songs were. He popularized the style referred to as talking blues, a genre of storytelling and social commentary in song.

The protest music of the '60s was partly spurred by Woody Guthrie, and his friend Pete Seeger, and Millard Lampell, Bess Lomax, Arthur Stern, and Sis Cunningham, who formed the Almanac Singers in the early '40s. The group, based in New York City's Greenwich Village, wrote and performed songs for labor and political rallies as well as antiwar songs. They had a great impact on the folk revival, having used traditional, simple folk songs with basic accompaniments and untrained voices to create new songs of contemporary social significance that were conducive to audience participation—an important element of folk music. The Almanac Singers were the predecessors of the highly influential group the Weavers.

Guthrie died during the 1960s, the decade when the folk singer-songwriter scene exploded in Greenwich Village, inspired by his legacy. He had become a legendary model for singer-songwriters of the next generation, most notably Bob Dylan, who paid homage to Guthrie in one of his first original songs, "Song to Woody" ("Hey, Hey Woody Guthrie"). Dylan

Woody Guthrie, 1943. Courtesy of the Library of Congress.

continued the folk tradition of incorporating introspective lyrics, politics, and poetry into his songs, thus contributing to his reputation as one of the best singer-songwriters of all time. Guthrie continues to influence many rock and roll musicians with his large body of simple songs telling important stories; among them is Bruce Springsteen, who has performed and recorded covers of Guthrie's songs.

Charles Seeger, a folklorist, ethnomusicologist, and pedagogue, and his family played an important part in the folk revival in America. His son Pete Seeger, a gifted banjo player, was greatly influenced by Lead Belly and Woody Guthrie. In 1938, Pete Seeger became Alan Lomax's assistant at the Archive of American Folk Song in Washington, D.C., prior to heading to New York City, the nucleus of folk song activity and the seat of left-wing political activism. After Woody Guthrie's departure from the Almanac Singers in 1948, Lee Hays, Ronnie Gilbert, and Fred Hellerman joined the group and they became known as the Weavers—Pete Seeger's very popular group. Seeger became a target of Senator Joseph McCarthy's witch hunts in the 1950s, which destroyed the Weavers. With such songs as "If I Had a Hammer," "Where Have All the Flowers Gone?" and "We Shall Overcome," Seeger's musical activity in the '60s continued to be important for protest songs and the Civil Rights Movement. In 1996, Pete Seeger was inducted into the Rock and Roll Hall of Fame.

The Weavers paved the path for folk groups. Many groups—trios and quartets—and some solo acts continued in their style throughout the 1950s and 1960s, such as the Kingston Trio; the New Lost City Ramblers; the trio of Peter, Paul, and Mary; Simon & Garfunkel; Joan Baez; Harry Belafonte; and Bob Dylan. Folk concerts and

 WOODY GUTHRIE (1912–1967)

Born into simple and poor circumstances in Oklahoma, Woody Guthrie inherited his love for music from his parents. His father had played guitar and banjo in cowboy bands, and his mother sang British ballads and songs to him. In the early '30s, Guthrie's uncle taught him to play guitar, and Guthrie began to perform with his uncle at dances and parties while they were living in Pampa, Texas. In the mid-1930s Woody began writing songs, such as "Dusty Old Dust" ("So Long, It's Been Good to Know You"), about the April 1935 Pampa dust storm. Realizing that music was his love, he moved to Los Angeles in 1937, along with thousands of other Dust Bowl refugees. There he worked with his cousin, Jack Guthrie, on a radio station KFVD show and met Cisco Houston, who became his friend and singing partner, and was one of the first folk singers to popularize Guthrie's compositions.

In 1939, Guthrie published his first collection of protest songs, including "Do Re Mi" and "Talking Dust Bowl Blues." After meeting many unionists and political activists, he wrote a column, "Woody Sez," for the West Coast Communist daily, *People's World.* The next year Guthrie moved to New York City, where he checked himself into a hospital. He spent the last twelve years of his life battling the degenerative disease that took his mother's life, Huntington's chorea.

Guthrie and his songs are still influential today. He left nearly 1,000 compositions: patriotic songs that celebrate America, "This Land Is Your Land" and "Pastures of Plenty"; tribute songs to fallen heroes, "Reuben James" and "Plane Wreck at Los Gatos"; social commentary songs, "Jesus Christ" and "Do Re Mi"; labor union songs, "Union Maid" and "Ballad of Harry Bridges"; Dust Bowl ballads, "Tom Joad" and "Dusty Old Dust"; Columbia River Power Project songs, "Roll On, Columbia" and "Grand

WOODY GUTHRIE (1912–1967)
(continued)

Coulee Dam"; and children's songs, "Put Your Finger in the Air" and "Car Car Song." Artists of the folk revival performed these songs throughout the 1950s and 1960s, and Americans still sing many of them.[13] Guthrie's songs have become woven into American life, and his influence can be detected in many contemporary performers. Artists from Suzanne Vega to Tracy Chapman and Dan Bern to Ani DiFranco have acknowledged Guthrie's impact and recorded his songs. In 1998, the album *Mermaid Avenue* was released when Billy Bragg set newly discovered Guthrie lyrics to music.

festivals became popular in the '50s and '60s, as did folk appearances in coffee-houses. Small- and large-scale folk festivals took place throughout the country; the most popular of them was the Newport Folk Festival in Rhode Island, which was inaugurated in 1959, giving tremendous exposure to the artists and their music. These musicians played simple music with only three or four chords, playable and singable by the general public.

The simplicity of folk music helped create straightforward rock and roll songs with clear-cut formal structure and basic harmony, as can be seen in most early rock songs of the '50s. In addition, folk music contributed lyrics to rock and roll, especially in the 1960s, when rock lyrics began

The Kingston Trio. Courtesy of Photofest.

to have more substance. Instead of the simple, rhyming, love lyrics common in '50s songs, the lyrics of the '60s had more depth and meaning, and became a vehicle for social commentary and protest. The public looked to folk music and folk-inspired rock music and the musicians for lyrics with deeper meaning and, in the 1960s, for information about domestic and world events.

Country Music

In the 1920s, country music came of age, along with blues, jazz, and gospel music. In many ways, country music was an outgrowth of folk music, derived from the traditional oral music brought to America by nonliterate immigrants from the British Isles. It evolved to telling in song tales of the people of rural America (from West Virginia and Kentucky to areas of the Deep South). English and Scottish popular ballads survived in the Appalachian Mountains, and new songs emerged that recounted events and took a point of view as

Hank Williams (center) at Grand Ole Opry 1951 with Chet Atkins (left) and Ernie Newton. Courtesy of Photofest.

well as entertained. The ballad tradition continued even after the rise of literacy and the development of newspapers, radio, and television.

In its early days, country music was referred to as "hillbilly music," named after the Hillbillies, a popular recording group from near Galax, Virginia. In 1949, the genre took the name "country music" when *Billboard* magazine started to describe the music with that designation. At first, the music mixed old narrative ballads brought to America by immigrants with newer American ballads accompanied by banjo, fiddle, guitar, or some combination of these instruments. Country music also consisted of dance music played with one or more fiddles, sometimes accompanied by banjo or guitar. After the introduction of the guitar in the late nineteenth century, Blue Ridge Mountains musicians started to play the guitar and added it to the classic string band that until then had often consisted of just the banjo and fiddle. In time, subgenres of country music evolved, from the mountain style and western swing to honky-tonk and bluegrass, each with its distinct sound and influence on rock and roll. The Carter Family, Jimmie Rodgers, and Uncle Dave Macon were among the pioneers of country music.

Its commercialization helped make country music a career option for musicians and made its performance more solitary, separating performers from their audiences. Following the lead of OKeh artists and repertoire (A&R) man Ralph Peer, who discovered local talent among working-class musicians in Georgia, record companies began scouting the South for talented singers, fiddlers, banjo players, and gospel quartets to record on location. Participatory music that had been passed down within families and communities for generations was now being recorded. In August 1927, Peer recorded on location for Victor in a temporary studio in a hat factory in Bristol, Tennessee. There he discovered two acts that were to dominate country music's first decade: the Carter Family and Jimmie Rodgers.

The Carter Family, from Clinch Valley in the Bristol, Tennessee, area, launched a career on that August day in 1927—one that would thrive until 1941 and include approximately 300 recordings of traditional ballads, folk songs, gospel songs, and the blues recorded for every major record company. They recorded dozens of songs that became country and bluegrass standards, among them "Wildwood Flower," "Wabash Cannonball," "Worried Man Blues," and "Will the Circle Be Unbroken." Alvin Pleasant Carter and his group became very popular for their Appalachian Mountain style. Their music reflected the sound of the mountains with a nasal vocal quality accompanied by acoustic instruments. According to Johnny Cash, Mother Maybelle Carter was very influential with her guitar playing, even more so than John Lennon or Bob Dylan. She picked the melody on the lower strings of her guitar while she strummed chords on the higher strings, creating the most influential guitar style in country and folk music.[14] Her guitar playing in their 1928 song "Wildwood Flower" is the most copied guitar solo in country music. With its strophic form and lyrics based upon "I'll Twine 'mid the Ringlets" (written by Maud Irving and J. P. Webster in 1860), this song is representative of the sound of the Carters: the Appalachian timbres of Sara Carter's plain vocals with a strong country twang and Maybelle's acoustic guitar solo repeated between every verse. The simplicity of mountain country songs (from their balanced, four-phrase verses and verse-refrain format to their simple, repetitive melodies and harmonies) was passed on to rock and roll, and can be seen in a wide variety of music by such early artists as Buddy Holly and the Everly Brothers and by later musicians such as John Mellencamp and Bruce Springsteen.

The Carter Family was honored for their contributions to country music when they were inducted into the Country Music Hall of Fame in 1970. In 1958, the country music industry's leading trade organization, the Country Music Association (CMA), was formed in Nashville to improve, market, and publicize country music and to make it more appealing. In 1961, the CMA established the Country Music Hall of Fame to recognize the contributions of those who have advanced country music and influenced others, and chose its first three inductees. Two years later, the state of Tennessee chartered the Country Music Foundation and announced plans for a Country Music Hall of

Fame and Museum to be built in Nashville. One of the Foundation's functions has been to operate the Country Music Hall of Fame and Museum, first opened in 1967 on Music Row in Nashville, and in May 2001 reopened on the west bank of the Cumberland River in downtown Nashville. According to the Country Music Hall of Fame and Museum's Web site, the mission of the Foundation is to identify and preserve the history and traditions of country music and to educate its audiences. It is a local history museum and an international arts organization that serves fans, students, scholars, members of the music industry, and the general public not only in the Nashville area, but throughout the nation and the world.[15]

Another leading country music artist and the Father of Country Music, Jimmie Rodgers was a railroad worker known as the Singing Brakeman who linked black and white music styles in his songs and became country music's first star. Hailing from Mississippi, Rodgers combined in his music all the types he had heard—black work chants, jazz, blues, Hawaiian music, and vaudeville songs. He recorded 110 songs between 1927 and his death in 1933—blues, hillbilly and parlor songs, some with jazz elements, and many of them incorporating the twelve-bar blues pattern that he learned from African Americans while working on the railroad. Rodgers was well known for his signature vocal style of yodeling in a falsetto voice, which gained him the nickname America's Blue Yodeler. His repertoire set the standard in country music, and he popularized songs that were covered many times over the years.

Rodgers was most famous for "Blue Yodel" and twelve sequels to it, including "Blue Yodel No. 8 (Muleskinner Blues)" in 1930, which clearly displays his virtuoso yodeling technique. Louis Armstrong joined him for "Blue Yodel No. 9," making Rodgers one of the first white stars to work with black musicians. His 1928 classic "Waiting for a Train" featured his famous train whistle imitation. This song, with instrumentation consisting of Hawaiian steel guitar mixed with a Dixieland jazz band (acoustic guitar, steel guitar, cornet, clarinet, and string bass) and his unique vocal sounds, displays a unique blending of instruments. Rodgers's recordings introduced new sounds and styles into country music. Such Jimmie Rodgers songs as "In the Jailhouse Now," "Travelin' Blues," and "T for Texas" set the stage for honky-tonk music.

By late 1932, the Depression had taken its toll on record sales and theater attendance. Rodgers's health was failing, and he died of tuberculosis in May 1933, the most influential country musician in history. His records influenced not only generations of country singers but also African Americans (many of whom did not know he was white) and rock and roll musicians. Jimmie Rodgers was honored by folk rocker Bob Dylan, whose first release on Egyptian Records was a Rodgers tribute. In 1961 Rodgers was inducted into the Country Music Hall of Fame, and in 1986 into the Rock and Roll Hall of Fame, a member of the first group of inductees for each organization.

Country music spread from the South to other areas of the country—to the Midwest, Southwest, New England, and the Far West—as commercial radio sprouted. Many radio stations popularized the music and its performers (WSB in Atlanta, WSM in Nashville, WBAP in Fort Worth, and WLS in Chicago). The *Grand Ole Opry*, which went on the air in 1925 as a barn dance feature and in 1927 took its present name, was broadcast on Saturday nights by Nashville's radio station WSM. It proved to be a springboard for country music's most important artists, from Roy Acuff and Hank Williams to Loretta Lynn.

Uncle Dave Macon, from rural Tennessee, was one of the earliest to find fame via the *Opry*. In addition to playing sentimental songs at hoedowns, family gatherings, and tent shows, he performed over the airwaves, establishing the *Grand Ole Opry* as one of the most popular radio programs in United States history. Macon became one of country music's first celebrities and helped define the genre. Eventually, rural country musical sounds thrived in Nashville, where the country music industry flourished and several major record companies established studios. In 1926, the *Opry* expanded from a regional radio show on WSM to nationwide broadcasts of live concerts from the Ryman Auditorium, which helped establish Nashville as a commercial center of country and western music.

Country music evolved with the changing culture, resulting in new subgenres. Experimental electric guitars had been around since the 1920s, though they did not appear in country music until 1934, when Milton Brown's guitarist, Bob Dunn, began using an amplified steel guitar. Its immediate acoustic predecessor was the Dobro—a guitar with a large metal resonating disk beneath the strings instead of a hole. When electric instruments were adopted, they became the defining feature of Southwestern country music; the Dobro and other acoustic string instruments remained associated with the more conservative country music of the Southeast. The development of the electric guitar allowed new styles of western music to surface in country music, such as the rise of western swing and honky-tonk styles in the 1930s and 1940s; other developments (such as cowboy western music of the same era, and the Nashville style of the late 1950s and 1960s) were motivated by the music industry and borrowed elements from established pop music styles.

Western Swing

In the Southwest and on the West Coast, a regional country version of big-band dance music evolved in the '30s, known as western swing. This country music subgenre blended ragtime, New Orleans jazz, blues, Mexican songs, big-band swing, and traditional fiddling. When mixed with the strings of country music, the horns of jazz combined the sounds of the swing big band with that of the country string band. It borrowed the improvisatory spirit of jazz big bands and the country instrumentation of honky-tonk (electric guitar, steel guitar, and fiddles) while adding smooth pop vocals to the mix. The Light Crust Doughboys, Bob Wills's Texas Playboys, and Milton Brown's Musical Brownies pioneered the style, and numerous other groups thrived in the late

1930s. Western swing music displayed the increasing importance of the jukebox in determining the record market, since jukebox distributors were major purchasers of records. Tens of thousands of customers who relaxed in bars and taverns in the South, Midwest, and working-class sections of cities listened and danced to Texas swing music, which had a significant impact on the jukebox trade, as did honky-tonk music.

James Robert Wills (Bob Wills), a major figure in the development of western swing and a bandleader, fiddler, singer, and songwriter, was highly influenced by African American folk blues and jazz. Like many poor whites, he had worked side by side with blacks in the cotton fields. There he learned their music, which is evident in the vocal and instrumental performance styles on his recordings. Texas-raised in an area famous for African American music (Scott Joplin, Victoria Spivey, and Blind Lemon Jefferson), Wills regularly listened to race records and was impressed with blues queen Bessie Smith. He originally formed the Light Crust Doughboys and hired white blues singer Milton Brown, though after managerial disputes, Wills and Brown went their own ways. Wills formed the Texas Playboys and Brown formed the Musical Brownies. Wills and his Playboys performed daily on a program on KVOO in Tulsa, Oklahoma, and were the most popular act in the Southwest. The Texas Playboys recorded approximately 140 songs for Columbia Records and became the most famous of the western swing bands.

Between 1935 and 1947, Wills was one of Columbia's biggest stars. His compositions are still the staples of the western swing repertoire and standards of country and pop music: "San Antonio Rose," "Faded Love," "Maiden's Prayer," and "Take Me Back to Tulsa." Songs by Bob Wills and his Texas Playboys band are saturated with characteristic elements of the genre: timbres consisting of drums, bass, electric rhythm guitar, electric steel guitar, at least two fiddles, banjo, piano, and sometimes an accordion mixed with big-band instruments (trumpet and saxophone) and smooth vocals; rhythms consisting of the backbeat supplied by drums and guitars; and form consisting of instrumental introductions with verse-refrain format and instrumental interludes.

As a result of their success, Wills and his band began appearing in movie westerns, thus adding cowboy songs to their repertoire as so many other country-cowboy singers, such as Gene Autry, had done. As Hollywood created cowboy movies, Tin Pan Alley composers wrote many cowboy songs for them. World War II brought an end to the western swing style because the draft decimated band personnel, resulting in smaller groups; the electric guitar and electric steel guitar had to compensate for the missing horns. As Wills downsized his band, he often had one tenor saxophone simulate a brass section, an important and innovative technique that influenced such early rock and roll bands as Bill Haley and the Comets. Recognized for his musical contributions to country music and rock and roll, Bob Wills was inducted into the Country Music Hall of Fame in 1968, and he and his Texas Playboys were inducted into the Rock and Roll Hall of Fame in 1999.

Honky-Tonk

Another style of western music that emerged in the 1930s was honky-tonk, named after the taverns where patrons gathered to listen and dance. The Texas oil boom brought rural dwellers to remote oil towns in search of work during the Depression. After the repeal of Prohibition in 1933, honky-tonks, where workers drank and danced on weekends, multiplied on the edges of these towns. In the bar atmosphere, country music changed its lyrics. Song themes were no longer sweet and gentle, about religion or family; they reflected self-pity and remorse. Country songs became known as cry-in-your-beer music—unfaithful love, broken hearts, and rowdy lifestyles. Since honky-tonks were loud places where people went to dance, out of necessity the music needed more volume to be heard and required a more insistent beat for dancing. While the piano (and sometimes the fiddle and rarely the drums) was often used to supply the dance beat, the acoustic guitar most often supplied the rhythm of honky-tonk songs. Their harmony consisted mostly of the simple chord progression of the tonic (I), subdominant (IV), and dominant (V) chords passed on from the blues. Honky-tonk song structure consisted of balanced, four-line phrases, with songs often in verse-refrain format. The electric and steel guitars flourished in honky-tonk music: the electric guitar took on a lead role, alternating solo verses with strong vocals. The guitar—especially the sound of the steel guitar—was borrowed from country music by rock and roll. The guitar eventually became *the* instrument of rock and roll music. Rock and roll bands later used it in the same manner as a lead instrument, alternating with a lead singer's vocals.

A 1965 Country Music Hall of Fame inductee and *Grand Ole Opry* star, Ernest Tubb was one of the first great honky-tonkers. A Jimmie Rodgers imitator with years of experience in the honky-tonks and dance halls of Texas, Tubb, called the Texas Troubadour, created the first widespread honky-tonk hit in 1941, "Walking the Floor over You." Tubb and his band, the Texas Troubadours, contributed greatly to the shaping of honky-tonk music with this song and such others as "I'll Always Be Glad to Take You Back," "Try Me One More Time," and "Driving Nails in My Coffin." After World War II, when the honky-tonk style was firmly established, a wave of singers emerged in the style. Among these major recording artists were Hank Williams, Clarence Eugene Snow (Hank Snow), William Orville Frizzell (Lefty Frizzell), and Webb Pierce.

Hank Williams, one of the biggest stars in country music, was from Alabama. He performed in honky-tonks for years prior to embarking on his successful career. It was after the Nashville music publisher Fred Rose asked Williams to write songs for Molly O'Day that his recording career began. The popularity of his 1948 classic, "Lovesick Blues," contributed to Williams's joining the *Grand Ole Opry* one year later. Having experienced such personal problems as marital distress, drug addiction, and alcoholism, Williams wrote country songs that were very real to many people: songs about family, drinking beer, religion, love, and love failures: "I Just Told Momma Goodbye," "Honky Tonkin'," "I Saw the Light," "Settin' the Woods on Fire," "Hey Good Lookin'," "There'll Be No Teardrops Tonight," "You Win Again," "I'm So Lonesome I Could Cry," "Cold, Cold Heart," and "Your Cheating Heart."

When Williams died in 1953, country music was at the peak of its postwar commercial surge, and his songs had crossed into pop music. Beginning with "Honky Tonkin'," a song resembling early rock and roll, many of his compositions became major pop hits when covered by other musicians, such as Tony Bennett, Guy Mitchell, Frankie Laine, and Mitch Miller. Williams's influence on rock music was enormous; such early artists as Chuck Berry and Elvis Presley listened to him on the radio. In 1987, Williams was inducted into the Rock and Roll Hall of Fame. In 1961, he had been honored for his country music influence by the Country Music Hall of Fame when he was one of its first three members.

Other country musicians, such as Hank Snow, Lefty Frizzell, and Webb Pierce, greatly influenced Elvis Presley, Ray Charles, Chuck Berry, and Carl Perkins. Snow, a 1979 Country Music Hall of Fame inductee known as the Yodeling Ranger, rose to fame in 1949 with "Brand on My Heart." Snow's many successes included the No. 1 "I'm Moving On" (1950), "Golden Rocket," and "Rhumba Boogie." Frizzell, a 1982 Country Music Hall of Fame inductee, monopolized the charts in 1951 with Hank Williams. Frizzell was one of the greatest stars of postwar honky-tonk and one of the most imitated singers in country music. Pierce, who dominated the country charts during the early '50s, introduced the pedal steel guitar to country music; it became the defining sound of modern honky-tonk and a major ingredient of some forms of rock. Pierce was inducted into the Country Music Hall of Fame in 2001.

Bluegrass

One last country subgenre to impact rock and roll music was bluegrass. With its fast tempos and virtuosic displays, bluegrass was formed from mountain music, square dance tunes, parlor songs, jazz, sacred music, and the blues. Played on fiddle and guitar or banjo, it was a style of hillbilly music that grew out of the music of string bands performing at barn dances in the '20s. Once the subgenre was standardized, bluegrass groups featured four to seven musicians: a rhythm section of guitar and string bass and a mix of such melodic instruments as the banjo and any combination of fiddle, mandolin, Dobro or another type of guitar, and, rarely, drums. Vocals consisted of a high voice singing above the melody with other voices in harmony below it. Melodic instrumentalists and vocalists frequently alternated solos while improvising and displaying virtuosic technique. The influence of bluegrass on rock and roll was noted a bit later— during the 1960s and 1970s, when folk rock and country rock groups, such as the Byrds, the Eagles, and the Charlie Daniels Band, arose.

A singer, songwriter, and bandleader, William Smith Monroe (Bill Monroe) was a pivotal influence on the sound of bluegrass. Some scholars argue that he was responsible for inventing the entire subgenre even before it was referred to as bluegrass, in the mid-1950s, to differentiate it from Nashville's commercial music after the onset of rock and roll. Monroe performed and recorded over 500 bluegrass songs, many of his original compositions complete with pulsing drive and intense high-pitched vocals—elements that gave country music a fresh new sound. During World War II, Monroe added the banjo and sometimes the accordion, jug, and harmonica to his band that consisted of mandolin, guitar, fiddle, and bass. He named the band the Blue Grass Boys, after his native Kentucky, the Bluegrass State.

Monroe, known as the Father of Bluegrass Music, had an extensive repertoire including sacred and secular music as well as songs and instrumentals. Many of his original compositions became bluegrass standards, such as "Uncle Pen," "Raw Hide," "I Want the Lord to Protect My Soul," and "Blue Moon of Kentucky." While shaping the bluegrass genre, Monroe gave the mandolin a new role as a lead instrument in country, pop, and rock and roll. He served as an inspiration for future musicians and set standards for such diverse performers as the Everly Brothers, Elvis Presley, George Jones, and Jerry Garcia. Monroe was inducted into the Country Music Hall of Fame in 1970 and into the Rock and Roll Hall of Fame in 1997.

Throughout the '50s, bluegrass music flourished as an acoustic alternative to honky-tonk and rockabilly (one of the early styles of rock and roll), especially in the Appalachian region and in cities with many Appalachian migrants. The Foggy Mountain Boys band was formed by Earl Scruggs, Monroe's banjo player, who popularized the three-finger picking style, and Lester Flatt, Monroe's lead vocalist. The Flatt and Scruggs duo went on to surpass Bill Monroe and became the most popular bluegrass act. They were chosen to sing "The Ballad of Jed Clampett," the title song of one of the most successful television shows in the '60s, *The Beverly Hillbillies*. Other bluegrass groups kept the genre active, such as the Stanley Brothers, the Clinch Mountain Boys, and the Osborne Brothers. A resurgence of the style occurred in the late 1990s and it became more popular in 2000 with the multiple Grammy-winning sound track recording, *O Brother, Where Art Thou?*, from the feature film of the same title, and in 2002, when *Billboard* magazine established a bluegrass chart.

The Nashville Sound

The arrival on the music scene of Elvis Presley and other rockabilly artists in the mid-1950s (Jerry Lee Lewis, Carl Perkins, Johnny Cash, Conway Twitty, Buddy Holly, and the Everly Brothers) threatened country music. As a result, in the late '50s, country music lost its popularity and its mostly young audience to the new, exciting sound of rockabilly. This serious commercial setback caused country musicians to develop a new sound, though some country artists created songs that displayed the influences of rockabilly, such as the 1955 No. 1 country and pop hit of Tennessee Ernie Ford, "Sixteen Tons," with its continuous rocking beat. The result was the Nashville crossover sound, which blended country music with the far more lucrative pop music. Nashville successfully won over new country music fans in the 1950s and the early 1960s, when country music recaptured much of its old audience and gained some new followers through the development of the new subgenre, which altered the older country sound by softening it in an attempt to reach a larger and more diverse audience. The smoother, more commercial Nashville sound included a string section, horns, and background voices. Chester Burton Atkins (Chet Atkins), country A&R director for RCA Records, and other record producers played a major role in the development of the style. Country music's raw edges were toned down, and the music was given a more uptown sound by avoiding the hillbilly vocal twang and rough-sounding fiddles and steel guitars; instead, lush vocal arrangements, bright piano embellishments, and relaxed string and horn arrangements were used. Referred to by some as country pop, the Nashville sound engulfed the country music field. Such artists as Richard Edward Arnold (Eddy

Undated portrait of Bob Wills. Courtesy of the Library of Congress.

Arnold), Jim Reeves, Virginia Patterson Hensley (Patsy Cline), George Morgan, Faron Young, Charlie Rich, and Tammy Wynette sang in the style.

The Nashville sound has been extremely popular ever since the '60s. It brought country singers who appealed to pop audiences closer to their country roots, such as Johnny Cash, Harold Jenkins (Conway Twitty), and Marty Robbins. Many artists and vocal groups rose to prominence in the style, with their songs topping both the country and the pop charts. With the huge success of the *Grand Ole Opry*, first as a radio show and then as a live performance show, Nashville became known as Music City, U.S.A. The *Opry* attracted country music stars the country audience wanted to hear; after the stars moved to Nashville, the music industry followed, from the Acuff-Rose Publications firm to the CMA. After Decca began recording in the city in the mid-1940s, an explosion of country music recording activity occurred there. Nashville's entertainment industry has expanded to include television and film production, recording and publication of national jingles and contemporary Christian music, and a booming convention and tourism business.

Country music was a great influence on rock and roll. The above-mentioned subgenres, especially western swing and honky-tonk, brought country music to

Johnny Cash, 1959. Courtesy of Photofest.

the verge of rock and roll; then Bill Haley, Elvis Presley, and other rockabilly artists took the next step. As Carl Perkins once put it, rockabilly was blues with a country beat. Even blues artists said that early country music influenced them. It was more than a matter of rock and roll borrowing the simple storytelling lyrics with simple harmonies and the formal structure of country music. As Colin Escott writes in *Lost Highway: The True Story of Country Music*, "The goofiness of rockabilly owed much to Hank Snow. Rock 'n' roll attitude owed much to Webb Pierce's flamboyance. The Everly Brothers drew on the sound of the country brother duets. Roy Orbison wanted to be Lefty Frizzell. The fierce confrontationalism of bluegrass gave rockabilly its fire."[16]

The borrowing of elements between country music and rock and roll occurred in the 1960s and 1970s when groups (such as the Flying Burrito Brothers, the Allman Brothers Band, the Band, Lynyrd Skynyrd, and the Eagles) developed the country-rock style. A similar crossover flourished in the 1990s and 2000s with such artists as Garth Brooks, Trisha Yearwood, Shania Twain, and Faith Hill. In country's earlier days, a blending with the pop music style occurred when musicians such as Uncle Dave Macon crossed styles and appeared in Hollywood films. As Tin Pan Alley and Hollywood pop composers wrote the songs for western movies that became most associated with cowboy music in the 1930s and 1940s, western music became very popular. Singing cowboy movie stars who blended pop and country tastes (such as Gene Autry, Roy Rogers, and Tex Ritter) influenced countless country artists and even pop singers, such as Bing Crosby, who included western songs in their recorded repertoires.

Pop Music

The phrase "pop music," short for "popular music," is a complicated term generally used to describe music that appeals to masses—it is not considered art music, and can be enjoyed and understood by the general public, not just by educated musicians. Prior to the mid-1950s quite often music of this sort is referred to as pop music, and music from after the 1950s is generally called rock and roll. America's history of popular music began with songs and dances

brought to the New World by European settlers. Once American composers began to
write and publish their own music, they
provided the nation with popular songs
that specifically represented American life.
In time New York City, with its Tin Pan Alley (TPA) and Broadway neighborhoods,
became an important source for many styles
of popular music. The genre discussed here
is the important predecessor of rock and
roll, American popular song, which filled
radio airwaves, record stores, and jukeboxes
until halfway through the '50s. Consisting
of sentimental ballads, novelty songs, and
instrumentals, this popular music reflected
the tastes of white adults. In the 1950s, pop
music songs by such artists as Bing Crosby,
Frank Sinatra, Nat "King" Cole, Perry
Como, Doris Day, and Debbie Reynolds
shared the charts with the new rock and
roll songs until the latter became the general public's taste.

Tin Pan Alley Repertoire

Irving Berlin, 1948. Courtesy of the Library of Congress.

Tin Pan Alley (TPA) was a nickname for
the popular songwriting and sheet-music industry based in New York City from
the 1890s to the 1950s. The name came from the tinny sound of upright pianos
in music publishers' offices in downtown Manhattan. Originally near the theater district on East Fourteenth Street and around Union Square, the industry
moved uptown to around West Twenty-eighth Street, between Fifth Avenue
and Broadway. The sheet music produced by the publishing firms was crucial to
the spread of popular music. By association, "Tin Pan Alley" came to mean the
general type of song created by the industry, first in America and then in Europe,
until the rise of the singer-songwriter movement in the mid-1960s.

The vast amount of music required for vaudeville shows helped New York
publishers gain control of the industry because of the many vaudeville houses
there and touring shows that, set out from the city. Songwriters played their
songs for publishers, hoping to get them performed in shows as well as printed,
distributed, and sold to audiences. First generation TPA composers wrote simple late nineteenth-century and early twentieth-century sentimental ballads often in waltz-like triple meters with a predictable formal structure. By the 1910s
and 1920s, a young, talented group of songwriters assumed the leadership of
American popular song, including Irving Berlin, Jerome Kern, George Gershwin, Cole Porter, and Richard Rodgers. New media to circulate the music had

emerged, such as the player piano, the phonograph, radio, and, in the late '20s, the sound film. These new media formats expanded popular music's audience and contributed to a huge revolution in pop music; the music began to change from an active consumption through performance to a passive consumption by simply listening. Prior to this time, one heard and enjoyed music by attending live performances. With the explosion of technology and recording methods, one could enjoy music simply by playing a recording at his or her convenience.

With the rise of ragtime music and its popularity, TPA composer Irving Berlin wrote songs such as "Alexander's Ragtime Band," which defined the era. Berlin and other TPA composers frequently wrote their songs in the AABA format, known as song form, which had emerged as a popular form. The storytelling concept of the verse-chorus waltz ballad had given way to the more concise thirty-two-measure chorus with a phrase structure consisting of either two halves of sixteen measures each or four groups of eight measures each—two A sections and a contrasting B section followed by another A section. The repetition of the A melody with just the one refreshing contrast of the B melody helped drill the tunes into listeners' ears and produced more hits.

These composers and their popular music benefited from the technology of mass media. Since early music could be presented only in print and in live performance, the media innovations helped spread the music. Thriving in the early twentieth century, automatic player pianos helped spread musicmaking to the home. The expansion of sheet music production resulted from the demand from vaudeville and the popularity of dancing, especially after World War I. Used for commercial entertainment at the turn of the twentieth century, the phonograph found its way into America's homes, increasing the demand for recordings of popular music. This caused an extraordinary growth of record production of mostly popular music genres. In 1920, the first commercial radio station (KDKA, in Pittsburgh) began broadcasting, transmitting music from both recordings and live performances. In 1925, record companies introduced electrical recording, using microphone technology that transformed sound quality and increased the appeal of the new media, replacing the old, primitive acoustical recording. By the late 1920s, the sound film was introduced, creating a demand for movie musicals, which became an important showcase for new songs. Thus, many TPA songwriters and lyricists divided their time between New York City and Hollywood.

Flourishing during the Great Depression while other media struggled for survival, radio was in virtually every household by 1950. Adults listened to pop songs that grew out of the TPA style, which were very popular at that time. Such musicians as Bing Crosby, Ella Fitzgerald, Perry Como, Judy Garland, and Frank Sinatra created hit after hit in this mainstream music style played on white radio stations. Some writers have described the genre as a white-bleached and pop-edged music style that engulfed America. With electrical recording, capturing a wide range of subtle sounds on records became possible, thus allowing singers to sing in a more conversational, intimate manner than before and bringing them closer to their audience. A generation of singers known as crooners, performing in this style, arrived on the pop music scene.

Crooners

The crooning style of singing with microphones had different requirements than the older style of theater singing. Singers didn't have to apply much breath to the vocal cords because the sensitive amplification of microphones favored lower-pitched voices. Often singers with swing big bands, crooners frequently slid into notes rather than attacking them directly on pitch, and they varied rhythms and melodies while singing. Some early crooners were "Scrappy" Lambert, Smith Ballew, "Whispering" Jack Smith, Rudy Vallee, and Gene Austin. After World War II and the demise of swing bands, solo singers emerged, such as Dick Haymes, Perry Como, Dean Martin, Frank Sinatra, Billy Eckstine, and Nat "King" Cole. The best crooners of the day were Crosby, Cole, and Sinatra.

Bing Crosby best exemplified the new crooning sound as he revolutionized popular singing in the late 1920s, setting the standard for crooning with the sensitive electronic microphone as an extension of his voice. Originally from Tacoma, Washington, Crosby sang for four years as one of the Rhythm·Boys (with Harry Barris and Mildred Bailey's brother, Al Rinker) with the Paul Whiteman Orchestra before beginning to work independently around 1930. In 1931, he began his career in radio and film. Crosby mastered the use of the microphone, not just for singing but also for talking over a melody. His innovative singing techniques included using less breath on the vocal cords; singing in a head voice (a register of the voice that produces a light tone quality) when in his low register; using forward production for clear enunciation; singing on consonants (as black singers did); and making subtle use of embellishments (decorations of the melody with appoggiaturas and mordents) and articulations (performance nuances, such as slurs) to emphasize the text. Almost all later popular singers imitated him. Crosby's 1931 recordings "Out of Nowhere" and "I'm Through with Love," and his 1932 "Brother, Can You Spare a Dime?" (the unofficial theme song of the Depression) reflect his unique use of these influential vocal techniques. The most popular singer of his generation, Crosby introduced the new singing technique to America with his many brilliant interpretations of American popular song.

Nat "King" Cole, from Montgomery, Alabama, was an African American popular singer and jazz pianist who moved to Chicago as a child and played the organ and sang in the church where his father was a minister. Cole formed his influential King Cole Trio in Los Angeles in 1937, and quickly won over a white audience with his perfect diction and smooth vocal style. Gradually he appeared less frequently with his trio, and in 1948, he became one of the first black artists to host his own weekly radio show. In 1956, he had a weekly show as a soloist on television, and throughout the '40s and '50s, Cole appeared in

Frank Sinatra and Bing Crosby in *High Society*, 1956. Courtesy of Photofest.

several films, including *St. Louis Blues*, in which he portrayed W. C. Handy. Cole's 1946 hit recording, "The Christmas Song," was the first of his solo recordings to be accompanied by a studio orchestra instead of his trio, and marked the start of his rise as an internationally acclaimed popular singer. Cole achieved success with a long list of hits, including "Straighten Up and Fly Right," "Embraceable You," "Star Dust," "Nature Boy," "Mona Lisa," and "Unforgettable." Well known for his emotive and sophisticated style, Cole toured until his death in 1965 and has remained popular, partly because his daughter, pop singer Natalie Cole, reworked his most famous recording, "Unforgettable," and released it as a duet in 1991, winning Grammys for Best Album and Best Song. Nat "King" Cole was inducted into the Rock and Roll Hall of Fame in 2000.

Bing Crosby's singing inspired Frank Sinatra to pursue a career in music. Sinatra learned from him and other early crooners, and became one of the best. Like Crosby, Sinatra was a master of the microphone and carried its use to a new level by realizing its potential for achieving a wide range of dynamics and for magnifying the expressive effects of singing at a medium volume in the recorded song. The most important voice of the 1940s and the most important link between TPA and the rise of rock and roll, Sinatra was the first real heartthrob—a sex symbol in American popular song. His stage appeal made each female member of his audience feel as if the song were meant just for her. Sinatra inspired a succession of male singers who copied his style, such as Dean Martin, Vic Damone, Steve Lawrence, Bobby Darin, and Jack Jones. Even early rock artists such as Elvis Presley used Sinatra's sexy and emotional performance style as a model for their own.

Often referred to as "The Voice," Sinatra had a dreamy quality to his vocals. The lightness of breath, forward vocal production, and extraordinarily clear enunciation in his singing allowed him to concentrate on shading and nuance while using phrasing that allowed for intensely personal renderings. His highly sophisticated interpretations were clearly guided by the music's content, as exemplified in his classic renditions of "I've Got You Under My Skin" (a Cole Porter song, and one of Sinatra's most memorable vocal performances), "I Only Have Eyes for You," and "Here's That Rainy Day." In the '60s, even though rock and roll was a major popular music force, the industry was still able to count on recordings by Frank Sinatra and other crooners, such as Andy Williams and Jack Jones, to sell as well as those by most rock artists. These pop artists dominated music variety shows on television, with Sinatra appearing in many specials.

Sinatra's singing career was augmented by an acting career. He appeared in fifty-eight films, in both singing and nonsinging roles. In his 1960s films, he played light-hearted playboys with the Rat Pack—a group of friends that included Sammy Davis Jr. and Dean Martin. Throughout his long career, Frank Sinatra's name was synonymous with "American popular singer," since as a performer he created somewhat of a new collaborative art form—songs that were created not only by

 FRANK SINATRA (1915–1998)

Remembered as Ol' Blue Eyes, Frank Sinatra, from Hoboken, New Jersey, is the most celebrated popular male vocalist of his generation. Having dropped out of high school in his senior year, he formed a singing group, the Hoboken Four. Later, Sinatra was a staff singer on WNEW's *Dance Parade* when he caught the attention of bandleader Harry James, who signed him as band vocalist in 1939. He sang with the Tommy Dorsey Orchestra from 1940 to 1942, which led to his first hit record. During this time, he reached celebrity status among young people on a scale matched only by Benny Goodman before him and by Elvis Presley and the Beatles after him. Beginning in 1953, after leaving Dorsey's orchestra, Sinatra was constantly in demand as a soloist, and recorded classic performances of popular standards with Capitol Records for eight years before forming his own record company, Reprise Records, in the early '60s.

When the music industry organized against rock and roll in the '50s, Sinatra testified before Congress in 1958. He and other crooners whose careers had plunged as the result of the success of rock and roll (such as Sammy Davis Jr. and Dean Martin) condemned it. Sinatra referred to rock music as a brutal, ugly, and vicious form of expression, and he labeled rock and roll musicians as abnormal, referring to their music as mentally deficient, with vulgar, dirty lyrics. During the congressional hearings, he also accused rock musicians of being delinquents. Pop song performers were not the only ones protesting rock and roll. Having lost listeners from their pop music programs to rock and roll stations, radio station disc jockeys also spoke out against their competition, as did the large record companies that recorded pop artists and were losing money, and ASCAP songwriters who had lost work because rock and roll performers usually wrote the new music themselves. Despite the disapproval of rock and roll in the 1950s, the

FRANK SINATRA (1915–1998)
(continued)

popularity of the new music continued. (See chapter 9 for further information.)

Though other crooners were threatened by rock and roll, Sinatra's career did not take the nosedive that so many others experienced. He continued to produce remarkable hits from the '60s until his death in spite of the popularity of Elvis Presley, the Beatles, and other newer stars. Sinatra was a respected and convincing song stylist, live show performer, and film and television star. In 1969 his incredible hit, "My Way," summed up the lifestyle of this popular song icon. Perhaps today he is best known for his 1977 cover of the theme song "New York, New York," from the movie of the same title. In 1993, Sinatra teamed up with other popular singers and, ironically, some rock musicians, when he recorded his biggest-selling album, *Duets*, old favorites sung with singers from Tony Bennett, Bono (from U2), and Julio Iglesias to Aretha Franklin, Carly Simon, and Kenny G. He followed it up the next year with *Duets II*, a collection of standards with such partners as Jimmy Buffet, Neil Diamond, Chrissie Hynde (from the Pretenders), Gladys Knight, Stevie Wonder, and Linda Ronstadt; it won the 1995 Grammy for Traditional Pop Performance.

the composer and the lyricist, but by the performer as well.

By the late '50s and early '60s, Tin Pan Alley, which catered to the white, middle-aged, middle-class audience, began to disappear as the up-and-coming youth audience demanded rock and roll. The rock idol was the best phenomenon that pop music lent to rock and roll. As crooners utilized the new recording technology, they became the first superstars of the radio era. His great sex appeal made Frank Sinatra the first great teen idol. He and other pop singers were concerned with the creation of a private space for listening to their music. These singers established a teen-based, predominantly female market for recorded popular music centered on an individual male. This significant concept carried over into rock and roll in the late 1950s and early 1960s with such artists as Francis Avallone (Frankie Avalon), Fabiano Forte Bonaporte (Fabian), and Robert Ridarelli (Bobby Rydell), and is still alive. Another role that pop music played in helping create rock and roll was the lending of song formats to the new genre. Song structures and forms from TPA songs carried forward to rock and roll songs. The eight- and sixteen-measure phrase structure in verse-chorus form remains common in rock and roll songs today. A third important contribution of pop music to rock and roll was the fact that the crooners and their music, so adored and listened to by adults, helped pave the way for rock and roll to be born. America's youths were bored with the pop music of their parents (the calm, strict-tempo dances and sterile hits of the crooners, such as Frank Sinatra's "I Only Have Eyes for You"); they needed exciting, new music that spoke directly to them. As teenagers discovered the thrilling music originally called rhythm and blues, and later referred to as rock and roll on race radio stations in the '50s, the generation gap between parents and their offspring widened. For the post–World War II baby boom generation, rock and roll music was addicting. It was about unleashing inhibitions and having fun, unlike the pop music that drove America's youngsters to the bold, new sound.

NOTES

All chart positions referred to in the chapter are based on Joel Whitburn's Record Research publications, which compile *Billboard* charts information of the rock and roll era.

1. Meredith E. Rutledge, *Rock My Soul: The Black Legacy of Rock and Roll* (Cleveland, OH: Arts League of Michigan and Rock and Roll Hall of Fame and Museum, 2003), 6.

2. Robert Palmer, *Deep Blues* (New York: Viking Press, 1981), 44.

3. Bill Wyman and Richard Havers, *Bill Wyman's Blues Odyssey: A Journey to Music's Heart & Soul* (New York: DK, 2001), 54–55.

4. Robert Santelli, "A Century of the Blues," in *Martin Scorsese Presents the Blues: A Musical Journey*, ed. Peter Guralnick, Robert Santelli, Holly George-Warren, and Christopher John Farley (New York: Amistad, 2003), 12–14.

5. Robert Santelli, *The Big Book of Blues: A Biographical Encyclopedia*, updated and rev. ed. (New York: Penguin, 2001), 254.

6. Blues Foundation, "Hall of Fame Introduction," Blues Foundation Blues Hall of Fame, http://www.blues.org/halloffame/index.php4.

7. Palmer, *Deep Blues*, 16–17.

8. Peter Guralnick, *Feel like Going Home: Portraits in Blues and Rock 'n' Roll* (New York: Outerbridge & Dienstfrey, 1971), 46.

9. Arnold Shaw, *Black Popular Music in America: From the Spirituals, Minstrels, and Ragtime to Soul, Disco, and Hip-Hop* (New York: Schirmer Books, 1986), 129.

10. Robert Palmer, "Rock Begins," in *The Rolling Stone Illustrated History of Rock & Roll*, 3rd ed., ed. Anthony DeCurtis, James Henke, and Holly George-Warren (New York: Random House, 1992), 7.

11. Claudia Perry, "Hallelujah: The Sacred Music of Black America," in *American Roots Music*, ed. Robert Santelli, Holly George-Warren, and Jim Brown (New York: Harry N. Abrams, 2001), 87.

12. Guralnick, *Feel like Going Home*, 61.

13. Norm Cohen, "The History of the Folk Song Revival," in *Folk Song America: A 20th Century Revival* (Washington, DC: Smithsonian Institution Press, 1991), 21–22.

14. Johnny Cash with Patrick Carr, *Cash: The Autobiography* (San Francisco: HarperSanFrancisco, 1997), 137.

15. Country Music Foundation, "Introduction to the New Country Hall of Fame and Museum," Country Music Hall of Fame and Museum, http://www.countrymusic halloffame.com/about/museum.html.

16. Colin Escott, *Lost Highway: The True Story of Country Music* (Washington, DC: Smithsonian Books, 2003), 85.

3

ROCK AND ROLL IS BORN: "LET THE GOOD TIMES ROLL"

THE NEW MUSIC ARRIVES

Determining the beginning of rock and roll is similar to identifying beginning or ending dates for most music genres (and eras). Changes in music styles do not occur quickly and noticeably, but evolve inconspicuously. The blending of American popular music styles in the late '40s and early '50s has made it difficult to pinpoint exactly when rock and roll started. Some music scholars claim it began in 1951, when Jackie Brenston and Ike Turner's Kings of Rhythm recorded "Rocket 88," while others maintain it began in 1954, when Elvis Presley recorded "That's All Right." Some say it began in 1955, when Bill Haley and the Comets' "Rock Around the Clock" became the best-selling record of the year, yet others claim other important early rock songs as marking the beginning of the new genre.

Since rock and roll's evolution was not a single event, it is tricky to identify its arrival with a specific song. It was a gradual process in which multiple popular music styles mixed together in a music melting pot during the first half of the twentieth century. As acknowledged in the "Rave On" exhibit in the Rock and Roll Hall of Fame and Museum, rock and roll's birth occurred throughout rural and urban America: "Somewhere between a rural juke joint and an uptown jukebox was born a music that legendary disc jockey Alan Freed labeled 'rock and roll.' From Philadelphia to Los Angeles, Lubbock to New York and New Orleans to Memphis came the voice of a new generation."[1]

Roots Genres Intertwine

The new music by Elvis Presley, Carl Perkins, Chuck Berry, Fats Domino, and a host of other '50s artists was built on the solid foundation of twentieth-century American roots music: blues, jazz, gospel, rhythm and blues, folk, country, and pop. One clear fact about the birth of rock and roll is that each of its roots lent certain characteristics to the new music, contributing in a unique and different way. Rock and roll was a culmination of virtually every innovation of its roots. Muddy Waters's assertion that "the blues had a baby and they called it rock and roll" was only part of the story; the other music roots played major roles in the evolutionary process as well.

The new music came from all over America, and was composed of Mississippi Delta blues with its complex, percussive guitar style and lyrics that spoke to the dark side of life; Kansas City boogie-woogie piano blues as perfected by Big Joe Turner and Pete Johnson; Chicago electric blues with its amplified guitars and use of harmonicas; and Los Angeles jump blues exemplified by saxophone great Louis Jordan. Rock and roll borrowed the sounds of traditional country music from the Appalachian-style folk ballads of the Carter Family, the country blues of Mississippian Jimmie Rodgers, the technically demanding bluegrass of Kentuckian Bill Monroe, the danceable western swing refined by Texan Bob Wills, and the emotional honky-tonk of Texan Ernest Tubb. The new genre employed the sounds of the socially conscious folk ballads of Woody Guthrie, the fiery and emotional gospel of Thomas A. Dorsey, and the calm, sweet classic pop of the great songwriters of the '30s and '40s. Though strongly rooted in the past, rock and roll wove together the sounds of its predecessors as it spoke to the future via '50s teenagers.

The rock era's pioneers brought further unique elements to the new conglomerate music. Chuck Berry became the premier musical poet with his four-chord, three-minute stories of kids, cars, and guitars; Elvis Presley changed the concept of the teen idol with his exciting music, charismatic looks, and daring actions; Little Richard delivered messages (often sexual) to teens while pounding excitedly on the piano; and the Drifters sang passionately while perfecting the gospel vocal ensemble style referred to as R&B. Rhythm and blues provided the template for nearly all rock and roll with its driving beat, fashion consciousness, minimalist instrumentation, and independent spirit.[2]

Most musicologists agree that rhythm and blues musicians (early rockers such as Bo Diddley) added more energy and a stronger backbeat than was typical of earlier R&B to create one of the first rock and roll music styles. Also agreed upon is that another early type of rock and roll music was created when musicians who grew up playing and singing the blues, R&B, and gospel (early African American rockers, such as Fats Domino, Chuck Berry, and Little Richard) added country elements to their music. Since much '50s rock and roll was a combination of blues and country music, another point of agreement among musicologists is that the early rock sound was created when country-trained musicians (early rockers such as Bill Haley, Elvis Presley, and Buddy Holly) not only played (and covered) songs in the blues format, but also added blues characteristics, such as blue notes and swing rhythms, to their playing and singing. Peter Guralnick cites Elvis Presley's quote while discussing the importance of the blues in early rock and roll in *Lost Highway: Journeys and Arrivals of American Musicians*: "As Elvis Presley said, in neat summation: 'Rock 'n' roll music stems basically from gospel music or rhythm 'n' blues. That's where I actually got my style of singing from, was rhythm 'n' blues and gospel mixed with country and western.'"[3]

In *The Story of Rock*, Carl Belz claims that until the advent of rock and roll in 1954, popular music consisted of three general fields: pop, R&B, and country and western—each with its own artists and record companies, radio stations, and audience. Each of the three fields exhibited a distinct music style and tradition. As rock and roll evolved, distinctions among these fields became increasingly unclear as their previously separate artistic elements blended and the songs crossed over on the three charts.[4]

First Rock and Roll Record

The origin of rock and roll in blues, jazz, gospel, rhythm and blues, folk, country, and pop music is clear; however, it is difficult to determine exactly which early rock recordings represent roots styles (especially R&B, because it sounded so similar to early rock and roll) and which represent rock music. Many '40s blues and R&B recordings have been considered rock and roll. Also clouding the issue is Alan Freed's first use of the phrase "rock and roll" in conjunction with the R&B sound and, previously, "rocking and rolling"—a euphemism for having sex (in blues and R&B circles). Nonetheless, many specific recordings have been considered the first rock and roll record, a hot topic that has caused much debate not only among music scholars but among the general public as well.

One of the most popular choices in this regard is Jackie Brenston's "Rocket 88" (1951), which he cut as a member of Ike Turner's band, the Kings of Rhythm. Two other records often thought to have been the first rock and roll song are Elvis Presley's "That's All Right" (1954) and Bill Haley and the Comets' "(We're Gonna) Rock Around the Clock" (1955). Other recordings that have been referred to as the first rock and roll record include R&B songs: Fats Domino's "The Fat Man" (late 1949), Lloyd Price's "Lawdy Miss Clawdy" (1952), Ruth Brown's "(Mama) He Treats Your Daughter Mean" (1953), Big Joe Turner's "Shake, Rattle and Roll" (1954), the Chords' "Sh-Boom" (1954), the Crows' "Gee" (1953), the Dominoes' "Sixty Minute Man" (1951), and the Orioles' "It's Too Soon to Know" (1948).

"Rocket 88"

Jackie Brenston's 1951 classic, "Rocket 88," is widely considered the first rock and roll record. It was produced by the legendary Sam Phillips (March

1951) at his tiny Memphis Recording Service a year before he formed Sun Records, the label that soon became synonymous with the birth of rock and roll. Phillips subsequently leased the recording to Chess Records. With its automobile lyrics aimed at teens, and featuring vocals by Kings of Rhythm baritone saxophonist Jackie Brenston, the song maintained a boogie-woogie rhythm (featuring jazzy New Orleans-style piano playing by Ike Turner) and incorporated the blues progression in a driving Memphis jump blues style. It used a heavily amplified guitar (the all-important rock and roll instrument borrowed from blues and country music) played by Willie Kizart. The blending of different roots characteristics in the song supports the claim that "Rocket 88" was the first rock and roll record. However, since it included an impassioned and prominent saxophone solo (featuring Kings of Rhythm tenor saxophonist Raymond Hill), many scholars have argued that the song belongs in the R&B style, and is not a rock and roll record. Rhythm and blues songs employed prominent saxophone use, replaced by the guitar in rock and roll—a determining factor that musicologists use to differentiate between the two genres.

It is fascinating that this historic record's label states it was recorded by Brenston and His Delta Cats instead of Ike Turner's Kings of Rhythm, who actually recorded it, and that it was written by Jackie Brenston instead of Ike Turner, who largely wrote it. Jackie Brenston was a one-hit wonder; after this song he released a few more singles between 1951 and 1953, but none of them came close to matching the success of "Rocket 88." After Chess Records released the record, it shot to No. 1 on the R&B charts (June 1, 1951), becoming the label's first No. 1 hit and one of the most successful R&B records of 1951 (second only to the Dominoes' "Sixty Minute Man"). The income from the song prompted Sam Phillips to establish his Sun label in Memphis the following year; Elvis Presley recorded for Sun two years later. Whether "Rocket 88" was indeed the first rock and roll record is subject to discussion; however, the song sounded and felt like a rock and roll song, and it provided an important link to the black R&B records that preceded it. Memphis deejay Dewey Phillips played the recording of "Rocket 88" on his *Red, Hot and Blue* radio show—the first time race music was played on a white station. This record was one of the first (R&B) hits to inspire a cover version. Bill Haley and the Saddlemen (Haley's group before they were known as the Comets) recorded it that same year, and their version is often referred to as the first rock and roll recording by a white artist.

Sun Records recorded a number of blues and R&B performers (including Rosco Gordon and Howlin' Wolf) before working with local country artists. Sam Phillips understood the new music needed a charismatic white performer, and was determined to find a white entertainer to bridge the gap between black and white music—one who could naturally feel the passion of black music (the blues). In 1954, Phillips found that artist in Elvis Presley.

"That's All Right"

In 1954, at Sun Records, Elvis Presley recorded a rousing cover, "That's All Right," of Mississippi bluesman Arthur "Big Boy" Crudup's 1946 Delta blues hit, "That's All Right Mama." The single's other side featured a lively version of "Blue Moon of Kentucky," written and originally recorded as a melancholy bluegrass song by country artist Bill Monroe. Presley's "That's All Right" is considered by many musicologists to be the first rock and roll song; however, as with "Rocket 88," there are many differences of opinion. Presley's choice of songs for the record (black blues and white country ballad) and the actual music of the two sides represented the coming together of blues, country music, pop, and gospel elements, revealing Presley as an eclectic musician. Crudup's original recording consisted of rough blues vocals and an out-of-tune guitar (Mississippi Delta-style performance), whereas Presley's slicked-up white cover displayed country influences in his guitar-picking style, which helped make the song accessible to a white audience.

On July 5, 1954, Sam Phillips recorded Presley's interpretation of "That's All Right" with guitarist Scotty Moore and bassist Bill Black, two country musicians with whom Phillips had paired Presley in the studio a few months prior. Memphis deejay Dewey Phillips immediately introduced the Sun single on the air, playing it fourteen times in a row. The blending of guitars, string bass, and vocals on the record helped shape a sound that crossed the barriers of roots music styles. Throughout the song the acoustic guitar and bass supplied rhythm and the electric guitar imitated Presley's vocals (in the honky-tonk country style). The string bass also provided harmony consisting of a walking bass line with simple chords (tonic, subdominant, and dominant, borrowed from the blues progression). The song's structure used the blues call-and-response technique with vocal antecedent phrases followed by guitar consequent phrases; its format was the typical verse-refrain sequence from folk and country music roots. Most captivating of all was Presley's electrifying voice, which displayed the quality of a black bluesman, the exciting sound Phillips was in search of—the black sound and feel created by a white man. Presley's vocal quality on this recording has been enough to cause many rock historians to call it the first rock and roll record. "That's All Right" has arguably been considered the first rock and roll recording because it assimilated American roots musics while presenting a white artist combining black and white performance practice on a black blues song—an extremely powerful mix.

With guidance from Phillips and in collaboration with Moore and Black, Presley used his natural talent, steeped in gospel music, country music, and the blues, to create his hybrid sound that shook the world. From July 1954 to August 1955, he released five singles for Sun Records, each featuring an R&B standard on one side and a spruced-up country song on the other. While his country songs helped define rockabilly, those in the blues style held the key to rock and roll, having blended all the right ingredients. When white Southern-ers heard Presley's "That's All Right," the first of these R&B records, many of them assumed they were listening to a black singer. By the time of his second record, "Good Rockin' Tonight," a heavily suggestive version of Roy Brown's "Good Rocking Tonight," they knew not only that Presley was white, but that it was time to lock up their daughters.

"(We're Gonna) Rock Around the Clock"

In *The Rockin' '50s*, Arnold Shaw alludes to the difficulties in determining the first rock and roll record and stresses the importance of "(We're Gonna) Rock Around the Clock" by William John Clifton Haley Jr. (Bill Haley):

> If one had to pick the recording session at which rock 'n' roll was born, it would be the date on April 12, 1954 at Pythian Temple on Manhattan's West Side at which Bill Haley and the Comets cut "Rock Around the Clock." It would not be an easy choice because the '55 session in Chicago at which Chuck Berry recorded "Maybellene" could not be dismissed. Nei-ther can one minimize the importance of "Ain't It A Shame," cut in New Orleans by Fats Domino, or of "Only You," recorded in Los Angeles by the Platters. I mention the localities to suggest that the development was be-ginning to assume national proportions. In the final analysis, Haley's disk would get the nod because of his style and impact.[5]

Having previously led a singing group called the Four Aces of Western Swing and then the Saddlemen, deejay Bill Haley blended the country sound with that of R&B in "Rock This Joint" in 1952. The Saddlemen became the Comets in 1953 and their first chart hit, "Crazy Man, Crazy," was the first rock and roll record to appear on the charts (1953, No. 12 pop hit). Bill Haley and the Comets (Danny Cedrone, guitar; Billy Guesack, drums; and Al Rex, bass) recorded "(We're Gonna) Rock Around the Clock" on April 12, 1954, in New York City. Haley had recorded for the independent Essex label, but recorded this song for Decca, one of the major labels. Also recorded in 1954, their cover of Big Joe Turner's "Shake, Rattle and Roll" was considered by many people to be the first rock and roll record.

Written for Haley by Max Freedman and Jimmy DeKnight (a pseudonym for Jimmy Myers, a New York songwriter and music publisher), "Rock Around the Clock," reflected the singer's unmistakably white voice with a country twang. It used repetitive choral chants from swing bands, specifically Bob Wills and His Texas Playboys. A significant feature of Haley's song was its relentless rhythm (from black music styles), with singers and instrumentalists heavily ac-centing every other beat. Recordings of this sort with an insistent dance beat were in great demand.

Upon its initial release, "Rock Around the Clock" was only mildly success-ful, so songwriter Jimmy Myers promoted it by sending copies to Hollywood. In the spring of 1955, MGM released the movie *The Blackboard Jungle* (based upon a novel by Evan Hunter published in 1954), which helped establish the connection between rock and roll and teenage rebellion with its plot about a teacher's experience with violent students in a vocational high school in the Bronx, New York. With "Rock Around the Clock" playing during the opening credits, the film was a huge success. There were riots in theaters and on streets as America's teens were drawn to the new music's sound. The song came to be associated with teenage alienation and hostility, and the ground was laid for the older generation to associate the new music with violence and juvenile delinquency. After the movie Haley's song was re-released; it stayed in the Top 10 for nineteen weeks and was the first rock and roll song to reach No. 1 (July 9, 1955), where it stayed for eight weeks and became the first international rock and roll hit. "Rock Around the Clock" was again a Top 40 hit in 1974, when it was used as the opening theme of the *Happy Days* television show.

The following year, movie producer Sam Katzman booked Haley and the Comets to star with Little Richard, Chuck Berry, and Alan Freed in a film titled *Rock Around the Clock*, which established a new trend in uniting rock and roll with the silver screen. Haley never again matched the success of his No. 1 single, but he was very popular and did concert tours all over the world. Known as the Father of Rock and Roll, he may not have had a career that reached the stratospheric heights of Elvis Presley, but he brought the new music to the consciousness of America and the world. Although much of the public considers "Rock Around the Clock" to be the first rock and roll record, it is the first significant rock and roll hit. It created a sensation marking the beginning of the rock and roll era.

Other Firsts

Out of the great piano-driven music from New Orleans came Fats Domino's "The Fat Man," which has been referred to as the first rock and roll song. Domino recorded the song in 1949 (when only seventeen years old), the first of his remarkable series of records for the Imperial label. Influenced by the Storyville piano tradition in New Orleans, Domino used a prominent and distinctive boogie-woogie-inflluenced acoustic piano style (playing chords with both hands). The song displayed not only Domino's piano skills but also his remarkably confident singing. On this early recording, Domino's high, energetic tenor voice engaged in scat singing imitating a trumpet. Other timbres in the song were the string bass, which along with the piano supplied rhythm, and the saxophone and trumpet (from New Orleans jazz). The bass also provided harmony consisting of a prominent walking (New Orleans-style) bass line on the twelve-bar blues progression. Since Domino did not use the guitar (considered the main element of rock and roll), many musicologists said the song had no white elements and consisted only of black characteristics, and would not place it in the rock and roll genre. (Many believe rock and roll was a coming together of black and white elements.) Charlie Gillett refers to "The Fat Man" as one of

Ruth Brown, 1955. © Frank Driggs Collection/Getty Images.

the biggest R&B hits of the period and does not consider it a rock and roll song.[6] Yet others claim that the plump and friendly-looking Domino, who created an upbeat, exhilarating brand of R&B and was a favorite of young white people, made the first rock record and that rock and roll was born in New Orleans.

Also from the New Orleans R&B tradition came Lloyd Price, who in 1952 recorded the No. 1 R&B hit "Lawdy Miss Clawdy" for Specialty Records. Though Price's voice was more intense than Fats Domino's (using a vocal style and tone from gospel music and blues), the song had a prominent New Orleans piano style throughout (played by Domino). Though it is considered by some to be the first rock and roll song, most music scholars have referred to "Lawdy Miss Clawdy," with its prominent rhythm and blues-styled saxophone solo, as an R&B song. Charlie Gillett states that the song was a huge hit in the R&B market and had incalculable effects both on rock and roll and on the growing tendency for singers to adopt gospel-influenced styles.[7] Arnold Shaw claims that Price made the transition from R&B to rock and roll in 1959.[8]

In 1953, Ruth Brown recorded "(Mama) He Treats Your Daughter Mean" with a band led by Ray Charles for Atlantic Records. Though largely considered an R&B artist, Brown has been cited as the creator of the first rock and roll record, "Mama." Musicologists have argued that the song holds true to its R&B origins, and is not rock and roll. Aside from Brown's repetitive, soft vocal screech (from gospel music), the song consisted of R&B elements such as saxophone and trumpet instrumental timbres and bluesy piano fills. With "Mama" (which she often had to perform multiple times to satisfy audiences) Brown became a sensation. The song was No. 1 on the R&B charts for five weeks and, with four other No. 1s, helped make Brown one of the top-selling artists of the '50s.

Recorded in 1954 by Big Joe Turner and written by Atlantic Records' arranger Jesse Stone (using the name Charles Calhoun), "Shake, Rattle and Roll" has been considered the first rock and roll song. The recording used a prominent R&B combo consisting of saxophone, piano, and drums in conjunction with a heavy R&B backbeat (provided by the drums). "Shake" used call-and-response (from the blues) between vocals and instruments, and its lyrics used the sexual metaphor "shake, rattle, and roll." The song displayed rhythm and blues characteristics and topped the R&B charts on June 12, 1954. References to Turner's "Shake, Rattle and Roll" as a rock and roll record are seemingly unfounded, since the music was conceived in the R&B genre. As Big Joe Turner's original version was about to hit No. 1 on the R&B charts, the cover version of the song, recorded on June 7 by Bill Haley and the Comets, was made. Haley's cover made more sense being called the first rock song, since it represented a white group singing a black R&B song.

Of the four doo-wop songs often cited as the first rock and roll record ("Sh-Boom," "Gee," "Sixty Minute Man," and "It's Too Soon to Know"), the Chords' "Sh-Boom" has had the strongest case for the distinction, as presented by Carl Belz. In *The Story of Rock*, Belz states that the original version of "Sh-Boom," as recorded on the Cat label (a subsidiary of Atlantic Records) in 1954 by the Chords, "occupies a unique position in the history of popular music: It not only heralded the style of the new music, but the history of its success established the pattern followed by nearly all of the successful rock records between 1954 and 1956." Belz stresses the importance of "Sh-Boom" because of its crossover appeal, as shown by its positions on both the R&B and pop charts in the summer of 1954. He makes it clear, however, that the Chords' single was not the first R&B record of 1954 to achieve such a distinction, and that the Crows' "Gee," another song named as the beginning of the rock and roll era, had done so previously (though "Gee" never reached the Top 10, as "Sh-Boom" did after only three weeks on the charts). Belz points out that "Gee" was not as popular as "Sh-Boom" because there were many cover versions of the Chords' song (by such groups and artists as the Crew-Cuts, Billy Williams, Sy Oliver, and Bobby Williamson) but not of the Crows'.[9]

In 1951, the Dominoes recorded for the Federal label what became an enormous R&B doo-wop hit, the crossover classic "Sixty Minute Man." It incorporated sexual imagery in its lyrics, which caused a stir in the gospel community (which had strongly influenced the group). The song featured the bass voice of Bill Brown boasting of his sexual prowess: being able to satisfy his "girls" with fifteen minutes each of "kissin'," "teasin'," and "squeezin'" before his climactic fifteen minutes of "blowin'" his "top." In the background, Clyde McPhatter sighed "don't stop" throughout the song. Whereas earlier songs used "rock" or "roll," "Sixty Minute Man" used the whole phrase, "rockin' and rollin'" and met with unprecedented white acceptance. Reebee Garofalo lists three definitions of the phrase "rock and roll": the actual musical genre, the more acceptable term for R&B music, and the sexual metaphor. He asserts that "Sixty Minute Man" fulfilled all three definitions while being a popular R&B release that crossed over to the mainstream audience; records that did this were often called rock and roll to obscure their origins.[10]

Known as the Vibranaires until Jerry Blaine (founder of Jubilee Records) renamed the group, the Orioles recorded "It's Too Soon to Know" in 1948. Greil Marcus is among the many pop music historians who have considered this piece as the first rock and roll song, having referred to it as the "new sound" and citing it as a contender for the title.[11] The Orioles' manager, Deborah Chessler, wrote "It's Too Soon" for this unique group that she discovered in Baltimore. It became their first recording (a No. 1 R&B hit), followed by a string of R&B classics such as "Forgive and Forget," "Baby Please Don't Go," and "Crying in the Chapel." The Orioles are one of the most important of the early R&B early vocal groups. They set the standards and established the showmanship that would be borrowed by 1950s doo-wop groups and therefore, arguably, are worthy of the first rock record distinction, having been so influential, especially throughout the period 1948–1954.

As "race music" (the term used for music intended for distribution in the African American community) became more popular throughout the 1940s, the number of songs employing the words "rock" and "roll" in their titles gradually rose. Their titles alone have caused many to cite these songs as the first of the new rock and roll genre. In 1948, blues shouter Wynonie Harris's No. 1 hit on the race charts, "Good Rockin' Tonight," was another of the several releases identified as the first rock and roll record. This cover of Roy Brown's 1947 song ("Good Rocking Tonight") was one of the first big hits using the term "rock." According to Charlie Gillett, "This was one of the songs that fired the imaginations of young people bored with white popular music; and several rock 'n' roll singers, including Elvis Presley, Buddy Holly, and Frankie Lymon, testified to its influence by recording their versions."[12] After Harris's hit, records that used the word "rock" sold in great numbers, and by 1950 more than a dozen R&B songs a year had either "rock" or "rockin'" in their titles. In 1948, Wild Bill Moore's "We're Gonna Rock, We're Gonna Roll" was recorded; it is often named as the R&B song from which Alan Freed coined the term "rock and roll." The next year Jimmy Preston's "Rock the Joint" was released, and in 1950 Muddy Waters recorded "Rollin' and Tumblin'."

Rock and Roll Spreads

The new music emerged and spread throughout the world as racial discrimination began—very slowly—to collapse. Black music finally entered mainstream society as whites demanded records by African American artists, a sign of rock and roll's association with young people's growing antiracism. Deejays were already promoting the driving beat of rhythm and blues music by 1951 as they noted the growing number of young white people discovering the more invigorating world of African American music. With its harsh vocals, more daring lyrics, and electric guitar and saxophone solos, R&B contrasted with the reserved white pop music. Bill Haley's western swing and Elvis Presley's hillbilly-boogie style had already incorporated the lively rhythms of African American music, thus contributing to the birth of rock and roll. Teenagers had money to buy records in the late '40s, and an environment for the two races to mingle developed as white teenagers bought black records in large quantities. It was the massive changes in American culture after World War II that made the birth of rock and roll possible in the '50s; it could not have happened earlier because the country was not ready for it.

The new music became the new criterion for the young generation distancing itself from adults. Rock and roll became one of the secret codes of a world that belonged exclusively to young people, where adults were not allowed and where drive-in movies and cruising around town with rock and roll playing on the car radio were their activities. The classic novel by American writer J. D. Salinger, *The Catcher in the Rye* (about the adventures of a gifted and sensitive young man incapable of adjusting to the rules at school, at home, and in society), was published in 1951, contributing to the growing generation gap. Salinger created one of the models for 1950s American teenagers who dared to reject mainstream American values and behaviors. As the decade progressed, "rock and roll" carried additional meaning, referring to a style of music as well as to a rebellious identity (similar to the term "jazz" in the 1920s, when it connoted that jazz fans smoked, drank, and frequented speakeasies where jazz was performed).

Dance, the physical element of R&B, was an essential characteristic of African music that became a major part of rock and roll. Thanks to Alan Freed and other deejays, America was dancing to the new sound, and within a few years R&B and rock and roll records began to soar on the national charts. *Billboard* magazine's charts at the time divided music into categories corresponding to audiences: pop, country and western (favored by Southern whites), and race music or R&B (originally targeted to an exclusively African American public). The new music frequently crossed over on the charts—it was on the R&B charts, sometimes crossing over to the pop charts. Bill Haley and the Comets' recording of "Rock Around the Clock" became the first rock and roll song to reach No. 1 on the pop charts, in July 1955.

Like the influences of rock and roll, the artists of this era who were featured on the charts came from all over America. Philadelphia was the home of former cowboy singer Bill Haley; the plains of Texas had been the homes of Buddy Holly and Roy Orbison; Memphis provided a launching pad for Johnny Cash, Carl Perkins, Jerry Lee Lewis, and Elvis Presley; New Orleans presented Little Richard, Fats Domino, and a generation of amazing musicians, such as Allen Toussaint, Earl Palmer, and Red Tyler. From Central Avenue in Los Angeles to Harlem's 125th Street, rock and roll was the rallying cry for the postwar generation.[13]

Many musicologists firmly believe the rock and roll culture was born in Cleveland, where races were integrated at Alan Freed's Moondog Coronation Ball in 1952. James Henke, editor of the *Rock and Roll Hall of Fame and Museum Guidebook*, claims that rock and roll music was born in Memphis, the Southern musical and cultural magnet at the northernmost edge of the Mississippi Delta. He maintains that the first stop of African American sharecroppers heading north during the Great Migration allowed transients with diverse influences and styles to congregate in the city where Sam Phillips recorded such legendary musicians as B. B. King, James Cotton, Howlin' Wolf, Elvis Presley, Carl Perkins, Johnny Cash, Roy Orbison, and Jerry Lee Lewis. As chief curator of the Rock and Roll Hall of Fame and Museum, Henke declares, "What transpired in Memphis changed popular music and ignited a revolution in popular culture."[14]

NOTES

All charts positions referred to in the chapter are based on Joel Whitburn's Record Research publications, which compile *Billboard* charts information of the rock and roll era.

1. "Rave On: Rock and Roll in the Fifties," permanent exhibit (Cleveland, OH: Rock and Roll Hall of Fame and Museum, November 21, 2003).

2. Ibid.

3. Peter Guralnick, *Lost Highway: Journeys and Arrivals of American Musicians* (Boston: David R. Godine, 1979), 9.

4. Carl Belz, *The Story of Rock* (New York: Oxford University Press, 1969), 16–25.

5. Arnold Shaw, *The Rockin' '50s: The Decade That Transformed the Pop Music Scene* (New York: Hawthorn Books, 1974), 136.

6. Charlie Gillett, *The Sound of the City: The Rise of Rock and Roll*, 2nd ed., enl. (New York: Da Capo Press, 1996), 139.

7. Ibid., 140.

8. Shaw, *The Rockin' '50s*, 95.

9. Belz, *The Story of Rock*, 26.

10. Reebee Garofalo, *Rockin' Out: Popular Music in the USA*, 3rd ed. (Upper Saddle River, NJ: Prentice Hall, 2005), 77.

11. Greil Marcus, "Is This the Woman Who Invented Rock & Roll?: The Deborah Chessler Story," *Rolling Stone*, June 24, 1993, 43.

12. Gillett, *The Sound of the City*, 131.

13. "Rave On," permanent exhibit, November 21, 2003.

14. James Henke, ed., *Rock and Roll Hall of Fame and Museum Guidebook* (Cleveland, OH: Rock and Roll Hall of Fame and Museum, 2000), 27.

4

RHYTHM AND BLUES–BASED ROCK AND ROLL: "GOOD GOLLY, MISS MOLLY"

THE RHYTHM AND BLUES SOURCE

Rhythm and Blues Styles

In its infancy, rock and roll borrowed greatly from its roots: blues, jazz, gospel, folk country, pop, and, most important, rhythm and blues. As the new music developed its own energetic style with pounding backbeats and loud guitars, it was based upon the music of the roots' masters—from Louis Armstrong and Marion Williams to Jimmie Rodgers and Bessie Smith. Rhythm and blues pioneers drew upon the roots music they grew up with in the '30s and '40s while devising the fresh, exhilarating sound of the '50s. When rock and roll began to emerge as a distinct entity in the early '50s, it was comprised of different styles developed independently of each other, but dependent on the rhythms (and beat) of black music. Rhythm and blues music helped stir happy emotions in its audience with its harsh vocal styles, explicit lyrics, and wailing instruments (saxophone, piano, guitar, and drums) playing loudly with a vigorous dance rhythm. Rhythm and blues was an extremely important source of early rock and roll music.

Many rock historians today consider the blues and R&B recordings of the '40s to be rock music, basing their theory on the fact that Alan Freed used the term "rock and roll" to identify rhythm and blues music. The large, varied R&B repertoire of many artists (including such '50s musicians as Bo Diddley, Chuck Berry, Fats Domino, and Little Richard) displayed a number of rhythm and blues styles constituting some of the very earliest rock and roll. Rhythm and blues honkers (such as Big Jay McNeely and Maxwell Davis) and shouters and leaders of the jump blues combos (such as Big Joe Turner and Wynonie Harris), as well as the creators of the quieter nightclub blues, laid the foundation for the early blues-based rock music. Rhythm and blues crier Roy Brown inspired many '50s musicians, including B. B. King, James Brown, Little Richard, Jackie Wilson, and Ernest Evans (Chubby Checker), and performers of the quieter club-style blues, such as Nat "King" Cole, Charles Brown, and Ray Charles, influenced other '50s rockers.

With its powerful rhythms and backbeats, R&B dance music expressed the enjoyment of life, performed with excitement and energy by artists and groups that put on dynamic stage shows. Saxophonists often played on the floor or in the audience, rolling around on their backs, and singers shouted their often sexually suggestive lyrics while gyrating on stage. These frenzied performance activities formed the basis of much '50s rock music and its performance, while also helping to contribute to the criticism of rock and roll that immediately arose. (See chapter 2 for more discussion on this musical style.)

Rhythm and Blueswomen

Numerous blueswomen laid the R&B foundation for rock and roll, among them Dinah Washington, Little Esther Phillips, and LaVern Baker. (See chapter 2 for further information.) Ruth Brown, Etta James, and Big Mama Thornton were also significant founders. Along with their significant male colleagues Louis Jordan, Big Joe Turner, Wynonie Harris, Ike Turner, Hank Ballard, and Ray Charles, these exceptionally talented ladies set the stage for 1950s rhythm and blues-based rock and roll. The sounds of first-class rockers Bo Diddley, Chuck Berry, Fats Domino, and Little Richard came from their R&B roots, as they shaped what came to be known as some of the first rock music in the '50s. Many secondary artists joined them, and R&B and rock and roll musicians influenced each other in profound ways, as the musicians themselves have asserted. Hank Ballard, composer of the dance classic "The Twist," declares that the melody for that song was based on the earlier Drifters' tune "What'cha Gonna Do?" Little Richard claims that his trademark phrasing in "Lucille" ("Lucille-*uh*") was taken from Ruth Brown's high-pitched vocal articulations ("Mama-*uh*") on her hit "(Mama) He Treats Your Daughter Mean."[1]

Ruth Brown.   Ruth Brown achieved immense success as an R&B singer, rivaling Dinah Washington as the '50s' leading black female singer. Born Ruth Weston in 1928 in Portsmouth, Virginia, Brown emerged from the gospel tradition; she began singing in her local church, where her father was choir director. After Lucky Millinder (whose band accompanied Wynonie Harris and many blues artists) hired her for a short time, Brown, who sang in the West Coast blues ballad R&B style, performed at Blanche Calloway's (the sister of bandleader Cab Calloway) club, the Crystal Caverns, in Washington, D.C. Her performances there led to a recording contract with Atlantic Records. In 1948, she signed a record deal with Atlantic's founders, Ahmet Ertegun and Herb Abramson, and in 1949 she gave the label its second hit, "So Long," which reached No. 4 on the R&B charts. The next year, she recorded her second single for Atlantic, "Teardrops from My Eyes," which became a No. 1 hit on the R&B charts. This song was the beginning of a string of twenty Top 10 hits, including No. 1's "5-10-15 Hours" (1952); "(Mama) He Treats Your Daughter Mean" (recorded with a band led by Ray Charles in 1953); "Mambo Baby" (1954); and "Oh What a Dream" (1954). Her hits firmly established Brown as a top-notch R&B singer, and her series of successful records secured Atlantic its place in the record industry; it was referred to as "The House That Ruth Built." Throughout the '50s, Brown recorded numerous songs for the label; she was its most prolific and best-selling musician of the period. In 1956, she began attracting a white audience while performing in Alan Freed's rock and roll shows. Brown crossed over to the pop charts in 1957, beginning with the success of "Lucky Lips," written for her by the songwriting team of Jerry Leiber and Mike Stoller (Leiber and Stoller), and "This Little Girl's Gone Rockin'" (1958), written for her by Bobby Darin. Known as Miss Rhythm, Brown was inducted into the Rock and Roll Hall of Fame in 1993.

Etta James.   Etta James (born Jamesetta Hawkins in Los Angeles in 1938, and nicknamed "Miss Peaches"), a 1993 Rock and Roll Hall of Fame inductee, began singing in church. As a teenager she was singing in a group, the Peaches, when they auditioned in 1954 for R&B bandleader Johnny Otis in San Francisco. In 1955, James (still with the Peaches) and Johnny Otis wrote and worked up a reaction song, "Roll with Me Henry," to Hank Ballard and the Midnighters' 1954 No. 1 R&B hit, "Work with Me Annie." James changed the title of "Roll with Me Henry" to the less suggestive "The Wallflower," and her first single was released on Modern Records in 1955; it hit No. 1 on the R&B charts. That year, pop performer Georgia Gibbs had a No. 1 pop hit with a cover of James's song, "Dance with Me Henry," the title that James later gave to her version. James spent the next few years touring with Otis and enjoyed further success with such R&B hits as "Good Rockin' Daddy" and "All I Could Do Was Cry." In 1960, James moved to Chess Records and recorded for its subsidiary labels Argo and, later, Cadet (followed by Chess). She had many R&B and pop charts hits throughout the '60s, including her career-defining "At Last." She overcame heroin addiction and has remained a popular concert performer. The powerful, emotionally expressive vocalist opened concerts for the Rolling Stones in 1978 and continued to tour and record throughout the '80s. In 1984, James sang at the opening ceremonies of the Olympic Games in Los Angeles, and in the '90s she continued to record very successful albums, such as *The Right Time*, called a masterpiece by *Rolling Stone*.

Big Mama Thornton.   Another blueswoman significant to '50s rhythm and blues-based rock and roll was blues belter Big Mama Thornton, who came from the tradition of classic blues singers. Born Willie Mae Thornton in 1926 in Montgomery, Alabama, she proved to be a direct descendant of Memphis Minnie, whose style Thornton's strongly resembled. At the age of fourteen, she moved to Atlanta to dance in a variety show, and gained experience as a singer and dancer by touring with a road show, Sammy Green's Georgia-based Hot Harlem Revue, until 1948, when she settled in Houston, Texas, and began recording for Peacock Records. Thornton also frequently played harmonica and drums for a variety of R&B bands. She became a featured artist with the Johnny Otis Rhythm and Blues Caravan in Los Angeles, and in the early '50s debuted at the Apollo Theater in New York, quickly progressing from opening act to headliner.

Big Mama Thornton recorded one of the seminal records in rock and roll history for the Peacock label, "Hound Dog," which was one of her most successful '50s hits on the R&B charts. Written for her by Leiber and Stoller, it was a No. 1 R&B song for seven weeks in 1953 but never made it to the pop charts, as did Elvis Presley's hit cover version of the song three years later (which was one of the biggest hits of the rock era). The lyrics of her original version emphasized that a hound dog was African American slang for a man who cheated on his woman, whereas Presley's cover of the song had lyrics that criticized a woman by saying she was of no more use than a hound dog who couldn't catch rabbits. Presley's slight change of text gave the song a completely different meaning, one that was suitable for his early tough-guy image. Thornton's original, black blues version had the rough vocal quality of the classic blues (complete with vocalized howling dogs) and elements of the country blues, while Presley's was a cleaned-up, polished white cover of the song in the urban blues style.

Big Mama Thornton's original "Hound Dog" recording had a slow blues tempo and implemented the classic blues progression. It also had country blues guitar-improvised solo lines and improvised vocal responses. Presley's cover of the song accelerated the beat and replaced the blues instruments and blues-oriented instrumental improvisations with country-styled ones. In 1956, Presley's recording was No. 1 for eleven weeks on the pop charts and No. 1 on the R&B charts for six weeks; he made the song a million-selling rock and roll hit. By this time, Presley was already publicized as the ultimate crossover artist who sounded black, although he was white, allowing him to perform R&B material with credibility and gain exposure through media that were still closed to most black performers, such as television and Top 40 radio.[2] In response to Thornton's "Hound Dog," Memphis blues and R&B singer and WDIA disc jockey Rufus Thomas recorded "Bear Cat" (credited to Rufus Hound Dog Thomas Jr.). Thomas was the first Sun Records artist to have a national hit when the song climbed to No. 3 on the R&B charts in 1953.

After appearing on '50s R&B package tours with such artists as Little Junior Parker, Bobby "Blue" Bland, Little Esther Phillips, and Johnny Ace, Thornton moved to California, where she recorded for a succession of labels and performed in several blues clubs in Los Angeles and San Francisco. In the mid-1960s, when Janis Joplin moved to California, the gutsy, throaty Thornton greatly influenced Joplin's blues vocal style and served as the link between classic blues singers and Joplin. One of Joplin's most memorable songs, "Ball and

Chain," was written and first recorded by Thornton in the early '60s. After interest in the blues was rekindled in the 1960s, Thornton enjoyed performing with blues legends Muddy Waters, B. B. King, and Eddie "Cleanhead" Vinson, and at blues and jazz festivals around the world. She continued releasing records until her death in 1984, the year she was inducted into the Blues Foundation's Hall of Fame.

Rhythm and Bluesmen

Louis Jordan.   Louis Jordan, a 1983 Blues Foundation Hall of Famer from Brinkley, Arkansas, was one of the fathers of rock and roll. Taught to play the saxophone by his father, and with deep roots in swing jazz, he pioneered the exciting jump blues R&B style that emphasized honking (saxophone solos) and screaming (vocal shouting) effects. Louis Jordan and His Tympany Five (which usually had eight or nine members) were often described as a jump band, with timbres of the R&B combo: saxophone, trumpet, bass, piano, drums, and vocals. Their music was very danceable with a fast rhythmic beat and the twelve-bar blues pattern, and was, often referred to as shuffle boogie, jumpin' jive, or jump blues. Music historians agree that white rockers, such as Bill Haley (whose music is referred to as Northern band rock and roll with a heavy boogie rhythm, a strong backbeat, and happy feelings), imitated Jordan's shuffle beat style in the early '50s. Jordan was a major influence on B. B. King, Ray Charles, Little Richard, and Chuck Berry, and was instrumental in transitioning big-band swing and early R&B to the '50s rock and roll sound.

Jordan reigned as the King of Jukeboxes with his series of catchy, boogie-woogie-influenced hits that he recorded for Decca Records; between 1942 and 1951, with fifty-seven of their singles on the R&B charts, the wildly popular Louis Jordan and His Tympany Five had eighteen No. 1 hits. The appeal of Jordan's songs (which reflected his great sense of humor), such as the No. 1 hits "Caldonia" (1945), "Choo Choo Ch'Boogie" (1946), "Ain't Nobody Here but Us Chickens" (1946), and "Saturday Night Fish Fry" (1949), was the lively evocation of good times and the swinging sounds (from hot jazz to shuffling boogie blues) of his band. Jordan supplied rock music with much of the slang used in its lyrics, and directly influenced the freewheeling spirit of early rockers, such as Chuck Berry, who acknowledges that he greatly identifies himself with Jordan.[3] Jordan's stage personality was so engaging that his records were as popular with whites as they were with blacks. He sold millions of records and appeared in such movies as *Meet Miss Bobby Socks* and *Swing Parade of 1946*. By the late '40s, Jordan was a major star; his jump blues convincingly left its mark on popular music. His classics, with jumping beats and clever lyrics, were the inspiration for the Broadway musical based on his music, *Five Guys Named Moe*, written in 1990 by Clarke Peters and bearing the title of Jordan's "Five Guys Named Moe" (1943). The lasting influence of this R&B pioneer who died of a heart attack in 1975 continues to be evident in rock music. Having held a record of 113 weeks at the No. 1 position on

Billboard's R&B charts, Louis Jordan was inducted into the Rock and Roll Hall of Fame in 1987.

Big Joe Turner.   At the same time Jordan was recording hit after hit, Kansas City native Big Joe Turner helped create the strand of R&B developed from blues shouters, which was featured by many bands of the late swing era. One of the founding voices of rock and roll, Turner, with his big, husky voice and nicknamed the Big Boss of the Blues, was a critical link between R&B and rock music. Referred to as a blues shouter because of his rousing performances in which he made his voice match the honking sounds of saxophones, he recorded jump blues for the African American market while retaining credibility in the jazz world (having sung jazz since the late '20s). Turner sang with boogie-woogie pianist Pete Johnson and with Kansas City big bands led by Benny Moten, Andy Kirk, and Count Basie. With such classics as "Roll 'Em Pete," he and Johnson sparked the boogie-woogie craze that swept the country in the late '30s and early '40s. When the craze passed, Turner changed to R&B music. While recording for Atlantic Records, he recorded a series of rhythm and blues hits from 1951 to 1956 that dominated the R&B charts and led straight into rock and roll. His hits included the No. 1s "Honey Hush" (1953) and "Shake, Rattle and Roll" (1954), and "Chains of Love," "Sweet Sixteen," "Flip Flop and Fly," "Corrine Corrina," and "Lipstick, Powder and Paint."

As was common in jazz and blues, Turner's songs often contained sexual references, as is evident in his most famous and No. 1 hit, "Shake, Rattle and Roll," recorded in 1954 for Atlantic Records. Atlantic's arranger Jesse Stone, under the name Charles Calhoun, wrote this classic rock song that was at No. 1 on the R&B charts for three weeks. Turner's original recording became the first standard of rock and roll.

Shortly after Turner's release in 1954, Bill Haley and the Comets covered "Shake, Rattle and Roll," establishing Haley as the first white artist to truly cross the line to rock. Because white singers who wanted their music played on the radio in the '50s had to remove lyrics with sexual references, the words in Haley's version were toned down to be more acceptable to a broader audience. The two versions of "Shake" display other differences between the blues and early rock music based on the blues: Haley's recording was faster than Turner's, contained fewer jazz characteristics, and repeated the classic twelve-bar blues pattern fewer times than Turner's; it had a less obvious backbeat than the original, and the cover's instrumental passages lacked the improvised solos in Turner's. Haley's recording reached No. 7 on the pop charts.

Popular with the young white audience, Turner appeared in the 1956 movie *Shake, Rattle and Rock!* and toured with Alan Freed's rock and roll shows. His ability to adapt and change as popular music changed explains the longevity of his career, which lasted from the 1930s until his death in 1985, and explains how he made successful transitions from boogie-woogie to R&B and then early rock and roll—an accomplishment that has given Turner a unique place in twentieth-century music history. Big Joe Turner was inducted into the Blues Hall of Fame in 1983 and the Rock and Roll Hall of Fame in 1987.

Wynonie Harris.   Another prominent R&B shouter, Wynonie Harris was also an architect of rock and roll. Known as Mr. Blues, Harris was born in 1913 (his year of birth is often given as 1915, but 1913 is attested by school records) in Omaha, Nebraska, and began his career as a dancer and comedian before moving to Los Angeles in 1939. In the early '40s, he performed in clubs in Los Angeles, Kansas City, and Chicago, and sang and toured with Lucky Millinder's band and Johnny Otis's band while recording. His recordings for the King label brought him considerable commercial success. Harris toured regularly with package shows during the early 1950s and staged battles of the blues with Big Joe Turner, Roy Brown, and others. Harris's recordings were powerful examples of R&B's sexual suggestiveness. He used many risqué stage moves that were later copied by Elvis Presley. Harris was an R&B pioneer whose exciting vocals, sharp stage moves, and handsome looks made him Big Joe Turner's most serious rival in the late 1940s and early 1950s. He appeared in several films, including *Cabin in the Sky*, *Hit Parade of 1943*, and *Mister Rock and Roll*. Harris had two No. 1 R&B hits: the seminal "Good Rockin' Tonight," a 1948 precursor of the rock and roll sound (the 1947 original recording, "Good Rocking Tonight," by Roy Brown was widely covered by other artists, including Elvis Presley in 1954), and the 1949 song "All She Wants to Do Is Rock." Harris made many successful R&B records, many of them centering on alcohol and sex, that helped pave the way for numerous rock artists. In 1969, Harris died of cancer in Los Angeles.

Jackie Brenston and Ike Turner.   The Memphis jump-blues style was incorporated into "Rocket 88" (1951), often cited as the first rock and roll record, by Jackie Brenston and Ike Turner and His Kings of Rhythm (credited on the record as Jackie Brenston and His Delta Cats), who achieved great success with the chugging R&B sound. (See chapter 3 for further information.) "Rocket 88," which sounded and felt like a rock and roll record, was an important link to the black R&B records that preceded it. Brenston, born in Clarksdale, Mississippi, in 1930, was a one-hit wonder, releasing only a few more singles between 1951 and 1953. He played saxophone in both Lowell Fulson's and Ike Turner's (Fulson's cousin) bands until 1962, then faded from the music scene.

Born Izear Luster Turner in 1931, also in Clarksdale, Ike Turner, the leader of the Kings of Rhythm, played a critical role in the early '50s Memphis music world. He worked with great bluesmen (including Little Junior Parker, Howlin' Wolf, B. B. King, and Johnny Ace) as a session musician and talent scout. Turner sent many artists to the Sun, Chess, RPM, and Modern labels, and performed on and produced many of the records of musical acts he discovered in the '50s. Turner and his Kings of Rhythm were performing in St. Louis when he met his future wife, Anna Mae Bullock (Tina Turner). She eventually fronted his group, which included female backup singers, the Ikettes, and

Ray Charles. Courtesy of Photofest.

changed its name to the Ike & Tina Turner Revue. The Revue performed many R&B hits throughout the '60s and disbanded in 1974. Two years later, the couple divorced. One of the significant originators of rock and roll music, Ike Turner was inducted into the Rock and Roll Hall of Fame in 1991.

Hank Ballard. Another Rock and Roll Hall of Fame inductee (1990), Hank Ballard combined sexually explicit lyrics with the rough sound of gospel music in the early '50s. Ballard and his backup group, the Midnighters (formerly known as the Royals), recorded several successful songs for the Federal and King labels, including what is referred to as the Annie Trilogy (1954)— "Work with Me Annie," "Annie Had a Baby," and "Annie's Aunt Fannie." All three were Top 10 R&B hits (the first two were No. 1's), and each sold more than a million copies, despite being banned from radio. Their success, along with other Top 10 hits, including "Sexy Ways" (No. 2 in 1954), made Ballard an R&B star. Ballard composed and recorded the novelty dance song "The Twist," which became the first rock and roll dance craze in the early '60s after Chubby Checker covered it in 1960 and it became one of rock and roll's early best-selling singles. Influenced by such other R&B musicians as Roy Brown and the Drifters, Ballard and the Midnighters were one of the mid-1950s' most popular R&B groups.

Ray Charles. Alongside these R&B styles (including blues shouters), Nat "King" Cole and his King Cole Trio, who influenced the style of blues ballad singing that developed on the West Coast (sometimes categorized as club blues), produced such artists as Cecil Gant, Charles Brown, and Roy Brown. It also produced a major disciple in Ray Charles. Born Ray Charles Robinson in Albany, Georgia, in 1930, this brilliant R&B singer, pianist, and composer transformed '50s music by injecting black gospel music into his songs, as did R&B singers Ruth Brown and LaVern Baker. Charles combined the emotional fervor of gospel music with the secular lyrics and stories of blues and country music, along with swing jazz and improvisational techniques from all genres, thus inventing the highly innovative and sophisticated soul genre of rock music in the mid-'50s, a decade prior to soul's heyday.

As a five-year-old in Greenville, Florida, Charles contracted glaucoma and was blind by the age of seven. He learned to read and write music in braille at the St. Augustine School for the Deaf and the Blind. Orphaned in 1945,

Charles formed a music combo and began to tour Florida before moving to Seattle, Washington, in 1947. Influenced by West Coast club bluesmen and performing in a crooning, soothing nightclub style with his jazz-blues trio (first called the McSon Trio and then the Maxine Trio), Charles began his recording career in 1949 at the invitation of Swing Time Records' Jack Lauderdale. His first R&B hits were "Confession Blues" (1949, No. 2), "Baby Let Me Hold Your Hand" (1951, No. 5), and "Kiss-a Me Baby" (1952, No. 8). After Atlantic Records acquired his Swing Time contract in 1952, Charles established himself in the R&B tradition and created his most memorable songs, such as the No. 1's "I've Got a Woman" (1955), "A Fool for You" (1955), "Drown in My Own Tears" (1956), and "What'd I Say (Part I)" (1959). Peter Guralnick describes Charles's stylistic change in his essay "Ray Charles":

> "I've Got a Woman," cut in Atlanta, was the consummate marriage of all the elements which up till then had simply failed to coalesce in Ray Charles's musical makeup. It featured, of course, his strong gospel-based piano, a seven-piece group (sans guitar) that cooked, and a vocal which, in the studio version of the song, only begins to suggest the change that had taken place in Ray Charles; with a full-throated rasp, sudden swoops, falsetto shrieks and a sense of wild abandon, Charles totally removed himself from the polite music he had made in the past. There was an unrestrained exuberance to the new Ray Charles, a fierce earthiness that, while it would not have been unfamiliar to any follower of gospel music, was almost revolutionary in the world of pop. Big Bill Broonzy was outraged: "He's crying, sanctified. He's mixing the blues with the spirituals. He should be singing in a church." Only Roy Brown, in the Forties, had even suggested this mix of styles, though Little Richard was soon to follow and raise a hopped-up version of the same hybrid to undreamt-of heights.[4]

With the incorporation of highly intense gospel vocal techniques (utilizing his female backup singers, the Raelettes, as a gospel choir) into his explicitly sexual songs, Charles created extremely successful hits throughout the '50s; his signature song, "What'd I Say," was an important link between blues, R&B, soul, and rock music. With this recording, Charles culminated the creation of the soul music sound. It served as a secular rendition of a church service, complete with moans and groans and a congregation speaking in tongues. Charles's first million-seller, the song was banned by many radio stations. Charles's clever combination of emotions mixed with brilliant musical virtuosity allowed him to move R&B music to unprecedented levels, and he was established as one of the most successful black artists in the music business. Audiences of all types accepted and adored him; white pop singer Frank Sinatra referred to him as a genius. His 1958 live recording, *Ray Charles at Newport*, made at the Newport Jazz Festival (that year the Festival inaugurated its first Blues Night), confirmed Charles as a leader of the new rock and roll genre.

In 1959, Charles, feeling confined by the R&B and jazz atmosphere of Atlantic Records and desiring more control over his recordings, began recording for ABC-Paramount Records, owned by the ABC television network. As he branched into country music in the early '60s, Charles released successful R&B hits with ABC, including "Georgia on My Mind," an update of Hoagy Carmichael's song that became one of Charles's signature songs (1960 No. 3 R&B hit; his first No. 1 pop hit that established his credentials in the pop mainstream and won him two 1961 Grammys; in 1979 it became the official song of the state of Georgia); "One Mint Julep," "Hit the Road Jack" (another No. 1 pop hit), and "Unchain My Heart" (all three 1961 No. 1 R&B hits); and "I Can't Stop Loving You" (1962 No. 1 R&B and pop hit). Added to his first decade of monumental hits, these newer recordings made Charles a major influence on numerous '60s rock artists, including James Brown, Stevie Wonder, the Righteous Brothers, Aretha Franklin, Joe Cocker, Steve Winwood, and Eric Burdon (of the Animals).

To this day, many musicologists debate that Ray Charles was the principal creator of soul music from R&B music. Without doubt, scholars agree that Charles, who died in June 2004, was one of the most original musicians of the '50s and one of the most important post–World War II American musicians. In 1980, Charles was inducted into the Blues Foundation's Hall of Fame, and in 1986, into the Rock and Roll Hall of Fame as a member of the founding class, presented by Quincy Jones (to whom Charles had taught music in Seattle). In 1988, Charles received a Lifetime Achievement Award at the Grammy Awards, and was referred to as the Father of Soul. Five years later, he was given a Lifetime Achievement Award by the Songwriters Hall of Fame, presented by Billy Joel, and in 1995 he was presented the Lifetime Achievement Award at the Rhythm & Blues Foundation's annual Pioneer Awards Ceremony.

RHYTHM AND BLUES–BASED ROCK AND ROLL

All of the styles embraced by the phrase "rhythm and blues" played a part in the development of mid-'50s rock and roll. As African American artists adapted to their new teenage audience by simplifying their music and eliminating adult themes from their lyrics (which Alan Freed began to call "rock and roll"), the musical distinctions between the two idioms became minute, as can be seen in the music of early rockers Chuck Berry and Little Richard. As the genre became more of a hybrid of R&B and country music, distinctions became greater. Rock and roll stars drawn from country music, such as Buddy Holly, Carl Perkins, and Jerry Lee Lewis, created the rockabilly subgenre. Nonetheless, rock and roll music developed from R&B styles thriving in the '50s in various areas of the country. Chicago and New Orleans were two cities where the new music was highly concentrated.

The Chicago Sound

Chicago's South Side black district was home to many musicians as the Great Migration continued throughout the first half of the twentieth century and blacks steadily moved north during and between the two world wars to find work in the city's factories. Many jazz artists, country bluesmen, and blues and boogie-woogie pianists called the Windy City home. As country blues changed and reflected its new urban environment in loud taverns where black patrons enjoyed and danced to it (as in the white honky-tonks of the Southwest), the music became heavily amplified with drums adding a prominent dance beat. Many blues artists became celebrities among the patrons of the South Side bars and were recorded on race record labels for the black market. As white teens began to display interest in rhythm and blues (race music), indies began to cash in on their business.

The most famous R&B record label in Chicago was Chess Records (started in 1947 as Aristocrat Records and renamed Chess in 1949) and its subsidiary, Checker Records (started in 1953), both founded by white bar owners Leonard and Phil Chess. Chess Records started as an extension for entertainers appearing in Chicago clubs owned by the Chess brothers, just as Peacock Records (started in 1949), owned by Don Robey, began in Houston, Texas. Blues artists on the Chess roster included Muddy Waters, Howlin' Wolf, Little Walter, Elmore James, and Sonny Boy Williamson #2, all influential in the development of rock and roll. With their rougher, more growling, sometimes gloomy and unsophisticated style of blues, these artists were not able to make the transition from the black R&B market to the youth pop market in the '50s; however, once British Invasion bands popularized their urban blues in the '60s, they received due recognition for their music. After 1964, the young rock audience accepted most of Chess and Checker's songs through interpretations presented by British rock artists who based their own styles on the recorded performances of the original blues artists. Chess and Checker Records broke into the pop market with Bo Diddley and Chuck Berry, two musicians who bridged the gap between the blues and rhythm and blues-based rock and roll, and whose influence on Chicago R&B was profound. As Arnold Shaw states, 1955 was the year when the great prophets of the new music walked the charts and electrified the airwaves: Bill Haley and Ray Charles, Bo Diddley and Little Walter, and Fats Domino and Chuck Berry.[5]

Bo Diddley

Born Otha Ellas Bates McDaniel in McComb, Mississippi, in 1928, Bo Diddley was one of the most original of the first generation of rock and roll musicians. A lover of string instruments, as a child Diddley moved to Chicago, where he took violin lessons for twelve years and played classical music before switching to the guitar, a more acceptable instrument in his rough Chicago neighborhood. Diddley grew up with black gospel music and the music of Chicago's South Side Delta blues players. His adoptive parents legally changed

Bo Diddley, 1955. © Frank Driggs Collection/Getty Images.

his name to Ellas McDaniel, which he used as a songwriter. Differing stories have surfaced about the source of his stage name, Bo Diddley. One account states that he claimed his friends named him Bo Diddley because of his originality in creating fighting tricks as a boxer in his youth; another states that his friends chose the name for him based on the diddley bow, a single-stringed instrument of African origin that was played by African Americans in the South.

Diddley received his first guitar as a Christmas gift at the age of ten, and formed his first band, the Hipsters, while in high school; they played on Chicago street corners in the late '40s. In 1951, after several years of street performing, Diddley began playing at the 708 Club in a rough neighborhood on Chicago's South Side, after which he became a regular performer in the neighborhood. He changed the name of his group to the Langley Avenue Jive Cats, named after the street he lived on. At various times, Diddley's band included drummers Clifton James and Frank Kirkland; pianist Otis Spann; guitarist and vocalist "The Duchess" (Diddley's half sister); harmonica player William Arnold (Billy Boy Arnold); guitarist Peggy Jones (Lady Bo); and long-time sidekick, bassist and percussionist Jerome Green.

A self-professed Muddy Waters fanatic, Diddley was also greatly influenced by John Lee Hooker, Jimmy Reed, Nat "King" Cole, and Louis Jordan. He was the author of classic songs that represent the earliest examples of rock music stemming from its R&B source material: "Bo Diddley," "I'm a Man," and "Diddley Daddy" (1955); "Pretty Thing" and "Who Do You Love?" (1956); "Hey Bo Diddley" and "Mona (I Need You Baby)" (1957); "Say Man" (1959); and "Road Runner" (1960). In 1955, Diddley signed a recording contract with the Checker label. His first single, "Bo Diddley" (1955 No. 1 R&B hit that he performed on the *Ed Sullivan Show* on November 20, 1955), which was originally called "Uncle John," became an instant hit after he reworked it for the Chess brothers and used his stage name in it. In the song, composed of simple harmony based on a single chord throughout, Diddley used a bottleneck to slide between frets on his guitar, giving the effect of more chord changes during breaks in the melody. The song utilized Diddley's distinctive rhythmic sound (which originated from his church music roots), as did many of his songs. The African-based rhythmic pattern, known as the "Bo Diddley beat" (because of the energy with which he strummed it and the fact that he popularized it) recurred throughout the song. The famous rhythm was in a meter of 4 and consisted of a quarter note followed by two eighth notes, an eighth rest and another eighth note, and a final quarter note. A rhythm fanatic who played the guitar as a percussion instrument strummed in a constant, throbbing style, Diddley created songs reflecting his unique and primitive guitar playing, his irresistible rhythmic patterns, and his resourceful songwriting.

After his pairing of "Bo Diddley" with "I'm a Man," his bluesy and largely autobiographical hit, a string of classic records followed. Diddley released albums with memorable titles, such as *Bo Diddley Is a Gunslinger* (1960), *Bo Diddley Is a Lover* (1961), and *Bo Diddley Is a Twister* (1962), that appealed to the rock and roll audience. When the surf craze swept the country and influenced rock music in 1963, Diddley released surf albums: *Surfin' with Bo Diddley* and *Bo Diddley's Beach Party*. In the '50s, Diddley performed regularly at the Apollo Theater in Harlem and at other R&B venues. Late in the decade and in the early '60s, he toured with rock and roll package shows. Known for his trademark square guitar (designed by Diddley while he was attending Foster Vocational School in Chicago), Diddley moved to Washington, D.C., in 1958. Along with Chuck Berry, he represents the fine line that existed between blues and rhythm and blues-based rock and roll in the 1950s.

Diddley earned his place as a founding father of rock and roll and has received much of the credit due for his musical success. After exerting considerable influence on many American rock musicians during the '50s, he also influenced those of the '60s, such as Jimi Hendrix, the Beatles, the Rolling Stones, and the Yardbirds. His legacy was enhanced considerably in the mid-1960s when cover versions of his songs were recorded by many American and English groups (especially by British blues revival rock groups): the Yardbirds covered "I'm a Man"; the Rolling Stones revised "Mona"; and the Animals redid "Bo Diddley." In addition to covering Diddley's songs, in 1964 the Animals recorded a tribute to him, "The Story of Bo Diddley." The Bo Diddley beat has been used in many rock songs, including Buddy Holly's "Not Fade Away," Johnny Otis's "Willie and the Hand Jive," the Who's "Magic Bus," Bruce Springsteen's "She's the One," U2's "Desire," and the Pretenders' "Cuban Slide," to name a few. Diddley continued to tour in the '70s and '80s, and in 1979 he opened concerts for the British punk group the Clash. Inducted into the Rock and Roll Hall of Fame in 1987, Diddley, still performing, writing, and recording in the '90s and the new century, has reached younger blues musicians with his rhythmic and blues-based style, as is apparent in the music of George Thorogood. Diddley received the Rhythm & Blues Foundation Lifetime Achievement Award and, in 1998, the Grammy (National Academy of Recording Arts & Sciences) Lifetime Achievement Award.

Chuck Berry, 1957. Courtesy of the Library of Congress.

Chuck Berry

A highly imaginative and creative pioneer of rock and roll, Chuck Berry is considered by many to be the first great rock star. He put the essential music pieces together in the '50s to help invent rock and roll, and was one of Chicago-based Chess Record's most successful artists in the mid-to-late '50s. Berry was one of rock music's first great lyricists, having written numerous songs with brilliant lyrics about American culture, especially teenagers' lives: cars, school, and young love. He gave rock and roll some of its first trademark guitar licks, such as the riff in "Johnny B. Goode," a staple of every rock guitarist's repertoire. Berry grafted blues, R&B, country music, and swing jazz into his music and became one of rock and roll's first great stylistic innovators. He combined country and western with the blues in his first hit, "Maybellene" (1955), and overcame the racial divide of the '50s while allowing rock music to acknowledge its black roots. In his autobiography, Berry states his marketing intentions: "The songs of Muddy Waters impelled me to deliver the down-home blues in the language they came from, Negro dialect. When I played hillbilly songs, I stressed my diction so that it was harder and whiter. All in all it was my intention to hold both the black and the white clientele by voicing the different kinds of songs in their customary tongues."[6]

Born in 1926 into a black working-class family in St. Louis, Charles Edward Anderson Berry was active in the Baptist Church, where he sang in the choir. The guitar fascinated him at an early age. As a teenager, he was taught to play a four-string acoustic guitar by St. Louis jazz guitarist Ira Harris. In the mid-1940s, he served three years of a ten-year sentence for robbery. In prison he began a gospel quartet and blues group whose performances brought them occasional performance privileges outside the gates. After marrying Themetta Suggs in 1948, Berry studied cosmetology and worked a variety of jobs, including beautician, prior to embarking on his music career. In 1950, he purchased his first electric guitar from Joe Sherman, who had a show on radio station WEW, where Berry was caretaker. Berry began performing professionally in St. Louis clubs with the Stevens Trio and then Sir John's Trio (also known as the Johnnie Johnson Trio) in 1952. Led by pianist Johnnie Johnson and with drummer

Eddie Hardy, this trio became one of the top mid-1950s club bands in the St. Louis area. While performing mainly blues with the combo, Berry incorporated country music characteristics from his background as a child listening to country radio stations. The trio's unique sound made many take notice of their music and caused their original black audience to become desegregated. Originally bluesmen at heart, Berry and Johnson took the blues into previously uncharted territory with this unique blend of blues and country styles, turning it into the new rock and roll sound.

Rooted in swing jazz and urban blues, Berry's definitive guitar style was as widely imitated as his witty lyrics. He was one of the first brilliant guitarists of rock and roll; his expert playing set the standard by which later guitarists have been judged. Famous for his duckwalk, one of the most recognizable stage moves in rock and roll, Berry has performed it for years, sliding in a crouched position while playing his guitar. Though he claims he started doing the move to cover wrinkles on his only suit during a multinight booking at Brooklyn's Paramount Theater in 1956, it soon became his trademark. Berry was highly influenced by T-Bone Walker, Howlin' Wolf, Muddy Waters, Jimmy Reed, and Louis Jordan, and particularly by Jordan's guitarist, Carl Hogan; and through Ira Harris' teaching, Berry was indirectly exposed to Charlie Christian's guitar style. Muddy Waters, who thought highly of Berry's talent, introduced him to Leonard Chess, head of Chess Records. Berry traveled to Chicago to perform for Chess, but it was a song on his audition tape, "Ida Red," that convinced Chess to sign Berry to the label. Berry later reworked the song into "Maybellene," the first of his string of hits from the 1950s, and followed with other classics, such as "Roll Over Beethoven" (1956), "School Day" (1957), "Rock and Roll Music" (1957), "Sweet Little Sixteen" (1958), and "Johnny B. Goode" (1958).

Consisting of witty lyrics full of clever insinuations about cars and girls, "Maybellene" helped lay the groundwork not only for the new rock and roll sound, but also for the new music's stance. Released on August 20, 1955, "Maybellene" became a No. 1 hit (for eleven weeks) on the R&B charts and a No. 5 hit on the pop charts, allowing Berry to cross over successfully to the largely white pop charts, a rarity for black artists at that time. Berry claims that he was able to make the transition to the pop charts because of his clear diction, which allowed the white pop audience to understand what he was saying (unlike other black artists). He also attributes his crossover success to his knack for language, since his songs depicted the experience of being a teenager in the changing '50s society, whether he was describing boredom in the classroom, as in "School Day," or the liberating appeal of rock music, in "Rock and Roll Music."[7]

Accompanied by pianist Johnnie Johnson and members of the Chess Records house band (including bassist Willie Dixon), Berry utilized his trademark double-string guitar licks in "Maybellene." "Ida Red" was based on a traditional country tune from the Anglo-Irish folk song tradition (recorded in 1938 by

Bob Wills and His Texas Playboys, a recording familiar to Berry while he was growing up); Berry modified the song to appeal to the car-worshipping teens of the 1950s and renamed it "Maybellene." Considered by many to be a pure rock and roll song (even more than Elvis's "That's All Right" because it was sung by an African American with much country music influence), "Maybellene" contained the raw, urgent sound of black blues. Berry's prominent lead guitar, complete with a stunning and influential solo, carried the entire song, accompanied by a heavy drum backbeat throughout. Lyric- and musicwise, "Maybellene" represented the integrative forces at work in Berry's music. It set the standard for his legendary style—the combination of uptempo, blues-based music with country rockabilly elements driven by a guitar rhythm. An excellent example of his early recordings that dealt with teen themes applicable to any race, "Maybellene" also displayed his clearly enunciated lyrics (a country music characteristic) that often led his white audience to think he was white because they could understand him so easily. With Berry on its label, Chess Records attracted a wider audience in the '50s. He was selling more records than anyone else on the label by the end of 1956 because white teens adored his infectious sound and his records routinely crossed over to the pop charts.

Berry's success on the charts continued throughout the '50s with such other classics as the No. 1 R&B hits "School Day" and "Sweet Little Sixteen." With lyrics about the boredom and frustration of the routine of school, "School Day" became very popular with teenagers as it cashed in on their desire to escape and hear music on the jukebox. Recorded at Chess on January 21, 1957, the song used the twelve-bar blues pattern and call-and-response with guitar fills imitating the voice throughout, thus establishing Berry not only as an R&B or a rock and roll musician, but also as a true pop star. "School Day" was an excellent demonstration of Berry's ability to write for an audience half his age—the new rock and roll generation. It was No. 1 on all three R&B charts (Most Played by Jockeys, Best Sellers in Stores, and Most Played in Juke Boxes) and No. 3 on the pop charts. As big a breakthrough as "Maybellene," "School Day" inaugurated a period when every single by Chuck Berry made the charts, an achievement that carried him successfully into the next decade. "Sweet Little Sixteen," released in February 1958, was Berry's biggest hit to date. It reached No. 1 on the R&B charts and No. 2 on the pop charts. Inspired by a young girl he noticed attempting to obtain singers' autographs while he was performing with a rock and roll package show at the Ottawa Coliseum, Berry once again captured the excitement of teenagers with the song. It was another striking demonstration of his ability to think like audiences half his age. The song's lyrics cleverly referred to Boston, Pittsburgh, San Francisco, St. Louis, and New Orleans, in the hope that residents of those cities would identify with the song. In addition, Berry shrewdly mentioned *American Bandstand* and was booked by Dick Clark to perform it on the show—one of his many *Bandstand* appearances over the years.

As Berry combined his rockabilly-style guitar with a lively backbeat rhythm and high, youthful, clear tenor voice, he enjoyed multiple mid-1950s hits that became rock and roll standards, including "Johnny B. Goode," with which he gave the new music an archetypal character in addition to a classic sound. The song is about a talented country guitarist from Louisiana (the original lyrics contained the words "colored boy," but Berry changed the words so racism would not get in the way of the song's commercial success) who makes it in the big city and pursues a dream of musical fame. The song is claimed by some critics to have been autobiographical, though Berry has disputed the claim. Others maintain the song (a No. 2 R&B hit and a No. 8 pop hit) is about Berry's pianist and sidekick, Johnnie Johnson. With an urgent, fast-paced tempo and strong rhythmic emphasis, "Johnny B. Goode" utilized blues elements: bent pitches (especially during the guitar introduction and solo); call-and-response (with his trademark interplay between guitar and exciting piano parts); and twelve-bar blues pattern. "Johnny B. Goode," a highly influential song, became one of the first anthems of rock and roll. Its guitar-solo introduction has been one of the most copied riffs in rock and roll history.

Berry's classic songs, numerous cross-country tours with rock and roll package shows, and appearances in early rock and roll films—*Rock, Rock, Rock!* (1956), *Mister Rock and Roll* (1957), and *Go, Johnny, Go!* (1958)—made Berry a major star. In the early '60s, young musicians overseas, such as Keith Richards and John Lennon, were mastering his songs. The Beatles, the Rolling Stones, and many other British Invasion groups covered them in the early '60s while Berry served two years in prison for allegedly violating the Mann Act. After his release, he continued with yet more rock classics while more groups, among them the Beach Boys, used his songs for inspiration. Berry sued for and won songwriting credit when the Beach Boys' 1963 hit, "Surfin' U.S.A.," was determined to have clearly borrowed the melody and rhythm of Berry's "Sweet Little Sixteen." In 1972, Chuck Berry achieved a No. 1 pop hit with a risqué novelty song, "My Ding-a-Ling"; at the time he had stopped touring with a band, instead recruiting pickup musicians in each performance locale.

Chuck Berry's music defined rock and roll in the '50s. He profoundly influenced many musicians who followed, including some of the most popular rock and pop artists and groups: the Beach Boys, the Beatles, the Rolling Stones, Bruce Springsteen, and Bob Dylan. Over the years, having greatly influenced many of the best rock and roll guitarists, including Buddy Holly, Carl Wilson, George Harrison, and Keith Richards, Berry is sometimes referred to as the Father of Rock Guitar. He received a Grammy Lifetime Achievement award in 1984 and was cited as one of the most influential and creative innovators in the history of American popular music. Inducted into the Blues Foundation's Hall of Fame in 1985, Berry was the first musician inducted into the Rock and Roll Hall of Fame at the inaugural induction ceremony in 1986; his longtime pianist and friend, Johnnie Johnson, was inducted in 2001 in the Sidemen category. On September 2, 1995, backed by Bruce Springsteen and the E Street Band, Berry performed at the opening concert for the Rock and Roll Hall of

Fame and Museum in Cleveland, Ohio. He released *Chuck Berry: The Autobiography*, in 1987, and that same year a documentary film, *Hail! Hail! Rock 'n' Roll*, was released. It included guest appearances by Rolling Stones guitarist Keith Richards and heartland rocker Bruce Springsteen. President Bill Clinton acknowledged Berry, who on occasion still performs today, as one of the twentieth century's most influential musicians and presented him the prestigious Kennedy Center Honors Award in December 2000.

The New Orleans Sound

Since much of America's popular music (jazz, blues, country, rhythm and blues, and gospel) was born in the South, many of the characteristics of rock and roll's roots came from the music of the black Southern Baptist Church, where many musicians honed their singing skills. Many of the best rock and roll singers have known and experienced this black tradition that went hand in hand with the branch of rock music known as the New Orleans sound—one that combined the city's distinctive music traditions. A rich diversity of ethnic groups and cultures helped contribute to the New Orleans sound. French, Italians, Africans, English, Spanish, Canadians, western Indians, Cajuns, and Creoles settled there because of its prime location near the outlet of the Mississippi River. After being both a French and a Spanish settlement, it joined the United States as part of the Louisiana Purchase of 1803. In the nineteenth century, African slaves helped shape New Orleans music. Slaves were allowed and encouraged to assemble and sing tribal chants, play instruments, and dance on Sunday afternoons in Congo Square. The practice preserved African music traditions that filtered into New Orleans music as slaves began to play European music with European instruments. Eventually, the city's rich tradition of Dixieland jazz became rhythm and blues. Its reputation as a significant music and entertainment center was supported by many live music venues: numerous dance halls, auditoriums, social clubs, and parks served as the fertile breeding ground for R&B music. The city's unique culture and history have been preserved by the New Orleans Jazz & Heritage Festival, which has become one of the most important music festivals in America, attracting major artists from jazz, blues, R&B, folk, gospel, Cajun, zydeco, rock, and country music.

In the '40s, the tradition of rhythm and blues in New Orleans caused R&B record label personnel to scout for new talent and to record there. Through the efforts of such '50s producers, bandleaders, and engineers as Dave Bartholomew, Paul Gayten, and Cosimo Matassa, the distinctive New Orleans rock and roll sound was recorded and preserved. A national recognition of New Orleans R&B came in 1947 with Roy Brown's "Good Rocking Tonight," followed in 1949 by Fats Domino's "The Fat Man." In the mid-1950s, as R&B began its transformation into rock and roll, Domino became one of the first and most successful African American artists to cross over to the popular market and attract a much broader audience than was previously reached with R&B music. During the '50s, an abundance of talented artists were leading practitioners of this distinctive local music sound in New Orleans, characterized by its swinging shuffle beat and blending of Dixieland jazz and jump blues. Among those who crafted the New Orleans sound were Professor Longhair, Huey "Piano" Smith, Guitar Slim, Shirley & Lee, Lloyd Price, Fats Domino, and Little Richard.

Masters of the Sound

Dave Bartholomew.   One of the most significant individuals to emerge from the New Orleans music scene was Dave Bartholomew, who helped develop and define the sound of '50s R&B. He was an important figure in the transition from jump blues and swing jazz to R&B and rock and roll. Bartholomew was responsible for bringing the big beat of the New Orleans sound (which became later known as rock and roll) to the world with Fats Domino's "Ain't That a Shame." The multitalented Bartholomew was a trumpeter (he studied with Peter Davis, who also taught Louis Armstrong), singer, bandleader, songwriter, arranger, producer, talent scout, and businessman. Born in 1920 in Edgard, Louisiana, he learned how to arrange music while in the army. After World War II, he returned to New Orleans and formed his band that included drummer Earl Palmer (a 2000 inductee of the Rock and Roll Hall of Fame) and saxophonists Lee Allen and Red Tyler. In the late '40s, the band became one of the most popular in the city.

Bartholomew started his career as a recording artist for the DeLuxe label in 1947 with "She's Got Great Big Eyes (and Great Big Thighs)," but turned his attention to producing and arranging when Lew Chudd, owner of Imperial Records, hired him in 1949. Thereafter, spending most of his time in the studio, Bartholomew produced songs for such early rock and roll artists as Overton Amos Lemons (Smiley Lewis) ("I Hear You Knocking," 1955), Lloyd Price, and Shirley & Lee. He also worked with Earl King, Roy Brown, Huey "Piano" Smith, Chris Kenner, Robert Parker, Frankie Ford, James Booker, Jewel King, James "Sugar Boy" Crawford, and Tommy Ridgley. Bartholomew discovered Fats Domino and teamed up with him through the early '60s. The Bartholomew-Domino team produced a stunning string of hits, including "The Fat Man," "Goin' Home," "Ain't That a Shame," "Blueberry Hill," "Blue Monday," and "I'm Walkin'." One of the most successful tunesmiths of all time, Bartholomew composed dozens of best-selling melodies. He produced records of the highest quality that had startling sales and established himself as a major architect of the 1950s New Orleans sound. After Liberty Records purchased Imperial Records in 1963, he retired from record producing and returned to his role as a jazz musician and bandleader. Bartholomew was inducted into the Rock and Roll Hall of Fame in 1991.

Paul Gayten.   Another popular New Orleans bandleader, Paul Gayten was the nephew of renowned barrelhouse piano (a style of piano playing, similar to boogie-woogie, that developed in barrooms known as barrelhouses) player Eurreal "Little Brother" Montgomery. Gayten influenced not only Dave Bartholomew, but Fats Domino, Professor Longhair, and many others. Though his main contribution was as a producer, arranger, and talent scout, he recorded for the DeLuxe and Regal labels in the late '40s and had a handful of hits, including "Since I Fell for You" and "True." Because of Gayten's mastery of the New Orleans blues and R&B scene, Chess Records hired him to work as A&R man in New Orleans when the label wanted to join the success of Imperial, Specialty, and Aladdin Records in the city. He discovered new artists (Clarence "Frogman" Henry, Bobby Charles, Eddie Bo, and Charles Williams) and produced and arranged their records for Chess. Gayten produced Henry's 1956 hit, "Ain't Got No Home," which showcased his froggy voice and gave him his famous nickname. Gayten promoted new releases to distributors and radio stations all over the South. He proved to be such a valuable promotion man that Chess moved him to Los Angeles in 1958 to expand and run the company's West Coast operation, where he was one of the first black record executives. Gayten remained with Chess until the label was sold to GRT in 1969 and he formed his own jazz record label, Pzazz.

Cosimo Matassa.   Another crucial figure in the New Orleans sound was Cosimo Matassa, owner and chief engineer of the legendary J&M Studio, where scores of '50s artists and groups recorded. Matassa originally owned an appliance, jukebox, and used record business in New Orleans. When his customers requested new records, he realized the need for a new record shop in the city, and he opened J&M Music Shop. The record store prospered until 1946, when Matassa realized that New Orleans, with its abundance of music, needed an outlet for recording music, so he opened the J&M Recording Service. By the early '50s, he was out of the jukebox and record business and involved solely in recording. Matassa had a simple formula for recording, with no overdubbing or electronic manipulation—he set the dials at one level, turned the machine on, and let performers do their job. He developed a special sound referred to as the "Cosimo Sound" consisting of strong drums, heavy bass, light piano, heavy guitar, light horns, and a strong vocal lead. It eventually became known as the New Orleans sound, with the guitar, baritone, and tenor doubling the bass line, making it a very strong sound.[8]

Before long, indies began using the New Orleans studio, looking for the Cosimo Sound. In 1947, DeLuxe Records was the first to bring in Dave Bartholomew, Paul Gayten, and Annie Laurie for recording sessions, resulting in Gayten's successful ballad, "True," which was followed by hits including Roy Brown's "Good Rocking Tonight." Throughout the '50s, record labels (Chess, Aladdin, Atlantic, Savoy, Imperial, and Specialty) came from all over the country to record at J&M. All the best artists (Tommy Ridgley, Guitar Slim, Professor Longhair, Big Joe Turner, Little Richard, and Ray Charles) from near and far flocked to Matassa's studio in search of the spectacular sound that resulted from a combination of the New Orleans sessionmen, the studio's acoustics, and the simplicity of Matassa's technique. J&M was the catalyst for the sound of New Orleans. Many of the best records from the late '40s to the early '70s (including Fats Domino's) were engineered by Matassa and made under his tutelage at J&M.

Crescent City Musicians

Professor Longhair.   An artist who recorded at Matassa's studio and had a profound influence on New Orleans pianists, Henry Roeland Byrd (Professor Longhair) created an idiosyncratic style of music that combined barrelhouse boogie-woogie piano with Caribbean rhythms and parade band music, transforming it into the foundations for a bass-centered R&B. Born in Bogalusa, Louisiana, Longhair spent most of his life in New Orleans; he began performing in the city's clubs in the late '40s and had an immediate impact on local audiences and musicians. He recorded for the Mercury, Star Talent, and Atlantic labels and became one of the most important R&B pianists to influence rock and roll. Longhair's powerful and carefree rolling bass riffs represented the Crescent City's freewheeling, good-time spirit. He contributed the solid bass foundation to the New Orleans sound, over which the city's musicians added contrast with higher timbres, such as a tenor saxophone or the voice of an R&B shouter. His rollicking boogie-woogie bass lines became essential elements in the rock styles of Fats Domino, Huey "Piano" Smith, Mac Rebennack (Dr. John), and Allen Toussaint, to name a few. To this day, Longhair's anthem, "Mardi Gras in New Orleans," is played every year as the theme song of the famous Mardi Gras carnival in the city. The Professor was inducted into the Rock and Roll Hall of Fame in 1992.

Huey "Piano" Smith.   The popular New Orleans R&B pianist Huey "Piano" Smith, influenced by Professor Longhair, accompanied Frank Guzzo (Frankie Ford), who recorded "Sea Cruise" (1959) for the Louisiana-based Ace Records. The song, which became a No. 11 R&B hit and a No. 14 pop hit, is an excellent example of New Orleans rock and roll, with its active horn (foghorn-like timbres) and boogie-woogie piano parts. With Smith, the Clowns accompanied Ford on "Sea Cruise," which Smith claims was originally his song and was stolen by Johnny Vincent (founder of Ace Records) and given to Ford to record.[9] Humor was not lacking in New Orleans' rhythm and blues-based style of rock music; Huey and the Clowns were a favorite with rock and roll audiences. They were popular for their rollicking live shows in which they presented lighthearted comedy routines as part of their stage act, often using call-and-response, with various group members taking turns singing lead. Smith played with an exciting boogie-woogie-based piano on his two hits, the 1957 rock classic "Rocking Pneumonia and the Boogie Woogie Flu" and "Don't You Just Know It" (1958). He was a popular session musician who worked with Earl King, Lloyd Price, Little Richard, and Smiley Lewis.

Guitar Slim.   Before going solo, Smith was a keyboard player in Guitar Slim's band. Born Edward Jones and raised in the Mississippi Delta, Guitar

Slim moved to New Orleans in 1950 and teamed up with Smith in a blues trio. In 1954, Slim released the million-selling No. 1 R&B hit, "The Things That I Used to Do" (with Ray Charles on piano), which became the best-selling R&B record of 1954 and was one of the most influential songs to come out of New Orleans' early R&B period. A pioneering rock and roll performer, Guitar Slim dressed and acted the part; he engaged in thrilling performances during which he worked his audiences, leaving fans screaming for more.

Shirley & Lee.   A history of female singers in New Orleans can be traced back to Annie Laurie and her early R&B hit records, such as 1947's "Since I Fell for You." Many female vocalists, provided by the flourishing R&B combos and orchestras of the time, followed Annie Laurie's late '40s hits. The female half of the duet Shirley & Lee, which provided some of New Orleans' biggest-selling records, Shirley Goodman continued the female R&B tradition in the early '50s. Known as the Sweethearts of the Blues and later as the Sweethearts of Rock and Roll after their hits crossed over to the pop charts, Shirley & Lee (Leonard Lee; born 1935) burst onto the record scene in 1952 with "I'm Gone" (recorded first with numerous friends and then re-recorded with just the two of them). Their recording reached No. 2 on the R&B charts and was followed by other R&B songs, including "Keep On" (1953), "Feel So Good" (1955, No. 2 R&B hit), and "I'll Do It" (1955). Born in 1936, Goodman began singing in church and was greatly influenced by Dinah Washington. After Cosimo Matassa allowed Goodman and her friends to make a record at his studio (on which she and Lee sang lead), Eddie Mesner, owner of Aladdin Records, who was in town to record Lloyd Price, heard the recording, pursued Goodman, and located Lee to sing with her. The young pair (ages fifteen and sixteen when they started singing together) were popular with the teenage audience for their many songs about teenage romance. Their clever song lyrics were presented to fans as if they were chapters in a young couple's life, such as "Let the Good Times Roll" (1956, million-seller No. 1 R&B hit that peaked at No. 20 on the pop charts) and "I Feel Good" (1956, No. 3 R&B hit and No. 38 pop hit). The duo worked with producer Dave Bartholomew and was backed by some of the finest New Orleans instrumentalists, including keyboardists James Booker, Huey "Piano" Smith, and Allen Toussaint. Shirley & Lee toured for the remainder of the '50s and performed until parting ways in 1963.

Lloyd Price.   Lloyd Price was a major figure in New Orleans rock and roll. Born in the city in 1933, he was influenced as much by gospel music as by R&B. His late '50s recordings "Stagger Lee" (1958) and "Personality" (1959) displayed elements of black gospel singing: elaborate vocal embellishments and a call-and-response vocal background group. In 1952, Price recorded his original "Lawdy Miss Clawdy," a New Orleans–flavored R&B hit produced by Dave Bartholomew, and featuring Fats Domino on piano, for Specialty Records. This No. 1 R&B classic hit that has been called the first rock and roll song had a tremendous influence on New Orleans records and helped give birth to rock and roll. (See chapter 3 for further information.) It was widely covered in the '50s and later by Elvis Presley, the Buckinghams, John Lennon, and Elvis Costello.

After Price's career was interrupted for a few years by his Korean War army duty, he began recording for ABC-Paramount and had an immediate hit in 1957 with "Just Because." After forming the KRC label with Harold Logan and Bill Boskent, he returned to ABC-Paramount and created a No. 1 hit on both the R&B and pop charts, "Stagger Lee," in late 1958. His greatest success, it was an arrangement of the traditional folk song "Stagolee" (also known as "Stack-O-Lee"), which had been recorded in various versions since the 1920s. John Broven claims that after "Stagger Lee," Price was considered a pop star, especially with the success of his 1959 No. 1 R&B hits "I'm Gonna Get Married" and "Personality."[10] Price had extraordinary entrepreneurial talents; he was an executive of two more record labels, Double-L and Turntable, in addition to owning a New York City nightclub, Lloyd Price's Turntable. In 1994, this exceptionally talented musician, bandleader, and songwriter received the Pioneer Award from the Rhythm & Blues Foundation, and in 1998 he was inducted into the Rock and Roll Hall of Fame.

In the early-to-mid-1950s, rockabilly and doo-wop joined the New Orleans sound as distinct early rock styles. (See chapters 5 and 7 for further information.) By mid-decade, Hollywood began embracing rock and roll with movies featuring rock stars performing their songs. Film was a very powerful medium that reached people all over the nation, including those in rural areas, who now had the opportunity to see rock artists on movie screens. Fats Domino and Little Richard were two of the major New Orleans '50s artists who, along with Bo Diddley and Chuck Berry, helped blur the line between R&B and rock and roll. They both appeared in films spreading the new music's sound to America: *The Girl Can't Help It* (1956, Domino and Little Richard), *Don't Knock the Rock* (1956, Little Richard), *Shake, Rattle and Rock!* (1956, Domino), and *Mister Rock and Roll* (1957, Little Richard).

Fats Domino

When Imperial Records' Dave Bartholomew and Lew Chudd discovered rhythm and blues pianist and singer Antoine Domino among the local talent at the Hideaway Club in New Orleans in 1949, they knew they had found an amazing talent. The most popular of all the New Orleans R&B artists, Domino had a relaxed and mellow tenor voice that, combined with his embraceable personality and constant smile, made a winning combination. With his warm and charming Creole vocals, Domino delighted America's youth, and because of his leisurely ways and wholesome personal life, he did not threaten their parents. Domino was a musical and visual opposite of his coarse and flashy '50s contemporaries (Chuck Berry, Little Richard, Elvis Presley, and Jerry Lee Lewis), which made him the perfect human being and musician for much of the public. After launching his career with the late 1949 recording of "The Fat Man" at J&M

Fats Domino (at the piano), in a scene from the film *The Big Beat*, 1958. Courtesy of the Library of Congress.

with Cosimo Matassa, Domino worked with producer Dave Bartholomew for many years, creating a long string of classic hits for the Imperial label, including the extremely popular "Ain't That a Shame" and "Blueberry Hill." In "Fats Domino," author Peter Guralnick affirms Domino's success: "He was simply the most consistent, predictable hitmaker of them all over a period of nearly twenty years, selling more than 65 million records, earning—depending on whose claim you believe—more gold records (fifteen, eighteen, twenty-two) than anyone except Elvis and the Beatles."[11]

Born into a musical family in New Orleans in 1928, Domino began playing the piano as a child. He was nine years old when his brother-in-law, Harrison Verrett (who later played guitar in Domino's band for years) taught him to play. Like the piano greats Professor Longhair and Amos Milburn, Domino began performing for small change in local honky-tonks while working odd jobs. By the time he was a teenager, he had developed his boogie-woogie piano technique and was playing in New Orleans clubs. In 1947, he was hired at the Hideaway Club, where bandleader Bill Diamond nicknamed him "Fats," a name that would stay with him. That year, Domino married his childhood sweetheart, Rose Mary Hall, and eventually raised a family of eight children. By 1949, Domino was a fixture at the Hideaway Club.

Though boogie-woogie pianists Albert Ammons, Pete Johnson, and Meade Lux Lewis influenced Domino, after rhythm and blues music became more accessible, Domino listened to and was influenced by the latest R&B artists, such as Charles Brown, Amos Milburn, Big Joe Turner, and Louis Jordan. In New Orleans clubs, Domino performed alongside legends Professor Longhair and Amos Milburn, who were both very strong influences on him. After Diamond encouraged him to start singing during their sets at the Hideaway, Domino met Bartholomew and Chudd in 1949, while the two were seeking talent and visiting the club to hear him. That same year, Bartholomew became Domino's producer, bandleader, and collaborator, a partnership that yielded many New Orleans R&B hit records. Throughout the '50s and '60s, Domino had sixty-one R&B hits and sixty-six pop hits. Among his most popular songs were "Ain't That a Shame" (1955), "Blueberry Hill" (1956), "Blue Monday" (1956), "I'm Walkin'" (1957), "Valley of Tears" (1957), "Whole Lotta Loving" (1958), "I Want to Walk You Home" (1959), and "Walking to New Orleans" (1960). With his impressive string of successful hits, Fats Domino was second only to Elvis Presley in terms of charts success during the first decade of rock and roll.[12]

 FATS DOMINO'S ROCK ERA HITS

Fats Domino's amazing rock era charts success is illustrated in the following select list (representative hits between 1950 and 1960), based upon Joel Whitburn's Record Research publications.[13] The listed position represents the song's peak location on the charts; the listed year represents the song's first chart date. All recordings were released by Imperial Records.

Title	Year	R&B Charts	Pop Charts
"The Fat Man"	1950	2	N/A
"Every Night About This Time"	1950	5	N/A
"Rockin' Chair"	1951	9	N/A
"Goin' Home"	1952	1	N/A
"How Long"	1952	9	N/A
"Going to the River"	1953	2	N/A
"Please Don't Leave Me"	1953	3	N/A
"Rose Mary"	1953	10	N/A
"Something's Wrong"	1953	6	N/A
"You Done Me Wrong"	1954	10	N/A
"Don't You Know"	1955	7	N/A
"Ain't That a Shame"	1955	1	10

FATS DOMINO'S ROCK ERA HITS *(continued)*			
"All by Myself"	1955	1	N/A
"Poor Me"	1955	1	N/A
"Bo Weevil"	1956	5	35
"I'm in Love Again"	1956	1	3
"My Blue Heaven"	1956	5	19
"When My Dreamboat Comes Home"	1956	2	14
"Blueberry Hill"	1956	1	2
"Blue Monday"	1956	1	5
"I'm Walkin'"	1957	1	4
"Valley of Tears"	1957	2	8
"Wait and See"	1957	7	23
"Sick and Tired"	1958	14	22
"Little Mary"	1958	4	48
"Whole Lotta Loving"	1958	2	6
"Telling Lies"	1959	13	50
"I'm Ready"	1959	7	16
"I Want to Walk You Home"	1959	1	8
"Be My Guest"	1959	2	8
"Walking to New Orleans"	1960	2	6
"Three Nights a Week"	1960	8	15
"My Girl Josephine"	1960	7	14

Domino's studio band featured a thick bass sound developed by Professor Longhair. Domino's music had a rhythmic feel that was looser and more relaxed than other styles of early rock music, and featured a horn section with a saxophone solo approximately two-thirds of the way through. As was common in New Orleans rock and roll, his band played more of a subordinate role to the singer, which allowed Domino's expressive, warm voice to dominate performances, a contrast to the exciting rhythmic drive and effect of the bands of other contemporary rock groups, such as Bill Haley and the Comets.

Upon asking Domino to make a record, Bartholomew rewrote "Junker Blues" into "The Fat Man" with Domino and produced the December 1949 recording that became a No. 2 R&B hit (and is often cited as the first rock and roll record). (See chapter 3 for further information.) "Junker Blues" was a song based on barrelhouse piano player William Thomas Dupree's (Champion Jack Dupree) 1940 recording. The new Bartholomew-Domino recording displayed the trademark Domino sound with smooth, bluesy piano rhythms accompanied by Bartholomew's band, featuring saxophonist Red Tyler and drummer Earl Palmer. Typical of the period, the record's instrumentation consisted of saxophone, trumpet, bass, drums, piano, and Domino's falsetto voice imitating the sound of a trumpet. The style of "The Fat Man" remained a trademark sound for Domino, and the recording's musicians performed on almost all of Domino's hits for the next twenty years. Domino was Imperial Records' most successful '50s artist. He spurred interest in other New Orleans artists and played an important role in shaping the city's rock and roll sound.

In 1955, Domino recorded "Ain't That a Shame" (also known as "Ain't It a Shame"), which established his identity with white teenagers. The single was his first crossover hit of many, reaching No. 1 on the R&B and No. 10 on the pop charts—an unusual feat for a '50s R&B song. With this song, Domino and Bartholomew broke the color line that had prevented R&B records from attracting pop audiences, partially because Domino was thought of as a country and western singer. With his soft, understated singing style, he had a wider appeal than any other R&B artist at the time, even though the black audience preferred a rougher blues sound. Domino's pleasant voice, with its calm quality that attracted both black and white listeners, was a perfect contrast to the powerful saxophone riffs of Bartholomew's band. White parents allowed their teenagers to listen to him. "Ain't That a Shame," featuring Domino's very smooth tenor voice (often referred to as sexy), was followed by a series of 1956 hits that were a mixture of new songs and revised standard pop songs: "My Blue Heaven," "When My Dreamboat Comes Home," "Blueberry Hill," and "Blue Monday." These classic hits and his immense popularity throughout the '50s placed Domino as a founder of rock and roll, alongside Chuck Berry, Little Richard, Elvis Presley, and Jerry Lee Lewis, even though the wholesome performer lacked the sexual appeal of his colleagues.

Domino established the piano as a rock instrument, and his thorough musicality in recordings and live performances endured throughout the '50s and '60s. For many years, the Domino-Bartholomew music partnership continued in the studio and the authorship of songs. Domino wrote and recorded hits into the '60s; he remained with Imperial until 1963, when the New Orleans sound began to fade on the pop charts as the public's musical tastes changed to surf, pop, and soul music. He had a fresh start with ABC-Paramount Records; however, the records he made there in 1963 and 1964, along with those he made with Mercury and Reprise Records later in the decade, never matched the success of those from his Imperial years. Though Domino and Bartholomew were one of the most successful songwriting teams in pop music history, by 1964 their music had lost much of its original charm and their audience dwindled. After working in nightclubs and casinos in Las Vegas and Reno, Nevada, Domino performed as a headlining act on rock and roll package tours and toured Europe many times in the '70s and '80s. The talented Domino was inducted into the Rock and Roll Hall of Fame in 1986 as a member of the first class of inductees. In 1987, he received a Lifetime Achievement Award at the annual Grammy Awards, where he was noted as one of the most important links between R&B and rock and roll. In 1995, Domino received the Rhythm & Blues Foundation's Lifetime Achievement Award, and in 1998, the National Medal of the Arts from President Bill Clinton.

After '50s society decided that rock and roll music was acceptable and cover artists began to thrive, Pat Boone recorded a cover of "Ain't That a Shame," which became a No. 1 pop hit the same year as Domino's version. Though Boone attempted to incorporate the exciting black sound into his recording, he did not know the sound as well as other '50s artists (such as Elvis Presley), and is thought by many critics to have failed at re-creating the tune. Nonetheless, the white listening audience flocked to purchase the cover record. Boone and other white artists recorded many covers of black songs that became popular with white teenagers, since they were allowed to listen to them but not to most of the original black artists. These cover artists not only captured the spotlight from the original artists but reaped profits as well, as major record companies pushed cover versions. Fats Domino's songs, with their clean arrangements, simple melodies, casual feel, and catchy lyrics, easily lent themselves to cover recordings. Pat Boone, Ricky Nelson, and Elvis Presley were among '50s cover artists who recorded arrangements of original songs by black R&B artists.

Little Richard

Little Richard, often claimed to be the '50s artist who turned rhythm and blues into rock and roll, was a dramatic contrast to Fats Domino. The singer, songwriter, and pianist lived the rebellious spirit of rock and roll with an outrageous appearance and frantic performance style. With his six-inch-high pompadoured hairstyle, liberal use of makeup, and extravagant jewelry and clothing (baggy, sparkling suits), Little Richard introduced cross-dressing and ambiguous sexuality to society at a time when they were unthinkable. He performed in a hysterical manner, frequently banging on piano keys and often leaving the piano to dance exuberantly (occasionally on top of the instrument); he was considered not merely a shouter but a screamer (his excited vocal style stemmed partially from his background in gospel shout singing). Little Richard, along with his white counterpart, Jerry Lee Lewis, and blues singer Jalacy J. Hawkins (Screamin' Jay Hawkins, who regularly engaged in such histrionics as vampire-and-coffin routines in performance), established rock musicians as aggressive extroverts engaging in outrageous performance behavior.

Born Richard Wayne Penniman in Macon, Georgia, in 1932, Little Richard came from, and was greatly influenced by, the gospel music tradition. Growing up in a religious household that frowned upon R&B music, he learned to sing and play the piano in church. In search of a performing career and seeking to

Little Richard, 1957. © Frank Driggs Collection/Getty Images.

flee troubles resulting from his homosexuality, he left home at the age of fourteen and performed in clubs throughout the South and with traveling minstrel shows. In 1951, he won an Atlanta radio station WGST audition that earned him a recording contract with RCA-Victor. For the next two years, Little Richard toured and made several recordings in the jump blues style before meeting Eskew Reeder (Esquerita), an R&B pianist and singer popular in the '50s and '60s Southern black gay community. It is thought that Esquerita influenced Little Richard with his flamboyant mannerisms and high pompadour, his pumping piano style, wild vocal technique (complete with falsetto screams and whoops), and racy song lyrics.

Little Richard's recording career continued in 1953 in Houston, Texas, with the Peacock label, where he recorded with the Tempo Toppers and the Deuces of Rhythm as his backup groups, and then in 1955 with the Johnny Otis Orchestra. Since none of his early recordings were very successful, he sent a demo tape to Art Rupe at Specialty Records in Los Angeles, who paired him with producer Robert Blackwell (Bumps Blackwell) and a backup band of New Orleans session players. Langdon Winner asserts that Little Richard's "Tutti Frutti" recording session on September 14, 1955, at Cosimo Matassa's J&M Studio was a crucial turning point in American music—the beginning of rock and roll, along with Elvis Presley's early recording sessions at Sun Records.[14]

Little Richard's music, greatly influenced by such artists as Marion Williams, Ruth Brown, Roy Brown, Louis Jordan, and other jump and urban blues musicians of the late '40s, was all over the R&B and pop charts from 1955 to 1957, with an audience of both white and black teenagers. "Tutti Frutti" sold more than 3 million copies and kicked off a string of classics that made Little Richard a star for Specialty Records: "Long Tall Sally" (1956), "Rip It Up" (1956), "Lucille" (1957), "Jenny, Jenny" (1957), "Keep a Knockin'" (1957), and "Good Golly, Miss Molly" (1958). His exciting music style, exemplified in "Tutti Frutti," consisted of the New Orleans boogie-woogie bass over which pounding piano chords and nonsense syllables emanated in disconnected phrases. The song's fast tempo, high energy level, and classic twelve-bar blues format were typical Little Richard. The use of storming R&B combo instruments in "Tutti Frutti"—rhythm piano (derived from the boogie-woogie style) emphasized the backbeat and supplied glissandos, growling saxophones imitated the rough vocals, and pulsing drums provided the forceful backbeat—was characteristic of Little Richard's music. His vocals, performed in a gospel-influenced voice with high-powered expressive intensity, produced the melody that consisted of disjunct octave leaps of nonsense syllables in a high tessitura. This unusual and wild vocal technique became a trademark of Little Richard's music.

Little Richard released risqué recordings, some of them very erotic, such as "Rip It Up," "Long Tall Sally," "Keep a Knockin'," and "Send Me Some Lovin'." "Tutti Frutti" also contained sexual lyrics; it was originally an obscene song that was sung in Southern black homosexual communities. The lyrics of the hit record version were cleaned up and merely suggested rocking (black slang for sexual activity) with girls (Sue and Daisy) who were driving him crazy and knew how to love him. When Pat Boone recorded a cover of "Tutti Frutti," its lyrics were cleaned and varied even more than Little Richard's recording. As in his other covers, Boone's recording was missing the exciting characteristics of black music—not only the erotic, sexual lyrics but also the black R&B music. Nonetheless, Boone's recording had great charts success. In 1956, it peaked at No. 12 and was on the charts for eighteen weeks, whereas Little Richard's recording peaked at No. 17 for twelve weeks on the pop charts. Little Richard was left with bitter feelings of exploitation by the successes of white cover versions of his (and others') original black recordings, even though his biggest hit, "Long Tall Sally," a No. 1 R&B hit, peaked on the pop charts at No. 6, beating Pat Boone's cover version, which peaked at No. 8.[15]

At the pinnacle of his career, Little Richard abandoned rock and roll in 1957 and was ordained a minister in the Seventh Day Adventist Church. He returned to music in 1964, enticed by the sounds of the British Invasion. He toured with the Beatles and the Rolling Stones, recorded intermittently (several recordings, including three albums in the early '70s), returned to preaching in the '70s, and appeared on television shows and in commercials and children's videos. Always flamboyant and outspoken, he continues to capture the spotlight after more than fifty years of performing. Still touring, he delivers his music with the same explosive energy, complete with his unique, frantic singing and piano-playing styles.

One of the key figures in the transition from R&B to rock and roll, Little Richard claims to this day that he was the first rock and roll artist and that he invented the genre by combining boogie-woogie and R&B music. His influence on his contemporaries was considerable. Elvis Presley imitated his songs, and Jerry Lee Lewis copied not only his music—evident in his racing piano style and wild vocal technique—but also his eccentric stage mannerisms, banging the keys of his rhythm piano while standing up and sitting down, bouncing on the keyboard with different body parts. Little Richard's extrovert and energetic style made him one of the most successful '50s rock and roll performers, and his music influenced subsequent black artists including Otis Redding, James Brown, Wilson Pickett, and Aretha Franklin.[16] In 1986, Little Richard was inducted into the Rock and Roll Hall of Fame as a member of the first class of inductees. In 1993, he received a Lifetime Achievement Award at the annual Grammy Awards, and in 1994, a Lifetime Achievement Award from the Rhythm & Blues Foundation. He remains an active performer and a living part of rock and roll history.

As the '50s ended, the rock and roll audience lost interest in the New Orleans sound created by these first-generation artists. Producer Allen Toussaint, among others, helped transform and renew the New Orleans sound in the next decade. The piano and saxophone that were essential in '50s New Orleans rock and roll lost their importance in the '60s as groups featured guitars as both lead and rhythm instruments (inspired equally by Chicago R&B and Memphis rockabilly). The '50s rhythm and blues–based rock and roll that emerged, from artists Ruth Brown to Big Joe Turner, Etta James to Chuck Berry, and Big Mama Thornton to Little Richard, played a tremendous role in the beginning of the new rock and roll genre—one that forever changed American popular music.

NOTES

All charts positions referred to in the chapter are based on Joel Whitburn's Record Research publications, which compile *Billboard* charts information of the rock and roll era.

1. James Henke, ed., *Rock Facts* (New York: Universe Publishing, 1996), 30.

2. Gillian G. Gaar, *She's a Rebel: The History of Women in Rock & Roll*, 2nd ed., enl. (New York: Seal Press, 2002), 4.

3. Rock and Roll Hall of Fame Foundation, "Louis Jordan," Rock and Roll Hall of Fame and Museum, http://www.rockhall.com/hof/inductee.asp?id=136.

4. Peter Guralnick, "Ray Charles," in *The Rolling Stone Illustrated History of Rock & Roll*, 3rd ed., ed. Anthony DeCurtis, James Henke, and Holly George-Warren (New York: Random House, 1992), 131–132.

5. Arnold Shaw, *The Rockin' '50s: The Decade That Transformed the Pop Music Scene* (New York: Hawthorn Books, 1974), 122.

6. Chuck Berry, *Chuck Berry: The Autobiography* (New York: Harmony Books, 1987), 90–91.

7. James Henke, ed., *Rock and Roll Hall of Fame and Museum Guidebook* (Cleveland, OH: Rock and Roll Hall of Fame and Museum, 2000), 74.

8. John Broven, *Rhythm & Blues in New Orleans* (Gretna, LA: Pelican, 1974), 13.

9. Jeff Hannusch, *I Hear You Knockin': The Sound of New Orleans Rhythm and Blues* (Ville Platte, LA: Swallow, 1996), 41.

10. Broven, *Rhythm & Blues in New Orleans*, 40.

11. Peter Guralnick, "Fats Domino," in *The Rolling Stone Illustrated History of Rock & Roll*, 3rd ed. (see note 4), 48.

12. "Rave On: Rock and Roll in the Fifties," permanent exhibit (Cleveland, OH: Rock and Roll Hall of Fame and Museum, November 21, 2003).

13. Joel Whitburn, *Joel Whitburn Presents Top R&B/Hip-Hop Singles, 1942–2004* (Menomonee Falls, WI: Record Research, 2004), 167–168; and *Joel Whitburn's Top Pop Singles, 1955–2002* (Menomonee Falls, WI: Record Research, 2003), 202–203.

14. Langdon Winner, "Little Richard," in *The Rolling Stone Illustrated History of Rock & Roll*, 3rd ed. (see note 4), 55.

15. Joel Whitburn, *Joel Whitburn's Top Pop Singles, 1955–2002* (see note 13), 72, 417.

16. Arnold Shaw, *Black Popular Music in America: From the Spirituals, Minstrels, and Ragtime to Soul, Disco, and Hip-Hop* (New York: Schirmer Books, 1986), 211.

ROCKABILLY: "GOODNESS, GRACIOUS, GREAT BALLS OF FIRE"

THE ROCKABILLY SOUND

Rock and roll launched another new sound in the '50s as it evolved into the rockabilly subgenre, which took its place alongside the New Orleans sound. As white music blended with immensely popular black music, the influential sounds of such country pioneers as Jimmie Rodgers, Bob Wills, Bill Monroe, and Hank Williams played an integral part in the emergence of rockabilly. White singers and instrumentalists, mostly Southerners, were attracted to the blues and African American musicians, to country music, resulting in a cross-pollination of musicians such as Elvis Presley and Chuck Berry. The rockabilly sound permeated the music of many '50s rock and roll artists, from Jerry Lee Lewis and Carl Perkins to Buddy Holly and Roy Orbison. It was referred to as country rock, but its fans and the music industry labeled it "rockabilly" to signify the merger of blues and hillbilly styles. As with many rock and roll subgenres, there are differing views as to when the sound was born, but in the late '40s and early '50s the rockabilly sound was already established in honky-tonks, long before it acquired a name.

Incorporating the twelve-bar blues progression and boogie-woogie rhythms from rhythm and blues, the new subgenre, to an extent, was similar in sound to the R&B of Bo Diddley and Chuck Berry. Other formal structures were borrowed from country and pop music, such as the eight- and sixteen-bar song forms. One specific characteristic that distinguished rockabilly was the use of agitated, fast tempos and a feeling of exuberance. Though backbeats were not as prominent as in R&B, rockabilly music was exciting. The new sound was a popular alternative for those who wanted to hear rock and roll without dealing with racial issues; rockabilly offered the excitement and appeal of rock music without the raucous qualities of R&B music.

Having borrowed the electric guitar from country music, rockabillies were highly indebted to the country genre for their instrumentation. They used the guitar as the main solo instrument in their songs, often playing with the twangy (honky-tonk) timbre of country music. This was a substantial change from the saxophone and piano solos of the African American R&B. In the '50s, rockabilly vocalists were accompanied by a slapped upright bass that supplied rhythm but later in the decade was replaced by drums (an R&B influence). Sometimes other instruments, such as the piano (after Jerry Lee Lewis), thickened song textures, but for the most part, rockabilly instrumentation took its cue from Elvis Presley's original trio: rhythm guitar, lead guitar, and string bass. Small backup groups were a trademark of this subgenre, and rockabilly singers employed unpredictable vocal inflections, such as gasps, hiccups, and stutters, in addition to nonsense syllables, though overall their lyrics were clearly enunciated and their melodies were sung cleanly on pitch (a country music influence). Quite often they sang lyrics about sexual themes (Jerry Lee Lewis's "Whole Lot of Shakin' Going On") and love themes (Buddy Holly's "Peggy Sue"), though the sky was the limit, with song topics ranging from clothes (Carl Perkins's "Put Your Cat Clothes On") to outer space (Billy Riley and His Little Green Men's "Flying Saucer Rock and Roll").

These artists performed with great intensity and developed wild and sexy personas, making them very popular with audiences. With few exceptions, rockabilly musicians were white Southern males (who attracted largely female audiences) steeped in the country and western music tradition. The rockabilly sound is often traced back to the 1954 recordings of the genre's most successful singer, Elvis Presley, who, like most of rockabilly's stars, recorded at Sam Phillips's legendary Sun Studio in Memphis.

SAM PHILLIPS AND SUN RECORDS

Born in 1923, Sam Phillips was raised on a tenant farm near Florence, Alabama. With deep Southern roots, he understood people from the region and acquired interpersonal skills useful for his future as a record entrepreneur. After being forced to leave high school to help support his family by working in a supermarket and a funeral home, Phillips realized his interest in music, especially styles of his rural upbringing (gospel, blues, and country music), and entered the music business. His music journey began as an announcer at radio station WMSL in Decatur, Alabama, then at WLAC in Nashville, and finally at WREC in Memphis, where he and his wife moved in 1945. Hosting *Songs of the West*, a daily country music show at WREC, Phillips developed his recording engineer skills (back then, radio engineers prerecorded programs onto acetate discs and duplicated and circulated them to other stations) and sound effect talents. At WREC, he had to locate records for the station's library, which familiarized him with artists and their repertoires. Phillips also hosted *Saturday Afternoon Tea Dance*, a show on which he spun jazz, blues, and pop discs, and discussed the music. In 1949, he decided to open a recording studio not only to serve as an outlet for his expertise and creativity, but also to fill the need for a studio in the South.

Phillips leased a small storefront property at 706 Union Avenue, near downtown Memphis, and opened his Memphis Recording Service in January 1950. He lived up to his new business slogan, "We record anything—anywhere—anytime," by recording many weddings, funerals, and other social events in addition to walk-ins aspiring to press a disc. Initially, Phillips's principal objective

Sam Phillips working with recording equipment at Sun Records. Courtesy of the Library of Congress.

was to record blues artists who were underexposed.[1] He saw the need for a recording service to record blues, gospel, and country music singers and musicians from the local area, and was concerned with preserving their music. Knowing a larger audience for the blues than just Southern blacks existed, Phillips wanted to reach large cities, where he knew whites were listening to black music. Hence, he began recording such blues artists as B. B. King, Jackie Brenston, Rosco Gordon, and Howlin' Wolf, and leased the recordings to indies (such as Brenston and Ike Turner's "Rocket 88," leased to Chess Records). After an initial unsuccessful experience launching the Phillips record label in 1950 (a joint venture with disc jockey friend Dewey Phillips), Sam Phillips opened his own label because there were many opening in town, some of them seizing his artists. In March 1952, Phillips opened Sun Records, which became instrumental in the development of the rockabilly style. Many music scholars and fans maintain that rock and roll was born at this renowned recording studio. Undoubtedly, some of the greatest records in the history of rock and roll were made there.

As many of the best black Sun recording artists moved to Chicago in the early '50s, Phillips experienced a decline in business, but he was insistent on reaching both young whites and young blacks in addition to the older African American audience already enjoying his blues recordings. Phillips confided to his assistant, Marion Keisker: "If I could find a white man who had the Negro sound and the Negro feel, I could make a billion dollars."[2] Shortly after, Elvis Presley entered his studio, and Phillips found the artist he sought. Together, they made rock and roll history. After Sun released Presley's recording of "That's All Right" (often cited as the first rock and roll record) in 1954, Phillips rarely recorded black artists; Presley's success led him to switch to white artists. Rockabilly musicians flocked to his studio, hoping to audition, record, and release the next big hit. Phillips maintained an impressive roster of recording artists who, at different times, included Presley, Carl Perkins, Johnny Cash, Jerry Lee Lewis, and a host of others, among them Roy Orbison, Malcolm Yelvington, Sonny Burgess, Warren Smith, Billy Riley, Carl Mann, and Charlie Rich.

With the very first Sun release, "Drivin' Slow," by saxophonist Johnny London (March 1952), the trademark sound of Phillips's studio was born. The un-refined sound, dark texture, experimental quality, and deep echo for which Sun Records became famous were present in this first recording. Sun recordings generously used echo (initially created by Phillips with a makeshift system of sewer pipes and bathroom acoustics), which became characteristic of the Sun sound. The recordings focused on feeling; Phillips responded to the feeling he heard in artists' music, not to their technical expertise as other producers did. If he had been looking for totally trained musicians, Phillips would have re-jected both Elvis Presley and Johnny Cash, but he saw much potential in their rough and unpolished sounds and allowed them the freedom to record music that represented who they were. Always in search of distinctive and sponta-neous sound, Phillips was adamant about capturing the perfect sound in a recording, no matter how many takes it required. He often rolled the tape con-tinuously, recording multiple versions of songs while waiting for the right take with the distinct sound he was seeking.

Phillips recorded his most important music with, by today's standards, simple and antiquated equipment. It originally consisted of a portable (since he recorded many events on location) Presto five-input mixing board and a portable Presto tape recorder. Wary of magnetic tape, Phillips recorded directly to disc, using a Presto cutting lathe and a Presto turntable to create an acetate master disc. In 1954, Phillips upgraded his equipment to two Ampex 350 tape recorders (one console model and another mounted on a rack behind his head to supply the famous Sun echo), on which he recorded Presley's first Sun single. Soon after, he upgraded the mixing board to the RCA 76-D radio console (with inputs and outputs coupled through transformers, yielding a distinctive warm sound), and by 1956 he recorded on tape. Phillips used this equipment to cut records, making some of the most important recordings in rock history. (He did not upgrade his facilities and equipment again until 1960, when he opened his new studio.) Phillips used few postproduction techniques, merely executing limited overdubs and edits, adding echoes, and changing tape speeds. He did not intend to change an artist's sound; he believed he was merely a facilitator who brought out an artist's native abilities. And he firmly believed in simplicity.

This philosophy of record production and its application made Phillips one of the most important innovators in the music business.[3]

The Sun studio was so small that Phillips did not have a desk in the office. He relied on the restaurant next door for business meetings and on his assistant, Keisker, to manage the office as well as maintain daily contact with distributors and pressing plants. With Sam and his brother, Jud Phillips, Keisker took care of the distribution network and radio contacts that helped launch Sun Records. Others who worked regularly at Sun included a staff band, three of whom were members of Sun's recording artist Billy Riley's Little Green Men: Roland Janes (guitar), J. M. Van Eaton (drums), and Jimmy Wilson (piano). Not a musician himself, Phillips was fortunate to have a backing band that instinctively knew the sound he sought in recordings. Saxophonist Bill Justis was the studio musical director; Jack Clement was a composer and arranger; steel guitarist Stan Kesler was a staff composer; and Bill Fitzgerald was general manager. The contributions of these dedicated colleagues allowed Phillips to achieve immense success.

 MONUMENTAL SUN RECORDINGS

This select list of a handful of the classic Sun singles is representative of the hundreds recorded by Phillips. These records, revealing the label's revolutionary nature and bold diversity, are documented by Colin Escott and Martin Hawkins in *Good Rockin' Tonight: Sun Records and the Birth of Rock 'n' Roll.*[4] Song and artist descriptions (and spellings) reflect initial pressings. The few recorded on Phillips's subsidiary label, Phillips International, are noted as such. Most of these recording artists, discovered by Phillips (he rarely recorded a musician who had recorded for another company), brought the '50s rockabilly sound to America via these and many more legendary records.

Sun Artist	Single	Release Date
Rufus "Hound Dog" Thomas Jr.	"Bear Cat"/"Walkin' in the Rain"	March 1953
Elvis Presley (Scotty and Bill)	"That's All Right"/"Blue Moon of Kentucky"	July 1954
Elvis Presley (Scotty and Bill)	"Good Rockin' Tonight"/ "I Don't Care If the Sun Don't Shine"	September 1954
Elvis Presley (Scotty and Bill)	"Milkcow Blues Boogie"/ "You're a Heartbreaker"	January 1955
Elvis Presley (Scotty and Bill)	"I'm Left, You're Right, She's Gone"/"Baby Let's Play House"	April 1955

⊙ MONUMENTAL SUN RECORDINGS (continued)

Johnny Cash (Tennessee Two)	"Cry! Cry! Cry!"/"Hey! Porter"	June 1955
Elvis Presley (Scotty and Bill)	"Mystery Train"/"I Forgot to Remember to Forget"	August 1955
Johnny Cash (Tennessee Two)	"So Doggone Lonesome"/ "Folsom Prison Blues"	December 1955
Carl Perkins	"Blue Suede Shoes"/ "Honey, Don't!"	December 1955
Johnny Cash (Tennessee Two)	"Get Rhythm"/"I Walk the Line"	April 1956
Roy Orbison (Teen Kings)	"Ooby Dooby"/"Go! Go! Go!"	May 1956
Carl Perkins	"Boppin' the Blues"/ "All Mama's Children"	May 1956
Carl Perkins	"I'm Sorry I'm Not Sorry"/"Dixie Fried"	August 1956
Billy Riley (and His Little Green Men)	"Flying Saucer Rock and Roll"/"I Want You Baby"	January 1957
Jerry Lee Lewis	"It'll Be Me"/"Whole Lot of Shakin' Going On"	March 1957
Bill Justis (and His Orchestra)	"Raunchy"/"Midnight Man"	September 1957 (Phillips International)
Jerry Lee Lewis (and His Pumping Piano)	"Great Balls of Fire"/"You Win Again"	November 1957
Johnny Cash (and the Tennessee Two)	"Ballad of a Teenage Queen"/"Big River"	December 1957
Jerry Lee Lewis (and His Pumping Piano)	"Down the Line"/"Breathless"	February 1958
Jerry Lee Lewis (and His Pumping Piano)	"High School Confidential"/ "Fools Like Me"	April 1958
Carl Mann	"Mona Lisa"/"Foolish One"	March 1959 (Phillips International)
Charlie Rich	"Lonely Weekends (The Gene Lowery Chorus)"/"Everything I Do Is Wrong"	January 1960 (Phillips International)

Of the dozens of artists on the Sun Records roster, the big four were Elvis Presley, Carl Perkins, Johnny Cash, and Jerry Lee Lewis. One day in December 1956, when Lewis was still just a studio hand (accompanying Perkins and his band while they recorded "Matchbox"), these musicians, dubbed the "Million Dollar Quartet," met at the studio and engaged in an impromptu, informal jam session. They performed and recorded gospel, country, and pop standards, such as the traditional "Down by the Riverside" (not surprising, since Presley, Perkins, and Lewis discovered music in church), which was released in the mid-'80s. Sam Phillips's path to commercial success was made clear by the success of one of these artists in particular: Elvis Presley, who, like Phillips, intuitively understood black music and quickly synthesized both a musical style and an image that would enable Phillips to take Sun Records into uncharted territory.

Elvis Presley

In the summer of 1953, for $4.00, a shy, young Elvis Presley recorded at the Memphis Recording Service two songs as a birthday present for his mother, "My Happiness" and "That's When Your Heartaches Begin." Phillips liked what he heard, realized that Presley had a good feeling for ballads, and invited him back. What Phillips did not know was that this unconfident singer would soon transform himself into a dazzling performer sought by every major record label in America. Thus country singer Presley became rock and roll singer Presley with his blending of pop, gospel, country, and R&B music styles.

The following spring, the introverted Presley was invited to return to Sun and record a new song, "Without You." Phillips matched him up with guitarist Scotty Moore (a 2000 Rock and Roll Hall of Fame inductee) and bassist Bill Black (from the Starlite Wranglers country group) and had them work up some songs. In a recording session on July 5, 1954, they recorded "That's All Right" after unsuccessfully attempting other songs. During a session break, Presley abruptly began singing the old blues song while hopping around and acting foolish. Black began playing his bass and doing the same, and Moore soon joined them. Phillips came out of the control booth and asked them to repeat the song. The famous Presley version was based on Delta bluesman Arthur "Big Boy" Crudup's song "That's All Right Mama." This recording preserved the black blues (swing) feel of the original and is often cited as the first rock and roll record. (See chapter 3 for further information.) The next day, Phillips recorded the trio performing Bill Monroe's 1947 country bluegrass waltz, "Blue Moon of Kentucky," for the B-side of the record. Drastically changing the feel of the country song with the black blues sound, Presley and the trio completed his debut single. Their exceptional blending of elements from country music and R&B, without the songs being identifiable as either, created the blueprint for rockabilly and rock and roll.

Phillips was ecstatic to have found a white man who sang like a black man.

He created a few demo tapes and circulated them to key disc jockeys in Memphis: WHHM's John Lepley (Sleepy-Eyed John), WMPS' Bob Neal (who later became Presley's manager), and WHBQ's Dewey Phillips. By interviewing Presley on the air and playing the disc numerous times, Dewey Phillips created a local demand for the record, which Sam Phillips released as Sun #209 on July 19, 1954. The recording received a favorable audience reaction and had a good review in *Billboard* magazine that summer. Knowing that Presley needed exposure, Phillips booked him as a warm-up attraction for a Slim Whitman show that summer, and on July 28, 1954, Presley received his first mention in the local newspaper (the Memphis *Press Scimitar*) along with his first publicity photo (featuring the young artist with a brush cut and bow tie). During his evening show on July 30, Presley began to shake his legs, causing the crowd to scream for more. The Presley legend began that evening when musical and visual elements came together for the first time. To this day, historians are not certain if his shaking was from nerves or from the influence of flamboyant R&B singers. Presley's momentum immediately grew after the release of his record. Scotty Moore became his manager and booked local performances for him. Some Dallas-area radio stations began to play the single, and Alta Hayes (from Big State Record Distributors) lobbied his record in the jukebox market. Soon after, Presley was invited to perform on the two most influential country music radio shows, *Grand Ole Opry* (broadcast from Nashville) and *Louisiana Hayride* (broadcast from KWKH in Shreveport, Louisiana). Having signed a year's contract with *Hayride*, Presley became a regular performer on the show, which gave him great exposure. At this early stage in his career, many (including Sam Phillips, Scotty Moore, Dewey Phillips, and Marion Keisker) believed in Presley, even before he believed in himself.

Following his debut record, Presley released four more singles with Sun, each featuring a blues or R&B song backed with a country-styled song. Each documented Presley's increasing confidence and was more commercially successful than the preceding one. Released on September 22, 1954, his second record combined two songs with very different themes: a cover ("Good Rockin' Tonight") of Roy Brown's "Good Rocking Tonight," which was a sexually suggestive R&B tune, and "I Don't Care if the Sun Don't Shine," from Walt Disney's children's film *Cinderella*. Presley's third single, consisting of "You're a Heartbreaker" and "Milkcow Blues Boogie," was released on January 8, 1955 (his twentieth birthday), and his fourth record, "I'm Left, You're Right, She's Gone" with "Baby Let's Play House," was released on April 25, 1955. His last Sun single, "Mystery Train" with "I Forgot to Remember to Forget" (his first No. 1 country hit), was released on August 1, 1955. With the success of these five groundbreaking singles, Presley's performances on package show tours and his growing popularity attracted the attention of promoter Col. Thomas Parker, with whom Presley signed a management contract that same month.

The success of Presley's "Mystery Train" (along with that of Johnny Cash's first single) created financial problems for Phillips. His small company was financially burdened by the practice of distributors ordering massive numbers of records and not paying for them until months later. Obliged to pay the manufacturers of discs, music publishers, and trade papers, Phillips was low on cash. He was also in debt to his brother, Jud, from the buyout agreement when Jud left Sun in 1954. (Jud had little faith in Presley, so he had tried to sell his Sun contract to Decca Records, but Decca and others, such as Columbia and MGM, declined, citing Sam Phillips's asking price of approximately $20,000 as too high.) In October 1955, after clearing his financial slate with his brother (which left him broke) and realizing that Presley's five Sun singles failed to achieve much charts success, Sam Phillips had no option but to consider selling Presley's contract. Unhappy that Presley was with the small label, Parker made the sale of Presley's contract simple for Phillips. He negotiated with Phillips and Julian and Jean Aberbach (owners of Hill & Range Music Publishing) and secured a deal with New York–based RCA Records. The next month, despite Presley's growing popularity, Sam Phillips sold Presley's contract for $35,000 to RCA, Hill & Range, and Parker. Presley received $5,000 in back royalties and Parker replaced Bob Neal as Presley's manager. It was a very good deal for Phillips.

Phillips was the first to perceive Presley's potential. He was impressed with Presley's intelligence and especially his knowledge of varied music types. He nurtured the young Presley's talents, allowing him to grow from his very humble background into the successful artist who left Sun for RCA. Phillips and Presley are credited with creating and popularizing the new rockabilly rock and roll sound around the world. (See chapter 6 for further information.)

Carl Perkins

Inspired by Presley's first record, rock and roll pioneer Carl Perkins was drawn to Sun Records and became one of the principal recording artists there in the '50s. His rural upbringing exposed Perkins to the blues, which profoundly marked his guitar style. A fan of black R&B spirituals heard in the fields, the young Perkins mixed the blues and country roots styles. He claimed that rockabilly music (rock and roll) was country music with black rhythm.[5] Unlike Presley, Perkins, a composer and gifted guitarist, wrote his own songs. His recordings had the urgent sound of R&B music, similar to those of Little Richard. With such classic compositions and recordings as "Blue Suede Shoes," "Put Your Cat Clothes On," and "Boppin' the Blues," Perkins made a major contribution to the foundation of rock and roll.

Born in 1932 into a sharecropping family in Tiptonville, Tennessee, Carl Lee Perkins listened to the *Grand Ole Opry* on the radio and to a black sharecropper, John Westbrook, establishing his affection for both country and blues music. In 1953, he bought his first guitar and began to develop his unique style, married Valda Crider, and began a family. A fan of Bill Monroe, John Lee Hooker, and Muddy Waters, Perkins played Hooker's blues songs in Monroe's country style. Accompanied by the Perkins Brothers Band, which included his siblings Jay (guitar) and Clayton (bass) and W. S. "Fluke" Holland (drums), Perkins often put his own lyrics to these songs, resulting in music that sounded very much like Presley's. The group performed at church socials, country dances, and honky-tonks. After Valda had him listen to Presley's recordings on a local radio program, Perkins realized that his band could be successful in the record business, so he approached Sam Phillips at Sun Records. Because of his fondness for the blues and R&B, Perkins decided to pattern his style after Presley's, and his group performed rock and roll, mixing blues, country, and pop elements. Perkins may not have had Presley's good looks and charm, but his music had a great sound and, unlike Presley, he played lead guitar. By 1954, Perkins had developed his unique style that borrowed feeling, phrasing, and rhythm from black music; he accented the rhythm of the bass and drums by striking the bass strings of his electric guitar; and he played lead guitar fills answering his voice in the manner of blues call-and-response.

In the fall of 1954, only a few weeks after hearing Presley's first single, Perkins and his band auditioned for Sun and were signed to a recording contract by Phillips, who was very impressed by Perkins's country-styled emotive voice. Phillips believed that Perkins could revolutionize the country end of his business. He released Perkins's first single, "Movie Magg," backed by "Turn Around," a Hank Williams–influenced country song, on his new Flip subsidiary label in February 1955. His second single, released on the Sun label that August (the same day Presley's last Sun record was released) paired "Let the Jukebox Keep on Playing," another Williams-like country tune, with "Gone, Gone, Gone," a rhythm and blues-styled song. By the time Perkins was ready to record his third single, Presley had left Sun, and Phillips was able to concentrate on Perkins's newest composition.

His new song, "Blue Suede Shoes," known as the signature song of the rockabilly genre, was released with "Honey, Don't" in December 1955 and became a smash hit, launching Perkins's career. With elements borrowed from all three roots genres (blues, country, and pop), the song crossed over into the pop market. It has been referred to as the first true rock and roll hit because it made history by becoming the first across-the-board chart hit, simultaneously reaching the Top 5 on the pop, country, and R&B charts (it was a No. 2 pop, No. 1 country, and No. 2 R&B hit). "Blue Suede Shoes" became Sun's first million-seller record (bringing Perkins a new Cadillac from Phillips, who had sworn that the first artist to sell a million copies of a Sun record would receive a Cadillac) on May 1, 1956. With this song, Perkins became the first country artist to reach the national R&B charts; he was followed by Presley with "Heartbreak Hotel" three weeks later. Later that year, when Presley recorded "Blue Suede Shoes," he turned Perkins's song into even more of a rock and roll anthem through his cover's immense success.

In March 1956, on his way to New York for the taping of the *Perry Como Show*, on which he would receive a gold record for his recording of "Blue Suede

Shoes," Perkins and his band were in an automobile accident near Dover, Delaware, that seriously injured all three Perkins brothers at the height of their success. For Perkins the accident was the beginning of a personal and professional struggle; in addition to his physical injuries, the following months at Sun were musically disappointing. After recovering, Perkins resumed his career at Sun, but despite writing songs that were even better than his big hit, he could not recapture the success of "Blue Suede Shoes." He recorded classic rockabilly records, including "Boppin' the Blues" (1956), which demonstrated his country roots; "Dixie Fried" (1956), which displayed Perkins's exceptional talent as a composer; and "Matchbox" (1957), an old blues standard. Frustrated that he could not repeat the success of "Blue Suede Shoes," in January 1958 Perkins signed a contract with Columbia Records, where he had several minor rockabilly hits.

Inducted into the Rock and Roll Hall of Fame in 1987, Perkins successfully assimilated all of the music he heard while growing up into his handful of rock and roll masterpieces. Though he never attained Presley's stardom, he created the new rockabilly sound along with Presley. After Presley's cover of "Blue Suede Shoes" hit the charts, Perkins worked in Presley's shadow, becoming known more for songwriting than for performing. He was a major influence on the Beatles (especially guitarist George Harrison), who paid him tribute by recording more covers of Perkins's songs than any composer other than themselves. In the mid-1960s, Perkins toured and recorded as a member of fellow Sun Records alumnus Johnny Cash's band, and, in the 1970s, Cash featured Perkins as a regular on his television variety show. His impact was evident in the '80s when Paul McCartney featured Perkins on his post-Wings album, *Tug of War*, and when Brian Setzer's rockabilly revival band, the Stray Cats, displayed his influence. In 1985, Perkins reunited with Sun recording artists Johnny Cash, Jerry Lee Lewis, and Roy Orbison to record an album titled *Class of '55*. His final recordings were issued on the 1996 album *Go, Cat, Go!*, which featured duets with such admirers as Harrison and McCartney, Paul Simon, Tom Petty, and Willie Nelson. Perkins died in 1998. His fans still celebrate his accomplishments, surrounded by his career memorabilia, at his restaurant, Suede's, in Jackson, Tennessee.

Johnny Cash

Born in Kingsland, Arkansas, in 1932, country singer and songwriter John Ray Cash spent his early days as a rockabilly singer recording for Phillips at Sun. While growing up during the Depression, Cash was exposed to country music as a cotton picker and was inspired by Roy Acuff and Ernest Tubb; later he was attracted to the blues and influenced by the music of Robert Johnson, Howlin' Wolf, and Muddy Waters. Cash drew together elements of folk, country, and gospel music in the more than 400 songs he composed and performed. They were simple stories about workingmen in America (coal miners, sharecroppers, prisoners, cowboys, family men). These song themes, in line with those of Woody Guthrie, later appeared in the works of Bob Dylan and Bruce Springsteen. One of Phillips's most important recording artists in the '50s, Cash was present at the birth of rock and roll. He recorded a string of rockabilly hits for Sun that included the classics "Folsom Prison Blues," "I Walk the Line," and "Cry! Cry! Cry!"

Cash joined the U.S. Air Force in 1950 after having left home as a teenager to work in the auto plants in Pontiac, Michigan. Stationed in Germany with other Southern musicians, he formed the Landsberg Barbarians and began writing songs. After his discharge in 1954, he married Vivian Liberto and settled in Memphis, working as an appliance salesman before becoming a full-time musician. While in Memphis, Cash was exposed to black music and grew fond of the blues. Although he hoped to become a radio announcer, he was unable to abandon his desire to become a singer. Since he passed Sun Records on his daily route from broadcasting school, he attempted to meet Phillips. He finally secured an audition and signed a contract with Phillips in June 1955.

Later that month, Cash released his debut single, "Cry! Cry! Cry!" backed with "Hey! Porter" and accompanied by the Tennessee Two, featuring guitarist Luther Perkins and bassist Marshall Grant. Cash and his group's originality was apparent in their unique sound. Perkins maintained the beat in a simple guitar accompaniment to Cash's distinctively stark, low vocals; Grant provided prominent walking bass lines; and they used Cash's distinct "boom-chicka-boom" rhythmic motif. Phillips thickened the sound of Cash's vocals and the rhythm track with the Sun echo. In December 1955, Phillips released Cash's recording of "Folsom Prison Blues" with "So Doggone Lonesome." That month, Cash toured with Presley and Perkins, and in January he was offered a regular Saturday-night spot on *Louisiana Hayride*, providing him with invaluable radio exposure. Phillips released Cash's monumental "I Walk the Line," a love song he wrote for Vivian, in April 1956. This recording launched his career nationally and was the first of his No. 1 country hits as well as his first pop hit. After signing with Bob Neal's new booking agency, Stars, Inc., Cash was offered a regular spot on *Grand Ole Opry* in July 1956. Sun composer Jack Clement wrote "Ballad of a Teenage Queen," which in April 1958 became Cash's biggest Sun Records success (a No. 1 country and No. 14 pop hit). Cash wrote rockabilly songs for his labelmates Elvis Presley, Warren Smith ("Rock 'n' Roll Ruby"), and Roy Orbison ("Little Woolly Booger (You're My Baby)") before leaving Sun when his contract expired in August 1958. Soon after he began recording for Columbia (with a higher composer royalty rate of 5 percent), Cash left Memphis and the *Grand Ole Opry* for California, where he hoped to expand his career to include movies (though he mostly received roles in lesser films). He recorded hits for Columbia, including the No. 1s "Don't Take Your Guns to Town" (1959), "Ring of Fire" (1963), "Understand Your Man" (1964), and "A Boy Named Sue" (1969). With Columbia, Cash was the first to create country concept albums with collections of western songs.

For several years, Cash was one of the most popular acts in American entertainment. Never forgetting his country roots and known as the Man in Black (for his black concert attire), he overcame a serious drug problem in the 1960s and married his second wife, June Carter (of the influential Carter Family), reinforcing his relationship with country music. Recorded at Folsom and San Quentin prisons, Cash's late '60s live prison albums presented some of his best work. In 1969, Cash recorded with Bob Dylan on the latter's album *Nashville Skyline*, and in June of that year, Dylan appeared in the first segment of Cash's top-rated television program, *The Johnny Cash Show* (which ran from 1969 to 1971). In the 1970s, he also made several film appearances. His powerful album from the mid-1990s, *American Recordings*, accompanied only by his guitar, is considered by many to be his finest album. It contained old and new songs and gospel songs, much the same mixture he had brought to Sun Records years earlier. Cash was inducted into the Country Music Hall of Fame in 1980 and into the Rock and Roll Hall of Fame in 1992. He died in September 2003, just four months after the death of his wife, June Carter Cash.

Jerry Lee Lewis

The last of the four main rockabilly artists to find a home at Phillips's Sun label was singer and pianist Jerry Lee Lewis. An entertainer gifted with intuitive flair, Lewis had creativity and impact that reached far beyond his few hits. He carried his effortless command of music with a tremendous amount of energy; his performances were stunning. Nicknamed The Killer for his treatment of the piano and his audience, this defiant and untiring music icon has lived a life marked by controversy and personal tragedy. Lewis wrote little music himself but recorded covers of blues songs (as did fellow rockabillies Elvis Presley and Bill Haley). He transformed others' songs into unrestrained rock and roll. However, unlike Presley, Lewis did not mix hymns or ballads in performance. He referred to his wild music as the Devil's music and felt it shouldn't be mixed with God's music. With his merging of various music styles (including western swing, boogie-woogie, R&B, and Delta blues) with a brash temperament, Lewis was a natural rock and roller, considered by many to be the ultimate rock and roll rebel. Lewis himself once boasted: "I'm a rock and rollin', country & western, rhythm & blues singin' mothe—!"[6]

Born in Ferriday, Louisiana, in 1935, Lewis learned to play the piano by ear. Although he also absorbed gospel music and R&B from the local black community, his early influences were Al Jolson, Jimmie Rodgers, and Hank Williams. A rebel from the beginning, Lewis was expelled from Southwestern Bible Institute in Texas at age fifteen, the same year he began performing music professionally. In September 1956, after hearing Presley's Sun recordings, Lewis traveled to Memphis with his father, hoping to audition for the label. With Sam Phillips out of town, he performed his country-styled audition for engineer Jack Clement, who suggested he learn some rock and roll similar to

Jerry Lee Lewis, right, in *Jamboree*. Courtesy of the Library of Congress.

Presley's. However, when Phillips heard the tape, he was greatly pleased and invited Lewis back, because he had been considering using instruments other than the guitar for backup on recordings.

For Lewis's first Sun single in late 1956, "Crazy Arms" (a cover of Ray Price's country hit) paired with "End of the Road," Clement rounded up Roland Janes and J. M. Van Eaton to provide accompaniment. The record immediately established Lewis as the only artist who could rival Presley, and was credited to Jerry Lee Lewis and His Pumping Piano. It was followed by a string of explosive hits including "Whole Lot of Shakin' Going On," "Great Balls of Fire," "Breathless," and "High School Confidential."

Lewis's second single and first hit was "Whole Lot of Shakin' Going On," recorded in February 1957. It had charging tempo and incessant piano backbeat over which Lewis delivered his characteristic frenzied vocals. Lewis inserted a talking segment (when he couldn't recall the words of the original version) that had a suggestive tone but was not explicitly obscene. It was, however, enough to have the record banned in many cities. Lewis combined his uninhibited, rowdy vocals with a ferocious, boogie-woogie instrumental style incorporating his flashy piano technique. The backbone of Lewis's sound was his piano playing, using not only boogie-woogie figures but exhilarating glissando runs as well. He played the instrument with an undisciplined and uncontrolled technique (hammering right-hand triplet chords against prominent, forceful bass lines with his left hand) matching his vocal unpredictability. Arrogant and talented, Lewis engaged in flamboyant stage antics. While singing, he pounded and jumped on the piano, and often pushed the bench away and danced while banging the piano keys with his feet. The ferocity was startling and sensational. It was a trademark of his performances and his being.

Released in March 1957, "Whole Lot of Shakin' Going On" was a cover of a blues song recorded by Big Maybelle in 1955. Though the song was full of sexual references, Lewis did not sanitize its lyrics. The public loved the record and the wild artist; some felt he was the successor to Presley. Suddenly the country kid from Louisiana was crossing the country on package tours and appearing on Dick Clark's *American Bandstand*. This record sold 6 million copies, topped both the country and R&B charts, and became a No. 3 pop hit. It remained on the pop charts for twenty-nine weeks, experiencing a boost when Lewis performed it in July on the *Steve Allen Show*. The success of "Whole Lot of Shakin' Going On" catapulted Lewis into prominence, making him an international celebrity. His subsequent hits, "Great Balls of Fire," "Breathless," and "High School Confidential," followed effortlessly.

Unlike Presley, Lewis did not offer performances that were rehearsed and had vocal inflections properly placed; he sang with spontaneity. Songs were never performed the same way twice. There were clear, audible differences of nuance and phrasing between different recording takes, as was the case in his next single, "Great Balls of Fire." The recording of this Otis Blackwell (composer of Presley's "Don't Be Cruel") and Jack Hammer composition featured Lewis's pounding, prominent rhythm piano with glissandos and repetitive eighth notes, along with bass, guitar, drums, and Lewis's vocals full of exciting inflections. The melody consisted of a repetition of only a few notes and large (and uncharacteristically vocal) melodic pitch leaps. A simple but exciting piano solo consisted of multiple bars of just one repeated note. A catchy, repetitive rhythmic motif, consisting of three short (eighth) notes followed by one longer (quarter) note supplied by the drums, bass, and piano, was prominent throughout the song. With its use of repeated harmonies consisting of tonic, subdominant, and dominant chords (borrowed from the blues progression) and walking bass lines, this piano-pounding rockabilly hit was a masterpiece. Released in November 1957, "Great Balls of Fire" sat atop most national charts and became the best-selling record in Sun's history.

The year 1958 was a promotional whirlwind. Lewis was booked with an Alan Freed tour, a Phillip Morris tour, and a tour of Australia and England. His outlandish behavior during performances continued. Jim Miller cites an alleged occurrence on the Alan Freed tour in March:

> During his heyday in the late Fifties, Lewis used to demand that he close any package tour he appeared on. As writer John Grissim tells the story, "One exception came during a concert tour with Chuck Berry, emceed by Alan Freed. Both Berry and Lewis had million-seller hits on the charts at the same time and one night Freed flat-out insisted that Jerry Lee perform first. After a furious argument, Lewis obeyed. The story has it that he blew

nonstop rock for a brutal thirty minutes and, during the final "Whole Lot of Shakin'," poured lighter fluid over the piano and threw a match to it. As he stomped off the stage he hollered to the stage crew: 'I'd like to see *any* son of a bitch follow that!'"[7]

In 1958, Lewis had two more big hits. Released by Sun in February, "Breathless," another Blackwell composition, became Lewis's third Top 10 single. "High School Confidential" followed in April. It was the title track for the teenage movie of the same title, in which Lewis had a role.

A few months prior, in December 1957, Lewis had sneaked off to Hernando, Mississippi, and married his cousin, Myra Gale Brown, the daughter of his bass player and cousin, J. W. Brown. Though she claimed to be twenty years old on the marriage certificate, Myra was only thirteen. Once the news of the marriage hit the press, a scandal erupted as Lewis began his short British tour in May 1958. The tour was canceled after only three shows when Lewis returned to the States amid controversy. He was blacklisted; industry leaders were aghast (only Alan Freed defended Lewis). No amount of payola could change the situation. Overnight, The Killer's career as a rock and roller took a precipitous tumble when the press discovered that he had married his barely teenage relative. Lewis endured a ten-year drought on the charts, then had a successful career as a country music artist.

In 1961, Lewis recorded his last Top 40 hit of the rock and roll era, a blazing version of Ray Charles's 1959 hit "What'd I Say." He left Sun Records in 1963 for Smash Records, a Mercury subsidiary. Though Lewis achieved great success with honky-tonk country music in the '60s, in 1972 he returned to rock and roll with his album *The "Killer" Rocks On*. Not only did Lewis's drinking and drug abuse catch up with him, but the Internal Revenue Service, searching for back taxes, did as well. In 1989, the biographical film *Great Balls of Fire* was released, starring Dennis Quaid as Lewis. Celebrating his sixtieth birthday in 1995 with an exciting rock and roll album, *Young Blood*, Lewis continued to influence the rock genre. Responsible for defining the rock tradition in the '50s and beyond with his outlandish personal and ferocious performance styles, Jerry Lee Lewis was inducted into the Rock and Roll Hall of Fame at the first induction ceremony in 1986. He performed on September 2, 1995, backed by Bruce Springsteen and the E Street Band, at the opening concert for the Rock and Roll Hall of Fame and Museum in Cleveland, Ohio.

Other Sun Artists

Roy Orbison

Another of the original Sun Records rockabilly artists more like labelmates Perkins and Cash than Presley and Lewis, Roy Orbison was well known for his original music compositions. He wrote songs that have never gone out of style and have been covered by such musicians as Glen Campbell, Don McLean,

Linda Ronstadt, and Van Halen. Born in 1936 in Vernon, Texas, Orbison began playing the guitar at age six, learning from both his father, who taught him country music, and his uncle, who played the blues. During high school, Orbison formed his first band, the Wink Westerners, which performed at dances and jamborees in West Texas. After seeing his friend and fellow North Texas State College student, Pat Boone, achieve great pop music success, Orbison, who boasted an operatic tenor voice with an extremely versatile vocal range, re-formed his band, naming them the Teen Kings. They auditioned "Ooby Dooby" at Norman Petty's studio in Clovis, New Mexico, before sending it to Sun Records. Phillips recorded the song in 1956, and it became Orbison's first hit.

Roy Orbison. Courtesy of Photofest.

Because of his desire to sing ballads, Orbison was not happy at Sun. He was at odds with Phillips, who wanted him to capture an audience (especially the young market)—which, according to Phillips, required appropriate and uptempo songs, not ballads. Shortly after "Ooby Dooby," his almost two-year Sun tenure came to an end. Orbison moved on to create masterpieces for the Monument label, such as "Only the Lonely," one of the most original and effective pop records of 1960 (a No. 2 hit), and "Oh, Pretty Woman," which topped the pop charts in 1964. Between these two classics, he achieved seven hits in the Top 10 at the peak of his career in the early '60s. In the late 1980s, along with Bob Dylan, George Harrison, Tom Petty, and Jeff Lynne, Orbison became a member of the extremely successful Traveling Wilburys. He inspired many rock and rollers through the years, including the Beatles. In 1987, one of his greatest admirers, Bruce Springsteen, inducted Orbison into the Rock and Roll Hall of Fame. After Orbison's death from a heart attack in 1988, his album *Mystery Girl*, with songs written by Elvis Costello, U2, Orbison, and Orbison's son, was released. Also following his death, two movies were released that appropriated his songs for their sound tracks and titles: *Pretty Woman* and *Only the Lonely*.

Others

Many others as talented as Orbison experienced a brilliant record or two at Sun Records and Phillips International, the subsidiary label formed by Phillips in 1957. Such one- and two-hit wonders included Malcolm Yelvington's

"Drinkin' Wine Spo-Dee-o-Dee" (Malcolm Yelvington and the Star Rhythm Boys, 1954); Sonny Burgess's "Red Headed Woman" (1956); Warren Smith's "Rock 'n' Roll Ruby" and "Ubangi Stomp" (both 1956); Billy Riley and His Little Green Men's "Flying Saucer Rock and Roll" (1956, with Jerry Lee Lewis on piano) and "Red Hot" (1957); Bill Justis's "Raunchy" (1957, Phillips International); Onie Wheeler's "Jump Right out of This Jukebox" (1957, released 1959); and Carl Mann's "Mona Lisa" (1959, Phillips International). The Arkansan songwriter Charlie Rich was one of Phillips's greatest late-period artists. According to Phillips, Rich was one of the most talented artists at Sun, where he played session piano and became a staff writer. He composed songs for Lewis, though their success was terminated when The Killer's marriage scandal erupted. Rich's "Lonely Weekends," recorded in 1959 (released 1960, Phillips International), was his first hit in 1960. His career peaked in the '60s.

These artists and others combined with the production team of Sam Phillips to play a profound role in the creation of rock and roll. Having come a long way from its first national hit, Rufus Thomas's "Bear Cat," to the overwhelming success of best-selling Jerry Lee Lewis's "Great Balls of Fire," Sun Records produced more rock and roll records than any other label in the '50s—297 (226 of them with Sun; 71 of them with Phillips International).

As his cramped studio on Union Avenue became obsolete and could no longer accommodate the larger groups Sun was recording in the late '50s, Phillips knew he had to move his recording operation to a new location, which would also allow him to rent studio time for custom recording and develop Phillips International into an album label. These new ventures would require more space, personnel, and updated equipment than was possible at the old studio. In September 1960, Phillips opened a modern, state-of-the-art facility—complete with two recording studios, A&R and promotion offices, a tape storage vault, and (finally) his own office—at 639 Madison Avenue in Memphis. Shortly after opening the new Memphis studio, he opened a studio for custom recording in Nashville (where Jerry Lee Lewis recorded "What'd I Say" in 1961). The Nashville site remained open only until 1964 because Phillips could not supervise it to his liking; Nashville musicians followed the American Federation of Musicians guidelines, which did not allow Phillips to bring in his own musicians from Memphis. Fred Foster, of Monument Records, bought the facility and later recorded some of Roy Orbison's biggest hits there. With Sun's golden age ended in 1959 and his business winding down, Phillips bought radio stations, Holiday Inn stock, and other properties. With fellow Memphis businessman Kemmons Wilson (owner of the Holiday Inn chain), Phillips briefly launched Holiday Inn Records in 1968, two months after the last Sun record was issued, but the company never really got off the ground. In 1968, Phillips ceased recording and sold Sun to Shelby Singleton, who reissued numerous Sun rockabilly and rock and roll classics.

The legendary Sam Phillips possessed not only acute ears but also an idea and formula that worked, and the ingenuity to discover and produce musicians' best. As he played his highly significant role in the birth of rock and roll pioneering rockabilly music, he brought some of the most talented artists of a single generation into his tiny studio, one at a time, and knew exactly what to do to invent the new music, helping change the course of American popular music. Sam Phillips was inducted into the Rock and Roll Hall of Fame with the first class of inductees in 1986; he was inducted into the Country Music Hall of Fame in 2001.

ROCKABILLY ACROSS THE LAND

After Sun's switch from recording black blues to white country rock artists, dozens of white singers began to perform not only for Sun but also for other record labels. As the rockabilly sound swept the nation, major record companies needed to compete with Sun Records for the rockabilly market. Decca took the lead, signing Bill Haley and the Comets, and other companies followed with more of the leading rockabilly performers. Like Sun artists, they mostly had grown up with heavy doses of country music (and some of them with R&B) in their environment. As these mostly white Southern males—Bill Haley, Buddy Holly, the Everly Brothers, Gene Vincent, Eddie Cochran, and Ricky Nelson—applied their country techniques to the rhythm and blues-oriented sound, they created masterpieces of rock and roll history. Though rockabilly was generally a male-dominated genre, female artists Brenda Lee, Wanda Jackson, Cordell Jackson, and others contributed to the style. Regardless of gender, all these artists lightened and cleaned up the hard-driving popular R&B style and incorporated country music elements into it, making their rock music more acceptable to a general audience.

Bill Haley

Bill Haley was one of the earliest rockabilly artists. Originally a mild-mannered country musician, Haley changed American popular music in the '50s with his landmark rock and roll recording of "(We're Gonna) Rock Around the Clock," which marked the beginning of the rock era. It was the first rock and roll record to reach No. 1 on the pop charts, a position it held for eight weeks in 1955. It remained on the pop charts for nearly half a year and sold 22 million copies worldwide. "Rock Around the Clock" was the first internationally known rock and roll recording. In Britain alone, it reentered the charts seven times. When Haley modified this black rhythm and blues song (originally recorded by R&B musician Sunny Dae) to a more mainstream rock and roll beat in 1954, he proved that country-rooted musicians could use R&B to create rock music. Influenced by the western swing of Bob Wills (which incorporated elements of blues, boogie-woogie, swing jazz, and country music), Haley fused country and R&B sounds in the early '50s. Though an

Bill Haley and the Comets performing in the movie *Don't Knock the Rock*, 1956. Courtesy of the Library of Congress.

unlikely rock and roll hero, he nonetheless was crucial to establishing the new music.

Born in Highland Park, Michigan, in 1925, William John Clifton Haley Jr. grew up in a musical family. His mother was a church organist and piano teacher, and his father, originally from Kentucky, was a mandolinist who taught his son country music. When he was seven, Haley's family moved to Wilmington, Delaware, and he began playing a homemade cardboard guitar. He became active as a yodeler and guitarist, and after making his first record, "Candy Kisses," at the age of eighteen, Haley traveled the country, singing and playing guitar with various country music bands.

In 1948, Haley became a disc jockey and hosted a show on radio station WPWA in Chester, Pennsylvania. Known on the air as the Ramblin' Yodeler, he formed a band, the Four Aces of Western Swing, that regularly performed on the radio show and, along with his other bands, the Down Homers and the Saddlemen, recorded country music. In 1950, Haley began making records for the independent Essex label in Philadelphia, and the following year released a cover version of Jackie Brenston's "Rocket 88." Though this record did not have great success, it revealed how much white teenagers enjoyed the beat and vivacity of R&B music. It led Haley to drop his country image, change the name of his group to the Comets, and begin recording blues and R&B music.

Haley's early Essex recordings are considered some of the first rock and roll songs on record.

After a minor success in 1952 with "Rock This Joint," followed in 1953 by their first song to make it on the charts, "Crazy Man, Crazy" (a No. 12 pop hit), Bill Haley and the Comets signed a contract with Decca Records in 1954. Elvis Presley benefited from Haley's music, since the climate for rhythm and blues-based music in the pop market was improving after Haley's hits (especially after "Rocket 88"). After he moved from the small Essex to the major Decca label, he immediately sold 3 million records. Haley covered two blues songs, "(We're Gonna) Rock Around the Clock" and Joe Turner's "Shake, Rattle and Roll." He and his band combined country swing music with the R&B boogie-woogie jump beat of Louis Jordan on these recordings. Their Decca producer, Milt Gabler, had them use Louis Jordan's shuffle rhythm but augment it with short guitar and tenor saxophone riffs, resulting in the high-spirited sound (containing the drive of Jordan's Tympany Five mixed with the flavor of country music) that some authors, such as Charlie Gillett, have labeled Northern band rock and roll.[8] When first released by Decca in the spring of 1954, "Rock Around the Clock" was only a minor hit. After this simple song was included on the sound track of the 1955 movie *Blackboard Jungle*, it was re-released that year, and became an international sensation. (See chapter 3 for further information.)

Haley's next Decca release, "Shake, Rattle and Roll," was a cover of Big Joe Turner's 1954 recording of the same title. The two versions demonstrate some of the differences between '50s R&B and rock and roll. Haley's cover is representative of his style: faster tempo, classic twelve-bar blues format, and rhythm section (piano and drums) supplying a shuffle beat pattern with the bass player snapping the strings of his instrument (country music slapping bass technique) over a less prominent backbeat (than Turner's). The saxophone and guitar play the melody in unison with no improvisation in Haley's version, whereas in Turner's, improvisation is evident. One major difference between the two styles lies in the lyrics. Turner's version included several sexual references, as expected in R&B songs. In the first verse the singer and the woman to whom he sings are in bed together; in the second, he expresses his appreciation for seeing the sun shine through her dress; and in the fourth, he expresses his appreciation for her being a woman. Haley cleaned up the lyrics and removed references to bed and woman's sexuality, making them more acceptable to a broader audience. However, he didn't change the third verse, about the one-eyed cat in the seafood store because he thought it was subtle enough to get by listeners who were easily offended, and that it would please those who listened for sexual innuendos. Haley's lyric changes helped account for the charts success of his recording. Turner's version was a No. 1 R&B hit but did not make the pop charts; Haley's was a No. 7 pop hit.

Throughout the '50s, Haley made his presence known, especially in mid-decade, when he had thirteen Top 40 records, including "Dim, Dim the

Lights (I Want Some Atmosphere)" (1954), "Burn That Candle" (1955), "Razzle-Dazzle" (1955), "See You Later, Alligator" (1956), and "R-O-C-K" (1956). Like Presley, he appeared in movies featuring his music: *Rock Around the Clock* and *Don't Knock the Rock.* Though he predated Elvis and achieved the first rockabilly success, Haley never stole the limelight from Presley. He gave audiences a smoother sound than the rougher music of Presley, and he and his Comets offered a tamer stage show (though his band members engaged in a few stage antics). Haley felt that the music was stimulating enough without creating additional excitement. In 1957, Haley's age (thirty-two) and appearance (chubby and balding) did not compare with that of the young, hip-gyrating Presley in the eyes of teenage rock fans with raging hormones. Nonetheless, it was Haley's significant music that deserved and received the attention. After Presley and the other Memphis rockabillies appeared, Haley remained a favorite of those who could not handle the wildness of Presley and others.

When innovative bandleader Bill Haley merged R&B music with his country sound, he laid the foundation not only for rock and roll but also for rockabilly. He is credited with having brought rock and roll to the consciousness of America and the world. Though his career did not reach the stratospheric heights of Presley's, Bill Haley holds the title of Father of Rock and Roll. He died from a heart attack in 1981. In 1987, he was inducted into the Rock and Roll Hall of Fame.

Buddy Holly

Buddy Holly, inducted as a charter member into the Rock and Roll Hall of Fame in 1986, had a profound influence on rock and roll's development. Though he participated in rock and roll for only two years, the wealth of his output recorded in that time made a major and lasting impact on popular music. Greatly influenced by Elvis Presley, Holly incorporated the latter's style into his unique sound. He was a seminal singer-songwriter who integrated country and R&B elements to produce brilliant music that demonstrated artistic maturity beyond his years. By 1957, Holly had perfected a light, bright rockabilly sound and pioneered and popularized the standard rock and roll band of two guitars, bass, and drums. This very talented innovator was a gifted composer and one of the first to use advanced studio techniques, such as double tracking. His playful, innocent singing style, which displayed his falsetto voice and trademark hiccup, was a major influence on Bob Dylan and Paul McCartney. His recorded standards continue to be covered: "Not Fade Away," "Rave On," "That'll Be the Day," "Peggy Sue," and "Oh, Boy!" No other founding father of rock and roll exerted a greater influence than Holly over the '60s British Invasion. Both the Hollies and the Beatles derived their names from Holly's Crickets; and the Rolling Stones' first major British hit was a cover of his "Not Fade Away."

Charles Hardin Holley was born in Lubbock, Texas, in 1936. Buddy was a childhood nickname, and his last name was amended later to Holly. As a child, he learned to play the piano, guitar, fiddle, and banjo. Like other rockabillies, Holly was influenced by white country music (especially bluegrass and western swing) and listened to such performers as Hank Snow and Hank Williams. He heard R&B on radio programs broadcast from Shreveport, Louisiana (which ultimately influenced his use of blue notes and the twelve-bar blues pattern). While still in school, Holly formed a duo (Buddy and Bob) with his friend Bob Montgomery, and regularly played on a Sunday afternoon program, *The Buddy and Bob Show*, on radio station KDAV in Lubbock. Eventually adding bass player Larry Welborn to the country group, they called themselves the Western and Bop Band. By his sixteenth birthday, Holly

Buddy Holly, 1958. Courtesy of the Library of Congress.

was considering a career in country music and dreaming of stardom; however, the new rock and roll sound changed his country music plans. In 1955, when Elvis Presley came to Lubbock for an engagement at the Cotton Club, Holly and Montgomery drove him around, and their group opened for Presley's concert. By their next radio performance, Holly was singing Presley's songs. He idolized Presley and began to sound like him, signifying his move from country music to rockabilly. With Bill Haley already on its roster, in 1956 Decca Records signed Holly after a Decca talent scout in Lubbock heard Holly and his group perform when they opened a concert for Haley. Holly went to Nashville with Sonny Curtis (guitar) and Don Guess (bass) and recorded such unnoticed singles as "Blue Days, Black Nights," "Midnight Shift," and an early version of "That'll Be the Day." Decca executives didn't like, and wouldn't release, the latter.

In January 1957, Holly's contract with Decca expired. Frustrated with the outcome in Nashville and impressed with Norman Petty's production of Southwestern rockabilly artist Buddy Knox's "Party Doll" (a 1957 No. 1 pop hit), Holly and the newly named Crickets took their distinctive music to Petty's small studio in Clovis, New Mexico. In February 1957, with Petty's assistance, the Crickets recorded "That'll Be the Day," the title taken from a phrase in the John Wayne movie *The Searchers*. Managing Holly and the Crickets, Petty negotiated a contract with Coral and Brunswick Records (oddly enough, two Decca subsidiaries). "That'll Be the Day," characteristically Holly, reflected the Crickets' innovative use of standard rockabilly instrumentation—two guitars (lead and rhythm), bass, and drums. Brunswick released the song credited to the Crickets, since producer and manager Petty had negotiated an unusual arrangement that their songs released on Brunswick were credited to the Crickets and those released on Coral were credited to Holly. This distinction was insignificant because Holly and the Crickets always recorded together. Nonetheless, the group, which, at various times consisted of Sonny Curtis (guitar), Don Guess (bass), Jerry Allison (drums), Niki Sullivan (guitar), Joe Mauldin (bass), Tommy Allsup (guitar), Glen Hardin (piano), Jerry Naylor (vocals), and Waylon Jennings (guitar), achieved great success after the release of this recording. It rose to the top of the pop charts later that year and to No. 2 on the R&B charts. During the next year, Holly and the Crickets continued their success with a series of five Top 40 rockabilly tunes, most featuring Holly's innovative guitar solos, including such rock and roll classics as "Peggy Sue," "Rave On," "Maybe Baby," and "Oh, Boy!"

Bo Diddley inspired Holly's 1957 follow-up record to "That'll Be the Day." With its frenetic and repeated rhythms played on the tom-tom throughout, "Peggy Sue" burst into the No. 3 position on the pop charts (No. 2 on the R&B charts). This song was in the Tex-Mex sound: Holly sang in a nasal, high-pitched Hank Williams–type voice, with hiccups, stretched syllables, and a feeling of nervous excitement. Arnold Shaw states that singers from the old school found this style disconcerting, but what was important was the agitation, tension, and energy of Holly's delivery as he created the new rock and roll sound: "Here in a large sense was the dividing line between the eras of the Big Ballad and the Big Beat."[9]

This skinny young musician from Lubbock who wore thick-rimmed glasses and a shy grin always maintained a clean-cut image, performing in suit and tie. He aroused hysteria among teenagers with his many love songs but was not reviled by disapproving parents. Holly appeared on the *Ed Sullivan Show* in late 1957 and performed on various '50s package tours, including Alan Freed's Big Beat Show (on which he played craps at the back of the bus with Chuck Berry). Major changes occurred in 1958 when he married Maria Elena Santiago, moved to New York City, and, after the Biggest Show of Stars tour, decided to leave both Petty and the Crickets. Jerry Allison, Joe Mauldin, and Niki Sullivan remained with Petty, and Holly recruited Jennings and Allsup as new Crickets. After moving to New York, he recorded his beautiful "True Love Ways" and his last studio track, "It Doesn't Matter Anymore," written for him by Paul Anka (which became a posthumous hit in March 1959). These ballads placed his distinctive voice in the innovative context of an orchestral string arrangement, yielding powerful recordings filled with a promise that was never fulfilled because of the accident that claimed his life.

In the winter of 1959, because of legal and financial problems resulting from his split with Petty, Holly reluctantly agreed to perform on the Winter Dance Party bus tour of the Midwest. Following a concert in Clear Lake, Iowa, Holly chartered a private plane to fly him and his band (Jennings and Allsup) to

Fargo, North Dakota, so they could get their laundry done and have a good night's sleep. Two of the tour's other featured performers, Richard Stephen Valenzuela (Ritchie Valens) and Jiles Perry Richardson (the Big Bopper) joined him to avoid taking the uncomfortable bus. (Valens and the Big Bopper wanted to travel by plane, so Valens tossed a coin with Allsup for his seat and won the toss; the Big Bopper had a cold and talked Jennings into trading places with him and taking the bus.) Their plane left the Mason City, Iowa, airport in the early morning hours of February 3, 1959, flew into a snowstorm, and crashed in a cornfield a few minutes later, killing all on board (the three singers and the pilot). Like James Dean, Johnny Ace, and Hank Williams, Holly had his career cut short and became a legend. Years later, singer-songwriter Don McLean immortalized the twenty-two-year-old Holly. In his 1971 No. 1 hit, "American Pie," he labeled that winter day as the day the music died.

It is difficult to comprehend that Buddy Holly, the genius behind the large body of indispensable, imperishable '50s rock and roll music that influenced almost every major artist of the rock era (especially the Beatles, the Rolling Stones, Bob Dylan, Elton John, Linda Ronstadt, John Denver, Bobby Vee, Tommy Roe, Elvis Costello, and a list too long to present in full here), died so young. Musicologists contemplate what more Holly would have contributed to the world if not taken at such a young age. Not only was he one of the first white rock and roll musicians to write his own material almost exclusively, and the Crickets probably the first white group to feature the future rock band instrumentation lineup, but Holly was also the first rock and roll singer to double track his voice and guitar in recording and the first to use strings on a rock and roll record.

Buddy Holly and Chuck Berry were the major influences on the rock music of the '60s. Though Holly's contribution is often underestimated, he was the main inspiration for the Beatles. His well-crafted songs provided a template for the early writing of John Lennon and Paul McCartney. In 1976, McCartney purchased the rights to the Buddy Holly song catalogue and inaugurated an annual weeklong tribute, Buddy Holly Week, in England, where Holly and the Crickets were immensely popular. Two years later, the motion picture *The Buddy Holly Story* was released, and in 1989 the musical *Buddy: The Buddy Holly Story* opened in England (it ran on Broadway in 1990). In 1993, Holly was honored with a postage stamp, and in 1996 MCA released *Not Fade Away: Remembering Buddy Holly*, featuring Waylon Jennings, Los Lobos, the Band, the Crickets, and others, as well as a duet between Holly and the Hollies. Three years later, the Buddy Holly Museum opened in Lubbock. Today, Buddy Holly remains an enduring icon, and his songs continue to be recorded.

The Everly Brothers

Another rockabilly act that preferred to sing about romantic love was the Everly Brothers. More than any others, Don and Phil Everly defined what love and affection meant in rock and roll with their songs about adolescent romance, teenage devotion, and heartbreak. One of the most influential rockabilly groups, these brothers transformed the country sounds (Appalachian Mountain and bluegrass music) of their Kentucky upbringing into a lavishly harmonized form of rock and roll as they sang flawlessly in tight harmony. Between 1957 and 1962, the Everly Brothers released a steady stream of hit records that crossed over from country to pop and to the R&B charts, including "Bye Bye Love," "Wake Up Little Susie," "All I Have to Do Is Dream," and "Bird Dog." The duo's expressive harmonic vocal style influenced the Beatles, the Hollies, the Beach Boys, the Mamas and the Papas, Simon and Garfunkel, the Byrds, and countless others.

The sons of highly respected country musicians and radio stars, Ike and Margaret Everly, Don (born in 1937 in Brownie, Kentucky) and Phil (born in 1939 in Chicago) grew up on country music and toured with their parents. The boys appeared on their parents' radio show from the time they were nine and seven years old, respectively, thus absorbing a strong country music background. With their high tenor voices, they sang in very close harmony supported by the sound of their acoustic guitars, influenced by the country groups the Delmore Brothers and the Louvin Brothers. With Elvis Presley as a model, they eventually turned toward rockabilly, creating a uniquely mixed sound and becoming immensely popular. Their sound consisted of Don singing melody with Phil harmonizing above him, usually at an interval of a third, as in bluegrass music. In 1955, the teenage duo went to Nashville, where they sold some of their songs to a country music publishing firm. That same year, they signed a contract with Columbia Records and released two singles; the first was "The Sun Keeps Shining." With their clean-cut good looks, they were the opposite of other chart-topping rockabilly crossover artists such as Jerry Lee Lewis.

The Everlys rose to prominence with New York–based Cadence Records, recording songs written for them by the husband-and-wife team of Felice and Boudleaux Bryant, who worked for the publishing/management company owned by Wesley Rose and Roy Acuff in Nashville. In February 1957, Rose persuaded the label to sign them. The owner of Cadence, Archie Bleyer, had gone to Nashville to establish a country music division to boost Cadence's sales. As songwriters under contract to Cadence, the Everly Brothers sold Don's "Thou Shalt Not Steal" to Kitty Wells. One of the Bryants's songs, "Bye Bye Love," which the brothers persuaded Bleyer they should record at their first session, proved to be a huge success, reaching No. 2 on the pop charts and No. 1 on the country charts in 1957. Shortly after, Rose became the duo's producer and manager.

"Bye Bye Love" established the musical model that the Everly Brothers followed for the rest of their tenure with Cadence. Unlike the spontaneity experienced in Sam Phillips's Sun Record studio, their recording sessions were scrupulously run with all arrangements carefully worked out before entering the studio (the Everlys rehearsed their vocals with a tape recorder). The sessionmen included Nashville's finest—professionals capable of adapting to any performers—usually Chet Atkins on guitar and Floyd Cramer on piano (both Rock and Roll Hall of Fame inductees in the Sidemen category, 2002 and 2003, respectively). The Everly Brothers' sound remained intact during their stay with Cadence; the only later change was placing greater emphasis on drums and electric guitar as they became more comfortable as rock and rollers. Both rhythm guitarists, Atkins and Don Everly admired Bo Diddley and increasingly attempted to incorporate his R&B guitar style into their playing, as is apparent in the "Bye Bye Love" introduction. This song melded country music's sense of order with the energy of rock and roll. With a pair of acoustic guitars and a rhythm section of bass, drums, and piano, the brothers' close and warm country harmonies soared above the rocking beat. The Everly Brothers' trademark sound was created. In May 1957, "Bye Bye Love," the first of many songs by Felice and Boudleaux Bryant made famous by the Everly Brothers, became their first big hit. Following the success of this song, the Bryants began tailoring songs specifically to the Everly Brothers' range, harmonies, and audience. The Bryants assumed that what that audience wanted was songs about love—romantic, tender, and sensitive love songs. Also crucial to the brothers' success was an abundance of creative uses of strong hooks and catchy melodies, which were always Bleyer's first priorities.

After participating in tours (such as 1957's Biggest Show of Stars with Chuck Berry, Buddy Holly and the Crickets, Paul Anka, Frankie Lymon and the Teenagers, the Drifters, and Clyde McPhatter, among others), appearing on the *Grand Ole Opry*, and accepting engagements on television shows including the *Ed Sullivan Show* and variety shows hosted by Perry Como, Alan Freed, and Patti Page, the Everlys followed their first million-seller hit with such other classics as "Wake Up Little Susie" (1957), "All I Have to Do Is Dream" (1958), and "Bird Dog" (1958, No. 1 pop and country hit). The follow-up to "Bye Bye Love" was "Wake Up Little Susie," another Bryant song that displayed their influential vocal style and incorporated electric lead guitar. With a strong backbeat supplied by guitars and drums and a syncopated rhythmic motif throughout, the song's structure prominently displayed R&B aspects such as the use of call-and-response between voices and instruments. The lyrics, however, sung in their usual soft, crisp, and clear vocals, caused controversy. Though probably intended as simple, sweet, and innocent, they insinuated that the girl in the song had been sleeping with her boyfriend at the drive-in. The record was banned by some radio stations for its suggestive lyrics, but it nonetheless became the Everly Brothers' first No. 1 single. In October 1957, "Wake Up Little Susie" topped the pop charts for four weeks, becoming their second million-seller.

Between 1957 and 1960, The Everlys placed eleven hits in the Top 10 (averaging one every four months), including four No. 1 pop songs (and four No. 1 country hits and three No. 1 R&B hits); in fact, they were rarely off the charts until 1963. Their 1958 No. 1 hit, "All I Have to Do Is Dream," was their top hit and the only song by someone other than Elvis Presley to reach the No. 1 position on the pop, R&B, and country charts. Their 1961 album, *A Date with the Everlys*, remains a milestone in pop history, featuring their biggest-selling single, "Cathy's Clown" (written by the brothers themselves). During the late '50s and early '60s, the Everlys began to achieve Top 10 success with their original songs, such as Don's "('Til) I Kissed You" (1959, with the Crickets as accompaniment) and Phil's "When Will I Be Loved" (1960). After new contract negotiations left them unhappy with their low royalty rate, the Everlys departed Cadence for Warner Brothers Records. In 1960, they signed a ten-year contract with Warner Brothers, for which they recorded prolifically during the following decade. With Warner, the pair released "Cathy's Clown," which sold more than 2 million copies and was their all-time best seller. Despite their commercial success with Warner, the change in labels and the breakup of their production team (they fired Wesley Rose) marked the beginning of their decline.

Despite personal (drug and marriage) and professional (failed albums) problems during the '60s, the Everly Brothers continued to churn out records, such as the 1967 autobiographical hit "Bowling Green," before their tense relationship resulted in a split during a concert in California in 1973. At that point, with the Everlys' career floundering, the Beach Boys, the Beatles, and the Byrds, all of whom acknowledged their debt to the brothers, surpassed them. In 1983, ten years after parting ways, the duo reunited onstage for two concerts at London's Royal Albert Hall, resulting in a live album and a home video released as *Reunion Concert*. The Everly Brothers inspired musicals, including 1998's biographical *Bye Bye Love: The Everly Brothers Musical* and 2000's *Dream, Dream, Dream*. This most important vocal duo in rock and roll history was inducted into the Rock and Roll Hall of Fame at the inaugural induction ceremony in 1986, and the Country Music Hall of Fame in 2001.

Other Rockabillies

Gene Vincent

As record companies searched for acts to enter the rockabilly market, Capitol Records signed Gene Vincent, a Korean War veteran born Eugene Vincent Craddock in Norfolk, Virginia, in 1935. Signing Vincent was the most immediate and successful response to Elvis Presley's RCA recordings by any major company. With his rockabilly stutter and hiccup, Columbia heard an Elvis sound-alike in Vincent, who was discovered through the label's talent search. Vincent and his band, the Blue Caps, recorded prolifically for Capitol in the '50s, producing such hits as "Be-Bop-a-Lula" (1956), "Bluejean Bop" (1956), "Lotta Lovin'" (1957), and "Dance to the Bop" (1957). The original Blue Caps included guitarists Cliff Gallup and Willie Williams, bassist Jack Neal, and drummer Dickie Harrell. In the mid-to-late '50s, Vincent and the Blue Caps were among the most popular rock and roll groups. Between 1957 and 1960, Capitol released six of their albums, including *Bluejean Bop!* (1956) and *Gene Vincent Rocks! And the Blue Caps Roll* (1958), which are some of the most collectible and priciest albums of the rock and roll era.

Having grown up listening to country music, Vincent performed on the Norfolk radio station WCMS's *Country Showtime*, a *Grand Ole Opry*–type show that aired live on Friday evenings. While recuperating from a serious leg injury sustained in a motorcycle accident while serving in the navy, Vincent purchased "Be-Bop-a-Lula" from another patient for $25 and recorded a demo tape of it that won him a recording contract with Capitol Records in 1956. Another account of the song's origin claims that Vincent wrote the song himself, inspired by Little Lulu, a character in a comic book. Regardless, "Be-Bop-a-Lula," Vincent's first single for Capitol, is today considered one of the rock and roll anthems of the '50s. It perfectly exemplifies the rockabilly sound, complete with two guitar solos and use of the blues progression, and ranks alongside Presley's "That's All Right," Perkins's "Blue Suede Shoes," and Eddie Cochran's "Summertime Blues." Vincent's recording copied the unique Sun Records rockabilly sound by incorporating an echo to distort his gentle voice and by having the accompanying musicians play simple arrangements. His high-pitched, erotic voice didn't sound like either a country singer or an R&B singer, as so many other rockers could be categorized. The B-side of the single, "Woman Love," was overtly sexual, earning him an obscenity conviction and a $10,000 fine in his home state of Virginia. "Be-Bop-a-Lula" rose to No. 7 on the pop charts, followed by "Bluejean Bop," written by Vincent, and "Lotta Lovin'," written by Bernice Bedwell.

Vincent sounded like Presley but made him look tame. The slick, good-looking rocker perfectly embodied rock and roll rebellion with his appearance and menacing stage presence styled in the James Dean tough-guy tradition. He looked darker, tougher, and greasier than Presley and dressed in black leather and blue denim, his costume in the 1956 movie *The Girl Can't Help It*, in which he appeared alongside Little Richard, Fats Domino, Eddie Cochran, and other rockers, singing "Be-Bop-a-Lula." Because of his leg injury, he couldn't perform the sexy hip movements that Presley did, but he made up for it with his breathy vocals conveying sexual desperation. The Blue Caps performed with frenzied energy that was unmatched by their contemporaries. Though he toured and recorded ceaselessly, Vincent's popularity waned as the rockabilly sound gave way to that of the teen idols. In 1960, while touring Europe, he was seriously injured in the accident that claimed fellow rockabilly Eddie Cochran's life when their limousine ran off the road en route to London's Heathrow Airport. Vincent remained a revered star in Britain and Europe throughout the '60s, and rock and rollers still profoundly admire the Blue Caps' music. The talented Vincent, who died of a stomach ulcer in 1971, was inducted into the Rock and Roll Hall of Fame in 1998.

Eddie Cochran

Appearing with Vincent in *The Girl Can't Help It*, Eddie Cochran, another James Dean/Marlon Brando tough-guy type, performed an exhilarating version of his "Twenty Flight Rock." Though he died when only twenty-one, Cochran left a lasting mark on rock and roll with his thick, aggressive rhythmic guitar sound and his defiant attitude, which made him an icon (especially in England) for several generations of rockers, from the Beatles, the Rolling Stones, the Who, and the Kinks to such punk rockers as the Sex Pistols. His songs, including "Summertime Blues," "C'mon Everybody," and "Somethin' Else," are among the gems that, along with those of Chuck Berry and the Coasters, tell the '50s teenage story.

Born in Oklahoma City in 1938, Cochran grew up in Minnesota and California, and began his music career in Los Angeles as a country music singer in the mid-'50s. Initially, he teamed up with singer and guitarist Hank Cochran (no relation), touring and recording as the Cochran Brothers before finding a manager and collaborator in songwriter Jerry Capehart, who worked with Cochran for the remainder of his career. After being influenced by Presley, Cochran changed from his country style to a harder rock and roll style. He recorded his first rock and roll song, "Skinny Jim," for the Crest label in 1956.

Eddie Cochran, 1956. Courtesy of the Library of Congress.

That same year, Capehart secured Cochran a recording contract with Liberty Records, enabling the label to join the rockabilly field. Cochran perfected his rock and roll sound with acoustic and electric guitars, handclaps, and tambourines, and his first hit was "Sittin' in the Balcony" (1957). He followed it in 1958 with "Summertime Blues" and "C'mon Everybody," and in 1959 with "Somethin' Else," co-written by his fiancée, Sharon Sheely.

Cochran recorded his most successful record, "Summertime Blues," in late 1958, and it became a No. 8 pop hit. In this anthem of teen disenchantment, he alternated whimper- and growllike vocal qualities. This and his next hit, "C'mon Everybody," were the result of Cochran's experiments with overdubbing, a recording technique invented by Les Paul in the early '50s, in which Cochran played and sang all the parts himself. He was among the first rockabilly musicians to use overdubbing extensively, though it had been used before and would soon become common recording practice. The innovative Cochran used techniques that produced sounds which were customarily associated with rock musicians only later—sounds that influenced such musicians as Pete Townshend and New Wave rockers. "Summertime Blues" featured a staccato rhythm guitar (reminiscent of Presley's "Jailhouse Rock") and harsh vocals, including some phrases spoken in a very low bass voice. This, and "C'mon Everybody" and "Somethin' Else," helped define the experience of young people in the 1950s. Cochran's exhilarating tenor voice was a key element in the success of these songs, though he is known more for the intensity of his guitar playing.

Cochran toured steadily in the mid-to-late '50s as a member of package tours, such as 1957's Biggest Show of Stars and 1958's Alan Freed Christmas Rock 'n' Roll Spectacular. The Kelly Four, consisting of bassist Connie Smith (replaced by Dave Schreiber), drummer Gene Ridgio, and various pianists and saxophonists, accompanied Cochran. In 1959, he was so deeply affected by the deaths of Holly, Valens, and the Big Bopper that he recorded a version of Tommy Dee's tribute song, "Three Stars," and avoided airplanes. During his lifetime, Cochran released only one album, *Singin' to My Baby*. His last recording, "Three Steps to Heaven," recorded in January 1960, was released at the time of his death. The song reflected more of a new pop sound, not rockabilly, perhaps because Cochran realized the rockabilly style was dying with the rise of teen idol pop stars, and was trying to alter his style to accommodate the change. He never got the chance to establish himself in this new style because his career was abruptly cut short. In April 1960, Eddie Cochran did not survive the limousine accident in which his fiancée and his friend Gene Vincent were seriously injured en route to Heathrow Airport at the end of his British tour.

Cochran, who was more popular in England than in America, epitomized the sound and stance of the '50s rebel rocker. His influence was greater than one would think—for instance, in June 1957, it was his "Twenty Flight Rock" that brought John Lennon and Paul McCartney together when McCartney taught Lennon the chords of the song while Lennon's Quarrymen were playing at a church picnic in England. An exceptionally talented guitarist and energetic stage performer, Cochran was inducted into the Rock and Roll Hall of Fame in 1987.

Ricky Nelson

Eddie Cochran's fiancée, Sharon Sheely, wrote Ricky Nelson's 1958 No. 1 pop hit, "Poor Little Fool." Nelson, who had the advantage of being introduced to the world on his family's popular television series, *The Adventures of Ozzie and Harriet*, practically grew up in the nation's living rooms. Ricky, as he was known until his twenty-first birthday, when he changed his name to Rick, was a handsome, gentle-voiced teen idol long before he made records. However, unlike most late '50s teen idols, Nelson was very talented. A good singer with a smooth, very pleasing voice, he had a band that always featured excellent musicians, such as the brilliant guitarist James Burton (a 2001 Rock and Roll Hall of Fame inductee), who later played for Elvis Presley. Nelson was a singer-guitarist with an instinctive feel for the country side of rockabilly. His records were exceptionally tough, exciting, and mostly free of the orchestration and studio gimmicks of other late-decade teen idols.

Born in 1940, the son of bandleader Ozzie Nelson and singer-actress Harriet Hilliard, Eric Hilliard Nelson longed to be a recording artist. He was a huge fan of the Sun Records artists and especially idolized Carl Perkins. From October 1952 until 1966, Nelson played himself on his parents' television show. At the age of sixteen, he began his singing career, performing weekly on the series to a massive audience. In April 1957, Nelson covered Fats Domino's "I'm Walkin'" on the show, and after a wild teenage response to the program, he released the song, backed with "A Teenager's Romance," on Verve Records. The songs became No. 4 and No. 2 pop hits, selling 60,000 copies in three days. Pushed by his success and the business wisdom of his father, Nelson sang one song on each subsequent episode of the show, usually belting out a song at the sock hop of his television high school. After Verve withheld royalties, Imperial Records, the label that featured Fats Domino as its star, snagged Nelson, who scored a lengthy series of hits for the label.

One of the few non-Southerners to be associated with rockabilly, Nelson developed a softer, more pop-oriented style as he recognized a shift toward pop music in the late '50s. He had a series of hits between 1957 and 1963, with thirty-two Top 40 hits, twelve of them in the Top 10 before the end of the decade. They included "Be-Bop Baby" (1957), "Stood Up" (1957), "Poor Little Fool" (1958), "Lonesome Town" (1958), and "It's Late" (1959). In 1961, he had yet more classic hits—"Travelin' Man" and his signature song, "Hello Mary Lou," a record that topped the pop charts. As the maturing Nelson's appeal with the teenage audience diminished, he began to develop a country rock style that proved influential years later, while continuing to develop his song-writing skills.

With his band, Nelson earned critical praise as a live act and released one of the biggest hits of his career, "Garden Party," in 1972, a personal anthem rejecting the notion that he allowed himself to be relegated to a nostalgia act. In the 1970s, he formed the Stone Canyon Band, one of the first country rock groups, which included future Eagle bassist Randy Meisner and then current Little Feat drummer Richie Hayward. Nelson died in a plane crash on December 31, 1985, along with his fiancée, Helen Blair; his sound engineer, Clark Russell; and band members Bobby Neal, Patrick Woodward, Rick Intveld, and Andy Chapin, when a chartered DC3 carrying them between concerts crashed near DeKalb, Texas. Until his death, he remained a hardworking musician, performing up to 200 concerts a year. One of the first teen idols of the rock era and a rockabilly sensation, Ricky Nelson left a worthy musical legacy, and was inducted into the Rock and Roll Hall of Fame in 1987.

Brenda Lee

Another young teen idol who achieved exceptional popularity via television was rockabilly singer Brenda Lee, who had much in common with Ricky Nelson. Born Brenda Mae Tarpley in Atlanta, Georgia, in 1944, she became a versatile teen idol in the late '50s, able to sing rockabilly, country music, and pop standards equally well. Though she grew up in the South, where country music had a strong presence, Lee's influences instead included pop singers such as Judy Garland and Frank Sinatra. With teenage themes very popular in '50s rock and roll music, teenage stars became particularly attractive. Brenda Lee was the most successful. She began her career at age six, appearing on a local radio show and, at age seven, on a Saturday afternoon television show before joining Red Foley's *Ozark Jubilee*, a Missouri-based country music television program. In May 1956 (at age eleven), she signed a contract with Decca Records, inaugurating her pro-

Brenda Lee sits with photos and albums to autograph for fans, 1959. © Hulton Archive/Getty Images.

lific and hit-filled recording career. Nicknamed Little Miss Dynamite, Lee recorded material in different styles. "Jambalaya," her first single (1957), was a rockabilly cover of a Hank Williams song; others, such as "One Step at a Time" and "Dynamite" (from which she acquired her nickname), were in gospel and harder rock styles. The young Lee presented a schoolgirl image, always dressed in pretty dresses, and occasionally falsified her age. Her first Top 40 hit, "Sweet Nothin's" (1959), which rose to No. 4 on the pop charts, capitalized on this image, while her later hits proved that she could sing with the emotional authority of an adult. In 1960, "I'm Sorry" became her first No. 1 pop hit, and was followed the same year by her second, "I Want to Be Wanted." In 1958, she recorded "Rockin' Around the Christmas Tree," which became an international hit that is still seasonally on the charts.

Lee's advanced musicality and emotional quality suggested wisdom and talent beyond her years. Because of her ability to belt out tunes, Lee impacted rock and roll in the late '50s and early '60s (John Lennon felt she had the greatest rock and roll voice). Her career was a very long and consistent one. From

1958 to 1976, she recorded almost exclusively with country producer Owen Bradley. She was a sensation in Europe and performed in concert with such artists as Elvis Presley, the Beatles (who opened for her), Gene Vincent, Duane Eddy, and Patsy Cline. When Lee toured Europe with Vincent, they were billed as the King and Queen of Rock and Roll. By the time she was twenty-one, Lee had recorded 256 sides for Decca, though her later hits never matched her late '50s hit, "Sweet Nothin's," and she returned to country music in the '70s and '80s. With her exceptional talent, Brenda Lee achieved great success and accomplished feats no other woman musician had—she sold more than 100 million records worldwide, and her hits appeared on more charts categories (country, pop, R&B, rock, and easy listening) than all others in the history of recorded music. In 1997, she was inducted into the Country Music Hall of Fame, and three years later she celebrated her fiftieth year in show business. In 2002, she published her autobiography, *Little Miss Dynamite: The Brenda Lee Story*, and was inducted into the Rock and Roll Hall of Fame.

Other Female Rockabillies

Wanda Jackson.   Another very gifted female rockabilly artist, Wanda Jackson, was born in Maud, Oklahoma, in 1937. When she was growing up in Oklahoma and California (with strong country influences, western swing and honky-tonk), Jackson's father taught her guitar and piano. She began singing professionally at age nine, and at thirteen her strong, impressive voice brought Jackson her own radio program. Soon after, she started performing with such country musicians as Hank Thompson. Jackson's compositional gifts and dynamic stage presence won her a record deal with Decca in 1954, and she achieved her first hit with the country song "You Can't Have My Love," a duet with the Brazos Valley Boys (Thompson's band) member Billy Gray. While on tour in the South, she met (and toured with) Elvis Presley, who aroused her interest in rockabilly music. Jackson quickly added the music to her repertoire in the mid-1950s after Presley raved that her strong voice was perfect for the style and urged her to change her act. Presley's colorful wardrobe so impressed Jackson that she abandoned her cowgirl outfits for skintight dresses accented with fringe and sparkly rhinestones that glistened while she danced on stage. Jackson was dubbed the Queen of Rockabilly.

In 1956, when she switched to Capitol Records, Jackson's repertoire became aggressive, and her raw and feisty voice shone through. Released that year, her recording of "I Gotta Know" alternated between the country sound and the rockabilly sound, complete with hiccups. Influenced by Gene Vincent and Presley, she added a defiant quality to the rough quality of her voice. She recorded such songs as "Hot Dog! That Made Him Mad" (about keeping one's man in line), "Fujiyama Mama" (in which she compares herself to atomic weaponry), and "Mean, Mean Man" (in which she dismisses any notion of submissiveness when her man won't give Jackson a goodnight kiss). "Cool Love" centered on her lover's tendency to treat her as a square, instead of being eager to party with her. This was a recurring theme in a number of rockabilly tunes recorded by women, who made their demands known in their songs (such as Donna Dameron's "Bopper 486609," an answer record to the Big Bopper's "Chantilly Lace," and Janis Martin's "Just Squeeze Me"). Presley's influence continued with Jackson's cover of "Let's Have a Party" (featured in Presley's movie *Loving You*). It became her first Top 40 (and biggest) hit in 1960, and featured accompaniment by Gene Vincent's Blue Caps.

Even after interest in the rockabilly sound declined, Jackson recorded rock and roll songs, including covers of Little Richard's "Long Tall Sally," the Coasters' "Yakety Yak," and Jerry Lee Lewis's "Whole Lot of Shakin' Going On." She had two more Top 40 hits in 1961 with country-styled ballads she wrote herself, "Right or Wrong" and "In the Middle of a Heartache," before returning to her country music roots. Jackson's long career included gospel music and songs performed in foreign languages (Japanese, German, and Dutch); she was very popular overseas and continued to tour throughout the world. In the mid-1990s, Jackson toured with Rosie Flores, introducing herself to a new generation of fans. With her unique voice and dynamic stage presence, the Queen of Rockabilly broke the barriers that had prevented women musicians from being as successful as their male counterparts. In the mid-1950s, when women in rock were not common, she proved to the world that women could rock.

Jean Chapel and Janis Martin.   Though they found little success on the charts, other female rockers included Jean Chapel, Janis Martin, and Cordell Jackson, among a host of regionally popular performers. Chapel appeared on the *Grand Ole Opry* as Mattie O'Neill, though she was credited with her given name (Jean Chapel) when she recorded such songs as "Oo-Ba La Baby" at Sun Records. Martin, hailing from Virginia, began playing the guitar at age four, and at eleven she became a member of the WDVA *Barndance* in Danville. She later performed on the *Old Dominion Barndance*, based in Richmond (at that time it was the third largest show of its kind in America). In 1956, she began recording for RCA, billed as The Female Elvis, and later recorded "My Boy Elvis" as a tribute. Released in 1956, her first single, "Willyou, Willyum," was backed with "Drugstore Rock and Roll," one of her own compositions. The record was so successful (in the Top 40), selling 750,000 copies, that *Billboard* voted Martin the Most Promising Female Artist of 1956. She toured with Carl Perkins and Johnny Cash, but after the birth of her son in 1958, she limited her live performances with her band, the Marteens, to local appearances in order to spend time with her family.

Cordell Jackson.   Cordell Jackson began composing songs and recording demo tapes at the Memphis Recording Service in the early '50s. Born Cordell Miller in Pontotoc, Mississippi, in 1923, she began her career by performing with her father's band, the Pontotoc Ridge Runners. While living in Memphis in the mid-1950s, Jackson composed songs and sought a recording career. When Sam Phillips turned her down, she founded her own label, Moon Records, in 1956. She recorded her first single that year, "Rock and Roll Christmas," one of her original songs, backed with "Beboppers Christmas." Jackson recorded such songs as "High School Sweater" and "Football Widow" for Moon Records between 1955 and 1959, in addition to producing records by other local performers. Jackson—guitarist, engineer, publisher, and promoter—proved that women not only could rock and roll, but that they also could succeed in all spheres of the music business.

Moon Records, along with many other indies kept the emerging music industry in line. With Sun Records, Sam Phillips proved to the world that with dedication, perseverance, and hard work, independents could make a difference. In fact, the major labels scrambled to keep up with them in order to benefit from the emerging rock and roll subgenres. Without doubt Phillips's discovery of rockabilly artist Elvis Presley forever changed America's and the world's popular culture—visually, aurally, and sociologically. As Presley captured the world's attention, he crystallized the rockabilly style, paving the way for its commercial success in rock and roll's first decade. Greil Marcus summarizes the rockabilly phenomenon in his book *Mystery Train*: "Rockabilly was a very special music. For all of its unchained energy and outrage, it demanded a fine balance between white impulses and black, country and city, fantasies of freedom and the reality that produced those fantasies."[10]

NOTES

All charts positions referred to in the chapter are based on Joel Whitburn's Record Research publications, which compile *Billboard* charts information of the rock and roll era.

1. "Memphis Recording Service," permanent exhibit (Cleveland, OH: Rock and Roll Hall of Fame and Museum, May 26, 2003).

2. David P. Szatmary, *Rockin' in Time: A Social History of Rock-and-Roll*, 5th ed. (Upper Saddle River, NJ: Prentice Hall, 2004), 33.

3. Colin Escott and Martin Hawkins, *Good Rockin' Tonight: Sun Records and the Birth of Rock 'n' Roll* (New York: St. Martin's Press, 1991), 14–18, 155–157.

4. Ibid., 250–267.

5. Katherine Charlton, *Rock Music Styles: A History*, 4th ed. (Boston: McGraw-Hill, 2003), 58.

6. "Rave On: Rock and Roll in the Fifties," permanent exhibit (Cleveland, OH: Rock and Roll Hall of Fame and Museum, May 31, 2004).

7. Jim Miller, "Jerry Lee Lewis," in *The Rolling Stone Illustrated History of Rock & Roll*, 3rd ed., ed. Anthony DeCurtis, James Henke, and Holly George-Warren (New York: Random House, 1992), 76.

8. Charlie Gillett, *The Sound of the City: The Rise of Rock and Roll*, 2nd ed., enl. (New York: Da Capo Press, 1996), 23.

9. Arnold Shaw, *The Rockin' '50s: The Decade That Transformed the Pop Music Scene* (New York: Hawthorn Books, 1974), 187.

10. Greil Marcus, *Mystery Train: Images of America in Rock 'n' Roll Music*, 4th rev. ed. (New York: Penguin, 1997), 290.

ELVIS PRESLEY: "ALL SHOOK UP"

THE MAN AND HIS MUSIC

Elvis Presley is the most celebrated individual not only in '50s rock and roll, but perhaps in the history of the genre. He was the first rock and roll superstar. With his extravagant lifestyle and innovative music performances, he shattered both societal and musical barriers, changing American culture forever. Presley revolutionized American popular music by brilliantly melding country, gospel, pop, and blues while fusing these black and white genres to create his unique sound. With his music, he blurred racial borders that dissolved as if they never existed in music, while performing with a natural sexuality that made him a teen idol and a role model for generations of rockers.

Perhaps the most controversial musician in rock history, Presley not only thrilled but also threatened American society by journeying to the greatest extremes with his ability to imitate black blues singers and his nerve to cross color borders, combined with his flamboyant, uninhibited performance behaviors. His love of roots music and respect for the past, along with his rejection of it and his demand for uniqueness, combined with his desire to raise his financial and social status to give him an intense drive to succeed. Presley signaled to '50s society that it was time to be liberated, that it was okay to listen to and partake in exciting rock and roll music. He helped launch the '50s youth culture as teenagers acquired their own radios and record players. With Presley, popular music began to challenge conventional tastes, and exhilarating rock and roll music began to dominate society.

Ever since his amazing ascendance in the mid-1950s, every rock and roll performer has been measured against Presley. Today, many years after his death, his image and influence remain undiminished. Though he is not credited with inventing rock and roll, he has nonetheless held the title King of Rock and Roll. Presley's accomplishments as a recording artist are unparalleled. He is credited with having sold more than 1 billion records worldwide, and the Recording Industry Association of America has awarded him the most gold, platinum, and multiplatinum awards of any artist in history. As documented by *Billboard*, his chart performance is also unmatched. Throughout his career, Presley had 114 Top 40, 38 Top 10, and 18 No. 1 pop hits, many of which crossed to the R&B and country charts.[1]

Early Years

Born to Gladys and Vernon Presley on January 8, 1935, in East Tupelo, Mississippi, Elvis Aron Presley was an only child. His twin brother, Jesse Garon, was stillborn, which instilled intense feelings of guilt that remained with Elvis throughout his life. The loss of his brother and the inability to have more children made his mother overprotective of Elvis, and his father barely kept the family above the poverty level with erratic employment. The Presleys lived in a small, simple house built by Vernon with borrowed money on land they did not own; they later moved often, renting various properties. When he was growing up, Presley's ambition was to lead his parents out of poverty and to protect them, though he was plagued by feelings of inferiority. The family struggled to preserve its dignity and keep from being called white trash. While his father was in prison for altering a check (he was sentenced to three years but served eight months because of good behavior), Presley and his mother lived with cousins after losing their house. His childhood poverty and resulting shame created Presley's continual desire for love and attention; he sought a life that would authenticate him as someone special.

Presley found both peace and excitement in music; he had an instinctual love and passion for it that lasted throughout his life. His family attended the Assembly of God Church, where he became comfortable with expressive, fervent gospel music and joined the choir. Growing up near Shake Rag, the black section of Tupelo, he was exposed to rhythm and blues music and heard blues and spirituals on streets, in churches, and at tent revivals. He listened to gospel quartets and on the radio heard classical, swing jazz, pop, and country music (*Grand Ole Opry* on Saturday nights). From the Delta, he heard songs of heartache, desperation, and longing that dominated white Southern culture. Presley went to courthouse jamborees (live radio broadcasts of local performers) to hear musicians such as Mississippi Slim. He absorbed these and other music styles, including field hollers and work songs of black farmworkers and prisoners at Parchman State Penitentiary, where his father served his prison sentence. His family regularly engaged in music at church (singing) and for fun; Gladys was a notorious buck dancer, performing dance moves consisting of hip swivels and rotations with astonishing looseness and talent; some cite her as the source of her son's later hip gyrations. In 1945, Presley was a finalist in a statewide singing contest at the Mississippi–Alabama Fair and Dairy Show at the Tupelo Fairgrounds, singing "Ole Shep," a heartbreaking Red Foley song about a man forced to shoot his old dog. The next year, for his eleventh birthday, he received his first guitar and learned to play from his uncles, who were country musicians. Presley was ridiculed in school when he claimed he would someday perform on the *Grand Ole Opry*.

In 1948, seeking better prospects, the Presleys moved to Memphis, where all music came from the Delta. Living in a subsidized housing project, the thirteen-year-old Presley had the opportunity to hear expressive black music that he could relate to because he felt it reflected his sense of worthlessness. He spent much of his spare time in the black section of town, where on Beale Street he heard such bluesmen as Furry Lewis and B. B. King perform. With his cousin Gene Smith, he listened to spirituals and gospel music in church and to R&B on jukeboxes. He wore flashy clothing from Lansky's, a Beale Street store that outfitted R&B artists. In Memphis, Presley felt closer to black people, with whom he had cultural similarities. This lonely, shy, and awkward boy often twitched; his hands, legs, and feet continuously beat rhythmic patterns. He was ridiculed at school, where, surprisingly, he did not excel in music since his music teachers did not support his preference in music styles.

Music Years

The Rockabilly Juncture

After graduating from L. C. Humes High School in Memphis in 1953, Presley passionately wanted to be a singer. Though his early employment included working in a machine shop, on an assembly line (manufacturing rocket shells), and at Crown Electric Company (driving a truck), and though his father tried to discourage him from a career in music, Presley never lost his dream of becoming a star. After his talent was discovered and realized in July 1954, during the history-changing recording session of "That's All Right" at Sam Phillips's Sun Records Studio, Presley became an overnight phenomenon in Memphis and a regional success. Though listeners couldn't classify his first record as

The acetate disc recorded by Elvis Presley as a demo for Sun Records owner Sam Phillips is shown. It is among the items that were sold as part of an auction of rock 'n' roll memorabilia in 1995. © AP/Wide World Photos.

Elvis Presley, mid-1950s. Courtesy of Photofest.

either R&B or country music, they knew it sounded black though the singer was white. When Presley crossed racial lines with this first single, creating his unique sound complete with wailing voice, sexual energy, and rollicking drive, Southern poor folks (both black and white) felt he authenticated their lives. They believed he was speaking directly to them as he captured the qualities of both blues and country music—roots styles forever after blended in rock and roll. As Charlie Gillett states in *The Sound of the City*, Jimmie Rodgers sang white blues in the '20s, but it was Presley who made it work as pop music in the '50s.[2] (See chapter 3 for further information.)

Realizing how important music was to the bright, young Presley, Phillips especially enjoyed the singer's creative energy and rebellious streak that exploded in performance. In the second half of 1954 and throughout 1955, while recording the remainder of his classic Sun singles, Presley toured the South with Scotty Moore and Bill Black (as the Blue Moon Boys; Presley quickly stole the show). Phillips also secured him national exposure on the *Grand Ole Opry* and the *Louisiana Hayride*. Presley underwent an astounding transformation—the shy, reserved young man became a natural showman, developing a great rapport with his audiences. He developed his performance stance, moving spontaneously and extravagantly on stage. With sideburns and long hair in a pompadour, colorful shirts, and baggy pants, he engaged in histrionics like those of his role model, Jim "Big Chief" Wetherington, a member of his favorite gospel group, the Statesmen. Presley's performance movements were unmistakably sensual and shocking to '50s society, causing swooning girls to scream for more. He shook and rotated his legs (one stunt consisted of pretending his leg had a mind of its own while trying to make it behave), and with sensual rhythm moved freely to his music. In his early days, Presley spat, told crude jokes, and gestured lewdly on stage, but most important, he established his performance stance. He created what became the standard performance pose of rock and roll musicians—singing with guitar across hips, standing with feet far apart and knees bent. It is thought that this stance evolved from an African American dance in which one stood wide-legged in the position of laborers (workers spread their legs and bent their knees while rhythmically swaying to lift heavy loads, referred to as "rocking").

It has been assumed that Presley adapted this position into a sexual dance while performing music to signify his leaving poverty. By performing their music, Presley identified with black people, with whose cultural heritage he had much in common. While his mostly white, Southern working-class audience identified with Presley's music, his sound appealed to teenagers, bringing them a sense of joyous freedom from the constraints of conservative '50s society.

Since each of Presley's five Sun singles consisted of a blues song backed with a country tune, most were already familiar to their respective audiences and each sold better than its predecessor. From his first Sun single, "That's All Right," to his fifth and final, "Mystery Train," Presley developed a personal version of the music styles he had absorbed, singing in his high, clear tenor voice. He frequently used hiccups and intervallic leaps (similar to country musician Jimmie Rodgers's yodels in his 1928 "Waiting for a Train") on drawn-out syllables, as in "Baby Let's Play House," thus creating a sense of breathless desperation while allowing his usually clear enunciation to meld into the instrumental accompaniment at the ends of phrases (a Delta blues performance technique). And "Mystery Train" incorporated a countrylike vocal yelp in its final bars, similar to the "aw-haws" of Bob Wills in his 1940 classic, "New San Antonio Rose." Presley's impatient singing in "Mystery Train" matched the urgent and continuous rhythmic motion of a train created by the accompanying bass and guitar that emphasized the backbeat (a rock and roll trademark).

Showing an extraordinary talent for a white singer, Presley innovatively applied remarkable rhythmic emphasis to songs. His sound suggested a young white man celebrating freedom—he usually performed songs (covers) with a much quicker tempo than their originals. The beat was splendidly supplied in these early recordings by the bass and guitars, as in his second single, "Good Rockin' Tonight," where the plucked walking string bass arpeggiated chord tones of the three simple harmonies borrowed from the blues progression— tonic, subdominant, and dominant chords. Also borrowed from the blues in this song (and in "Baby Let's Play House") was the use of stop-time and call-and-response blues techniques. Unlike R&B songs, these early Presley recordings moved away from the blues by their use of lead guitar solos instead of the saxophone solos that were found in '50s songs by rhythm and blues-based musicians such as Little Richard. Though simple, the guitar solos in such early recordings as "That's All Right," "Good Rockin' Tonight," "Baby Let's Play House," and "Mystery Train" represented the new rock and roll sound. Musicologists claim that this significant use of guitar allows them to classify these as true rock and roll songs. This theory supports the strong argument made by many that Presley's "That's All Right" was the first rock and roll record.

Presley's 1955 cover of "Mystery Train," written by Little Junior Parker and first recorded by him and his Blue Flames for Sun Records in 1953, exemplifies the rockabilly sound, representing the balancing act between blues and country music. Presley's version is very different from the original, for each of these artists had his own sound. Both had outstanding voices, but Parker's was a definite R&B sound with low-register glissandi and melismas. Conversely, Presley used his distinctive country-oriented vocal style saturated with broken syllables and vibrato. In addition, his cover was faster and used the rhythmic guitar differently. Parker's original had a lead guitar solo played by bluesman Pat Hare that was stylistically different from that played by Moore in the cover (even though Moore bent notes in the blues style). Presley sang Parker's song in his own manner, retaining, to a point, the blues sound, complete with call-and-response. The song's lyrics contained a message to which many could relate: having to say goodbye to a loved one, wondering if she would be back. Released on August 1, 1955, "Mystery Train" displayed the same natural exuberance that Presley and his group first showed in "That's All Right" (though they had a better knowledge of themselves and their musical techniques than in 1954) and was a national hit (No. 11 on the country charts). Phillips realized that Presley achieved the sound he had been seeking. Phillips invested much effort in perfecting Presley's recordings in the studio, making them flawless, emotional, and spontaneous.

Presley moved in other musical directions after being pursued by Col. Thomas A. Parker (whose title was honorific), a country music promoter who had managed the careers of Eddy Arnold and Hank Snow. Believing that Presley could be a superstar, Parker was determined to manage the upcoming musician's career even though Bob Neal already represented him. In a shockingly manipulative manner, Parker moved in on Presley, offering to facilitate bookings for him. Though many have criticized the shrewd and relentless Parker (who arranged business contracts to his financial advantage) for having taken advantage of Presley (who knew he and his parents needed guidance even though Gladys didn't trust Parker), he was the one to advance Presley to national status. In spite of Parker's swindling him as Presley realized financial success, he still earned what was to him and his family a fabulous fortune. Parker acquired Presley's contract at Sun Records, dismissing the label as small-time, and initiated the deal with RCA-Victor to buy Presley's contract from Sun. Though Phillips detested Parker, financial strains forced him to accept the deal; he couldn't properly produce and market Presley's records and stay abreast of his growing fame. Thus Presley's contract was sold to RCA on November 21, 1955. (See chapter 5 for further information.)

The Fifties at RCA

The week of his twenty-first birthday, in January 1956, Presley began recording for RCA in Nashville. He experienced major changes during his time at the new label that affected him for the remainder of his life. Not only were the large company's recording techniques and business attitudes different from what he was used to at Sun Records, but Presley rose to national superstar status after the release of his first RCA record, "Heartbreak Hotel." While continuing to book Presley (who was then performing not only with Moore and

Black but also with drummer D. J. Fontana) for performances throughout the South, Parker decided to introduce him to the North via television. Thanks to appearances on network television programs in the first half of the year, Presley gained powerful publicity, placing him in the public's eye and helping him reach a major turning point in his career.

Most '50s television shows that included rock and roll singers were general entertainment shows, among them programs of Arthur Godfrey, Jackie Gleason, Steve Allen, and Ed Sullivan. Godfrey presented rock and roll (and R&B) to an audience that hadn't heard the music much on the radio. Gleason's show featured rock and roll less often, but nonetheless made a crucial contribution to the genre, and to Presley's career in particular, by having him appear six successive weeks (on the *Tommy and Jimmy Dorsey Stage Show*, the lead-in to Gleason) at the time of his first RCA release. Presley also appeared on the *Milton Berle Show*, the *Steve Allen Show*, and the *Ed Sullivan Show*. These appearances introduced him to large, appreciative national audiences while initiating a debate about the artistic value of rock and roll music. The singer's exceptional manners, good looks, and sincerity charmed the public; hordes of teenage fans adored him and his music. At the other end of the spectrum were the many critics who began to attack Presley, ridiculing both his performance behavior and his music. In a 1956 article about the future of rock and roll music, *Billboard* magazine, which generally gave Presley's recordings favorable reviews, gave the genre some negative publicity. This ignited a wave of rock and roll popularity, with small radio stations, indies, and musicians all responding enthusiastically in favor of rock and roll. Also at this time, Alan Freed's promotion of rock and roll, coupled with increasing numbers of fans rallying for it, made the music a commercial entity. Both good and bad elements of rock and roll acted as a catalyst for the music while thousands of fans purchased Presley's records each day.

The controversy steadily grew, but after Presley's performance of "Hound Dog" on the *Milton Berle Show* in June 1956, a national furor erupted. At the end of the song, he engaged in what were then considered horrendous and threatening actions. With outspread arms he fluttered his fingers, dragged the microphone to the floor while staggering to his knees, and circled the mike sensuously while jackknifing his legs. These movements horrified adults and delighted teenagers. Presley amplified teens' dissatisfaction with postwar America and greatly assisted in revamping '50s society. James Dean in *Rebel Without a Cause* had been their rebel hero until this point, when they chose Presley as their new youth rebellion icon. The show was a hit despite outbursts of criticism that referred to Presley as vulgar, indecent, and threatening to America's youth. Some branded him untalented and without formal training or restraint. His wild performance stance brought Presley many labels, among them Elvis the Pelvis and the Hillbilly Cat. Hurt and angered by the attacks, he proclaimed his innocence, stating he wasn't attempting to be sexy and was merely expressing feelings. Nonetheless, he was a distinct target, as Peter

Guralnick states in *Last Train to Memphis*: "Juvenile delinquency, a widespread breakdown of morality and cultural values, race mixing, riots, and irreligion all were being blamed on Elvis Presley and rock 'n' roll by a national press that was seemingly just awakening to the threat, the popularity of the new music among the young, and, of course, the circulation gains that could always be anticipated from a great hue and cry."[3]

Though television host Steve Allen was warned not to have the singer on his show, he invited Presley to appear on the *Steve Allen Show* on July 1, 1956. To eradicate rumors that Presley was a sexual danger, NBC announced that Allen would present a new, sanitized Presley, and an attempt was made to calm down the wild performer. On the program, clad in a tuxedo, Presley was required to sing "Hound Dog" to a basset hound dressed in a bow tie and top hat. The humiliated artist didn't appear on national television again until that September. Dave Marsh gives an account of the experience in *Elvis*: "Elvis cringed, but he never quit; he proved that he really was a trouper. As a result, Allen's contempt and condescending attitude backfired. Elvis became bigger than ever after this appearance."[4]

Originally resistant to having him on his show, television host Ed Sullivan finally relented because of Presley's immense popularity, booking the singer, who was paid the then astounding sum of $50,000 for three appearances: September 9 and October 28, 1956, and January 6, 1957. Gaining huge visibility from the *Ed Sullivan Show*, Presley was launched into national consciousness. His first appearance attracted over 82 percent of the viewing audience (the highest ratings in television history) when Presley performed such songs as "Don't Be Cruel," "Love Me Tender," "Love Me," "Too Much," and a cover of Little Richard's 1956 "Ready Teddy." As unrelenting charges of vulgarity and lewdness persisted, for his third appearance Presley was televised only from the waist up, in order not to subject America to his wild stage moves below the belt. This third time Presley performed many songs on the air, including "Don't Be Cruel" and "Peace in the Valley" (written by black gospel composer Thomas A. Dorsey and popularized by country singer Red Foley), with the Jordanaires supplying background vocals. After this last appearance, Sullivan endorsed Presley to his audience: "Elvis, ladies and gentlemen . . . I wanted to say to Elvis Presley and the country that this is a real decent, fine boy, and . . . we want to say that we've never had a pleasanter experience on our show with a big name than we've had with you."[5]

While attempting to prove his musical worthiness to the world that summer, Presley traveled to New York City and recorded "Don't Be Cruel," "Hound Dog," and "Any Way You Want Me," all of which became enormously popular and displayed his exuberant spirit. The young, unseasoned artist was perplexed by his newfound celebrity. He had quickly been swept up in fame and fortune, and his records moved beyond the Southern working class to middle-class young America, who responded favorably to his energy and musical beat. Presley's financial difficulties disappeared forever. He purchased his parents a home in Memphis complete with a pink Cadillac in the driveway (a gift for his mother even though she didn't drive) and began to live a new, extravagant life.

Known as the Year of Elvis, 1956 was Presley's biggest year. As he became accustomed to his new roles with RCA and his new lifestyle as a rock and roll superstar, *Variety* bestowed the title King of Rock and Roll upon him. That spring, his first RCA single, "Heartbreak Hotel," which caused raging hysteria among his audiences, became a No. 1 hit where it remained for eight weeks on the pop charts and seventeen weeks on the country charts, and his first album, *Elvis Presley*, peaked at No.1 and stayed there for ten weeks. Presley signed a contract appointing Parker his manager and paying him 25 percent of his earnings, projected to continue through Presley's lifetime and beyond. That year, while transforming himself into the King, the young artist underwent significant changes personally and professionally. His Sun days were behind him, and he was in the big leagues with a major record label and a national career. Presley became isolated in a protective cocoon, an aura of secrecy and suspicion encircling him; Parker kept people (even friends and accompanying musicians) away from him. A compulsive perfectionist, Presley spent much time in the recording studio, but eventually realized he couldn't recapture his Sun Records sound with the new RCA technology and accepted his new sound. Also at that time, he developed an instinct for commercial songs, showing an intuitive knack for recording appropriate pop songs (which he had relied on Sam Phillips to provide earlier). He continued to tour more widely and to perform at larger venues. In addition, with plans to remove Presley from the rock and roll controversy, introduce him to a wider audience, and to give him a more wholesome image, Parker sent him to Hollywood for a screen test that spring. Presley was awarded a multimovie contract with Paramount Pictures. Parker's strategy had paid off.[6]

After "Heartbreak Hotel," many of Presley's 1956 singles were big hits: "I Was the One," "Blue Suede Shoes," "I Want You, I Need You, I Love You," "My Baby Left Me," "Don't Be Cruel," "Hound Dog," "Love Me Tender," "Anyway You Want Me (That's How I Will Be)," "Love Me," and "When My Blue Moon Turns to Gold Again." Quickly becoming the idol of millions of teenagers, Presley was the first rock and roll musician to appear in films with consistent commercial success. He starred in the first of his thirty-one movies, *Love Me Tender*, which premiered at the New York Paramount Theater on November 15, 1956, and was a box office smash, recouping its $1 million production cost in three days. This black-and-white Civil War drama featured the young, vibrant, and sexy Presley singing the title song, which he had performed on his first appearance on the *Ed Sullivan Show* to a record viewing audience estimated at 54 million. This No.1 song was released in December on the album *Love Me Tender*. Presley starred in three more movies before the end of the decade: *Loving You* (1957), *Jailhouse Rock* (1957), and *King Creole* (1958)—the four films often considered his best.

In 1957, as his popularity soared and he became the most famous young man in the world, Presley purchased Graceland, a mansion on the outskirts of Memphis, where he and his parents could have privacy from the fans who were becoming unbearable. On the large estate, Gladys returned to her simple life of gardening and raising chickens; in this huge house, isolated with servants, her health deteriorated. Depressed and nervous about her son, she always worried for his safety. Presley, constantly away filming movies and touring, occasionally returned to Graceland for visits, though not often enough for his mother. Also in 1957, his friends and backup musicians, Scotty Moore and Bill Black (already excluded from future royalties thanks to Parker) were phased out, eventually resigning because of financial stress. They recorded with him only sporadically during the 1960s. Although the two were essential to developing Presley's musical style and sound, Parker and RCA preferred to hire studio musicians to accompany Presley (though drummer D. J. Fontana continued to perform with him through 1968). The King's impressive list of 1957 hits included "Poor Boy," "Too Much," "Playing for Keeps," "All Shook Up," "(There'll Be) Peace in the Valley (for Me)" (his first gospel re-

Elvis Presley in *Jailhouse Rock*, 1957. Courtesy of the Library of Congress.

lease), "(Let Me Be Your) Teddy Bear," "Loving You," "Jailhouse Rock," and "Treat Me Nice."

Drafted into the U.S. Army in December 1957, Presley reported for duty in March 1958, unhappy and fearing his career would end during his two-year absence. However, Parker, who urged Presley to enter regular military duty to display patriotism, intentionally kept Presley out of Special Services (which would have used his talents as an entertainer). He took measures to maintain Presley's career and make sure he was not forgotten, promoting Presley as a patriotic, honorable man performing his duty and fostering an all-American image for him. Parker occasionally released singles recorded by Presley before he entered the army (that sold millions) and would not allow him to perform while in the army (to create even more of a demand for him). After basic training, Private Presley settled at Fort Hood, Texas, and rented a house for his parents, his friend Lamar Fike (his bodyguard), and his cousins Gene and Junior Smith to live with him. That summer, Gladys returned home to Memphis in poor health; she was hospitalized, and died of a heart attack on August 14. The loss of his mother (whom he referred to as his main girl) devastated Presley, though it also liberated him from the double life of sexual icon-rebel rocker and polite, caring mama's boy. Without her moral authority, restraints on his life were gone. He engaged in outrageously impulsive, extravagant, and domineering actions as he entered a new phase of his life.

Germany was Presley's next military assignment; for seventeen months he completed his army duty while his father, grandmother, and two of his Memphis friends lived with him, satisfying his increasing need to surround himself with many

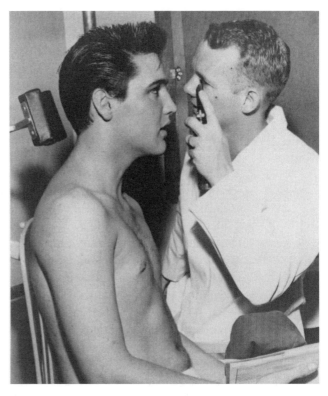

Elvis Presley being examined as part of induction into the army, 1957. Courtesy of the Library of Congress.

people for companionship and security. Homesick and depressed during his time overseas, Presley began self-destructive behavior patterns in Germany that continued for the rest of his life. He was introduced to drugs by his army superiors, came to rely on pills for physical strength and courage, and became a night person, engaging in all-night activities with friends. Presley fell in love with Priscilla Beaulieu, a fourteen-year-old army officer's stepdaughter who eventually became his wife. Before entering the army in 1958, Presley had had two hit singles, "Don't" and "I Beg of You," which, along with others released while he was on active duty, became hits in absentia: "Wear My Ring Around Your Neck," "Doncha' Think It's Time," "Hard Headed Woman," "Don't Ask Me Why," "One Night," "I Got Stung," "(Now and Then There's) A Fool Such as I," "I Need Your Love Tonight," "A Big Hunk o' Love," and "My Wish Came True." Upon his release from the military in March 1960, his new single, "Stuck on You," quickly reached No. 1, and he appeared on Frank Sinatra's television program performing "Witchcraft" as a duet with Sinatra and "Love Me Tender" as a solo. At first, the new, restrained Presley feared Sinatra because of the latter's previous derogatory remarks about rock and roll (and especially after Steve Allen had mocked Presley on television), but to his surprise Sinatra enjoyed the performance, and the King made a triumphant return.

As Presley swept the nation with his RCA hits, his musical style changed from his earlier Sun sound. With Steve Sholes (RCA's Southern A&R representative) as his producer in Nashville, Presley immediately reached a massive audience, in part assisted by the new Top 40 format. While thoroughly impressed by the novelty of the singer's vocal style, his uninhibited stage movements, and his electrifying effects on audiences, Sholes was committed to recouping RCA's investment in Presley. Presley's RCA records, on which he sometimes performed with country great Chet Atkins (and sometimes was produced by Atkins), featured vocal groups, heavily electrified guitars, and drums, all of which were considered taboo by both country music and country rock audiences; his backup vocal groups included the Jordanaires. In reaction to these new and unfamiliar accompaniments, Presley's voice became deeper, more theatrical, and increasingly self-conscious as he sought to create excitement and emotion (which he achieved naturally on his Sun records) in his recordings. A self-pitying tone quality entered his vocal style, as opposed to the sound of impatient enjoyment, which was a common mood on his Sun recordings. Presley vocally interpreted a succession of themes with admirable conviction and an increasingly mannered style in his early RCA releases: "Heartbreak Hotel" required a voice of despair; "Hound Dog" required a curt, sarcastic, and tough voice; "Don't Be Cruel" required a breathy, light vocal style; and "Love Me Tender" required the calm, soothing voice of a ballad singer. His subsequent releases had similar vocal expressions, and emotions were also supplied in backup accompaniments.

Presley was swept up in one of the most fabulous success rides any musician has ever experienced. His recording accomplishments are unparalleled in the history of rock and roll music. Having achieved a groundbreaking number of hits, in 1956 he had his first No. 1, "Heartbreak Hotel," backed with "I Was the One." Like his Sun releases, this record coupled modified country and blues, attempting to re-create the Sun sound. In these records from his first recording sessions, RCA supplemented the typical bare Sun instrumental accompaniments of slapped bass and rhythm guitar with a much fuller orchestral sound, complete with echo, while keeping the guitar prominent and adding piano filler (Floyd Cramer) and drums (D. J. Fontana). With its relaxed tempo, "Heartbreak Hotel" contained a simple rockabilly electric guitar solo similar to those created at Sun Records, though here it traded off with a blueslike piano solo while accompanied by a walking bass (as at Sun) supplying simple harmonies from the blues progression. Sung in Presley's new deeper and desperate-sounding voice, in a melodramatic, sexual style complete with reverberation, the song's lyrics spoke directly to teenagers who were feeling lonely and desperate in their quest for independence from parents and society in general. With its desperate, gloomy sound, "Heartbreak Hotel" had sales that quickly spread from the country to the pop and then the R&B markets. With this first RCA hit that remained at the top of *Billboard*'s charts, Presley proved that rock and roll could appeal simultaneously to audiences of all three styles of music.

Presley brought "Hound Dog" into his repertoire after seeing Freddie Bell and the Bellboys perform it in Las Vegas, even though he knew the original recording by Big Mama Thornton, a No. 1 R&B hit in 1953. Though based upon Bell's version, Presley's very distinctive and popular cover caused the song thereafter to be associated with him. He used a much quicker tempo than Thornton's original, along with prominent drums accenting a strong backbeat, stop-time technique, and polyrhythms resulting from the addition of hand-claps. Provided by a male chorus singing sustained-note harmonies of the twelve-bar blues pattern (repeated eight times, as in the original), backup vocals figured prominently in the two solo guitar sections. As in the blues, electric guitar fills answered the voice's melody throughout, and the guitar solos reflected the honky-tonk country style. The bass provided a riff pattern styled after those played by the saxophone in Bill Haley's version of "Shake, Rattle and Roll." Presley's singing talent was evident as he blended the different strains of American popular music into one rebellious voice. He sang "Hound Dog" in a polished, urban blueslike style and tone quality, whereas the original by Thornton consisted of rough, classic blues-styled vocals, complete with her voice imitating a barking dog. In the cover, Presley drastically changed the song's lyrics, singing them as a man singing to a woman who has no more value to him than a hound dog that cannot catch rabbits, whereas Thornton's lyrics were sung by a woman to a man who had cheated on her. Presley's version, backed with "Don't Be Cruel," reached the No. 1 position on all three charts; it remained in the peak position for eleven weeks on the pop, ten weeks on the country, and six weeks on the R&B.

Following the "Hound Dog" and "Don't Be Cruel" single, RCA released records that were cover versions of previous R&B hits (some of them probably recorded with Sam Phillips for release on Sun before the RCA contract), such as his cover of Lloyd Price's "Lawdy, Miss Clawdy." Charlie Gillett claims in *The Sound of the City* that Presley's style began to change with his early 1957 No. 1's, "Too Much" and "All Shook Up," which displayed a modified vocal style with the dragging of vowels and the unnecessary accenting of every other beat, and that some of the songs for Presley's films (*Loving You* and *Jailhouse Rock*) also allowed him to exaggerate his feelings and begin his transformation toward more dramatic and pop-styled songs. According to Gillett, Presley's "It's Now or Never" (1960; No. 1 pop hit) displayed the inevitable change with its operatic vocal quality resulting from Presley's abandonment of the culture that produced his original style, making him essentially a competent and charismatic pop music singer with a devoted audience.[7]

THE TOP 40 HITS

With his lengthy string of hits, Elvis Presley set in motion the rock and roll style of music that dominated the world for the rest of the twentieth century. Of his 114 Top 40 hits, thirty-two of them were between 1956 and 1959. The list below shows each of these hits with its highest chart position, in chronological order by the date it debuted in the Top 40.[8]

Title	Date	Position
"Heartbreak Hotel"	March 10, 1956	1
"I Was the One"	March 17, 1956	19
"Blue Suede Shoes"	April 28, 1956	20
"I Want You, I Need You, I Love You"	June 2, 1956	1
"My Baby Left Me"	June 9, 1956	31
"Don't Be Cruel"	August 4, 1956	1
"Hound Dog"	August 4, 1956	1
"Love Me Tender"	October 20, 1956	1
"Anyway You Want Me (That's How I Will Be)"	November 10, 1956	20
"Love Me"	November 24, 1956	2
"When My Blue Moon Turns to Gold Again"	December 29, 1956	19
"Poor Boy"	January 5, 1957	24
"Too Much"	January 26, 1957	1
"Playing for Keeps"	February 9, 1957	21
"All Shook Up"	April 6, 1957	1
"(There'll Be) Peace in the Valley (for Me)"	April 29, 1957	25
"(Let Me Be Your) Teddy Bear"	June 24, 1957	1
"Loving You"	July 8, 1957	20
"Jailhouse Rock"	October 14, 1957	1
"Treat Me Nice"	October 21, 1957	18
"Don't"	January 27, 1958	1
"I Beg of You"	February 3, 1958	8
"Wear My Ring Around Your Neck"	April 21, 1958	2
"Doncha' Think It's Time"	May 5, 1958	15

THE TOP 40 HITS (*continued*)

"Hard Headed Woman"	June 30, 1958	1
"Don't Ask Me Why"	July 14, 1958	25
"One Night"	November 10, 1958	4
"I Got Stung"	November 10, 1958	8
"(Now and Then There's) A Fool Such as I"	March 30, 1959	2
"I Need Your Love Tonight"	March 30, 1959	4
"A Big Hunk o' Love"	July 13, 1959	1
"My Wish Came True"	July 13, 1959	12

Of these extremely powerful songs, twelve were No. 1's, and five were No. 1 on all three charts—pop, country, and R&B: "Don't Be Cruel," "Hound Dog," "All Shook Up," "(Let Me Be Your) Teddy Bear," and "Jailhouse Rock." Presley continued his success, achieving a total of eighteen No. 1 pop hits in his career, along with numerous other No. 1's on other charts. In the history of the world, few artists have achieved so much.

Presley's immense success dominated the music industry from 1956 to 1963; in the '50s alone, he had multiple gold, platinum, and multiplatinum singles. According to Whitburn's Record Research publications, in his first two years with RCA, Presley had the best-selling record in 61 of 104 weeks. His reign over the charts testifies not only to his popularity but also to effective promotion by the record label and careful management by Parker. In the '60s and '70s, when his production of No. 1's slowed down, Presley's recordings were nevertheless million-sellers throughout the world. Realizing that the singer's versatile voice allowed people of all types and interests to identify with him, and anxious to retain that audience and enlarge it, RCA gradually transformed Presley's vocal style to more of a croon. This soft pop sound was apparent in such songs as "Can't Help Falling in Love" (1961).

After returning from military duty in March 1960, Presley had five more No. 1 hits in the early '60s: "Stuck on You" (1960), "It's Now or Never" (1960), "Are You Lonesome Tonight?" (1960), "Surrender" (1961), and "Good Luck Charm" (1962). Though he had a host of other Top 10 singles in the early '60s, he left the concert stage and concentrated on starring in movies, most of which had concurrently released sound track albums (some became No. 1's, such as G. I. Blues and Blue Hawaii, and others became Top 10s), and also recorded sacred songs, his favorite type to sing. As most American rock and rollers were swept away by the British Invasion in the '60s, Presley did not disappear. When the

Beatles (great fans of Presley) dominated the airwaves, the King continued recording, and many records became Top 40 hits. In 1967, Presley married Priscilla Beaulieu (they divorced in 1973), and the next year their only child, Lisa Marie, was born. In 1969, he began performing in Las Vegas, and as a result of his revival as a performer, he released a series of successful singles, some considered to be the most mature and satisfying music of his career, including the 1969 No. 1 hit, "Suspicious Minds." In addition to Las Vegas performances in the '70s, he toured the country, playing to capacity crowds until his death; his last concert was in Indianapolis, Indiana, on June 26, 1977. Just prior to embarking on a new tour, Presley died of heart failure at Graceland on August 16, 1977, at the age of forty-two. His stature as a cultural icon has continued to grow even after his death.

THE IMPACT

Elvis Presley's celebrity was an amazing phenomenon that gripped the entire nation. This rock and roll singer impacted '50s society like no other. Teenagers went wild with excitement. Their parents became exceedingly anxious over his overt sexuality. And Presley mania swept the world. After the advertising industry great Hank Saperstein joined Parker's team in mid-1956, Presley's name and picture appeared on all types of products. By 1957, the American market was saturated with Presley promotional material, from bobby socks and shoes to charm bracelets and lipstick. Presley purses, pencils, soft drinks, skirts, blouses, and pants inundated America. There were seventy-eight products that grossed approximately $55 million by the end of the year. In the midst of this popularity, the national press attacked Presley. Not only newspaper (such as the *New York Times*) and magazine (including *Time*) writers blasted him, but government officials (among them Congressman Robert MacDonald of Massachusetts) and religious leaders (such as Rev. Robert Gray of Trinity Baptist Church in Jacksonville, Florida, who warned the youth in his congregation not to attend an upcoming Presley concert) did, too. Because of his street-tough image and exciting performances, Presley was continuously accused of spurring juvenile delinquency, a major topic of concern as the generation gap widened between '50s teens and their parents. Repeatedly dismissed as vulgar, incompetent, and a negative influence, the King of Rock and Roll nonetheless reigned supreme and rose above these reactions.

The King of Rock and Roll was, and still is, one of the most popular modern heroes. He was the first rock and roll idol. He virtually invented the sound, demeanor, and stance of the rock and roll star. This trailblazer had an enormous impact on society and influence on future rock and roll music in both America and Britain. For young American musicians, his influence was far-reaching, even though he was perceived by the industry as a mere teen idol, the marketing approach applied to most of his contemporaries. Like the pop teen idols,

Presley relied on songwriters and producers to supply his repertoire of songs, whereas the trend of 1960s rock and roll (with such groups as the Beatles and the Rolling Stones in the forefront) was for groups to compose, arrange, and perform their own songs. Presley's influence reached both professional and amateur musicians, including such extremes as rocker Bruce Springsteen and saxophonist President Bill Clinton. Of Presley's September 9, 1956, performance on the *Ed Sullivan Show*, Pamela Clarke Keogh comments in *Elvis Presley: The Man. The Life. The Legend.* that when Presley performed, the crowd was beside themselves, screaming and carrying on, "This was most of young America's introduction to Elvis Presley. Bruce Springsteen was nine years old, sitting in front of the TV, and his mother had *Ed Sullivan* on, and on came Elvis. 'I remember right from that time, I looked at her and I said, "I wanna be just . . . like . . . that."' In Hope, Arkansas, ten-year-old Billy Clinton and his mom were watching, too."[9]

With the spontaneous music that flowed from his soul, the extraordinary output of this vivacious artist sparked the teen idol craze in the late '50s. After Sam Phillips's discovery of Presley, every record producer across the country looked for young singers with potential, particularly if they came from Memphis. While attempting to re-create him, they sought the characteristics (dark features, greasy black hair, and surly expression) that would make musicians look good in pictures in teen magazines and exaggerated the elements that made Presley so popular. By 1957, Presley proved that once the array of catchy novelty and suitable R&B songs had been exhausted, new types of songs were necessary for rock and roll. The music needed a strong beat, captivating chorus, and relevance to adolescent life. In 1957, while teen songs were popular as many teen idols entered popular music, producers in Philadelphia took Presley's image and repackaged it in such artists as Frankie Avalon and Fabian. Producers began to record music that had worked for Presley, using electric guitars, piano, harmonica, saxophone, and vocal groups to embellish arrangements and give records more teenage appeal.

The undisputed King of Rock and Roll who rose from humble circumstances, launched the rock and roll revolution, and became a superstar whose like the world had never seen before, has had enduring power as a cultural force. The charismatic, impassioned singer embraced the celebrity brought him by a host of hit records and movies, and for millions of people he embodied the rebel spirit in spite of his personal fears. The soft-spoken, working-class Southern boy who walked into Sam Phillips's recording studio in 1953 could never have been prepared for the unprecedented magnitude of his success or the fiery controversies he would arouse. With his ascendance from regional to national music star and Hollywood actor occurring so swiftly, and with a talent and impact that defied category in the mid-'50s, Elvis Presley became a mythical figure. He continues to be revered by music fans and has been studied in a number of works by authors including Dave Marsh, Greil Marcus, and Peter Guralnick. The number of books that have been published about him reveals Presley's unparalleled impact on the world; by 2001, in the United States alone there were more than 300 books. Presley received several honors and awards, among them the 1971 Grammy Lifetime Achievement Award and his 1998 induction into the Country Music Hall of Fame. In 1986, this sensation who defined rock and roll music's experience was among the first ten performers inducted into the Rock and Roll Hall of Fame.

NOTES

All charts positions referred to in the chapter are based on Joel Whitburn's Record Research publications, which compile *Billboard* charts information of the rock and roll era.

1. Joel Whitburn, *The Billboard Book of Top 40 Hits* (New York: Billboard Books, 2000), 500–504.

2. Charlie Gillett, *The Sound of the City: The Rise of Rock and Roll*, 2nd ed., enl. (New York: Da Capo Press, 1996), 27.

3. Peter Guralnick, *Last Train to Memphis: The Rise of Elvis Presley* (Boston: Little, Brown, 1994), 285.

4. Dave Marsh, *Elvis* (New York: Times Books, 1982), 106.

5. Guralnick, *Last Train to Memphis*, 379.

6. Howard A. DeWitt, *Elvis, the Sun Years: The Story of Elvis Presley in the Fifties* (Ann Arbor, MI: Popular Culture, Ink., 1993), 264–265.

7. Gillett, *The Sound of the City*, 55.

8. Whitburn, *The Billboard Book of Top 40 Hits*, 500–502.

9. Pamela Clarke Keogh, *Elvis Presley: The Man. The Life. The Legend* (New York: Atria Books, 2004), 88.

DOO-WOP: "OH WHAT A NITE"

THE VOCAL GROUP SOUND

Emerging from the rhythm and blues tradition early in the '50s, the softer, gentler doo-wop sound took its place alongside other rock and roll subgenres. Similar to rockabilly, doo-wop was mostly spontaneous and informal music created by amateur but determined musicians. Impromptu performances abounded in this very popular style, many of them preserved on recordings that are now collectors' dreams. With its roots in gospel, jazz, blues, and R&B, the doo-wop sound was performed by vocal groups of three to six (mostly four or five) members, consisting of a lead and background singers performing in close harmony, often a cappella, though usually recorded with background instrumental accompaniment (supplied by musicians active in other areas of R&B) obscured by the power of the voices. Scads of vocal groups performing in this style emerged in the 1950s, including such prominent ensembles as the Moonglows, the Flamingos, the Chords, the Five Satins, and Frankie Lymon and the Teenagers. Especially popular doo-wop groups were the Drifters, the Platters, and the Coasters, creating rock and roll concurrently with the sounds of Bo Diddley, Chuck Berry, Fats Domino, Little Richard, and Elvis Presley.

Often referred to as rhythm and blues, this urban subgenre was popular in large cities such as New York, Philadelphia, and Boston, where white ensembles who admired and emulated black groups became enormously popular later in the '50s and early '60s. At first consisting of Italian Americans (then followed by Anglo-Americans and Hispanics), many white vocal groups, such as Dion and the Belmonts, the Capris, the Diamonds, and Danny & the Juniors, sang in a slightly different style from contemporary black groups, one closer to the Tin Pan Alley pop sound. Nonetheless, all doo-wop ensembles sang songs with general similarities—simple music with a gentle beat, light instrumentation, and group harmony created by a range of voice types from bass to falsetto. For these groups of usually inexperienced teenage musicians, singing on street corners was a fun pastime and a way to attract girls.

With roots in the late nineteenth-century barbershop singing style, doo-wop incorporated similar voice types. A lead vocalist, sometimes a tenor or high tenor (such as the Ravens' Maithe Williams [Maithe Marshall]), a young high tenor (such as the Teenagers' Frankie Lymon), or a regular tenor (such as the Capris' Nick Santamaria), sang the melody and lyrics while lower background voices (second tenor, baritone, and bass) resounded underneath. Sometimes groups featured a low baritone or bass voice as lead (as in the El Dorados' "Bim Bam Boom" or the Coasters' "Zing Went the Strings of My Heart"); others used double leads—for example, the Orioles' tenor, Earlington Tilghman (Sonny Til), occasionally yielded to baritone George Nelson to lead during a song's bridge. No matter what the lead's voice type, the influence of gospel music was apparent in melismatic, expressive singing throughout the repertoire. Singers often embellished melodies with ornaments and extra syllables, as in the Platters' "Only You," when lead singer Tony Williams gently stretched out the syllables of the word "only" (comparable to rockabilly's hiccup technique). When applied by background singers, this vocal practice (referred to as blow-harmony technique) resulted from syllabic sounds formed by blowing air out of the mouth (for example, "ah-*hoo*"). At the low end of the pitch spectrum, the bass singer often provided the introduction to a song, as in the Continentals' "Fine, Fine Frame," and punctuated between verses of a song, as in the Hi-Fives' "Dorothy." Sometimes basses blended with the other voices' harmony, and other times they freely sang their own line, as in Dion and the Belmonts' "I Wonder Why."

Two other common bass characteristics in doo-wop were providing a talking bridge in which the bass singer dramatically talked his way through a section of the song (as in the Checkers' "My Prayer Tonight") and providing a percussive beat, imitating a string bass. With the human voice as the main component of the style, doo-woppers sang songs with mostly romantic lyrics (usually lead singers on the melody) while utilizing nonsense syllables (mostly the background singers in harmony). This repertoire represented a more conservative approach to love songs with topics of tender love and valentine relationships, whereas other rhythm and blues-influenced rock and roll songs voiced urgent sexual activity, such as those by Little Richard.

The use of nonsense syllables proliferated in the style, eventually giving the subgenre its label. The syllables "doo-wop" were heard as background filler (a black gospel influence) in recordings starting in the '30s, though the term was not applied to the music until after the subgenre's heyday; it was simply referred to as rock and roll or R&B in the '50s. In response to the lead, background singers performed meaningless vocalizations, such as "doo-wah" and "doo-wop," sometimes as simple monosyllables ("boom") and occasionally as complex multisyllables ("ting-a-ling" and "oodly-pop-a-cow"). At times, background singers repeated syllables or a few words from the lead singer's lyrics, but the use of meaningless vocal sounds prevailed. Originating in African American music (specifically West African chants), the use of syllables surfaced in jazz subgenres with Louis Armstrong and others vocally improvising (scatting) to imitate their instruments. In the doo-wop style, with much of the music created a cappella on street corners in African American and Italian American neighborhoods by musicians too poor to afford musical instruments, the syllables were used to replace instruments (such as the string bass), while handclaps and finger snaps supplied rhythm (in place of drums). Appealing to the ear, by the turn of the '50s, nonsense syllables became essential to the signature doo-wop sound. By the mid-1950s, they were found in abundance in classic doo-wop songs, such as the Crows' "Gee" and the Spaniels' "Goodnite Sweetheart, Goodnite."

Another signature musical characteristic of the doo-wop sound was a basic harmonic progression. Commonly referred to as the doo-wop progression, it consisted of the tonic followed by the submediant-seventh, supertonic-seventh, and dominant-seventh chords (I-vi7-ii7-V7; for example, the C, Am7, Dm7, and G7 chords in the tonality of C), as found in the Chords' 1954 song, "Sh-Boom." Sometimes varied with the subdominant (IV) substituted for the supertonic-seventh (ii7) chord, this progression was the harmonic basis of many songs in the doo-wop style. Its customary use in approximately the same harmonic rhythm made doo-wop songs sound alike. A distinctive rhythmic characteristic of the repertoire was the use of triplet patterns, often appearing as repeated chords (three per beat) in accompaniments with bass and melody lines using uneven beat subdivisions (as in boogie-woogie and swing jazz) to complement them, as in the Penguins' "Earth Angel."

Carried mainly by the human voice, instrumentation was relegated to a secondary role as accompaniment in these songs—a major difference between the doo-wop sound and other '50s rock and roll styles. However, there were exceptions, most notably in bridges when a saxophonist performed a solo for a few measures before singers reentered. Saxophonists such as Curtis Ousley (King Curtis, a favorite R&B session soloist and bandleader and a 2000 inductee of the Rock and Roll Hall of Fame) were famous for their brief instrumental interludes in this otherwise primarily vocal music. Sometimes guitars were played in doo-wop song bridges, especially on recordings of the small record labels. The common AAB phrase structure of many uptempo doo-wop songs was borrowed from the urban blues and ultimately from the Delta blues.

In addition to being influenced by the barbershop singing style, the doo-wop sound was inspired by the secular music of gospel-influenced black vocal groups of the early twentieth century, such as the Mills Brothers, who sang four-part harmony in a smooth, sophisticated style during the 1920s and 1930s; the Ink Spots, whose high tenor lead voice often yielded to the bass singer for spoken lyrics accompanied by the rest of the group humming chord tones during the 1930s; the Ravens, whose pianist played a constant triplet pattern behind the group's vocals during the 1940s; and the Orioles, who during the '40s inspired a number of groups named after birds that appeared in the early and mid-1950s (among them the Larks and the Flamingos). These four innovative vocal ensembles paved the way for the thousands of doo-wop groups that emerged across America from the late 1940s through the early 1960s.

Doo-Wop Forerunners

Black vocal group harmony existed in America well before the Civil War. Always a spontaneous and unrehearsed sound, it was first sung by slaves while completing tasks on Southern plantations and then by early groups, such as the Dinwiddie Colored Quartet (the first black group to record on the flat disc format), at the turn of the twentieth century. Following the black gospel and barbershop quartet music that flourished during the first two decades of the twentieth century were songs of the Mills Brothers and the Ink Spots, whose unique sounds (musical arrangements and vocal imitations of musical instruments) made these groups tremendously popular. Many others copied their sound and capitalized on the new R&B (race) music, such as, in the '40s, the Delta Rhythm Boys, the Cats and the Fiddle, and the Deep River Boys. During the late 1940s, the Ravens and the Orioles made recordings that are often considered the beginning of R&B vocal group harmony, and they are credited with fathering the subgenre's groups, since an overwhelming majority of those that followed were in some way influenced by them.

Emerging in 1931 from Piqua, Ohio, the Mills Brothers—Herbert, Harry, Donald, and John Jr. (replaced after his death by his father, John Sr.)—were one of the first groups to achieve great commercial success and among the earliest African American ensembles to attract a nationwide following with many hit songs. They accompanied their vocal arrangements with vocally imitated musical instruments, as in their 1931 No. 1 pop song, "Tiger Rag." According to

The Mills Brothers, 1951. Courtesy of the Library of Congress.

legend, this innovative vocal technique began when they forgot their kazoos (their trademark accompanying instrument) for a performance, so they used improvised vocalizations instead (cupping their hands). This pleased their audience so much that they incorporated the technique into their act. Thus the human orchestra, complete with horn and string bass imitations, was invented. The vocally imitated instrumental timbres were so convincing that the Brunswick label printed an announcement on their record labels stating that no musical instruments other than guitar were used on the recordings.[1] The Mills Brothers were the first black group to attain widespread popularity with white audiences and they were role models for the many vocal groups recording in the early-to-mid-1950s.

In addition to mimicking instruments, the Mills Brothers are credited with the first incorporation of a talking bridge into a song (as in 1932's "Rockin' Chair"), though there may have been earlier examples of this vocal practice. Nevertheless, the Ink Spots' bass, Orville "Hoppy" Jones, was best known for talking bridge solos in hit ballads beginning in 1939 (as in "If I Didn't Care"). Following choruses of their lead tenor, Bill Kenny, the Spots provided humming backgrounds over which Jones delivered powerfully recited emotional love messages, followed by Kenny singing the final chorus. Talking bridge solos maintained their popularity throughout the 1950s in such songs as the Drifters' "Someday You'll Want Me to Want You." In addition to Jones and Kenny, the original Ink Spots included Ivory "Deek" Watson (lead), Jerry Daniels (first tenor, replaced by Kenny in 1936), and Charlie Fuqua (second tenor). Formed in Indianapolis, Indiana, in the '20s, the Spots performed sentimental ballads in their unique, close harmonic style. They were extremely popular in the '40s and provided the blueprint for doo-wop groups of the next decade. One of the first popular African American groups, the Spots, with their improvised vocal harmonies and simulated vocal wind instruments, influenced many black vocal groups, including the Orioles and the Ravens, and such major artists as the Impressions' Jerry Butler and the Drifters' Clyde McPhatter. One of the first groups to break racial barriers by performing at previously all-white Southern venues, the Ink Spots were inducted into the Rock and Roll Hall of Fame in 1989.

With the Spots having popularized the practice of using two leads in vocal ballads, the Ravens continued the practice with tenors Maithe Marshall and Joe Van Loan and bass Jimmy Ricks. Formed in New York City in 1945, the Ravens were originally led by tenor Ollie Jones (replaced in 1947 by Marshall), but Ricks's remarkably deep voice thrust him to the foreground. Throughout the late 1940s and 1950s, there were personnel changes in the group, including Joe Van Loan replacing Marshall in 1951. Other original musicians were Leonard Puzey (second tenor) and Warren "Birdland" Suttles (baritone). Ricks frequently led the Ravens on both sentimental ballads and uptempo tunes (including a 1947 recording of "Ol' Man River" from the Broadway musical *Showboat*, which drew attention to the bass voice). Influenced by the Mills Brothers' John Jr., the Ink Spots' Orville Jones, and the Delta Rhythm Boys'

Lee Gaines, Ricks used his mellifluous delivery of ballads to help pave the way for the next generation of bass singers (the Robins' and the Coasters' Bobby Nunn; the Dominoes' and the Checkers' Bill Brown; the Drifters' Bill Pinkney; the Swallows' Norris "Bunky" Mack; the Cadets' and the Jacks' Will "Dub" Jones; the Du Droppers' Bob Kornegay; and the Spaniels' Gerald Gregory). Also, with his sophisticated jazz- and rhythm and blues–based phrasings, Ricks allowed the group to sound black, unlike earlier African American vocal groups (including the Mills Brothers and Ink Spots) who attempted to sound white and were targeting white audiences. With Ricks's lead, the Ravens changed that practice, allowing future black groups to sound like themselves and receive due credit as African American ensembles.

The Ravens toured nationally and recorded for many record labels (including King, Columbia, OKeh, and Mercury). Their Top 10 R&B hits included "I Don't Have to Ride No More" (1949) and "Rock Me All Night Long" (1952). The group inspired dozens of vocal ensembles named after birds, including the Robins, the Crows, and the Penguins.

The Orioles, originally formed in 1946 as the Vibranaires, continued the practice of using two leads on late '40s recordings, with George Nelson (baritone) performing second lead behind Sonny Til (second tenor). Other original members of the group were Alexander Sharp (tenor) and Johnny Reed (bass). Because they were from Baltimore, Maryland, one of the cornerstones of R&B, the group took its name from the Maryland state bird, following the emerging trend of black vocal groups naming themselves after birds. Their 1948 No. 1 R&B hit, "It's Too Soon to Know," is considered by many to be the first R&B vocal group harmony recording. It is often cited as the first rock and roll record. (See chapter 3 for further information.) After recording with New York's Jubilee label for seven years, the Orioles achieved their greatest success with "Crying in the Chapel" (August 1953). Ironically, this cover of a white country song (originally recorded by country artist Darrell Glenn in July 1953 and composed by his father, Artie Glenn) was one of the first recordings by African American artists to be successful on the pop charts. The Orioles' recording (with Gaither replaced by Ralph Williams and Nelson replaced by John Gregory Carroll) was not the first cover of this song; however, it surpassed most other versions on the charts—a No. 1 R&B hit and No. 11 pop hit until Elvis Presley's 1965 cover, which was much closer in style to the Orioles' than to Glenn's, and became a No. 3 hit on the pop charts. The Orioles' cover was very different from the Glenn original: the white version used a steady beat with even beat subdivisions and country instrumental practices, while the black cover used a shuffle rhythm and backbeat with vocal improvisation (melismatic embellishments) by a backup chorus. The original Orioles disbanded in 1954 when Til replaced them with an extant group, the Regals. The new Orioles switched to the Vee Jay label two years later. Though Til recorded with various groups into the late '70s, "Crying in the Chapel" remained his and the Orioles' finest achievement. Having influenced many other vocal groups with their sound, the Orioles were inducted into the Rock and Roll Hall of Fame in 1995.

Shortly after these doo-wop pioneers laid the R&B foundation, other groups followed in their footsteps. In late 1950, the Blenders released "I'm Afraid the Masquerade Is Over," and the Four Buddies, considered the first group to sing totally in the doo-wop style (from the beginning of their recording career), issued "Just to See You Smile Again." These were followed in 1951 by recordings of the Larks, the Dominoes, the Clovers, the Swallows, the Five Keys, and the Cardinals. Many musicologists agree that the doo-wop era began in 1948 with the Orioles; however, debates continue regarding the first doo-wop record. Some consider the Ravens' "Lullaby" (1946) or "Count Every Star" (1950) to be the first. Jim Dawson and Steve Propes discuss this in *What Was the First Rock 'n' Roll Record?*, narrowing the first rock and roll record down to fifty songs from 1944 to 1956, with no definitive answer.[2] It is, however, agreed and understood that the Ravens and the Orioles were the most important catalysts of the early doo-wop sound and that by 1950 the doo-wop era was in full force.

Vocal Groups

These predecessors created consistently romantic music with moderately slow and danceable tempos while incorporating the sounds of the blues, R&B, gospel, and pop. As doo-wop groups emerged in the early '50s, such significant vocal ensembles as the Moonglows, the Flamingos, the Dells, the Drifters, the Platters, and the Coasters began their careers. Roots musical characteristics could be heard in songs ranging from the Clovers' "Good Lovin'" (blues) to the Drifters' "Money Honey" (R&B) and from the Dominoes' "Sixty Minute Man" (gospel) to the Platters' "Only You" (pop): several lead singers used gospel singing techniques, including repeated breath punctuations emphasizing words and stylized embellishments ending phrases. Since the doo-wop subgenre was born from the combination of these early styles, the artists were almost all African American; whites appeared mainly as record company executives and deejays.

By mid-decade, hundreds of young African American males, most of whom were teenagers and recent high school graduates, harmonized on the streets of urban America to impress girls in their neighborhood. Many vocal groups thrived on the East Coast, with the New York City area (including New Jersey and Connecticut), and specifically Harlem, Brooklyn, and the Bronx, as the mecca of the subgenre. The Apollo Theater showcased established groups, such as the Orioles, the Ravens, the Five Keys, the Dominoes, and the Cardinals. Teenagers congregated on street corners and in hallways, alleys, and subways to imitate those celebrities whose recordings were available in local stores. Several pioneering indies based in the city specialized in doo-wop groups: Red Robin (the city's first major independent black label), Whirling Disc, Bruce, Old Town, Rama, Gee, Jubilee, Josie, and Rainbow. Among the region's ensembles were the Chords, the Paragons, the Jesters, the Hearts, the Jive Five, the Heartbeats, the Nutmegs, the Monotones, the Fiestas, and the Five Satins. Other prominent metropolitan areas that served as home bases for doo-wop's important groups were Chicago, whose groups included the Dells, the El Dorados, the Flamingos, the Spaniels, the Moonglows, the Orchids, and the Gems; Los Angeles, with such groups as the Platters, the Penguins, the Jay-hawks, the Medallions, and the Hollywood Flames; and Philadelphia, with the Castelles, the Belltones, the Buccaneers, the Angels, the Dreams, and the Sil-houettes. In addition, Cincinnati, Baltimore, Pittsburgh, and numerous other cities across the country had their groups. Countless members of these groups never received royalties for their songs (especially from the many indies), and several of them achieved one-time-only hits, a common event in the doo-wop subgenre.

Groups took their names not only from birds, but also borrowed them from mammals (the Jaguars, the Lions, the Beavers, and the Colts), invertebrates, and insects. Many named themselves after flowers (the Orchids, the Daffodils, the Marigolds, and the Blossoms), and precious stones (the Gems, the Dia-monds, the Crystals, the Emeralds, the Opals, and the Pearls) abounded as well. Very popular group names came from automobiles passing doo-woppers on street corners, such as the El Dorados, the Cadillacs, the Edsels, the Impalas, the Imperials, the Rivieras, and the Belvederes. Some named themselves after the urban streets where they lived (the Belmonts were named after Belmont Avenue in the Bronx), and the sky was the limit for other group names: games (the Checkers and the Dominoes), geography (the Orients and the Trinidads), and even cigarettes (the Kents and the Kool Gents).

 FIFTIES DOO-WOP GROUPS

This representative list serves merely as an introduction to the thousands of di-verse vocal groups that arose during the doo-wop era. For each ensemble, a sig-nature song with its year of recording is provided. As documented by Bob Hyde and Walter DeVenne, compilers of *The Doo Wop Box* discography, this style de-veloped between 1948 and 1955 and swelled to massive proportions from 1955 to 1957, reaching its golden age between 1957 and 1959.[3]

Group	Song	Year
The Ravens	"Count Every Star"	1950
The Crows	"Gee"	1953
The Drifters	"Money Honey"	1953
The Orioles	"Crying in the Chapel"	1953
The Chordettes	"Mr. Sandman"	1954

FIFTIES DOO-WOP GROUPS (continued)

The Chords	"Sh-Boom"	1954
Shirley Gunter and the Queens	"Oop Shoop"	1954
The Moonglows	"Sincerely"	1954
The Penguins	"Earth Angel"	1954
The Spaniels	"Goodnite Sweetheart, Goodnite"	1954
The Wrens	"Come Back My Love"	1954
The Cadillacs	"Speedoo"	1955
The Clovers	"Devil or Angel"	1955
The El Dorados	"At My Front Door"	1955
The Hearts	"Lonely Nights"	1955
Frankie Lymon and the Teenagers	"Why Do Fools Fall in Love"	1955
The Nutmegs	"Story Untold"	1955
The Platters	"The Great Pretender"	1955
The Bop Chords	"When I Woke Up This Morning"	1956
The Cadets	"Stranded in the Jungle"	1956
The Cleftones	"Little Girl of Mine"	1956
The Dells	"Oh What a Nite"	1956
The Dell-Vikings	"Come Go with Me"	1956
The Five Satins	"In the Still of the Night"	1956
The Heartbeats	"A Thousand Miles Away"	1956
The Schoolboys	"Please Say You Want Me"	1956
The Bobbettes	"Mr. Lee"	1957
The Chantels	"Maybe"	1957
Danny & the Juniors	"At the Hop"	1957
The Diamonds	"The Stroll"	1957
The Gladiolas	"Little Darlin'"	1957
The Hollywood Flames	"Buzz-Buzz-Buzz"	1957
The Jesters	"I'm Falling in Love"	1957
The Mellokings	"Tonite, Tonite"	1957
The Monotones	"Book of Love"	1957
The Silhouettes	"Get a Job"	1957
The Teenchords	"I'm So Happy"	1957
The Tuneweavers	"Happy, Happy Birthday Baby"	1957

> ### ⊛ FIFTIES DOO-WOP GROUPS (continued)
>
> | | | |
> |---|---|---|
> | The Capris | "There's a Moon Out Tonight" | 1958 |
> | The Coasters | "Yakety Yak" | 1958 |
> | The Crests | "Sixteen Candles" | 1958 |
> | Dion and the Belmonts | "I Wonder Why" | 1958 |
> | The Elegants | "Little Star" | 1958 |
> | The Fiestas | "So Fine" | 1958 |
> | The Impressions | "For Your Precious Love" | 1958 |
> | Little Anthony and the Imperials | "Tears on My Pillow" | 1958 |
> | The Matadors | "Vengeance" | 1958 |
> | The Shirelles | "I Met Him on a Sunday" | 1958 |
> | The Skyliners | "Since I Don't Have You" | 1958 |
> | The Eternals | "Rockin' in the Jungle" | 1959 |
> | The Flamingos | "I Only Have Eyes for You" | 1959 |
> | The Fleetwoods | "Come Softly to Me" | 1959 |
> | The Impalas | "Sorry (I Ran All the Way Home)" | 1959 |
> | The Passions | "Just to Be with You" | 1959 |

Many of these vocal groups were teenagers who came together for a brief moment of glory to sing, make records, and win the attention of their female audience, rather than to embark upon a career in music. Such groups as the Teenagers, the Teenchords, and the Schoolboys represented the youthful doo-wop substyle that emerged in the mid-'50s when boys heard older groups, formed their own ensembles, and attempted to duplicate the sound. A distinct musical characteristic of these teenage groups was the use of a high tenor lead sung mostly by a male. The Teenagers' Frankie Lymon was the best-known lead singer in this style, though his brother, Lewis (the Teenchords), and Leslie Martin (the Schoolboys) were also very talented. Other young groups, such as the Jesters, the Matadors, and the Bop Chords, sang in this style with more of a tough, urban quality to their sound. Teenage gangs and clubs in large cities (especially in New York's Harlem) engaged in such social activities as singing rumbles (sing-offs), resulting in doo-wop with a rough twist. Though they still included falsetto vocal emphasis, these songs also exploited the bass voice and displayed much intricate harmony with pounding beats.

Prior to 1958, more than 90 percent of doo-wop group members were African American; as the decade progressed, however, that changed as white interest in R&B music rose. Many white vocal groups began singing in the doo-wop style later in the decade, such as the Diamonds, Danny & the Juniors, and Dion and the Belmonts. Some of these groups deviated from the prominent love song theme and sang of other topics, such as the Eternals' "Rockin' in the Jungle" and the Skyliners' "Pennies from Heaven" (covers of standard pop songs became common in this later vocal group substyle). Two very successful doo-wop groups of young adults, the Moonglows and the Flamingos, sang in a more sophisticated style and sought serious careers in music, and the Dells have been one of the longest-lived vocal groups in rock and roll history.

The Moonglows

The Moonglows consisted of Bobby Lester (lead) and Harvey Fuqua (first tenor), both from Louisville, Kentucky, who moved to Cleveland, Ohio, because of the success of Alan Freed's WJW radio show. There they met Danny Coggins (second tenor) and Prentiss Barnes (bass), added them to their jazz-oriented group (initially called the Crazy Sounds), and toured the Midwest. They recorded for Alan Freed's Champagne label and the deejay renamed them the Moonglows after his popular radio show, *The Moondog Rock 'n' Roll Party*. When Champagne closed its doors in 1953, with Freed's assistance they began their illustrious career in Chicago, recording five singles for Chance Records before securing more favorable royalty arrangements with Chess Records.

Their first Chess release in 1954, "Sincerely," became the Moonglows' trademark song; it was the group's biggest success (a No. 1 R&B hit and a No. 20 pop hit), despite the McGuire Sisters' winning white cover (which was quickly recorded and became a 1955 No. 1 pop hit) and other competing versions. This vocally innovative song exemplified the Moonglows' exquisite vocal blend with a unique abundance of minor chords and major seventh chords utilizing the blow-harmony technique. With the doo-wop triplet rhythmic pattern, its instrumental accompaniment supplied the song's steady beat. Whether as a sign of friendship or as a necessity of '50s music industry practice, Alan Freed received co-composer credit for "Sincerely."[4] This captivating recording was the beginning of a series of superb Moonglows singles released by Chess, including "Most of All" (1955), "See Saw" (1956), "Over and Over Again" (1956), and "Please Send Me Someone to Love" (1957).

By 1958, with guitarist Billy Johnson accompanying them and the group's name changed to Harvey and the Moonglows, "Ten Commandments of Love" was recorded, yet another illustration of the group's superb harmonic and innovative style (in 1956 they recorded one of the first doo-wop records featuring string instruments). This last hit for the Moonglows highlighted spoken recitation by Fuqua's soulful voice, detailing the commandments of ideal romantic love, while group members solemnly sang the commandment numbers in the background, making an unusual romantic recording that became very popular in both black and white markets (reaching No. 9 on the R&B charts and No. 22 on the pop charts). Though there had been prior songs with spoken recitations in bridges, "Ten Commandments" was almost all recitation. Following the practice of the '50s rock and roll music business, this song credited M. Paul, the son of one of the Chess brothers, as co-writer, though it was composed solely by Fuqua. "Ten Commandments" was their last recording of significance.

To capitalize on the Moonglows' success, the Chess brothers allowed Bobby Lester to form a side group, the Moonlighters, who released such recordings as "Shoo-Do-Be-Do" on their Checker subsidiary label. The Moonglows starred in Freed's rock and roll movies *Rock, Rock, Rock!* (1956) and *Mister Rock and Roll* (1957). In 1959, the group dissolved, though a new version of the Moonglows, including Marvin Pentz Gay Jr. (Marvin Gaye), continued for a few more years. Lester moved to Chicago, where he opened a nightclub; Fuqua moved to Detroit, formed the Tri-Phi label with his wife (Gwendolyn, the sister of the Motown label founder, Berry Gordy), and discovered the Spinners and the Dells. He became a producer and talent scout for Motown, and produced the Supremes, Marvin Gaye, and Steveland Judkins Morris (Stevie Wonder). In 1972, Lester and Fuqua reunited with some new members and recorded an album for RCA, *The Return of the Moonglows*, which included their last recording to place on the charts, an arrangement of their huge hit, this time titled "Sincerely '72." In the 1990s, Fuqua became a trustee of the Rhythm & Blues Foundation, an organization that offers assistance to R&B veteran musicians, such as financial support, the receipt of songwriting and performance credits, personal assistance, and medical treatment. In 2000, *Harvey & the Moonglows 2000* was released on Fuqua's Resurging Artist label and the Moonglows were inducted into the Rock and Roll Hall of Fame.

The Flamingos

The Flamingos, another mature doo-wop group that recorded for Art Sheridan's Chance Records and appeared in Freed's *Rock, Rock, Rock!*, are widely regarded as one of the best vocal groups in music history. The group consisted of Earl Lewis (lead), who was replaced by Sollie McElroy before their first recording, and two sets of cousins: Zeke (second tenor) and Jake Carey (bass), who knew the Orioles' Sonny Til in Baltimore, and Johnny Carter (first tenor) and Paul Wilson (baritone). The Flamingos' elegant, intricate, and flawless vocal technique and use of melodies in minor tonalities reflected their church choir background (Wilson, Carter, and the Careys) at the black Jewish Church of God. Singing in diverse styles, they successfully aimed their irresistible songs at the white market. Initially called the Swallows, then the Five Flamingos, and finally just the Flamingos, they formed in Chicago in 1952, were spotted by Sheridan while performing at a local club, were signed to a recording contract, and in January 1953 recorded their first single, "Someday, Someway," backed with "If I Can't Have You." The remainder of their memorable recordings for the small, troubled Chance label included their third single, "Golden

Teardrops" (1953). Featuring their impeccable vocal harmonies with McElroy's falsetto vocals looming in the background, this classic has been acknowledged as the most perfect-sounding single of all time—even though it didn't reach the national pop charts upon its first release. Along with almost all others on the Chance label (and especially early Flamingos recordings), this classic is one of the recordings most desired by rock and roll record collectors.

The Flamingos' short tenure with Parrot Records (1954–1955) was marked by the addition of Nate Nelson (lead), who became one of the latter-day Platters when McElroy left the Flamingos (and later sang with the Moroccos, the Nobels, and the Chanteurs). With Parrot, the Flamingos released three records before their move in 1955 to Chess's Checker subsidiary, where they achieved great success with their stunning ballad "I'll Be Home" (1955), featuring Nelson's beautiful lead and the group's flawless, smooth vocal harmonies, complete with a recited bridge and minimal instrumental accompaniment. "I'll Be Home," their first national hit, sold well in the teenage market and was followed in 1956 by "A Kiss from Your Lips" and "Would I Be Crying?"

Members of the Flamingos went their own ways when Carter and Zeke Carey were drafted in 1956, then regrouped the following year with Tommy Hunt (who replaced Nelson as lead). Guitarist and singer Terry Johnson joined the group in 1958. They recorded with Decca for a short while (1957–1958), and in 1958 they signed a contract with the ultimate entrepreneur of teen marketing, George Goldner, owner of End Records in New York City. At End, they achieved record successes blending pop and doo-wop, with "Lovers Never Say Goodbye" (1958) and "I Only Have Eyes for You" (1959). Their first release for End, "Lovers Never Say Goodbye," originally titled "Please Wait for Me" (after the opening line of the song), is considered one of the most beautiful and charming doo-wop ballads, with the group's elegant vocal harmonies set in a soft triplet rhythmic-patterned slow tempo. Goldner, who had an ear for the teenage record market, and was possibly the largest manufacturer of doo-wop records, next produced the Flamingos' signature song, "I Only Have Eyes for You." He had a knack for "package goods," as albums were called by '50s trade journals. In late 1956, he released one of the first doo-wop albums by the Teenagers, on the Gee label, and followed with 1959 releases by the Chantels and Little Anthony and the Imperials.

While at End, the Flamingos released four albums, including *Flamingo Serenade* (1959, an album of pop standards by Cole Porter, George Gershwin, and others), in the doo-wop style. Complete with echo techniques and instrumental accompaniments, this production yielded the single "I Only Have Eyes for You," a 1934 Ben Selvin hit. With its nonsense syllables ("doo-bop sh-bop") and smooth, mature harmonies, the single became a huge hit (No. 3 on the R&B charts and No. 11 on the pop charts) and has remained one of the most enduring vocal group recordings. With their polished vocals and impressive choreography, these doo-wop pioneers influenced many groups, including some of Motown's greatest stars—the Temptations, the Supremes, the Jackson

5, and the Miracles. Though their popularity waned with the rise of the British Invasion, the ensemble continued performing and recording until the deaths of the Carey cousins in the late '90s. Regarded by many as the finest vocal group in R&B history, the Flamingos were inducted into the Rock and Roll Hall of Fame in 2001.

The Dells

In the late 1950s, Johnny Carter left the Flamingos and joined the Dells, a group that formed from the El Rays and was mentored by the Moonglows. The El Rays began in 1952 in the Chicago suburb of Harvey, Illinois, when six high school friends—Johnny Funches (lead), Marvin Junior (first tenor), Verne Allison (second tenor), Michael "Mickey" McGill (baritone), Chuck Barksdale (bass), and Lucius McGill (bass)—created the street corner a cappella doo-wop group. By 1955, after recording a single for Checker, the group consisted of five members (minus Lucius), renamed themselves the Dells, and began recording for the Chicago–based R&B label Vee Jay. They had only one personnel change throughout their existence, when ex-Flamingo falsetto Johnny Carter replaced Funches. During their doo-wop years, they recorded several records for Vee Jay, including "Oh What a Nite" (1956), and later had numerous hits for several labels in the '60s and '70s, including "Stay in My Corner," "There Is," and "Give Your Baby a Standing Ovation." These are just a few examples of many songs (they placed more than forty singles on the R&B charts and eight on the Top 40 charts) that enabled the Dells to remain a premier vocal group for years.

One of their early Vee Jay releases, "Oh What a Nite," was a huge hit and marked the beginning of the Dells' success. It became a Top 10 R&B hit (eventually peaking at No. 4) right after the group dissolved in frustration over their previously unsuccessful recordings. Though their first two Vee Jay records, "Tell the World" and "Dreams of Contentment," were not successful, these and their first recording as the El Rays are now revered by doo-wop enthusiasts. The Moonglows informed them of their new hit, and they quickly regrouped. "Oh What a Nite" fueled the group for years to come, complete with typical doo-wop ingredients of the basic chord progression, persistent triplet rhythmic pattern, and saxophone solo.

In 1958, en route to a performance, the Dells were in an auto accident that seriously injured McGill, forced Funches to retire, and placed the Dells out of commission for almost two years. When they started performing again, Johnny Carter replaced Funches, and they continued their success throughout the next two decades. In 1969, they recorded a soul version ("Oh, What a Night") of "Oh What a Nite" that placed on the pop charts (No. 10 hit), which the original had not, and also topped the R&B charts. By the mid-1960s, their sound progressed naturally to the soul subgenre. Over their more than fifty-year existence, the Dells recorded and performed with, and backed up singers including Jerry Butler and Dinah Washington, and greatly influenced younger vocal groups, such as Boyz II Men, the Backstreet Boys, and 'N Sync. In 2002, the Dells celebrated their fiftieth anniversary, and in 2004, recognized for their remarkable talent and perseverance, they were inducted into the Rock and Roll Hall of Fame.

The Drifters

For inspiration, doo-wop groups looked to Clyde McPhatter and the Drifters, a vocal group that hailed from the gospel tradition and, unlike the Dells, evolved with changing members. Like most doo-woppers, McPhatter first joined (in 1950) a gospel vocal group, Billy Ward and the Dominoes, which mastered the smooth, sophisticated sound of the Ravens. After their television debut in 1950 on *The Arthur Godfrey Show*, the Dominoes mastered and recorded the rhythm and blues-based sound, as in their 1951 classic, "Sixty Minute Man." With lead tenor McPhatter, the Dominoes became one of the best-regarded R&B ensembles. In 1953, after differences with Ward, McPhatter left the group and the equally talented Jackie Wilson replaced him, remaining

The Drifters, 1959. © Frank Driggs Collection/Getty Images.

with the Dominoes until becoming a solo act (in 1957) and one of the premier singers of the late 1950s. At that time Atlantic Records was the most famous of the indies; its fresh sounds and savvy marketing sent major record labels scrambling during the early stages of rock and roll. Thoroughly impressed with McPhatter's radiant, gospel-trained tenor voice, Ahmet Ertegun of Atlantic Records encouraged him to form his own group and offered him a recording contract and star billing. Gathering his musician friends together, McPhatter formed his new group, and because members drifted in and out of the ensemble, McPhatter settled on the Drifters as their name.

Formed in New York City in 1953, the Drifters included McPhatter (lead) and David Baughan (first tenor), William "Chick" Anderson (second tenor), David Baldwin (baritone), and James Johnson (bass). Though not the classic Drifters group, this lineup was the first to record (as the Atlantic Drifters). Thereafter, numerous personnel changes occurred; no one stayed with the ensemble throughout its existence. The era of Clyde McPhatter and the Drifters (1953–1954) refers to the first classic lineup of singers: McPhatter, Andrew and Gerhart Thrasher, Bill Pinkney, William Ferbie, and Walter Adams. This group recorded their first Atlantic release, "Money Honey," in 1953. McPhatter was drafted and left the group in July 1954; Baughan sang lead until Johnny Moore joined the group. Ferbie and Adams also left; Pinkney was fired and replaced by Tommy Evans; Jimmy Oliver replaced Adams; and Bobby Hendricks replaced Moore, who was drafted. Other additions included Dee Ernie Bailey, Billy Kennedy, and Charlie Hughes (who replaced Andrew Thrasher, who left with Pinkney). Later, Hughes was drafted and replaced by Jimmy Milner.

The McPhatter and the Drifters era yielded "Money Honey," "Such a Night" (1954), "Honey Love" (1954, a No. 1 R&B hit), "Bip Bam" (1954), and "White Christmas" (1954), a revolutionary doo-wop version of the seasonal song that has remained second in popularity only to Bing Crosby's version. The Drifters achieved immediate success with "Money Honey," a No. 1 R&B hit. It was the best-selling R&B record of 1953, turned the Drifters and gospel-trained lead singer McPhatter into major R&B stars, and constituted the first of dozens of hits for the group. Atlantic's outstanding session players—guitarist Mickey Baker, pianist Van Walls, and saxophonist Sam Taylor—accompanied the song. With its prominent, powerful R&B backbeat supplied by the drums, and embellishing boogie-woogie-styled filler supplied by the piano, the song incorporated a rhythm and blues-flavored saxophone solo in addition to the blues progression and blues stop-time technique. The Drifters sustained the song's melodic hook, consisting of unison "ah-ooms" (as a drone introducing melodic phrases) with the saxophone (a technique used the following year in Hank Ballard and the Midnighters' hit "Work with Me Annie"), while McPhatter, with his radiant, gospel-trained and high-pitched voice, and the background Drifters sang exhilarating vocals, including screams from the gospel and R&B tradition.

Upon his discharge from the army, McPhatter resumed his career as a solo artist with Atlantic in 1956, achieving a number of hits (among them the 1958 No. 1 R&B hit "A Lover's Question"). This talented singer enjoyed another great solo hit in 1962 with "Lover Please" but, partially because of the British Invasion, his popularity faded. McPhatter was one of the brightest stars to burn out prematurely in the world of rock and roll; in 1972, beset with alcohol and money problems, he died from a heart attack. With his fervent voice and passionate delivery, McPhatter influenced many other singers: Jackie Wilson and Smokey Robinson, to name just two. For his innovative contributions as an R&B (and later a soul) singer, in 1987 Clyde McPhatter was inducted into the Rock and Roll Hall of Fame as a solo artist.

Meanwhile, in 1958, due to the lack of record sales and drinking problems of the current members of the Drifters, manager George Treadwell became impressed with the Crowns, another group that was performing at the Apollo Theater, and signed them as the new Drifters (he retained the copyright on the group's name). These King era Drifters included lead singer Ben E. King, Charlie Thomas (tenor), Dock Green (baritone), and Elsbeary Hobbs (bass). The first release of this new lineup was "There Goes My Baby" (1959), a song that reflected a music style different from previous Drifters' songs. Their sound became more pop-oriented, incorporating fewer R&B elements, and was more in line with late '50s rock and roll fashion. King's lead vocals and the orchestral accompaniment led this record to achieve sales never attained by the earlier Drifters. The new Drifters followed with other hits, such as "Dance with Me" and "(If You Cry) True Love, True Love" (1959); "This Magic Moment" and "Save the Last Dance for Me" (1960); "Up on the Roof" (1962), "On Broadway" (1963), and "Under the Boardwalk" (1964).

Beginning their work with Jerry Leiber and Mike Stoller in 1959, the King era Drifters recorded "There Goes My Baby," written and produced by their new songwriting team, which mixed R&B and pop elements. A studio experiment, this classic recording employed a string accompaniment (complete with swirling violins) and is credited with having put string instruments into rock and roll music, even though it was not the first to use orchestral strings. Buddy Holly had done this earlier in 1959, in his last hit, "It Doesn't Matter Anymore." However, the Drifters' recording was the first R&B record that incorporated a full, thick-textured background. In addition to male voices, other timbres included timpani drums and the use of heavy reverberation as an echo technique. The song had a Latin (Brazilian) rhythm with the drums accenting beats (though lacking the powerful rhythm and blues-accented backbeat) and uneven beat subdivisions throughout. Its form consisted of eight-bar phrases, sometimes blurred, without contrasting sections, and the harmony consisted of a variation of the doo-wop progression (the popular alternative that replaced the supertonic-seventh with the subdominant chord), with each of the four chords lasting for two bars (resulting in the chord progression I-I-vi7-vi7-IV-IV-V7-V7). Though the melody and harmony were repeated throughout, the song did not sound repetitious because the vocals and background instruments were varied. The melody, sung as a bass solo by King, was sometimes accompanied by soft backup voices providing harmony with syncopated rhythmic syllables (such as "doo-doo-doo-doo"); at other times no backup vocals were present, but lower string instruments supplied a dramatic accompaniment in call-and-response to the lead voice.

The lyrics of "There Goes My Baby" reflected the popular love song theme: the singer's lover goes away brokenhearted, not saying whether she loves him, and the singer wishes he could tell her of his love for her. In addition to the innovative strings, this pioneering song utilized a new technique whereby its ending faded out. All of these musical elements combined to form a magnificent hit that set the successful course for the new Drifters and heavily influenced rock and roll production for the next few years. Though the old Drifters had recorded songs that were successful on the R&B charts, the new group went to the No. 2 position on the pop charts with "There Goes My Baby." They followed with other hits, including "Save the Last Dance for Me" (their only single to top both the pop and R&B charts) and "This Magic Moment," before King departed for a solo career; he later recorded the classics "Spanish Harlem" and "Stand by Me."

More drifting occurred among ensemble members with the addition of Rudy Lewis, who replaced King and fronted the group for its third million-seller, "Up on the Roof." Dock Green left and was replaced by Eugene Pearson. When Lewis died in 1964 and the group once again lost a brilliant voice, Johnny Moore (who sang with an earlier version of the Drifters) returned as lead singer, and the group recorded the best-seller "Under the Boardwalk" with the Moore, Charlie Thomas, Pearson, and Tommy Evans lineup. Their former manager, Lover Patterson, formed another Drifters group made up of Charlie Hughes, Green, and Evans (who had just left the other group). Also, Bill Pinkney created a group called the Original Drifters, with David Baughan, Andrew and Gerhart Thrasher, and himself. Amazingly, the next several years witnessed even more personnel changes with Drifters groups.

No matter who sang lead—McPhatter, Moore, King, Thomas, or Lewis—the Drifters created what are considered to be some of the most charming vocal hits of the '50s and early '60s: "Money Honey" (McPhatter); "There Goes My Baby," "This Magic Moment," and "Save the Last Dance for Me" (King); "Sweets for My Sweet" (1961, Thomas); "Up on the Roof " and "On Broadway" (Lewis); and "Under the Boardwalk" (Moore). With the finest craftsmen behind the scenes, the Drifters recorded phenomenal hits for Atlantic, epitomizing the vocal group sound of New York City that combined the sweet, streetwise R&B sound with gospel influences, linking '50s rhythm and blues with '60s soul music. Their producers included Leiber and Stoller, who introduced Latin rhythms and accompanying strings into the vocabulary of popular music. Burt Bacharach and the New York–based songwriting teams of Leiber and Stoller, Carole King and Gerry Goffin, and Doc Pomus and Mort Shuman composed songs about romance and everyday life in the city for the Drifters, who proved to be an ideal vehicle for their convincing delivery.

A consistently high standard was maintained throughout the Drifters' recording tenure with Atlantic Records (from late 1953 to early 1966). The label's cofounder, Ahmet Ertegun, has claimed that the Drifters were the all-time greatest Atlantic Records group, having achieved No. 1 singles with three different lead singers (McPhatter, Moore, and King).[5] The Drifters were among the first inductees into the Vocal Group Hall of Fame in 1998. Ten years earlier, the Drifters—McPhatter, King, Lewis, Moore, Pinkney, Thomas, and Gerhart Thrasher—were inducted into the Rock and Roll Hall of Fame.

The Platters

Considered the most successful rock and roll vocal group of the '50s, the Platters also initially had a shifting lineup. The group was founded in Los Angeles in 1952, and the original members were Tony Williams (lead), David Lynch (second tenor), Alex Hodge (baritone), and Herb Reed (bass); songwriter Buck Ram was their manager and producer. After several personnel changes, the Platters received a recording contract with Federal, one of the larger indies; however, the lack of success of their first two records led Ram to

The Platters, 1958. © Frank Driggs Collection/Getty Images.

make adjustments to the group; Zola Taylor (from Shirley Gunter and the Queens) joined in 1954, causing Hodge to depart and Paul Robi to replace him. This lineup created a pop doo-wop style (a sound that spent much time on the charts in the late '50s and early '60s and was performed by such other vocal groups as the Avalons, the Fidelities, the Skyliners, and the Duprees) that descended from the balladry of the Mills Brothers and the Ink Spots. Ram is credited with having coached the group to become a newer version of the Spots (for whom he had composed songs in the '40s). Like the Ink Spots in the '40s, the Platters were the most popular black group of the '50s. With their polished, pop-oriented sound, they had the first No. 1 doo-wop song to appear on the pop charts in 1955, "The Great Pretender." The ensemble released a series of other hallmark hits, including "Only You" (1955, No. 5 pop hit), "(You've Got) The Magic Touch" (1956, No. 4 pop hit), "My Prayer" (1956, remake of an earlier Ink Spots hit and a No. 1 pop hit), "Twilight Time" (1958, No. 1 pop hit), and "Smoke Gets in Your Eyes" (1958, No. 1 pop hit).

In his essay "Doo-Wop," Barry Hansen acknowledges the importance of the Platters, claiming that their emergence was the second biggest rock event of 1955, second only to the success of the influential hit "Rock Around the Clock," which moved the rock and roll audience from a minority to the majority.[6] In 1954, after switching to Mercury, one of the major labels of the '50s, the Platters became an enormously popular act and had remarkable recording successes with both songs written specifically for them and pre-existing pop tunes. At this time, wanting to bolster its R&B division, Mercury was pursuing the Penguins, also managed by Ram, who had just had a hit for Dootone Records with "Earth Angel." Ram arranged a deal such that if Mercury wanted to record the Penguins, the company also had to sign the Platters. After hesitating about the Platters (who at the time were considered an ordinary-sounding group with previously unsuccessful records), Mercury finally signed both groups. Since Federal wanted to record only R&B groups, its owner, Sydney Nathan (who didn't like the original Federal recording of the Platters' "Only You"), allowed the Platters to switch to Mercury. Ironically, the Penguins recorded no hits for Mercury, while the Platters became the most successful vocal group of the decade.

Written by Ram and recorded in April 1955, "Only You (and You Alone)" was the Platters' first recording for Mercury. Though they had recorded an unsuccessful version of the song for Federal, this time it became a milestone of the '50s doo-wop sound. In his gospel-influenced voice, complete with his trademark high-note hiccups, Williams delivered smooth, clearly enunciated vocals while declaring undying devotion in the song's lyrics; this rendition was softened by the addition of the female vocalist Zola Taylor. "Only You" used a steady rhythm section with backbeats supplied by drums and an abundance of piano triplets (played by Ram), bringing this more pop-sounding music up to date and making it able to hold the rock and roll audience. Though the recording took a few months to be noticed, it eventually climbed to the upper levels of both the R&B (No. 1 hit) and pop (No. 5 hit) charts, establishing lead singer Tony Williams as one of the most popular crooners of the era. As a result of this recording, Mercury had a black artist singing in a crooning style whom it could market as part of a pop group that would be accepted by white America. The label marketed the Platters as a white act but wasn't sure whether the group was just a one-hit wonder, which would be determined by their next recording.

Composed by Ram specifically to showcase Williams's exceptional voice, "The Great Pretender" is generally considered a better song than "Only You" and is one of the popular representatives of the doo-wop era. According to rock folklore, before this song was written, Ram promised Mercury executives a new Platters record that would outsell "Only You." When asked the name of it, Ram quickly responded, "The Great Pretender," and soon afterward composed the song. Recorded in November 1955, the single topped both the pop and the R&B charts and set the Platters up for a long career. This was the first No. 1 pop hit recorded by an R&B vocal group. The success of this recording also realized Ram's declared ambition to launch a modern-day Ink Spots group. With Williams's soaring vocals delivering the melody with great purity and precision, accompanied by crisp, rich harmonies of the background voices, this single showcased all the classic elements of doo-wop, complete with prominent piano triplets and saxophone. The record attracted a mixed audience of not only white and black teenagers, but adults, as well.

Having achieved great success through their choice of repertoire alone (adult ballads and standards that predated rock and roll), the Platters became the most popular black group of their time. They continued to record hits for Mercury throughout the decade, created a series of albums (including *The Platters*, *The Flying Platters*, and *Remember When?*), and appeared in the rock and roll movies *Rock Around the Clock* and *The Girl Can't Help It*. Williams left to pursue a solo career in 1960, and personnel changes commenced in the early '60s. Sonny Turner assumed the lead responsibility; and Zola Taylor departed and was replaced by Sandra Dawn. In 1966, the Platters left Mercury for Musicor and continued to be successful with a soul music sound. Three years later, Herb Reed departed and Nate Nelson (who formerly sang lead with the Flamingos) replaced him. By 1970, more personnel changes had occurred, and groups with little or no relation to the original group began calling themselves the Platters. By 2000, original member Herb Reed was leading the only official version of the ensemble, whose name and trademark he had been granted. With an abundance of landmark records, this ensemble accomplished a major feat—it outsold all other doo-wop era vocal groups. A global sensation during the second half of the '50s, the Platters were inducted into the Rock and Roll Hall of Fame in 1990, and into the Vocal Group Hall of Fame among the first inductees in 1998.

The Coasters

Another extremely successful '50s vocal group originally from Los Angeles, the Coasters recorded music very different from that of the Platters. Instead of singing songs of romantic love with beautiful harmonic arrangements, the Coasters took a humorous approach to music, creating recordings with a less polished sound, emphasis on spoken bass parts, and lyrics about teenage life. Known for their chain of comical R&B hits sung in a catchy, uptempo doo-wop style, by the late '50s the Coasters ranked among the most popular American groups. Sung with vitality and humor, and accompanied by vigorous honking saxophone solos by King Curtis, their recordings incorporated exciting R&B musical characteristics. The Coasters helped define rock and roll by appealing to and reflecting America's teens with such classic singles as "Searchin'" (1957), "Young Blood" (1957), "Yakety Yak" (1958), "Charlie Brown" (1959), "Along Came Jones" (1959), "Poison Ivy" (1959), and "That Is Rock & Roll" (1959; cited as the recording that best defines 1950s rock music).

The history of the group dates back to 1947, when the Robins formed in San Francisco. Members included Ty Tyrell (lead), Billy Richard (baritone), Roy Richard (baritone), and Bobby Nunn (bass); changes to the group included the addition and subtraction of Grady Chapman (replaced by Carl Gardner). After moving to Los Angeles in 1949, the Robins performed at Johnny Otis's Barrelhouse Club and had success with R&B hits on Jerry Leiber and Mike Stoller's Spark Records label, "Riot in Cell Block Number 9" (1954) and "Smokey Joe's Café" (1955). In 1955, the ailing Spark label was sold to Atlantic's Atco subsidiary. Having attracted a regional audience with "Riot" and "Smokey Joe's," Leiber and Stoller were offered a contract by Atlantic Records to produce similar records for Atco. This was the first independent production arrangement; before this, staff members of the record labels produced almost all records. Shortly afterward, Leiber and Stoller moved to New York City. Gardner and Nunn followed them, and the remainder of the Robins stayed in California. In New York, Gardner and Nunn joined with Billy Guy and Leon Hughes, and named themselves the Coasters for their West Coast heritage. Thus the original Coasters lineup consisted of Gardner (lead), Hughes (tenor), Guy (baritone), and Nunn (bass). Various others sang with the group at different times, including Obie "Young" Jessie, Leroy Binns, Cornelius Gunter (brother of Shirley Gunter of Shirley Gunter and the Queens), Earl Carroll, Ronnie Bright, Teddy Harper, Jimmy Norman Scott, Bobby Sheen, Bobby Steger, and Nathaniel Wilson. However, the classic Coasters lineup materialized when tenor Cornelius Gunter and bass Will "Dub" Jones replaced Hughes and Nunn.

After signing with Atco Records, the Coasters had their first R&B hit with "Down in Mexico" in 1956, followed by even greater success the next year with their double-sided hit, "Searchin'" and "Young Blood," both No. 1 R&B hits and in the Top 10 on the pop charts; both displayed the group's trademark comic strip scenarios and clownlike vocals. "Young Blood" opened the way for later short, cartoon-type dramatic songs, and during the late '50s the group achieved its greatest successes with Leiber and Stoller's sequence of comic songs (called playlets by the composers) portraying teenage life. The Coasters sang about youthful rebelliousness in "Yakety Yak" (No. 1 hit on both the R&B and pop charts), a skin rash in "Poison Ivy" (No. 1 R&B hit and No. 7 pop hit), Hollywood movie clichés in "Along Came Jones" (No. 14 R&B hit and No. 9 pop hit), and a class clown in "Charlie Brown" (No. 2 R&B and pop hit).

These novelty recordings spoke to teenagers everywhere, not only with their lyrics on familiar topics, but also with exhilarating elements of R&B music: up-beat tempos with strong backbeats supplied by the drums; stop-time technique featuring the lead singer (and sometimes a duet) singing (or speaking) an important phrase; call-and-response with prominent saxophone filler; exciting saxophone solos in the R&B tradition; rough and playful vocal qualities; repeated bass riffs; and boogie-woogie-style piano playing. Featuring a lead voice accompanied by background voices in harmony, these novelty songs incorporated amusing vocal inflections by both the lead and background singers. The Coasters' popularity was inevitable, given the lyrics of these songs. Not only was "Yakety Yak" one of the largest and funniest hits of 1958 (with its hilarious litany of parental demands, such as taking out the trash, and comical representation of the oppressive conditions of an adolescent's life), it was also proof that America's teen culture had found its voice in rock and roll.

Guided by Leiber and Stoller, the Coasters made some of the wittiest recordings of the rock and roll era, achieving phenomenal success in the late 1950s. The ensemble reunited occasionally in the late 1960s and early 1970s, and later in the '70s Leiber and Stoller produced material by a re-formed version of the group, and Gunter kept the Coasters performing during the 1980s. The group influenced early '60s English bands, including the Hollies and the Rolling Stones, who recorded their hits. In 1987, the Coasters were inducted into the Rock and Roll Hall of Fame; in 1994, they were presented the Pioneer Award at the annual Rhythm & Blues Foundation Awards.

White Groups

White groups singing in a preppy pop style, such as the Ames Brothers and the Four Aces, had been performing since the late 1940s, but white groups singing in the doo-wop style did not appear until the second half of the '50s and continued their popularity through the early '60s. The white group sound appeared late in the decade (many musicologists agree on 1958) as white ensembles entered the doo-wop scene in large numbers. Sometimes referred to as the second generation of vocal groups, many were white only and some were interracial. Taking their inspiration from sounds they heard on street corners, these groups thrived mostly in large urban areas, though they were active throughout the country. Dion and the Belmonts are considered to have been the first successful white group with their record "I Wonder Why" (1958). Other contenders included the Elegants ("Little Star," 1958), Danny & the Juniors

("Dottie," 1958), and the Capris (original recording of "There's a Moon Out Tonight," 1958). As record after record with the white-styled sound started to inundate the market, numerous releases of several groups emerged.

Dion and the Belmonts. Considered by many to be the greatest of these groups, Dion and the Belmonts were formed in 1958 by Dion DiMucci in the Bronx, New York. Dion, known only by his first name, gathered a few of his friends together and named his group after Belmont Avenue, a street in their neighborhood. Having perfected four-part harmony singing, the group earned a reputation as the best street corner singers in the area. Consisting of Dion

Dion and the Belmonts, 1958. © Frank Driggs Collection/Getty Images.

(lead), Angelo D'Aleo (first tenor), Fred Milano (second tenor), and Carlo Mastrangelo (bass), the Belmonts combined the doo-wop sound with rock and roll influences from Bo Diddley, Fats Domino, Jerry Lee Lewis, and Elvis Presley. After a couple of unsuccessful attempts on the Mohawk label (later Laurie Records), the quartet recorded their first Top 40 hit, "I Wonder Why." In the doo-wop tradition with falsetto singing, the song exploited nonsense syllables masterfully sung by bass Mastrangelo with the Belmonts adding chord tones (arpeggiating harmonies) above, on nonsense syllables, while Dion delivered the melody. After this classic single, a deluge of white, predominantly Italian American, groups emerged, singing in what has been labeled neo-doo-wop style.

With their highly recognizable sound perfectly complementing Dion's voice, the Belmonts achieved a number of late '50s hits, including "A Teenager in Love," a 1959 international hit (No. 5 on the pop charts). Composed by Doc Pomus and Mort Shuman specifically for the group, this song featured Dion's lead voice with the Belmonts supplying very smooth background vocals consisting of the doo-wop progression harmonies. Flowing from beginning to end, "A Teenager in Love" represented the change in the group's style to what has been labeled a more syrupy sound, the late-'50s pop-oriented sound, evident in the song's message of the agony of young love and its soft rock blend of street corner doo-wop and teen idol balladry.

Dion and the Belmonts toured frequently and were on the Winter Dance Party package tour in February 1959; they declined a ride on the chartered plane that later crashed, killing Buddy Holly, Ritchie Valens, and the Big Bopper. In 1960, after their largest hit, "Where or When," and unhappy with the direction in which the group was being steered (toward the polished, adult pop sound), Dion left the Belmonts and pursued a solo career to reclaim his rock and roll roots. He had multiple solo hits, such as "Runaround Sue" and "The Wanderer" (1961, No. 1 and No. 2 pop hits, respectively; the songs were not truly solos, since the Del Satins provided background vocals). The Belmonts also achieved moderate success recording without Dion in the early '60s (two Top 40 singles and an album that has received much critical acclaim, *Cigars Acapella Candy*), and in the early '70s Dion joined them for a tremendous reunion concert at Madison Square Garden. Rising victoriously from personal problems (including heroin addiction) and his diminished popularity due to the British Invasion, over the years the versatile Dion ingeniously altered his style to adapt to changing musical times, as is evident in his popular 1968 folklike, singer-songwriter-styled ballad "Abraham, Martin and John" (a No. 4 pop hit), a tribute to Abraham Lincoln, Martin Luther King Jr., and John Kennedy. He also added Christian music to his doo-wop, folk, and R&B styles. For his longevity, significant contributions to the music, and influence on many other rockers (including Paul Simon, Billy Joel, and Lou Reed), Dion was inducted into the Rock and Roll Hall of Fame in 1989.

The Elegants. Another early white doo-wop group, the Elegants consisted of Vito Picone (lead) and Carmen Romano (baritone), who originally joined the Crescents in 1956. When that group disbanded the following year, they recruited Arthur Venosa (first tenor), Frank Tardogna (second tenor), and James Moschella (bass). In 1958, by rearranging Mozart's "Twinkle, Twinkle, Little Star" and recording it for Apt Records, this Staten Island, New York, group (which took its name from a whiskey advertisement) had the No. 1 pop and R&B hit, "Little Star"—one of the all-time largest doo-wop hits. However, extensive touring and lack of studio time prevented the group from regaining momentum after their one triumphant recording.

Danny & the Juniors.   Unlike the one-hit-wonder Elegants, Danny & the Juniors succeeded with a handful of hits in the late '50s on ABC-Paramount Records, among them "Dottie" (1958). This white vocal group from Philadelphia benefited from exposure on Dick Clark's *American Bandstand*. Members Danny Rapp (lead), David White (first tenor), Frank Maffei (second tenor), and Joe Terranova (baritone), known as the Juvenairs, began singing on Philadelphia street corners. Artie Singer, owner of Singular Records, discovered them, became their vocal coach, and suggested their name change to Danny & the Juniors. During the summer of 1957, when the bop was the most popular dance on *American Bandstand*, White, Singer, and John Medora wrote a song about this dance craze, "Do the Bop," which Dick Clark suggested they change to "At the Hop"; it was immediately a huge hit. This landmark single was the first No. 1 record of 1958 (it topped the charts for seven weeks on the pop charts and five weeks on the R&B charts), and though it is considered by some to have been more pop rock and roll than doo-wop or R&B, it was a vocal group creation. Its flip side, "Sometimes," was a strong early white-styled doo-wop recording. The Juniors' next single, "Rock and Roll Is Here to Stay" (1958), was written in response to attacks against rock and roll, including a records-smashing event sponsored by St. Louis radio station KWK. Along with songs of Chuck Berry ("Roll Over Beethoven" and "Sweet Little Sixteen"), "Rock and Roll Is Here to Stay" became an anthem for the new generation. Danny & the Juniors toured frequently (including Alan Freed's package tours), appeared on *Bandstand* and in the 1958 movie *Let's Rock*, and continued to place records on the Hot 100 until early 1963.

The Capris.   Another one-hit group, the Capris, consisted of Nick Santamaria (lead), Mike Mincelli (first tenor), Vinny Narcardo (second tenor), Frank Reina (baritone), and John Apostol (bass). They recorded "There's a Moon Out Tonight" in 1958 for Planet Records. Following the single's failure, this street corner high school-aged group from Queens, New York, disbanded. However, a year and a half later, in Irving "Slim" Rose's New York City subway arcade record shop, employee Jerry Greene (one of the key figures in collecting of original 1950s discs in this subgenre) bought a copy of this record from a customer for store credit. He brought it to deejay Alan Fredericks for airplay on radio station WHOM; it met instant response, with people rushing to buy copies of the record. In time, Greene and some friends bought the master recording and leased it to Old Town Records' Hy Weiss. On that label, with the support of disc jockey Murray "the K" Kaufman, "There's a Moon Out Tonight" became a No. 3 pop hit in early 1961, two and a half years after it was recorded. Needless to say, the Capris quickly re-formed and recorded more singles for Old Town, though scoring only minor hits. By 1963, the Capris faded from the music scene and did not revive their career until the 1980s, when they enjoyed more performing and touring than ever.

The Diamonds.   A very popular white vocal group active in the second half of the decade was the Diamonds, from Toronto, Canada, known as a cover group because of the many records by black ensembles they covered and usually outsold. Recording for the Mercury label, the Diamonds were able to achieve such Top 40 hits as "Ka-Ding-Dong," "The Church Bells May Ring," "Little Darlin'" (1957, No. 2 pop hit originally an R&B hit by the Gladiolas), and "The Stroll," a 1958 No. 4 pop hit (recorded late 1957), which was popularized on *American Bandstand* and became the first rock and roll group dance. Their white sound, though progressive compared with the pop music parents were listening to in the '50s (such as Doris Day and Perry Como), did not meet much opposition from parents because the Diamonds were Caucasian. The group was accepted more quickly than black groups.

The Four Seasons and Others.   Other readily received white groups included the Teardrops ("The Stars Are Out Tonight"), the Neons ("Angel Face"), the Mellokings ("Tonite, Tonite"), and the Three Chuckles ("Runaround"). Groups with both white and black lead singers that arose in the mid-1950s included the Crests ("Sixteen Candles"), the Heartbreakers ("Without a Cause"), the Rob Roys ("Tell Me Why"), Don Julian and the Meadowlarks ("Heaven and Paradise"), the Jaguars ("Be My Sweetie"), and the Dell-Vikings ("Come Go with Me"). Of the many other groups, the most notable was the Four Seasons, from Newark, New Jersey, which formed in 1956 and became the longest-lived and most successful white doo-wop group. Lead singer Francis Casteluccio (Frankie Valli) initially sang with the Varietones, who later changed their name to the Four Lovers. After achieving a hit in 1956 with "You're the Apple of My Eye," the Lovers became the Four Seasons. This group's trademark sound was Valli's strong falsetto and wide-ranged voice, combined with the Seasons' immaculate doo-wop harmonies on songwriter/group member Bob Gaudio's songs, which were recorded with arrangement and production techniques ranging from Phil Spector's Wall of Sound to Berry Gordy's Motown sound. Their string of hits came from 1962 to 1968 and included No. 1 hits "Sherry," "Big Girls Don't Cry," "Walk like a Man," and "Rag Doll." In addition to Valli and Gaudio, the Four Seasons' lineup was singer-guitarist Tommy DeVito and bass vocalist Nick Massi (later replaced by Joe Long). Having sold over 100 million records worldwide during their nearly forty-year career, the Four Seasons were inducted into the Rock and Roll Hall of Fame in 1990.

One-Hit Wonders

By the mid-1950s, when doo-wop music prospered with vocal groups named for birds, cars, and other things pouring into the market, it was common for a group to have one or two hits and then disappear from the scene. Throughout rock and roll history, there have always been artists associated with only one song. Sometimes the hit was the debut recording; in other cases, it came at the end of a career. Of all rock and roll subgenres, few possessed as many one- or two-hit wonders as the doo-wop style. Some of the most popular vocal group songs fell into the one-hit category: the Five Satins' "In the Still of the Night," the Chords' "Sh-Boom," Frankie Lymon and the Teenagers' "Why Do Fools Fall in Love," and the Penguins' "Earth Angel." Many of these songs (and performers) enjoyed immense popularity for a brief moment; a fine example is the Monotones' "Book of Love" (1957), a major hit by a talented group that, like the Elegants, have just one song attached to their name even though they recorded a number of fine novelty songs and ballads later in the decade.

 DOO-WOP ONE- AND TWO-HIT WONDERS

Following is a select list of '50s doo-wop one- and two-hit wonders. Representative vocal groups are listed, each with its associated hit and the year it was recorded.

Song	Group	Year
"Gee"	The Crows	1953
"Earth Angel"	The Penguins	1954
"Sh-Boom"	The Chords	1954
"At My Front Door"	The El Dorados	1955
"Why Do Fools Fall in Love"	Frankie Lymon and the Teenagers	1955
"Come Go with Me"	Dell-Vikings	1956
"Eddie My Love"	The Teen Queens	1956
"In the Still of the Night"	The Five Satins	1956
"Priscilla"	Eddie Cooley and the Dimples	1956
"Alone (Why Must I Be Alone)"	The Shepherd Sisters	1957
"Book of Love"	The Monotones	1957
"Get a Job"	The Silhouettes	1957
"Happy, Happy Birthday Baby"	The Tuneweavers	1957

DOO-WOP ONE- AND TWO-HIT WONDERS (continued)

"Mr. Lee"	The Bobbettes	1957
"Silhouettes"	The Rays	1957
"Born Too Late"	The Poni-Tails	1958
"Down the Aisle of Love"	The Quin-Tones	1958
"Little Star"	The Elegants	1958
"Oh Julie"	The Crescendos	1958
"Since I Don't Have You"	The Skyliners	1958
"So Fine"	The Fiestas	1958
"There's a Moon Out Tonight"	The Capris	1958
"You Cheated"	The Shields	1958
"Sorry (I Ran All the Way Home)"	The Impalas	1959

The Five Satins.   The hit associated with the Five Satins, "In the Still of the Night" (1956), was another of the most popular doo-wop songs. Formed in New Haven, Connecticut, in 1955, the Five Satins were one of the best-known '50s vocal groups. The four original members, Fred Parris (lead), Al Denby (tenor), Ed Martin (baritone), and Jim Freeman (bass), recorded this first record, with "The Jones Girl" on its flip side, for the tiny local Standord label; a fifth Satin, Jessie Murphy, played piano. Written by Parris (who previously sang with the Scarlets), the single was brought to the attention of Al Silver, who purchased the master for his Herald/Ember Records in New York. After steady exposure, it entered both the charts, though it was not as big a hit as one would expect, considering the long-time popularity of the song (No. 3 R&B hit and No. 24 pop hit). Interest was revived in "In the Still" after it appeared on the first *Oldies But Goodies* album and was re-released in the late 1950s and early 1960s. Silver had a talent for picking vocal groups, and in addition to the Five Satins, his label recorded the Nutmegs, the Turbans, and the Mellokings—four of the most admired vocal groups of the day.

Because of its crude sound and muffled and distorted quality, this original recording, made in the basement of a church, received unfavorable reviews; however, it is considered a magnificent doo-wop record. The title has been listed in different ways, sometimes as "(I'll Remember) In the Still of the Night" or "I'll Remember (In the Still of the Night)" to distinguish it from the Cole Porter standard. This classic recording utilized the common doo-wop characteristics of triplet rhythmic pattern in the piano accompaniment, use of a saxophone solo, innocent lyrics with a love theme, and background voices singing nonsense syllables (though roughly and loudly for a vocal group recording). The Five Satins recorded a number of records for Herald/Ember over the next couple of years, having success with "To the Aisle" (1957), featuring lead vocalist Bill Baker, who temporarily replaced Parris while in the army. Other personnel changes within the group were the additions of Lou Peebles and Stanley Dortch. The Five Satins appeared in many of Dick Clark's road revues in the late 1950s and were featured on his *American Bandstand*; they also toured Europe, performing and recording as Black Satin in the 1970s.

The Crows.   George Goldner, originally a New York City garment district wholesaler, recorded not only the Flamingos but also several doo-wop groups influenced by the Ravens and the Drifters. Interested in Latin music, in 1948 he founded Tico Records and recorded popular Latin performers prior to embarking upon the doo-wop sound. While recording the Crows in 1953, Goldner struck gold with their landmark record, "Gee," which attracted both R&B and pop audiences. Formed at a Manhattan high school in 1951, the Crows performed at school, on street corners, and in subways before being discovered by one of Goldner's talent scouts at an Apollo Theater amateur night. Originally consisting of Daniel "Sonny" Norton (lead), Jerry Wittick (tenor), Harold Major (tenor), William Davis (baritone), and Gerald Hamilton (bass), the Crows experienced a personnel change in 1952 when Wittick left to join the service and was replaced by Mark Jackson (prior to their recordings). Davis wrote the highly successful "Gee" and its flip side, "I Love You So," which became a 1958 hit for the Chantels.

"Gee" was one of the first crossover records by a black group, reaching No. 2 on the R&B charts and No. 14 on the pop charts. This was unexpected because R&B songs hadn't yet infiltrated the almost exclusively white charts, but soon other records (such as the Chords' "Sh-Boom") followed suit, changing the nature of popular music in America. Despite their success with "Gee," which in 1956 prompted Goldner to establish the Gee subsidiary label, the Crows had a handful of failed singles, and after 1954's "Sweet Sue" they parted company (Davis joined the Continentals for their only record, 1955's "You're an Angel"). "Gee" has been cited as a contender for the title of first rock and roll record. (See chapter 3 for further information.)

Frankie Lymon and the Teenagers.   Among the legendary harmonizers that Goldner signed to his Gee label, the Teenagers, an even younger group than the Crows, was led by twelve-year-old Frankie Lymon, who with his junior high school friends practiced on street corners, in backyards, and on the roofs of Harlem apartment buildings. In 1954, Herman Santiago (first tenor), Jimmy Merchant (second tenor), Joe Negroni (baritone), and Sherman Garnes (bass) formed a vocal quartet called the Premiers, adding Lymon (who made the transition from sacred to secular songs, having previously sung in his father's gospel group, the Harlemaires) after meeting him at a talent show. Richard Barrett, the lead singer of another Goldner group, the Valentines, overheard the Premiers and brought them to Gee Records for an audition. Re-named the Teenagers, in late 1955 they recorded "Why Do Fools Fall in Love" (initially titled "Why Do Birds Sing So Gay"), which has the status of a vocal group classic because of Lymon's innocent and charming performance. The success of the song made Lymon the first black teenage pop star. Released in early 1956, it became a tremendous hit, climbing to the top of the R&B charts and to No. 6 on the pop charts. Today, "Why Do Fools" remains one standard by which the doo-wop style is defined. Goldner followed the Teenagers' success with recordings by such other doo-wop groups as the Wrens, the Harptones, the Flamingos, and the Cleftones.

In the mid-1950s, Frankie Lymon and the Teenagers popularized the doo-wop style with youngsters (young teens and preteens), whereas previously groups sang songs with texts targeting an adult audience. Their "Why Do Fools" hit presented the typical schoolboy doo-wop sound, featuring Lymon's clear falsetto lead voice that became the group's trademark sound, accompanied by background voices harmonizing lyrics of innocent love. In *The Sound of the City*, Charlie Gillett claims this notable recording represents the late '50s novelty sound:

> "Why Do Fools Fall in Love" was in many ways the definitive fast novelty vocal group record of the period, combining an unforgettable web of back-up noises with a classic teenage-lament lyric. Bass singer Sherman Garnes kicked the song off: "Ay, dum-da di-dum dah dum . . ." and in came Frankie, wailing high in his little boy's cry: "Ooh-wah, oo-ooh wah-ah." And then, with the rest of the group weaving in and out, and saxman Jimmy Wright honking along with them, came the song itself, as simple as a nursery rhyme, and as effective, but sung with such heartfelt conviction that it sounded—like the group's name—teenage, not kindergarten.[7]

On the success of this record, the Teenagers toured frequently, influencing others with their clean-cut, innocent image and tightly choreographed performances that included turns, pivots, and kicks while tugging their shirt cuffs, all with coordinated precision. In 1956 and 1957, they followed with five more R&B Top 10 singles, including "I Want You to Be My Girl," "Who Can Explain?," and "The ABC's of Love." The Teenagers were featured singing their fifth single, "I'm Not a Juvenile Delinquent" (1956), in the Alan Freed movie *Rock, Rock, Rock!*, helping defend the new rock and roll genre. In 1957, after appearing in Freed's *Mister Rock and Roll*, Lymon attempted an unsuccessful solo career (with only one modest pop hit, "Goody Goody") and the Teenagers continued for a short time without him. Lymon died in 1968 of a heroin overdose at age twenty-five. Although acknowledged almost solely for his one hit, "Why Do Fools," he greatly influenced future rock and rollers. As the first black teen idol, he was an inspiration to many '60s artists, including Ronnie Spector, Diana Ross, Marvin Gaye, Stevie Wonder, and Michael Jackson. Though his group's output was small, their recordings are some of the finest of the rock and roll era. Frankie Lymon and the Teenagers were inducted into the Rock and Roll Hall of Fame in 1993.

The Chords.   The Chords recorded their famous song, "Sh-Boom," in March 1954, on Atlantic Records' Cat subsidiary. This is another recording that has stirred the ongoing debate among rock enthusiasts as to which was the first rock and roll record, since it has been cited as another contender for the title, along with the Crows' "Gee." (See chapter 3 for further information.) Chronologically, the Crows' single was recorded first, but both songs peaked in the summer of 1954. With the Chords' having reached more people, the recording became the first black doo-wop record in the Top 10 on the pop charts. Nonetheless, both songs had a tremendous impact on the doo-wop sub-genre, rock and roll's development, and '50s society. Hailing from the Bronx, New York, the Chords consisted of Carl Feaster (lead), Jimmy Keyes (first tenor), Floyd McRae (second tenor), Claude Feaster (baritone), and William "Ricky" Edwards (bass). The group formed from previous ensembles: the Tune-toppers (the Feaster brothers), Buddy McRae's Keynotes, and Jimmy Keyes's Four Notes joined Ricky Edwards, who came from a group called the Chords. In 1951, the four groups merged, first named the Keynotes and then the Chords. All of the previous groups had been performing "Sh-Boom," so it was the logical first release for the newly formed Chords.

This landmark record featured the quintet's voices throughout, beginning in the four-bar introduction with characteristic doo-wop a cappella vocals followed by a soft rhythm section (guitar, string bass, and drums) instrumental accompaniment and tenor saxophone improvisatory solo. With an exuberant beat, the song had a very balanced structure of eight-bar periods, each consisting of two four-measure phrases. Most sections included group vocals in harmony (the chord tones of the doo-wop progression) on both lyrics and nonsense syllables while a bass solo constituted the bridge section, reflecting the Ink Spots' influence. The song's title represented the syllables sung by the group, both behind the soloists and as filler during breaks in the song's lyrics (whose message was about dreaming of a future with someone to whom the singer was attracted). With its song theme, it was no surprise that the recording appealed to teenagers and adults alike.

"Sh-Boom" ranked high on both black (No. 2) and white (No. 5) charts despite an immediate cover version by a Canadian white vocal group, the Crew-Cuts. The Crew-Cuts' rendition triggered a flood of R&B covers by white pop artists; it was common for white groups to cover black songs and change lyrics and instrumentation, making them more marketable to white audiences than the black originals. Though the Crew-Cuts did not change this song's lyrics (other than a few nonsense syllables), they removed African American musical characteristics and cleaned up the sound by replacing the singers' small R&B combo accompaniment with a large swing band including several saxophones, brass instruments, and a rhythm section with a timpani drum. Shortly after the

Chords' "Sh-Boom" release, Atlantic Records was served a restraining order by another group called the Chords, making the company rename its new hit group the Chordcats, after which they again changed their name to the Sh-Booms in hopes that the song reference would remind deejays of the group's past hit. It didn't work, however, and the ensemble's popularity faded, though not before they enjoyed a brief moment of glory and created an exciting doo-wop gem.

The Penguins.   Along with the Five Satins' "In the Still of the Night" and the Flamingos' "I Only Have Eyes for You," the Penguins' "Earth Angel" is another of the most popular doo-wop songs. Recorded in 1954, this simple and innocent love song sung by a high lead voice with background vocals providing "oohs" and "wahs" in thick harmony, accompanied by the doo-wop triplet rhythmic figure in the accompanying piano, was a No. 1 R&B and No. 8 pop hit. As was the case with the Five Satins, this recording has been criticized as amateurish because of its crude recording techniques. The single was created in a garage studio with drums muffled by pillows in an attempt not to overpower the young vocalists. Nevertheless, "Earth Angel" remains one of the most popular oldies, if not the absolute all-time favorite. For ten years after its release, group after group covered the recording.

The Penguins consisted of Cleveland Duncan (lead), Dexter Tisby (second tenor), Curtis Williams (baritone), and Bruce Tate (bass). They were students at Fremont High School in Los Angeles and took their name from the image on the Kool cigarettes package. After Dootone's president, Dootsie Williams, heard the group, they began recording for the label. A rough demo of "Earth Angel" was brought to John Dolphin's Dolphins of Hollywood store, where the in-store deejay, Dick "Huggy Boy" Hugg, gave it immediate airplay (broadcast from the front window of the record store), ensuring quick exposure. As listeners began requesting the song, Williams was forced to manufacture the record as quickly as possible. Group personnel changes occurred when Teddy Harper and Randolph Jones replaced Tate and Williams, respectively. The group moved to the Mercury label when manager Buck Ram acquired the package recording deal for them and the Platters. Unsuccessful at Mercury, they switched to Atlantic Records and then back to recording for Dootsie Williams. The Penguins never achieved success equal to that of "Earth Angel." A Crew-Cuts pop cover of this landmark record proved successful a year later, ranking No. 3 on the pop charts.

The Silhouettes.   The Silhouettes' "Get a Job," another instant winner, was recorded in late 1957 for Junior Records and released on Herald/Ember in 1958. The recording shot to the top of both the R&B and the pop charts. With its nonsense syllables ("byip byip byip byip" and "sha-na-na") creating the rhythmic background over which the breathtakingly fast verses were provided by the lead singer, this song written by Richard Lewis was about the group's true-life situation of making a living, at the time an unusual topic for a doo-wop song. It incorporated a honking rhythm and blues-flavored saxophone solo and boogie-woogie-style piano accompaniment with handclaps and a strong backbeat provided by the drums. The song was immensely popular that year. Originally from Philadelphia, the Silhouettes were named the Gospel Tornados until their need for work made them switch to secular music in 1955. After being spotted performing in a small club by Philadelphia disc jockey and owner of Junior Records, Kae Williams, they recorded "Get a Job" on the label and changed their name to the Silhouettes, the title of an earlier hit by the Rays. The vocal ensemble consisted of William Horton (lead), Richard Lewis (tenor), Earl Beal (baritone), and Raymond Edwards (bass). Once Dick Clark heard the recording, he realized its hit potential. However, knowing Junior was too small a label to support a national hit, he did not play it on *American Bandstand* until Al Silver of Herald/Ember Records arranged a lease arrangement with Junior. Shortly after "Get a Job" was first played on the television show, it became a sensation. Although the Silhouettes recorded throughout the early '60s, they never had another hit.

Other Doo-Woppers

There were many other interesting and captivating doo-wop delights made in the late '50s. Little Anthony and the Imperials' "Tears on My Pillow" (1958) and "Shimmy, Shimmy, Ko-Ko-Bop" (1959) were two doo-wop hits, the latter a wild novelty song. This group served as a role model for numerous future artists during the late '50s. The integrated Impalas' irresistible "Sorry (I Ran All the Way Home)" (1959) represents the quintessential late '50s rock and roll group song, with its opening spoken "ut-oh" by lead singer Joe "Speedo" Frazier, intoned as if a little boy had been caught doing something naughty, and orchestral timbres accompanying the quartet. The Fiestas' "So Fine" (1958), with its enticing backbeat and welcoming vocal harmonies, was representative of the group's output that ventured into soul music. The Clovers, performers of "Devil or Angel" (1955), consistently achieved hits for Atlantic Records, both beautiful ballads and uptempo R&B songs. Originally formed at a Washington, D.C., area high school, they were one of the most successful R&B groups, blending R&B and gospel-style vocals and helping lay the groundwork for soul music. Their last major hit was Jerry Leiber and Mike Stoller's "Love Potion No. 9" (1959). The Fleetwoods (Gary Troxel, Barbara Ellis, and Gretchen Christopher), a vocal trio initially called Two Girls and a Guy, had an angelic, mellow sound, displayed in their very popular debut single, "Come Softly to Me" (1959). This song reflected the spontaneous air of doo-wop songs and initially was recorded a cappella, with only shaken car keys in the background; instruments were added later. The recording reached both white and black audiences (No. 1 on the pop charts and No. 5 on the R&B charts), and was followed by another pop charts-topper by the group, "Mr. Blue" (1959).

Lady Doo-Woppers

Although the '50s rock and roll doo-wop subgenre consisted mostly of male performers, side by side with such gender-mixed groups as the Fleetwoods were female vocal ensembles. Females were at a cultural disadvantage during the '50s because they weren't permitted to spend time singing on street corners, as did their male counterparts. If girls formed groups, it was usually at school with their music teachers. In addition, the music industry felt that female groups wouldn't be profitable, since women were the buyers of most records. This scarcity of the female group sound also occurred partly because women were at a musical disadvantage since the voices of women's groups were relatively uniform. Male groups had a wide range of voice types, from falsetto to bass. Nevertheless, three kinds of female vocal groups emerged in the '50s: all-female groups, female leads fronting male ensembles, and groups with female members in supporting roles. Doo-wop sung by female groups is considered to have begun with the Bobbettes and the Chantels in 1957, but the sound made no impression on the music world until the '60s girl groups. However, the earlier (mid-1950s) influential female groups cannot be overlooked: all-female groups, such as Shirley Gunter and the Queens, the (West Coast) Dreamers, the Hearts, and the Cookies; those with female leads fronting male groups, such as the Charmers, the Sensations, the Kodaks, and the Tuneweavers; and groups with female members in supporting roles, such as the Platters, the Fleetwoods, the Lovenotes, and the Skyliners.

Shirley Gunter and the Queens was one of the first all-female R&B groups. Hailing from Los Angeles, the group consisted of Shirley Gunter (lead, sister of Coasters member Cornelius Gunter), Lula Bee Kinney (first tenor), Lula Mae Suggs (second tenor), and Blondine Taylor (baritone). Their first release, "Oop Shoop" (1954), is considered the first all-female doo-wop recording. They followed with other recordings, such as "You're Mine" (1955) and "What Difference Does It Make?" (1955). The Dreamers were referred to as the West Coast Dreamers so as not to be confused with other vocal groups with the Dreamers name. This group, consisting of Gloria Jones (tenor), Nanette Williams (tenor), Annette Williams (second tenor), and Fanita Barrett (baritone), had modest success when they backed up Richard Berry on the "Bye Bye" and "At Last" single (1955), and became famous when they changed their name to the Blossoms and added Darlene Love (of the Crystals and Bob B. Soxx and the Blue Jeans 1960s fame). The Hearts are considered to have been the premier female group of the mid-1950s for their "Lonely Nights" (1955) recording, which has been named the best female group R&B recording. With members Joyce West (lead), Hazel Anderson (tenor), Florestine Barnes (tenor), and "Ena" Louise Harris Murray (baritone), this group had a wider harmonic range than most female groups because of Murray's low voice. Featuring Jeannette "Baby" Washington (who embarked upon a successful solo career in 1957) and sometimes joined vocally by piano accompanist Rex Garvin, the Hearts followed with "All My Love Belongs to You" (1955) and "She Drives Me Crazy" (1956). The Cookies were the female trio that later evolved into the Raelettes, Ray Charles's backup group. They did much female background singing for Atlantic's artists, such as Joe Turner and Chuck Willis. Margie Hendricks (lead),

Ethel McCrae, and Dorothy Jones began recording as the Cookies in 1954 with "Don't Let Go" and "All Night Mambo" before releasing "In Paradise," which was on the R&B charts (No. 9 hit) in 1956.

Of the vocal groups with females in fronting roles, the Charmers featured Lucille "Vicki" Burgess (lead) for two highly treasured recordings in 1954, "The Beating of My Heart" and "Tony My Darling." A friend of Clyde McPhatter and his family, Burgess was the inspiration for the Drifters' "Lucille" that same year. Afterward, the Charmers became the Chorals, and Burgess then sang lead for the all-girl Joytones in 1956. The Sensations, originally called the Cavaliers, formed in Philadelphia in 1954. Recording for Atlantic's Atco subsidiary, Yvonne Mills Baker led the male group with her spry, strong voice. Since Atco's management regarded their sound as sensational, the group received its new name. After releasing their first two singles, "Yes Sir, That's My Baby" (1955) and "Please Mr. Disc Jockey" (1956) (both on the R&B charts), the Sensations had some very successful hits in the early 1960s. Making their debut in 1957, the Kodaks, known for their schoolgirl doo-wop sound, featured Pearl McKinnon. Of all the singers influenced by Frankie Lymon, McKinnon came the closest in quality to Lymon's voice with her high tenor. This almost-all-male group recorded a series of classics, including their first single, "Teenager's Dream" and the flip side "Little Boy and Girl" (1957), "Oh Gee, Oh Gosh" (1957), and "Runaround Baby" (1958). Though popular in the New York City area, the Kodaks never had any national hits. After the group parted company, McKinnon joined the Deltars. The Tuneweavers' lead singer, Margo Sylvia, had a sweet, smooth voice. She joined her brother, Gilbert Lopez's, group called the Toneweavers, and they performed her original "Happy Happy Birthday" in their live shows. After a Boston area deejay incorrectly introduced their record as by the Tuneweavers, that became their name. Sylvia's song, known as "Happy, Happy Birthday Baby" (1957), became a huge hit (No. 4 on the R&B charts and No. 5 on the pop charts), and has been one of the most popular oldies dedication songs ever since.

One of the vocal groups with female members in supporting roles, besides the Platters and the Fleetwoods, was the Lovenotes. Formed in 1956 in New York City, the group included Lucy Cedeño (also known as Lucy Anderson, wife of Gary "U.S." Bonds) singing second tenor. Their R&B hit, "United" (1957), became part of the doo-wop repertoire. Another group, the Skyliners, was formed by Jimmy Beaumont (lead), Wally Lester (second tenor), and Jack Taylor (bass) after they left the Crescents, with the addition of high school friends Janet Vogel (first tenor) and Joe VerScharen (baritone) in 1958. The group began recording for Calico Records, a Pittsburgh label. Their first single, "Since I Don't Have You" (late 1958), was a No. 3 hit on the R&B charts and a No. 12 hit on the pop charts. Featuring Beaumont's irresistibly smooth and versatile voice, complemented by Vogel's astonishingly high soprano, this elaborately produced recording had sophisticated and tight doo-wop harmonies with supporting orchestral accompaniment. It expanded doo-wop's horizons, influencing Phil Spector (of the Teddy Bears and '60s girl group production fame) and the early '60s girl group rock subgenre. Recording into the mid-1960s with additional Top 40 hits, the Skyliners never again achieved the success of their first record.

Other female doo-woppers included the Miller Sisters, the Deltairs, the Joytones, and the Rosebuds. The Bonnie Sisters ("Cry Baby," 1956), the Poni-Tails ("Born Too Late," 1958), and the Chordettes ("Mr. Sandman," 1954; "Lollipop," 1958) had high-ranking pop hits as more acceptable female white pop groups in the mid-1950s. Other groups in the pop realm that catered to adults and had many hits with covers of male doo-wop songs included sister combos, such as the Fontane Sisters ("Hearts of Stone," 1954) and the McGuire Sisters ("Goodnight, Sweetheart, Goodnight," 1954; "Sincerely," 1955).

The Bobbettes.   One of the most influential '50s all-girl groups, the Bobbettes was the first female vocal group to have a No. 1 R&B hit and a Top 10 hit. Formed in 1956 and known as the Harlem Queens until manager James Dailey changed their name, all members were between the ages of eleven and fourteen. These talented young women—Emma Pought (lead tenor), Reather Dixon (lead baritone), Laura Webb (tenor), Helen Gathers (tenor), and Janice Pought (tenor), composed a number of the songs they recorded. Brought to the attention of Atlantic, with which they began their recording career in 1957, they had an enormously popular debut single, "Mr. Lee" (No. 1 R&B hit and No. 6 pop hit), released that year. It was originally a derisive song about their fifth grade teacher, and Atlantic insisted they change its lyrics before releasing the record. Though this was their only Top 40 hit, the girls continued to perform, tour, and record through the mid-1960s and, occasionally, the mid-1970s. When they were on the road, they were the only girl group on the tour bus, so singers such as Ruth Brown and LaVern Baker befriended them, helping the teenagers adjust to their new way of life. With frequent label changes hindering their success and achieving only minor hits in the early '60s, the Bobbettes recorded their sequel Mr. Lee song, "I Shot Mr. Lee," about Mr. Lee being shot in the head because of his unfaithfulness. Originally recorded in 1959 by Atlantic, which chose not to release it, the record was released by Triple-X Records in 1960 (immediately followed by an Atlantic release of it), the same year as their single "Dance with Me, Georgie" and "Have Mercy Baby."

The Chantels.   Another significant early female group, and one of the most popular, the Chantels were teenagers from the Bronx, New York. They were one of the first all-girl vocal groups to have more than one hit. Schoolmates who sang together in their Catholic school choir, Arlene Smith (lead), Sonia Goring, Rene Minus, Jackie Landry, and Lois Harris took their name from another Catholic school in the Bronx (St. Francis de Chantelle). Influenced by the vocals of Frankie Lymon and the Teenagers' big hit on Gee Records, the girls began recording for George Goldner's End label with the assistance of Richard Barrett (the Teenagers' manager). Rehearsed, mentored, and produced by Barrett, they recorded their first single, "He's Gone" with "The Plea" (1957), both songs written by Smith and featuring her soulful lead voice, then recorded "Maybe," their second single, the same year. Featuring Smith's attractive and powerful voice, "Maybe" became their biggest hit, reaching No. 2 on the R&B charts and No. 15 on the pop charts (it recharted in 1969 after Janis Joplin's cover) and earning the group an appearance on *American Bandstand* and inclusion on one of Alan Freed's package tours. The Chantels followed with other favorites, including "Every Night (I Pray)" (1958) and "I Love You So" (1958). The group experienced financial tensions and personnel changes; Smith and Harris departed in 1959, and Annette Smith (no relation) replaced Arlene Smith as lead on the group's next hits in 1961, "Look in My Eyes" and "Well, I Told You" (an answer song to Ray Charles's "Hit the Road Jack"). The group recorded for several labels throughout the '60s. Arlene Smith went on to a solo career in the '60s, became a teacher, and re-formed the group, continuing to perform with new members throughout the '90s. Though there were R&B all-girl groups before the Chantels, none of them had such a run of popular records or offered such a distinctive sound. The Chantels greatly influenced the girl groups that flourished in the early 1960s, such as the Shangri-Las, the Ronettes, and the Crystals.

The Shirelles and Others.   Among other late 1950s vocal groups with females were the Aquatones ("You," 1958), the Quin-Tones ("Down the Aisle of Love," 1958), the Teddy Bears ("To Know Him, Is to Love Him," a 1958 No. 1 pop hit), the Tonettes ("Oh What a Baby," 1958), and the Shirelles. Originally called the Poquellos, the Shirelles formed in 1957 when four schoolmates in Passaic, New Jersey, were inspired by the Chantels to start their own group: Shirley Owens (lead), Addie "Micki" Harris, Doris Coley, and Beverly Lee. The Shirelles wrote their own songs, such as "I Met Him on a Sunday," which they allegedly composed to perform at their school's talent show in 1958 (some sources credit the Five Royales as the composers of the tune). A classmate invited them to sing for her mother, Florence Greenberg, owner of Tiara Records (which changed its name to Scepter), and they began their recording career. The group had many more hits, such as "Dedicated to the One I Love" (1959) and "Tonights the Night" (1960). Their classic recording, "Will You Love Me Tomorrow," an instant success with its inviting combination of Alston's lead vocals, background voices in harmony, and ingenious orchestral accompaniment, was the first No. 1 pop hit by an all-female rock and roll group. Recorded in late 1960 and charting in early 1961, it was also a No. 2 R&B hit. "Tomorrow" not only established the popularity of the Shirelles, but also became an influential template for girl group recordings. Gillian Gaar proclaims the significance of this song in *She's a Rebel*: "After the success of previous hits like the Bobbettes' 'Mr. Lee' and the Chantels' 'Maybe,' the Shirelles' 'Will You

Love Me Tomorrow' heralded the true start of the girl group era."[8] One of the greatest female vocal groups, the Shirelles thrived during the emergence of the girl group subgenre; their other No. 1 on the pop charts was "Soldier Boy" (1962). In 1996, the Shirelles were inducted into the Rock and Roll Hall of Fame for their important contributions to the genre.

Sometimes considered to be overlooked and underrated, the '50s vocal group rock and roll sound flourished into the early '60s, when doo-wop elements blended with other styles and appeared in new rock and roll subgenres. The sound of such girl groups as the Chiffons, the Crystals, and the Ronettes wasn't alone in borrowing doo-wop characteristics. The thrilling new sounds of soul music did as well; both the more pop-oriented Motown and the Memphis-style soul groups (including the Four Tops, the Supremes, the Impressions, and the Falcons) received their inspiration from, and sometimes their start with, '50s vocal groups. The rise of '60s surf music witnessed the borrowing of harmonic tendencies, as is evident in the singing of the Beach Boys, influenced by the Four Freshmen and other '50s vocal groups. Even when the music of '50s doo-wop groups became dated as the evolution of rock and roll progressed (complete with new political and societal influences), this sweet, harmonic style reflecting '50s American life continued to resound. Long after doo-wop's popularity diminished, several '50s vocal groups continued to perform in rock and roll revival shows, especially during the '80s and '90s, when some still released records. The sound was revived by such '90s groups as Boyz II Men, the Backstreet Boys, 98 Degrees, and 'N Sync, who performed similar music in the barbershop quartet tradition and sang covers of doo-wop classics. This was a well-deserved tribute to the subgenre that established vocal virtuosity and background harmonies as viable elements of rock and roll.

NOTES

All charts positions referred to in the chapter are based on Joel Whitburn's Record Research publications, which compile *Billboard* charts information of the rock and roll era.

1. Anthony J. Gribin and Matthew M. Schiff, *The Complete Book of Doo-Wop* (Iola, WI: Krause, 2000), 26.

2. Jim Dawson and Steve Propes, *What Was the First Rock 'n' Roll Record?* (Boston: Faber and Faber, 1992).

3. Bob Hyde and Walter DeVenne, "Track Lineup" and "Compiler's Notes" for Rhino Collection of Recordings, *The Doo Wop Box: 101 Vocal Group Gems from the Golden Age of Rock 'N' Roll* (Los Angeles: Rhino Records, 1993), 4–11.

4. "Alan Freed: King of the Moondoggers," temporary exhibit (Cleveland, OH: Rock and Roll Hall of Fame and Museum, May 10, 2003).

5. Rock and Roll Hall of Fame Foundation, "The Drifters," Rock and Roll Hall of Fame and Museum, http://www.rockhall.com/hof/inductee.asp?id=94.

6. Barry Hansen, "Doo-Wop," in *The Rolling Stone Illustrated History of Rock & Roll*, 3rd ed., ed. Anthony DeCurtis, James Henke, and Holly George-Warren (New York: Random House, 1992), 97.

7. Charlie Gillett, *The Sound of the City: The Rise of Rock and Roll*, 2nd ed., enl. (New York: Da Capo Press, 1996), 32.

8. Gillian G. Gaar, *She's a Rebel: The History of Women in Rock & Roll*, 2nd ed., enl. (New York: Seal Press, 2002), 32.

8

ROCK AND ROLL MUSIC BUSINESS: "MONEY HONEY"

THE MUSIC INDUSTRY

In the '50s, rock and roll artists helped change America by reshaping its popular music with new sounds. The stable, conservative life Americans led after World War II became increasingly infiltrated with rock and roll music as the decade progressed, resulting in the emergence of a popular culture complete with developing industries to support it. Early in the decade, as more and more white teenagers became aware of rhythm and blues music, society took note of youths beginning to purchase the music not only in the South and the west but eventually all over the country. The Civil Rights Movement and its desegregation of schools have been credited with making possible the acceptance of African American–style music by white teens. Black and white youths danced together at increasingly integrated rock and roll concerts. The new music helped break racial barriers. Prior to the '50s, black music had been nearly totally segregated from white music (*Billboard* referred to R&B music as "race music" until 1949), had not been played on network radio, and had been sold only in black record stores. In the '50s, along with those involved in the emergent music industry (record executives, disc jockeys, and songwriters), parents noticed that millions of white teens flocked to R&B music, by then called rock and roll, and made it their own. America's youth listened to their favorite music not only on transistor and car radios but also on recordings, which they began to purchase in droves.

During this prosperous time, most record sales were made to girls desiring songs they listened to on the radio and purchasing them with their allowances. Steve Chapple and Reebee Garofalo illustrate society's change of musical appetite in *Rock 'n' Roll Is Here to Pay* with statistics from the famous Dolphin Record Store in Los Angeles, which specialized in R&B records. By 1952 the store reported that 40 percent of its sales were to whites, whereas a few months prior, sales were almost exclusively to blacks. The store's most popular R&B records with both whites and blacks were Fats Domino's "The Fat Man"; Jackie Brenston's "Rocket 88"; Lloyd Price's "Lawdy Miss Clawdy"; Big Joe Turner's "Chains of Love," "Sweet Sixteen," and "Honey Hush"; and Stick McGhee's "Drinkin' Wine Spo-Dee-o-Dee," all recorded by indies.[1]

Rock and roll is credited not only with helping to integrate America racially but also with the reinvigoration of the recording industry as music in recorded format supplanted printed sheet music. As the teen market blossomed, record companies thrived and a new music industry evolved—one that catered to the audience of the exhilarating new music. Tin Pan Alley publishing houses, which previously dominated the music business by supplying pop songs for the tastes and conservative cultural values of white, middle-aged America, no longer reigned. Side by side with TPA publishers were a handful of major record companies (majors) that had established themselves with the creation of a predictable, polite product that refrained from giving offense. It was not customary in that pop music for black musicians to flourish as performers; few of them were accepted into the mainstream, and when they were, it was usually because they either sustained a humorous, minstrel-type black image (such as Louis Jordan) or removed African American musical characteristics from their performing style (such as the Mills Brothers and Nat "King" Cole). The resulting pop music included conservative and inoffensive material that was more popular than black music, primarily because whites performed it. While rock and roll changed the pop music industry with its unprecedented content of music by African Americans and black music performed by young whites, music industry leaders battled this threat, though eventually they accepted rock and roll on their own terms.

The entertainment industry felt threatened by rock and roll in three chief ways, and initiated a counterattack on the new music. First, in the recording business, since an abundance of indies supported rock and roll, the majors that specialized in classical, jazz, and pop music—and initially rejected rock and roll music as inferior (such as Columbia, RCA, Capitol, and Decca)—were outnumbered. As indies greatly increased their market share in the 1950s, majors experienced a substantial loss of sales. The exception was Columbia; its A&R man, Mitch Miller, resisted rock and roll in favor of easy listening music into the late 1960s—yet the company still had good sales.

A second industry problem arose in the publishing business because most rock artists composed their own music, causing ASCAP (which represented professional TPA songwriters) to suffer for its earlier arrogance of shutting out R&B and rock and roll songwriters. Those represented by ASCAP missed out on the financial rewards of the new '50s music. Having accepted all songwriters (including rock and rollers) that ASCAP rejected, its competitor, Broadcast

Music, Incorporated (BMI) flourished. These organizations collected royalty payments for artists. Because rock and roll songs frequently were not written down and existed only in musicians' heads, a change occurred in the music industry: the performance of a song (recorded or not) was more important than the composition itself. This helped lessen the importance of TPA's long-standing sheet music industry.

Third, with the rise of television and its important visual display of rock and roll via variety shows, another threat to the established music industry was a violation of the accepted artist image and performance style. With polite society accustomed to the likes of Perry Como and Frank Sinatra, such rock and roll artists as Little Richard and Elvis Presley shocked the establishment by displaying what was considered outlandish performance attire and gestures, let alone what was deemed poor vocal technique. While rock musicians were labeled crude and amateurish, TPA began to lose ground with the youthful audience's demand for rock and roll.

To place all this in historical context, during the '30s, the publishing and broadcasting facets of the music industry and the American Federation of Musicians (AFM) expanded, and ASCAP tried to double its licensing fees to the National Association of Broadcasters (NAB). In response, the NAB banned all ASCAP material from the airwaves and formed BMI (a less pop-oriented organization than ASCAP) as its own licensing group in 1940, thus providing for the needs of minority songwriters and performers excluded by ASCAP's elitism. This was important to the music industry outside the closed association of TPA writers and publishers, and resulted in huge royalty profits once rock and roll became popular. Many radio stations would not sign agreements with ASCAP at this time (including the CBS and NBC networks). Catastrophe struck when the AFM went on strike in 1942, preventing union musicians from recording. At the same time, during this swing jazz era, big bands featured a singer in mostly instrumental arrangements. Once the AFM strike was settled, popular taste had shifted to these singers, such as Perry Como, Peggy Lee, Jo Stafford, and Frank Sinatra.

Ed Ward succinctly sums up the 1950s rock and roll–caused TPA turmoil in *Rock of Ages* by pointing out how the new music infiltrated the songwriter's trade and that most veteran songwriters had no clue how to write rock and roll songs, simple though they were. The pop market hadn't entirely surrendered to rock music, and deejays across America swore their allegiance to what they referred to as "good music" and adult-oriented programming; however, rock and roll hits brought in better profits more quickly. Ward makes it clear that the industry understood that TPA had missed out and that, if the traditional songwriting industry was to survive, it had to incorporate rock and roll into its production. Ward concludes that the salvation of professional songwriters came in late 1957, when they began to craft professionally written pop songs with the rock and roll feeling for new pop idols, such as Paul Anka, Frankie Avalon, and Fabian.[2]

Concurrent with the emergence of rock and roll, a changed music industry arose from necessity. As the '50s progressed and more teenagers were attracted to rock and roll, they wanted records, record players, and radio programming of the music. The music industry quickly produced responses, because for companies to remain on the leading edge, change was imperative. Businesses were required to engage in methods and practices they initially did not approve of but had to use in order to stay afloat. The first main change occurred in the record industry. Record companies were central to the '50s music business as the source of the product. As transformation of record production and distribution activities occurred, other industry divisions became affected, and the '50s witnessed enormous music industry growth. Chief among these was radio, which had already reserved its place of importance in America's homes and took on a new role in the '50s as a major promoter of the new music. Before long, other aspects of the business evolved, including television's role providing exposure not only to the sounds of rock and roll but also to its visual aspects. As the decade progressed, songwriters, producers, managers, and concert promoters found their niche as rock and roll matured from infancy to established music genre; however, each facet of the music business was dependent on the record companies that produced the most important product, the music.

RECORD PRODUCTION AND DISTRIBUTION

By the mid-'50s, it was evident that Americans were enjoying entertainment and spending more money on it than ever before. An important development affecting the music industry was the trend toward home entertainment. Between 1945 and 1950, the number of home record players had doubled to more than 25 million.[3] With a phonograph in nearly every home, whether a large console or a portable model, some consumers indulged in the new expensive high fidelity craze: amplifiers, FM tuners, speakers, and tape recorders. However, the source product was still the record. The music recording industry experienced vast improvements with technological breakthroughs after World War II, from high fidelity to stereo sound and tape recording to the album.

Ever since Thomas Edison invented the phonograph (wax cylinder) in 1877, the recording industry had expanded, from spoken word and classical music to the day's pop music—on cylinders of wax. In 1894, Emile Berliner began selling discs that were a great improvement over the cylinder, in that molding from a master could produce multiple copies; meanwhile, Eldridge R. Johnson developed a method of cutting a groove in a solid wax disc. In 1901, Johnson and Berliner formed the Victor Talking Machine Company, which, with the Columbia Graphophone Company, dominated early record production in the United States. They recorded show tunes by TPA and other New York City composers, and in the '20s competed with smaller independent companies, such as OKeh, the source of the first black musician's record (blueswoman Mamie

The Christmas window display of L.A. May Co. in New York City, showing television set, phonograph, Christmas tree, and other music paraphernalia, 1952. Courtesy of the Library of Congress.

Smith's 1920 "Crazy Blues"), discoverer of the black market, and labeler of "race records" (by Smith's producer, Ralph Peer).

Record sales thrived, exceeding all other leisure-time spending until the early '20s, when commercial radio became popular and, by 1922, had drawn the public's attention away from the phonograph, causing sales to plummet until the Great Depression (when they were almost nonexistent). After the 1929 stock market crash, most of the small record companies went out of business or were bought by larger ones. Even Victor was purchased by the Radio Corporation of America (RCA) in 1929. Years later, the record label was changed to RCA-Victor; part of RCA was bought by Edward Noble, who renamed it the American Broadcasting Company (ABC) and opened its record division in the '50s. In these early days, the growth of commercial radio broadcasting allowed the record business to be mostly financed by radio profits from RCA network radio and the Columbia Broadcasting System (CBS), formed in 1927 by Arthur Judson as a rival network of twelve radio stations (before he purchased other labels in 1934 and started a record division). Rivalry between the two large companies began to extend beyond radio to records. In the 1950s, the rivalry expanded to television, and during the 1960s, RCA and CBS emphasized the more profitable television medium.

Following the Depression, the jukebox helped save the record industry. Though the device had been around early in the century (first developed in 1908), it fell by the wayside as phonographs and records moved into America's

Dr. Frances O. Kelsey, passing phonograph records to her daughters Christine (left) and Susan, at their home in Maryland, 1959. Courtesy of the Library of Congress.

homes. However, after Prohibition was repealed in 1933 and bars opened by the thousands, tavern owners looked to the coin-operated jukebox for an additional source of revenue and low-cost entertainment for their patrons. Manufactured by such companies as Wurlitzer, Rockola, and Seeburg, by 1935 jukeboxes were a thriving business in the United States; 150,000 were in operation, accounting for 40 percent of the record trade. The machines became a major source of public entertainment, providing a guaranteed market for record companies and a valuable promotional vehicle for recording artists. In addition, jukeboxes stocked with a variety of music styles allowed the public to decide what to listen to. With a jukebox record play costing only 5 cents (and records costing 35 cents to purchase), the new machines were very profitable and helped revitalize the industry.[4]

With the ten-inch shellac 78-RPM record disc having become the norm in the '30s, that record speed was the worldwide vehicle for the spread of music. This format remained the primary recording medium until after World War II, when advances were made with microgroove recording and long-playing (LP) records. In 1948, Columbia introduced the twelve-inch vinyl phonograph disc with a playing speed of 33 ⅓ RPM, which provided superior sound quality, was more durable, and could hold more musical information—eventually about twenty-five minutes of music per side. RCA-Victor followed with the 1949 introduction of the 45-RPM disc, considered a compromise between fidelity and duration that chose convenience over longer playing time. A seven-inch vinyl disc with a wide center hole, the 45 eventually replaced the 78—it had a similar playing time of three to four minutes per side. In time, two 45-RPM discs appeared: the seven-inch extended play (EP) disc, which had two tracks on each side and ran for twice as long as a single, and the twelve-inch single, which ran for up to twelve minutes per side. In the late '40s, American record companies waged what is referred to as the "battle of the speeds," which required three-speed record players: Capitol produced records at all three speeds; RCA-Victor began producing LPs in addition to 45s; and Columbia began to produce single discs at 45 RPM. The 78s gradually disappeared from the market; the LP became the format for album sets in all categories of music (no longer only for classical music, as initially was the case), and 45s became the standard for popular songs.

This record progress coincided with other recording industry developments from the '20s to the '50s: electrical recording and electronic amplification, which became standard, and greatly improved recorded sound; magnetic tape, which was used for commercial master recordings beginning in late 1949; home tape recorders (for recording and playback), which appeared in 1947; multitrack recording, which mixed multiple tracks and made possible new and complex editing techniques in the recording studio, introduced in the late 1950s; and stereophonic sound (although stereo recordings were made as early as the '30s, the technique became important with the arrival of high-fidelity microgroove records), which was introduced by the recording industry in 1957 and used by most

THE JUKEBOX

Helping to revitalize not only the record business but also the entire music industry, the jukebox became big business itself in the '50s. Jukebox operators in locations with a white teenage business were among the first to notice the growing desire of their patrons for black R&B music before local record retailers recognized the trend. With this demand, jukeboxes, which cost an operator approximately $1,000, were stocked with black records purchased at a discount, supplied free by record labels and distributors, or acquired as payola (to feature certain songs in preference to others). The hundreds of millions of dollars generated by jukeboxes were customarily divided equally between jukebox owners and owners of establishments where they were housed—bars, soda shops, restaurants, and other favored teenage places. During the '50, this division of profits changed to a minimum-guarantee system whereby a 60–40 split (with the operator getting the larger share; and sometimes even an 80–20 split) became common. Jukebox operators earned up to $15,000 annually. Establishment owners often supplemented their jukebox income with earnings from other coin-operated machines, such as games, children's rides, and cigarette, food, or drink vending. During the '50s, mobsters purportedly used jukeboxes to support and establish certain artists by dictating the play of their records. Operators were told to give these musicians' selections the No. 1 or No. 2 position on their jukes, thus turning their records into best-sellers. With reports of racketeering in the jukebox industry, investigations were initiated, and Congress introduced a bill in 1956 proposing an annual $52 tax on each jukebox. Also, by decade's end, the overwhelming success of these machines spurred efforts to collect money for performances of recorded music from their operators.

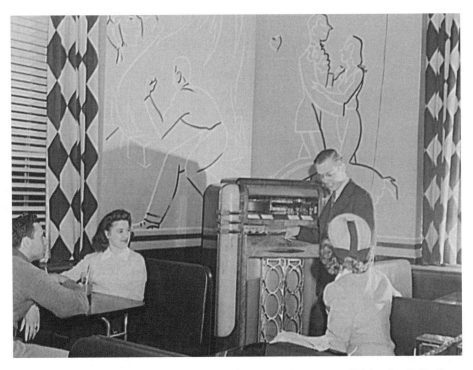

Jim Tillma at the jukebox in the grill at the student union, University of Nebraska, 1951. Courtesy of the Library of Congress.

companies by 1958, with stereo recordings rapidly replacing monophonic records in the '60s. Amid these numerous technological advances, most '50s R&B and early rock and roll record labels used the singles format—the 45.

The third of the large pre–World War II companies, Decca, a British record company, formed its American branch in 1934. Immediately building an impressive roster, Decca label head Jack Kapp helped the company succeed when he slashed record prices to 35 cents or three for a dollar, causing Victor and Columbia to lower their 75-cent records to the same price. As a result, sales climbed as records became an entertainment bargain, and the recording industry was financially rejuvenated. At this time, many of the records manufactured by Decca, RCA-Victor, and Columbia went into jukeboxes, and these record manufacturers, along with song publishers, led the music industry. Publishers derived their income from sheet music sales and from live performances over network radio (royalties) for their copyrighted songs. The music industry's power was a combination of major publishers and major record companies; publishers chose songs they thought should be the next hits and brought them to the record firms to record (sometimes they brought songs to several companies for recording; it was not unusual for multiple renditions of one song to be on the charts simultaneously). When their songs were purchased in record stores and sold as sheet music, publishers' royalties were guaranteed. With so

Gordon MacRae with Dinah Shore on ABC's *The Railroad Hour with Dinah Shore*, c. 1951. Courtesy of the Library of Congress.

many people playing records at home, record company A&R men were elevated to power. Next to them were radio deejays, usually the first to be approached by publishers. Once disc jockeys pushed a record and it was climbing the charts, publishers turned to a second line of plugging that was common at this time—live radio and television performances.

In the early 1950s, the handful of majors that dominated the recording industry included RCA-Victor, Columbia, Decca, Capitol, Mercury, MGM, and ABC-Paramount. These labels represented mostly the mainstream pop market in the late 1940s and early 1950s, yielding the majority of the top hits—such songs as Dinah Shore's "Buttons and Bows" (Columbia), Vaughn Monroe's "Riders in the Sky (A Cowboy Legend)" (RCA-Victor), and Patti Page's "The Tennessee Waltz" (Mercury). Even though these labels dominated race music during the Depression, when they bought out the smaller labels (such as OKeh, absorbed by Columbia in 1926), during World War II, with the shortage of shellac, a chief ingredient of 78-RPM discs, the majors decided to abandon the specialty fields of hillbilly, race, and gospel music, and instead opted to record mainstream commercial pop music. Espousing the general belief that rock and roll was a passing fad, the majors were reluctant to get involved with it, partly from executive dislike and lack of interest in the music, partly from the industry-established patterns of signing artists for multiple years (and artists' being adaptable for long-term appeal), and partly from believing rock and rollers were inflexible, one-style novelty singers.

The Emergence of Indies

America's cultural climate brought about an explosion of new record labels in the '50s, due in part to the majors' shunning of other music styles. The thriving economy increased people's leisure time and income while teenagers figured prominently in American society's consumption of popular culture. Many factors accounted for the recording industry's expansion after 1950—from new technologies improving operations efficiency to the decrease in costs of materials, manufacturing, and distribution, making recordings more afford-able. With favorable economic conditions and new music consumers, innova-tive record labels arose and competed with the established majors. World War II helped change the public's consumption of music with the extensive migration of rural job seekers to cities, allowing different racial and ethnic groups to mix, and the growth in jobs led to growth in disposable income. Par-allel changes occurred in the music industry. Not only were social and musical

Chess Recording Studio, 2005. Courtesy of the Chicago City of Tourism.

aspects of life intermingling, but record sales reflected working-class society's attitudes and tastes. Song messages began to depict the daily life of average people more than they had in commercial pop music. This change was accompanied by the diffusion of power from New York City to other geographic areas of the country, and from major labels to independent entrepreneurs who recorded music and performers the working-class public appreciated. These companies included Sydney Nathan's King Records (Cincinnati, Ohio), Herman Lubinsky's Savoy Records (Newark, New Jersey), Phil and Leonard Chess's Chess Records (Chicago), Don Robey's Duke/Peacock Records (Houston, Texas), and Ahmet Ertegun, Herb Abramson, and Jerry Wexler's Atlantic Records (New York City). With their open minds and sense of what the public wanted to hear, these entrepreneurs were willing to record musicians whom the majors would not.[5]

Whereas the majors consisted of corporate structures complete with executives, producers, A&R men, and pluggers, and recorded large ensembles with choruses as background to solo voices in studios, the indies relied on the ingenuity of their owners, recording simply (and often in garages). Indies were at an advantage because they had low overheads; usually just one person (the owner) served as talent scout, producer, business manager, promotion man, distributor, and even receptionist and mailroom clerk. Their only financial responsibilities often were office rent, payments to record manufacturers (often owned by the majors, who thus earned money from the success of indies), and gifts for deejays in return for playing their records. Few of these labels hired union musicians, and kept costs down by using a small number of performers on recording sessions. There usually were no royalty agreements with artists, who were pleased to receive a small flat fee.

Selling a few thousand records usually covered these expenses, whereas majors had to sell tens of thousands to cover their costs. Most independents raised their profits by working regionally, and thus were not required to know the whole record market in order to do business. Owners distributed their product by car, peddling their newest singles to record stores, radio stations, and wholesalers themselves, often covering their territory in a day or two. Trying to capture a share of the market where no one else had gone, indies kept an open mind about music, venturing where majors did not—usually into R&B, rockabilly, and rhythm and blues-based rock and roll. In the Northeast, significant New York City–based labels included Jubilee, Atlantic, Herald/Ember, and Rama. In the Midwest, King/Federal/DeLuxe, Chess/Checker, and Vee Jay thrived; and in the West such indies as Aladdin, Modern, Specialty, and Imperial served their audience.

By the time deejay Alan Freed moved to New York City in 1954, there were dozens of independent rhythm and blues–based record companies operating on the West Side of Manhattan in an area known as the "Street of Hope"—the area from Forty-second to Fifty-sixth Street and from Tenth Avenue to Broadway. John Jackson states in *Big Beat Heat*, "Each 'indie' label owner harbored aspirations that he might become the next to produce the surprise pop hit to intrude on a field dominated by the few major companies. The area's aura of shirtsleeve-style entrepreneurship contrasted starkly to the more formal midtown zone just a few blocks to the east, which housed RCA Victor, Columbia, Mercury, and Decca." Jackson continues, "What there was was a group of innovative and energetic hustling optimists who hoped the combination of long work hours, a lot of luck, and whatever else it might take would somehow be enough to overcome the long odds of becoming the 'street's' next surprise hit maker."[6]

Formed in 1948 by Jerry Blaine (a co-owner of Cosnat, an R&B label distributor), Jubilee and its subsidiary label Josie were indies that recorded the vocal groups the Orioles, the Four Tunes, and the Cadillacs ("Speedoo" and "Rudolph the Red-Nosed Reindeer") in addition to Bobby Freeman ("Do You Want to Dance") and the instrumental group the Royaltones ("Poor Boy"). Jubilee was one of the first indies to reach a white audience with a black vocal group when the Orioles' "Crying in the Chapel" crossed over to the pop charts in 1953.

Also formed in 1948 as one of the largest of the indies, Atlantic was started by Ahmet Ertegun, the son of a Turkish diplomat, and Herb Abramson, a dentist who worked as an A&R man for National Records in the '40s. Jerry Wexler, who previously worked at *Billboard*, joined as A&R man in 1953 when Abramson began military duty. The three constituted an extraordinary, ingenious, and talented team. Atlantic reached the national level with its outstanding artists, who included Big Joe Turner, Ray Charles, Clyde McPhatter, Chuck Willis ("C. C. Rider" and "What Am I Living For"), and Ivory Joe Hunter ("Since I Met You Baby"), as well as female artists LaVern Baker and Ruth Brown, and vocal groups the Clovers, the Drifters, and the Cardinals ("The Door Is Still Open"). Atlantic's subsidiary labels, Atco and Cat, recorded the Coasters and the Chords, pop singer Walden Robert Cassotto (Bobby Darin; "Splish Splash" and "Dream Lover"), and Ben E. King ("Stand by Me"). Atlantic used outstanding sessionmen on recordings, including pianists and session leaders Jesse Stone, Howard Biggs, and Henry Van Walls, guitarist Mickey Baker, and saxophonists King Curtis and Sam Taylor. By the mid-1950s, Atlantic and its subsidiaries had at least one record on the charts at all times. Atlantic became a dominant R&B label and made the transition from R&B to rock and roll. In 1987, Ahmet Ertegun and Jerry Wexler were inducted into the Rock and Roll Hall of Fame.

Also in New York City, Al Silver formed Herald/Ember in 1952 when his Herald label merged with his brother-in-law Jack Angel's Ember, a label that specialized in vocal groups. The indie recorded some of the most admired ensembles, even though they were mostly one-hit wonders. Silver recruited mainly from outside the metropolitan area: the Nutmegs, the Five Satins, the Turbans, the Mellokings, and the Silhouettes. The next year, George Goldner formed Rama Records and recorded many vocal groups from the streets of New York, such as the Crows, the Harptones, and the Valentines. His subsidiaries included Gee, which recorded the Cleftones and Frankie Lymon and the Teenagers, and Gone/End, which featured the Chantels, the Flamingos, and Little Anthony and the Imperials. Other significant New York indies were Apollo, formed in 1942 by Ike and Bess Berman, and Savoy, formed the same year by Herman Lubinsky (across the Hudson River in Newark, New Jersey). Apollo featured Wynonie Harris's early recordings and the vocal groups the Five Royales and the Larks; Savoy's roster included Johnny Otis, Little Esther ("Double Crossing Blues"), Big Jay McNeely ("The Deacon's Hop"), Napoleon Brown Culp (Nappy Brown; "Don't Be Angry"), and the vocal group the Four Buddies ("I Will Wait"). Other New York indies were Old Town, formed about 1955 by Hy Weiss; Baton, founded in 1955 by Sol Rabinowitz; and Red Robin/Robin, started in 1953 by Bobby Robinson.

In the Midwest, Sydney Nathan formed King Records in Cincinnati in 1945. King and its subsidiaries, which included DeLuxe, Federal, and Queen, provided country music to whites who had moved to the Midwest from Appalachia and R&B to black urban dwellers who had moved from the South. Working with these different styles and artists, Nathan helped lay the groundwork for the hybrid rock and roll. Highly innovative in the '50s, with R&B singers recording versions of country songs and introducing novelty songs in the new rock and roll style, these labels featured R&B instrumentalists, such as Bill Doggett ("Honky Tonk") and Earl Bostic ("Flamingo"), and R&B singers including Wynonie Harris, Bullmoose Jackson, and Eddie "Cleanhead" Vinson. Being the only indies to have country singers on their rosters, these labels recorded such artists as Moon Mullican and the Delmore Brothers, and numerous vocal groups enjoyed success as well, including the Platters (early recordings), the Midnighters, and the Dominoes. In addition, Hank Ballard and Charlie Feathers created memorable recordings with these indies, whose geographic location made them accessible not only to artists from the South, but also to those crossing the nation on tour. As with Atlantic, King's success thrust the label from regional status to national attention (beginning with Hank Ballard's smash hit, "Work with Me Annie"). For his numerous accomplishments and his support of rock and roll, Sydney Nathan, who launched the careers of James Brown, Hank Ballard, and many other R&B greats, was inducted into the Rock and Roll Hall of Fame in 1997.

The other prominent Midwest independent label was Chess Records and its subsidiaries, Checker and Argo, in Chicago. Formed in 1947 by Polish immigrants Leonard and Phil Chess, the label was first named Aristocrat, then Chess in 1949. After concentrating on such blues artists as Muddy Waters, Howlin' Wolf, and John Lee Hooker, the label branched out to vocal groups: the Moonglows, the Flamingos (both of which had recorded for Art Sheridan's Chance Records until it folded), the Tuneweavers, and the Monotones. Other artists included Bo Diddley, Chuck Berry, Robert Charles Guidry (Bobby Charles; "Later Alligator"), Dale Hawkins ("Susie-Q"), and Clarence "Frogman" Henry ("Ain't Got No Home"). With Diddley and Berry on its roster, Chess had great success in the '50s, partly assisted by deejay Alan Freed, who received co-composer credit on the Moonglows' "Sincerely" and Chuck Berry's "Maybellene" and promoted the records and artists on his radio shows. With Chuck Berry, Chess Records attained its peak success and made its major mark on music history. Leonard Chess was inducted into the Rock and Roll Hall of Fame in 1987.

Along with King and Chess, another Midwest indie of note was Vee Jay, formed in 1953 by Vivian Carter and James Bracken in Chicago. Jimmy Reed, John Lee Hooker, and Rosco Gordon were among the R&B artists recorded by this indie, and the vocal groups the Spaniels, the El Dorados, the Dells, and the Impressions created their memorable doo-wop hits for the label. Even though Vee Jay had very successful hits on the pop charts with Gene Chandler ("Duke of Earl") and the groups the Four Seasons and the Beatles, the label was generally committed to black music styles.

On the West Coast, in 1945 Eddie and Leo Mesner formed Aladdin Records, an R&B indie that employed producers Maxwell Davis and Dave Bartholomew. Rhythm and blues artists Amos Milburn and Charles Brown recorded for Aladdin, and the label achieved pop success with the duos Gene & Eunice (Forest Gene Wilson and Eunice Levy; "Ko Ko Mo") and Shirley & Lee. The Five Keys ("The Glory of Love") recorded for the indie before switching to Capitol, which was trying to break into the rock and roll market. Thurston Harris ("Little Bitty Pretty One" and "Do What You Did") was one of the last rock and rollers to create hits for Aladdin, which folded in the late '50s, unable to promote its artists on the national level. Also formed in 1945 in the West was Modern Records, originally an R&B label. Jules and Saul Bihari established the indie in Los Angeles and followed with the subsidiaries RPM (1950) and Flair (1953). The Biharis became known for often covering R&B hits. Among the many talented performers on their roster were Lightnin' Hopkins, Johnny Moore's Three Blazers, Etta James (early recording "The Wallflower"), and B. B. King, and the vocal groups the Teen Queens, the Cadets, and the Jacks. Modern began to concentrate on manufacturing budget albums on its Crown label before the company went bankrupt and Kent took over its catalogue.

Another Western label founded in 1945 was Art Rupe's Specialty Records. Robert "Bumps" Blackwell was among the producers employed by Specialty, along with Salvatore Bono (later Sonny Bono of Sonny & Cher) producing in Los Angeles and Harold Battiste doing likewise in New Orleans. Technology made it possible to place studios in remote locations to capture local sounds unattainable in the three cities where the bulk of recording activity occurred: New York, Los Angeles, and Nashville. Little Richard was the label's most important discovery in the Southeast, and others on its roster were Joe and Jimmy Liggins, Lloyd Price, Guitar Slim, the Soul Stirrers, and Larry Williams ("Bony Moronie" and "Short Fat Fannie," a 1957 No. 1 R&B and No. 5 pop hit whose lyrics quoted titles of the best recent rock and roll hits). In 1947 Lew Chudd founded Imperial Records, another Los Angeles indie that was active in New Orleans with producer Dave Bartholomew. Recording the legendary Fats Domino for several years, Imperial achieved enormous success with his string of '50s hits. The New

Orleans vocal group the Spiders had a number of R&B hits for the label, and Imperial also recorded Smiley Lewis and Ricky Nelson, whose Verve contract was purchased by Imperial when it sought a singer who could reach the young rock and roll audience and not upset adults. Domino's and Nelson's hits fueled the company into the early '60s, when it was taken over by Liberty Records.

Numerous other significant independents opened in the '50s. In the South were the famous and ever important Sun Records (where Elvis Presley first recorded) and its subsidiary, Phillips International. (See chapter 5 for further information.) Lester Bihari formed Meteor in Memphis in 1952, and Ernie Young launched Excello in Nashville the same year. In Houston, Duke/Peacock was founded in 1949 by nightclub owner Don Robey, and in Jackson, Mississippi, Johnny Vincent established Ace in 1955. Dot Records, begun in 1951 by Randy Wood in Gallatin, Tennessee (moved to Hollywood in 1956), did so well that it rivaled the majors in the '50s, along with Liberty, founded in 1955 in Hollywood, with Al Bennett as vice president. Dot recorded cover artist Pat Boone and the vocal group the Dell-Vikings, and Liberty featured the novelty group David Seville and the Chipmunks ("Witch Doctor" and "The Chipmunk Song"), the pop singer Bobby Vee ("Take Good Care of My Baby"), the R&B group Billy Ward and the Dominoes, and rockabilly artist Eddie Cochran.

After recording with the Soul Stirrers at Specialty, Sam Cooke began his solo recording career with Keen, which was hastily formed in 1957 in Hollywood by Bob Keene with Bumps Blackwell as A&R man (after Rupe dismissed him from Specialty). His first record was the 1957 No. 1 R&B and pop hit, "You Send Me," followed by an impressive string of others that eventually won him a contract with RCA-Victor. Era Records, formed in Hollywood in 1955 by Herb Newman and Lew Bidell, recorded the Teddy Bears ("To Know Him Is to Love Him"), and surf-rock duo Jan & Dean ("Baby Talk") on its subsidiary, Dore. Later, Teddy Bears member Phil Spector opened his Philles label with Lester Sill. During this time, a plethora of other indies appeared: Challenge, Rendezvous, Class, Ebb, London, Monument, Hi, Cameo, Chancellor, Cadence, Roulette, Laurie, and Swan and its subsidiary, Hunt. In addition, in Hollywood in 1959, Warner Brothers Pictures launched Warner Brothers Records.

With majors constantly seeking repertoire, indies sent their records to them in hopes they would use a song for one of their artists to record—it was common practice among majors to release multiple versions of a song, a tradition that didn't change until the 1960s, when the Beatles ushered in the age of composing performers in place of the industry owning (controlling and profiting from) their material. Earlier in pop music, those expecting to make money from a hit song copyrighted and published it, but they were very rarely the artist or the songwriter. Routinely, independents' owners took songwriting credit in order to maximize profits (for example, Chess Records). Sometimes they assigned composer credit to a family member or friend so as not to appear greedy, and often they sold the copyright to a major publisher. Many musicians were exploited in this manner, but especially poor, uneducated bluesmen and blueswomen, who received small fees (sometimes as low as $5.00) or a token (such as a bottle of whiskey) for their recorded music. While discussing the Chantels, whose recording career was with indies End and Gone, Gillian Gaar reveals in *She's a Rebel* that often artists were not compensated for their hits in spite of their success on the charts, partly because of income being absorbed by recording-related expenses:

> The lack of monetary compensation was an unfortunate fact of life for many recording artists, particularly black performers, for haphazard accounting procedures, along with frequent disregard for an artist's welfare, kept artists from earning money no matter how substantial a hit was. "In those days we paid for everything," explains Ruth Brown. "The recording studio, the scores being written, all the records given out for promotions, the musicians. So you thought you were doing all right with advances and whatnot, but all that money came back off the top before you saw a dime, and you always ended up in debt. We were just out there taking you at your word if you said, 'Okay, you're going to make $700.' I look for $700, no questions asked. I don't know what happened to that other $7,000 over there, but the $700 was what I was promised."[7]

These and multiple other indies emerging in the early 1950s dominated the market at the dawn of rock and roll; these industry structures were in place to sustain the new music genre and support its innovative artists. With astonishing success, they released records of the new musical genre that sold incredibly well while climbing the charts. Indies proved to be profoundly influential in the rock era: instrumental in the new music's birth in the early '50s, nourishing it throughout the decade, and ultimately dictating its fate. Though many indies were out of business by the decade's end, they nonetheless covered musical territory the majors ignored, depriving the majors of huge profits and shaking them up to the point of retaliation with cover artists and new marketing and distribution networks.

The Majors Retaliate

The majors had not totally ignored R&B and rock and roll, though RCA-Victor, Columbia, and Capitol initially hoped the music would vanish. Some acquired race labels (partly to disguise their connections to the music) and issued releases, such as RCA-Victor's R&B label, Groove (formed in 1953), which recorded Mickey and Sylvia (McHouston "Mickey" Baker and Sylvia Vanderpool; "Love Is Strange") and the Du Droppers. These artists could not compete with performers on indies. Frustrated by the lack of hits, RCA closed Groove and its other subsidiary, X Records. When RCA signed Elvis Presley and he quickly climbed all three charts, it proved that his fusion of country, pop, and R&B styles appealed to America's tastes. However, the label did not record many other rock and rollers other than Janis Martin and R&B artists Jesse Belvin, the Isley Brothers (debut recording, "Shout"), and Sam Cooke (in the '60s). Columbia was happy as the most successful of all the majors in the early '50s, recording such artists as Frankie Laine, Guy Mitchell, Rosemary Clooney, and Doris Day. The company recorded Johnny Mathis and country musicians Gene Autry and Marty Robbins, and the race label it had acquired during the Depression, OKeh, released records by Johnnie Ray ("Cry"), Chuck Willis's early recordings, and Screamin' Jay Hawkins ("I Put a Spell on You"). Capitol made a swift response to RCA's Elvis Presley by signing rockabilly Gene Vincent and his group, the Blue Caps, and also responded to wild Little Richard with Esquerita, the flamboyant R&B artist who created some of the most frantic rock and roll records ever made for the company. Others recorded by Capitol were Johnny Otis, Nat "King" Cole, Tennessee Ernie Ford ("Sixteen Tons"), and such groups as the Five Keys ("Ling, Ting, Tong"), the Four Freshmen, the Four Preps, and the Kingston Trio ("Tom Dooley").

Because of Decca founder Jack Kapp's tastes, the company had interest in black dance music and recorded the Mills Brothers and Ink Spots, rhythm and bluesmen Louis Jordan and Lucky Millinder, and

Pat Boone rehearsing at the London Palladium in 1956. © AP/Wide World Photos.

gospel artist Sister Rosetta Tharpe. Country artists on its roster included Red Foley, Ernest Tubb, and Webb Pierce, as well as Bobby Helms ("Jingle Bell Rock") and Brenda Lee. Decca signed Bill Haley and the Comets to its roster in an effort to join the ranks of rock and roll, and its subsidiaries Coral and Brunswick recorded Jackie Wilson and Buddy Holly and the Crickets. Mercury was successful with many covers of R&B hits with such artists and groups as Fredda Gibbons (Georgia Gibbs), the Crew-Cuts, and the Diamonds, but also attempted to release true R&B and rock and roll records with the Big Bopper and groups such as Freddie Bell and the Bellboys, the Penguins, and the Platters. Formed in 1946 as a division of the film company, MGM (and its subsidiary Cub Records) recorded country artist Hank Williams and black pop singer Tommy Edwards ("It's All in the Game") in addition to the Impalas, Conway Twitty ("It's Only Make Believe"), and teen idol Concetta Rosa Maria Franconero (Connie Francis; "Who's Sorry Now"). ABC-Paramount, formed in Hollywood in 1955, sported composer and teen idol Paul Anka ("Lonely Boy") and R&B artist Lloyd Price, whose success caused the label to recruit rhythm and bluesman Ray Charles. The vocal group Danny & the Juniors recorded on its roster, and its subsidiary Apt recorded the Elegants.

Regarding '50s recording industry success, as Steve Chapple and Reebee Garofalo illustrate in *Rock 'n' Roll Is Here to Pay*, by 1954's end, the independents had nearly total control of the R&B market. Atlantic, Cat, Federal, DeLuxe, Herald, Chess, Imperial, Rama, and Vee Jay had twenty-three of the Top 30 hits that year; majors Columbia (Epic and OKeh subsidiaries) and Mercury represented the remainder. Chapple and Garofalo state that by 1956, the majors had nearly given up on R&B.[8] In addition, Charlie Gillett points out in *The Sound of the City* that between 1955 and 1959, just under half of the Top 10 hits could be classified as rock and roll (with either vigorous backbeats or other obvious rhythm and blues-influenced elements, such as vocal style). Of those considered rock hits, more than two thirds were on indie labels. Gillett states that of the ten artists who had three or more hit records in the Top 10, only Elvis Presley and Lloyd Price recorded for major companies.[9] This overwhelming success of the indies made the large companies feel very threatened by rock and roll.

The majors engaged in a counterattack by producing cover versions of songs originally recorded by black R&B artists. To accomplish this, they used reserved, wholesome white pop artists, who for a few years successfully covered numerous songs that the majors considered rock and roll. These pop renditions, which generally lacked the feeling and sense of the originals, nonetheless consistently outsold original recordings. This cover practice reflected the cultural, economic, and political realities of the '50s that discriminated against African Americans not only in the music industry but also in America as a whole. The RCA label began this trend with Perry Como covering Gene & Eunice's "Ko Ko Mo," and Columbia's Tony Bennett did the same. During the early days of covering, the white teenage audience (and parents) enjoyed these covers of black songs. Some versions kept the integrity and excitement of the originals and were musically justifiable, such as Bill Haley and the Comets' cover of Big Joe Turner's "Shake, Rattle and Roll" or Presley's cover of Big Mama Thornton's "Hound Dog," but most covers lacked the feeling and excitement that the originals

Perry Como. Courtesy of the Library of Congress.

conveyed. Mercury's list of covers included recordings by the Crew-Cuts and Georgia Gibbs. The Crew-Cuts recorded a cover of the Chords' "Sh-Boom" that became a huge 1954 pop hit (No. 1 for nine weeks), and followed with a version of Nappy Brown's "Don't Be Angry" and the Penguins' "Earth Angel." Gibbs covered Etta James's "The Wallflower" with a sanitized version called "Dance with Me Henry," a 1955 No. 1 pop hit. Decca's female vocal group, the McGuire Sisters, covered the Moonglows' "Sincerely" on its Coral subsidiary, and it was a No. 1 pop hit for ten weeks in 1955 (the Moonglows' recording was a No. 1 R&B hit for two weeks in 1954 and reached only No. 20 on the pop charts in 1955).

 '50s COVERS

This list of '50s covers is intended as an introduction to the cover phenomenon that flourished during the rock era. Songs are listed alphabetically with their original recording artist(s)/group and their cover artist(s)/group(s). Only '50s cover recordings are included; others covered later—for example, Dion's 1960 rendition of "In the Still of the Night" or the Four Seasons' 1963 version of "Ain't That a Shame"—are not on the list.

Song	Original Artist(s)/ Group	Cover Artist(s)/ Group(s)
"Ain't That a Shame"	Fats Domino	Pat Boone
"At My Front Door"	The El Dorados	Pat Boone
"Crying in the Chapel"	The Orioles	June Valli
"Earth Angel"	The Penguins	The Crew-Cuts
"Eddie My Love"	The Teen Queens	The Fontane Sisters The Chordettes
"Fever"	Little Willie John	Peggy Lee
"Goodnite Sweetheart, Goodnite"	The Spaniels	The McGuire Sisters
"Good Rocking Tonight"	Roy Brown Wynonie Harris	Pat Boone Elvis Presley
"Hound Dog"	Big Mama Thornton	Elvis Presley
"I Hear You Knocking"	Smiley Lewis	Gale Storm

'50s COVERS *(continued)*

"I'll Be Home"	The Flamingos	Pat Boone
"I'm in Love Again"	Fats Domino	The Fontane Sisters Ricky Nelson
"I'm Walkin'"	Fats Domino	Ricky Nelson
"Lawdy Miss Clawdy"	Lloyd Price	Elvis Presley
"Little Darlin'"	The Gladiolas	The Diamonds
"Long Tall Sally"	Little Richard	Pat Boone Elvis Presley
"Money Honey"	Clyde McPhatter and the Drifters	Elvis Presley
"Mystery Train"	Little Junior Parker's Blue Flames	Elvis Presley
"Ready Teddy"	Little Richard	Elvis Presley
"Rip It Up"	Little Richard	Bill Haley and the Comets Elvis Presley
"Rock Around the Clock"	Sonny Dae	Bill Haley and the Comets
"The Wallflower (Roll with Me Henry)"	Etta James	Georgia Gibbs
"Shake, Rattle and Roll"	Big Joe Turner	Bill Haley and the Comets Elvis Presley
"Sh-Boom"	The Chords	The Crew-Cuts
"Sincerely"	The Moonglows	The McGuire Sisters
"That's All Right"	Arthur "Big Boy" Crudup	Elvis Presley
"Tutti Frutti"	Little Richard	Pat Boone Elvis Presley
"Tweedlee Dee"	LaVern Baker	Georgia Gibbs
"Why Do Fools Fall in Love"	Frankie Lymon and the Teenagers	The Diamonds Gale Storm

Cover artist Pat Boone was the most commercially successful '50s teen idol, achieving a string of thirty-two Top 40 hits, sixteen of them Top 10s and five of them No. 1's (with four of them crossing over to the R&B charts), between 1955 and 1959 alone. He built his reputation and career by covering black R&B songs. His several polished and refined renditions of songs originally recorded by such artists as Fats Domino, Little Richard, Roy Brown, and a host of others allowed him to place hit after hit on the pop charts and become one of the biggest-selling pop singers in popular music history. While participants in such an exploitative practice would normally be condemned, in this case historians and musicians claim that cover artists such as Boone did rock and roll a favor by providing accessible, filtered presentations of songs approved by parents as wholesome, eventually paving the way for the white audience to accept the originals. Having publicly expressed his dislike for the unfair and exploitative cover tradition, Little Richard has nevertheless acknowledged that although original artists did not receive their due rewards, the overall process helped rock and roll in the long run.

Boone recorded for the Dot label, which was the most successful cover company. In the '40s, Tennessee entrepreneur Randy Wood opened a record store and mail order company before forming Dot to record local groups that performed R&B music. After realizing the white market's demand for R&B, Wood concentrated on pop music covers of R&B. He recorded Boone's renditions of Fats Domino's "Ain't That a Shame," the Five Keys' "Gee Whittakers," Ivory Joe Hunter's "I Almost Lost My Mind," Little Richard's "Tutti Frutti" and "Long Tall Sally," and Big Joe Turner's "Chains of Love." At the height of his success, these

 PAT BOONE (B. 1934)

Born Charles Eugene Boone on June 1, 1934, in Jacksonville, Florida, this descendant of American pioneer Daniel Boone two years later moved to Tennessee, where he grew up and recorded country songs while in high school. Host of his own radio show on WSIX in Nashville, *Youth on Parade*, Boone graduated from Columbia University with a degree in English and married country musician Red Foley's daughter, Shirley, in 1953. He released his first Dot recording two years later—"Two Hearts," a rendition of the Charms' "Two Hearts," the first of his covers of R&B originals that defined his early career—and appeared in concert with Elvis Presley in Cleveland, Ohio. At the height of his singing career, this calm, parent-approved alternative to exuberant rockers, who became known for his trademark white buck shoes, wrote many books filled with wholesome teenage advice, including *The Care and Feeding of Parents*.

In 1956, Boone signed a million-dollar contract with Twentieth Century Fox to begin his parallel movie career, and the next year he filmed his first of fifteen movies, *Bernardine*; in later films he appeared with such actors and actresses as Bobby Darin, Shirley Jones, Ann Margret, Debbie Reynolds, and Tony Curtis. Boone hosted a weekly ABC television music show, *The Pat Boone-Chevy Showroom*, from 1957 to 1960. Later he performed and toured with his gospel-based Pat Boone Family Show, which included his wife and four daughters, Cherry, Linda, Laura, and Debby (who became a music star in 1977 with her No. 1 pop hit, "You Light Up My Life"). Though he remained in the public's eye as a television personality through the years, Boone, who recorded compilations of hymns during the '50s and '60s and hosted a nationally broadcast Christian radio program in the '80s, shocked the nation when, at age sixty-two, he released his 1997 album *In a Metal Mood: No More Mr. Nice Guy*, which contained

PAT BOONE (B. 1934) *(continued)*

big band arrangements of songs by Led Zeppelin, Van Halen, and Metallica. In the media stir of his wild style transformation, complete with appearances in heavy metal black leather attire with dog collar and tattoos, Boone lost his weekly *Gospel America* television show, though he was reinstated after convincingly defending himself.

recordings and several more allowed parents to consider Boone a rock and roller. Deemed the calm alternative not only to Chuck Berry and other black rockers but also to such thrilling white artists as Elvis Presley and Jerry Lee Lewis, Boone earned his welcome in teenagers' homes. As his career progressed, he moved toward soft ballads and won the status of teen idol. Singing in the pop tradition of Perry Como and Bing Crosby, he achieved further successes with very effective songs aimed at the teen market, such as "Don't Forbid Me" and "Love Letters in the Sand."

The profitable cover practice continued for the majors until songs by original artists began to appear on the pop charts in significant numbers in 1956. With covers now less popular, the majors made adjustments and planned strategies to regain the market, such as their attempt to establish calypso music as a hot trend to oust rock and roll. In 1957, Harry Belafonte recorded "Banana Boat (Day-O)" for RCA, Nat "King" Cole recorded "When Rock and Roll Come to Trinidad" for Capitol, and Terry Gilkyson and the Easy Riders recorded "Marianne" for Columbia. Though rock and roll–seeking teenagers overlooked calypso, the music satisfied adults as yet another pop music sound. Still trying to win over the rock audience, the majors next presented folk music, such as Capitol's vocal group the Kingston Trio, though the style proved popular mostly among college students and did not become an active rock subgenre until the '60s. Other approaches by the majors included the introduction of clubs by Columbia and Capitol, such as the Columbia Record and Tape Club (established in 1955). These tactics were augmented by, for example, the use of seven-inch vinyl 45-RPM records, which were lighter, more durable, and more convenient for consumers (smaller in diameter and easier to mount on phonographs) than the prevailing 78-RPMs. With the discs quicker and easier to manufacture and ship, this was one successful line of attack with which many indies could not compete financially. A distribution and marketing tactic of the majors also proved successful when they realized the sales potential by placing their products in large stores. The first to do this, RCA (shortly followed by Decca) displayed records on racks near checkout counters in drugstores and supermarkets, thus capitalizing on impulse buying. Also, RCA and Columbia began using color record jackets with liner notes and enclosed LPs in cellophane to preserve them.

Along with TPA, the majors finally succeeded in displacing the first generation of rock artists with their carefully groomed late 1950s singers and entertainers. Considered to have cleaned up rock and roll by making it presentable to the general public, the majors offered new pop-sounding music changed to the point that it was no longer recognizable as rock music. Referred to as teen idols, the new artists were primarily from the Philadelphia area and were given national television exposure by *American Bandstand*. These wholesome and handsome teenager performers—such as Fabian, Paul Anka, Frankie Avalon, Brenda Lee, and Connie Francis—sang inoffensive music with overwhelming success in the late 1950s. For the first time since the emergence of the indies, in 1959 the majors outgrossed the independents. Also at this time, indies became prominent targets of the payola investigations and were swiftly going out of business. (See chapter 9 for further information.)

RADIO'S NEW ROLE

The development of American popular music in the twentieth century was inseparably connected with radio broadcasting. Developed by Guglielmo Marconi, the radio was used for communication during World War I. The first continuous public radio transmission came in 1920, when the

Harry Belafonte, mid-1950s. Courtesy of the Library of Congress.

first commercially licensed radio station, KDKA in Pittsburgh, Pennsylvania, broadcast the results of the Harding-Cox presidential election. Radio spread rapidly across America, with stations owned by individuals and companies, such as Chicago's WLS, owned by Sears (WLS for "World's Largest Store") and Nashville's WSM, owned by the National Life and Accident Insurance Company (WSM for "We Shield Millions"). By the mid-1920s, most major cities boasted a radio station, and with the uncluttered airwaves, people regularly picked up stations hundreds of miles away. The record industry was well developed by this time, and the two media benefited one another, with records promoting sales over the airwaves. Radio had a powerful influence on people's record-buying habits. In the '20s and '30s, when many records became commercially available, those introduced to the public through radio sold the best. Coincidentally, with the founding of RCA and its pooling of technical patents with other companies (such as General Electric and Westinghouse), inexpensive receivers were manufactured and sold in abundance to the public.

Radio was the main medium of entertainment before World War II; practically all families owned a large console to which the entire family listened in their living room. Parents decided which programs to listen to, leaving children little say in the matter until the transistor radio arrived and radios became smaller, more portable, and less expensive. Families soon owned more than one radio as teenagers bought the battery-powered transistors, which gave them freedom to listen to whatever they desired. During the post–World War II era, parents preferred the television. As television became a more practical medium, the networks essentially abandoned radio, which returned to community programming, usually featuring local music (such as country or R&B). Local radio became the most accessible and effective way for indies to promote artists. Rock and roll and radio became mutually dependent in the 1950s, as radio took on its new role of bringing the exciting sound to the public. Deejays became stars, linking themselves with rock and roll and its musicians that they featured on the air.

Reflecting the postwar explosion of black music throughout the nation, the radio was receptive to the popularity of R&B records among white teenagers and promoted the music over the airwaves. With the rise of television and the decline in network radio, owners of independent radio stations and of the emerging small chains of stations had room to experiment with specialized record programming and accommodated a diversity of musical preferences. These stations played the roots music of rock and roll—race music ranging from blues to jazz and gospel. These genres and country music were usually broadcast at the times of day when they would offend the fewest people. Country music aired very early in the morning, when farmers had time to listen while eating breakfast, and the blues were broadcast either early in the morning or late at night. This did not stop America's teens, who were enjoying their radio independence and listening any time they wanted, especially at night, when exciting R&B music aired. These rock and roll radio stations were of primary importance, eventually pushing aside the unadventurous network stations and helping indies thrive.

A live coast-to-coast Saturday night radio music program that debuted in 1935, *Your Hit Parade*, also boosted the record industry. The popular show was a summation of TPA pop music. It centered on the ten top songs each week, revealed on the air amid an aura of anticipation. Originally a radio program, *Parade* shaped the popular music tastes of the American public for over two decades. It was one of the first radio shows to transfer to television (1950), where it ran until 1959, when it succumbed to rock and roll and the changed music industry. Sponsored by Lucky Strike cigarettes, in its heyday *Parade* was a winning music show complete with writers, choreographers, set designers, costumers, and producers; Ray Charles served as the show's choral director and vocal music arranger from 1949 to 1958. Once America's teenagers knew exciting rock and roll, they did not want to hear the show's singers perform arrangements of songs; they wanted to hear rock and roll performed by the stimulating bands who made the records. Not only did *Your Hit Parade* suffer (especially after Top 40 radio programming provided its own hit parade for listeners), but talk shows, news broadcasts, and other radio programs ended as television took over, and teens listened to their favorite music played by their favorite disc jockeys on their favorite radio stations. Hundreds of independent stations, free of network constraints, identified with local listeners' preferences. They gave birth to a new breed of broadcast entertainer, the disc jockey. The more a deejay played their music, the more teenagers would listen to that jockey's station. This resulted in the emergence of on-air personalities who engaged in flamboyant and provocative behaviors tolerated by program directors because outrageous actions translated into profits. America's teens respected and adored their deejays, and the more eccentric they were, the better.

Disc Jockeys and Stations

As economical record programming on local independent stations replaced live entertainment (such as costly studio orchestras) on network radio by the early 1950s, disc jockeys became prominent figures. The term "disc jockey" was first used early in the decade to describe those who played and helped select the popular hits for broadcast. Their rise to prominence went hand in hand with the growth of early 1950s rock and roll. One of the most influential deejays of the rock era, Alan Freed helped introduce black R&B to the mainstream white audience, and with his unique on-air identity he helped to launch the era of personality radio. As many more disc jockeys joined the field, these powerful personalities became crucial factors in the promotion of rock and roll, as is evident in the late 1950s payola scandal that exposed the practice of influential deejays being assigned co-composer credit on songs in exchange for playing the records on their shows. Though considered illegal, payola was in full force during this period of disc jockey

Handbill for one of Alan Freed's music extravaganzas in Cincinnati, 1958. Courtesy of the Library of Congress.

dominance as they popularized indies' records and assisted in the birth of rock and roll.

Before the '50s, radio announcers introduced much classical and swing music to the public. After the success of two Southern radio stations showed the broadcasting industry the commercial viability of programming R&B music, these presenters came to the forefront as the market for black music expanded and increasing numbers of stations began playing race music. On Nashville's WLAC, white deejay "Daddy" Gene Nobles broadcast black music in the '40s. He and fellow deejay "John R" Richbourg, who joined the station after World War II, began to fill requests for blues records manufactured and sold in the South. Richbourg is credited with having introduced numerous performers to a national audience, among them B. B. King, Bo Diddley, Chuck Berry, Little Richard, and Jackie Wilson. By the late 1940s, every weeknight Nobles and Richbourg played R&B to a huge audience stretching from Texas to Canada and to the East Coast. In 1949, deejay and wild man Bill "Hoss" Allen joined them; together, these three announcers were responsible for transmitting much black music to America. With its massive transmitting power, in the early 1950s WLAC became a major station for developing R&B hits. Record companies targeted WLAC and other influential stations, bringing them new releases in hopes of "breaking in" new hits. The other influential Southern station was WDIA in Memphis, which had catered to a white audience before switching to meet the demands of the area's huge black population. The station used an all-black format complete with black deejays, including B. B. King and Rufus Thomas, who were better known for performing than announcing. Very quickly, WDIA became a commercial success and started a trend toward black programming. Martha Jean "The Queen" Steinberg, who, unlike other female announcers, played hot music, deejayed on WDIA before she was recruited by a Michigan station, WCHB, and became the mother of Detroit radio. Initially mostly in the South, race stations with white owners and black disc jockeys, such as WDIA, multiplied in the late 1940s and early 1950s.

During the '50s, deejays began to invent their own slang and catchphrases for use on the air. The white jockeys Richbourg of Nashville's WLAC and Freed of Cleveland's WJW modeled themselves on their black counterparts, mimicking black speech so well that listeners didn't know if they were white or black. WLAC's Allen grew up with a black nanny and effectively used black jive talk on the air. For example, on the streets something good was labeled "tight like that," so Hoss would use the phrase on the air to describe good records and performances. To introduce his show, he used slang from black pimps, such as "git down time" (which referred to the time of night when prostitutes hit the streets): "It's git down time with Hoss Allen." These deejays also adopted nicknames used by black deejays who broadcast under such names as Dr. Jive, Jet Pilot of Jive, Satellite Papa, and Daddy-O Hot Rod. At the peak of the personality deejay era, at each of their stations, chains created disc jockey personalities and used nicknames to show they were hip, resulting in multiple

Dr. Jives (and others) broadcasting with different voices all over the country. And though male deejays were more common, female announcers took to the air, such as WDIA's Steinberg and Atlanta station WAOK's Zilla "Dream Girl" Mays. Since '50s society had not yet learned to listen to its increasingly sophisticated teenagers, disc jockeys served not only as music announcers but also as teens' advocates (for example, they successfully lobbied for student rates at movie theaters), and provided entertainment by staging opportunities for teenagers (such as teen talent shows, teenage guest deejay hours, and record hops) throughout the country. As Wes Smith notes in *The Pied Pipers of Rock 'n' Roll*, it was significant that many '50s deejays had nicknames such as "Daddy" or "Uncle," and that such jockeys as Chicago station WLS's Dick Biondi provided male teenagers with step-by-step shaving instructions during commercials for Gillette razors: "The disc jockeys, then, were to the airwaves what Holden Caulfield and *Catcher in the Rye* were to literature and Marlon Brando and James Dean were to the movies—sources of identification for the stirring teenage rebellion of post–World War II."[10]

Though there were black deejays in the '50s, they were outnumbered by whites who entertained African Americans with R&B music. They were generally very hip and accepted in black communities, and especially by R&B musicians, who were grateful for the exposure given their music. Noteworthy white deejay Hunter Hancock began hosting his very popular R&B program, *Huntin' with Hunter*, on KFVD in Los Angeles in 1948, and gained a reputation as a hit-maker. With his growling, shaking voice, he carried on like a wild man in a style his black audience adored. Another, Dick "Huggy Boy" Hugg, began announcing in the late night hours for station KRKD in 1951, calling himself the "West Coast Alan Freed" and working out of a front window of the Dolphin Record Store in Los Angeles' black neighborhood. Also in California, beginning in the late 1940s, "Jumpin'" George Oxford was among the first white deejays to broadcast R&B on KSAN, KDIA, and KWBR in the San Francisco and Oakland area, regularly dropping on-air innuendos about his lust for his female listeners.

Among the many other early 1950s white deejays spinning R&B music was Zenas "Daddy" Sears on Atlanta's WGST (and WAOK, another important Southern R&B outlet), where he was one of the first to play Little Richard and Ray Charles. Tom "Big Daddy" Donahue, who began his career in 1949, worked on WIBG in Philadelphia in the '50s. While at KYA in San Francisco, Donahue had been a kingpin disc jockey, concert promoter, and tipsheet publisher. Known as the godfather of FM progressive radio in the '60s, he pioneered "free form" radio on FM and revolutionized radio broadcasting in America. For his support of rock and roll, Donahue was inducted into the Rock and Roll Hall of Fame in 1996. Present when Elvis Presley entered the rock and roll scene and responsible for breaking in his records in the Memphis region, Dewey Phillips played R&B for his primarily black audience on WHBQ and WDIA. Conservative white deejay Bill Randle of Cleveland's station

WERE is credited with having introduced Presley to Northern audiences. His legendary Cleveland colleague, Freed, promoted the new rock and roll sound more than any other. One of the sharpest improvising poets of radio, Pete "Mad Daddy" Myers, also announced in Cleveland, at station WHK, before moving to WINS in New York City. Possessed of two radio personalities, he was a calm, smooth-talking deejay in the afternoon, and at night he was a wacko "Mad Daddy" who took part in wild stunts (such as his parachute jump into Lake Erie in the early 1960s) before committing suicide at age forty, despondent over a shift in time of his radio show.

The East Coast lagged behind other regions of the country in playing R&B; however, the important Philadelphia radio market possessed Joe Niagara of WIBG. Between 1947 and 1957, he boasted the highest disc jockey rating in the city. Porky Chedwick began on Pittsburgh's WAMO in 1949. Fluent in jive talk, he referred to himself as the "Daddio of the Raddio" and as "a porkulatin' platter-pushin' poppa" with "more jams than Smuckers," and claimed he graduated from the University of Spinner Sanctum with a doctorate in insanity—and parents in the Pittsburgh and tri-state area felt it was true. In New York City, "Symphony Sid" Torin ruled the airwaves at station WHOM and later at station WOV. Having received his nickname while moonlighting at the Symphony Shop, a New York record store, this influential deejay inspired Dick Clark, who was one of his listeners. Another pioneering Big Apple deejay, Tommy Smalls, known as "Dr. Jive," was on WWRL and one of the first jocks involved in packaging R&B shows at the Apollo Theater and other venues. Hired by CBS television variety show host Ed Sullivan in 1956, Smalls arranged and emceed an R&B show; he also oversaw a segment of rock and roll talent on Sullivan's television show, showcasing LaVern Baker, Bo Diddley, the Five Keys, and other black musicians. Smalls, Jocko Henderson, and Freed were perhaps the most powerful rock and roll promoters of their day. Smalls presented six or seven shows a day over two-week periods; thousands of fans came to see and hear live the artists they regularly listened to on the radio. As was Freed, high-profile disc jockey Smalls was ruined as a result of the payola scandal in the late 1950s.

In New Orleans, WMJR's Vernon Winslow rhymed jive for white disc jockeys and created the "Poppa Stoppa" character. He renamed himself "Doctor Daddy-O" and franchised that character to other stations. His success inspired others, such as New Orleans white deejay Ken "Jack the Cat" Elliott. In Austin, Texas, Lavada Durst, also known as "Dr. Hepcat," announced on station KVET throughout the '50s. Durst was a Texas boogie-woogie and blues piano player who thickly laid the jive talk on, so as to be different from white deejays. To help his listeners understand his speech, Dr. Hepcat wrote and published his own dictionary, *The Jives of Dr. Hepcat*, which has become a collector's item among rock and roll fans and folklorists.

Not all early jive-talking R&B deejays came from the South. Among those from the Midwest was Al Benson, who dominated black-oriented radio in Chicago in the '40s and '50s. Reaching the peak of his popularity in the late

1950s, Benson was famous for his undecipherable speech. This often incoherent disc jockey promoted blues and R&B performances at Chicago's Regal Theater that were similar to those sponsored by Freed and Smalls. Another significant deejay was Dick Biondi, who spent time in Chicago at stations WLS, WJMK, WCFL, and WBBM, and had a reputation of being a rebel. Considered one of the first bad boys of radio, he was one of the most admired and most fired deejays of his time. He began his career in 1951 in Corning, New York, near his native Endicott, followed by stations around the country, including KYSO in Alexandria, Louisiana (his all-black show *Jammin' Jive*), WKBW in Buffalo, New York (where he replaced George "Hound Dog" Lorenz), WHOT in Youngstown, Ohio, WSAI in Cincinnati, KRLA in Los Angeles, and WNMB in North Myrtle Beach, South Carolina. This pioneering radio disc jockey, considered one of the greatest in rock radio history, was kept on the move by a combination of successes and controversies. This advocate of R&B and early rock and roll went on to introduce talent in concerts and befriended Buddy Holly, Jerry Lee Lewis, and Elvis Presley, among many others. Rated the No. 1 deejay in the country at different times and often No. 1 in most major markets, Biondi was known by several titles: "The Big Noise from Buffalo," "The Screamer," "The Wild Eye-Tailian," and "The Supersonic Spaghetti Slurper."

Perhaps the most renowned black deejay of the early rock era was Baltimore-based Douglas "Jocko" Henderson on WSID. Known as a quick-rhyming talker, he was lured to Philadelphia's WHAT and quickly became the hottest jock in the city with his *Rocket Ship Show* before moving to one of the biggest and most powerful stations in the city, WDAS. Henderson remained at WDAS for twenty years while commuting to New York City, where his radio shows on stations WLIB and WADO were even more popular. In addition to broadcasting, Henderson hosted more than 100 live shows at the Apollo Theater and was just as big an attraction at concerts as the musical acts. Of the deejays to emerge from the City of Brotherly Love, Henderson and Dick Clark were two of the most famous. The influential Georgie Woods, "the guy with the goods," was one of the biggest deejays in Philadelphia at WHAT and later at WDAS. He staged concerts at the Uptown Theater. Dick Clark relied upon Woods (and Hy Lit at station WHAT and Jocko Henderson at WDAS) to inform him which records were hot in the black community, especially when he first took over *Bandstand*. Known as a breakout market, Philadelphia was a strong radio town in the late '50s. It had huge radio personalities and powerful stations, and if a record hit on local radio, it would likely make it to network television on Clark's show.

George "Hound Dog" Lorenz

One of the most important pioneering disc jockeys was George "Hound Dog" Lorenz in Buffalo, New York. Born near the suburb of Cheektowaga and having grown up in Buffalo, Lorenz began his announcing career on WBTA in nearby Batavia, New York. In 1947, he started broadcasting on WXRA in

Buffalo, only to be fired for playing risqué R&B records; he then moved to WJJL in Niagara Falls. Lorenz's black Buffalo audience gave him his Hound Dog nickname—short for one of the jive expressions popular then, "doggin' around," which meant you were "hangin' around the corner"—because when Lorenz came on the air, he always greeted his audience with "Here I am to dog around for another hour." While presiding over the Northeast and Canada, in 1953 the very popular Lorenz received an offer from Cleveland, the hottest radio market in the country. He accepted the offer of WSRS, and then two of the most influential deejays, the Hound Dog and the Moon Dog, simultaneously broadcast from Cleveland for a short while before Freed moved to New York (1954) and Lorenz returned to Buffalo (1955). On Buffalo's WKBW, Lorenz hosted a Saturday morning show, *Hound Dog Hit Parade*, but it was his late-night show, often broadcast from a booth at Club Zanzibar in the city, that was most popular. Hound Dog's fans regularly filled the club, and members of his huge fan club attended rock and roll shows at Memorial Auditorium in downtown Buffalo that he hosted—some with his Cleveland friend, Freed—featuring top-notch rock and roll performers of the day: Chuck Berry, Fats Domino, Little Richard, Elvis Presley, Jerry Lee Lewis, Bill Haley and the Comets, and Buddy Holly.

An innovative deejay whose actions pushed rock and roll radio to its heights, Hound Dog Lorenz is considered the first to "rock the pot," a phrase that refers to turning the volume controls up and down with the beat of the music. Never one to let the music stop, Lorenz was one of the first jocks to use instrumentals so he could speak and read commercials on the air with records still spinning. The Hound Dog understood the music and artists he played, and enjoyed telling listeners the history behind the songs. A protector of black artists, Lorenz fought to keep their music on the air. In 1958, when WKBW adopted the Top 40 format, the Hound Dog left in order to maintain his on-air freedom and helped pioneer the FM market with R&B and rock and roll music. He syndicated a show taped in a Buffalo studio that was sold to stations all over the country, and in 1965 he purchased WBLK-FM, the only full-time black music station outside of New York City in New York State. For his new station, Lorenz hired black deejays and, thanks to his long-time connections with rock and roll record companies, introduced records to the black community before they appeared on AM radio. Lorenz died of a heart attack in 1972, at age fifty-two. His sons stepped in to run WBLK, which is still thriving. Hound Dog Lorenz's influence on listeners and disc jockeys (including Dick Biondi, who replaced him at WKBW) along the East Coast was enormous. Lorenz is considered by many rock and roll historians to rank with Alan Freed as one of the most influential deejays of the '50s.

Alan Freed

Born Albert James Freed in 1922 in Johnstown, Pennsylvania, this devoted preacher of rock and roll was the most significant '50s radio personality. After

Southerners found work in the North and black music worked its way with them to Cleveland from the Mississippi Delta through Nashville, Louisville, Cincinnati, and Columbus, Freed began announcing at various stations in Pennsylvania and Ohio before settling at Cleveland's WJW. On his show, *The Moondog Rock 'n' Roll Party*, he howled along with records to his initial nearly all-black audience, bringing the music to local teens who realized it had a good dance beat. Attracting white listeners without losing his black audience, Freed was attacked by ministers and parents, and was watched by organizations ranging from the Mafia and the Ku Klux Klan to the Federal Bureau of Investigation and the Roman Catholic Church, to those looking for Communists. The powers of the music industry watched him, and everybody listened to him. Teenagers danced while Freed, known as the Moondog, turned songs into instant hits, gaining Cleveland the reputation with record companies as an excellent place to break in a new record. In 1954, he moved to station WINS in New York City and also began his association with the silver screen, appearing in and producing many films that promoted rock and roll to a wider audience between 1956 and 1958. Though not the first to play rock and roll, he was the first to neatly package and market it to a huge integrated audience.

As Freed took the music out of the studio and onto the road, packing concert halls with racially mixed crowds at his organized shows featuring the biggest stars of the era (including Chuck Berry, LaVern Baker, Buddy Holly and the Crickets, and Jerry Lee Lewis), he changed American (and world) culture with the sound of American popular music. As did other crusading deejays, many of whom he influenced, Freed refused to play cover versions of rock and roll songs. He contributed greatly to breaking down segregation, and as a result of the mystery of his identity that arose from his on-air persona, he was referred to as a white Negro (to describe the cultural blend). Freed's firing from station WINS detrimentally affected rock and roll; concert venues withered as promoters (including Dick Clark and his Caravan of Stars) retreated. Always playing music he thought teens would like, this legendary deejay who adored rock and roll was a star of radio, the concert hall, and the silver screen—a disc jockey who lived the music while playing it and spreading its good news. Having accepted payments from

 ALAN FREED (1922–1965)

"Often dubbed the 'Pied Piper of Rock and Roll,' Alan Freed was one of the first and most influential champions of rock and roll. As a disc jockey, first in Cleveland and then in New York, Freed introduced millions of white listeners to 'race' music, or rhythm and blues. As the music evolved, Freed dubbed it 'rock and roll,' and as rock and roll swept the country, Freed became its primary promoter."[11]

Cleveland record store owner Leo Mintz witnessed firsthand the emerging pattern of white customers buying records by black artists in his store, the Record Rendezvous. This caused Mintz to convince Freed to start his R&B show, *The Moondog Rock 'n' Roll Party*, on local radio station WJW. Combining Todd Rhodes's "Blues for the Red Boy" as his theme song with his own nutty on-air persona as the Moondog, the disc jockey brought black R&B music to America's teenagers calling it "rock and roll," a phrase from the lyrics of black songs.

ALAN FREED (1922–1965)
(continued)

After he presented the Cleveland Moondog Coronation Ball on March 21, 1952, Freed realized the potential of live concerts with multiple acts. He hosted several dance shows featuring R&B artists prior to his arrival in New York. Mostly African Americans attended these early shows, though gradually white teenagers began to appear. By the time Freed had his first concert in New York in 1955, the audience was completely integrated. On April 12, 1955, Freed presented his first show at the Brooklyn Paramount in downtown Brooklyn. Tickets cost 90 cents, and the show included both black and white artists. There were several shows every day at the Paramount, each with artists who performed two songs each. From 1955 to 1959, the Paramount was Freed's New York venue for rock and roll shows that set many musical and cultural precedents. In the '60s, deejay Murray "the K" Kaufman held a series of concerts that featured the Who, Cream, Wilson Pickett, Mitch Ryder, Smokey Robinson, and the Blues Project. Other rock festivals featuring multiple acts and the excitement of those early Freed shows have included Ozzfest, Lollapalooza, and Summer Sanitarium.

record companies throughout his career, he was ruined by the payola scandal that erupted in late 1959. Alan Freed, a 1986 Rock and Roll Hall of Fame inductee, died from cirrhosis of the liver in 1965. (See chapter 1 for further information.)

These masters of their craft were stars themselves—many deejays as popular as the records they spun. Disc jockeys were there between all the songs and stayed with their listeners for hours each night, in both the background (accompanying listeners' homework) and the foreground (providing gossip, information, and contest prizes). Their sociable voices were accessible by phone, at hops, and at concerts. As Ed Ward proclaims in *Rock of Ages*, jockeys turned their work into an art by howling, screaming, and playing records that people thought they could get only on the wrong side of town while telling them where they could get them on the right side of town. These pioneers of the airwaves stirred up hormones while bonding and uniting with America's teenagers—the chosen ones who heard the news: There's good rockin' tonight.[12]

The Creation of the Top 40

As Ben Fong-Torres states in *The Hits Just Keep on Coming*, the exact origin of Top 40 radio is debatable: "Some say it was born in a bar in Omaha, Nebraska, or at a station in New Orleans. Others say it was born in Texas, where Gordon McLendon brought the format, with splashy promotional pizzazz, to his stations in Dallas, San Antonio, and Houston. Still others maintain it was created by radio programming consultant Bill Gavin, who weaved [sic] playlist reports from stations around the country into a chart."[13] Most historians have labeled the birthplace of formula radio as that tavern in Nebraska, sometime between 1953 and 1955, when the operator of station KOWH and the owner of a small chain of stations, Todd Storz, discovered the concept that would become known as Top 40. While Storz was discussing television's negative impact on radio and trying to devise a way to improve his station's ratings with program director Bill Stewart, the two noticed interesting jukebox activity:

customers played the same few songs repeatedly over the course of four or five hours. Then, after most customers left, a waitress continued to select the same songs. Stewart wrote down the approximately thirty song titles they had heard played all evening, and with Storz's approval applied this jukebox theory to KOWH, eliminating its classical, country, and other current programs and focusing on pop songs, targeting homemakers. With soaring ratings, their daytime AM station was soon turned around.

Though this jukebox brainstorm allegedly occurred in 1955, Storz is thought to have created a similar program at his New Orleans station, WTIX, in 1953 when station manager George "Bud" Armstrong heard *The Top 20 at 1280*, a show on rival station WDSU. Trying to outdo the competition, WTIX created a similar show starting an hour earlier and lasting an hour longer than the rival station's. With an extended record list, WTIX called the program *Top 40 at 1450*. Adding even more complexity to the mystery of the beginnings of the format, Todd Storz stated in an interview with *Television* magazine in 1957 that he realized while in the army during World War II that people demanded their favorites over and over. Whatever the case, this concept that Gordon McLendon was also reported using as early as 1953 was applied, and the result was Top 40 radio.[14]

In its early days, radio's first music format consisted of deejays following a playlist that was not aimed at teenagers; they played pop, country, blues, jazz, sound tracks, and rock and roll. The concept involved the constant rotation of the forty top-rated recordings determined by *Billboard* magazine and assured listeners that they would always hear something they enjoyed. This radio practice made broadcasting access very competitive for record companies and increased the power of disc jockeys. Radio station program managers and deejays were then in a position to influence the next big hit, further diminishing the concept of popular music as a sheet music industry while enraging other facets of the music industry. To get their music on the air, agents and record companies resorted to bribing deejays and station managers for airplay, until the Federal Trade Commission (FTC) investigated this payola practice in 1959 and 1960.

The mantra of Top 40's founding fathers, Todd Storz, Gordon McLendon, and Bill Stewart, was "play the hits," as they created their on-air jukebox. McLendon also developed another aspect of Top 40 radio. While airing local groups live on the air, his Dallas KLIF station music director, Bill Meeks, started having their house band sing and record what became known as jingles in 1947, allowing time to switch musicians and setups between programs. In addition to playing the most popular records of the day, Top 40 eventually became a nonstop flurry of broadcast activities, including commercials, time checks, news, weather, and sports, as well as contests, listener requests, and dedications mixed with jingles repeating the station's call letters and frequency. Many pioneering deejays, such as Tom Donahue, were bothered by the new format, upset that it squashed their originality and no longer allowed them to be themselves or freely choose what music to play on the air.

OTHER INDUSTRY-RELATED BUSINESS

As rock and roll began its ascendancy to big business in the '50s, other facets of the industry became vital, such as the booking agency, talent management, and concert production, along with the emergence of rock and roll songwriters and producers. As television began to promote the new music, trade magazines and music charts assisted with its organization. Artist and group appearances became very popular during the decade, making television a highly effective promotional tool used by record companies to sell records.

Television and *American Bandstand*

Television's 1950s progression from novelty to common household item accompanied the trend toward home entertainment. Such television variety shows as those of Jackie Gleason and Ed Sullivan broadcast musical talent into America's homes that network radio used to, adding the visual component of the music. Rock and roll was spread with this new medium that was found in more homes as the decade progressed, and fewer people were turning to the radio for news and entertainment. Since fewer radio listeners meant fewer

Entertainers (left to right) Conway Twitty, Chubby Checker, and Dick Clark, doing the Twist, 1959. Courtesy of the Library of Congress.

sponsors and lower advertising revenue, stations faced going out of business or finding a new audience—ironically, at the time when teenagers were tuning in to the radio in large numbers. As their parents gathered in front of television sets, teens had access to radios somewhere else in their homes, invariably in the evenings, when the exciting R&B programs were broadcast. Advertisers pushed to buy airtime on television. Bothered by the direction in which America's disc jockeys (and BMI's growing share of the music) were leading society, ASCAP's TPA publishers found hope in television, which was bringing what was considered more quality music to the viewing public. The established music industry looked to television for salvation, seeking pop standards that television producers lavishly produced on the highly rated shows of Milton Berle, Perry Como, and Dinah Shore. Meanwhile, rock and roll supporters very quickly learned that widely viewed television plugs were potent, and as people began to realize the rock and roll phenomenon was not going to disappear as quickly as originally thought, such television hosts as Ed Sullivan, a respected columnist for the *New York Daily News* with his own television program that drew a huge viewing audience on Sunday nights, began inviting rock and rollers to perform on his show. In addition, he hired deejay Tommy "Dr. Jive" Smalls to present a fifteen-minute sample of his live Harlem shows.

Philadelphia deejay Dick Clark's national television show *American Bandstand* was even more influential with its delivery of music to America's homes. Born Richard Wagstaff Clark on November 30, 1929, in Bronxville, New York, Dick Clark, who graduated from Syracuse University with a business degree and held positions in upstate New York at Utica's WRUN and Syracuse's WOLF, became a television newscaster in November 1951 at Utica-Rome's WKTV. This promising young entrepreneur's big break was being hired by radio station WFIL in Philadelphia on May 13, 1952, one month before he married his high school sweetheart, Barbara "Bobbie" Mallery. Clark became a commercial announcer on WFIL-TV in addition to hosting his daily radio program, *Dick Clark's Caravan of Music*, which featured easy listening standards.

Later that year, WFIL-TV instituted its daily *Bandstand* show, hosted by Bob Horn and Lee Stewart on October 7, 1952. The television show consisted of an informal dance party for local teens, originally modeled after Philadelphia radio station WPEN's *950 Club* and WFIL-TV's jazzman-turned-disc jockey Paul Whiteman's *TV-Teen Club*, a Saturday evening dance and talent show. The station's Tony Mammarella was appointed producer of the show. Though *Bandstand* was primarily a mainstream pop music venue (that eventually offered R&B music), Bill Haley and the Comets performed their hit, "Crazy Man, Crazy," on the show the following spring, and in the summer of 1954, Horn began to program black R&B on the previously all-white pop *Bandstand*, beginning with the Chords' "Sh-Boom." Stewart was removed from the show the following year, leaving Horn as the only host until he was fired in 1956. On July 9, 1956, Dick Clark began as the new host.

The genial Clark kept Horn's *Bandstand* format intact. Two components of the show were Rate-a-Record, in which selected teenage guests offered numerical evaluations of new songs, and the popular daily lip-synched performances by guest singers that occurred between records. Airing every weekday immediately after school and attracting a huge audience of teenagers, *Bandstand* became so popular in the Philadelphia area that after Clark convinced ABC, it went nationwide on the network. The American Broadcasting Company had already experimented with rock and roll, having launched Ricky Nelson's career on its popular *The Adventures of Ozzie and Harriet* sitcom and aired Alan Freed's television show, *Big Beat*, a thirty-minute program consisting of artists lip-synching their latest hit records (which lasted only three episodes and was dropped one week before *American Bandstand* made its network debut). On August 5, 1957, *American Bandstand* made its national debut to millions of viewers. With its calm and controlled atmosphere and safe and jovial host, the show was a huge success with its well-groomed and well-behaved teenage guests. The program's regulars (teen dancers) became instant celebrities who established the grooming and fashion trends of the day. *American Bandstand*'s immense popularity with teens (and, surprisingly, with housewives) across the nation broadened the show's promotional capability to propel featured singers to the top of the charts. The show created instant national hits ranging from Paul Anka's "Diana" and Danny & the Juniors' "At the Hop" (both 1957 No. 1 pop and R&B hits) to the Silhouettes' "Get a Job" (1958 No. 1 pop and R&B hit) and the Royal Teens' "Short Shorts" (1958 No. 3 pop and No. 2 R&B hit).

Meanwhile, Clark embarked upon various music business projects. He was part owner of several local companies, including the Cameo, Jamie, Swan, and Chancellor record labels, and began to feature these indies' artists on *American Bandstand*. He formed the Click Corporation to handle his song publishing and record hop revenues, and the Binlark Company (with Bob Marcucci and Bernie Binnick) to bankroll the rock and roll movie *Jamboree*, in which Charles Graci (Charlie Gracie) and other artists appeared with deejays, including Clark himself. In 1957, Clark formed Sea-Lark Enterprises, a BMI-affiliated song publishing firm, and Chips Distribution (with Harry Chipetz and Bernie Lowe), a record distributorship. As John Jackson states in *American Bandstand*, "By using *Bandstand* to introduce young white singers less offensive than 'Elvis the Pelvis,' the show's host did more than any

AMERICAN BANDSTAND TELEVISION DEBUTS

After ABC nationally broadcast *American Bandstand*, musicians had more access to national television than ever before. Whereas traditional television shows such as Ed Sullivan's allowed only one featured rock and roll artist per week, *American Bandstand* had several spots available each day, five days a week. This format created an unprecedented number of performing opportunities and allowed numerous performers who perhaps never would have been given the opportunity to be on television the chance to do so. This show that predated MTV by twenty-five years introduced a formidable array of pioneering rock and roll artists to America. The following '50s recording artists and groups are among those who made their network television debut on *American Bandstand*.[16]

other non-performer to change the face of rock 'n' roll—and amassed a personal fortune in the process."[15]

Among the many singers from the Philadelphia area who appeared on *American Bandstand* were Bobby Rydell ("We Got Love"), Frederick Picariello (Freddie Cannon; "Tallahassee Lassie"), Frankie Avalon ("Venus"), and Fabian ("Tiger"). These locals were joined by a host of others, such as Paul Anka, Bobby Darin, and Johnny Tillotson ("Dreamy Eyes"), all of whom appeared regularly and sounded alike, singing a diluted version of rock music that resembled the style of the earlier pop crooners more than rock and rollers (referred to by many writers as "Philadelphia schlock rock"). This commercially successful music dominated the charts until the Beatles and other early 1960s groups replaced it. The more pop-oriented teen idol music did not affect the financially successful Clark, who capitalized on the growing industry of rock and roll music.

Seeking to capitalize on Clark's success, ABC began televising *American Bandstand* during prime time on Monday evenings,

AMERICAN BANDSTAND TELEVISION DEBUTS *(continued)*	
Paul Anka	Frankie Avalon
Chuck Berry	Freddy Cannon
Johnny Cash	The Chantels
Chubby Checker	The Coasters
Eddie Cochran	Sam Cooke
Bobby Darin	Dion and the Belmonts
The Drifters	The Everly Brothers
Fabian	The Flamingos
Connie Francis	Annette Funicello
Buddy Holly and the Crickets	Jerry Lee Lewis
Little Anthony and the Imperials	Johnny Mathis
Bobby Rydell	Neil Sedaka
Simon & Garfunkel (as Tom and Jerry)	Jackie Wilson

beginning October 7, 1957, but without teenagers and housewives available to watch at that hour, the show's ratings were disastrous and it was canceled. After both the show and the evening it aired (to Saturday night), were changed, and Clark and Mammarella were given total control over guest artists, *The Dick Clark Show* debuted on February 15, 1958, broadcast from ABC's Little Theatre in New York City. Artists on the first show included the Royal Teens, Jerry Lee Lewis (who refused to lip-synch), and Connie Francis.

As his popularity rose, Clark's power within the music business increased. His holdings expanded in 1958 with his organization of the Globe Record Corporation, and the forming of Kincord Music Publishing and a new Hunt record label. At this point, with his own record pressing plant and talent management company, Clark was a one-man music conglomerate, and could have a hand in every facet of an artist's career, as can be seen in his shared management of rock guitarist Duane Eddy ("Rebel-'Rouser"), one of the most promising artists to appear on his show. As Clark's reputation as the nation's premier song plugger within the popular music industry increased, ABC was delighted with the success of its young star. Among the many deejays affected in 1959 by the payola scandal, ABC supported Clark, but he had to sell his music companies in order to remain on the air.

Perhaps Clark's *American Bandstand* softened rock and roll somewhat as the late 1950s teen idol phenomenon arose, but by playing R&B records by the original artists on his show, the television host helped stop the long-standing practice of white artists sanitizing black artists' records. *American Bandstand* was the hottest show on daytime television; *The Dick Clark Show* almost overnight boasted a waiting list of seven months to attend and quickly became ABC's hottest program overall. These shows played an integral role in establishing rock and roll. They allowed the new music to flourish and helped shape its future. The underlying factor in the phenomenal success of these television programs was indeed Dick Clark. A television personality who recognized the need to showcase rock and roll as a safer, more accessible music, he brought the sound to America, spreading the word throughout the entertainment industry that rock and roll was not a fluke while also playing a major role in creating the late 1950s teen idol phenomenon. Having transformed the record business into an international industry, Dick Clark was rightfully honored for his rock and roll contributions by his induction into the Rock and Roll Hall of Fame in 1993.

Songwriters, Producers, and Others

While *American Bandstand* was providing rock and roll musicians more national exposure than ever before, behind-the-scenes individuals, songwriter- and producer-creators of the music influenced the production of rock and roll, and artist managers and concert promoters helped publicize the new music. The path to high-production rock and roll opened in the '50s as records progressed from creation in rustic locations to sophisticated recording studios. With TPA's efforts to raise songwriting and production standards, the quality of rock recordings improved, with professional songwriters and producers influencing record production and even creating new acts to exhibit their talents. Industry greats Jerry Leiber, Mike Stoller, Doc Pomus, Milt Gabler, Dave Bartholomew, and Cosimo Matassa were among the important behind-the-scenes industry figures emerging in the '50s.

One of the first and finest of the songwriter-producer teams, Leiber and Stoller, teenage prodigies with an interest in R&B, moved to Los Angeles in 1950. Born in 1933, lyricist Leiber was raised near Baltimore's black ghetto, and composer Stoller, born the same year, hailed from Queens, New York. This duo wrote some of the most vigorous, enduring rock and roll songs, including "Hound Dog" (Big Mama Thornton and Elvis Presley), "Jailhouse Rock" and "Treat Me Nice" (Elvis Presley), "Love Potion No. 9" (the Clovers), "Searchin'" and "Yakety Yak" (and most other major hits by the Coasters), "Kansas City" (Wilbert Harrison, a 1959 No. 1 pop and R&B hit that had a number of cover versions by artists as diverse as Little Richard, Peggy Lee, and the Beatles),

The songwriting team of Leiber and Stoller (Mike Stoller, left, Jerry Leiber, right) with Elvis Presley during the filming of *Jailhouse Rock*, 1957. Courtesy of Photofest.

"On Broadway" (the Drifters), "Ruby Baby" (Dion), and "Stand by Me" (Ben E. King), one of the duo's most recorded compositions. After their early string of hits, in 1956 Atlantic Records signed Leiber and Stoller as independent producers—the first production deal of this sort in rock history. This pioneering songwriting team set the standard for novelty doo-wop songs and expanded rock and roll orchestration and recording techniques (as in the Drifters' "There Goes My Baby"). For propelling the early popularity of rock and roll with their astounding catalogue of well-crafted songs and professional recordings, Jerry Leiber and Mike Stoller were inducted into the Rock and Roll Hall of Fame in 1987.

Jerome Solon Felder (Doc Pomus), a 1992 Rock and Roll Hall of Fame inductee, and his partner, Mort Shuman, were another '50s songwriting team with an impressive repertoire. Born in Brooklyn in 1925, Pomus wrote some of the greatest songs in rock and roll history: "Boogie Woogie Country Girl" (Joe Turner), "Young Blood" (the Coasters; written with Leiber and Stoller), "Lonely Avenue" (Ray Charles), "Turn Me Loose" (Fabian), "A Teenager in Love" (Dion and the Belmonts), "This Magic Moment" (the Drifters), and "Save the Last Dance for Me" (Ben E. King). In addition, Elvis Presley recorded approximately twenty Pomus originals, including "Viva Las Vegas." Despite being confined to a wheelchair from polio, Pomus composed over a thousand songs, many with Shuman, until his death in 1991. Most early 1960s charts hits were written in or near the Brill Building in New York City (a newer version of Manhattan's TPA), where composers wrote in small cubicles with pianos. Don Kirshner and Al Nevins's publishing company, Aldon Music, was located across the street from the Brill Building on Broadway before moving into the famous edifice. In 1958, Kirshner and Nevins hired Pomus and Shuman along with the team of Neil Sedaka and Howard Greenfield. Sedaka-Greenfield hits included "Oh! Carol" and "The Diary" (Neil Sedaka) and "Frankie" and "Stupid Cupid" (Connie Francis). In 1960, the prolific Carole King-Gerry Goffin team joined the firm, and was later followed by the Barry Mann and Cynthia Weil team, and Neil Diamond. This talented stable of the best songwriters around created what became known as "Brill Building Pop" in the early 1960s. Rather than send simple piano-vocal demonstration tapes (or records) of his writers' material for consideration, Kirshner invested in high-quality production, using an orchestra to perform arrangements as he thought they should be done.

Other successful songwriting teams included Felice and Boudleaux Bryant. Composer and violinist Boudleaux and his lyricist wife, Felice, began writing songs together for enjoyment, but after achieving a country hit in 1949 the couple moved to Nashville. In 1957, publisher Wesley Rose introduced the Bryants to the Everly Brothers, who recorded their "Bye Bye Love," "Wake Up Little Susie," "All I Have to Do Is Dream," "Bird Dog," and "Devoted to You." Philadelphia's Bernard Lowenthal and Kalman Cohen (Lowe and Mann) were another '50s songwriting team. By 1956, this duo had several of their compositions published and recorded, including "(Let Me Be Your) Teddy Bear" (Elvis Presley; 1957 No. 1 pop, R&B, and country hit), which, because of a deal with the powerful New York-based Hill and Range music publishing company, they were forced to relinquish to the company. Approximately twenty artists (including Andy Williams) covered Lowe and Mann's "Butterfly" (the original artist was Charlie Gracie). With Clark's plugging on *American Bandstand*, the original "Butterfly" became a huge success (a 1957 No. 1 pop and No. 10 R&B hit) and one of 1957's biggest sellers. In addition to the songwriting teams and many songwriting rockers (such as Bo Diddley, Chuck Berry, and Ray Charles), numerous other composers wrote rock and roll songs in the '50s, among them Berry Gordy. This founder of the Motown recording empire began writing songs for such '50s artists as Jackie Wilson ("Lonely Teardrops," "That's Why (I Love You So)," and "I'll Be Satisfied").

As Leiber and Stoller set the precedent for the songwriter-producer and pioneered the '50s concept of freelance producer, they blazed a trail for such others as Lee Hazlewood, Bob Crewe, Phil Spector, and Bert Berns. Majors traditionally had staff members who supervised records (such as A&R men, music directors, or house producers), and indie owners usually did this themselves, whereas in the mid-1950s independent producers were jacks of all trades. They did everything from composing songs to locating singers, financing recordings, supervising recording sessions, and leasing recordings to record companies. Another kind of producer emerged, serving more as a manager and supporting artists all the way to finished recordings. Such a pioneer was Norman Petty. Based in Clovis, New Mexico, Petty owned a studio where he recorded members of the Rhythm Orchids, Buddy Knox ("Party Doll"), and Jimmy Bowen ("I'm Stickin' with You")—recordings released on Roulette Records—and Buddy Holly demos. In Phoenix, Arizona, disc jockey Lee Hazlewood mixed country and blues and located local singers and musicians to perform his music, such as guitarist Al Casey. Using rhythmic riffs and echo devices, Hazlewood created songs with appealing lyrics, though his greatest 1950s successes were instrumental recordings of Duane Eddy and others.

Milt Gabler, with a background in jazz, was hired by Decca in 1941 as an A&R man, which allowed him to branch out to R&B and rock and roll music. Having produced such founding fathers as Louis Jordan ("Caldonia" and "Choo Choo Ch'Boogie") and Bill Haley and the Comets ("Shake, Rattle and Roll"), Gabler became one of the strongest forces in popular music for much of the twentieth century. When he changed his production style from Jordan's jump blues sounds with a balanced swing-band-type rhythm section to the forceful backbeat of Haley's songs, Gabler helped in the birth of rock and roll. For his impact on the genre, Milt Gabler was inducted into the Rock and Roll Hall of Fame in 1993.

Dave Bartholomew was another significant figure in the transition from jump blues to R&B and rock and roll. A chief proponent of the New Orleans sound, this talented songwriter, producer, arranger, and talent scout spent much of his time in the studio recording Imperial's artists, such as Smiley Lewis, Lloyd Price, and Shirley & Lee. Bartholomew discovered Fats Domino and produced his lengthy string of hit records. Another significant figure in New Orleans was Paul Gayten, who produced, arranged, and served as talent scout; he discovered Clarence "Frogman" Henry and others as A&R man for Chess Records. The master of the New Orleans sound, Cosimo Matassa attracted many '50s R&B artists to his J&M Studio to record, from Big Joe Turner to Little Richard and Ray Charles. (See chapter 4, for further information.)

Another '50s producer, Bob Marcucci, made a name for himself in Philadelphia as a scout and promoter of teen idols; he discovered Frankie Avalon. Ralph Bass enjoyed a lengthy career as a producer and talent scout for the influential Savoy, King/Federal, and Chess indies. Born in the Bronx in 1911, Bass recorded many of the greatest artists in black music, including T-Bone Walker ("Call It Stormy Monday") and Hank Ballard and the Midnighters ("Work with Me Annie"). In addition to recording many extraordinary blues, gospel, R&B, and rock and roll musicians—from Clara Ward, the Soul Stirrers, and Etta James to Howlin' Wolf and Muddy Waters—Bass discovered James Brown and brought him to the Federal label. For his impact on rock and roll, Ralph Bass was inducted into the Rock and Roll Hall of Fame in 1991. Another Rock and Roll

Hall of Famer, Johnny Otis, was inducted in 1994 for his outstanding skills as a producer, talent scout, and songwriter. Otis, a percussionist and bandleader, scouted talent for Sydney Nathan's King and Federal labels, and discovered the Midnighters (then known as the Royals). His R&B stage revues, numerous recordings made under his name (including those by Little Esther, Big Mama Thornton, Etta James, and the Robins-turned-Coasters), and various other achievements made the multitalented Otis a key figure in the rise of R&B and rock and roll in the 1950s. Producer and engineer Sam Phillips created history at Sun Records with his '50s series of recordings by Johnny Cash, Elvis Presley, Jerry Lee Lewis, and many others who gave their finest performances in his studio. Between his ability to reveal artists' emotions in recordings and the excitement generated by their records, this producer, considered the greatest by many, ensured his stature among the most important in popular music. (See chapter 5 for further information.)

Phil Spector, a teenage prodigy, apprenticed with Leiber and Stoller in the 1950s. Under their tutelage, the young Spector began producing hits for Atlantic before forming his own Philles label in the early 1960s and going on to produce a string of hits by artists including the Crystals ("He's a Rebel" and "Da Doo Ron Ron [When He Walked Me Home]"), the Ronettes ("Be My Baby"), and the Righteous Brothers ("You've Lost That Lovin' Feelin'" and "Unchained Melody"). The multiple achievements of this 1989 Rock and Roll Hall of Fame inductee included creation of the rock and roll girl group. Though female vocal groups had previously been present in popular music, Spector freshened up the doo-wop subgenre by replacing male vocal ensembles with girl groups in the early 1960s; these groups became models for others, such as the Marvelettes and the Supremes. Attempting to control all aspects of his musical product, Spector explored all possibilities of the studio and developed what is referred to as the "Wall of Sound," which used many instruments (and overdubbing) as well as echo, resulting in a loud, busy sound. Considered one of the greatest producers of rock and roll for his production sophistication, Spector helped redefine and revitalize rock and roll in the late 1950s and early 1960s. His innovations allowed producers to become known by their sound and to receive as much respect and appreciation as the artists whose records they produced.

The '50s rock and roll music market not only changed the recording industry and radio, it also established the importance of other industry-related persons, such as managers, agents, and concert promoters. The structure for promoting artists and groups previously existed, but in the '50s it was changed to accommodate the new music and its huge audience. Managers rose to the forefront. Colonel Tom Parker, the Nashville-based industry veteran and manager of Eddie Arnold, practically adopted Elvis Presley. He devoted himself to Presley and planned the commercial life of the young artist by moving him in and out of various entertainment media and from rock and roll to the army and

Colonel Tom Parker and Elvis Presley on the set of *Love Me Tender*, 1956. Courtesy of Photofest.

several movies. Their relationship helped establish the manager/agent role in the music industry. Managers protected and spoke for artists, and dealt with lawyers, record companies, and booking agencies, giving musicians freedom from business affairs to develop artistically. In the 1950s, many managers were businessmen with little respect for their artists as musicians, and they frequently took financial advantage of their R&B clients. This situation changed in time, as did the role of managers.

During the '50s, concert promotion occurred through disc jockeys, who had unlimited access to the power of radio, had daily contact with musicians and managers, and were often celebrities themselves. Alan Freed's successful concerts encouraged nightclubs and dance halls to book R&B acts, and such other deejays as Dick Clark and Murray "the K" Kaufman became active in concert promotion. Clark's Caravan of Stars package show toured extensively on the East Coast; Kaufman's concerts at the Brooklyn Fox Theater drew huge crowds. These promoters paid their acts very little, and most shows were package deals consisting of five to ten artists and groups. Each act performed only a few songs, and the deejays often spent time entertaining on stage as well. Several shows were performed daily, reaping huge profits.

Trades and Charts

Before the music industry became a large complex of corporations, there was a newsletter circulated by Bill Gavin, a trusted report on radio requests and airplay referred to as a "tipsheet" for radio stations, deejays, record companies, and record retailers. *Billboard* and *Cashbox* were weekly music trade magazines. Each provided basic coverage of industry events and compiled the charted hits in different categories. Considered a leading voice of the music business, *Billboard* is the most influential, largest, and oldest trade publication. According to Fred Bronson, "*Billboard* began publishing on November 1, 1894, 'devoted to the interests of advertisers, poster printers, billposters, advertising agents and secretaries at fairs.' Over more than 100 years, *Billboard* has evolved from a trade paper covering those 19th-century issues to the 'international newsweekly of music, video and home entertainment' that it is today."[17]

Industry executives still regularly follow *Billboard*'s charts. The trade magazine chronicles news within the music industry: current artists; music genres and markets; radio, jukebox, and television programming; music research, development, and marketing; developments in the recording business; new companies and executives within the industry; international news and markets; and, its most important and popular feature, the charts of record sales. A very important development in the history of *Billboard* was the July 20, 1940, premier of the first "Music Popularity Chart," which reported Tommy Dorsey's "I'll Never Smile Again" (vocals by Frank Sinatra) as the very first No. 1 record. Ever since then, *Billboard* has weekly reported the best-selling records in America. Once Bill Haley and the Comets' "(We're Gonna) Rock Around the Clock" became the first rock and roll record to top the charts in 1955, a chronological boundary divided all previous records from rock and roll records. This song was an

Advertisement for Jerry Lee Lewis' "Great Balls of Fire" as seen in a November 1957 edition of *Billboard* magazine. Courtesy of the Library of Congress.

indication that those to follow would be different from earlier hits by such artists as Bing Crosby, Perry Como, and Rosemary Clooney. *Billboard* published more than one pop chart each week until 1958, including Best Sellers in Stores, Most Played in Juke Boxes, Most Played by Jockeys, and the Honor Roll of Hits. A Top 100 chart (the first 100-position pop chart) was published as early as November 12, 1955. *Billboard* introduced the Hot 100 chart on August 4, 1958 (the first chart to fully integrate the hottest-selling and most-played pop singles), a survey that remains the definitive industry chart. The first song to top the Hot 100 chart was "Poor Little Fool" by Ricky Nelson. Beginning with this record, the Hot 100 became the source for all No. 1 singles.[18]

To better reflect the hottest songs of the radio and record industries, over the years *Billboard* has made major adjustments in the compilation of its many charts. There have been separate listings for music subgenres ranging from country music to easy listening and from disco to R&B. For example, in the R&B category, there have been multiple singles charts: the Harlem Hit Parade (the first R&B singles sales chart, 1942) evolved into the Most-Played Juke Box Race Records chart (1945); the Best Selling Retail Race Records chart was introduced in 1948, and the next year "rhythm and blues" was substituted for "race" in the chart name of both the Best Selling and the Juke Box charts; and in 1955 the Most Played by R&B Disk Jockeys debuted. Each of these weekly charts focused on a specific area of the music trade. The Juke Box chart was discontinued on June 17, 1957, and on October 20, 1958, the Best Seller and Disk Jockey charts were replaced by one all-inclusive Top 30 R&B singles chart, Hot R&B Sides. Since the mid-1960s, this chart has changed in name and size, and today is known as the Hot R&B/Hip-Hop Singles & Tracks chart.[19]

Trade magazines of the '50s set precedents for future rock journalism. From 1943 to 1973, Paul Ackerman served as music editor of *Billboard* magazine. He was among the first journalists to tackle rock and roll, and felt that music was the most important of the arts. A superb writer who charted the rise of R&B, country music, and rock and roll, documenting their impact on the world of popular music, Ackerman was inducted into the Rock and Roll Hall of Fame in 1995. With his guidance, *Billboard* became the music industry's premier trade publication. At first, whether in newspapers or magazines (such as *16* and *Hit Parader*), rock journalism was aimed at teenagers. Though it concentrated on artists' looks rather than on their music, this early writing eventually became more music-oriented as rock and roll became prominent. The practice of writing liner notes for albums began when Atlantic's Jerry Wexler hired Jon Landau to write notes for an Otis Redding record. Journalists of such publications as *Mojo Navigator*, *Crawdaddy*, and *Creem* began to discuss the music. When Jann Wenner founded *Rolling Stone* in the '60s, it became the first significant publication to reflect the tremendous importance and impact of rock and roll on society, treating rock and roll and its artists as subjects worthy of critical discourse.

As America's pop culture surfaced in the '50s and rock and roll music earned its place in society, consumers boosted the economy by purchasing the product, allowing the music industry to grow immensely. Innovative entrepreneurs with small companies recognized the importance of the new music, which thoroughly shook up established business patterns. Revenues generated by rock and roll have made this genre financially more important than others. Drawing huge crowds since Alan Freed's first live shows, rock concerts have always produced great profits. Rock and roll fans still attend rock shows in great numbers; it is not uncommon nowadays to see three generations of a family at a Rolling Stones concert. Today, baby boomers are active consumers of the music, buying compact and digital video discs. And the huge record conglomerates have specific divisions devoted to these consumers, creating neatly packaged boxed sets of specialized music products aimed at these customers who are acquiring recordings of their favorite songs more than fifty years after the birth of rock and roll.

NOTES

Record label statistics referred to in the chapter are based on Charlie Gillett's *The Sound of the City* and Joel Whitburn's Record Research publications; all charts positions referred to in the chapter are based on Whitburn's publications, which compile *Billboard* charts information of the rock and roll era.

1. Steve Chapple and Reebee Garofalo, *Rock 'n' Roll Is Here to Pay: The History and Politics of the Music Industry* (Chicago: Nelson-Hall, 1977), 30–31.

2. Ed Ward, Geoffrey Stokes, and Ken Tucker, *Rock of Ages: The Rolling Stone History of Rock & Roll* (New York: Rolling Stone Press, 1986), 165–166.

3. Russell Sanjek, updated by David Sanjek, *Pennies from Heaven: The American Popular Music Business in the Twentieth Century* (New York: Da Capo Press, 1996), 318.

4. Reebee Garofalo, *Rockin' Out: Popular Music in the USA*, 3rd ed. (Upper Saddle River, NJ: Prentice Hall, 2005), 49–50.

5. David Sanjek, "They Work Hard for Their Money: The Business of Popular Music," in *American Popular Music: New Approaches to the Twentieth Century*, ed. Rachel Rubin and Jeffrey Melnick (Amherst: University of Massachusetts Press, 2001), 15–17.

6. John A. Jackson, *Big Beat Heat: Alan Freed and the Early Years of Rock & Roll* (New York: Schirmer Books, 1991), 109–110.

7. Gillian G. Gaar, *She's a Rebel: The History of Women in Rock & Roll*, 2nd ed., enl. (New York: Seal, 2002), 28.

8. Chapple and Garofalo, *Rock 'n' Roll Is Here to Pay*, 35.

9. Charlie Gillett, *The Sound of the City: The Rise of Rock and Roll*, 2nd ed., enl. (New York: Da Capo Press, 1996), 64.

10. Wes Smith, *The Pied Pipers of Rock 'n' Roll: Radio Deejays of the 50s and 60s* (Marietta, GA: Longstreet Press, 1989), 22–26.

11. "Alan Freed: King of the Moondoggers," temporary exhibit (Cleveland, OH: Rock and Roll Hall of Fame and Museum, May 10, 2003).

12. Ed Ward, *Rock of Ages*, 71.

13. Ben Fong-Torres, *The Hits Just Keep on Coming: The History of Top 40 Radio* (San Francisco: Backbeat Books, 2001), 37.

14. Ibid., 38–39.

15. John A. Jackson, *American Bandstand: Dick Clark and the Making of a Rock 'n' Roll Empire* (New York: Oxford University Press, 1997), 41.

16. Ibid., 289–290.

17. Fred Bronson, *The Billboard Book of Number One Hits*, 4th ed. (New York: Billboard Books, 1997), xxiii.

18. Ibid.

19. Joel Whitburn, *Joel Whitburn Presents Top R&B/Hip-Hop Singles, 1942–2004* (Menomonee Falls, WI: Record Research, 2004), 9.

9

FIFTIES POSTLUDE: "ROCK AND ROLL IS HERE TO STAY"

ROCK AND ROLL IS A MAJOR FORCE

As the '50s progressed and rock and roll gained momentum, it left a remarkable mark on society as Americans embraced and adored the powerful new music and its creators. By decade's end, both parents and their children were enjoying rock and roll sounds in one form or another—teenagers enjoyed "Splish Splash" and parents, "Mack the Knife." After *The Blackboard Jungle* and its 1955 rock and roll introduction by Bill Haley and the Comets' profoundly influential "Rock Around the Clock," America's youth were drawn to the fresh, invigorating sounds. Shortly after, they discovered the sounds of Chuck Berry, Fats Domino, Little Richard, Elvis Presley, and the rest. As these talented musicians shared their brilliance with American teens who welcomed their music with open arms, initially parents were threatened by the music. As rock music permeated society and the music industry softened the music with more acceptable sounds, parents eventually came around, accepting and embracing versions of it.

By the mid-1950s, there was no stopping the rise of rock and roll. America's popular music was no longer segregated; the music had crossed racial barriers, and recordings from artists as diverse as LaVern Baker and the Penguins became hits with white listeners. Rock and roll, no longer exclusively the domain of black artists, became more popular than ever as it permeated American society.

The media popularized the new sound. Newspapers and magazines highlighted rock and roll with publicity that boosted record sales and polished the music's image. Radio promoted it with wild, fast-talking disc jockeys who kept pace with the vibrant new sounds. Television adopted the music not only on variety shows and situation comedies (to increase ratings), but also with Dick Clark and *American Bandstand*. The show's publicity caused millions of teenagers and their mothers to tune in every day after school. This daily meeting of teenagers with their peer group at a television record hop broadened the audience base for rock and roll. Rock music provided comfort in various ways. There were records about loneliness, such as Elvis Presley's "Heartbreak Hotel," the Elegants' "Little Star," and Jackie Wilson's "Lonely Teardrops"; and songs about alienation and oppression, including Eddie Cochran's "Summertime Blues," the Coasters' "Yakety Yak," and Link Wray and His Ray Men's "Rumble." Other songs provided release through happy and carefree sounds, such as Huey "Piano" Smith and the Clowns' "Rocking Pneumonia and the Boogie Woogie Flu" and Robert Byrd's (Bobby Day) "Rock-in' Robin"; and still others promised escape through magic, alcohol, and make-believe worlds, including Ross Bagdasarian's (David Seville) "Witch Doctor," the Champs' "Tequila," and the Cadets' "Stranded in the Jungle."

Hollywood promoted the new music in numerous rock and roll movies throughout the decade, helping shape the public's image of the music. Rock performers were usually portrayed as clean-cut American youth having fun with their music. These movies implied that rock and rollers were not into drugs, alcohol, or any other appalling activities; they reassured parents that rock and roll was harmless by displaying Frankie Lymon and the Teenagers' performance of "I'm Not a Juvenile Delinquent" and Elvis Presley's righteous path to success. After *The Blackboard Jungle*'s startling success, film's power to create a national hit record was capitalized on. To exploit the rock and roll craze, the low-budget film *Rock and Roll Revue* appeared in theaters later that year as a series of stage performances featuring Big Joe Turner, Ruth Brown, and the Larks, and such nonrock artists as Count Basie, Lionel Hampton, and Sarah Vaughan. Poorly distributed, the movie quickly disappeared from theaters; however, it spurred B-movie specialist Sam Katzman to improve on the film's format by adding a story line to performing rock and rollers. He persuaded Alan Freed to portray himself and signed Bill Haley to perform "Rock Around the Clock" for the quickly produced film with that title.

A typical '50s rock and roll film, *Rock Around the Clock* had a minimal story centered around whether or not the new music (as sung in the film by such artists as Haley, the Platters, and Freddy Bell and the Bellboys) would overcome traditional music and win the minds of adults as well as the hearts of their children (which the plot proved true). A pro-rock and roll editorial aimed at adult society as well as for teenage entertainment, the movie was released in April 1956 and featured rock and rollers on screen for approximately half its length. *Rock Around the Clock* attained instant notoriety largely because of postscreening riots around the world as rock and roll-crazed teens rampaged through cities from America to Ireland and from Egypt to Great Britain. It influenced a young John Lennon, who attended its showing in Liverpool. England's Queen Elizabeth changed a scheduled Buckingham Palace

A scene from the film *Rock Around the Clock*, 1956. © Columbia/The Kobol Collection.

showing of *The Caine Mutiny* to one of *Rock Around the Clock*. The movie grossed almost five times its production costs and became the prototype for subsequent rock and roll films, all of which highlighted major music acts and promoted their songs. *Rock, Rock, Rock!* featured Frankie Lymon and the Teenagers, LaVern Baker, Chuck Berry, the Moonglows, and the Flamingos; *Don't Knock the Rock* included Bill Haley and the Comets, Alan Freed, and Little Richard. *Mister Rock and Roll* highlighted Alan Freed, Frankie Lymon and the Teenagers, Chuck Berry, LaVern Baker, Clyde McPhatter, Little Richard, and the Moonglows; and *Go, Johnny, Go!* featured Alan Freed, Jimmy Clanton, Chuck Berry, Ritchie Valens, Jackie Wilson, and Eddie Cochran. Although rockers received few speaking parts in these movies and their appearances had little relevance to the films' stories, they helped introduce rock and roll to the world.[1]

These and many more rock movies linked rock and roll to the emerging youth culture: *Love Me Tender*, *The Girl Can't Help It*, *The Big Beat*, *Jamboree*, *Loving You*, *Rock Around the World*, *Rock Pretty Baby*, *High School Confidential*, *King Creole*, and *G. I. Blues*. This ceaseless promotion made rock and roll all the stronger and resulted in hit after hit, allowing fans to view rock and rollers on the large screen when they could not attend concerts. Along with rock movies, concert tours served as promotional vehicles for the new music. Such concert promoters as Alan Freed and Irving Feld (who is thought to have created rock and roll's first successful large tour, an eighty-day 1957 excursion around the United States starring top recording artists) popularized the music still further and helped establish the rock and roll concert tour business. As rock and roll blossomed, two trends flourished simultaneously along with the major subgenre hits performed by these major touring artists: the novelty song and the instrumental.

Novelty Songs

Some of the most popular '50s records were novelty songs, a staple of the pop music industry. Among the many novelty hits on the charts during the '50s and early '60s (especially 1958), these songs sported simple messages and usually included irresistible phrases, such as "gooba-gooba-gooba-gooba" in Huey "Piano" Smith and the Clowns' "Don't You Just Know It." In 1956, Buchanan & Goodman (Bill Buchanan and Richard Goodman) originated the novelty break-in recording, featuring bits of the original versions of Top 40 hits woven throughout a recording of their "The Flying Saucer (Parts 1 & 2)," a No. 3 pop and a No. 4 R&B hit.

The book *Duel with the Witch Doctor* inspired David Seville's "Witch Doctor" No. 1 pop and R&B hit, 1958's sixth biggest recording. Written and produced under Seville's real name, Ross Bagdasarian, the vocals of this song were recorded at different speeds. The text detailed the singer's troubles with his girlfriend and his going to a witch doctor friend for advice that consisted of such nonsense syllables as "ooh, eeh, ooh ah-ah" and "ting tang walla-walla bing-bang." Seville also recorded vocals with different speeds for his other No. 1 novelty song that year, "The Chipmunk Song" (at the top of the pop charts for four weeks). Inspired by a stubborn chipmunk who refused to move from the middle of the road, Bagdasarian devised the group called the Chipmunks while driving through Yosemite Park in California. He named the three of them after Liberty Records executives Alvin Bennett (Al), Simon Waronker (Sy), and Theodore Keep (Ted), and modeled Alvin after his youngest son, who always kept asking if it was Christmas yet. To move "Witch Doctor" off the charts, country music singer-songwriter and actor Shelby Wooley (Sheb Wooley) created "The Purple People Eater," ranked the highest of the novelties in 1958, at No. 5 on the Hot 100. Wooley auditioned it for MGM Records, and within three weeks of its release it was the No. 1 pop song in the country, and stayed there for six weeks. A Beaumont, Texas, station KTRM disc jockey known as the Big Bopper, Jiles Perry Richardson participated in the novelty craze with his "Purple People Eater Meets Witch Doctor," but it was the flip side of this 1958 record, "Chantilly Lace," that became a big hit at No. 6 (pop) and No. 3 (R&B). Known for his trademark Stetson hat and wild striped suit, the Big Bopper was a flamboyant and jovial personality whom teens loved, famous for his phrase "Oh, baby, that's-a what I like!" He died in the 1959 plane crash that also took the lives of Buddy Holly and Ritchie Valens.

Even '50s vocal groups participated in the novelty craze. Recorded by a vocal trio from Waterbury, Connecticut, known as the Playmates, another huge 1958 hit, "Beep Beep," held the No. 4 position on the pop charts. Its lyrics, about a drag race between a Cadillac and a Nash Rambler, caused Roulette Records to decide not to issue the song in 45-RPM format because it mentioned commercial products and changed tempo (making it nondanceable); however, the label released it as a single after deejays played the tune from its album. The doo-wop group the Cadets recorded the humorous "Stranded in the Jungle" (1956), and the Silhouettes had a 1958 No. 1 hit with novelty "Get a Job." Little Anthony and the Imperials' "Shimmy, Shimmy, Ko-Ko-Bop" also depicted the popular jungle atmosphere and was an immediate hit in early 1960. "Shimmy" found its place in rock history as the last song played by Alan Freed on WABC in New York before he resigned in 1960 after the payola hearings ruined him. The New Jersey–based quintet the Royal Teens (Bob Gaudio's group before the Four Seasons) recorded "Short Shorts" in 1958 as a studio improvisation of one of their instrumentals, with two teenage girls singing the phrase, "Who wears short shorts?" The song rose to No. 3 on the pop charts and No. 2 on the R&B charts. Another novelty, recorded by the R&B vocal group the Olympics, "Western Movies" was a No. 8 pop song that year (and a No. 7 R&B song). Sounding similar to songs by the Coasters, the song's text referred to popular television westerns, such as *Maverick*, *Cheyenne*, and *Sugarfoot*. In addition to the many other doo-wop groups who sang these songs, the Coasters left their mark with numerous novelties, including "Yakety Yak," "Charlie Brown," "Poison Ivy," and "Along Came Jones." (See chapter 7 for further information.)

Rock Instrumentals

Along with novelties, instrumentals came of age in 1958. Disc jockeys loved instrumentals because they were able to talk over them on the air and not have any dead air space in the background. They were perfect pieces of music for this late 1950s sock hop age, the ideal way to keep teens on the dance floor. Somewhat simpler in style, instrumentals were uncomplicated by lyrics. The first instrumental smash, jazz and R&B keyboardist Bill Doggett's "Honky Tonk (Parts 1 & 2)" was a No. 2 pop hit in 1956. This innovative piece featured a very attractive and wild saxophone solo with a prominent rock and roll backbeat. The Champs attained the first No. 1 rock instrumental with their first single, "Tequila," which stayed at the top of the pop charts for five weeks (and at the top of the R&B charts for four weeks), became 1958's biggest instrumental hit and the No. 8 song of the year, and won a Grammy Award for Best R&B Record. This very catchy tune featured a honking saxophone solo, accompanied by a Latin rhythm that retained rock's important backbeat; the only word was "Tequila," shouted at the end of refrains. The Champs, formed in 1957 in Los Angeles, recorded for Gene Autry's Challenge label and named

Les Paul working in his studio, 1952. Courtesy of the Library of Congress.

themselves after his famous horse; they included, at different times, Jimmy Seals and Dash Crofts (of Seals & Crofts fame) as well as Glen Campbell. Another instrumental featuring the popular saxophone was Bill Justis's "Raunchy," a No. 2 pop hit in 1957; the composer played the saxophone and the guitarist was Sid Manker. Justis was a session saxophonist-arranger and producer who led the house band for Sun Records in Memphis.

Without the instruments of rock and roll, the music that audiences know today would not exist. Two significant innovators, Leo Fender and Les Paul, were responsible for the invention of rock and roll's most popular instrument, the electric guitar. Born in 1909 near Anaheim, California, Fender was an electronics fanatic and radio repairman who turned his attention to the guitar. In 1948, he invented the Fender Broadcaster, the first solid-body electric guitar to be mass-produced. Two years later, he introduced his Precision bass, the first electric bass. It brought not only new freedom to bass players by eliminating the large standup bass, but also gave a new sound to band rhythm sections. In 1954, Fender unveiled the Stratocaster, a classy instrument with a contoured body that became a favorite of many virtuoso rock guitarists over the years. After these inventions, guitarists no longer had to attach pickups to the surface of their hollow-bodied guitars. Fender also designed some of the music industry's most desired amplifiers. Responsible for revolutionizing popular music, and specifically rock and roll, with his creations, Leo Fender was inducted into the Rock and Roll Hall of Fame in 1992.

Les Paul was born Lester Polfus in Waukesha, Wisconsin, in 1915. This musician and inventor created the first solid-body electric guitar and introduced modern recording techniques, such as close microphone positioning, electronic echo, and studio multitracking. A country music performer in his teens, Paul appeared on the radio for Chicago's WLS and WJJD. After he formed the Les Paul Trio and they moved to New York City, the group performed with Fred Waring's Pennsylvanians Orchestra on NBC radio in the late 1930s. Interested in revolutionizing the guitar, by 1941 Paul had built the first solid-body electric guitar as his musical taste changed to jazz. He experienced a lengthy and successful pop-jazz career and played with many jazz greats, including Louis Armstrong, Art Tatum, and Charlie Christian. After he was drafted, Paul performed with Bing Crosby, Rudy Vallee, Johnny Mercer, and many more while working for the Armed Forces Radio Service. After he married singer Colleen Summers (Mary Ford), they recorded numerous hits together that are among the earliest multitracked pop songs, featuring what is referred to as Paul's "talking" guitar and Ford's vocal answers to it, including "How High the Moon" and "Vaya con Dios" (1951 and 1953 No. 1 pop hits, respectively). Paul created instrumental hits as well, such as "Nola" (1950), "Whispering" (1951), "Tiger Rag" (1952), and "Meet Mister Callaghan" (1952).

Paul launched the Les Paul Recording Guitar in 1952 and used it for his recordings, later allowing Gibson to build and market that model in 1971. First marketed in May 1952, Les Paul Gibsons received a reputation for their "hot" pickups, "fatter" tone, and sustaining capacity, compared with the twangier Fender electric guitars. Paul also created the first eight-track tape recorder in 1952 (which helped pioneer multitrack recording), and he invented "sound-on-sound" recording, nowadays known as overdubbing. He also invented the floating bridge pickup, the electrodynamic pickup, the dual-pickup guitar, the fourteen-fret guitar, and various types of electronic transducers used in both guitars and recording studios. For his achievements that helped define rock and roll and refine sound technology, in 1988 Les Paul was inducted into the Rock and Roll Hall of Fame. The Rock and Roll Hall of Fame and Museum featured Paul, who continues to perform in New York City, with a major exhibit in 2004 and 2005.

Duane Eddy

One of the first to explore the potential of the electric guitar as a solo voice in rock and roll, Duane Eddy was the originator of the twangy guitar sound and became the most successful instrumentalist in rock and roll history. Born April 26, 1938, in Corning, New York, Eddy began playing guitar at age five. In his teens he moved to Arizona and became a friend of disc jockey Lee Hazlewood in Phoenix (who turned to producing and songwriting in the mid-1950s). Recorded and mentored by Hazlewood at his Phoenix studio, Eddy and his band, the Rebels (including such revered session musicians as saxophonist Steve Douglas, a 2003 Rock and Roll Hall of Fame inductee, and keyboardist Larry Knectel), released their '50s recordings on Jamie Records, one of Dick Clark's business interests in Philadelphia, and also performed on Clark's 1957 Caravan of Stars tour.

In 1958, beginning his impressive string of hits with "Moovin' 'n' Groovin'," Eddy introduced his trademark twangy guitar sound to the world, recording the bass strings with tremolo on his Gretsch guitar through an echo box (using

Hazlewood's novel drainpipe echo chamber). He followed in 1958 and 1959 with the impressive hits "Rebel-'Rouser," "Ramrod," "The Lonely One," and "Forty Miles of Bad Road," all Top 40 hits with catchy rhythms and melodies. As was typical of the day, composer credits were shared by Hazlewood and Eddy. As had instrumentals of Bill Justis and Link Wray, Eddy's "Rebel-'Rouser" climbed to the upper echelons of the charts. This simple, repetitive song, with its powerful backbeat, honking saxophone solo, and rebel yells (performed by the Sharps, later known as the Rivingtons) featured Eddy's guitar melody throughout. After Eddy's first *American Bandstand* appearance, "Rebel-'Rouser" became a No. 6 pop and No. 8 R&B hit and was his first million-seller record. In the fall of 1958, Eddy followed with "Cannonball," and after he plugged it on Clark's Saturday night show, it became a big hit. He and Hazlewood followed with hit records for the Jamie label at an unprecedented pace, aided by Eddy's regular appearances on Clark's national television shows. His friendship with Clark grew so strong that the television host named his second son Duane. Eddy was extremely successful in the late 1950s, and recorded hits throughout the early 1960s. With fifteen Top 40 hits on the charts (twenty-eight on the Hot 100 overall) and appearances in five movies (the first of which in 1960, *Because They're Young*, featured his "Because They're Young" theme song, which became a No. 4 pop hit), Eddy inspired teenagers all over the world to play the guitar as a rock and roll instrument. He also influenced many fellow rockers, including the Ventures, the Beatles, Creedence Clearwater Revival, and Bruce Springsteen. For his widespread influence on rock and roll, Duane Eddy was inducted into the Rock and Roll Hall of Fame in 1994.

Other rock and roll instrumentalists included the guitar duo Santo & Johnny (brothers Santo and Johnny Farina) from Brooklyn, New York, who created another of the decade's biggest instrumentals, 1959's "Sleep Walk," a No. 1 hit that featured their dreamy steel guitar sound with a slow dancelike tempo using the doo-wop harmonic progression. Another rock and roll guitarist, Link Wray (of Link Wray & His Ray Men), and his band recorded the popular hits "Rumble" (1958) and "Raw-Hide" (1959; credited to Link Wray and the Wraymen). Johnny and the Hurricanes, hailing from Toledo, Ohio, were a late 1950s instrumental rock and roll group that produced such hits as "Crossfire" and "Red River Rock" (both 1959). The Ventures, from Seattle, Washington, and one of the finest and most enduring rock instrumental groups, recorded "Walk—Don't Run" in 1959, which became a No. 2 hit the next year. Prominent drums with metallic and twangy-sounding guitars playing catchy tunes created this guitar-based rock combo's trademark sound. Predating and influencing the early 1960s surf craze, the Ventures brought their exciting guitar-drum instrumental sound into the '60s and became famous for their 1969 "Hawaii Five-O" theme song for the television series of that title. Having experienced multiple personnel changes, the Ventures continue to perform today.

THE FORCE WEAKENS

Knocking the Rock

Opposition to rock and roll flared up as fast as the new sound swept the nation. Society in the '50s was offended by the music's sexual and suggestive lyrics (often referred to as "leerics") and artists' risqué stage behavior. Rockers were considered indecent and were perceived by the establishment as challenging the system. As '50s teen culture developed, rock and roll was accused of distancing young people from their stable family lives. Adults were horrified by and attacked this music that America's youth loved, claiming it corrupted morals and instigated juvenile delinquency and violence. Enraged by rock music and feeling that it allowed teens to defy and ridicule their elders, parents were determined to undermine and combat rock and roll.

The anti-rock sentiment was widespread. *Variety* magazine and ASCAP writers and publishers condemned the music's smutty and suggestive lyrics, and *Billboard* sided with ASCAP against BMI and rock and roll, demanding that the music industry clean up lyrics without hindering pop music in general. James Henke, editor of *Rock Facts*, cites a variety of accounts from rock and roll opponents. First, he mentions a 1955 issue of *Downbeat* where Ruth Cage reported, "The screaming is mostly that R&B is driving our young people to some unwholesome passion. We are being told that this is a narcotic on wax that is taking them from the path of righteousness to the highways of iniquity." Henke continues with a 1956 account by Ben Gross of the *New York Daily News*: "Elvis, who rotates his pelvis, was appalling musically. Also he gave an exhibition that was suggestive and vulgar, tinged with the kind of animalism that should be confined to dives and bordellos." Of the numerous religious leaders condemning the music, Henke cites the views of the Catholic Youth Center in Minneapolis in its teen newspaper *Contacts* in 1958: "Smash the records you possess which present a pagan culture and a pagan concept of life. Phone or write a disc jockey who is pushing a lousy record. Switch your radio dial when you hear a suggestive song. Some songwriters need a good swift kick. So do some singers. So do some disk jockeys."[2]

Since society viewed rock and roll as a dangerous new music form, religious leaders not only spoke out against the music, they also arranged record burnings to "save their youngsters from Satan." Some non-rock and roll disc jockeys spoke out against the music, referring to it as "junk." Taking an anti-rock stance, St. Louis radio station KWK announced the start of its Record Breaking Week on January 12, 1958; the station played each rock and roll record once, followed by the deejay breaking it on the air. Lists of banned songs circulated as radio stations screened recordings before airing them. In Houston, Texas, the Juvenile Delinquency and Crime Commission created a subcommittee, the Wash-Out-the-Air Committee, which prepared a twenty-six-song list of objectionable records to ban from radio (mostly due to their sexually oriented lyrics). Included on the list were Ray Charles's "I've Got a Woman," Hank Ballard and the Midnighters' "Annie Had a Baby," the Dominoes' "Sixty Minute Man," and Roy Brown's "Good Rocking Tonight" and Elvis Presley's "Good Rockin' Tonight." The committee then monitored the airwaves until all stations complied.

Anti-rock events included establishing bans on live rock and roll shows and on jukebox rock and roll plays. Bridgeport and New Haven, Connecticut, enforced the first bans on such events in March 1955, after a rock and roll teenage dance in New Haven resulted in a brawl and several teens were arrested. Though overcrowding or poor stage arrangement often caused riots at rock concerts and dances, undoubtedly the main blame fell on the music and the emcees—disc jockeys. Frequently, riots began with teens dancing in the aisles at concerts and police chasing them back to their seats, turning these events into scuffles that spilled onto the streets. As Linda Martin and Kerry Segrave write in *Anti-Rock*, "The jockey quickly came to be viewed as little more than a pimp for rock music, the prostitute of the industry. This image would help pave the way for the downfall of Alan Freed and would help establish a base for attacking the jockeys through the payola hearings."[3] Nationwide, the media focused on rock-related violence at concerts and record hops—as in Cleveland, Ohio, Birmingham, Alabama, and Cambridge and Boston, Massachusetts—prompting city officials to discontinue such events. *Look* magazine compared attending a rock and roll concert to attending the rites of an obscure tribe that communicated incomprehensibly, and *Time* compared rock and roll to a loud interruption (a motorcycle club at full throttle) on a quiet Sunday afternoon.[4] An interesting ban occurred in San Antonio, Texas, in 1956, when the Parks Department prohibited rock and roll records from jukeboxes at city swimming pools to avoid objectionable incidents that were blamed on the music. Teenagers were not to dance to rock and roll in their bathing suits, and people were not to loiter to listen to rock music with no intention of swimming.

In addition to opposition to lyrics and bans on live shows, rock and roll performers and their performances were targets. As white artists tried to reach a larger audience by cleaning up rock lyrics, by 1956 opponents found less to complain about, so they concentrated on performers instead, such as Elvis Presley. In the early years of rock and roll, Presley was attacked more than others because of his stage behavior. Society could not handle his flailing legs and knocking knees or shaking hips and gyrating pelvis (often reported in the media as "bumps" and "grinds"). His actions with the microphone, the expressions on his face, and his outfits all propelled adults into anti–Elvis mode. Presley was denounced after many a performance. In La Crosse, Wisconsin, the local newspaper labeled him obscene—his performance was a striptease with clothes on; in San Diego, California, the police warned him that if he wanted to appear there again, he must clean up his act and eliminate the bumps, which were not appropriate for young eyes; in other cities, authorities informed him that he could not move while singing. Individuals and organizations of all types—journalists, educators, politicians, and clergy—assailed Presley, considering him a cause of juvenile delinquency.

Such famous musicians as Percy Faith and Frank Sinatra (though he changed his rock music opinion later, to capitalize on Elvis Presley's popularity by inviting him on his television show) spoke out against the music, and others, such as Dr. Howard Hanson (then director of the Eastman School of Music in Rochester, New York) referred to rock and roll as "acoustical pollution." Criticism continued to the point of blaming a wide variety of youthful behavior on rock and roll; the music became a scapegoat for everything about teens that adults didn't like. Experts in all fields were summoned to express their opinions on the anti-rock movement. Newspapers and magazines attacked with editorials; in *America*, for example, people were warned to beware of Elvis Presley—his records were acceptable but not his lewd, suggestive, and obscene stage behavior. One final example of '50s anti-rock activity was the theatrical event staged by station WLEV in Erie, Pennsylvania. In September 1959, the station rented a hearse and packed the vehicle with its 7,000 rock records. After a mock funeral procession to Lake Erie, station personnel dumped all the discs into the water.

Eruption of the Payola Scandal

The 1959–1960 payola investigation was perhaps the greatest attack on rock and roll, as well as an attempt by ASCAP to rid the music industry of rival BMI (the organization that broke ASCAP's song-licensing monopoly). Despite payola's (play for pay) existence for decades (dating back to the vaudeville song-plugging tradition) as an accepted practice in the music industry, the payola investigation created the impression that payola was a recent phenomenon associated with rock and roll. The investigation began in November 1959 when television quiz show contestant Charles Van Doren revealed rigging of the show's outcomes to a House of Representatives Special Committee on Legislative Oversight assigned to investigate the alleged wrongdoings. The hearings became a media sensation, and the collapse of game shows quickly followed: *Twenty-One* and *The $64,000 Question*, then America's most popular television show, were canceled. In this climate, concern was also raised about the music business after allegations that at the May 1959 International Radio Programming Seminar and Pop Music Disk Jockey Convention in Miami Beach, fifty promotion people and record labels had spent approximately $250,000 to entertain approximately 2,500 disc jockeys. "Booze, Broads and Bribes" was the *Miami Herald*'s headline on its story about the weekend. Press reports horrified the public and reported that prostitutes, expensive gifts, and drugs were provided for deejays as payments for favoring particular records.[5] Concerned about such rock and roll artists as Chuck Berry, who wrote his own compositions, ASCAP's professional songwriters

Quiz show *Twenty-One* host Jack Barry turns toward contestant Charles Van Doren as fellow contestant Vivienne Nearine looks on, 1957. Courtesy of the Library of Congress.

and others saw this as an opportunity (especially in an election year) to involve their congressmen, and the payola scandal quickly attacked BMI and the rock music it licensed.

Claiming the public (especially innocent youth) was manipulated into liking rock and roll (referred to as "junk music" and "trash") by corrupt disc jockeys pushing the music—the traditional music (referred to as "good") did not require payola—the songwriters swiftly involved congressmen in the assault. Rock and roll deejays became the target of the House committee (headed by Oren Harris of Arkansas) that scrutinized many of them, including Boston disc jockey Norm Prescott, who claimed that bribery was the way for a record to get airplay. Prescott confessed to having received approximately $10,000 from record distributors, and another Boston deejay, Dave Maynard, admitted that a record distributor gave him more than $6,000 in cash and financed two of his cars. Many other rock and roll disc jockeys acknowledged having received money and items of value in return for record favoritism; 207 of them had accepted more than $263,000 in payola. Without delay, the profession suffered the consequences of the investigation; deejays were fired across the country. Even though record companies (such as Sydney Nathan's King Records) admitted paying disc jockeys to play their records, no action was taken against the labels because it was customary to prosecute only one party in an alleged bribery case. Thus, indies were given immunity for testifying, while most of the deejays were fired.

Among those fired, Alan Freed was one of payola's first fatalities. After admitting to having received more than $30,000 from record companies and pleading guilty in 1962 to two counts of commercial bribery, he was blackballed by the industry, fined $300, and given a suspended sentence. Still a target two years later, he was charged with income tax evasion and ordered to pay the Internal Revenue Service back taxes of almost $38,000. The other pillar of rock and roll, Dick Clark, maintained his innocence throughout the payola investigation. Although scrutinized, he avoided penalties, but was ordered by ABC to give up his music businesses or leave the network (and his enormously popular television shows). Clark liquidated his business holdings and ABC fully supported him.

Rock and roll did not escape the two-year investigative ordeal undamaged. Attendance at live concerts fell. Record companies and radio stations reacted to the media and political pressure by recording and playing less adventurous music. Some stations played only majors' recordings, deemed to be safer than those of indies. Others changed to the Top 40 format, taking power away from disc jockeys; some forbade deejays to choose records for airplay. Banning the use of the term "disc jockey," station WEOK in Poughkeepsie, New York, referred to its announcers as "musicasters." Other stations stopped airing rock and roll, such as Boston's WILD, Chicago's WMAQ, and Denver's KICN. Though it seemed both the music establishment and '50s society triumphed in the battle against rock and roll, neither BMI nor the music disappeared after the controversy.

Rock and Roll Begins to Fade

During the '50s, rock and roll emerged from its roots musics, experienced massive growth and power as it spread to the world in various subgenres, and somewhat faded away as the decade came to a close. The genre lost many of the first generation rockers in the late 1950s. Chuck Berry went to jail for alleged liaisons with young women. Little Richard found religion and felt that participating in the music was sinful. Elvis Presley was in the army, and upon discharge turned to such pop-oriented songs as "It's Now or Never" (1960) and "Are You Lonesome Tonight?" (1960). Jerry Lee Lewis married his underage cousin, was banned from concerts and the airwaves, and dropped from view. Carl Perkins never regained his recording momentum after his serious automobile crash, and was unable to follow his classic "Blue Suede Shoes" with another big hit. Buddy Holly, Ritchie Valens, and the Big Bopper perished in a plane crash in 1959—the day the music died. Many important rockabilly artists disappeared from the charts; Eddie Cochran's death in the automobile accident that Gene Vincent survived, affected Vincent to the point that he never regained his momentum. He performed abroad while his popularity waned.

Overall, each of these events contributed to a monumental loss of first generation rockers. This loss was devastating for rock and roll. Ed Ward sums up the late 1950s–early 1960s period in *Rock of Ages*:

> As America sailed into a new decade, rock and roll, the music of hooligans and streetcorner singers, the music of hillbillies who'd listened to too many R&B records, the music of misfits and oddballs, was dead. Just as teenagers, with their awesome purchasing power, were being courted by Hollywood and Madison Avenue, rock and roll had passed into the mainstream, fast becoming the province of established corporate interests rather than the renegade visionaries of the past. For a while, at least, the music would be in the hands of professionals, who knew what teens wanted and how to sell it to them. These developments might have outraged older rockers, who would hardly recognize the fruits of their creative vision. Still, as long as there were teenagers, those teenagers would want a special music that spoke to them. It's just that the language was going to change for a while.[6]

A widely accepted belief that musically rock and roll died at the end of the decade, and was not revived until the arrival of the Beatles, has appeared often in discussions of the music. A lull in rock and roll occurred between Elvis Presley and the Beatles. The period of approximately 1957 to 1962 has often been referred to as the years of schlock or homogenized rock. This period yielded music devoid of the kick and excitement of the first rock generation—music that has been criticized for not being authentic rock and roll (in reality, it was a newly emerged subgenre). Referred to as the "teen idol phenomenon," this music lacked the invigorating qualities of the first generation's repertoire—such elements as the exciting backbeat and rock band timbres—and producers created nonthreatening, easy listening sounds with a touch of rock and roll.

Teen Idols

Although rock and roll music did not disappear, as the established ASCAP composers had hoped it would, the payola investigation did impact the music. As radio stations looked for nonthreatening music to play, professional songwriters once again dominated American popular music at the turn of the decade. The late 1950s and early 1960s witnessed a new strain of tunesmiths evolving in New York City who cornered the teen market, writing what has been referred to as "watered-down rock." Still using the phrase "rock and roll," songwriters composed a different repertoire for the new teen idol trend. This lavishly orchestrated pop-oriented rock immediately filled the void created by the mass exodus of the first generation of unpredictable and exciting rock and rollers. Once again, the music establishment (promoters, radio programmers, record executives, and A&R men), those who had sought to bring rock and roll more in line with industry standards, controlled the music.

As the new, tame, and parentally palatable music appeared, a stable of glamorous pop stars emerged, their looks more important than their music. Rock and rollers Holly, Valens, and the Big Bopper were replaced with the attractive idols Robert Velline (Bobby Vee), Frankie Avalon, and Jimmy Clanton. Often criticized as less interpretive and artistic than the first generation, these new pop-rock artists were young singers performing in a Tin Pan Alley-influenced crooner style. Though the records were produced well and quite attractive to listeners, teen idol music lacked the authentic qualities associated with rock and roll's early subgenres. Unlike earlier '50s rockers who both sang and played instruments, teen idols usually specialized in singing. Their recordings were often diluted creations of true rock and roll. Nonetheless, the young rock audience accepted the teen idols, who mostly performed songs composed by professional songwriting teams targeting teen interests and emotions, and were perfectly groomed by their managers and producers.

Cover artist Pat Boone was an extremely popular teen idol and father figure, considered a very safe alternative to '50s hard rockers. (See chapter 8 for further information.) Though most teen idols were white, Chubby Checker was an exception. Born Ernest Evans in 1941 in Andrews, South Carolina, and raised in Philadelphia, Checker received his nickname from Dick Clark's wife, Bobbie, because of his resemblance to Fats Domino. Known for his impersonations of famous singers, Checker achieved only one '50s hit, 1959's "The Class," with imitations of other musicians, such as Fats Domino, the Coasters, Elvis Presley, and the Chipmunks. Checker's 1960 No. 1 smash, "The Twist," was a cover of Hank Ballard's song; Checker's version sparked the worldwide dance craze.

Often referred to as a teen idol, Latino rocker Ritchie Valens was a talented singer-songwriter and guitarist. Born Richard Stephen Valenzuela in 1941 in the Los Angeles suburb of Pacoima, he was only seventeen when he died in a plane crash with Buddy Holly and the Big Bopper. "Donna" (1958, No. 2 pop hit), a sweet, simple love song for a girl he knew at San Fernando High School, made Valens a star, but its flip side, "La Bamba," became the song with which he has been identified. This record is often referred to as one of the greatest '50s rock and roll singles. A vigorous arrangement of an old Mexican wedding song, "La Bamba" was a forerunner of simple rock and roll sounds and of the subgenres of garage rock and punk rock. With his rock arrangement of this folk song, complete with an exuberant guitar solo, Valens created Latino rock. Known as the Little Richard of the San Fernando Valley, Ritchie Valens was inducted into the Rock and Roll Hall of Fame in 2001.

Other popular late 1950s idols were Frankie Avalon, Bobby Rydell, Fabian, Bobby Vee, Annette Funicello (Annette), Connie Francis, and Brenda Lee. Also flourishing were the uniquely talented Paul Anka, Bobby Darin, Neil Sedaka, and Ricky Nelson. Frankie Avalon, discovered by talent scout-producer-owner of Chancellor Records Bob Marcucci, was born Francis Avallone in Philadelphia in 1939. In the mid-1950s, he performed on radio and television with Paul

Whiteman, sang and played trumpet with Rocco & His Saints in 1956, and costarred in movies with Annette. Avalon had many pop hits between 1958 and 1962, including the 1959 No. 1's "Venus" and "Why." Also a member of Rocco & His Saints, Bobby Rydell, born Robert Ridarelli in 1942, had more pop hits than Avalon, but no chart-toppers. A movie star known for his good looks, Rydell had popular hits that included "We Got Love" (1959), "Wild One," and "Volare" (both 1960). Because of his appealing looks and interesting name, Marcucci discovered fellow Philadelphia-based musician Fabiano Forte, better known as Fabian, at the age of fourteen. Among Fabian's late 1950s hits were "Turn Me Loose," "Tiger," and "Hound Dog Man," all from 1959. Fabian began his acting career that year with the movie *Hound Dog Man*. Bobby Vee, born Robert Velline in 1943 in Fargo, North Dakota, formed the rock group the Shadows while in high school. His career began the night after Buddy Holly's plane crash, when Vee filled in for Holly at the concert he had been scheduled to headline in Fargo. Vee's first hit, "Suzie Baby" (1959), was his only success on the charts during the '50s. Vee was a prolific hit maker of calm, studio-crafted teen songs throughout the '60s, and most popular was the No. 1 hit "Take Good Care of My Baby" (1961).

Most successful teen idols were males chosen to appeal to adolescent girls, the primary market for this music. However, female stars also arose, attracting young male fans. Born in Utica, New York, in 1942, Annette Funicello was a Mouseketeer on the '50s television series *The Mickey Mouse Club*. Known by her first name, Annette recorded between 1959 and 1961, her biggest success being 1959's "Tall Paul." An actress in several early 1960s teen movies, she starred with Frankie Avalon in many films, including the famous beach series. Perhaps the most prolific of all the teen idols, Connie Francis placed fifty-six hits on the pop charts during the '50s and '60s. Born Concetta Rosa Maria Franconero, in 1938, Francis, from Newark, New Jersey, enjoyed three No. 1 hits during the '60s and also appeared in movies. Her *American Bandstand* fans remember her best for "Who's Sorry Now" (1958) and "Where the Boys Are" (1961), both No. 4 pop hits. Brenda Lee, ranked as the No. 1 female singer of the '60s, began charting hits in the late 1950s with such songs as "Dynamite" (1957) and "Sweet Nothin's" (1959). Born Brenda Mae Tarpley in 1944 in Lithonia, Georgia, she has been celebrated for her rockabilly sounds. (See chapter 5 for further information.)

Among the very talented idols was Paul Anka, from Ottawa, Canada. This songwriter composed hits for others (such as Buddy Holly's "It Doesn't Matter Anymore") in addition to those he recorded himself. Anka had many hits on the pop charts during the 1950s, 1960s, and 1970s, two of them No. 1s from the late 1950s: "Diana" (1957), written for the family babysitter, and "Lonely Boy" (1959), written for the movie *Girls Town*, in which he starred that year. Another gifted idol and a very ambitious and versatile performer, Bobby Darin, was born Walden Robert Cassotto in 1936 in the Bronx, New York. He began his lengthy, prolific recording career in the mid-1950s, recording with the Jaybirds. Perhaps best known for his first hit, "Splish Splash," a 1958 novelty bathtub nonsense song (No. 3 pop and No. 1 R&B hit), Darin had over forty hits on the pop charts during his career that included nightclub singing. Other big successes from the '50s were "Queen of the Hop" (1958), "Dream Lover" (1959, No. 2 pop hit), and "Mack the Knife" (1959, No. 1 pop hit for nine weeks). In 1973, this gifted idol who also starred in films and on Las Vegas stages died of heart failure. A 1959 Grammy Award recipient for his signature song, "Mack the Knife," Darin was inducted into the Rock and Roll Hall of Fame in 1990.

Neil Sedaka was born in Brooklyn in 1939. A prolific hit songwriter, while still in high school he formed a songwriting team with lyricist Howard Greenfield and wrote numerous songs for other artists. Sedaka formed, and began recording with, the Tokens in the mid-1950s (they later recorded the hit "The Lion Sleeps Tonight"). A classically trained pianist, Sedaka composed "Oh! Carol" in 1959 for fellow singer-songwriter Carole King. Among Sedaka's hits that he both wrote and recorded were "Calendar Girl" (1960), "Happy Birthday, Sweet Sixteen" (1961), and "Breaking Up Is Hard to Do" (1962, No. 1 hit). Also promoted as a soft rocker teen idol, rockabilly Ricky Nelson became one of the first idols, and an enormously popular one, via television in the '50s. This exceptional musician had top caliber records in the late 1950s, including the 1958 No. 1, "Poor Little Fool." After Imperial Records bought his contract from Verve, he was endorsed as a calm alternative to Elvis Presley. (See chapter 5 for further information.)

NEW ARTISTS ENTER THE ROCK AND ROLL ARENA

Old and New Styles Flourish

As the teen idol music continued to thrive into the '60s reflecting the values, interests, and optimism of teenagers, many new artists and groups entered the rock and roll arena. As a solo artist, in 1961 Dion released "Runaround Sue" and "The Wanderer" (No. 1 and No. 2 pop hits, respectively), and rocker Charles Westover (Del Shannon) emerged that year with his No. 1 song, "Runaway," the beginning of his solid run of '60s hits. Gene Pitney followed in 1962 with his No. 2 song, "Only Love Can Break a Heart," and in 1963 Margaret Battivio (Little Peggy March) had the smash No. 1 "I Will Follow Him," which incorporated the period's teen idol-type lush string accompaniment. One of the first garage bands, the Kingsmen, arrived that year with "Louie Louie," a revised version of the 1957 Jamaican love song by the R&B vocal group Richard Berry & the Pharaohs. Lesley Gore ("It's My Party"), Johnny Tillotson ("Poetry in Motion"), and countless others continued the pleasing pop rock while some of the older subgenres were still thriving and some new styles were brewing.

A new subgenre that arose in the late 1950s and flourished in the early 1960s, surf music began with such groups as the vocal duo Jan & Dean (Jan Berry and Dean Torrence) from Los Angeles. They formed as the Barons while in high school, became Jan & Arnie (Arnie Ginsburg) when Dean was in the Army Reserves, and were Jan & Dean by 1959. They began recording in 1958, and the duo's output included such huge hits as 1963's "Surf City" (a No. 1 pop hit) and 1964's "Dead Man's Curve" and "The Little Old Lady (from Pasadena)." Several surf rock groups followed in the early 1960s, bringing an exciting instrumental-based sound and a return to the basic rock instrumentation. Among these groups were the Marketts, the Beach Boys, the Safaris, the Chantay's, and Dick Dale and the Del-Tones.

Girl groups, another early 1960s phenomenon, were rooted in '50s R&B vocal groups (such as the Bobbettes and the Chantels). As female vocal ensembles flourished in the early 1960s, the Shirelles continued their phenomenal success with such hits as the Carole King-Gerry Goffin team's "Will You Love Me Tomorrow," the first No. 1 pop song by an all-girl group. (See chapter 7 for further information.) With Berry Gordy's establishment of Motown Records and Phil Spector's production contributions, numerous girl groups emerged, such as the Marvelettes, Martha and the Vandellas, the Supremes, the Crystals, and the Ronettes, to name just a few.

While these new sounds were filling the airwaves at the turn of the decade, other established sounds were still around. On the rockabilly front, the Everly Brothers continued their outstanding accomplishments with impressive hits, such as "Cathy's Clown," a 1960 No. 1 pop and R&B hit. Roy Orbison achieved new highs with "Only the Lonely (Know How I Feel)" (1960, No. 2 hit), "Running Scared" (1961, No. 1 hit), and "Oh, Pretty Woman" (1964, No. 1 hit). Wanda Jackson's "Let's Have a Party" hit the charts in 1960. Conway Twitty continued his '50s successes, such as his 1958 No. 1 hit, "It's Only Make Believe." A surge of country artists crossed over to the pop charts, including Jim Reeves, Marty Robbins, Eddy Arnold, and Patsy Cline.

Late 1950s Rhythm and Blues Stars

Rhythm and blues music continued to thrive during this transitional period as the smooth, pop-oriented doo-wop sound gave way to gutsier African American styles in the late 1950s, and soul music broke forth. At first labeled "soul music" because of gospel groups stirring listeners' emotions, by the early 1960s the phrase referred to African American secular music in general. With Ray Charles having paved the way for the funky new sound, such groups as the Drifters helped create soul music by bringing gospel-styled vocals to secular songs. (See chapters 4 and 7 for further information.) Such earlier stars as Jesse Belvin, Lloyd Price, Fats Domino, Little Richard, the Platters, and the Coasters faded away, but they were replaced by such dynamic new talents as Sam Cooke, Jackie Wilson, James Brown, Wilson Pickett, Marvin Gaye, Ben E. King, the Isley Brothers, the Impressions, and the Miracles. Some of these musicians had already broadened the base of musical sounds in the '50s with their inspiring rhythm and blues-based rock and roll.

Sam Cooke

Sam Cooke, born in Clarksdale, Mississippi, in 1931 and raised in Chicago, where his father was a minister, began in the gospel realm and changed to pop and R&B music. His oeuvre consisted of both secular and gospel songs of all types, from ballads and lighthearted pop music to exciting, raspy R&B and rock and roll. At age fifteen, Cooke joined the gospel group the Soul Stirrers and served as lead vocalist from 1950 to 1956, when he left to begin his solo career. After recording his first pop song under a pseudonym (Dale Cook) so as not to jeopardize his standing in the gospel community, Cooke realized secular music suited him. His first solo success, "You Send Me" (1957), was a No. 1 pop and R&B hit. He followed with many other No. 1 R&B hits, including "I'll Come Running Back to You" (1957), "Twistin' the Night Away" (1962), "Another Saturday Night" (1963), and a string of pop hits until his death in 1964, when he mysteriously died from a gunshot. With his teen idol looks and blending of sensual and spiritual elements, and revered as the definitive soul singer, Sam Cooke was inducted into the Rock and Roll Hall of Fame as a member of the inaugural class in 1986. He was honored with a Grammy Lifetime Achievement Award in 1999.

Jackie Wilson

Known as Mr. Entertainment, Jackie Wilson created hit after hit from 1957 to 1975 and became one of the premier voices of the period. His hits, many of them No. 1 on the R&B charts, included two dozen Top 40 singles, such as "Lonely Teardrops" (1958), "You Better Know It" (1959), and "A Woman, a Lover, a Friend" (1960). Born in Detroit, Michigan, in 1934, Wilson was perhaps best known for his 1967 No. 1 R&B hit, "(Your Love Keeps Lifting Me) Higher and Higher." He sang in gospel groups before joining Billy Ward and the Dominoes as lead singer in 1953 (replacing Clyde McPhatter, who left to join the Drifters). In 1957, Wilson began his solo career with two of Berry Gordy's songs, "Reet Petite" and "To Be Loved." An incredibly dynamic performer, this gifted singer-showman radiated excitement at concerts. Wilson headlined a 1963 British concert with the Beatles as one of his opening acts. In the middle of a show in Cherry Hill, New Jersey, in 1975, Wilson suffered a stroke and fell into a coma; he remained hospitalized for more than eight years until his death in 1984. An athletic performer and former amateur boxer, Jackie Wilson was inducted into the Rock and Roll Hall of Fame in 1987.

James Brown

One of the most influential soul artists of all time, James Brown recorded his first successful records in the mid-to-late 1950s: "Please, Please, Please" (1956), "Try Me" (1958, No. 1 R&B hit and his first crossover to the pop charts), and "I Want You So Bad" (1959). Born into poverty in Barnwell, South Carolina, in 1933 and raised in Augusta, Georgia, Brown went from picking cotton

James Brown, 1955. © Frank Driggs Collection/Getty Images.

to dancing and shining shoes for small change. After being convicted of armed robbery at age sixteen, he spent three years in reform school, where he befriended Bobby Byrd, leader of a gospel group that performed in his prison. Inspired by Hank Ballard and Fats Domino, Brown and Byrd were attracted to secular music and formed a group of singers, dancers, and instrumentalists, the Flames (later known as the Famous Flames). Responsible for helping create soul music in the '60s, funk in the '70s, and rap in the '80s, Brown is known by many titles, such as Soul Brother Number One and The Hardest Working Man in Show Business. A prolific powerhouse musician and a captivating performer, Brown incorporated all types of theatrics into his shows (even false heart attacks) while blending emotionally explosive and intense R&B with the fervor of gospel music and redefining the direction of black music. The Godfather of Soul, James Brown was inducted into the Rock and Roll Hall of Fame in 1986 at the first induction ceremony. In 1992, he received a Grammy Lifetime Achievement Award, and in 2003 the Kennedy Center Honors.

The Fifties Yield to the Sixties

Musical changes after the 1963 assassination of President John F. Kennedy included artists as diverse as the Beatles and Bob Dylan. As the ideals and dreams of America's youth were shattered and teenagers mourned the death of the president, the music, like its listeners, began to question society. Social and political change required songs with meaning—substantial lyrics for a sophisticated audience who discovered folk music and looked to such artists as Bob Dylan for guidance. The gentle acoustic folk sounds of such groups as the Kingston Trio ("Tom Dooley," 1958 No. 1 pop hit) and Peter, Paul & Mary ("Blowin' in the Wind," 1963 No. 2 pop hit) met listeners' needs, and the immensely popular British Invasion group, the Beatles, returned to the basics of rock and roll's first generation, once again providing comfort with a musical backbeat.

Originally forging group identity among America's teens, rock and roll emerged in the 1950s as a distinct genre with its unique sounds resulting from the melting pot of the various roots musics. As teens identified their own songs, dance steps, and musical heroes separating them from adults, they embraced the new music completely, including its fashions. During rock and roll's first decade, the principal styles were diverse. From the New Orleans and Chicago sounds to the rockabilly and doo-wop sounds, these subgenres all shared a common thread as descendants of the roots of rock and roll—blues, jazz, gospel, rhythm and blues, folk, country, and pop music. Though unique in style and quality, the songs are valuable sources of social and cultural history, reflecting and influencing the beliefs, values, and actions of their audiences.

Although rock's first era is long gone, the '50s made its mark with musical treasures and a universal language of youth, and continues to affect later generations. Glenn Altschuler sums it up in *All Shook Up*: "In the half century since rock 'n' roll got its name, the music has taken many forms, including R&B, romantic rock, heavy metal, punk rock, grunge rock, Christian rock, and postmodern feminist rock. . . . The music that changed America in the 1950s and '60s, rock 'n' roll continues to solidify youth consciousness and bring meaning and order to the lives of millions of people."[7] This rich repertoire still regularly reaches new audiences, and America's current youth are exposed to the genius and talent of '50s artists—from Chuck Berry and Ray Charles to Fats Domino and Little Richard, and Elvis Presley and Buddy Holly to the Platters and the Drifters. The excitement is still present, both in the music and in the listeners' reactions. This body of big beat music has a perpetual pulse, not only in the '50s repertoire but also in that of the succeeding decades that it highly influenced. As one of the genre's own, Danny & the Juniors, expressed simply in 1958: "Rock and roll is here to stay."

NOTES

All charts positions referred to in the chapter are based on Joel Whitburn's Record Research publications, which compile *Billboard* charts information of the rock and roll era.

1. "Alan Freed: King of the Moondoggers," temporary exhibit (Cleveland, OH: Rock and Roll Hall of Fame and Museum, May 10, 2003).

2. James Henke, ed., *Rock Facts* (New York: Universe Publishing, 1996), 100.

3. Linda Martin and Kerry Segrave, *Anti-Rock: The Opposition to Rock 'n' Roll* (Hamden, CT: Archon Books, 1988), 28.

4. John A. Jackson, *Big Beat Heat: Alan Freed and the Early Years of Rock & Roll* (New York: Schirmer Books, 1991), 129.

5. Ben Fong-Torres, *The Hits Just Keep on Coming: The History of Top 40 Radio* (San Francisco: Backbeat Books, 2001), 98–100.

6. Ed Ward, Geoffrey Stokes, and Ken Tucker, *Rock of Ages: The Rolling Stone History of Rock & Roll* (New York: Rolling Stone Press, 1986), 224.

7. Glenn C. Altschuler, *All Shook Up: How Rock 'n' Roll Changed America* (New York: Oxford University Press, 2003), 192.

A-TO-Z OF ROCK, 1951–1959

Bold-faced terms refer to other entries in this A-to-Z chapter.

ABC-Paramount Records. Formed in Hollywood in 1955 and owned by the ABC television network, this label was the first **major** to be established during the heart of the **rock and roll** era. Label president Sam Clark and A&R men Don Costa and Sid Feller frequently licensed masters and released recordings by **indies**. The company's roster included **Paul Anka** ("Lonely Boy"), **Lloyd Price** ("Stagger Lee"), **Ray Charles** (recordings beginning in 1960), the Royal Teens ("Short Shorts"), Joe Bennett and the Sparkletones ("Black Slacks"), and **Danny & the Juniors** ("At the Hop"). Its subsidiary Apt Records recorded the Elegants ("Little Star").

Abramson, Herb. See **Atlantic Records**.

Ace Records. Formed in 1955 in Jackson, Mississippi, by Johnny Vincent, this indie produced several important **rock and roll** records. Its roster included Louisiana-based musicians Frankie Ford ("Sea Cruise"), Jimmy Clanton ("Just a Dream"), and **Huey "Piano" Smith** and the Clowns ("Rocking Pneumonia and the Boogie Woogie Flu").

Ackerman, Paul (1908–1977). Music editor of *Billboard* magazine from 1943 to 1973, this journalist was among the first to tackle **rock and roll**. A superb writer who charted the rise of **R&B**, country music, and rock and roll by documenting their impact on the world of **popular music**, Ackerman, inducted into the Rock and Roll Hall of Fame in 1995, helped *Billboard* become the music industry's premier trade publication.

"Ain't That a Shame" (1955). Recorded by **Fats Domino** on **Imperial Records** as "Ain't It a Shame," this recording produced by **Dave Bartholomew**

broke the color line that had prevented **R&B** records from attracting **pop** audiences. It also established Domino's identity with white teenagers and solidified the new **rock and roll** market. This single that brought the big beat of the **New Orleans sound** to the world was Domino's first crossover hit of many, reaching No. 1 on the R&B charts and No. 10 on the pop charts—an unusual feat for a '50s R&B song.

Aladdin Records. Formed by Eddie and Leo Mesner in Los Angeles in 1945, this important West Coast **R&B indie** was one of the first sources of **rock and roll** with Gene & Eunice's "Ko Ko Mo." Maxwell Davis and **Dave Bartholomew** produced songs for the label, such as **Shirley & Lee**'s "Let the Good Times Roll" and Thurston Harris's "Little Bitty Pretty One." Others who recorded with the label were **Charles Brown** ("Trouble Blues"), Amos Milburn ("Chicken-Shack Boogie"), and the Five Keys ("The Glory of Love"). Unable to promote its artists on the national level, Aladdin folded in the late '50s.

Aldon Music. This New York City publishing company owned by Don Kirshner and Al Nevins was located across the street from the Brill Building on Broadway before moving into the famous edifice. In 1958, Kirshner and Nevins hired the songwriting teams **Pomus and Shuman** and **Neil Sedaka**–Howard Greenfield. In 1960, the prolific Carole King–Gerry Goffin team joined the firm, later followed by the Barry Mann–Cynthia Weil team, and Neil Diamond. This talented stable of the best songwriters around created what became known as "Brill Building **Pop**" in the early 1960s.

American Bandstand. Originally a local show first broadcast in 1952 on Philadelphia station WFIL, Bob Horn's *Bandstand* was a popular radio program. Upon its move to television, this WFIL-TV program hosted by Bob Horn and Lee Stewart played filmed musical performances by conservative popular artists of the day. As **rock and roll** swept the nation, the show's format came to incorporate kids dancing to the new hit records live, and in 1956 **Dick Clark** became the show's host. It was broadcast every weekday immediately after school, attracting a huge teenage audience. *Bandstand* became very popular in the Philadelphia area and went nationwide on ABC in 1957 with a new title, *American Bandstand.* It became television's longest running (1952–1989) and most popular dance program. The show was extremely influential with youth; its immense popularity across the nation propelled featured performers to the top of the charts. It became the greatest promotional vehicle in **pop music** history, creating instant national hits for artists and groups.

Anka, Paul (b. 1941). Among the very talented late 1950s **teen idols** was this successful songwriter from Ottawa, Canada, who composed hit songs for others (including **Buddy Holly**'s "It Doesn't Matter Anymore," Frank Sinatra's "My Way," and Tom Jones's "She's a Lady") in addition to those he recorded himself. Though most of his huge hits on the **pop** charts came in the '60s and '70s, two of his No. 1's came from the late 1950s: "Diana" (1957) and "Lonely

Boy" (1959). Anka has enjoyed a long career in music and is mostly known for his songwriting skills and Las Vegas appearances.

Annette. See **Funicello, Annette.**

Apollo Records. A significant New York City indie, this label formed in 1942 by Ike and Bess Berman. It featured gospel artist **Mahalia Jackson** ("Silent Night, Holy Night") and an outstanding **R&B** roster, including **Wynonie Harris** (early recordings), and vocal groups the Five Royales ("Help Me Somebody") and the Larks ("Eyesight to the Blind").

Apt Records. See **ABC-Paramount Records.**

Argo Records. See **Chess Records.**

Aristocrat Records. See **Chess Records.**

Armstrong, Louis (1901–1971). Born Daniel Louis Armstrong in New Orleans and known by various nicknames, such as Satchmo and Pops, this 1990 Rock and Roll Hall of Fame inductee heightened the artistic merit of jazz in the 1920s with his trumpet playing; his extraordinary range and superb phrasing, combined with his expansion of improvisation left its mark on the music world. This improvisatory genius of jazz recorded monumental recordings of the classic jazz repertoire with his Hot Five and Hot Seven bands, including "West End Blues," "Hotter Than That," and "Potato Head Blues" with timbres of the typical New Orleans jazz band sound. In the absence of drums in hot jazz, the banjo often supplied rhythm, while the music usually consisted of an upbeat tempo with exciting syncopated rhythms and multiple instrumental solos and improvisation, a trademark that would carry on in **rock and roll** music. Another contribution to rock music by Armstrong was his singing with blues- and jazz-inflected interpretations, which broadened the expressive range of popular singing. His singing style not only influenced singers of the next generation, including Frank Sinatra, **Nat "King" Cole**, and Peggy Lee, but also musicians of the early era of rock and roll, such as **Ray Charles** and multiple members of **doo-wop** groups.

Atco Records. See **Atlantic Records.**

Atkins, Chet (1924–2001). Born Chester Burton Atkins in Luttrell, Tennessee, this revered guitarist and country music producer established the country subgenre known as the Nashville sound and brought country music to mainstream American **popular music.** After recording as a sessionman and solo artist, in the late 1950s he became vice president of **RCA-Victor**'s Nashville operations, serving as producer from 1957 through the mid-1970s. A country legend who designed a line of Chet Atkins signature guitars, he played on and produced numerous musicians' recordings, including those by Eddy Arnold, Perry Como, **Elvis Presley**, and **Roy Orbison**. Atkins was inducted into the Rock and Roll Hall of Fame in 2002.

Atlantic Records. Formed by Ahmet Ertegun (a 1987 Rock and Roll Hall of Fame inductee) and Herb Abramson in New York City in 1948, this was one of the most prominent and successful **indies**, with scores of hits on the charts throughout the '50s. Jerry Wexler (a 1987 Rock and Roll Hall of Fame inductee) joined the label as an A&R agent in 1953, Nesuhi Ertegun joined as an album supervisor in 1955, and **Leiber and Stoller** joined as freelance producers in 1956. With its subsidiary labels Atco and Cat, Atlantic went beyond the regional status of most indies, reaching the national level with its collection of outstanding '50s artists and groups, including **LaVern Baker** ("Tweedlee Dee"), **Ruth Brown ("(Mama) He Treats Your Daughter Mean")**, Chuck Willis ("C. C. Rider"), Ivory Joe Hunter ("Since I Met You Baby"), **Clyde McPhatter** ("A Lover's Question"), **Big Joe Turner** ("Honey Hush"), **Ray Charles** ("Drown in My Own Tears"), **Bobby Darin** ("Splish Splash"), the **Drifters** ("Money Honey"), the **Chords** ("Sh-Boom"), and the **Coasters** ("Searchin'"). Using outstanding sessionmen and leaders (including Jesse Stone, Howard Biggs, Henry Van Walls, Mickey Baker, **King Curtis**, and Sam Taylor), Atlantic became a dominant **R&B** label, advancing the evolution of **rock and roll** and making the transition from R&B to rock and roll. The label went on to become one of the most significant **soul music** labels, and was purchased in 1967 by Warner Brothers. It later branched out to jazz, classical, country music, and rock subgenres.

Avalon, Frankie (b. 1939). Discovered by talent scout-producer and Chancellor Records owner Bob Marcucci, this late 1950s **teen idol** was born Francis Avallone in Philadelphia. In the mid-1950s, he performed on radio and television with Paul Whiteman, sang and played trumpet with Rocco & His Saints (which included fellow idol **Bobby Rydell**), and starred in many movies with **Annette Funicello**. Known for his good looks and as a regular on **Dick Clark**'s *American Bandstand*, Avalon had many successful **pop** hits between 1958 and 1962, including 1959 No. 1's "Venus" and "Why."

Baker, LaVern (1929–1997). Born Dolores Williams in Chicago, this '50s **rhythm and blues** vocalist known as Little Miss Sharecropper was one of the most popular female R&B singers of the early rock era. With a background in gospel music, she had great success with **Atlantic Records**, where she recorded major R&B and crossover hits, including "Tweedlee Dee," "Jim Dandy," and "I Cried a Tear." This 1991 Rock and Roll Hall of Famer became a key artist with **Alan Freed**'s Rock 'n' Roll Jubilee shows and appeared in two of his movies, *Mister Rock and Roll* and *Rock, Rock, Rock!*. She was one of the most popular artists of '50s **rock and roll**.

Ballard, Hank (1936–2003). Born in Detroit, this rhythm and bluesman was a regular on the **R&B** charts throughout the '50s. Having combined sexually explicit lyrics with the rough sound of gospel music early in the decade, he and his backup group, the Midnighters (formed as the Royals in 1952; renamed in 1954), recorded several successful songs for the Federal and **King** labels, including what is referred to as the Annie Trilogy (1954)—"Work with Me Annie," "Annie Had a Baby," and "Annie's Aunt Fannie." All three were Top 10 R&B hits (the first two were No. 1's), and each sold more than a million copies, despite being banned from radio. Their success, along with the No. 2 hit "Sexy Ways," made Ballard an R&B star. He composed and recorded the novelty dance song "The Twist," which became the first **rock and roll** dance craze after Chubby Checker recorded it in 1960 and was one of rock and roll's early best-selling singles. Influenced by such other R&B musicians as **Roy Brown** and the **Drifters**, Ballard and the Midnighters were one of the mid-1950s most popular R&B groups. Hank Ballard was inducted into the Rock and Roll Hall of Fame in 1990.

Bartholomew, Dave (b. 1920). Born in Edgard, Louisiana, this top **R&B** producer was a chief designer of the **New Orleans sound** and a 1991 Rock and Roll Hall of Famer. A significant figure in the transition from jump blues to R&B and **rock and roll**, this talented songwriter, producer, arranger, and talent scout spent much of his time in the studio recording artists and groups including **Smiley Lewis**, **Lloyd Price**, and **Shirley & Lee**. Bartholomew discovered **Fats Domino**, wrote many songs for him, and produced his string of '50s hit singles on **Imperial Records**.

Bass, Ralph (1911–1997). Hailing from the Bronx, New York, this 1991 Rock and Roll Hall of Famer had a lengthy career as a producer and talent scout for the influential **Savoy**, **King**/Federal, and **Chess indies**. He recorded many of the greatest artists in black music, including **T-Bone Walker** ("Call It Stormy Monday"), **Hank Ballard** and the Midnighters ("Work with Me Annie"), and the **Dominoes** (**"Sixty Minute Man"**). In addition to recording many extraordinary blues, gospel, **R&B**, and **rock and roll** musicians—from Clara Ward, the Soul Stirrers, and **Etta James** to **Howlin' Wolf** and **Muddy Waters**—Bass discovered **James Brown** and brought him to the Federal label.

"Be-Bop-a-Lula" (1956). Recorded by **Gene Vincent** and His Blue Caps on **Capitol Records**, this is considered one of the greatest **rock and roll** anthems of the '50s. Perfectly exemplifying the **rockabilly** sound, complete with two guitar solos and use of the blues progression, this single that reached No. 7 on the **pop** and No. 8 on the **R&B** charts ranks alongside the greatest of the subgenre.

Berry, Chuck (b. 1926). Born Charles Edward Anderson Berry in St. Louis, this highly imaginative and creative pioneer of **rock and roll** is considered the first great rock star. He put the essential music pieces together in the '50s to help invent rock and roll and was one of Chicago-based **Chess Record's** most successful recording artists in the mid-to-late '50s; he also was active on the performance circuit, where he was famous for his duckwalk. One of rock music's first great lyricists, he wrote numerous songs with brilliant lyrics, especially about teenagers' lives. Berry gave rock and roll some of its first trademark guitar licks, as in **"Johnny B. Goode,"** a staple of every rock guitarist's repertoire. His string of '50s hits included the classic standards "Roll Over Beethoven," "School Day," "Rock and Roll Music," and "Sweet Little Sixteen." Rooted in swing jazz and urban blues, he was highly influenced by bluesmen **T-Bone Walker, Howlin' Wolf, Muddy Waters, Jimmy Reed,** and **Louis Jordan.** Berry grafted blues, **R&B,** country music, and swing jazz into his music and became one of rock and roll's first great stylistic innovators. He combined country and western with the blues in his first hit, **"Maybellene,"** and overcame the racial divide of the '50s while allowing rock music to acknowledge its black roots. His innovative music defined rock and roll, profoundly influencing most musicians who followed, including some of the most popular rock and **pop** artists and groups: the Beach Boys, the Beatles, the Rolling Stones, Bruce Springsteen, and Bob Dylan. Inducted into the Rock and Roll Hall of Fame in 1986, Berry is referred to as the Father of Rock Guitar for his great influence on many of the best rock and roll guitarists over the years, including **Buddy Holly,** Carl Wilson, George Harrison, and Keith Richards.

The Big Bopper (1930–1959). Born Jiles Perry Richardson in Sabine Pass, Texas, this **disc jockey** for radio station KTRM in Beaumont, Texas, participated in the late 1950s **novelty song** craze with his "Purple People Eater Meets Witch Doctor," but it was the flip side of this 1958 record, "Chantilly Lace," that became a big hit at No. 6 (**pop**) and No. 3 (**R&B**). Known for his trademark Stetson hat and wild striped suit, the Big Bopper was a flamboyant and jovial personality whom teens loved, famous for his phrase "Oh, baby, that's-a what I like!" He died in the February 3, 1959, plane crash near Clear Lake, Iowa, that also took the lives of **Buddy Holly** and **Ritchie Valens.**

Bihari, Jules. See Modern Records.

Bihari, Saul. See Modern Records.

Billboard. Considered a leading voice of the music business, *Billboard,* the most influential, largest, and oldest trade publication, began publication in 1894. Today it is an international newsweekly that covers music, video, and home entertainment. In the 1950s, *Billboard* provided coverage of industry events and compiled the charts of music hits in various categories. **Paul Ackerman** served as music editor from 1943 to 1973 and helped *Billboard* become the music industry's premier trade publication.

Bill Haley and the Comets. See Haley, Bill.

The Blackboard Jungle (1955). This movie that included **Bill Haley and the Comets'** **"(We're Gonna) Rock Around the Clock"** on its sound track gave teenage rebellion its first theme song. It helped launch this song as an international sensation and the first No. 1 **rock and roll** hit on the ***Billboard*** charts.

Bland, Bobby "Blue" (b. 1930). Born Robert Calvin Bland in Rosemark, Tennessee, just outside Memphis, Bland was active in the blues scene and was a member of the Beale Streeters. Known for his soul-blues voice and polished guitar riffs, along with **Sam Cooke, Ray Charles**, and Little Junior Parker he influenced many blues and rock vocalists and was one of the main creators of **soul music**, mixing gospel with the blues and **R&B**. Bland recorded such '50s classics as "Farther up the Road" and "I'll Take Care of You," and was inducted into the Rock and Roll Hall of Fame in 1992.

"Blue Suede Shoes" (1955). Known as the signature song of the **rockabilly** subgenre, this **Sun Records** smash hit written and recorded by **Carl Perkins** became the label's first million-seller and launched Perkins's career. It is referred to as the first true **rock and roll** hit because it was the first across-the-board chart hit, simultaneously reaching the Top 5 on the **pop**, country, and **R&B** charts.

The Bobbettes. Formed in 1956 (and known as the Harlem Queens until manager James Dailey changed their name), this highly influential '50s all-girl group was the first female vocal group to have a No. 1 **R&B** hit and a **pop** Top 10 hit. These talented young women—Emma Pought, Reather Dixon, Laura Webb, Helen Gathers, and Janice Pought—composed a number of the songs they recorded. They had an enormously popular debut single, the R&B No. 1 and pop No. 6 hit "Mr. Lee," and its sequel, "I Shot Mr. Lee." They were a great influence on the early 1960s **girl groups**.

"Bo Diddley" (1955). A No. 1 **R&B** hit originally called "Uncle John," this single had its title changed to the composer's stage name before **Bo Diddley** recorded it on Checker Records. With simple harmony and bottleneck guitar playing, it utilized Diddley's distinctive rhythmic sound, known as the Bo Diddley beat. (See also **Chess Records**.)

Boone, Pat (b. 1934). Born Charles Eugene Boone in Jacksonville, Florida, this descendant of American pioneer Daniel Boone was the most commercially successful '50s **teen idol**. A prolific cover artist, he built his reputation and career by covering black **R&B** songs by such artists as **Fats Domino, Little Richard**, and **Roy Brown**, placing hit after hit on the **pop** charts and becoming one of the biggest-selling pop singers. His renditions included Fats Domino's **"Ain't That a Shame,"** the Five Keys' "Gee Whittakers!," Ivory Joe Hunter's "I Almost Lost My Mind," Little Richard's **"Tutti Frutti"** and "Long Tall Sally," and **Big Joe Turner's** "Chains of Love." Deemed the calm alternative not only to **Chuck Berry** and other black rockers but also to such thrilling white artists as **Elvis Presley** and **Jerry Lee Lewis**, Boone earned his welcome in '50s teenagers' homes. As his career progressed, he moved toward soft ballads and won the status of teen idol. Singing in the pop tradition of Perry Como and Bing Crosby, this crooner achieved further successes with songs such as "Don't Forbid Me" and "Love Letters in the Sand."

Brenston, Jackie (1930–1979). In 1951, this singer and saxophonist in **Ike Turner**'s Kings of Rhythm sang lead vocal on the No. 1 **R&B** hit **"Rocket 88,"** often cited as the first **rock and roll** record (the record is credited to Jackie Brenston and His Delta Cats). Born in Clarksdale, Mississippi, he was a one-hit wonder, releasing only a few more singles between 1951 and 1953. He played saxophone in Lowell Fulson's and Ike Turner's bands until 1962, then faded from the music scene.

Brown, Charles (1922–1999). This 1999 Rock and Roll Hall of Famer, one of the most popular **R&B** artists of the late 1940s and early 1950s, popularized the blues ballad or nightclub strain of blues on the West Coast. With his mellow piano playing, this crooner from Texas City, Texas, created smooth, more urban arrangements of songs with calm vocals and small combos. With Johnny Moore's Three Blazers, he recorded such hits as "Driftin' Blues" and "Merry Christmas, Baby" before forming the Charles Brown Trio in 1949. His series of hits included R&B No. 1 classics "Trouble Blues" and "Black Night."

Brown, James (b. 1933). Born in Barnwell, South Carolina, and raised in Augusta, Georgia, the Godfather of Soul (as he is known) recorded his first successful records in the mid-to-late 1950s: **"Please, Please, Please,"** "Try Me," and "I Want You So Bad." Inspired by **Hank Ballard** and **Fats Domino**, Brown and Bobby Byrd formed the Flames, later known as the Famous Flames. Responsible for helping create **soul music** in the '60s, funk in the '70s, and rap in the '80s, this 1986 Rock and Roll Hall of Famer is known by many titles (such as "Soul Brother Number One" and "The Hardest Working Man in Show Business"). A captivating performer, he incorporated theatrics into his shows while blending emotionally explosive and intense **R&B** with the fervor of gospel music.

Brown, Roy (1925–1981). Originally from New Orleans, this **R&B** singer and piano player helped pave the way for **rock and roll** as one of the originators of the **New Orleans sound**. Having inspired many musicians—including **Elvis Presley**, Little Junior Parker, **B. B. King**, **Jackie Wilson**, and **James Brown**—he was very successful as a recording artist between 1949 and 1951. He had several Top 10 R&B hits, including "Hard Luck Blues" and "Love Don't Love Nobody." Brown is best known for his 1947 hit "Good Rocking Tonight," which was later covered by **Wynonie Harris**, Elvis Presley, and **Pat Boone**.

Brown, Ruth (b. 1928). Born Ruth Weston in Portsmouth, Virginia, this **R&B** singer emerged from the gospel tradition and achieved immense success, rivaling **Dinah Washington** as the '50s' leading black female singer. Known as Miss Rhythm, Brown had a string of Top 10 hits, including No. 1's "5-10-15 Hours," **"(Mama) He Treats Your Daughter Mean,"** "Mambo Baby," and "Oh What a Dream." Dominating the R&B charts in the '50s as **Atlantic**'s top-selling artist of the decade, she secured the label's place in the record industry and it was referred to as "The House That Ruth Built." In 1956, Brown began attracting a white audience while performing in **Alan Freed**'s rock and roll shows; she crossed over to the **pop** charts in 1957, beginning with the success of **Leiber and Stoller**'s "Lucky Lips" and **Bobby Darin**'s "This Little Girl's Gone Rockin'." Brown was inducted into the Rock and Roll Hall of Fame in 1993.

Bryant, Felice and Boudleaux. This successful '50s songwriting team consisted of composer Boudleaux and his lyricist wife, Felice, who began writing songs together for enjoyment. After achieving a country hit in 1949, the couple moved to Nashville and began tailoring songs specifically to the **Everly Brothers**' range, harmonies, and audience. The Everly Brothers recorded their **"Bye Bye Love,"** "Wake Up Little Susie," "All I Have to Do Is Dream," "Bird Dog," and "Devoted to You."

Buddy Holly and the Crickets. See Holly, Buddy.

"Bye Bye Love" (1957). The **Everly Brothers** recorded this **rockabilly** classic composed by **Felice and Boudleaux Bryant** on **Cadence Records**. With the Everlys' trademark close vocal harmonies, this recording established the musical model that the duo followed for the rest of their successes; it was their first million-seller hit and reached No. 1 on the country and No. 2 on the **pop** charts.

Cadence Records. Formed by Archie Bleyer in 1953, this New York City–based **indie** rivaled **Dot Records** and **Liberty Records** as one of the most successful new indies in the late 1950s. It boasted a roster including Bill Hayes ("The Ballad of Davy Crockett"), Andy Williams ("Butterfly"), the **Chordettes** ("Mr. Sandman"), Johnny Tillotson ("True True Happiness"), Link Wray ("Rumble"), and the **Everly Brothers** ("All I Have to Do Is Dream"). Bleyer closed the label in 1964.

Capitol Records. Founded by Glenn Wallichs, Buddy DeSylva, and Johnny Mercer in Los Angeles in 1942, this **major** label presented a swift response to **RCA-Victor Records**' **Elvis Presley** with **rockabilly Gene Vincent** and the Blue Caps (**"Be-Bop-a-Lula"**) and also responded to **Specialty Records**' **Little Richard** with **R&B** artist Esquerita ("Green Door"). Les Baxter, Billy May, and Nelson Riddle served as music directors; Ken Nelson, Voyle Gilmore, Dave Cavanagh, and Dave Dexter Jr. were A&R agents. Other '50s musicians recorded by Capitol included **Johnny Otis** ("Willie and the Hand Jive"), **Nat "King" Cole** ("Mona Lisa"), Tennessee Ernie Ford ("Sixteen Tons"), the **Kingston Trio** ("Tom Dooley"), the Five Keys ("Ling, Ting, Tong"), the Four Freshmen ("Graduation Day"), and the Four Preps ("Big Man").

Cash, Johnny (1932–2003). Born in Kingsland, Arkansas, this country singer, songwriter, and guitarist spent his early days as a **rockabilly** singer recording for **Sam Phillips** at **Sun Records**. Later he was attracted to the blues, influenced by the music of **Robert Johnson, Howlin' Wolf,** and **Muddy Waters**. A Rock and Roll Hall of Famer (inducted in 1992), he drew together elements of folk, country, and gospel music in the more than 400 songs he composed and performed in his baritone voice. They were simple stories about workingmen in America—in line with those of **Woody Guthrie** that later appeared in the works of such **rock and roll** artists as Bob Dylan and Bruce Springsteen. Cash recorded a string of rockabilly hits for the Sun label that included the classics "Folsom Prison Blues," "I Walk the Line," and "Cry! Cry! Cry!"

Cat Records. See **Atlantic Records**.

The Chantels. A significant early female vocal group, this ensemble from the New York City area, formed in 1956, consisted of teenagers Arlene Smith, Sonia Goring, Rene Minus, Jackie Landry, and Lois Harris. It was one of the first all-girl vocal groups to sustain success beyond one hit. Their biggest hit, "Maybe," was followed by other favorites, including "Every Night (I Pray)" and "I Love You So." Though there were **R&B** all-**girl groups** before this one, none of them had such a run of popular records or presented such a distinctive sound. The Chantels greatly influenced the girl groups of the early 1960s, such as the Shangri-Las, the Ronettes, and the Crystals.

Charles, Ray (1930–2004). Born Ray Charles Robinson in Albany, Georgia, this brilliant **R&B** singer, pianist, and composer transformed '50s music by injecting black American gospel music into his songs, combining its emotional fervor with the secular lyrics and stories of blues and country music, along with swing jazz and improvisational techniques. He thus invented the highly innovative and sophisticated **soul** subgenre of **rock** music in the mid-'50s, ten years prior to its heyday. Influenced by West Coast club bluesmen while performing in his crooning, soothing nightclub style with his jazz-blues trio, this blind musician established himself in the R&B tradition and created some of his most memorable songs in the '50s, such as the No. 1's "I've Got a Woman," "A Fool for You," "Drown in My Own Tears," and his signature **"What'd I Say (Part I),"** an important link between blues, R&B, soul, and rock music. With the incorporation of highly intense gospel vocal techniques into his explicitly sexual songs, Charles created hits throughout the decade; his clever combination of emotions and brilliant musical virtuosity allowed him to move R&B music to unprecedented levels. One of the most original musicians of the '50s and one of the most important post–World War II American musicians, this 1986 Rock and Roll Hall of Famer established himself as one of the most successful black artists in the music business.

Checker Records. See **Chess Records**.

Chess, Leonard. See **Chess Records**.

Chess, Phil. See **Chess Records**.

Chess Records. Founded by Leonard (a 1987 Rock and Roll Hall of Fame inductee) and Phil Chess as Aristocrat Records in 1947 and renamed Chess Records in 1949, this was a highly important and active '50s blues, **R&B**, and **rock and roll** Chicago–based **indie**. Chess and its subsidiary labels Checker (formed in 1953) and Argo (formed in 1956; later named Cadet) recorded legendary artists and groups: **Howlin' Wolf** ("How Many More Years"), **Muddy Waters** ("I'm Your Hoochie Coochie Man"), **Chuck Berry** ("Sweet Little Sixteen"), **Bo Diddley ("Bo Diddley")**, **Clarence "Frogman" Henry** ("Ain't Got No Home"), Bobby Charles ("Later Alligator"), Dale Hawkins ("Susie-Q"), the **Moonglows** ("Sincerely"), the Tuneweavers ("Happy, Happy Birthday Baby"), the Monotones ("Book of Love"), and the **Flamingos** ("I'll Be Home"). In the early '50s, Muddy Waters was the label's biggest and most influential artist, followed by harmonica wizard Little Walter ("Juke"); both were instrumental in the development of early Chicago blues, as were the label's producers, **Willie Dixon** and **Ralph Bass**. Recording mostly blues musicians, Chess/Checker eventually diversified with early rocker Chuck Berry, who had multiple hits, and the early **doo-wop** group the Moonglows, who created sentimental ballads for America's white audience. In addition to recording its own artists, Chess leased master recordings made by independent producers, such as **Sam Phillips**'s recording of **Jackie Brenston**'s **"Rocket 88,"** considered by many historians to be the first rock and roll record. With its roster of gifted artists, Chess achieved great success in the '50s and left its mark on music history. The label was sold in 1969 to GRT Corporation (General Recorded Tape), and MCA Records purchased the catalogue of Chess recordings in 1986. MCA then began a comprehensive reissue program, making the great Chess/Checker recordings of the past available on compact disc.

The Chordettes. Formed in 1946, this popular white female group from Sheboygan, Wisconsin, achieved **pop** charts success in the mid-1950s with "Mr. Sandman" and "Lollipop."

The Chords. Hailing from the Bronx, New York, and consisting of Carl Feaster, Jimmy Keyes, Floyd McRae, Claude Feaster, and William "Ricky" Edwards, this black vocal group recorded their landmark record, **"Sh-Boom,"** a **doo-wop** gem that has been cited as the first **rock and roll** recording, in March 1954.

Christian, Charlie (1919–1942). This jazz guitarist took the guitar out of the rhythm section and made it a lead instrument equal to the trumpet and saxophone. He had a profound influence on jazz, blues, and **rock and roll** musicians. Christian was inducted into the Rock and Roll Hall of Fame in 1990.

Chudd, Lew. See Imperial Records.

Clark, Dick (b. 1929). This Philadelphia **disc jockey** and host of the national television show **American Bandstand** was born Richard Wagstaff Clark in Bronxville, New York. Very influential through his delivery of **rock and roll** music to America's homes, this music entrepreneur helped establish many '50s artists and groups. He created numerous hits by using *Bandstand* to introduce music to America and change the face of rock and roll. In 1993 he was inducted into the Rock and Roll Hall of Fame.

The Coasters. An extremely successful '50s vocal group originally from Los Angeles, this **doo-wop** ensemble took a humorous approach to music, creating recordings with a less polished sound and an emphasis on spoken bass parts and lyrics about teenage life. The original Coasters lineup consisted of Carl Gardner, Leon Hughes, Billy Guy, and Bobby Nunn; others who sang with the group at various times included Obie "Young" Jessie, Leroy Binns, Cornelius Gunter, Earl Carroll, Ronnie Bright, Teddy Harper, Jimmy Norman Scott, Bobby Sheen, Bobby Steger, and Nathaniel Wilson. The classic Coasters lineup materialized when tenor Cornelius Gunter and bass Will "Dub" Jones replaced Hughes and Nunn. Known for their string of comical **R&B** hits, by the late 1950s the Coasters ranked among the most popular American groups. Sung with vitality and humor, and with vigorous, honking saxophone solos by **King Curtis**, their recordings incorporated exciting R&B musical characteristics. The Coasters helped define **rock and roll** by appealing to and reflecting America's teens with such classics as "Searchin'," "Young Blood," "Yakety Yak," "Charlie Brown," "Along Came Jones," and "Poison Ivy."

Cochran, Eddie (1938–1960). Inducted into the Rock and Roll Hall of Fame in 1987, Cochran had a brief career as a **rockabilly** artist. He left a lasting mark on **rock and roll** with his influential thick, aggressive rhythmic guitar sound and his defiant attitude that made him an icon, especially in England, for rockers from the Beatles, the Rolling Stones, the Who, and the Kinks to such punk rockers as the Sex Pistols. His songs, including **"Summertime Blues,"** "C'mon Everybody," and "Somethin' Else," are among the gems that, along with those of **Chuck Berry** and the **Coasters**, tell the '50s teenage story. In April 1960, Cochran died in a limousine accident in which his fiancée, Sharon Sheely, and friend, **Gene Vincent**, were seriously injured en route to Heathrow Airport at the end of his British tour. Cochran, who was more popular in England than in America, epitomized the sound and stance of the '50s rebel rocker.

Cole, Nat "King" (1919–1965). Born Nathaniel Adams Coles in Montgomery, Alabama, this African American popular singer and jazz pianist learned to play the organ and to sing in church. He formed his influential King Cole Trio in Los Angeles in 1937 and quickly won over a white audience with his perfect diction and smooth vocal style. In 1948, he became one of the first black artists to host his own weekly radio show; in 1956, he had a weekly television show as a soloist. Throughout the '40s and '50s, Cole appeared in several films, including *St. Louis Blues*, in which he portrayed W. C. Handy. Cole's

1946 hit recording, "The Christmas Song," was the first of his solo recordings to be accompanied by a studio orchestra instead of his trio, and marked the start of his rise as an internationally acclaimed popular singer. Cole achieved success with a long list of hits, including "Straighten Up and Fly Right," "Embraceable You," "Star Dust," "Nature Boy," "Mona Lisa," and "Unforgettable." Well known for his emotive and sophisticated style, this 2000 Rock and Roll Hall of Famer toured until his death in 1965, and has remained popular with the general public. (See also **Pop Music**.)

Columbia Records. Founded about 1885, this label was the most successful of all the **majors** early in the 1950s, recording such artists as Frankie Laine ("Moonlight Gambler"), Guy Mitchell ("Singing the Blues"), Rosemary Clooney ("Hey There"), and Doris Day ("Whatever Will Be, Will Be [Que Sera, Sera]"). Its '50s music director and A&R chief, Mitch Miller, rejected **rock and roll**, and Columbia recorded **pop** artist Johnny Mathis ("Chances Are") and country musician Marty Robbins ("El Paso"). Its race labels Epic and OKeh released records by Roy Hamilton ("Unchained Melody"), Johnnie Ray ("Cry"), Chuck Willis ("My Story"), and Screamin' Jay Hawkins ("I Put a Spell on You").

Cooke, Sam (1931–1964). Born in Clarksdale, Mississippi, and raised in Chicago, Cooke began in the gospel realm, then changed to **pop** and **R&B**. His oeuvre consisted of both secular and gospel songs of all types, ranging from ballads and lighthearted pop music to exciting, raspy R&B and **rock and roll**. He was the lead vocalist of the Soul Stirrers from 1950 to 1956, then left to begin his solo career; he achieved his first solo success in 1957 with "You Send Me," a No. 1 pop and R&B hit. He followed with many other No. 1's, including "I'll Come Running Back to You," "Twistin' the Night Away," and "Another Saturday Night." He died under mysterious circumstances in 1964, killed by a gunshot. With his **teen idol** looks and blending of sensual and spiritual elements, he is revered as the definitive soul singer. Sam Cooke was inducted into the Rock and Roll Hall of Fame in 1986. (See also **Soul Music**.)

"Crazy Man, Crazy" (1953). This **Bill Haley** recording was the first **rock and roll** record to appear on the **pop** charts; it was a No. 12 hit.

The Crew-Cuts. One of the first white vocal groups to cover **R&B** hits, these Canadians were originally called the Canadaires (they changed the name in 1954). In 1954, their cover of the **Chords' "Sh-Boom"** was a huge No. 1 hit, triggering a flood of R&B covers by white **pop** artists.

The Crows. Formed in 1951, this young **doo-wop** group originally consisted of Daniel "Sonny" Norton, Jerry Wittick, Harold Major, William Davis, and Gerald Hamilton. In 1952, Wittick left to join the service and was replaced by Mark Jackson. They performed at school, on street corners, and in subways before being discovered. Davis wrote their landmark song, **"Gee,"**

which attracted both **R&B** and **pop** audiences. One of the first crossover records by a black group, it has been cited as the first **rock and roll** record.

Danny & the Juniors. This white **doo-wop** group from Philadelphia succeeded with a handful of hits in the late '50s, among them "Dottie," "Rock and Roll Is Here to Stay," and their landmark No. 1 single, "At the Hop." Originally known as the Juvenairs, Danny Rapp, David White, Frank Maffei, and Joe Terranova began singing on street corners. The group toured frequently (including **Alan Freed**'s package tours), appeared on *American Bandstand* and in the 1958 movie *Let's Rock*, and continued to place records on the Hot 100 until early 1963.

Darin, Bobby (1936–1973). A gifted **teen idol** and ambitious, versatile performer, this 1990 Rock and Roll Hall of Famer was born Walden Robert Cassotto in the Bronx, New York. He began his prolific recording career in the mid-1950s, recording with the Jaybirds. Perhaps best known for his first hit, the 1958 **novelty** "Splish Splash," he had over forty hits on the **pop** charts during his lengthy career, including the big '50s successes "Queen of the Hop," "Dream Lover," and his signature song, "Mack the Knife."

Decca Records. Formed in 1934 as the American subsidiary of British Decca and purchased from UK Decca in the mid-1940s, this **major** label signed and recorded black artists because of president Jack Kapp's interest in black dance music. Personnel in the '50s included music directors Gordon Jenkins and Dick Jacobs, and A&R agents Dave Kapp, **Milt Gabler**, Jimmy Hilliard, and Bob Thiele, with Paul Cohen and Owen Bradley at the Nashville division. Ella Fitzgerald ("Smooth Sailing"), the Mills Brothers ("Till Then"), the **Ink Spots** ("Into Each Life Some Rain Must Fall"), **Louis Jordan** ("Choo Choo Ch'Boogie"), Lucky Millinder ("Who Threw the Whiskey in the Well"), and Sister Rosetta Tharpe ("Strange Things Happening Every Day") were recorded by Decca. Country artists on its roster included Red Foley ("Peace in the Valley"), Ernest Tubb ("Walking the Floor over You"), and Webb Pierce ("I Ain't Never"), as well as Bobby Helms ("Jingle Bell Rock") and **Brenda Lee** ("Sweet Nothin's"). Decca signed **Bill Haley** and the Comets (**"(We're Gonna) Rock Around the Clock"**) in an effort to join the ranks of **rock and roll**; its subsidiaries Coral and Brunswick recorded **Jackie Wilson** ("Lonely Teardrops") and **Buddy Holly** and the Crickets ("That'll Be the Day"). Its subsidiary London Records recorded Italian instrumentalist Annunzio Mantovani and His Orchestra ("Cara Mia").

The Dells. This vocal group formed from the El Rays, which began as a street corner a cappella **doo-wop** group in 1952 in the Chicago suburb of Harvey, Illinois: Johnny Funches, Marvin Junior, Verne Allison, Michael "Mickey" McGill, Chuck Barksdale, and Lucius McGill. By 1955, the group was pared down to five members (minus Lucius) and renamed. During their doo-wop years, they recorded the classic "Oh What a Nite," a huge 1956 hit that marked the beginning of their success. With their exceptional vocal talent, the Dells placed more than forty singles on the **R&B** charts and eight on the Top 40 charts. Over more than fifty years, these 2004 Rock and Roll Hall of Famers consistently recorded, performed, and backed up singers (including Jerry Butler and **Dinah Washington**) enabling them to remain a premier vocal group.

DeLuxe Records. See **King Records.**

Diddley, Bo (b. 1928). Born Otha Ellas Bates McDaniel in McComb, Mississippi, this most original of the first generation of **rock and roll** musicians and self-professed **Muddy Waters** fanatic was the author of a repertoire of classic songs that represent the earliest examples of rock music stemming from its **R&B** source material: **"Bo Diddley,"** "I'm a Man," "Diddley Daddy," "Pretty Thing," "Who Do You Love?," "Hey Bo Diddley," "Mona (I Need You Baby)," "Say Man," and "Road Runner." Famous for his distinctive sound and African-based "Bo Diddley beat" rhythmic pattern, as well as his trademark square guitar, he exerted considerable influence on many American rock musicians during the '50s and '60s, including Jimi Hendrix, the Beatles, the Rolling Stones, and the Yardbirds. His legacy was enhanced considerably in the mid-1960s when many American and English groups, especially British blues revival rock groups, recorded cover versions of his songs. His Diddley beat has been used in many rock songs, among them **Buddy Holly**'s "Not Fade Away," **Johnny Otis**'s "Willie and the Hand Jive," the Who's "Magic Bus," Bruce Springsteen's "She's the One," U2's "Desire," and the Pretenders' "Cuban Slide." Along with **Chuck Berry**, this founding father of rock and roll, who was inducted into the Rock and Roll Hall of Fame in 1987, personifies the fine line that existed between blues and rhythm and blues-based rock and roll in the 1950s.

DiMucci, Dion (b. 1939). In 1958 Dion formed the Belmonts, considered to have been the greatest white **doo-wop** group, in the Bronx, New York. Consisting of Dion, Angelo D'Aleo, Fred Milano, and Carlo Mastrangelo, Dion and the Belmonts combined the four-part harmony doo-wop sound with **rock and roll** influences from **Bo Diddley**, **Fats Domino**, and **Elvis Presley**. The quartet's 1958 classic single, "I Wonder Why," was followed by a number of late '50s hits, including **"A Teenager in Love,"** which caused many white, predominantly Italian-American groups to form. In 1960, unhappy that the group was being steered toward the polished, adult **pop** sound, Dion left the Belmonts and pursued a solo career to reclaim his rock and roll roots. An influence on many other rockers, including Paul Simon, Billy Joel, and Lou Reed, Dion had such solo hits as "Runaround Sue" and "The Wanderer." He was inducted into the Rock and Roll Hall of Fame in 1989.

Dion and the Belmonts. See **DiMucci, Dion.**

Disc Jockey. The term "disc jockey" was first used early in the '50s to describe those who played and helped select the popular hits for radio broadcast.

Their rise to prominence went hand in hand with the growth of **rock and roll**. As hundreds of independent radio stations identified with listeners' preferences, this new breed of broadcast entertainer appeared. The more a deejay played their music, the more teenagers would listen to that jockey's station; this resulted in the emergence of jockeys who engaged in flamboyant and provocative on-air behaviors. America's teens respected and adored their deejays, and the more eccentric they were, the better. Among the finest '50s jockeys were **Alan Freed**, **Dewey Phillips**, Hunter Hancock, Tom "Big Daddy" Donahue, Pete "Mad Daddy" Myers, Porky Chedwick, Tommy "Dr. Jive" Smalls, Dick Biondi, Douglas "Jocko" Henderson, and **George "Hound Dog" Lorenz**. These masters of their craft were stars, many of them just as popular as the records they spun.

Dixon, Willie (1915–1992). From Vicksburg, Mississippi, this extremely important behind-the-scenes Chicago bluesman who often played bass with **Muddy Waters**, helped define the **Chess Records** sound as producer, arranger, session musician, and performer. A composer of many classic songs, he led the house band at Chess, backing quite a few blues performers, including **Chuck Berry** and **Bo Diddley**. This 1994 Rock and Roll Hall of Famer influenced his contemporaries and numerous blues and **rock and roll** artists, including Led Zeppelin, the Doors, and Cream.

Domino, Fats (b. 1928). Born Antoine Domino in New Orleans, this legendary performer became one of the first and most successful African American artists to cross over to the **popular** market. He attracted a much broader audience than was previously reached with **R&B** music through his boogie-woogie piano and **New Orleans sound**. He was the most popular of all the New Orleans R&B artists; his relaxed and mellow tenor voice, combined with his impeccable piano playing, embraceable personality, and incessant smile, delighted America's youth without threatening their parents. A musical and visual opposite of his coarse and flashy contemporaries, he launched his career with the late 1949 recording **"The Fat Man,"** then worked with producer **Dave Bartholomew** for many years, creating a long string of classic hits for the Imperial label. Among his most popular songs were **"Ain't That a Shame,"** "Blueberry Hill," "Blue Monday," "I'm Walkin'," "Valley of Tears," "Whole Lotta Loving," and "Walking to New Orleans." Fats Domino was second only to **Elvis Presley** in terms of charts success during the first decade of rock and roll. With the sound of his easy-listening boogie-woogie piano and charming voice, he brought the New Orleans sound to **rock and roll** and established the piano as a rock instrument. Domino was inducted into the Rock and Roll Hall of Fame in 1986.

The Dominoes. This gospel vocal group, formed by Billy Ward in New York City about 1950, mastered and recorded the smooth, sophisticated **rhythm and blues**-based sound in their classic early '50s No. 1 hits **"Sixty**

Minute Man" (featuring the bass voice of Bill Brown) and "Have Mercy Baby." With lead tenor **Clyde McPhatter** and then **Jackie Wilson**, the Dominoes became one of the best-regarded R&B ensembles.

Don't Knock the Rock (1956). This **rock and roll** movie featured **Alan Freed**, **Bill Haley** and the Comets, and **Little Richard**.

Doo-Wop. Emerging from the **R&B** tradition early in the '50s, the softer, gentler doo-wop sound took its place alongside other '50s **rock and roll** sub-genres. Similar to **rockabilly**, doo-wop was mostly spontaneous and informal music created by amateur but determined musicians. Impromptu performances abounded in this very popular '50s style, many of them preserved on recordings that are now collectors' dreams. With its roots in gospel, jazz, blues, and R&B, the doo-wop sound was performed by vocal groups of three to six (mostly four or five), consisting of a lead and background singers performing in close harmony, often a cappella (though usually recorded with background instrumental accompaniment obscured by the power of the voices). Countless vocal groups performing in this style emerged in the '50s, including such prominent ensembles as the **Moonglows**, the **Flamingos**, the **Drifters**, the **Platters**, the **Coasters**, and **Frankie Lymon** and the Teenagers. The vocal group rock and roll sound flourished into the early '60s, when doo-wop elements blended with other styles and appeared in new rock and roll subgenres.

Dot Records. Founded by Randy Wood in 1951 in Gallatin, Tennessee, this **indie** moved in 1956 to Hollywood, and was known for its cover versions of **R&B** songs. In the '50s, with music director Billy Vaughn, Dot rivaled the **majors** with recordings by such artists as **Pat Boone ("Ain't That a Shame")**, Gale Storm ("I Hear You Knocking"), Tab Hunter ("Young Love"), and the Dell-Vikings ("Come Go with Me").

The Drifters. This vocal group came from the gospel tradition and helped create **soul music**. Formed in New York City in 1953, the Drifters included **Clyde McPhatter**, David Baughan, William "Chick" Anderson, David Baldwin, and James Johnson. Though not the classic Drifters group, this lineup was the first to record as the **Atlantic** Drifters. Thereafter, numerous personnel changes occurred; no one stayed with the ensemble throughout its existence. In the Clyde McPhatter era, the Drifters consisted of McPhatter, Andrew and Gerhart Thrasher, Bill Pinkney, William Ferbie, and Walter Adams; these singers recorded "Money Honey," "Such a Night," "Honey Love," "Bip Bam," and "White Christmas." The King era Drifters included lead singer **Ben E. King**, Charlie Thomas, Dock Green, and Elsbeary Hobbs. They sang in a more **pop**-oriented style than the previous Drifters, one more in line with late 1950s **rock and roll**: **"There Goes My Baby,"** "Dance with Me," "This Magic Moment," "Save the Last Dance for Me," "Up on the Roof," "On Broadway," and "Under the Boardwalk." The 1988 Drifters Rock and Roll Hall of Famers were McPhatter, King, Pinkney, Thomas, Rudy Lewis, Johnny Moore, and Gerhart

Thrasher, spanning the group's history. (See chapter 7 for further Drifters personnel information.)

Duke/Peacock Records. Founded in Houston in 1949 by nightclub owner Don Robey, this **indie** sported producers **Johnny Otis**, Bill Harvey, Joe Scott, and Johnny Board, and recording musicians **Big Mama Thornton ("Hound Dog")**, Clarence "Gatemouth" Brown ("Mary Is Fine"), and the Dixie Hummingbirds ("Loves Me Like a Rock"). Its subsidiaries Duke (formed by James Mattis in Memphis in 1952 and taken over by Peacock in 1953) and Black Beat (formed about 1956) recorded Johnny Ace ("Pledging My Love"), **Bobby "Blue" Bland** ("Farther up the Road"), and Norman Fox and the Rob Roys ("Tell Me Why").

Ed Sullivan Show. Hosted by Ed Sullivan, this general entertainment television show featured and introduced to the nation musicians of all types, including rock and rollers. **Elvis Presley** made three appearances on the show during the fall of 1956 and winter of 1957, and was launched into national consciousness.

Eddy, Duane (b. 1938). One of the first to explore the potential of the electric guitar as a solo voice in **rock and roll**, this originator of the twangy guitar sound became the most successful instrumentalist in rock and roll history. Born in Corning, New York, he and his band, the Rebels (including such revered session musicians as saxophonist and 2003 Rock and Roll Hall of Famer Steve Douglas, and keyboardist Larry Knectel), began an impressive string of hits in 1958 with "Moovin' 'n' Groovin'," followed by **"Rebel-'Rouser,"** "Ramrod," "The Lonely One," and "Forty Miles of Bad Road," all Top 40 hits. Having inspired innumerable teenagers to play the guitar as a rock and roll instrument as well as influenced many fellow rockers (including the **Ventures**, the Beatles, Creedence Clearwater Revival, and Bruce Springsteen), Eddy, considered rock and roll's No. 1 instrumentalist of all time, was inducted into the Rock and Roll Hall of Fame in 1994. (See also **Rock Instrumentals**.)

Ertegun, Ahmet. See **Atlantic Records**.

The Everly Brothers. This most important vocal duo in **rock and roll** history preferred to sing about romantic love; Don (b. 1937) and Phil (b. 1939). Everly defined what love and affection meant in their songs about adolescent romance, teenage devotion, and heartbreak. One of the most influential **rockabilly** groups, these brothers transformed the country sounds (Appalachian Mountain and bluegrass music) of their Kentucky upbringing into a lavishly harmonized form of rock and roll as they flawlessly sang in tight harmony. Between 1957 and 1962, these 1986 Rock and Roll Hall of Famers released a steady stream of hit records that crossed over from country to **pop** and to **R&B** charts, including **"Bye Bye Love,"** "Wake Up Little Susie," "All I Have to Do Is Dream," "Bird Dog," and "Cathy's Clown." The duo's expressive harmonic vocal style influenced many later pop musicians, including the Beatles, the Hollies, the Beach Boys, the Mamas and the Papas, the Byrds, and Simon and Garfunkel.

Fabian (b. 1943). Born Fabiano Forte Bonaparte in Philadelphia, this late 1950s **teen idol** discovered by manager Bob Marcucci was marketed alongside fellow Philadelphia-based idols **Frankie Avalon** and **Bobby Rydell**. After appearing on numerous national package show tours and *American Bandstand*, he followed his late 1950s hits, "Turn Me Loose," "Tiger," and "Hound Dog Man," with an acting career that began with the 1959 movie *Hound Dog Man* and continued with many movies, and television and commercial appearances.

"The Fat Man" (1949). The first of **Fats Domino**'s remarkable series of hits for the **Imperial** label and often cited as the first **rock and roll** record, with its prominent and distinctive boogie-woogie piano style, this recording was influenced by the New Orleans Storyville piano tradition (blues and jazz elements). It was originally titled "Junker Blues," a song based on barrelhouse piano player Champion Jack Dupree's 1940 recording; **Dave Bartholomew** and Domino rewrote the song. It became a No. 2 **R&B** hit for Domino in 1950. (See also **New Orleans Sound**.)

Federal Records. See **King Records**.

Fender, Leo (1909–1991). Along with **Les Paul**, Leo Fender was responsible for revolutionizing **popular music**, and specifically **rock and roll**, with the invention of the electric guitar. Born near Anaheim, California, in 1948 this electronics fanatic invented the Fender Broadcaster, the first solid-body electric guitar to be mass-produced; two years later, he introduced his Precision bass, the first electric bass, which brought new sound to band rhythm sections. Also a designer of some of the music industry's most desired amplifiers, in 1954 he unveiled the Stratocaster, a classy instrument with a contoured body that became a favorite of many virtuoso rock guitarists. Leo Fender was inducted into the Rock and Roll Hall of Fame in 1992.

The Flamingos. Initially called the Swallows, then the Five Flamingos, and finally just the Flamingos, this mature **doo-wop** group that is widely regarded as one of the finest vocal groups in music history, formed in Chicago in 1952. Elegant, intricate, and flawless vocal technique and a use of melodies in minor tonalities reflected their church choir background. The group consisted of Earl Lewis, Sollie McElroy, Johnny Carter, Paul Wilson, and Zeke and Jake Carey. Featuring their impeccable harmonies in diverse styles, their irresistible and memorable recordings were aimed at the white market; among them were "Someday, Someway," "If I Can't Have You," "Golden Teardrops" (one of the classics most desired by **rock and roll** record collectors), "I'll Be Home," "A Kiss from Your Lips," "Lovers Never Say Goodbye," and "I Only Have Eyes for

You." Inducted into the Rock and Roll Hall of Fame in 2001, the Flamingos have remained one of the most enduring vocal groups and have created some of the most beautiful and charming doo-wop ballads ever recorded. Their polished vocals and impressive choreography influenced many groups, including some of Motown's greatest stars—the Temptations, the Supremes, the Jackson 5, and the Miracles.

The Four Seasons. From Newark, New Jersey, this most successful white **doo-wop** group in **rock and roll** history formed in 1956 with lead singer Frankie Valli (he initially sang with the Varietones, who later changed their name to the Four Lovers). After achieving a hit in 1956 with "You're the Apple of My Eye," the Four Lovers became the Four Seasons and enjoyed a nearly forty-year career. Valli's strong falsetto and wide-ranged voice combined with the Seasons' immaculate doo-wop harmonies on group member Bob Gaudio's songs to produce a remarkable string of hits during the '60s incorporating many arrangement types and production techniques, including No. 1s "Sherry," "Big Girls Don't Cry," "Walk Like a Man," and "Rag Doll." In addition to Valli and Gaudio, the lineup of these 1990 Rock and Roll Hall of Famers included singer-guitarist Tommy DeVito and bass vocalist Nick Massi (later replaced by Joe Long).

Francis, Connie (b. 1938). Perhaps the most prolific of all the late 1950s **teen idols**, this singer placed fifty-six hits on the **pop** charts during the '50s and '60s. Born Concetta Rosa Maria Franconero in Newark, New Jersey, she is best remembered by *American Bandstand* fans for "Who's Sorry Now" (1958) and "Where the Boys Are" (1961), both No. 4 pop hits.

Frankie Lymon and the Teenagers. See **Lymon, Frankie.**

Freed, Alan (1922–1965). One of the first and most influential champions of **rock and roll**, this **disc jockey** known as the Moondog hosted *The Moondog Rock 'n' Roll Party* first at Cleveland's WJW and then New York's WINS. Through his show he introduced millions of white listeners to **R&B** music, and he was the first to call it "rock and roll." Freed, a lover of classical music, did more to spread the gospel of rock and roll during its infancy than any other; as the music swept the country, he became its primary promoter, bringing black R&B music to America's teenagers via radio, dance shows, and package tours. In 1952 Freed presented the Cleveland **Moondog Coronation Ball**, which is widely considered the first rock and roll concert. He offered many other shows, and assisted with racial integration at his concerts, which had black and white performers and audiences. A victim of the late 1950s–early 1960s **payola investigation**, the Father of Rock and Roll pleaded guilty to two counts of bribery in 1962 and was fined $300; three years later, he died a broken man. Today, the Rock and Roll Hall of Fame and Museum hosts a memorial to Freed, a permanent exhibit in which his ashes are housed. He was inducted into the Rock and Roll Hall of Fame in 1986.

Funicello, Annette (b. 1942). Born in Utica, New York, and a Mouseketeer on the '50s television series *The Mickey Mouse Club*, this **teen idol**, known by her first name, recorded between 1959 and 1961; her biggest success was 1959's "Tall Paul," a No. 7 **pop** hit. An actress in several early 1960s teen movies, Annette starred with **Frankie Avalon** in many films, including the famous beach series.

Gabler, Milt (1911–2001). Though his background was in jazz, this **Decca Records** producer branched out to **R&B** and **rock and roll** music and produced recordings of such founding fathers as **Louis Jordan** ("Caldonia" and "Choo Choo Ch'Boogie") and **Bill Haley** and the Comets (**"Shake, Rattle and Roll"**). When this 1993 Rock and Roll Hall of Famer changed his production style from Jordan's jump blues sounds with a balanced swing-band rhythm section to the forceful backbeat of Haley's songs, he helped in the birth of rock and roll. Gabler was one of the strongest forces in **popular music** for much of the twentieth century.

Gayten, Paul (1920–1991). An **R&B** bandleader and pianist who had a handful of successful hits with his orchestra and Annie Laurie, including "True" and "Since I Fell for You," this significant figure in New Orleans produced, arranged, and served as talent scout. As A&R man for **Chess Records**, he discovered **Clarence "Frogman" Henry** and others active with the **New Orleans sound**.

"Gee" (1953). This significant single recorded by the **Crows** on **Rama Records** was one of the first crossover records by a black group; in 1954, it reached No. 2 on the **R&B** charts and No. 14 on the **pop** charts. Since R&B songs hadn't yet infiltrated the almost exclusively white charts, this song and other crossovers that soon followed, helped change the nature of popular music in America. "Gee" has been cited as a contender for the title of first **rock and roll** record.

Gee Records. See **Rama Records**.

***The Girl Can't Help It* (1956).** This **rock and roll** movie featured **Gene Vincent, Little Richard, Fats Domino, Eddie Cochran**, and other '50s rockers.

Girl Groups. Rooted in '50s **R&B** vocal groups, the early 1960s girl group phenomenon began with such ensembles as the **Bobbettes**, the **Chantels**, and the **Shirelles**. As female vocal ensembles flourished in the early 1960s, groups such as the Shirelles continued their success with such hits as the Carole King-Gerry Goffin team's "Will You Love Me Tomorrow," the first No. 1 **pop** hit by an all-girl group. With Berry Gordy's establishment of Motown Records and **Phil Spector**'s production contributions, numerous girl groups emerged, including the Marvelettes, Martha and the Vandellas, the Supremes, the Crystals, and the Ronettes.

***Go, Johnny, Go!* (1958).** This **rock and roll** movie featured, among others, **Alan Freed**, Jimmy Clanton, **Chuck Berry**, Jackie Wilson, **Eddie Cochran**, and **Ritchie Valens** (in his first, and only, screen appearance).

Goldner, George. See Rama Records.

Gone/End Records. See Rama Records.

Goodman, Shirley. See Shirley & Lee.

Guitar Slim (1926–1959). Born Edward Jones and raised in the Mississippi Delta, this blues singer-guitarist with roots in gospel music moved to New Orleans in 1950 and teamed up with **Huey "Piano" Smith** as part of a blues trio. In 1954, Slim released the million-selling No. 1 **R&B** hit, "The Things That I Used to Do," with **Ray Charles** on piano. It became the best-selling R&B record of the year, and was one of the most influential songs to come out of New Orleans' early R&B period. A pioneering **rock and roll** performer, Guitar Slim dressed and acted the part; he engaged in thrilling performances during which he worked his audiences, leaving fans screaming for more. (See also **New Orleans Sound.**)

Guthrie, Woody (1912–1967). Folk musician-composer Woodrow Wilson Guthrie left his mark on America with his nearly 1,000 compositions: patriotic songs that celebrate America ("This Land Is Your Land" and "Pastures of Plenty"); tributes to fallen heroes ("Reuben James" and "Plane Wreck at Los Gatos"); social commentary songs ("Jesus Christ" and "Do Re Mi"); labor union songs ("Union Maid" and "Ballad of Harry Bridges"); Dust Bowl ballads ("Tom Joad" and "Dusty Old Dust"); Columbia River Power Project songs ("Roll On, Columbia" and "Grand Coulee Dam"); and children's songs ("Put Your Finger in the Air" and "Car Car Song"). Artists of the folk revival performed his songs throughout the '50s and '60s, and Americans still sing many of them. This 1988 Rock and Roll Hall of Famer's influence can be detected in many musicians, from Suzanne Vega to Tracy Chapman, Dan Bern to Ani DiFranco, and Bob Dylan to Bruce Springsteen; many have acknowledged Guthrie's impact and have recorded his songs.

Guy, Buddy (b. 1936). Born George Guy in Lettsworth, Louisiana, Guy was a popular session player and successful solo blues artist, and is noted for his blues guitar playing. Active in the late 1950s on the Chicago blues scene, he was a session guitarist for **Chess Records** and backed many noted bluesmen, including **Muddy Waters**, **Willie Dixon**, and Little Walter. He influenced many of the great **rock and roll** guitarists, among them Jimi Hendrix and Eric Clapton. Buddy Guy was inducted into the Rock and Roll Hall of Fame in 2005.

Haley, Bill (1925–1981). One of the earliest **rockabilly** artists and originally a mild-mannered country musician, William John Clifton Haley Jr. changed American **popular music** in the '50s with his landmark **rock and roll** recording of **"(We're Gonna) Rock Around the Clock,"** the first rock and roll record to hit No. 1 on the pop charts (in 1955, and marked the beginning of the rock era). When this innovative bandleader and his group, the Comets, merged **R&B** music with the country sound, they laid the foundation not only for rock and roll but also for rockabilly. This Father of Rock and Roll and 1987 Rock and Roll Hall of Famer and the Comets made their presence known throughout the decade with such hits as **"Shake, Rattle and Roll,"** "Dim, Dim the Lights (I Want Some Atmosphere)," "Burn That Candle," "Razzle-Dazzle," "See You Later, Alligator," and "R-O-C-K." Though he predated **Elvis Presley** and achieved the first rockabilly success, Haley never stole the limelight from the King; instead, he gave audiences a smoother sound, and he and the Comets offered a tamer stage show. Thus they remained a favorite of those who could not handle the wildness of Presley and others.

Harris, Wynonie (1913–1969). An architect of **rock and roll** whose stage act and songs were very suggestive, this prominent **R&B** shouter known as Mr. Blues offered exciting vocals, sharp stage moves, and handsome looks that made him **Big Joe Turner**'s most serious rival in the late 1940s and early 1950s. He regularly toured with package shows during the early 1950s and staged battles of the blues with Turner, **Roy Brown**, and others. Harris recordings were powerful examples of R&B's sexual suggestiveness. **Elvis Presley** later copied his risqué stage moves. Harris made many successful R&B records, centering on alcohol and sex, that helped pave the way for numerous rock artists. He had two No. 1 R&B hits, "Good Rockin' Tonight" (1948) and "All She Wants to Do Is Rock" (1949).

Hazlewood, Lee (b. 1929). This Phoenix, Arizona, songwriter, producer, and **disc jockey** who mixed country music and the blues, used local singers and musicians to perform his music. With rhythmic riffs and echo devices, he created songs with appealing lyrics; his greatest '50s successes were instrumental recordings of **Duane Eddy**. In the '60s he produced records for (and performed with) singer Nancy Sinatra.

"Heartbreak Hotel" (1956). This recording by **Elvis Presley** was his first release on **RCA-Victor** and his first No. 1 hit; it remained at the top of *Billboard*'s charts for eight weeks. Sung in Presley's new deeper and desperate-sounding voice, in a sexual, melodramatic style complete with reverberation, the song's lyrics spoke directly to teenagers who were feeling lonely and desperate in their quest for independence from parents and society in general. The record's sales quickly spread from the country to the **pop** and then the **R&B** market, proving that **rock and roll** could appeal simultaneously to audiences of all three styles of music.

Henry, Clarence "Frogman" (b. 1937). This native of Algiers, Louisiana, was a **New Orleans sound R&B** singer-pianist-songwriter who had a handful of popular crossover hits. Among them was his 1956 "Ain't Got No Home," which featured his froggy voice and brought him his nickname.

Herald/Ember Records. Al Silver formed this **indie** in New York City in 1952 by merging his Herald label with Jack Angel's Ember, a vocal group specialty label. Herald/Ember recorded some of the most admired **doo-wop** ensembles, many of them one-hit wonders: the Nutmegs ("Story Untold"), the Five Satins ("In the Still of the Nite"), the Turbans ("When You Dance"), the Mellokings ("Tonite, Tonite"), and the Silhouettes ("Get a Job").

Holly, Buddy (1936–1959). Born Charles Hardin Holley in Lubbock, Texas, this 1986 Rock and Roll Hall of Famer had a profound influence on **rock and roll**'s development. This seminal singer-songwriter integrated country and **R&B** elements to produce brilliant **rockabilly** music; popularized the standard rock and roll band of two guitars, bass, and drums; and was one of the first to use advanced studio techniques. His innocent singing style, complete with falsetto voice and trademark hiccups, was a major influence on such later artists as Bob Dylan and Paul McCartney. With his group, the Crickets, he recorded a catalogue of rock and roll classics, most of them featuring his innovative guitar solos: "Not Fade Away," "Rave On," **"That'll Be the Day,"** "Peggy Sue," and "Oh Boy!" No other founding father of rock and roll had a greater influence than Holly on the '60s British Invasion. Both the Hollies and the Beatles derived their names from Holly's Crickets; and the Rolling Stones' first major British hit was a cover of his "Not Fade Away." This gifted pioneer was one of the first white rock and roll musicians to write almost all of his own material, the first rock and roll singer to double track his voice and guitar in recording, and the first to use strings on a rock and roll record. With his thick-rimmed glasses and clean-cut image, he aroused hysteria among teenagers with his many love songs, without drawing the disapproval of their parents. His career was cut short when he, **Ritchie Valens**, and the **Big Bopper** perished in a February 3, 1959, plane crash while performing on the Winter Dance Party tour of the Midwest. Holly was immortalized in Don McLean's 1971 No. 1 hit, "American Pie," which labeled that winter day as "the day the music died." Today, Holly remains an enduring icon, and his songs continue to be recorded.

Hooker, John Lee (1917–2001). One of the great links between the blues and **rock and roll**, this legendary bluesman is known as the Father of the Boogie for his trademark sound—intense, one-chord guitar rhythm patterns and the rhythmic stomping of his feet. Born in Clarksdale, Mississippi, in 1943 he moved to Detroit. There this blues legend helped define post–World War II electric blues and was an enormous influence on many British and American blues and rock musicians, among them the Animals, the Rolling Stones, Canned Heat, Jimi Hendrix, John Mayall and the Bluesbreakers, Fleetwood Mac, Johnny Winter, George Thorogood, Bonnie Raitt, and Bruce Springsteen. Hooker began his recording career in 1948 with the No. 1 **R&B** hit "Boogie Chillen" (topped the charts in early 1949), followed by "Crawlin' Kingsnake" and "I'm in the Mood" (1951 No. 1 R&B hit). Hooker recorded extensively between 1949 and 1952, quite often under a number of pseudonyms to escape contractual obligations. The Motor City's most popular blues star, John Lee Hooker was inducted into the Rock and Roll Hall of Fame in 1991.

"Hound Dog" (1953). Written by **Leiber and Stoller** for **Big Mama Thornton**, who recorded it on Peacock Records, this song became one of the seminal records in **rock and roll** history. One of her most successful '50s hits on the **R&B** charts, it was the No. 1 song for seven weeks. However, it never made it onto the **pop** charts, as did **Elvis Presley**'s hit cover version of the song three years later, which topped the charts for eleven weeks and became one of the biggest hits of the rock era. (See also **Duke/Peacock Records**.)

Howlin' Wolf (1910–1976). Born Chester Arthur Burnett in West Point, Mississippi, this most electrifying performer in modern blues history helped shape **rock and roll** with his influential blues. Discovered by **Ike Turner** in West Memphis, Arkansas, the Wolf recorded "Moanin' at Midnight" and "How Many More Years" for **Sam Phillips** before moving to Chicago and making further recordings, such as "Spoonful," "Little Red Rooster," "Back Door Man," and "Superstitious." Though not known for his composition skills, this legendary blues singer-guitarist wrote some of his own songs, including "Smokestack Lightning" and "Killing Floor." A 1991 Rock and Roll Hall of Famer, the Wolf left his mark on the music world by having injected power and frustration into the blues with his wild performances, complete with whooping, howling, moaning, and groaning, in addition to his wild stage theatrics.

Imperial Records. In 1947, Lew Chudd founded this Los Angeles **indie**, which was active in New Orleans, with producer **Dave Bartholomew**. The firm recorded **Fats Domino ("Ain't That a Shame")**, and for several years achieved enormous success with his incredible string of '50s Top 10 hits. Other recording artists included the Spiders ("I Didn't Want to Do It"), **Smiley Lewis** ("I Hear You Knocking"), and **Ricky Nelson** ("Poor Little Fool"), who served as a soft rock alternative to **Elvis Presley**. Domino's and Nelson's hits fueled the company until it was taken over by **Liberty Records** in 1963.

Independent Record Labels. See Indies.

Indies. Referred to in the music industry as "indies," small, independent record labels recorded the majority of the best and most successful **rock and roll** records during the '50s. These small companies included **Aladdin, Atlantic, Apollo, Chess, Duke/Peacock, King**, Federal, **Imperial, Herald/Ember, Jubilee, Modern, Rama, Savoy, Sun**, and **Vee Jay**. By 1954's end, indies had nearly total control of the **R&B** market, with twenty-three of the Top 30 hits that year. Indies' overwhelming success made the **majors** (large companies) feel threatened by rock and roll, since most rock artists recorded for indies.

The Ink Spots. One of the first popular African American vocal groups, this highly influential ensemble, formed in the '20s in Indianapolis, Indiana, performed sentimental ballads in a unique and brilliant close harmonic style. During the '40s, their improvised vocal harmonies and simulated vocal wind instruments provided the blueprint for '50s **doo-wop** groups and influenced many black vocal groups, including the **Orioles** and the Ravens, and such major artists as the Impressions' Jerry Butler and the **Drifters' Clyde McPhatter.** These 1989 Rock and Roll Hall of Famers, who popularized the practice of using two leads and engaged in talking bridge solos in vocal ballads, were one of the first groups to break racial barriers by performing at previously all-white Southern venues.

Instrumentals. See **Rock Instrumentals**.

"It's Too Soon to Know" (1948). Composed by Deborah Chessler, who discovered **the Orioles** and became their manager, this No. 1 **R&B** hit was the first recording of this important R&B vocal group. Recorded on the It's a Natural label and reissued on **Jubilee**, it has been cited as the first **rock and roll** song by some music historians.

Jackson, Cordell (b. 1923). Born Cordell Miller in Pontotoc, Mississippi, this female **rockabilly** artist began performing with her father's band, the Pontotoc Ridge Runners. While living in Memphis, she composed songs and founded Moon Records (1956). Her '50s recordings included "Rock and Roll Christmas," "Beboppers Christmas," "High School Sweater," and "Football Widow." This guitarist, engineer, publisher, and promoter proved that women not only could **rock and roll**, but also could succeed in all spheres of the music business.

Jackson, Mahalia (1911–1972). Dubbed the Queen of Gospel Music and considered the greatest gospel singer of all time, this native of New Orleans who moved to Chicago absorbed the sounds of blues singers Ma Rainey and **Bessie Smith**, as is evident in her numerous hits, including "How I Got Over" and "Move On Up a Little Higher." These black gospel songs used call-and-response interactions of organ accompaniment and background choir, blueslike vocal qualities, and expressive melismas—techniques that profoundly influenced **rock and roll** music. Inducted into the Rock and Roll Hall of Fame in 1997, Mahalia Jackson greatly influenced such later rockers as Aretha Franklin.

Jackson, Wanda (b. 1937). Called the Queen of **Rockabilly**, this very gifted rockabilly artist and composer was born in Maud, Oklahoma. She toured with **Elvis Presley** and enjoyed a lengthy career thanks to her strong voice, dynamic stage presence, and aggressive repertoire (songs with lyrics that displayed the strength of a woman). Her recordings included "Hot Dog! That Made Him Mad," "Fujiyama Mama," "Mean, Mean Man," "Cool Love," "Right or Wrong," and "In the Middle of a Heartache," as well as a cover of "Let's Have a Party." With her unique voice and dynamic stage presence, Jackson broke barriers that had previously prevented women musicians from performing as successfully as their male counterparts. In the mid-1950s, when women were not common in **rock and roll**, she proved to the world that women could rock.

James, Elmore (1918–1963). Born Elmore Brooks in Richland, Mississippi, and considered to be the most important and influential slide guitar stylist of the postwar era, this disciple of **Robert Johnson** made his biggest mark on the blues with his successful 1952 recording, "Dust My Broom," his version of Robert Johnson's tune, "I Believe I'll Dust My Broom." James, a 1992 Rock and Roll Hall of Famer, bridged the gap between urban Chicago and rural Delta blues and influenced many musicians, from **B. B. King** and Eric Clapton to **Jimmy Reed** and Fleetwood Mac.

James, Etta (b. 1938). Born Jamesetta Hawkins in Los Angeles and nicknamed Miss Peaches, this 1993 Rock and Roll Hall of Famer recorded and co-wrote the 1955 No. 1 **R&B** hit and reaction song "Roll with Me Henry" (changed to the less suggestive "The Wallflower") to **Hank Ballard** and the Midnighters' 1954 hit, "Work with Me Annie." She enjoyed further success with R&B hits "Good Rockin' Daddy" and "All I Could Do Was Cry," and continued with many others throughout the '60s, including her career-defining "At Last." This powerful, emotionally expressive vocalist who helped lay the foundation for **rock and roll** overcame heroin addiction and has remained a popular concert performer.

Jan & Dean. See **Surf Rock**.

J&M Studio. See **Matassa, Cosimo**. (See also **New Orleans Sound**.)

"Johnny B. Goode" (1958). Composed and recorded by **Chuck Berry** on **Chess Records**, this classic that became one of the first anthems of **rock and roll** contained some of the first trademark rock guitar licks. A highly influential song, its famous guitar-solo introduction has been one of the most copied riffs in rock and roll history, and a staple of rock guitarists' repertoires.

Johnson, Robert (1911–1938). From Hazelhurst, Mississippi, this legendary bluesman, perhaps the most celebrated and mythic figure in Delta blues, is considered by most blues scholars and critics to be a musical genius who paved the path for other blues musicians. His style infiltrated modern blues and **rock** music. A virtuoso guitarist whose stunning technique was due in part to his extremely large hands, Johnson developed a unique finger-style approach to guitar playing. Legend has it that he made a pact with the Devil at the crossroads in order to become a better guitar player, exchanging his soul for his guitar virtuosity. Whatever is the case, Johnson's skills as both a guitarist and a blues singer-songwriter had a profound effect on many blues and rock musicians, including **Jimmy Reed, Muddy Waters, Elmore James, B. B. King,** Eric Clapton, Keith Richards, Jimi Hendrix, Stevie Ray Vaughan, and hundreds of others. He recorded twenty-nine tracks in 1936–1937, including "Cross Road

Blues," "I Believe I'll Dust My Broom," "Sweet Home Chicago," "Walkin' Blues," "Hell Hound on My Trail," and "Me and the Devil Blues." Inducted into the Rock and Roll Hall of Fame in 1986, Johnson recorded blues standards that have been covered by many rockers, including the Rolling Stones, Led Zeppelin, Cream, Eric Clapton, Steve Miller, and Cassandra Wilson.

Jordan, Louis (1908–1975). From Brinkley, Arkansas, this important **R&B** saxophonist, singer, and bandleader pioneered jump blues in the late 1940s. His stage personality was so engaging that his records were as popular with whites as they were with African Americans, and he sold millions of records. From 1941 to 1952, he reigned as King of Jukeboxes through his series of catchy, boogie-woogie-influenced hits with his band, the Tympany Five, including "I'm Gonna Move to the Outskirts of Town," "Five Guys Named Moe," "Choo Choo Ch'Boogie," "Saturday Night Fish Fry," "Let the Good Times Roll," "Is You Is, or Is You Ain't (Ma Baby)?" and "Caldonia." Instrumental in the transition of big band swing and early R&B to the '50s **rock and roll** sound of **Little Richard** and others, this 1987 Rock and Roll Hall of Famer inspired many future musicians, from **B. B. King** to **Chuck Berry**.

Jubilee Records. Formed in 1948 by Jerry Blaine, this **indie** and its subsidiary, Josie, recorded Bobby Freeman ("Do You Want to Dance"), the instrumental group the Royaltones ("Poor Boy"), and the vocal groups the **Orioles** ("Tell Me So"), the Four Tunes ("Marie"), and the Cadillacs ("Speedoo"). One of the first indies to reach a white audience with a black vocal group, Jubilee had its No. 1 hit by the Orioles, "Crying in the Chapel," cross over to the **pop** charts in 1953.

Jump Blues. See **Rhythm and Blues**.

Justis, Bill (1926–1982). This session saxophonist, arranger, and producer from Birmingham, Alabama, was the studio music director at **Sun Records** in Memphis. Featuring the composer on saxophone with guitarist Sid Manker, Justis's instrumental, "Raunchy," was a No. 1 **R&B** and No. 2 **pop** hit in 1957. (See also **Rock Instrumentals**.)

King, B. B. (b. 1925). Born Riley B. King near Indianola, Mississippi, this bluesman became the blues' most successful concert artist and ambassador, blending Delta blues, jazz, gospel, **rock**, and **pop music**. With a strong passion for the music, he elevated the blues guitar solo to an art form with his exquisite use of vibrato and pitch bending, mixed with eloquent treatment of solo passages. King brought the blues out of juke joints, clubs, and roadhouses, and earned it great respect by performing in concert halls and the world's most prestigious venues. Known in Memphis as the Beale Street Blues Boy (later shortened to B. B.), he has had an active performance career consisting of hundreds of blues performances every year since the 1950s. King's '50s recordings included the **R&B** No. 1's "Three O'Clock Blues," "You Know I Love You,"

"Please Love Me," and "You Upset Me Baby." A 1987 Rock and Roll Hall of Famer, King pioneered vibrato and note-bending techniques (used today by lead guitar players) on his beloved guitar, known as Lucille. He has had a more profound effect on rock guitarists than any other bluesman, having influenced such rockers as Eric Clapton, Jeff Beck, Jimmy Page, Johnny Winter, and Stevie Ray Vaughan. Since the '60s, when rock groups acknowledged King's influence, his audience has grown even larger, encompassing rock and roll fans. He has recorded with and performed alongside many rock and roll artists and groups, including the Rolling Stones, Stevie Wonder, the Marshall Tucker Band, and U2, all the while spreading rock and roll's most important root, the blues, throughout America and overseas.

King, Ben E. (b. 1938). Born Benjamin Nelson in Henderson, North Carolina, and raised in Harlem, New York, in 1957 this singer joined the Five Crowns (who became the new **Drifters** in 1958). He sang lead for the Drifters on such tunes as **"There Goes My Baby"** and "Save the Last Dance for Me." In 1960 he went solo with such classics as "Spanish Harlem" and the No. 1 "Stand by Me." As a member of the Drifters, Ben E. King was inducted into the Rock and Roll Hall of Fame in 1988.

King Curtis (1934–1971). Saxophonist Curtis Ousley, a favorite **R&B** session soloist and bandleader from Fort Worth, Texas, became famous for brief instrumental interludes in recordings, such as the **Coasters'** 1957 hit, "Yakety Yak." He backed well over 100 musicians, including the **Shirelles**, Wilson Pickett, Sam and Dave, Eric Clapton, and the Allman Brothers. King Curtis was inducted into the Rock and Roll Hall of Fame in 2000.

King Records. Sydney Nathan, a 1997 Rock and Roll Hall of Famer, formed this highly successful **indie** in Cincinnati in 1945. With its subsidiaries DeLuxe, Federal, and Queen, King produced country music and **R&B** recordings while simultaneously laying the groundwork for **rock and roll**. Highly innovative in the '50s, with R&B singers recording versions of country songs and introducing **novelty songs** in the new rock and roll style, these labels featured R&B instrumentalists Bill Doggett ("Honky Tonk [Parts 1 & 2]") and Earl Bostic ("Flamingo"), and many R&B singers including **Wynonie Harris** ("All She Wants to Do Is Rock"), Bullmoose Jackson ("I Can't Go on Without You"), and Eddie "Cleanhead" Vinson ("Somebody Done Stole My Cherry Red"). The only indies with country singers on their rosters, these labels made memorable country recordings in addition to those of numerous vocal groups, including the **Platters** (early recordings) and the **Dominoes** (**"Sixty Minute Man"**). King's success raised the label from regional status to national attention, beginning with **Hank Ballard** and the Midnighters ("Work with Me Annie") and continuing with **James Brown** ("Try Me").

The Kingston Trio. Formed in 1957 in San Francisco, this folk group influenced by **Woody Guthrie** and the Weavers had the 1958 No. 1 "Tom Dooley."

Precursors of the '60s folk music scene, this talented ensemble performed traditional American and English folk songs. (See also **Seeger, Pete.**)

"La Bamba" (1958). A vigorous arrangement of an old Mexican wedding song, this **Ritchie Valens** recording on the Del-Fi label was a forerunner of simple **rock and roll** sounds and the subgenres garage rock and punk rock. With his rock arrangement of this folk song, complete with an exuberant guitar solo, Valens created Latino rock. The record's flip side was the hit "Donna," and this double-sided record is often referred to as one of the greatest '50s rock and roll singles.

Lead Belly (c. 1885–1949). Also referred to as Leadbelly, this black folk singer born Huddie Ledbetter in Shiloh, Louisiana, played folk ballads, dance tunes, spirituals, **pop** songs, prison songs, and the blues. Known as the King of the Twelve-String Guitar for his rhythmic guitar playing, he had a very powerful voice and extensive repertoire of black folk songs. He lived the life of a bluesman, traveling the South, performing both alone and with others (most notably Blind Lemon Jefferson). His greatest contribution to American music was in folk music: such classics as "Goodnight Irene," "Rock Island Line," "The Midnight Special," and "Cotton Fields." Inducted into the Rock and Roll Hall of Fame in 1988, Lead Belly was a great influence on generations of musicians—from such other folk musicians as **Woody Guthrie** to **rock and roll** musicians **Little Richard**, Led Zeppelin, John Mellencamp, and Kurt Cobain.

Lee, Brenda (b. 1944). This 2002 Rock and Roll Hall of Famer was born Brenda Mae Tarpley in Lithonia, Georgia. A **rockabilly** performer known as Little Miss Dynamite, she was a very successful late 1950s **teen idol**, able to sing rockabilly, country music, and **pop** standards equally well. Her first big hit, "Sweet Nothin's," was followed by No. 1's "I'm Sorry" and "I Want to Be Wanted." In 1958, she recorded "Rockin' Around the Christmas Tree," which became an international hit that is still seasonally on the charts.

Lee, Leonard. See **Shirley & Lee.**

Leiber and Stoller. One of the first and finest of the songwriter-producer teams consisted of lyricist Jerry Leiber (b. 1933), raised near Baltimore's black ghetto, and composer Mike Stoller (b. 1933), who hailed from Queens, New York. This pioneering songwriting team wrote some of the most vigorous, enduring **rock and roll** songs, including **"Hound Dog" (Big Mama Thornton** and **Elvis Presley**); "Jailhouse Rock" and "Treat Me Nice" (Elvis Presley); "Love Potion No. 9" (the Clovers); "Searchin'" and "Yakety Yak" (and most other major hits by the **Coasters**); "Kansas City" (Wilbert Harrison, a 1959 No. 1 **pop** and **R&B** hit that had cover versions by artists as diverse as **Little Richard**, Peggy Lee, and the Beatles); "On Broadway" (the **Drifters**); "Ruby Baby" (**Dion**); and "Stand by Me" (**Ben E. King**, one of the duo's most recorded compositions). In 1956, **Atlantic Records** signed the team as independent producers—the first production deal of this sort in rock history. Propelling the early popularity of rock and roll with their astounding catalogue of '50s and early '60s well-crafted songs and professional recordings, they created the standard for **novelty doo-wop** songs and expanded rock and roll orchestration and recording techniques. Jerry Leiber and Mike Stoller were inducted into the Rock and Roll Hall of Fame in 1987.

Leiber, Jerry. See Leiber and Stoller.

Lewis, Jerry Lee (b. 1935). One of the four main **rockabilly** artists to find a home at **Sam Phillips's Sun Records**, this singer and pianist had an intuitive flair whose creativity and impact reached far beyond his few hits that reached the general public. His effortless command of music was presented with a tremendous amount of energy in stunning performances, and he justly deserved his nickname, the Killer, for his treatment of the piano and his audience. This defiant and untiring music icon has lived a life marked by controversy, including his 1957 marriage to his thirteen-year-old cousin, Myra Gale Brown, the daughter of his bass player and cousin, J. W. Brown. The marriage resulted in a scandal and the ruin of his career. Inspired by **Elvis Presley** and, like him and **Bill Haley**, Lewis recorded covers of blues songs, transforming others' songs into unrestrained **rock and roll**. He merged various styles of roots musics, including western swing, boogie-woogie, **R&B**, and Delta blues—which, combined with his brash temperament, made him a natural rock and roller, the ultimate rebel. Inducted into the Rock and Roll Hall of Fame in 1986, Lewis had a string of explosive '50s hits that included **"Whole Lot of Shakin' Going On,"** "Great Balls of Fire," "Breathless," and "High School Confidential."

Lewis, Smiley (1920–1966). Born Overton Amos Lemons in Union, Louisiana, this New Orleans **R&B** singer was best known for his 1955 "I Hear You Knocking," featuring **Huey "Piano" Smith** on piano, and 1952's "The Bells Are Ringing." Though Lewis achieved success on the R&B charts, he never crossed over to the **pop** charts. Those who covered his songs, including **Elvis Presley** and **Fats Domino**, achieved pop hits.

Liberty Records. Founded in Hollywood in 1955 with Al Bennett as vice president, this **indie** featured David Seville and the Chipmunks ("Witch Doctor"), **Bobby Vee** ("Suzie Baby"), Billy Ward and the **Dominoes** ("Star Dust"), and **Eddie Cochran ("Summertime Blues")**, who enabled the label to jump into the **rockabilly** field in 1956. Bennett distributed for other indies, including Dolton (formerly Dolphin) and Demon, and purchased **Imperial Records** from Lew Chudd in 1963.

Little Esther. See Phillips, Esther.

Little Richard (b. 1932). Born Richard Wayne Penniman in Macon, Georgia, this singer, songwriter, and pianist who came from, and was greatly influenced by, the gospel music tradition was one of the key figures in the transition from **R&B** to **rock and roll**. Along with **Fats Domino, Chuck Berry, Elvis Presley,** and **Buddy Holly,** he defined rock and roll in the '50s. He lived the rebellious spirit of rock and roll with an outrageous appearance and frantic performance style; along with his white counterpart, **Jerry Lee Lewis,** and blues singer Screamin' Jay Hawkins, Little Richard established rock musicians as aggressive extroverts engaging in outrageous performance behavior. His string of '50s classics, including risqué recordings, characteristically consisted of the New Orleans boogie-woogie bass over which pounding piano chords and nonsense syllables emanated in disconnected phrases: **"Tutti Frutti,"** "Long Tall Sally," "Rip It Up," "Lucille," "Jenny, Jenny," "Keep a Knockin'," "Send Me Some Lovin'," and "Good Golly, Miss Molly." With the backing of an R&B combo, his recordings often displayed fast tempos, classic twelve-bar blues formats, piano glissandos, growling saxophones, forceful backbeats with pulsing drums, and rough, wild vocals in falsetto. Inducted into the Rock and Roll Hall of Fame in 1986, Little Richard had considerable influence on his contemporaries; Elvis Presley imitated his songs, and Jerry Lee Lewis copied not only his music but also his eccentric stage mannerisms. His extrovert and energetic style made him one of the most successful performers of the rock and roll era, and his fervent music influenced subsequent black artists, including Otis Redding, **James Brown,** Wilson Pickett, and Aretha Franklin.

Lorenz, George "Hound Dog" (1920–1972). Hailing from Buffalo, New York, Lorenz was one of the most important pioneering **disc jockey**s; he presided over the Northeast and Canada, at radio stations including Buffalo's WKBW, Niagara Falls's WJJL, and Cleveland's WSRS. He hosted **rock and roll** shows at Memorial Auditorium in downtown Buffalo with his Cleveland friend, **Alan Freed,** featuring the top rock and roll performers of the day. An innovative deejay whose actions pushed rock and roll radio to its heights, he is considered the first to "rock the pot" (a phrase that refers to turning the volume controls up and down with the beat of the music), and use instrumentals so he could speak and read commercials on the air while records were spinning. A protector of black artists, he fought to keep their music on the air and understood their music; in 1958, when WKBW adopted the **Top 40** format, he left in order to maintain his on-air freedom and helped pioneer the FM market with **R&B** and rock and roll music. In 1965, he purchased Buffalo station WBLK-FM, the only full-time black music station outside of New York City in New York State. His influence on listeners and disc jockeys along the East Coast was enormous; Lorenz is considered by many rock and roll historians to rank with Alan Freed as one of the most influential '50s deejays.

Lymon, Frankie (1942–1968). This lead singer of the Teenagers previously sang in his father's gospel group, the Harlemaires. In 1954 he joined his junior high school friends' vocal quartet, the Premiers, consisting of Herman Santiago, Jimmy Merchant, Joe Negroni, and Sherman Garnes. Renamed the

Teenagers, in late 1955 they recorded **"Why Do Fools Fall in Love,"** a vocal group classic in which Lymon's clear falsetto lead was accompanied by background voices harmonizing lyrics of innocent love. Released in early 1956, it was a tremendous hit, climbing to the top of the **R&B** charts and to No. 6 on the **pop** charts, making Lymon the first black teenage pop star. This song by these 1993 Rock and Roll Hall of Famers remains one standard by which the **doo-wop** style is defined.

Major Record Labels. See **Majors.**

Majors. A handful of large record labels dominated the recording industry in the early 1950s: **RCA-Victor, Columbia, Decca, Capitol, Mercury, MGM,** and **ABC-Paramount.** These labels resisted **rock and roll** as it evolved, thus missing out on the new genre's success except for the recordings of a few rock and rollers (**Bill Haley, Elvis Presley,** and **Lloyd Price**). By 1954, when **indies** had nearly total control of the **R&B** market with twenty-three of the Top 30 hits, the majors engaged in a counterattack that resulted in the cover syndrome—the recording of R&B hits by **pop** artists on the majors' rosters. Late in the decade, the **teen idol** phenomenon was another attempt by the majors to regain control of the recording industry.

"(Mama) He Treats Your Daughter Mean" (1953). Recorded by **Ruth Brown** for **Atlantic Records** with a band led by **Ray Charles,** this recording has been cited as the first **rock and roll** record; it was No. 1 on the **R&B** charts for five weeks. With this song that she often had to perform several times at each concert to satisfy audiences, Brown became a sensation.

Matassa, Cosimo (b. 1926). A crucial figure in the **New Orleans sound,** this owner and chief engineer of the renowned J&M Studio was responsible for the scores of legendary recordings made there. With a simple recording formula (no overdubbing or electronic manipulation), he developed a special sound referred to as the Cosimo Sound: strong drums, heavy bass, light piano, heavy guitar, light horns, and a strong vocal lead, with the guitar, baritone, and tenor doubling the bass line. This sound became known as the New Orleans sound. Numerous **indies** and the best artists from near and far flocked to Matassa's studio in search of the spectacular sound that resulted from a combination of the New Orleans sessionmen, the studio's acoustics, and the simplicity of Matassa's technique. Many of the best records from the late '40s to the early '70s (including **Fats Domino**'s) were engineered by Matassa and made under his tutelage there.

"Maybellene" (1955). Based on a traditional country tune from the Anglo-Irish folk song "Ida Red," this song was modified by **Chuck Berry** to appeal to the car-loving teens of the '50s. He renamed it "Maybellene" and recorded it on **Chess Records.** The first of his string of hits from the 1950s, this No. 1 **R&B** (and No. 5 **pop**) hit helped lay the groundwork for the new

rock and roll sound, and allowed Berry to cross over to the largely white pop charts, a rarity for black artists at that time.

McPhatter, Clyde (1932–1972). Previously a lead singer of many hits for the **Dominoes** and the **Drifters**, upon his discharge from the army this talented singer from Durham, North Carolina, resumed his career as a solo artist with **Atlantic Records** in 1956. He had a number of hits as a soloist, among them the No. 1 **R&B** hits "Treasure of Love" and "A Lover's Question." With his fervent voice and passionate delivery, McPhatter influenced many other singers, including **Jackie Wilson** and Smokey Robinson. McPhatter was inducted into the Rock and Roll Hall of Fame as a solo artist in 1987, and as a member of the Drifters in 1988.

Memphis Recording Service. See Sun Records.

Mercury Records. This **major** label was formed in Chicago in 1946 with Irving Green as president. Its A&R agents included Mitch Miller (1948–1950), Art Talmadge, Arnold Maxin, and Clyde Otis; Shelby Singleton joined the team in the late 1950s. Successful with many covers of **R&B** hits by **pop** artists and groups, Mercury's roster included Georgia Gibbs ("Dance with Me Henry [Wallflower]"), the **Crew-Cuts** ("Earth Angel"), and the Diamonds ("Little Darlin'"). When covers became less acceptable, the label attempted to release true R&B and **rock and roll** records by recording the **Big Bopper** ("Chantilly Lace") and the groups Freddie Bell and the Bellboys ("Giddy-Up-a-Ding-Dong"), the **Penguins** (no major hits with Mercury), and the **Platters** ("My Prayer"). Others recording for Mercury in the '50s included R&B balladeers **Dinah Washington** ("Trouble in Mind"), Sarah Vaughan ("Broken-Hearted Melody"), and Brook Benton ("It's Just a Matter of Time").

Mesner, Eddie. See Aladdin Records.

Mesner, Leo. See Aladdin Records.

Meteor Records. See Modern Records.

MGM Records. MGM Records was formed in Hollywood in 1946 as a division of the film company, with A&R agents Frank Walker and Harry Meyerson; they were replaced by Arnold Maxin and Morty Craft in the mid-'50s. Nashville producer Jim Vienneau and music director Leroy Holmes also worked for the company. This **major** and its subsidiary, Cub Records, recorded country and **pop** artists and groups, including **Hank Williams** ("Your Cheating Heart"), Conway Twitty ("It's Only Make Believe"), Tommy Edwards ("It's All in the Game"), **Connie Francis** ("Who's Sorry Now"), and the Impalas ("Sorry [I Ran All the Way Home]").

Milton Berle Show. Hosted by Milton Berle, this general entertainment television show's featuring of **Elvis Presley** performing **"Hound Dog"** in June 1956 caused a national furor. While performing, at the end of the song Presley engaged in what were then considered horrendous and threatening actions. With outspread arms he fluttered his fingers, dragged the microphone to the floor while staggering to his knees, and circled the mike sensuously while jack-knifing his legs. These movements horrified adults but delighted teenagers, who sought a more expressive behavior than conservative '50s society permitted.

Mister Rock and Roll (1957). This **rock and roll** movie featured **Alan Freed, Chuck Berry, LaVern Baker, Clyde McPhatter, Little Richard**, the **Moonglows**, and **Frankie Lymon** and the Teenagers, among others.

Modern Records. Formed in 1945 in Los Angeles by Jules and Saul Bihari, Modern was a successful mid-1950s **indie** that regularly covered **R&B** hits, attempting to reach the popular market. Producers Joe, Jules, and Saul Bihari recorded many R&B and **rock and roll** artists and groups on the label and its subsidiaries, RPM (formed in 1950), Meteor (formed in 1952; managed by Lester Bihari), and Flair (formed in 1953): Johnny Moore's Three Blazers ("Dragnet Blues"), Roy Hawkins ("Why Do Things Happen to Me"), Lightnin' Hopkins ("Tim Moore's Farm"), **John Lee Hooker** ("Boogie Chillen"), **B. B. King** ("Three O'Clock Blues"), Rosco Gordon ("Booted"), **Elmore James, Etta James** ("The Wallflower"), Jesse Belvin ("Goodnight My Love (Pleasant Dreams)"), the Cadets ("Stranded in the Jungle"), and the Teen Queens ("Eddie My Love"). Modern later concentrated on producing budget albums on its Crown label before the company went bankrupt and Kent took over its catalogue.

Monroe, Bill (1911–1996). A singer, songwriter, and bandleader, William Smith Monroe was a pivotal influence on the sound of bluegrass country music, having combined elements of blues, jazz, gospel, and country music. He performed and recorded over 500 bluegrass songs, giving country music a fresh new sound; many of his original compositions became bluegrass standards, including "Uncle Pen," "Raw Hide," "I Want the Lord to Protect My Soul," and "Blue Moon of Kentucky." During World War II, Monroe added the banjo and sometimes the accordion, jug, and harmonica to his band, the Blue Grass Boys, which consisted of mandolin, guitar, fiddle, and bass. Known as the Father of Bluegrass Music, Monroe was inducted into the Rock and Roll Hall of Fame in 1997. He inspired and set standards for such diverse later musicians as the **Everly Brothers, Elvis Presley**, George Jones, and Jerry Garcia. Monroe gave the mandolin a new role as a lead instrument in country, **pop**, and **rock and roll.**

Monument Records. Formed in 1958 by Fred Foster in Andersonville, Tennessee, this **indie** was nationally distributed by London Records. Besides country **pop** artists Billy Grammer, Boots Randolph, and Charlie McCoy, the label recorded **rockabilly Roy Orbison**'s '60s hits "Only the Lonely (Know How I Feel)," "Running Scared," and "Oh, Pretty Woman."

The Moondog Coronation Ball (1952). Held on March 21, 1952, at Cleveland Arena in Cleveland, Ohio, this landmark event in the birth of **rock**

and roll was intended to be an **R&B** concert starring the **Dominoes**, Paul Williams, and Vanetta Dillard. Organized by **Alan Freed**, Leo Mintz, and Lew Platt, it attracted nearly 20,000 people; the police and fire departments closed down the show after the crowd became rowdy. An event that escalated Freed's popularity, the Ball is cited by many as the first rock and roll concert.

The Moonglows. Formed in 1950 and initially called the Crazy Sounds, this **doo-wop** group known for its exquisite vocal blend consisted of Bobby Lester, Harvey Fuqua, Danny Coggins, and Prentiss Barnes. Their 1954 No. 1 **R&B** song, "Sincerely," was their biggest success and the beginning of a series of superb singles released by **Chess**, including "Most of All," "See Saw," "Over and Over Again," "Please Send Me Someone to Love," and "Ten Commandments of Love." These 2000 Rock and Roll Hall of Famers influenced most later black R&B vocal groups.

Nathan, Sydney. See **King Records.**

Nelson, Ricky (1940–1985). A **rockabilly** sensation and one of the first **teen idols** of the **rock** era, this singer-guitarist, born Eric Hilliard Nelson in Teaneck, New Jersey, was introduced to the world on his family's popular weekly television series, *The Adventures of Ozzie and Harriet*. One of the few non–Southerners to be associated with rockabilly, he developed a softer, more **pop**-oriented style of rockabilly. His band always featured excellent musicians, such as the brilliant guitarist James Burton, a 2001 inductee of the Rock and Roll Hall of Fame, who later played with **Elvis Presley**. Nelson had a remarkable series of classic hits between 1957 and 1963, including "Poor Little Fool," "Travelin' Man," "Be-Bop Baby," "Stood Up," "A Teenager's Romance," and his signature song, "Hello Mary Lou." With an instinctive feel for the country side of rockabilly, Nelson created records that were exceptionally tough, exciting, and mostly free of the orchestration and studio gimmicks of other late-'50s teen idols. Ricky Nelson was inducted into the Rock and Roll Hall of Fame in 1987.

New Orleans Sound. This early **rock and roll** subgenre combined the city's distinctive music traditions, the result of a rich diversity of ethnic groups and cultures. In the '40s, the tradition of **rhythm and blues** in the city caused R&B record label personnel to scout for new talent and to record there. Through the efforts of such '50s producers, bandleaders, and engineers as **Dave Bartholomew, Paul Gayten**, and **Cosimo Matassa**, the distinctive New Orleans rock and roll sound was recorded and preserved at Matassa's famous J&M Studio. During the '50s, many talented artists were leading practitioners of this distinctive local music sound that was characterized by its swinging shuffle beat and blending of Dixieland jazz and jump blues. Among those who crafted these sounds were **Professor Longhair, Huey "Piano" Smith, Guitar Slim, Shirley & Lee, Lloyd Price, Fats Domino**, and **Little Richard**.

Novelty Songs. The late 1950s novelty craze brought forth some of the most popular '50s records that were a staple of the **pop music** industry. They sported simple messages and were usually comic, with irresistible phrases and nonsense syllables. Popular '50s novelties included David Seville's "Witch Doctor" and "The Chipmunk Song," Sheb Wooley's "The Purple People Eater," and the **Big Bopper**'s "Purple People Eater Meets Witch Doctor." Vocal groups contributed to the craze with such hits as the Cadets' "Stranded in the Jungle," the Silhouettes' "Get a Job," Little Anthony and the Imperials' "Shimmy, Shimmy, Ko-Ko-Bop," and the Royal Teens' "Short Shorts." Among the many **doo-wop** groups who sang these songs, the **Coasters** left their mark with novelties that spoke to teens, including "Yakety Yak," "Charlie Brown," "Poison Ivy," and "Along Came Jones."

OKeh Records. See **Columbia Records**.

"Only You (and You Alone)" (1955). Written by manager Buck Ram and recorded by the **Platters** on **Mercury Records**, this piece was the first of the group's string of huge '50s hits. The recording was a milestone of the **doo-wop** sound and a No. 1 **R&B** (and No. 5 **pop**) hit, establishing this highly influential, enormously popular, and most successful '50s vocal group.

Orbison, Roy (1936–1988). Originally a **Sun Records rockabilly** artist, Orbison was well known for his original music compositions. He wrote songs that have never gone out of style and have been covered by such artists as Glen Campbell, Don McLean, Linda Ronstadt, and Van Halen. Born in Vernon, Texas, this guitarist who boasted an operatic tenor voice with an extremely versatile range, recorded his first hit, "Ooby Dooby," in 1956, followed by "Only the Lonely" and "Oh, Pretty Woman." In the late 1980s, along with Bob Dylan, George Harrison, Tom Petty, and Jeff Lynne, Orbison became a member of the extremely successful Traveling Wilburys. He inspired many rock and rollers through the years, including the Beatles' and Bruce Springsteen. Roy Orbison was inducted into the Rock and Roll Hall of Fame in 1987.

The Orioles. Originally formed in Baltimore in 1946 as the Vibranaires, this group took their name from the Maryland state bird and, along with the Ravens, is considered one of the cornerstones of **R&B**. Various incarnations of this pioneering **doo-wop** group appeared over the years; original members included George Nelson, Sonny Til, Alexander Sharp, and Johnny Reed. With their light tenor lead and unique vocal styling, in 1948 they charted what many record collectors consider to be the first R&B vocal group harmony recording, **"It's Too Soon to Know."** Often cited as the first **rock and roll** record, it paved the way for the rise of the R&B vocal group. An influence on many other vocal groups, these 1995 Rock and Roll Hall of Famers achieved their greatest success with their 1953 landmark record, "Crying in the Chapel." One of the first recordings by African American artists to be successful on the **pop** charts, this crossover hit signaled the coming explosion of R&B music gracing the pop charts.

Otis, Johnny (b. 1921). Born John Veliotes in Vallejo, California, this talent scout, songwriter, producer, and bandleader was a key figure in the rise of **R&B** and **rock and roll** in the '50s. Inducted into the Rock and Roll Hall of Fame in 1994, the multitalented Otis scouted for the **King** and Federal labels and discovered the Midnighters (then known as the Royals). Numerous recordings were made under Otis's name, including those by **Little Esther, Big Mama Thornton, Etta James**, and the Robins-turned-**Coasters**.

Parker, Colonel Thomas A. (1909–1997). This Nashville-based country music promoter and manager of Eddie Arnold and Hank Snow practically adopted **Elvis Presley** when he became the King of Rock and Roll's manager. Born Andreas Cornelis van Kuijk in Holland, Parker devoted himself to Presley, planning and making possible the young artist's commercial life by moving him in and out of various entertainment media and from **rock and roll** to the army and several movies, gaining him national status. The Parker-Presley relationship helped establish the manager/agent role in the music industry.

Paul, Les (b. 1915). Born Lester Polfus in Waukesha, Wisconsin, this musician and inventor helped define **rock and roll** and refine the sound technology by creating the first solid-body electric guitar and by introducing modern recording techniques, such as close microphone positioning, electronic echo, and studio multitracking. He had a long, successful **pop**-jazz career and played with many jazz greats, including **Louis Armstrong**, Art Tatum, and **Charlie Christian**, and performed with Bing Crosby, Rudy Vallee, Johnny Mercer, and many more. After he married singer Mary Ford, they recorded numerous hits together that are among the earliest multitrack pop songs, including "How High the Moon" and "Vaya con Dios." This 1988 Rock and Roll Hall of Famer also recorded such instrumental hits as "Nola," "Whispering," "Tiger Rag," and "Meet Mister Callaghan."

Payola Investigation (1959–1960). Perhaps the greatest attack on **rock and roll**, this investigation of the music industry resulted from an attempt by ASCAP (the American Society of Composers, Authors, and Publishers) to rid the music industry of its rival BMI (Broadcast Music, Incorporated). Rock and roll **disc jockeys** became the target of a House of Representatives committee headed by Oren Harris of Arkansas that scrutinized many deejays accused of playing records for pay. Despite the fact that "play for pay" had been an accepted practice in the music industry for decades, this caused the downfall of disc jockeys. **Alan Freed** was among the many deejays ruined by the proceedings, and rock and roll was greatly affected by the investigation. Ironically, neither BMI nor rock and roll music disappeared after the controversy.

Peacock Records. See Duke/Peacock Records.

The Penguins. Formed in Los Angeles in 1954, this **doo-wop** group originally consisted of Cleveland Duncan, Dexter Tisby, Curtis Williams, and Bruce

Tate. That year they recorded their one big hit, the **R&B** No. 1 "Earth Angel" (a No. 8 **pop** hit), which remains one of the most popular oldies, if not the absolute all-time favorite.

Perkins, Carl (1932–1998). Born into a sharecropping family in Tiptonville, Tennessee, this **rock and roll** pioneer was one of the principal recording artists at **Sun Records** in the '50s. An exceptionally talented composer and gifted guitarist, he wrote his own songs, mixing the blues, **pop**, and country roots styles; his recordings contained the urgent sound of **R&B** music. With such classic compositions and recordings as **"Blue Suede Shoes,"** "Put Your Cat Clothes On," "Dixie Fried," "Matchbox," and "Boppin' the Blues," this **rockabilly** made a major contribution to the foundation of rock and roll. Known as the signature song of the rockabilly subgenre, his smash hit, "Blue Suede Shoes," launched his career and made Perkins the first country artist to reach the national R&B charts; despite writing songs that were better than this big hit, he never could recapture the success of it. Though he never attained **Elvis Presley**'s stardom, Perkins created the new rockabilly sound along with Presley and became known more for songwriting than for performing. Perkins was a major influence on the Beatles' (especially guitarist George Harrison), Paul Simon, Tom Petty, Willie Nelson, and Brian Setzer. Carl Perkins was inducted into the Rock and Roll Hall of Fame in 1987.

Petty, Norman (1927–1984). This pioneering manager-producer from Clovis, New Mexico, supported artists all the way to finished recordings. His Norm Petty Trio consisted of himself, his wife, Violet, and Jack Vaughn. At his famed studio, Petty recorded members of the Rhythm Orchids, Buddy Knox ("Party Doll"), and Jimmy Bowen ("I'm Stickin' with You"), and released their recordings on Roulette Records. He also recorded **Buddy Holly** demos.

Phillips, Dewey (1926–1968). Present when **Elvis Presley** entered the **rock and roll** scene and responsible for breaking in his records in the Memphis region, this pioneering **disc jockey** played **R&B** for his primarily black audience on Memphis radio station WHBQ. The wild and crazy Phillips hosted a daily evening show, *Red, Hot & Blue*, on which he played race music. The first disc jockey to air Presley's first single, "That's All Right," on the air after it was recorded by **Sun Records**, Daddy-O (as **B. B. King** called Dewey) served as the test market for many new record releases in the Memphis area. When he played songs on the air, teenagers listened; they not only paid attention to the music but also listened carefully to Phillips ramble between songs as he created their new street lingo.

Phillips, Esther (1935–1984). Born Esther Mae Jones in Galveston, Texas, this great **R&B** vocalist who learned how to sing in church was discovered by **Johnny Otis**. Called Little Esther, she became famous for her 1950 "Double Crossing Blues," recorded with the Johnny Otis Quintette and the Robins. With this recording, she became the youngest female vocalist to achieve a No. 1

record on the R&B charts. She followed with other '50s hits, including No. 1's "Mistrustin' Blues" and "Cupid Boogie," both duets with Mel Walker backed by the Johnny Otis Orchestra.

Phillips International Records. See Sun Records.

Phillips, Sam (1923–2003). This white **disc jockey** and engineer from Florence, Alabama, created history at **Sun Records** with his '50s recordings by **Johnny Cash, Elvis Presley, Jerry Lee Lewis, Carl Perkins,** and many others who gave their finest performances in his studio. Phillips opened the Memphis Recording Service in 1950 and formed his record label, Sun, in 1952; there he initially recorded such black urban blues singers as **Howlin' Wolf, B. B. King,** Little Junior Parker, and **Ike Turner**. Phillips pioneered the **rockabilly** music style at Sun by bringing several music styles together. His label produced more **rock and roll** records than any other of its time; legendary artists and groups made some of the greatest records in the history of rock and roll and set the foundation for rock and roll there. Phillips is credited with having discovered Presley, who helped make Sun Records one of the most significant **indies** in rock history. His ability to reveal artists' emotions in recordings, and the excitement generated by their records, made Phillips one of the most important figures in **popular music**. Sam Phillips was inducted into the Rock and Roll Hall of Fame in 1986.

The Platters. Considered the most successful **rock and roll** vocal group of the '50s, this ensemble was founded in Los Angeles in 1952 by Tony Williams, David Lynch, Alex Hodge, and Herb Reed. After several personnel changes, the addition of Zola Taylor in 1954 resulted in a stabilized lineup. This group created a **pop doo-wop** style that came from the formal balladry of the Mills Brothers and the **Ink Spots**. The Platters were the most popular black group of their time. With their polished and pop-oriented sound, they had the first No. 1 doo-wop song to appear on the pop charts in 1955, "The Great Pretender." In addition, the ensemble released a series of other hallmark hits, including **"Only You (and You Alone),"** "(You've Got) The Magic Touch," "My Prayer," "Twilight Time," and "Smoke Gets in Your Eyes." Their enormously popular recordings displayed Williams's soaring voice as he delivered melodies with great purity and precision, accompanied by crisp, rich harmonies by background voices. With all the classic elements of the doo-wop style, they created a sound proper for white and black teenagers and adults. With a number of landmark records, these 1990 Rock and Roll Hall of Famers outsold all other doo-wop vocal groups and became a global sensation during the second half of the '50s.

"Please, Please, Please" (1956). This early recording by **James Brown,** the Godfather of Soul, and the Famous Flames on the Federal label established what would become Brown's trademark sound and the foundation for **soul music**. Composed by Brown, this piece displayed his characteristic blending of gospel and **R&B** elements, which helped redefine the direction of black music and inspired numerous musicians.

Pomus and Shuman. Born Jerome Solon Felder in Brooklyn, New York, Doc Pomus (1925–1991) and his partner, Mort Shuman (1936–1991), were a successful '50s songwriting team with a highly impressive repertoire. Pomus wrote some of the greatest songs in rock and roll history: "Boogie Woogie Country Girl" (**Big Joe Turner**), "Young Blood" (the **Coasters**; written with **Leiber and Stoller**), "Lonely Avenue" (**Ray Charles**), "Turn Me Loose" (**Fabian**), **"A Teenager in Love"** (**Dion** and the Belmonts), "This Magic Moment" (the **Drifters**), and "Save the Last Dance for Me" (**Ben E. King**). In addition, **Elvis Presley** recorded approximately twenty Pomus originals, including "Viva Las Vegas." In 1958, the Pomus-Shuman team began writing for Don Kirshner and Al Nevins' New York City publishing company, **Aldon Music**. Doc Pomus was inducted into the Rock and Roll Hall of Fame in 1992.

Pomus, Doc. See **Pomus and Shuman**.

Pop Music. The phrase "pop music," short for "popular music," is generally used to describe music that appeals to masses—it is not considered art music, and can be enjoyed and understood by the general public. Quite often, prior to the mid-1950s music of this sort is referred to as pop music, while music from after the 1950s is generally called **rock and roll**. A major root of rock and roll that filled radio airwaves, record stores, and jukeboxes until halfway through the '50s, American popular song was an important predecessor of rock music; it consisted of sentimental ballads, **novelty songs**, and instrumentals, reflecting the tastes of white adults. In the '50s, pop songs by such artists as Bing Crosby, Frank Sinatra, **Nat "King" Cole**, Perry Como, Doris Day, and Debbie Reynolds shared the charts with the new rock and roll songs until the latter's popularity won the general public's taste. The rock idol was the best phenomenon that pop music brought to rock and roll; this significant concept carried over into rock music, as is apparent in the late 1950s and early 1960s with such **teen idols** as Frankie Avalon, Fabian, Bobby Rydell, Elvis Presley, and Bobby Darin.

Popular Music. See **Pop Music**.

Presley, Elvis (1935–1977). Born in East Tupelo, Mississippi, and known as the King of **Rock and Roll**, Presley was, and still is, one of the most popular modern music heroes. He was the first rock and roll idol and virtually invented the sound and demeanor of the rock and roll star. Discovered by **Sam Phillips**, Presley was a trendsetter with his good looks—dark features, greasy black hair, and surly expression. Though he was perceived by the industry as a mere **teen idol**, the influence of this charismatic, impassioned singer was far-reaching. He performed with bassist Bill Black and guitarist Scotty Moore (a 2000 inductee of the Rock and Roll Hall of Fame); Presley's managers were, first, Memphis **disc jockey** Bob Neal and, second, **Colonel Thomas A. Parker**. The King aroused fiery controversies and rose from regional to national music star and Hollywood actor very swiftly, demonstrating a talent that defied category in the mid-1950s. In 1954 he recorded **"That's All Right,"** widely regarded as the first rock and roll record, for **Sun Records**. He switched to **RCA-Victor** in 1956 and had unprecedented success with his recordings, including No. 1's **"Heartbreak Hotel,"** "Don't Be Cruel," **"Hound Dog,"** "All Shook Up," and "Jailhouse Rock." Presley embraced the celebrity brought him by a host of hit records and movies, and for millions of people he embodied the rebel spirit in spite of his personal fears. After his death, he became a mythical figure, and continues to be revered by music fans and to be studied by notable authors including Dave Marsh, Greil Marcus, and Peter Guralnick. Inducted into the Rock and Roll Hall of Fame in 1986, Presley helped define rock and roll music in the '50s.

Price, Lloyd (b. 1933). This exceptionally talented **R&B** musician, bandleader, and songwriter was a major figure in New Orleans **rock and roll**. In 1952, he recorded the No. 1 R&B classic "Lawdy Miss Clawdy," produced by **Dave Bartholomew** and featuring **Fats Domino** on piano, for **Specialty Records**. The recording had a tremendous influence on New Orleans records and helped in the birth of rock and roll; considered by some to be the first rock and roll song, it was widely covered in the '50s and later by such rockers as **Elvis Presley**, the Buckinghams, John Lennon, and Elvis Costello. His other '50s No. 1's, displaying elements of black gospel singing, included "Stagger Lee," "I'm Gonna Get Married," and "Personality." An extraordinary entrepreneur, he was also an executive of record labels and the owner of a New York City nightclub. Price was inducted into the Rock and Roll Hall of Fame in 1998. (See also **New Orleans Sound**.)

Professor Longhair (1918–1980). Born Henry Roeland Byrd in Bogalusa, Louisiana, this artist who recorded at **Cosimo Matassa's** J&M Studio had a profound influence on New Orleans pianists and was one of the most important **R&B** pianists to influence **rock and roll**. He created an idiosyncratic style of music that combined barrelhouse boogie-woogie piano with Caribbean rhythms and parade band music, transforming it into the foundations for a bass-centered R&B. The Professor contributed the solid bass foundation to the **New Orleans sound**, over which the city's musicians added contrast with higher timbres, such as a tenor saxophone or the voice of an R&B shouter. His rollicking boogie-woogie bass lines became essential elements in the rock styles of such New Orleans musicians as **Fats Domino**, **Huey "Piano" Smith**, Dr. John, and Allen Toussaint. The Professor, inducted into the Rock and Roll Hall of Fame in 1992, had as his anthem "Mardi Gras in New Orleans," which is the theme song of the Mardi Gras carnival in the city.

Rama Records. Formed by George Goldner in New York City in 1953, this **indie** was originally a subsidiary of his Tico label, which specialized in Latin music. Rama and its subsidiaries Gee (formed in 1956), Roulette (formed in 1956; sold in 1957), and Gone/End (formed in 1957) recorded many talented vocal groups from the streets of New York: the **Crows ("Gee")**, the Harptones ("Shrine of St. Cecelia"), the Valentines ("Don't Say Goodnight"), the Cleftones ("Little Girl of Mine"), **Frankie Lymon** and the Teenagers **("Why Do Fools Fall in Love")**, the **Chantels** ("Maybe"), the **Flamingos** ("I Only Have Eyes for You"), and Little Anthony and the Imperials ("Tears on My Pillow").

R&B. See **Rhythm and Blues**.

RCA-Victor Records. In 1901, Emile Berliner and Eldridge Johnson formed the Victor Talking Machine Company, which was taken over by the Radio Corporation of America (RCA) in 1929. During the '50s, this **major** label's A&R agents included Charlie Green, Manie Sachs, and Steve Sholes; the music director was Hugo Winterhalter; and the Nashville division head was **Chet Atkins**. During the decade, various **pop** and country artists, and a few rockers, recorded with the label and its subsidiaries Groove (formed in 1953; supervised by Bob Rolontz) and X (formed in 1953; renamed VIK Records in 1956): Perry Como ("Round and Round"), Harry Belafonte ("Banana Boat (Day-O)"), Eddy Arnold ("I Wouldn't Know Where to Begin"), Hank Snow ("I've Been Everywhere"), Mickey and Sylvia ("Love Is Strange"), the Du Droppers ("I Wanna Know"), Janis Martin ("Drugstore Rock 'n' Roll"), and **Elvis Presley** ("Don't Be Cruel"). By the late 1950s, the label attempted to address the **teen idol** phenomenon with **Neil Sedaka** ("Breaking Up Is Hard to Do") and **Sam Cooke** ("Twistin' the Night Away"). Presley's phenomenal success left these extremely talented artists in the shadows, however.

"Rebel-'Rouser" (1958). Recorded by **Duane Eddy** on Jamie Records, this pioneering **rock instrumental** smash hit was the guitarist's first million-seller record. Complete with Eddy's trademark twangy guitar sound, powerful backbeat, honking saxophone solo, and rebel yells, this recording, a No. 6 **pop** hit and a No. 8 **R&B** hit, inspired many to play the guitar as a **rock and roll** instrument and influenced numerous rockers.

Reed, Jimmy (1925–1976). A 1991 Rock and Roll Hall of Famer originally from Mississippi, this blues singer-guitarist had a laid-back singing style that appealed to a broad spectrum of people—white country and **rock and roll** fans as well as blacks who usually preferred blues with a more vigorous sound. Along with **B. B. King**, Reed sold the most blues records in the '50s and '60s. This Chicago musician had a profound impact on rock and roll artists and groups with his relaxed blues that regularly crossed over to the **pop** charts. His wife, Mary Lee (Mama Reed), wrote many of his songs. Reed's impressive string of hits included "You Don't Have to Go," "Ain't That Lovin' You Baby," "Baby What You Want Me to Do," and "Big Boss Man." Many rockers, including **Elvis Presley**, the Rolling Stones, and Aretha Franklin, have covered Reed's songs.

Rhythm and Blues. In 1949, *Billboard* reporter Jerry Wexler introduced the term "rhythm and blues" to replace "race music," which had been used for music intended for distribution in the African American community. Many of the styles embraced by this term played a part in the development of **rock and roll** when the music was marketed to teenagers in the mid-1950s. African Americans were listening to this black music on "race" radio stations; this was the music that **Alan Freed** referred to as rock and roll when he marketed it to the radio public. With time, many black artists began to simplify their music and eliminate adult themes from the lyrics, making it more accessible and acceptable to a wider audience that included whites. Many music historians agree that when this blending of black and white music and culture occurred, rock and roll was born. Of its major roots, rhythm and blues played the biggest role in forming rock and roll. This dance music expressed the enjoyment of life and displayed it in energetic stage shows, quite often with saxophone players engaging in fun-to-watch antics, pre-dating those of rock and roll bands. Rhythm and blues singers shouted out their frequently sexually suggestive lyrics with a high level of physical activity accompanied by the accented backbeats of the rhythm, and the excitement and energy of R&B formed the basis for '50s rock and roll. As the R&B genre developed, two tendencies appeared: emphasis on the saxophone (honking) and emphasis on the voice (shouting). In the '40s and '50s, different R&B subgenres existed, such as jump blues (the sound of **Louis Jordan**) and West Coast blues ballad R&B (the sound of **Charles Brown**). Other R&B artists flourishing at this time included **Johnny Otis**, **Big Joe Turner**, **Wynonie Harris**, **Roy Brown**, **Ray Charles**, **Dinah Washington**, **Ruth Brown**, **LaVern Baker**, **B. B. King**, and **Ike Turner**. As rock and roll supplanted R&B in the mid-1950s, such early rock and roll artists as **Bo Diddley**, **Chuck Berry**, **Fats Domino**, and **Little Richard** continued the R&B tradition.

Riley, Billy Lee (b. 1933). This **Sun Records** recording artist and studio session musician from Pocahontas, Arkansas, was among the most important early **rockabillies**. A talented guitar, harmonica, piano, and drum player, he backed label mates **Jerry Lee Lewis**, **Johnny Cash**, **Roy Orbison**, and others. Billy Riley's Little Green Men recorded "Flying Saucer Rock and Roll" and "Red Hot" with guitarist Roland Janes, drummer J. M. Van Eaton, and pianists Jerry Lee Lewis and Jimmy Wilson.

Robey, Don. See Duke/Peacock Records.

Rock. See Rock and Roll.

Rock and Roll. First and foremost, this term refers to the music genre that evolved in the '50s, a product of the blending of major roots music styles—blues, jazz, gospel, **rhythm and blues**, folk, country, and **pop music**—by such artists as **Bill Haley**, **Chuck Berry**, and **Elvis Presley**. It was used during the '50s as a more acceptable term for R&B music in order to obscure its race music origins. Also, "rock and roll" was used as a sexual metaphor in blues, R&B, and rock and roll songs to obscure the risqué messages of the music. As rock and roll evolved, subgenres developed, such as the **New Orleans sound**, **rockabilly**, and **doo-wop**.

Rockabilly. The rockabilly sound permeated the music of many '50s **rock and roll** artists, from **Jerry Lee Lewis** and **Carl Perkins** to **Buddy Holly** and **Roy Orbison**. Referred to as country rock, it was labeled by its fans and the music industry as rockabilly to signify the merger of blues and hillbilly (country) styles. As with many rock and roll subgenres, there are differing views as to when the sound was born, but in the late 1940s and early 1950s the rockabilly sound was already established in honky-tonks, long before it acquired a name.

***Rock Around the Clock* (1956).** A pro-**rock and roll** editorial aimed at adult society as well as a source of teenage entertainment, this movie, released in April 1956, featured rock and rollers, including **Bill Haley**, the **Platters**, and Freddy Bell and the Bellboys, on screen for approximately half its length. The film stirred unexpected controversy, and violence and riots occurred from America to Ireland and from Egypt to Great Britain. The movie grossed almost five times its production costs and became the prototype for subsequent rock and roll films, all of which highlighted major music acts and promoted their songs.

"Rock Around the Clock." See "(We're Gonna) Rock Around the Clock."

"Rocket 88" (1951). Widely considered the first **rock and roll** record and credited to **Jackie Brenston** and His Delta Cats, this No. 1 **R&B** hit was recorded by Jackie Brenston and **Ike Turner**'s Kings of Rhythm. It was produced by **Sam Phillips** at his Memphis Recording Service and released on the **Chess** label; it was Chess's first No. 1 hit and one of the most successful R&B records of 1951. This historic song's composer credit went to baritone saxophonist Brenston (its featured singer) instead of Turner, who largely wrote it. Whether "Rocket 88" was indeed the first rock and roll record is subject to discussion; however, the song sounded and felt like a rock and roll song, and it provided an important link to the black R&B records that preceded it. With its automobile lyrics, boogie-woogie rhythm, and blues progression in a driving Memphis jump blues style, this classic was one of the first R&B hits to inspire a cover version. **Bill Haley** and the Saddlemen recorded it that same year; their version is often referred to as the first rock and roll recording by a white artist.

Rock Instrumentals. Instrumentals came of age in 1958. Uncomplicated by lyrics, they were perfect music for the late 1950s sock hops. Bill Doggett's "Honky Tonk (Parts 1 & 2)" was the first instrumental smash, and the Champs' "Tequilla" was the first No. 1 rock instrumental. Others contributing '50s rock instrumentals were **Bill Justis**, **Les Paul**, Santo & Johnny, Link Wray, Johnny and the Hurricanes, the **Ventures**, and **Duane Eddy**, who is considered **rock and roll**'s No.1 instrumentalist.

Rock, Rock, Rock! (1956). This **rock and roll** movie featured **Alan Freed**, **Chuck Berry**, **LaVern Baker**, the **Moonglows**, the **Flamingos**, and **Frankie Lymon** and the Teenagers.

Rodgers, Jimmie (1897–1933). Hailing from Mississippi, James Charles Rodgers linked black and white music styles in his songs and became country music's first star. Dubbed the Father of Country Music, this railroad worker known as the Singing Brakeman combined in his music all the types he had heard—black work chants, jazz, blues, Hawaiian music, and vaudeville songs. His large output included blues, hillbilly and parlor songs, some with jazz elements and many of them incorporating the twelve-bar blues pattern: "Waiting for a Train," "In the Jailhouse Now," "Travelin' Blues," and the "Blue Yodel" series. His recordings played an important role in introducing new sounds and styles into country music; he was also one of the first white stars to work with black musicians. Well known for his signature vocal style of yodeling in a falsetto voice that gained him the nickname America's Blue Yodeler, this 1986 Rock and Roll Hall of Famer had a repertoire that set the standard in country music. He popularized songs that were covered many times over the years, influencing not only generations of country singers but also African Americans and **rock and roll** musicians.

Roulette Records. See Rama Records.

RPM Records. See Modern Records.

Rupe, Art. See Specialty Records.

Rydell, Bobby (b. 1942). Born Robert Ridarelli in Philadelphia, this late 1950s–early 1960s **teen idol** had an impressive string of **pop** hits; however, none were chart-toppers. A movie star well known for his good looks, this popular singer had hits that included "We Got Love," "Wild One," and "Volare."

Savoy Records. Herman Lubinsky formed this significant New York-based **indie** label in 1942 in Newark, New Jersey. Savoy's roster included **Johnny Otis** ("Double Crossing Blues"; 1950 No. 1 **R&B** hit by the Johnny Otis Quintette, the Robins, and **Little Esther**), Little Esther ("Mistrustin' Blues"; 1950 No. 1 R&B hit by the Johnny Otis Orchestra and Little Esther with Mel Walker), Big Jay McNeely ("The Deacon's Hop"; 1949 No. 1 R&B hit), Nappy Brown ("Don't Be Angry"; 1955 No. 2 R&B hit), and the vocal group the Four Buddies ("I Will Wait"; 1951 No. 2 R&B hit). **Ralph Bass** served as A&R man for the label.

Sedaka, Neil (b. 1939). A **teen idol** from Brooklyn, New York, while still in high school this prolific hit songwriter formed a songwriting team with lyricist Howard Greenfield and wrote numerous songs for other artists, eventually joining Al Nevins and Don Kirshner's **Aldon Music** team. Sedaka formed and began recording with the Tokens in the mid-1950s. A classically trained pianist, he composed "Oh! Carol" in 1959 for fellow singer-songwriter Carole King. Among his many hits that he both wrote and recorded were "Calendar Girl," "Happy Birthday, Sweet Sixteen," and "Breaking Up Is Hard to Do."

Seeger, Pete (b. 1919). This legendary folk singer and songwriter formed the Almanac Singers with **Woody Guthrie** in 1940, and the Weavers in 1948—a group that paved the path for folk-singing groups. Many groups (trios and quartets) and some solo acts continued in their style throughout the '50s and '60s, including the **Kingston Trio**, the New Lost City Ramblers, the trio Peter, Paul, and Mary, Simon & Garfunkel, Joan Baez, and Bob Dylan. With such songs as "If I Had a Hammer," "Where Have All the Flowers Gone?" and "We Shall Overcome," Seeger's musical activity in the '60s continued to be important in the area of protest songs and the Civil Rights Movement. A gifted banjo player and son of folklorist Charles Seeger, this 1996 Rock and Roll Hall of Famer played an important part in the folk revival in America.

"Sh-Boom" (1954). The **Chords** recorded this song that has been cited as the first **rock and roll** record on **Atlantic Records**' Cat subsidiary. The recording ranked high on both black (No. 2) and white (No. 5) charts, and thus the Chords were the first black **doo-wop** group to have a record in the Top 10 on the **pop** charts, despite an immediate cover version by the Canadian white vocal group, the **Crew-Cuts**. The Chords' record had a tremendous impact on doo-wop, rock and roll's development, and '50s society.

"Shake, Rattle and Roll" (1954). Recorded by **Big Joe Turner** and written by **Atlantic Records**' arranger Jesse Stone (using the name Charles Calhoun), this classic has been considered the first **rock and roll** song. Turner's most famous hit, this original reached No. 1 on the **R&B** charts in June 1954, the same month that **Bill Haley** and the Comets covered it, creating a No. 7 **pop** hit that also has been referred to as the first rock and roll record.

The Shirelles. Originally called the Poquellos, this influential **girl group** formed in 1957 in Passaic, New Jersey, consisted of Shirley Owens, Addie "Micki" Harris, Doris Coley, and Beverly Lee. The talented group wrote their own songs and had many hit recordings, such as "I Met Him on a Sunday," "Dedicated to the One I Love," "Tonight's the Night," and "Will You Love Me Tomorrow," the first No. 1 **pop** hit by an all-female **rock and roll** group. One of the greatest female vocal groups, the Shirelles thrived during the height of the girl groups, the late 1950s through early 1960s. They were inducted into the Rock and Roll Hall of Fame in 1996.

Shirley & Lee. Known as the Sweethearts of the Blues and later as the Sweethearts of **Rock and Roll** after their hits crossed over to the **pop** charts, Shirley Goodman (b. 1936) and Leonard Lee (1935–1976) provided some of

New Orleans' biggest-selling records after bursting onto the scene in 1952. This young duo was popular with the teenage audience for their many recordings about teenage romance: "I'm Gone," "I'll Do It," "Let the Good Times Roll," and "I Feel Good." Produced by **Dave Bartholomew** and backed by some of the finest New Orleans instrumentalists, Shirley & Lee were an influential **rhythm and blues**-based rock and roll duo who toured through the '50s and performed until parting ways in 1963. (See also **New Orleans Sound**.)

Shuman, Mort. See **Pomus and Shuman.**

"Sixty Minute Man" (1951). The **Dominoes** recorded this enormous **R&B doo-wop** hit and crossover classic that has been referred to as the first **rock and roll** record on the Federal label. Whereas earlier songs used the words "rock" or "roll," this one used the whole phrase, "rockin' and rollin'," and met with unprecedented white acceptance. The record sat in the No. 1 position on the R&B charts for fourteen weeks and was the most successful R&B record of 1951.

Smith, Bessie (1894–1937). This greatest and most influential singer to emerge from the classic blues era has influenced every female blues and blues-related artist since, including gospel great **Mahalia Jackson** and blues rocker Janis Joplin. Born in Chattanooga, Tennessee, the Empress of the Blues was one of the most prolific classic blues artists, recording more than 150 songs, including the classics " 'Taint Nobody's Bizness if I Do," "Back Water Blues," "Mama's Got the Blues," "Poor Man's Blues," and "Nobody Knows You When You're Down and Out," all songs that illustrate her blues vocal mastery and her ability to evoke feelings while explaining 1920s black culture. This 1989 Rock and Roll Hall of Famer dressed the part of a blues diva, performing in lavish gowns, and recorded with a number of noted musicians, such as **Louis Armstrong** on her hit "St. Louis Blues."

Smith, Huey "Piano" (b. 1934). This popular New Orleans **R&B** pianist worked with **Lloyd Price, Little Richard, Smiley Lewis**, and others before going solo. With his group, the Clowns, he had two hits, the classic "Rocking Pneumonia and the Boogie Woogie Flu" and "Don't You Just Know It." Smith and the Clowns were favorites with **rock and roll** audiences, especially for their rollicking live shows. They also accompanied Frankie Ford on "Sea Cruise"—a song that Smith claims was originally his—an excellent example of New Orleans rock and roll with its active horn and boogie-woogie piano parts. (See also **New Orleans Sound**.)

Soul Music. As **R&B** music continued to thrive throughout the '50s, it evolved into gutsier African American styles, resulting in the soul subgenre. First labeled soul music because of gospel groups stirring listeners' emotions, by the early 1960s the phrase referred to African American secular music in general. With **Ray Charles** having paved the way for the funky new sound, such groups as the **Drifters** helped create soul music by bringing gospel-styled vocals to secular songs. Such earlier stars as **Lloyd Price, Fats Domino, Little Richard**, the **Platters**, and the **Coasters** faded away, but they were replaced by such dynamic new talents as **Sam Cooke, Jackie Wilson**, Wilson Pickett, Marvin Gaye, the Isley Brothers, the Impressions, the Miracles, and **James Brown**, the Godfather of Soul.

Specialty Records. Founded by Art Rupe in Hollywood in 1945, this **indie** employed Rupe, Robert "Bumps" Blackwell, J. W. Alexander, and Johnny Vincent as producers, as well as Sonny Bono (Los Angeles) and Harold Battiste (New Orleans). **Little Richard** ("Long Tall Sally") was the label's most important discovery in the Southeast with his string of '50s hits. Others on its roster were Joe and Jimmy Liggins ("Pink Champagne" and "Drunk," respectively), **Lloyd Price** ("Lawdy Miss Clawdy"), **Guitar Slim** ("The Things That I Used to Do"), and Larry Williams ("Short Fat Fannie").

Spector, Phil (b. 1940). This writer-producer, who was also a member of the Teddy Bears, apprenticed with **Leiber and Stoller** in the '50s and produced early hits for **Atlantic Records**. He formed his own Philles label in the early 1960s and produced a string of hits by various musicians, including the Crystals, the Ronettes, and the Righteous Brothers. Considered one of the greatest producers of **rock and roll,** with his production sophistication Spector helped redefine and revitalize rock and roll in the late 1950s and early 1960s. The great achievements of this 1989 Rock and Roll Hall of Famer included creation of the rock and roll **girl group,** of studio recording known as the Wall of Sound, and of enabling producers to become known by their sound and to receive as much respect and appreciation as the artists whose records they produced.

Stoller, Mike. See Leiber and Stoller.

The Stroll. The first **rock and roll** group dance popularized on *American Bandstand*, the stroll was performed to the 1958 No. 4 **pop** hit "The Stroll," recorded late in 1957 by the Diamonds, a white cover vocal group from Toronto, Canada.

"Summertime Blues" (1958). **Eddie Cochran** recorded this exhilarating anthem of teen disenchantment on **Liberty Records**. With its harsh vocals (including some phrases spoken in a low bass voice), and staccato rhythm guitar, it struck a chord among teenagers and helped to define the experience of young people in the 1950s. Featuring Cochran's exhilarating tenor voice and intense guitar playing, this recording was his most successful and became a No. 8 **pop** hit.

Sun Records. **Sam Phillips** opened the Memphis Recording Service, where he recorded black urban blues singers, in 1950. The success of these recordings led him to form Sun Records in 1952, and he began recording the blues of

Howlin' Wolf, **B. B. King**, Little Junior Parker, and **Ike Turner**. Phillips, Jack Clement, and music director **Bill Justis** served as producers. A very significant label in the early development of **rockabilly**, Sun recorded **Jerry Lee Lewis, Carl Perkins, Johnny Cash, Roy Orbison**, and **Elvis Presley** (before he signed with **RCA-Victor**). Phillips pioneered rockabilly, bringing several '50s music styles together, while producing more **rock and roll** records on Sun than any other label of its time. Many of the songs that were the foundation for rock and roll were recorded there—ranging from Elvis Presley's **"That's All Right"** and Carl Perkins's **"Blue Suede Shoes"** to Jerry Lee Lewis's **"Whole Lot of Shakin' Going On"** and Roy Orbison's "Ooby Dooby." Other influential artists and groups who recorded at the label and its subsidiary, Phillips International Records (formed in 1957), included Charlie Rich, Frank Floyd, Sonny Burgess, Warren Smith, Carl Mann, "Sleepy" John Estes, James Cotton, Little Milton, Rosco Gordon, the Southern Jubilees, the Prisonaires, and Bill Justis & His Orchestra. Their rich and diverse Sun recordings helped change the course of **popular music**.

Surf Rock. A subgenre that arose in the late 1950s and flourished in the early 1960s, surf music began with such groups as the **Ventures** and the vocal duo Jan & Dean. Beginning in 1958, the duo's output included such huge hits as 1963's No. 1 "Surf City," and 1964's "Dead Man's Curve" and "The Little Old Lady (from Pasadena)." Bringing an exciting instrumental-based sound and a return to the basic **rock** instrumentation, other surf rock groups followed, including the Marketts, the Beach Boys, the Safaris, the Chantay's, and Dick Dale and the Del-Tones. (See also **Rock Instrumentals**.)

Teen Idols. Evolving in the late 1950s, teen idols flourished when a stable of glamorous **pop** stars emerged; their looks were more important than their music. These attractive idols included **Bobby Vee, Frankie Avalon, Annette Funicello, Bobby Darin, Connie Francis, Fabian, Brenda Lee, Bobby Rydell, Neil Sedaka**, and **Paul Anka**. Often criticized as less interpretive and artistic than the first generation, these new pop rock artists were young singers performing in a Tin Pan Alley-influenced crooner style. Though their records were produced well and were quite attractive to listeners, teen idol music lacked the authentic qualities associated with **rock and roll**'s early subgenres. Unlike earlier '50s rockers who both sang and played instruments, idols usually specialized in one aspect of performance, such as singing. Their recordings were often diluted creations of true rock and roll. Nonetheless, the young rock audience accepted teen idols who mostly performed songs composed by professional songwriting teams targeting teen interests and emotions. These artists were perfectly groomed by their managers and producers, and were given national exposure by *American Bandstand*.

"A Teenager in Love" (1959). Dion and the Belmonts recorded this international hit composed for the group by **Pomus and Shuman** for Laurie Records.

With its influential **doo-wop** harmony sounds, the recording represented the change in the group's style to the late 1950s **pop**-oriented sound, evident in the song's message of the agony of young love and its soft **rock** musical blend of street corner doo-wop and **teen idol** balladry. After this and other influential songs by Dion and the Belmonts, a deluge of white, predominantly Italian-American groups emerged, singing in what has been labeled a neo-doo-wop style.

"That'll Be the Day" (1957). Recorded by **Buddy Holly** and the Crickets for Brunswick Records, this **rock and roll** classic reflected the Crickets' innovative use of standard **rockabilly** instrumentation—two guitars (lead and rhythm), bass, and drums. Produced by their manager, **Norman Petty**, at his Clovis, New Mexico, studio, the record became a No. 1 **pop** and No. 2 **R&B** hit. Its title was taken from a phrase in the John Wayne movie *The Searchers*.

"That's All Right" (1954). With guitarist Scotty Moore and bassist Bill Black, **Elvis Presley** recorded this cover of bluesman Arthur "Big Boy" Crudup's 1946 Delta blues song, "That's All Right Mama," in July 1954 at **Sam Phillips**'s **Sun Records**. Featuring Presley's electrifying voice, the recording assimilated American roots musics while representing a white artist combining black and white performance practices on a black blues song—an extremely powerful mix. The single is considered by many to be the first **rock and roll** record.

"There Goes My Baby" (1959). The **Drifters** recorded for **Atlantic Records** this No. 1 **R&B** hit that is credited with having put string instruments into **rock and roll** music. Written and produced by **Leiber and Stoller** as the first release of the new lineup referred to as the King era Drifters, this record featured lead singer **Ben E. King**. With its orchestral string accompaniment and full, thick-textured background, the recording influenced early 1960s records. The single is noted for its producing techniques and is credited with reflecting a new music style of Drifters songs—a more **pop**-oriented sound with fewer R&B elements and more in line with late 1950s rock and roll fashion. This record set the successful course for the new Drifters and heavily influenced rock and roll production for the next few years.

Thomas, Rufus (1917–2001). Originally from Cayce, Mississippi, this radio station WDIA **disc jockey** was a regular on the **R&B** scene in Memphis, Tennessee. Known for his outrageous costumes in performance, he recorded for **Sun Records**. A reaction song to **Big Mama Thornton**'s **"Hound Dog,"** his 1953 "Bear Cat" (No. 3 on the R&B charts) became the label's first national hit. Thomas, who recorded throughout the '60s and '70s for Stax Records (sometimes with his daughter, Carla), is remembered for his hits "Walking the Dog" and "Do the Funky Chicken."

Thornton, Big Mama (1926–1984). A significant blueswoman in '50s **rhythm and blues**–based **rock and roll**, this blues belter who arose from the tradition of classic blues singers was born Willie Mae Thornton in Montgomery, Alabama. She frequently played harmonica and drums for R&B bands and became a featured artist with the **Johnny Otis** Rhythm and Blues Caravan in Los Angeles. After beginning her recording career in Houston, Texas, she recorded one of the seminal records in rock and roll history for the Peacock label, **"Hound Dog."** One of her most successful '50s hits on the R&B charts (a No. 1 hit in 1953), it was written for her by **Leiber and Stoller** and covered by **Elvis Presley** in 1956 (a version that became one of the biggest hits of the rock era).

Top 40 Radio. The exact origin of formula radio is debatable, but most historians believe that it was born between 1953 and 1955 when Todd Storz developed the concept that would become known as Top 40. Along with the format's other founding fathers, Bill Stewart and Gordon McLendon, Storz played the most popular records of the day, creating an on-air jukebox. Top 40 eventually became a nonstop flurry of broadcast activities, including commercials, time checks, news, weather, and sports, as well as contests, listener requests, and dedications mixed with jingles repeating the station's call letters and frequency. Many pioneering **disc jockeys** were bothered by the new format, upset that it stifled their originality and no longer allowed them to express their personality or freely choose what music to play on the air.

Turner, Big Joe (1911–1985). With his big, husky voice and nicknamed the Big Boss of the Blues, this singer was one of the finest blues shouters and an important link between **R&B** and **rock and roll**. A native of Kansas City, Missouri, he sang with boogie-woogie pianist Pete Johnson and with Kansas City big bands led by Benny Moten, Andy Kirk, and Count Basie, then successfully made the transitions from boogie-woogie to R&B to early rock and roll—an accomplishment that has given Turner a unique place in twentieth-century music. With classics like "Roll 'Em Pete," he and Johnson sparked the boogie-woogie craze that swept the country in the late 1930s and early 1940s. When the craze passed, Turner changed to R&B music. One of the first major figures in R&B and a founding father of rock and roll, this 1987 Rock and Roll Hall of Famer recorded a series of classics from 1951 to 1956 that dominated the R&B charts and led straight into rock and roll, including "Chains of Love," "Sweet Sixteen," "Honey Hush," "Corrine Corrina," "Flip, Flop and Fly," and his most famous hit, the original 1954 **"Shake, Rattle and Roll,"** which **Bill Haley** and the Comets covered a few months later.

Turner, Ike (b. 1931). Born Izear Luster Turner in Clarksdale, Mississippi, this leader of the Kings of Rhythm band played a critical role in the early 1950s Memphis music world. Working with many great bluesmen as a session musician and talent scout, he sent many artists to the **Sun**, **Chess**, RPM, and **Modern** labels, and performed on and produced many of the recordings of musical acts he discovered. One of the significant originators of **rock and roll** music, Turner, with his band, recorded the monumental **"Rocket 88"** in 1951 with **Jackie Brenston** on vocals (though the record is credited to Jackie Brenston and His Delta Cats); this single is widely regarded as the first rock and roll record. Turner was inducted into the Rock and Roll Hall of Fame in 1991.

"Tutti Frutti" (1955). **Little Richard** recorded this masterpiece at **Cosimo Matassa**'s J&M Studio. Released on **Specialty Records**, it sold more than 3 million copies, became a No. 2 **R&B** hit, and kicked off Little Richard's string of classics. This significant recording, exemplifying his exciting music style, provided a link between R&B and **rock and roll**. Originally an obscene song that was sung in Southern black homosexual communities, the lyrics of this hit record version were cleaned up and merely suggested rocking (sexual activity) with girls. When **Pat Boone** covered the tune, its lyrics were cleaned and varied even more, and that version had great charts success in 1956.

Valens, Ritchie (1941–1959). Born Richard Stephen Valenzuela in the Los Angeles suburb of Pacoima, California, and often referred to as a **teen idol**, this Latino rocker was a talented singer-songwriter and guitarist. Only seventeen when he died in a February 3, 1959, plane crash with **Buddy Holly** and the **Big Bopper** while on tour, this 2001 Rock and Roll Hall of Famer, known as the Little Richard of the San Fernando Valley, is credited with having created Latino rock. Forerunners of simple **rock and roll** sounds and of the subgenres garage rock and punk rock, his '50s classics "Donna" and **"La Bamba"** made him a star. This double-sided record is often referred to as one of the greatest '50s rock and roll singles.

Vee, Bobby (b. 1943). Born Robert Velline in Fargo, North Dakota, this **teen idol**'s career truly began the night after **Buddy Holly**'s death in a plane crash in 1959, when Vee and his rock group, the Shadows, filled in at the concert Holly had been scheduled to headline in Fargo. Vee's first hit, "Suzie Baby," was his only success on the charts during the '50s. He was a prolific maker of calm, studio-crafted hit teen songs throughout the '60s, the most popular being the 1961 No. 1 **pop** hit, "Take Good Care of My Baby."

Vee Jay Records. Formed in 1953 by Vivian Carter and James Bracken in Chicago, this **indie** was generally committed to black music styles in the '50s, though the company later had very successful '60s hits with the **Four Seasons** ("Big Girls Don't Cry") and the Beatles' ("From Me to You"). Producers Calvin Carter and Al Smith oversaw the recording of the label's roster, which included **R&B** artists **Jimmy Reed** ("Ain't That Lovin' You Baby") and **John Lee Hooker** ("I Love You Honey"), and the vocal groups the Spaniels ("Goodnite Sweetheart, Goodnite"), the El Dorados ("At My Front Door"), and the **Dells** ("Oh What a Nite"). In the early 1960s, the label once again topped the charts with Gene Chandler's "Duke of Earl."

The Ventures. One of the finest and most enduring **rock instrumental** groups, this ensemble from Seattle, Washington, predated and influenced the early 1960s **surf rock** craze. In 1959 they recorded "Walk—Don't Run," which became a No. 2 **pop** hit the next year. Having brought their exciting guitar-drum instrumental sound into the '60s, they became famous for "Hawaii Five-O," the theme song for the television series of the same title. Prominent drums with metallic and twangy-sounding guitars playing catchy tunes created this rock combo's trademark sound.

The Victor Company. See RCA-Victor Records.

Vincent, Gene (1935–1971). Born Eugene Vincent Craddock in Norfolk, Virginia, this **rockabilly** and his band, the Blue Caps, were among the most popular **rock and roll** groups during the mid-to-late '50s. A slick, good-looking rocker, Vincent perfectly embodied rock and roll rebellion with his appearance and menacing stage presence styled in the James Dean tough-guy tradition. The Blue Caps performed with frenzied energy that was unmatched by their contemporaries. Their hits included "Bluejean Bop," "Lotta Lovin'," "Dance to the Bop," and **"Be-Bop-a-Lula,"** which is considered one of the greatest rock and roll anthems of the '50s and a perfect example of the rockabilly sound. In 1960, while touring Europe, this 1998 Rock and Roll Hall of Famer was seriously injured in the car accident that claimed the life of fellow rockabilly **Eddie Cochran** when their limousine ran off the road en route to London's Heathrow Airport.

Walker, T-Bone (1910–1975). Born Aaron Thibeaux Walker in Linden, Texas, this outstanding bluesman and first-rate singer was a noted composer of blues tunes. His single most famous title and massive hit was "Call It Stormy Monday (But Tuesday Is Just as Bad)," generally considered one of the greatest blues songs of all time. Other seminal Walker hits included "T-Bone Shuffle," which became an essential song in every blues guitarist's repertoire, and "I'm Still in Love with You." This blues master had an immense impact on the course of blues guitar history and was a creator of modern blues; he was also a pioneer in the development of the electric guitar sound that shaped practically all postwar **popular music**. Walker created the electric blues guitar style and was the first blues artist to play the electric guitar in public. Inducted into the Rock and Roll Hall of Fame in 1987, he influenced nearly every major post-World War II guitarist, including **B. B. King**, **Buddy Guy**, Jimi Hendrix, Eric Clapton, and Stevie Ray Vaughan. He incorporated guitar-playing antics into his performances by playing the guitar behind his back and neck and between his legs, while doing splits and twists. Walker's showmanship strongly influenced **Chuck Berry** and Jimi Hendrix.

Washington, Dinah (1924–1963). Born Ruth Lee Jones in Tuscaloosa, Alabama, and raised in Chicago, this '50s singer who came from a gospel music background was one of the most successful **R&B** recording artists. She had forty-seven hits on the R&B charts, five of them No. 1 records. Her vocal legacy places her in the same category as **Bessie Smith**, Billie Holiday, and other great blues-based black female vocalists. With her bluesy and emotional voice, Washington influenced such other female artists as **LaVern Baker**, **Etta James**, **Ruth Brown**, and Little **Esther Phillips**. She was inducted into the Rock and Roll Hall of Fame in 1993.

Waters, Muddy (1915–1983). A brilliant blues artist from Rolling Fork, Mississippi, McKinley Morganfield moved to Chicago in 1943. He is considered the founder of post–World War II Chicago blues. A master guitarist, singer, songwriter, bandleader, and recording artist, he played a critical role in linking the Delta and the urban blues. Transforming the blues guitar sound with his innovative use of the electric guitar, he created a louder, harder-edged, and bigger sound. Waters shifted the blues from a lonely solo act to a lively group experience by playing it with a band. Many Chicago blues greats played in his band, including Little Walter, Junior Wells, James Cotton, **Willie Dixon**, and Otis Spann. Waters's recordings included "Louisiana Blues," "Long Distance Call," "Honey Bee," "I'm Your Hoochie Coochie Man," "Just Make Love to Me," "I'm Ready," and "Rollin' Stone." The latter inspired the name of the Rolling Stones, the title of *Rolling Stone* magazine, and songs by other rockers. His rhythmic innovations—the stop-time riff and strong backbeat—eventually permeated **rock and roll** music. Having redefined the blues, making it contemporary music with rhythmic excitement and flashy lyrics that was played in a flamboyant performance style, Waters, inducted into the Rock and Roll Hall of Fame in 1987, assisted in the birth of rock and roll in the early 1950s and inspired countless guitarists to play the blues, helping change American music.

The Weavers. See Seeger, Pete.

"(We're Gonna) Rock Around the Clock" (1954). Written by Max Freedman and Jimmy DeKnight (a pseudonym for Jimmy Myers), this anthem recorded for **Decca Records** by **Bill Haley** and the Comets became the first **rock and roll** song to reach No. 1 on the **pop** charts (July 9, 1955), a position it held for eight weeks. The best-selling record of 1955, it remained on the pop charts for nearly six months, sold 22 million copies worldwide, and became the first internationally known rock and roll recording. Only mildly successful upon its initial release, the record received a huge promotional boost when it was featured as the theme song in the 1955 movie *The Blackboard Jungle*. This song, one of the most famous in rock and roll history, marked the beginning of the rock era. It again became a Top 40 hit in 1974, when it was used as the opening theme of the *Happy Days* television show.

Wexler, Jerry. See Atlantic Records.

"What'd I Say (Part I)" (1959). With his highly intense gospel-influenced vocals, **Ray Charles** recorded this signature song for **Atlantic Records**—a performance that was an important link between blues, **R&B**, soul, and **rock** music. With this recording that served as a secular rendition of a church service, complete with moans and groans and a congregation speaking in tongues, Charles culminated the creation of the **soul music** sound. Though it was a No. 1 R&B hit and No. 6 **pop** hit and Charles's first million-seller, the song was banned by many radio stations.

"Whole Lot of Shakin' Going On" (1957). **Jerry Lee Lewis** recorded this monumental **rockabilly** tune, his first hit, for **Sun Records**. With its exhilarating sound, this cover of one of Big Maybelle's 1955 blues recordings was full of sexual references and was banned in many cities, though the public loved the record and the wild artist. The record sold 6 million copies and topped both the country and **R&B** charts. It was a No. 3 **pop** hit that remained on the pop charts for twenty-nine weeks and catapulted Lewis into prominence, making him an international celebrity.

"Why Do Fools Fall in Love" (1955). **Frankie Lymon** and the Teenagers recorded this vocal group classic in late 1955 for Gee Records. Initially titled "Why Do Birds Sing So Gay," this recording represented the typical schoolboy **doo-wop** sound, featuring Lymon's clear falsetto lead voice accompanied by background voices harmonizing lyrics of innocent love. Released in early 1956, the record was a tremendous hit, climbing to the top of the **R&B** charts and to No. 6 on the **pop** charts; it became a standard by which the doo-wop style is defined.

Williams, Hank (1923–1953). Alabama-born singer, songwriter, and guitarist Hiram Williams impacted the development of both country music and **rock and roll**. One of the biggest stars in country music, he performed in honky-tonks before embarking on his successful recording career. After experiencing marital distress, drug abuse, and alcoholism, he wrote songs to which many people could relate: songs about family, beer drinking, religion, love, and love failures: "Lovesick Blues," "I Just Told Momma Goodbye," "Honky Tonkin'," "Hey Good Lookin'," "I'm So Lonesome I Could Cry," "Cold, Cold Heart," and "Your Cheating Heart." His songs crossed into **pop music**, and some of them resembled early rock and roll. Many of his compositions became major pop hits when covered by such other musicians as Tony Bennett, Guy Mitchell, and Frankie Laine. A 1987 Rock and Roll Hall of Famer, Williams had an enormous impact on the development of rock and roll. Early rockers, including **Chuck Berry** and **Elvis Presley**, listened to him on the radio.

Wills, Bob (1905–1975). A major figure in the development of western swing as well as a bandleader, fiddler, singer, and songwriter, James Robert Wills was highly influenced by African American folk blues and jazz. In 1935, he formed the Texas Playboys, a group that became the most popular act in the Southwest and recorded approximately 140 songs. His compositions are still staples of western swing and standards of country and **pop music**: "San Antonio Rose," "Faded Love," "Maiden's Prayer," and "Take Me Back to Tulsa." As World War II brought an end to the western swing style and Wills downsized his band, he often had one tenor saxophone simulate a brass section, an important and innovative technique that influenced such early **rock and roll** bands as **Bill Haley** and the Comets. Inducted into the Rock and Roll Hall of Fame in 1999, Bob Wills and His Texas Playboys greatly contributed to the evolution of country music and rock and roll.

Wilson, Jackie (1934–1984). Known as Mr. Entertainment, this **R&B** singer from Detroit created hit after hit from 1957 to 1975 and became one of the premier voices of the period. His hits included No. 1's "Lonely Teardrops," "You Better Know It," "A Woman, a Lover, a Friend," and "(Your Love Keeps Lifting Me) Higher and Higher." With a background in gospel, he was lead singer of the **Dominoes** in the '50s. A dynamic performer, this 1987 Rock and Roll Hall of Famer was extremely popular; in 1963 he headlined a British concert with the Beatles as one of his opening acts. (See also **Soul Music**.)

Your Hit Parade. This live coast-to-coast Saturday night radio music program debuted in 1935 and boosted the record industry, specifically Tin Pan Alley **pop music**, by centering on the ten top songs each week. It shaped the music tastes of the American public and was one of the first radio programs to transfer to television in 1950. It ran until 1959, when it succumbed to **rock and roll** music and the changed music industry. In its heyday, *Parade* was a winning music show complete with writers, choreographers, set designers, costumers, and producers; **Ray Charles** served as the show's choral director and vocal music arranger from 1949 to 1958.

APPENDICES

List of Top-Selling Records, 1951–1959

Since '50s records were ranked on diverse charts, the top-selling records of the decade are provided in two lists to include all appropriate records with their proper rankings: Top 20 Rhythm and Blues and Rock and Roll Records, and Top 20 Pop and Rock and Roll Records. *Billboard* introduced its comprehensive Hot 100 chart on August 4, 1958, and this pop singles survey remains the definitive industry chart to this day. On October 20, 1958, *Billboard* introduced its comprehensive Hot R&B Sides chart, which is known today as Hot R&B/Hip-Hop Singles & Tracks. Prior to these dates, *Billboard* published multiple charts to archive record information. The statistics from these surveys were used to compile the two lists below. With its record label, each single is listed by rank. The year given is when the record peaked on the *Billboard* charts. The weeks at No. 1 column shows how many weeks the record was at the No. 1 position. All data are based on Joel Whitburn's Record Research publications, which compile *Billboard* charts information of the rock and roll era.

TOP 20 RHYTHM AND BLUES AND ROCK AND ROLL RECORDS

Rank	Title	Artist/Group	Peak Year	Record Label	Weeks at No. I
1	"Sixty Minute Man"	The Dominoes	1951	Federal	14
2	"Black Night"	Charles Brown and His Band	1951	Aladdin	14
3	"The Things That I Used to Do"	Guitar Slim and His Band	1954	Specialty	14
4	"Honky Tonk (Parts 1 & 2)"	Bill Doggett	1956	King	13
5	"Pink Champagne"	Joe Liggins and His Honeydrippers	1950	Specialty	13
6	"Searchin'"	The Coasters	1957	Atco	12
7	"Teardrops from My Eyes"	Ruth Brown	1950	Atlantic	11
8	"Blueberry Hill"	Fats Domino	1956	Imperial	11
9	"Ain't That a Shame"	Fats Domino	1955	Imperial	11
10	"Money Honey"	Clyde McPhatter and the Drifters	1953	Atlantic	11
11	"The Great Pretender"	The Platters	1956	Mercury	11
12	"Maybellene"	Chuck Berry and His Combo	1955	Chess	11
13	"Shake a Hand"	Faye Adams	1953	Herald	10
14	"Have Mercy Baby"	The Dominoes	1952	Federal	10
15	"Pledging My Love"	Johnny Ace	1955	Duke	10
16	"Double Crossing Blues"	Johnny Otis Quintette/The Robins/Little Esther	1950	Savoy	9
17	"My Song"	Johnny Ace with the Beale Streeters	1952	Duke	9
18	"I'm in Love Again"	Fats Domino	1956	Imperial	9
19	"Hearts of Stone"	The Charms	1954	DeLuxe	9
20	"It's Just a Matter of Time"	Brook Benton	1959	Mercury	9

TOP 20 POP AND ROCK AND ROLL RECORDS

Rank	Title	Artist/Group	Peak Year	Record Label	Weeks at No. 1
1	"Don't Be Cruel/ Hound Dog"	Elvis Presley	1956	RCA-Victor	11
2	"Singing the Blues"	Guy Mitchell	1956	Columbia	10
3	"Mack the Knife"	Bobby Darin	1959	Atco	9
4	"All Shook Up"	Elvis Presley	1957	RCA-Victor	9
5	"(We're Gonna) Rock Around the Clock"	Bill Haley and the Comets	1955	Decca	8
6	"The Wayward Wind"	Gogi Grant	1956	Era	8
7	"Sixteen Tons"	"Tennessee" Ernie Ford	1955	Capitol	8
8	"Heartbreak Hotel"	Elvis Presley	1956	RCA-Victor	8
9	"Love Letters in the Sand"	Pat Boone	1957	Dot	7
10	"Jailhouse Rock"	Elvis Presley	1957	RCA-Victor	7
11	"(Let Me Be Your) Teddy Bear"	Elvis Presley	1957	RCA-Victor	7
12	"At the Hop"	Danny & the Juniors	1958	ABC-Paramount	7
13	"Love Is a Many-Splendored Thing"	Four Aces	1955	Decca	6
14	"Rock and Roll Waltz"	Kay Starr	1956	RCA-Victor	6
15	"The Poor People of Paris"	Les Baxter	1956	Capitol	6
16	"The Yellow Rose of Texas"	Mitch Miller	1955	Columbia	6
17	"Memories Are Made of This"	Dean Martin	1956	Capitol	6
18	"April Love"	Pat Boone	1957	Dot	6
19	"The Battle of New Orleans"	Johnny Horton	1959	Columbia	6
20	"Young Love"	Tab Hunter	1957	Dot	6

List of Most Significant Rock Records, 1951–1959

This list consists of the '50s records most important to the genesis and evolution of the rock and roll genre. These groundbreaking recordings significantly contributed to the shaping of the new music during its first decade and considerably influenced its future. The reasons for including a record vary; however, each was musically innovative, profoundly influential, and critically important in redefining American popular music during the '50s. With its record label, each single is listed chronologically by the year it was recorded. (See "A-to-Z of Rock, 1951–1959" for further information.)

Title	Artist/Group	Record Year	Record Label
"Rocket 88"	Jackie Brenston and His Delta Cats [Ike Turner's Kings of Rhythm]	1951	Chess
"Sixty Minute Man"	The Dominoes	1951	Federal
"Gee"	The Crows	1953	Rama
"Hound Dog"	Big Mama Thornton	1953	Peacock
"Shake, Rattle and Roll"	Big Joe Turner	1954	Atlantic
"Sh-Boom"	The Chords	1954	Cat
"That's All Right"	Elvis Presley	1954	Sun
"(We're Gonna) Rock Around the Clock"	Bill Haley and the Comets	1954	Decca
"Ain't That a Shame"	Fats Domino	1955	Imperial
"Blue Suede Shoes"	Carl Perkins	1955	Sun
"Bo Diddley"	Bo Diddley	1955	Checker
"Maybellene"	Chuck Berry	1955	Chess
"Only You (and You Alone)"	The Platters	1955	Mercury
"Tutti Frutti"	Little Richard	1955	Specialty
"Why Do Fools Fall in Love"	Frankie Lymon and the Teenagers	1955	Gee
"Be-Bop-a-Lula"	Gene Vincent	1956	Capitol
"Heartbreak Hotel"	Elvis Presley	1956	RCA-Victor
"Please, Please, Please"	James Brown and the Famous Flames	1956	Federal

(continued)

Title	Artist/Group	Record Year	Record Label
"Bye Bye Love"	The Everly Brothers	1957	Cadence
"That'll Be the Day"	The Crickets [Buddy Holly and]	1957	Brunswick
"Whole Lot of Shakin' Going On"	Jerry Lee Lewis	1957	Sun
"Johnny B. Goode"	Chuck Berry	1958	Chess
"La Bamba"	Ritchie Valens	1958	Del-Fi
"Rebel-'Rouser"	Duane Eddy	1958	Jamie
"Summertime Blues"	Eddie Cochran	1958	Liberty
"A Teenager in Love"	Dion and the Belmonts	1959	Laurie
"There Goes My Baby"	The Drifters	1959	Atlantic
"What'd I Say (Part 1)"	Ray Charles	1959	Atlantic

REFERENCE GUIDE

PRINTED SOURCES

Books

Altschuler, Glenn C. *All Shook Up: How Rock 'n' Roll Changed America*. New York: Oxford University Press, 2003.

Amburn, Ellis. *Buddy Holly: A Biography*. New York: St. Martin's Press, 1995.

Aquila, Richard. *That Old Time Rock & Roll: A Chronicle of an Era, 1954–1963*. New York: Schirmer Books, 1989.

Belz, Carl. *The Story of Rock*. New York: Oxford University Press, 1969.

Berry, Chuck. *Chuck Berry: The Autobiography*. New York: Harmony Books, 1987.

Booth, Mark W. *American Popular Music: A Reference Guide*. Westport, CT: Greenwood Press, 1983.

Brewster, Bill, and Frank Broughton. *Last Night a DJ Saved My Life: The History of the Disc Jockey*. New York: Grove Press, 2000.

Bronson, Fred. *The Billboard Book of Number One Hits*. 4th ed. New York: Billboard Books, 1997.

———. *Billboard's Hottest Hot 100 Hits*. New York: Billboard Books, 2003.

Broven, John. *Rhythm & Blues in New Orleans*. Gretna, LA: Pelican, 1974.

Brown, James, with Bruce Tucker. *James Brown, the Godfather of Soul*. New York: Macmillan, 1986.

Brown, Ruth, and Andrew Yule. *Miss Rhythm: The Autobiography of Ruth Brown, Rhythm and Blues Legend*. New York: Da Capo Press, 1999.

Bruce, Chris, ed. *Crossroads: The Experience Music Project Collection*. Seattle, WA: Experience Music Project, 2000.

Campbell, Michael. *And the Beat Goes On: An Introduction to Popular Music in America, 1840 to Today*. New York: Schirmer Books, 1996.

Cash, Johnny, with Patrick Carr. *Cash: The Autobiography*. San Francisco: HarperSan-Francisco, 1997.

Chapple, Steve, and Reebee Garofalo. *Rock 'n' Roll Is Here to Pay: The History and Politics of the Music Industry*. Chicago: Nelson-Hall, 1977.

Charles, Ray, and David Ritz. *Brother Ray: Ray Charles' Own Story*. 3rd ed. Cambridge, MA: Da Capo Press, 2003.

Charlton, Katherine. *Rock Music Styles: A History*. 4th ed. Boston: McGraw-Hill, 2003.

Chilton, John. *Let the Good Times Roll: The Story of Louis Jordan and His Music*. Ann Arbor: University of Michigan Press, 1997.

Christgau, Robert. *Grown Up All Wrong: 75 Great Rock and Pop Artists from Vaudeville to Techno*. Cambridge, MA: Harvard University Press, 1998.

Clark, Dick, and Fred Bronson. *Dick Clark's American Bandstand*. New York: Collins, 1997.

Clark, Dick, and Richard Robinson. *Rock, Roll, & Remember*. New York: Crowell, 1976.

Clayton, Marie. *Elvis Presley: Unseen Archives*. New York: Barnes & Noble, 2004.

Clemente, John. *Girl Groups: Fabulous Females That Rocked the World*. Iola, WI: Krause, 2000.

Cohn, Nik. *Rock from the Beginning*. New York: Stein & Day, 1969.

Collis, John. *Chuck Berry: The Biography*. London: Aurum Press, 2004.

———. *The Story of Chess Records*. New York: Bloomsbury, 1998.

Cooper, B. Lee, and Wayne S. Haney. *Rock Music in American Popular Culture: Rock 'n' Roll Resources*. New York: Haworth Press, 1995.

Crampton, Luke, and Dafydd Rees. *Rock & Roll Year by Year*. New York: DK, 2003.

Dawson, Jim, and Steve Propes. *What Was the First Rock 'n' Roll Record?* Boston: Faber and Faber, 1992.

DeCurtis, Anthony, ed. *Present Tense: Rock & Roll and Culture*. Durham, NC: Duke University Press, 1992.

DeCurtis, Anthony, James Henke, and Holly George-Warren, eds. *The Rolling Stone Album Guide*. 3rd ed. New York: Random House, 1992.

———. *The Rolling Stone Illustrated History of Rock & Roll*. 3rd ed. New York: Random House, 1992.

DeWitt, Howard A. *Elvis, the Sun Years: The Story of Elvis Presley in the Fifties*. Ann Arbor, MI: Popular Culture, 1993.

Du Noyer, Paul, ed. *The Billboard Illustrated Encyclopedia of Music*. New York: Billboard Books, 2003.

Emerson, Ken. *Doo-Dah!: Stephen Foster and the Rise of American Popular Culture*. New York: Simon & Schuster, 1997.

Ennis, Philip. *The Seventh Stream: The Emergence of Rock 'n' Roll in American Popular Music*. Hanover, NH: University Press of New England, 1992.

Epstein, Jonathon S., ed. *Adolescents and Their Music: If It's Too Loud, You're Too Old*. New York: Garland, 1994.

Escott, Colin. *Lost Highway: The True Story of Country Music*. Washington, DC: Smithsonian Books, 2003.

Escott, Colin, and Martin Hawkins. *Good Rockin' Tonight: Sun Records and the Birth of Rock 'n' Roll*. New York: St. Martin's Press, 1991.

Fong-Torres, Ben. *The Hits Just Keep on Coming: The History of Top 40 Radio*. San Francisco: Backbeat Books, 2001.

Friedlander, Paul. *Rock and Roll: A Social History*. Boulder, CO: Westview Press, 1996.

Frith, Simon. *Sound Effects: Youth, Leisure, and the Politics of Rock 'n' Roll*. New York: Pantheon, 1981.

Frith, Simon, and Andrew Goodwin, eds. *On Record: Rock, Pop, and the Written Word*. New York: Pantheon, 1990.

Gaar, Gillian G. *She's a Rebel: The History of Women in Rock & Roll*. 2nd ed., enl. New York: Seal Press, 2002.

Gambaccini, Paul. *The Top 100 Rock 'n' Roll Albums of All Time*. New York: Harmony Books, 1987.

Garman, Bryan. *A Race of Singers: Whitman's Working-Class Hero from Guthrie to Springsteen*. Chapel Hill: University of North Carolina Press, 2000.

Garofalo, Reebee. *Rockin' Out: Popular Music in the USA*. 3rd ed. Upper Saddle River, NJ: Prentice Hall, 2005.

George, Nelson. *The Death of Rhythm and Blues*. New York: Pantheon, 1988.

George-Warren, Holly, and Rolling Stone Editors. *The Decades of Rock & Roll*. San Francisco: Chronicle Books, 2001.

George-Warren, Holly, and Patricia Romanowski, eds. *The Rolling Stone Encyclopedia of Rock & Roll*. New York: Fireside, 2001.

Gillett, Charlie. *Making Tracks: Atlantic Records and the Growth of a Multi-Billion-Dollar Industry*. New York: Dutton, 1974.

———. *The Sound of the City: The Rise of Rock and Roll*. 2nd ed., enl. New York: Da Capo Press, 1996.

Goldrosen, John, and John Beecher. *Remembering Buddy: The Definitive Biography of Buddy Holly*. New York: Penguin, 1986.

Gordon, Robert. *Can't Be Satisfied: The Life and Times of Muddy Waters*. Boston: Little, Brown, 2002.

———. *It Came from Memphis*. New York: Pocket Books, 1995.

Graff, Gary, and Daniel Durchholz, eds. *MusicHound Rock: The Essential Album Guide*. New York: Schirmer Books, 1999.

Gribin, Anthony J., and Matthew M. Schiff. *The Complete Book of Doo-Wop*. Iola, WI: Krause, 2000.

———. *Doo-Wop: The Forgotten Third of Rock 'n' Roll*. Iola, WI: Krause, 1992.

Guralnick, Peter. *Careless Love: The Unmaking of Elvis Presley*. Boston: Little, Brown, 1999.

———. *Feel Like Going Home: Portraits in Blues and Rock 'n' Roll*. New York: Outerbridge & Dienstfrey, 1971.

———. *Last Train to Memphis: The Rise of Elvis Presley*. Boston: Little, Brown, 1994.

———. *Lost Highway: Journeys and Arrivals of American Musicians*. Boston: David R. Godine, 1979.

———. *Sweet Soul Music: Rhythm and Blues and the Southern Dream of Freedom*. Boston: Little, Brown, 1999.

Guralnick, Peter, Robert Santelli, Holly George-Warren, and Christopher John Farley, eds. *Martin Scorsese Presents the Blues: A Musical Journey*. New York: Amistad, 2003.

Hagarty, Britt. *The Day the World Turned Blue: A Biography of Gene Vincent*. Vancouver, BC: Talonbooks, 1983.

Halberstam, David. *The Fifties*. New York: Villard Books, 1993.

Haley, John W., and John von Hoelle. *Sound and Glory: The Incredible Story of Bill Haley, the Father of Rock 'n' Roll and the Music That Shook the World.* Wilmington, DE: Dyne-American, 1990.

Hamm, Charles. *Yesterdays: Popular Song in America.* New York: Norton, 1979.

Hannusch, Jeff. *I Hear You Knockin': The Sound of New Orleans Rhythm and Blues.* Ville Platte, LA: Swallow, 1996.

———. *The Soul of New Orleans: A Legacy of Rhythm and Blues.* Ville Platte, LA: Swallow, 2001.

Haralambos, Michael. *Soul Music: The Birth of a Sound in Black America.* New York: Da Capo Press, 1974.

Hardy, Phil, and David Laing. *The Faber Companion to 20th Century Popular Music.* Boston: Faber and Faber, 2001.

Henke, James, ed. *Rock and Roll Hall of Fame and Museum Guidebook.* Cleveland, OH: Rock and Roll Hall of Fame and Museum, 2000.

———. *Rock Facts.* New York: Universe Publishing, 1996.

Hitchcock, H. Wiley, and Stanley Sadie, eds. *The New Grove Dictionary of American Music.* 4 vols. New York: Grove's Dictionaries of Music, 1986.

Hopkins, Jerry. *Elvis: A Biography.* New York: Simon & Schuster, 1971.

———. *Elvis: The Final Years.* New York: St. Martin's Press, 1980.

Iwaschkin, Roman. *Popular Music: A Reference Guide.* New York: Garland, 1986.

Jackson, John A. *American Bandstand: Dick Clark and the Making of a Rock 'n' Roll Empire.* New York: Oxford University Press, 1997.

———. *Big Beat Heat: Alan Freed and the Early Years of Rock & Roll.* New York: Schirmer Books, 1991.

Joyner, David. *American Popular Music.* 2nd ed. New York: McGraw-Hill, 2003.

Keil, Charles. *Urban Blues.* Chicago: University of Chicago Press, 1966.

Keogh, Pamela Clarke. *Elvis Presley: The Man. The Life. The Legend.* New York: Atria Books, 2004.

King, B. B., and David Ritz. *Blues All Around Me: The Autobiography of B. B. King.* New York: Avon Books, 1996.

Knight, Richard. *The Blues Highway: New Orleans to Chicago.* Hindhead, UK: Trailblazer, 2003.

Larkin, Colin, ed. *The Billboard Illustrated Encyclopedia of Rock.* New York: Billboard Books, 2003.

———. *The Guinness Encyclopedia of Popular Music.* 4 vols. Chester, CT: New England Pub. Associates, 1992.

Lehmer, Larry. *The Day the Music Died: The Last Tour of Buddy Holly, the Big Bopper, and Ritchie Valens.* New York: Schirmer Books, 1997.

Lewis, Myra, with Murray Silver. *Great Balls of Fire: The Uncensored Story of Jerry Lee Lewis.* New York: Morrow, 1982.

Lissauer, Robert. *Lissauer's Encyclopedia of Popular Music in America: 1888 to the Present.* New York: Paragon House, 1991.

Lomax, Alan. *The Land Where the Blues Began.* New York: Pantheon, 1993.

Malone, Bill C. *Country Music, U.S.A.: A Fifty-Year History.* 2nd rev. ed. Austin: University of Texas Press, 2002.

Marcus, Greil. *Mystery Train: Images of America in Rock 'n' Roll Music.* 4th rev. ed. New York: Penguin, 1997.

Marsh, Dave. *Elvis.* New York: Times Books, 1982.

Martin, Linda, and Kerry Segrave. *Anti-Rock: The Opposition to Rock 'n' Roll.* Hamden, CT: Archon Books, 1988.

McKeen, William, ed. *Rock and Roll Is Here to Stay: An Anthology.* New York: Norton, 2000.

Millar, Bill. *The Drifters: The Rise and Fall of the Black Vocal Group.* New York: Macmillan, 1971.

Nite, Norm. *Rock On: The Illustrated Encyclopedia of Rock 'n' Roll.* 2 vols. New York: Crowell, 1974.

Norman, Philip. *Rave On: The Biography of Buddy Holly.* New York: Simon & Schuster, 1996.

Ochs, Michael. *Rock Archives: A Photographic Journey Through the First Two Decades of Rock & Roll.* Garden City, NY: Doubleday, 1984.

Oliver, Paul. *Songsters and Saints: Vocal Traditions on Race Records.* New York: Cambridge University Press, 1984.

———. *The Story of the Blues.* London: Barrie and Rockcliff, 1969.

Palmer, Robert. *Baby, That Was Rock & Roll: The Legendary Leiber & Stoller.* New York: Harcourt Brace Jovanovich, 1978.

———. *Deep Blues.* New York: Viking Press, 1981.

———. *A Tale of Two Cities: Memphis Rock and New Orleans Roll.* I.S.A.M. Monographs, no. 12. Brooklyn, NY: Brooklyn College Institute for Studies in American Music, 1979.

Passman, Arnold. *The Deejays.* New York: Macmillan, 1971.

Pollock, Bruce. *When Rock Was Young.* New York: Holt, Rinehart and Winston, 1981.

Pruter, Robert. *Doowop: The Chicago Scene.* Urbana: University of Illinois Press, 1996.

Quain, Kevin, ed. *The Elvis Reader: Texts and Sources on the King of Rock 'n' Roll.* New York: St. Martin's Press, 1992.

Randel, Don Michael, ed. *The Harvard Biographical Dictionary of Music.* Cambridge, MA: Belknap Press of Harvard University Press, 1996.

———. *The Harvard Dictionary of Music.* 4th ed. Cambridge, MA: Belknap Press of Harvard University Press, 2003.

Rees, Dafydd, and Luke Crampton, eds. *Rock Movers and Shakers.* Rev. and enl. ed. New York: Billboard Books, 1991.

———. *Rock Stars Encyclopedia.* New York: DK, 1999.

Rock and Roll Hall of Fame and Museum Curators and Music Experts. *Five-Hundred Songs That Shaped Rock and Roll.* Cleveland, OH: Rock and Roll Hall of Fame and Museum, 1995.

Rosalsky, Mitch. *Encyclopedia of Rhythm & Blues and Doo-Wop Vocal Groups.* Lanham, MD: Scarecrow Press, 2002.

Rosen, Craig. *The Billboard Book of Number One Albums: The Inside Story Behind Pop Music's Blockbuster Records.* New York: Billboard Books, 1996.

Rubin, Rachel, and Jeffrey Melnick, eds. *American Popular Music: New Approaches to the Twentieth Century.* Amherst: University of Massachusetts Press, 2001.

Rutledge, Meredith E. *Rock My Soul: The Black Legacy of Rock and Roll.* Cleveland, OH: Arts League of Michigan and Rock and Roll Hall of Fame and Museum, 2003.

Sadie, Stanley, ed. *The New Grove Dictionary of Music and Musicians.* 20 vols. London: Macmillan, 1980. Also available online as *Grove Music Online.* Edited by L. Macy. http://www.grovemusic.com.

Sanjek, Russell. *Pennies from Heaven: The American Popular Music Business in the Twentieth Century*. Updated by David Sanjek. New York: Da Capo Press, 1996.

Santelli, Robert. *The Best of the Blues: The 101 Essential Blues Albums*. New York: Penguin, 1997.

———. *The Big Book of Blues: A Biographical Encyclopedia*. Updated and rev. ed. New York: Penguin, 2001.

Santelli, Robert, Holly George-Warren, and Jim Brown, eds. *American Roots Music*. New York: Harry N. Abrams, 2001.

Schuller, Gunther. *The Swing Era: The Development of Jazz, 1930–1945*. New York: Oxford University Press, 1989.

Segrave, Kerry. *Payola in the Music Industry: A History, 1880–1991*. Jefferson, NC: McFarland, 1994.

Shadwick, Keith. *The Encyclopedia of Jazz & Blues*. London: Quintet Publishing, 2002.

Shaw, Arnold. *Black Popular Music in America: From the Spirituals, Minstrels, and Ragtime to Soul, Disco, and Hip-Hop*. New York: Schirmer Books, 1986.

———. *Honkers and Shouters: The Golden Years of Rhythm and Blues*. New York: Macmillan, 1978.

———. *The Rockin' '50s: The Decade That Transformed the Pop Music Scene*. New York: Hawthorn Books, 1974.

Shore, Michael, with Dick Clark. *The History of American Bandstand*. New York: Ballantine, 1985.

Smith, Wes. *The Pied Pipers of Rock 'n' Roll: Radio Deejays of the 50s and 60s*. Marietta, GA: Longstreet Press, 1989.

Southern, Eileen. *The Music of Black Americans: A History*. 3rd ed. New York: Norton, 1997.

Southern, Eileen, comp. *Biographical Dictionary of Afro-American and African Musicians*. Westport, CT: Greenwood Press, 1982.

Stambler, Irwin. *Encyclopedia of Pop, Rock & Soul*. New York: St. Martin's Press, 1977.

Stokes, Geoffrey. *Star-Making Machinery: Inside the Business of Rock and Roll*. New York: Vintage Books, 1977.

Stuessy, Joe, and Scott Lipscomb. *Rock and Roll: Its History and Stylistic Development*. 4th ed. Upper Saddle River, NJ: Prentice Hall, 2003.

Sullivan, Robert, ed. *Rock & Roll at 50*. New York: Life Books, 2002.

Szatmary, David P. *Rockin' in Time: A Social History of Rock-and-Roll*. 5th ed. Upper Saddle River, NJ: Prentice Hall, 2004.

Tosches, Nick. *Hellfire: The Jerry Lee Lewis Story*. New York: Dell, 1982.

———. *Unsung Heroes of Rock 'n' Roll: The Birth of Rock in the Wild Years Before Elvis*. New York: Da Capo Press, 1999.

Ward, Ed, Geoffrey Stokes, and Ken Tucker. *Rock of Ages: The Rolling Stone History of Rock & Roll*. New York: Rolling Stone Press, 1986.

Wexler, Jerry, and David Ritz. *Rhythm and the Blues: A Life in American Music*. New York: Knopf, 1993.

Whitburn, Joel. *The Billboard Book of Top 40 Albums*. 3rd ed., rev. and enl. New York: Billboard Books, 1995.

———. *The Billboard Book of Top 40 Hits*. New York: Billboard Books, 2000.

———. *Billboard Top 10 Singles Charts, 1955–2000*. Menomonee Falls, WI: Record Research, 2001.

———. *Billboard Top 1000 Singles, 1955–2000*. Milwaukee, WI: Hal Leonard, 2001.

————. *Joel Whitburn Presents a Century of Pop Music*. Menomonee Falls, WI: Record Research, 1999.

————. *Joel Whitburn Presents Billboard #1s, 1950–1991*. Menomonee Falls, WI: Record Research, 1991.

————. *Joel Whitburn Presents Top R&B/Hip-Hop Singles, 1942–2004*. Menomonee Falls, WI: Record Research, 2004.

————. *Joel Whitburn's Top Pop Singles, 1955–2002*. Menomonee Falls, WI: Record Research, 2003.

————. *Pop Memories 1890–1954: The History of American Popular Music*. Menomonee Falls, WI: Record Research, 1986.

————. *Top Country Singles, 1944–2001*. Menomonee Falls, WI: Record Research, 2002.

Whitcomb, Ian. *After the Ball: Pop Music from Rag to Rock*. New York: Simon & Schuster, 1972.

White, Charles. *The Life and Times of Little Richard: The Quasar of Rock*. New York: Harmony Books, 1984.

Wicke, Peter. *Rock Music: Culture, Aesthetics and Sociology*. Translated by Rachel Fogg. New York: Cambridge University Press, 1990.

Wilder, Alec. *American Popular Song: The Great Innovators, 1900–1950*. Edited by James T. Maher. New York: Oxford University Press, 1972.

Wyman, Bill, and Richard Havers. *Bill Wyman's Blues Odyssey: A Journey to Music's Heart & Soul*. New York: DK, 2001.

Articles

Ackerman, Paul. "Tin Pan Alley Days Fade on Pop Music Broader Horizons." *Billboard*, October 5, 1955.

"Alan Freed: Breaking It Up at Brooklyn Paramount." *Billboard*, September 9, 1957.

"Alan Freed: Daddy of the Big Beat." *Hit Parader*, December 1958.

"American Bandstand." *TV Guide*, October 19, 1957.

"Bands Dug by the Beat: Louis Jordan." *Down Beat*, September 1, 1944.

Bunzel, Peter. "Music Biz Goes Round and Round: It Comes Out Clarkola." *Life*, May 16, 1960.

Chappell, Kevin. "How Blacks Invented Rock and Roll." *Ebony*, July 2001.

"Cleve. Cats Are Clipped by Cops' Crackdown on Jock's Jive Jamboree." *Variety*, February 9, 1955.

Davidson, Bill. "18,000,000 Teen-Agers Can't Be Wrong." *Collier's*, January 4, 1957.

"The Dick Clark Show." *Variety*, February 19, 1958.

"Dick Clark Talks to Teenagers." *Seventeen*, July 1959.

"Exhaustive Probe for Whole Music Industry on Way." *Billboard*, December 21, 1959.

"Facing the Music." *Time*, November 30, 1959.

Farley, Christopher John. "Forever Rockin'." *Time*, September 4, 1995.

Gilbert, Eugene. "Why Today's Teenagers Seem So Different." *Harper's Magazine*, November 1959.

"Goodbye, Ookie Dookie: Payola." *Newsweek*, February 22, 1960.

Harris, Wynonie "Mr. Blues." "Women Won't Let Me Alone." *Tan*, October 1954.

Hill, Trent. "The Enemy Within: Censorship in Rock Music in the 1950s." *South Atlantic Quarterly* 90, no. 4 (Fall 1991).

"The Immortals: A Fiftieth Anniversary Tribute to the Fifty Most Important Performers in Rock & Roll History, by the Artists They Inspired." *Rolling Stone*, April 15, 2004.

Jarman, Rufus. "Country Music Goes to Town." *Nation's Business*, February 1953.

"Jocks Junk Payola Platters." *Variety*, February 16, 1955.

Kamin, Jonathan. "Parallels in the Social Reactions to Jazz and Rock." *Black Perspective in Music* 3 (Fall 1975).

———. "Taking the Roll out of Rock and Roll." *Popular Music and Society* 2 (Spring 1972).

———. "The White R&B Audience and the Music Industry, 1952–1956." *Popular Music and Society* 6 (Summer 1978).

Kaye, Elizabeth. "Sam Phillips Interview." *Rolling Stone*, February 13, 1986.

Killmeier, Matthew A. "Voices Between the Tracks: Disc Jockeys, Radio, and Popular Music, 1955–1960." *Journal of Communication Inquiry*, October 2001.

"LaVern Baker Claims 15G Royalty Loss on Lifting of Song Arrangements." *Variety*, March 2, 1955.

"Letter Asks Clean-Up of Filth Wax." *Billboard*, December 18, 1954.

Liddell, Marlane A. "Roots of Rhythm." *Smithsonian*, November 2001.

Marcus, Greil. "Is This the Woman Who Invented Rock & Roll?: The Deborah Chessler Story." *Rolling Stone*, June 24, 1993.

"Moondog to WINS; Freed Freed of WJW to Start in N.Y. in Fall." *Billboard*, July 10, 1954.

Mooney, Hugh. "Just Before Rock: Pop Music 1950–1953 Revisited." *Popular Music and Society* 3 (Summer 1974).

Murray, Charles Shaar. "The Blues Had a Baby . . . and They Called It Rock 'n' Roll." *New Musical Express*, April 30, 1977.

"Music Biz Now R&B Punchy: Even Hillbillies Are Doing It." *Variety*, February 9, 1955.

"Newest Music for a New Generation: Rock 'n' Roll Rolls On 'n' On." *Life*, December 22, 1958.

"Now Freud Gets into Teen-Age R&R Act." *Billboard*, July 14, 1956.

Palmer, Robert. "The Fifties." *Rolling Stone*, April 19, 1990.

———. "Fifty from the Fifties." *Rolling Stone*, April 19, 1990.

Parshall, Gerald. "Bing and the King." *U.S. News & World Report*, June 1, 1998.

Peterson, Richard A. "Why 1955? Explaining the Advent of Rock Music." *Popular Music* 9, no. 1 (January 1990).

"Rock 'n' Roll." *Time*, July 23, 1956.

Rolontz, Bob. "Rhythm and Blues Notes." *Billboard*, October 9, 1954.

Rolontz, Bob, and Joel Friedman. "Teen-Agers Demand Music with a Beat, Spur Rhythm-Blues: Field Reaps $15,000,000; Radio, Juke Boxes Answer Big Demands." *Billboard*, April 24, 1954.

Rumble, John. "Roots of Rock & Roll: Henry Glover of King Records." *Journal of Country Music* 14, no. 2 (1992).

Sanjek, David. "One Size Does Not Fit All: The Precarious Position of the African American Entrepreneur in Post-WWII American Popular Music." *American Music* 15, no. 4 (Winter 1997).

Schipper, Henry. "Dick Clark." *Rolling Stone*, April 19, 1990.

Sheridan, Kevin, and Peter Sheridan. "T-Bone Walker: Father of the Blues." *Guitar Player*, March 1977.

Simon, Bill. "Indies' Surprise Survival: Small Labels' Ingenuity and Skill Pay Off." *Billboard*, December 3, 1949.

Spake, Amanda. "Sweet Rhythm and Hot Blues." *U.S. News & World Report*, November 30, 1998.

"Subcommittee Hooks Set for Payola Probe." *Billboard*, December 7, 1959.

"Teeners' Hero." *Time*, May 14, 1956.

"Top Names Now Singing the Blues as Newcomers Roll on R&B Tide." *Variety*, February 23, 1955.

Tucker, Bruce. "Tell Tchaikovsky the News: Postmodernism, Popular Culture, and the Emergence of Rock 'n Roll." *Black Music Research Journal* 8/9, no. 2 (1989).

Vito, R. "The Chuck Berry Style: A Modern Rocker Pays Tribute to the Master." *Guitar Player*, June 1984.

"A Warning to the Music Business." *Variety*, February 23, 1955.

"Yeh-Heh-Heh-Hes, Baby." *Time*, June 18, 1956.

WEB SITES

All Music Guide. *The Allmusic Website*. 2005. All Media Guide. http://www.allmusic.com.

Beale Street Corporation. *Beale Street: Home of the Blues/Birthplace of Rock & Roll Home Page*. 2002–2004. http://www.bealestreet.com.

Billboard. *Billboard Magazine Online*. 2005. VNU eMedia. http://www.billboard.com.

Blues Foundation. *The Blues Foundation Home Page*. 2003–2005. http://www.blues.org.

Center for Black Music Research. *Center for Black Music Research Home Page*. 2005. Columbia College, Chicago. http://www.cbmr.org.

Center for Popular Music. *Center for Popular Music Home Page*. 2001. Middle Tennessee State University. http://www.mtsu.edu/~ctrpopmu.

Center for Southern Folklore. *Center for Southern Folklore Home Page*. 2004. http://www.southernfolklore.com.

Country Music Hall of Fame and Museum. *Country Music Hall of Fame and Museum Website*. 2003–2005. Country Music Foundation. http://www.countrymusichalloffame.com.

Elvis Presley Enterprises. *Elvis Presley: The Official Site*. 2000–2005. http://www.elvis.com.

Experience Music Project. *Experience Music Project Website*. 2000–2004. http://www.emplive.com.

Hewston, Curtis. *The Blue Highway Home Page*. 1995–2004. http://www.thebluehighway.com.

Michael Ochs Archives. *Michael Ochs Archives Home Page*. 1999–2004. http://www.michaelochs.com.

Peneny, D. K. *The History of Rock 'n' Roll: The Golden Decade 1954–1963 Home Page*. 1998–2004. http://www.history-of-rock.com.

Pillsbury, Glenn. *The International Association for the Study of Popular Music, United*

States Branch Website. 2004. International Association for the Study of Popular Music, United States Branch. http://www.iaspm-us.net.

Rockabilly Music Preservation. *Rockabilly Hall of Fame Home Page.* 1997–2005. http://www.rockabillyhall.com.

Rock and Roll Hall of Fame and Museum. *Rock and Roll Hall of Fame and Museum Website.* 2005. Rock and Roll Hall of Fame Foundation. http://www.rockhall .com.

Rolling Stone. The Rolling Stone.com Website. 2005. Real Networks. http://www .rollingstone.com.

Sun Studio. *The Birthplace of Rock 'n' Roll: Sun Studio Home Page.* 2005. http://www .sunstudio.com.

Variety. Variety.com Website. 2005. Reed Business Information. http://www.variety .com.

Vulcan Productions/Experience Music Project. *Martin Scorsese Presents the Blues Website.* 2003. Public Broadcasting Service. http://www.pbs.org/the blues.

William and Gayle Cook Music Library. *Worldwide Internet Music Resources.* 1995–2004. Indiana University School of Music. http://www.music.indiana .edu/music_resources.

ORGANIZATIONS

Archives of African American Music & Culture
Smith Research Center
2805 E. Tenth Street
Indiana University
Bloomington, Indiana 47408
http://www.indiana.edu/~aaamc

> Collects, preserves, and disseminates materials for research and study of post-World War II African American music and culture; features a variety of holdings, including oral histories, photographs, musical and print manuscripts, audio and video recordings, and educational broadcast programs; provides reference services and outreach programs for scholars, students, and the general public, including live performances, exhibits, seminars, workshops, and summer music camps.

Country Music Hall of Fame and Museum
222 Fifth Avenue S.
Nashville, Tennessee 37203
http://www.countrymusichalloffame.com

> Identifies and preserves the history and traditions of country music and educates its audiences at the Country Music Foundation's museum; features public programs and permanent and special exhibits; houses country music artifacts: interactive exhibits, music, films, costumes, memorabilia, instruments, photographs, and manuscripts.

Delta Blues Museum
#1 Blues Alley
Clarksdale, Mississippi 38614
http://www.deltabluesmuseum.org

Explores the history and heritage of the blues and the Delta region and its music; features exhibits about the culture and people of the blues; houses blues artifacts: photos, instruments, and local pieces.

Elvis Presley Birthplace
306 Elvis Presley Drive
Tupelo, Mississippi 38801
http://www.elvispresleybirthplace.com
    Houses the Elvis Presley Museum, the Memorial Chapel, a gift shop, and a statue of Presley at the Mississippi landmark and birthplace of Presley located in Elvis Presley Park.

Experience Music Project
325 5th Avenue N.
Seattle, Washington 98109
http://www.emplive.com
    Celebrates and explores roots and genres of rock and roll music in an interactive music museum; features public programs and state-of-the-art exhibits; houses more than 80,000 artifacts that shaped music history: instruments, photographs, stage costumes, handwritten song lyrics, fanzines, and rare music sheets.

Graceland Estate
Graceland Plaza
Memphis, Tennessee 38186
http://www.elvis.com/graceland
    Features the Graceland mansion, Chapel in the Woods, and Sincerely Elvis Museum at Graceland Plaza, consisting of Elvis Presley's fourteen-acre estate; also automobile, custom airplane, and trophy museums as well as gift shops and restaurants; mansion tours and extensive displays of Presley career mementos: stage costumes, jewelry, photographs, gold records, and awards.

International Rock-A-Billy Hall of Fame Museum
105 N. Church Street
Jackson, Tennessee 38301
http://www.rockabillyhall.org
    Preserves and promotes rockabilly music; features memorabilia reflecting and recognizing the pioneers and heritage of rockabilly.

Memphis Rock 'n' Soul Museum
191 Beale Street
Memphis, Tennessee 38103
http://www.memphisrocknsoul.org
    Examines the history of Memphis music and its impact on American culture; houses the Smithsonian Institution's "Rock 'n' Soul: Social Crossroads" exhibit; features artifacts highlighting America's cultural and musical past.

The New York Public Library for the Performing Arts
Dorothy and Lewis B. Cullman Center
40 Lincoln Center Plaza
New York, New York 10023
http://www.nypl.org/research/lpa

Houses the world's most extensive collection of reference and research materials on music, dance, theater, recorded sound, and other performing arts; the Music Division boasts one of the world's finest music collections chronicling music genres from opera, spirituals, and ragtime to jazz, rock, and pop music; features collections, archives, materials, and exhibits.

Rock and Roll Hall of Fame and Museum
One Key Plaza
Cleveland, Ohio 44114
http://www.rockhall.com

Preserves the history and spirit of rock and roll music at the Rock and Roll Hall of Fame Foundation's museum; educates the public on the story of rock and roll from its roots to the present; honors and recognizes artists, composers, producers, and others who helped make rock and roll one of the most popular and influential art forms, including Hall of Fame inductees; features extensive collection of historic artifacts, pays tribute to the artists who played key roles in the evolution of the music, and utilizes the latest technology in permanent and special exhibits: films, video walls, and interactive computers.

Vocal Group Hall of Fame Museum
82 West State Street
Sharon, Pennsylvania 16146
http://www.vocalhalloffame.com

Honors the world's greatest vocal groups with more than 100 exhibits of inductee and potential inductee memorabilia.

EVENTS

Beale Street Music Festival
Memphis in May International Festival
Memphis, Tennessee
http://www.memphisinmay.org

Annual three-day spring festival featuring leading popular music artists; held prior to the W. C. Handy Awards in May as part of the Memphis in May International Festival.

Elvis Presley Week and Elvis Presley Birthday Celebration
Graceland Plaza
Memphis, Tennessee
http://www.elvis.com

Annual weeklong celebration of Presley occurring near the anniversary of his August 16 death; music, dance, sports, and social events commemorating the music, magic, and memories associated with the Presley legacy; near the anniversary of the King's January 8 birthday, there is a three-day Elvis Presley Birthday Celebration.

New Orleans Jazz & Heritage Festival
Fair Grounds Race Course
New Orleans, Louisiana
http://www.nojazzfest.com

Annual ten-day spring cultural festival; features cooks, craftspeople, and internationally renowned musicians; music encompasses every genre associated with New Orleans and Louisiana, from jazz, blues, R&B, folk, and gospel to Cajun, zydeco, rock, rap, and country music; considered one of America's premier musical events.

Rockabilly Fest
Carl Perkins Civic Center
Jackson, Tennessee
http://www.rockabillyhall.org

Annual summer rockabilly festival features regionally and nationally known rockabilly artists.

FILMS

Original theatrical release dates follow titles, when available; original film, videocassette (VHS), and digital videodisc (DVD) formats are included.

Blackboard Jungle (1955). Warner Home Video, 2005.
Don't Knock the Rock. Columbia Pictures, 1956.
Love Me Tender (1956). Fox Home Entertainment, 2004.
Rock Around the Clock. Columbia Pictures, 1956.
Rock, Rock, Rock! (1956). Koch Entertainment, 2003.
Shake, Rattle, and Rock! (1956). Dimension Home Video, 2003.
The Girl Can't Help It (1956). Twentieth Century Fox, 1985.
Jailhouse Rock (1957). Warner Studios, 2004.
Jamboree (1957). Warner Studios, 1997.
Loving You (1957). Lionsgate, 2003.
Mister Rock and Roll (1957). Hallmark Home Entertainment, 2000.
Go, Johnny, Go! (1958). Anchor Bay Entertainment, 1989.
High School Confidential (1958). Lionsgate, 2004.
King Creole (1958). Paramount Studios, 2003.
Chuck Berry: Rock & Roll Music (1969). Geneon Entertainment, 2002.
Little Richard: Keep on Rockin' (1969). Geneon Entertainment, 2002.
The Buddy Holly Story (1978). Columbia/Tristar Studios, 1999.
The Idolmaker (1980). MGM/UA Studios, 2001.
Rock 'n' Roll: The Early Days (1984). BMG Distribution, 1989.
Carl Perkins and Friends—Blue Suede Shoes: A Rockabilly Session (1985). Music Video Distributors, 2002.
A Tribute to Ricky Nelson (1986). K-Tel/DVD, 2000.
Fats Domino: Blueberry Hill (1986). K-Tel/DVD, 2000.
Chuck Berry: Hail! Hail! Rock 'n' Roll (1987). Universal/MCA, 1989.
Elvis '56: In the Beginning (1987). A Vision, 2004.
La Bamba (1987). Columbia/Tristar Studios, 2002.
Great Balls of Fire! (1989). MGM/UA Video, 2002.
Legends of Rock 'n' Roll Live (1989). Image Entertainment, 2000.
Dick Clark's Best of Bandstand (1990). Lionsgate, 1990.
Les Paul: Living Legend of the Electric Guitar (1992). BMG/BMG Video, 1993.
Deep Blues (1993). Fox Lorber, 2000.

Goin' to Chicago. University of Mississippi, 1994.

History of Rock 'n' Roll (10-episode set). Warner Studios, 1995.

Elvis: The Complete Story (1996). Passport Video, 2000.

Rock 'n' Roll Invaders: The AM Radio DJs (1998). Winstar Home Entertainment, 2001.

Hellhounds on My Trail: The Afterlife of Robert Johnson (1999). Windstar Home Entertainment, 2003.

Ritchie Valens: The Complete Ritchie Valens (1999). Whirlwind Media, 2000.

American Roots Music (4-episode set). Palm Pictures, 2001.

Good Rockin' Tonight: The Legacy of Sun Records (2001). Image Entertainment, 2004.

Blues Masters: The Essential History of the Blues. Wea Corporation, 2002.

Ed Sullivan's Rock 'n' Roll Classics (9-episode set). Warner/Elektra/Atlantic Video, 2002.

Elvis: The Great Performances (3-episode set). Warner/Elektra/Atlantic Video, 2002.

Elvis Presley (2002). Eagle Eye/Pioneer, 2002.

The Legends of New Orleans: The Music of Fats Domino (2003). Sony Music Entertainment, 2003.

Life Could Be a Dream: The Doo-Wop Sound. Kultur, 2003.

Martin Scorsese Presents the Blues: A Musical Journey (7-episode set). Sony Music Entertainment, 2003.

Elvis: The Birth of Rock 'n' Roll. Kultur, 2004.

Rock and Roll at 50. Sony Music Entertainment, 2004.

The Real Buddy Holly Story. Kultur, 2004.

Elvis by the Presleys. BMG Music, 2005.

RECORDINGS

Anthologies consist of various artists; all recordings refer to compact disc (CD) format.

The Aladdin Records Story (2-CD set). Capitol, 1994.

American Roots Music (4-CD set). Palm, 2001.

Atlantic Rhythm and Blues: 1947–1974 (8-CD set). Atlantic, 1991.

The Best of Doo Wop (2-CD set: *Ballads; Uptempo*). Rhino, 1989.

Billboard Top R&B Hits (5-CD set: *1955, 1956, 1957, 1958, 1959*). Rhino, 1989.

Billboard Top Rock 'n' Roll Hits (5-CD set: *1955, 1956, 1957, 1958, 1959*). Rhino, 1988–1990.

Bill Haley & His Comets: The Decca Years and More (5-CD set). Bear Family, 1994.

The Birth of Soul: The Complete Atlantic Rhythm & Blues Recordings, 1952–1959 (Ray Charles; 3-CD set). Atlantic, 1991.

Black & White Roots of Rock 'n' Roll (2-CD set). Indigo, 2004.

Blues Classics (3-CD set). MCA, 1996.

Chess Blues (4-CD set). Chess, 1993.

Chess Rhythm & Roll (4-CD set). MCA, 1994.

The Doo Wop Box: 101 Vocal Group Gems from the Golden Age of Rock 'n' Roll (4-CD set). Rhino, 1993.

The Doo Wop Box II: 101 More Vocal Group Gems from the Golden Age of Rock 'n' Roll (4-CD set). Rhino, 1996.

Elvis: The King of Rock 'n' Roll: The Complete 50s Masters (5-CD set). RCA, 2000.

The Golden Era of Rock 'n' Roll: 1954–1963 (3-CD set). Hip-O, 2004.

The King R&B Box Set (4-CD set). King, 1996.

The Legend and the Legacy (4-CD set; Les Paul). Capitol, 1991.

Let the Good Times Roll: The Anthology 1938–1953 (2-CD set; Louis Jordan). MCA, 1999.

Loud, Fast & Out of Control: The Wild Sounds of '50s Rock (4-CD set). Rhino, 1999.

Martin Scorsese Presents the Blues: A Musical Journey (5-CD set). Hip-O/Universal, 2003.

Oldies but Goodies: 250 Legendary Hits (15-CD set). Original Sound, 1996.

The R&B Box: 30 Years of Rhythm & Blues (6-CD set). Rhino, 1994.

Red White & Rock (3-CD set). Rhino, 2002.

Rock & Soul Instrumental Classics (3-CD set). Golden Stars, 2001.

The Rock 'n' Roll Era (7-CD set). Time-Life Music/BMG, 1988.

The Rock 'n' Roll Era: Elvis Presley (2-CD set). Time-Life Music/BMG, 1988.

The Rock 'n' Roll Era: Roots of Rock (2-CD set). Time-Life Music/Time Warner, 1990, 1992.

The Rock 'n' Roll Era: Teen Idols (2-CD set). Time-Life Music/Time Warner, 1990, 1992.

Rock, Rhythm and Doo Wop, Volume 1: The Greatest Songs from Early Rock 'n' Roll (3-CD set). Rhino, 2001.

Rock This Town: Rockabilly Hits (2-CD set). Rhino, 1991.

Roots of Rock 'n' Roll: 1946–1954 (3-CD set). Hip-O, 2004.

Say It Loud!: A Celebration of Black Music in America (6-CD set). Rhino, 2001.

The Specialty Story (5-CD set). Specialty, 1994.

The Sun Records Collection (3-CD set). Rhino/BMG, 1994.

When the Sun Goes Down: The Secret History of Rock & Roll Series (12-CD set). RCA-Bluebird, 2002–2004.

INDEX

About the Author

LISA SCRIVANI-TIDD is a professor of music in the State University of New York (SUNY) at Jefferson and is also the university organist at St. Lawrence University. Dr. Scrivani-Tidd has taught for the Education Department at the Rock and Roll Hall of Fame and Museum in Cleveland, Ohio, and has developed a music curriculum at SUNY Jefferson where she currently teaches courses in music theory, music appreciation, performance, and music history, including History of American Popular Music and History of Rock and Roll.